Cambridge International AS and A Level Accounting

D1613684

Harold Randall
David Hopkins

CAMBRIDGE
UNIVERSITY PRESS

CAMBRIDGE UNIVERSITY PRESS
Cambridge, New York, Melbourne, Madrid, Cape Town,
Singapore, São Paulo, Delhi, Tokyo, Mexico City

Cambridge University Press
4381/4 Ansari Road, Daryaganj, Delhi 110002, India

www.cambridge.org
Information on this title: www.cambridge.org/9781107690622

First published 2012
Reprinted 2012, 2013

Printed in India at Replika Press Pvt. Ltd.

A catalogue for this publication is available from the British Library

ISBN 978-1-107-69062-2   Paperback

Contents

Preface   *v*
Topics grid   *vi*
International Standards Terminology   *vii*

Part I.   The accounting system   **1**
   1. Double-entry bookkeeping: cash transactions   3
   2. Double-entry bookkeeping: credit transactions   9
   3. Books of prime (or original) entry   14
   4. Balancing accounts   21
   5. The classification of accounts and division of the ledger   23
   6. The trial balance   25

Part II. Financial accounting   **29**
   7. Income Statements for sole traders   31
   8. Statements of Financial Position for sole traders   39
   9. Accounting principles or concepts   42
  10. Accruals and prepayments (the matching concept)   47
  11. Provisions for the depreciation of non-current assets   52
  12. Bad and doubtful debts   61
  13. Bank reconciliation statements   67
  14. Control accounts   72
  15. Suspense accounts   81
  16. Incomplete records   89
  17. Non-profit-making organisations (clubs and societies)   99
  18. Departmental accounts   108
  19. Manufacturing accounts   114
  20. Valuation of inventory   120
  21. Partnership accounts   128
  22. Partnership changes   136
  23. An introduction to the accounts of limited companies   157
  24. Statement of cash flows   174
  25. Limited companies: more about share capital and debentures;
       capital reductions and reconstructions   188
  26. Business purchase   200
  27. Published company accounts   209

Part III. Financial reporting and interpretation   **223**
  28. Interpretation and analysis   225
  29. Company financing   245

Part IV. Elements of managerial accounting **253**

   30. Costing principles and systems: total (or absorption) costing   255

   31. Unit, job and batch costing   266

   32. Process costing   270

   33. Marginal costing   276

   34. Budgeting   289

   35. Standard costing   301

   36. Investment appraisal   313

   Appendix 1: Table showing net present value of $1   323

   Answers to exercises and multiple-choice questions   **325**

   Index   371

Preface

There have been a number of changes in the world of accounting since the first publication of this textbook, most notably the introduction of the **International Accounting Standards (IAS)**. These changes have resulted in the need for a re-write of the original work. The book is still aimed at AS and A level accounting students studying the CIE syllabus, who still face the problems by asking 'How do I do this?'

This textbook covers the entire Cambridge AS and A Level Accounting syllabus. Ideally, students should already have taken O level or IGCSE accounting before starting on AS Level or A level studies. Many do not have such a background and this text has such students in mind in the early chapters. The essentials of double-entry bookkeeping are covered in sufficient detail to equip students to progress to more advanced work. It must be emphasised, however, that thorough mastery of the basics is absolutely necessary if real progress is to be made with the subsequent chapters.

The text follows the order of the Cambridge AS and A Level Accounting syllabus but allows for some flexibility in the sequence in which the topics are studied. Whichever the order in which the chapters are taken, it is of paramount importance that the whole of the syllabus is covered before the examination. Every topic is likely to find its place in at least one of the papers each session. It is invariably the case that too many candidates enter the examinations inadequately prepared — with inevitably disappointing results. A grid is provided to show how the chapters cover the AS level and A level syllabuses. However, as the syllabus changes from time to time, both tutors and students need to assess the topics and their teaching and learning strategy in light of any changes.

I have been an examiner and lecturer for a number of years and also trained abroad on behalf of CIE. These experiences have given me a valuable insight into the challenges face by students and tutors overseas. In re-writing the text I hope that I have kept to the style which Harold Randall used so effectively.

New topics have been added and old ones deleted. Answers to exercises within chapters and answers to multiple-choice questions are provided at the end of the textbook. I have also retained and, in some cases expanded the section on 'Examination hints'. Despite numerous re-reads and re-working of questions any mistakes are solely down to me!

The study of accountancy can be extremely rewarding. I have been involved in it now for more years than I care to admit to and am still learning! To all my readers, both old and new, I send my best wishes for success.

David Hopkins

Topics grid

The grid below shows how the chapters of this text cover the topics in the syllabuses for AS level and A level accounting. The syllabuses do not present the topics or their contents in the order in which they should be taught, and the order in which the chapters are shown in the grid is intended only to show how the syllabuses are covered. Teachers will decide their own order to suit their particular teaching plans, which will usually follow, more or less, the chapters in sequence.

Some topics are either wholly or partly outside the AS level syllabus but none of the topics is outside the A level syllabus.

Syllabus	Chapter	AS level	A level
THE ACCOUNTING SYSTEM			
A. Recording Financial Information	1	All	All
	2	All	All
	3	All	All
	4	All	All
	5	All	All
	10	All	All
	11	All	All
	12	All	All
B. Accounting Principles	9	All	All
C. Control Systems	6	All	All
	13	All	All
	14	All	All
	15	All	All
FINANCIAL ACCOUNTING			
D. Preparation of Financial Statements	7	All	All
	8	All	All
	16	All	All
	17	All	All
	18	All	All
	19	All	All
	20	All	All
	21	All	All
	22	All	All
	23	All	All
	24	N/A	All
E. Capital	25	§§25.1–25.5	All
F. Business Purchase	26	N/A	All
G. Published Company Accounts	27	N/A	All
FINANCIAL REPORTING AND INTERPRETATION			
H. Interpretation and Analysis	28	§§ 28.1–28.6, 28.8, 28.9, 28.10	All
I. Company Financing	29	N/A	All
ELEMENTS OF MANAGERIAL ACCOUNTING			
J. Costing Principles and Systems	30	All	All
	31	All	All
	32	N/A	All
	33	All	All
K. Budgeting	34	N/A	All
L. Standard Costing	35	N/A	All
M. Investment Appraisal	36	N/A	All

International Standards Terminology

Given below is the list of international standards terminology used in CIE accounting syllabuses. Centres should use the new terminology in their teaching and learning materials so that candidates are familiar with the terms. Candidates will not lose marks for using different terms.

International Usage	Current/UK usage
Balance sheet (statement of financial position)	Balance sheet
Bank (and other) loans/Interest bearing loans and borrowing	Loans repayable after 12 months
Bank overdrafts and loans/Interest bearing loans and borrowing	Loans repayable within 12 months
Capital or equity/shareholders' equity	Capital
Cash (and cash equivalents)	Bank and cash
Cost of sales	Cost of goods sold
Current assets	Current assets
Current liabilities	Current liabilities/Creditors: amounts due within 12 months
Finance costs	Interest payable
Finance income/investment revenues	Interest receivable
Financial statements	Final accounts
Gross profit	Gross profit
Income statement (statement of comprehensive income)	Trading and profit and loss account
Intangible assets	Goodwill etc.
Inventory/inventories (of raw materials and finished goods)	Stock
Investment property	Investments
Non-current assets	Fixed assets
Non-current liabilities	Long term liabilities/Creditors: amounts falling due after more than one year
Other operating expenses	Sundry expenses (administration and distribution)
Other operating income	Sundry income
Other payables	Accruals
Other receivables	Prepayments
Plant and equipment	Plant and equipment
Profit (before tax) for the year	Net profit
Property	Land and buildings
Raw materials Ordinary goods purchased	Purchases
Revenue	Sales
Share capital	Share capital
Trade payables	Creditors
Trade receivables	Debtors
Work in progress	Work in progress

4

Part I
The accounting system

1 Double-entry bookkeeping: cash transactions

In this chapter you will learn:

- that every transaction has two aspects
- that double-entry bookkeeping records both aspects of a transaction
- what ledger accounts are
- the meanings of the terms 'debit' and 'credit'
- how to record cash transactions in ledger accounts.

1.1 What is double-entry bookkeeping?

Double-entry bookkeeping is a system of recording transactions that recognises that there are two sides (or aspects) to every transaction. For example, you give your friend $10 in exchange for his watch. This involves you giving him $10 (one aspect) and your friend receiving $10 (the other aspect). The transfer of the watch involves him giving you the watch (one aspect) and you receiving his watch (the other aspect). Every transaction involves giving and receiving. It is important that you *recognise* and *record* both aspects of every transaction in your bookkeeping.

1.2 Ledger accounts

Transactions are recorded in **ledger accounts**. An account is a history of all transactions of a similar nature. A ledger is a book that contains accounts. An account separates what is received from what is given. For example, a Cash account records cash received and cash paid, as shown:

Cash					
Debit			**Credit**		
		$			$
Mar 1	Cash received from customers	240	Mar 2	Cash paid to suppliers	80
Mar 4	Cash received from customers	118	Mar 3	Wages paid	116

The left-hand side of the account is called the debit side and is used to record cash received (that is, coming into the account). The right-hand side of the account is the credit side and shows cash paid (that is, going out of the account). All accounts have a debit side on the left to record what is received, and a credit side on the right to record what is given. In practice, the words 'debit' and 'credit' are not shown because bookkeepers do not need to be reminded of them.

1.3 How to record cash transactions

Bookkeeping treats businesses as 'persons' with separate identities from their owners. For example, if Abdul is a trader, all his business transactions are recorded as those of the business and not as Abdul's own transactions.

In the example that follows, some transactions are recorded in ledger accounts. Make sure you understand the bookkeeping entries, and observe the wording carefully. This is important as you must be able to record transactions in ledger accounts correctly.

Example

(Here all transactions are recorded from the point of view of Abdul's business, not from the point of view of the people with whom the business deals.)

Transaction 1 April 1. Abdul starts business as a trader by paying $10 000 into a Bank account which he opens for the business. Abdul gives, and the business receives, $10 000. An account for Abdul will be opened (his Capital account) and credited with his 'capital'. The business Bank account will be debited.

Bank			
	$		$
Apr 1 Abdul – Capital 10 000			

Abdul – Capital			
	$		$
		Apr 1 Bank	10 000

Note. Each entry is dated and shows the name of the other account in which the double entry is completed. Make sure you show these details for every entry you make in a ledger account.

Entries in ledger accounts are known as **postings**, and bookkeepers are said to 'post' transactions to the accounts.

Transaction 2 April 2. Abdul buys a motor vehicle for the business and pays $2000 from the business Bank account. A Motor Vehicles account must be opened.

Bank			
	$		$
Apr 1 Abdul – Capital 10 000		Apr 2 Motor Vehicles 2000	

Motor Vehicles			
	$		$
Apr 2 Bank	2000		

Transaction 3 April 3. Abdul buys goods which he will re-sell in the normal course of trade for $3000 and pays by cheque.

Bank			
	$		$
Apr 1 Abdul – Capital 10 000		Apr 2 Motor Vehicles 2000	
		Apr 3 Purchases 3000	

Purchases			
	$		$
Apr 3 Bank	3000		

Transaction 4 April 4. Abdul sells a quantity of the goods for $800 and pays the money into the bank.

Bank			
	$		$
Apr 1 Abdul – Capital 10 000		Apr 2 Motor Vehicles 2000	
Apr 4 Sales	800	Apr 3 Purchases 3000	

Sales			
	$		$
		Apr 4 Bank	800

Transaction 5 April 7. A customer returns some goods and receives a refund of $40.

Bank			
	$		$
Apr 1 Abdul – Capital 10 000		Apr 2 Motor Vehicles 2000	
Apr 4 Sales	800	Apr 3 Purchases 3000	
		Apr 7 Sales Returns 40	

Sales Returns			
	$		$
Apr 7 Bank	40		

Note. Goods returned are not debited to Sales account but to Sales Returns account. This account is also known as Goods Inwards or Returns Inwards account.

Transaction 6 April 8. Abdul returns some goods costing $100 to a supplier and receives a refund.

Bank			
	$		$
Apr 1 Abdul – Capital 10 000		Apr 2 Motor Vehicles 2000	
Apr 4 Sales	800	Apr 3 Purchases 3000	
Apr 8 Purchases Returns 100		Apr 7 Sales Returns 40	

Purchases Returns			
	$		$
		Apr 8 Bank	100

Note. Goods returned to a supplier are credited to Purchases Returns account. This account is also known as Goods Outwards account.

Transaction 7 April 10. Abdul buys another motor vehicle for the business and pays $4000 by cheque.

Bank			
	$		$
Apr 1 Abdul – Capital	10 000	Apr 2 Motor Vehicles	2000
Apr 4 Sales	800	Apr 3 Purchases	3000
Apr 8 Purchases Returns	100	Apr 7 Sales Returns	40
		Apr 10 Motor Vehicles	4000

Motor Vehicles			
	$		$
Apr 2 Bank	2000		
Apr 10 Bank	4000		

Note. As explained in §1.2, an account is a history of all transactions of a similar nature. Therefore, it is not necessary to open another account for the second motor vehicle. Similarly, all purchases of office equipment are posted to Office Equipment account, and all purchases of office furniture are posted to Office Furniture account. You will encounter other examples such as plant and machinery, and fixtures and fittings.

Transaction 8 April 11. Tania lends the business $5000. Abdul pays the money into the business bank account.

Bank			
	$		$
Apr 1 Abdul – Capital	10 000	Apr 2 Motor Vehicles	2000
Apr 4 Sales	800	Apr 3 Purchases	3000
Apr 8 Purchases Returns	100	Apr 7 Sales Returns	40
Apr 11 Tania – Loan	5 000	Apr 10 Motor Vehicles	4000

Tania – Loan			
	$		$
		Apr 11 Bank	5000

Transaction 9 April 12. Abdul pays rent on a warehouse by cheque, $1000.

Bank			
	$		$
Apr 1 Abdul – Capital	10 000	Apr 2 Motor Vehicles	2000
Apr 4 Sales	800	Apr 3 Purchases	3000
Apr 8 Purchases Returns	100	Apr 7 Sales Returns	40
Apr 11 Tania – Loan	5 000	Apr 10 Motor Vehicles	4000
		Apr 12 Rent Payable	1000

Rent Payable			
	$		$
Apr 12 Bank	1 000		

Transaction 10 April 14. Abdul sublets part of the warehouse and receives a cheque for $300 for the rent. This is paid into the bank.

Bank			
	$		$
Apr 1 Abdul – Capital	10 000	Apr 2 Motor Vehicles	2000
Apr 4 Sales	800	Apr 3 Purchases	3000
Apr 8 Purchases Returns	100	Apr 7 Sales Returns	40
Apr 11 Tania – Loan	5 000	Apr 10 Motor Vehicles	4000
Apr 14 Rent Receivable	300	Apr 12 Rent Payable	1000

Rent Receivable			
	$		$
		Apr 14 Bank	300

Note. Rent receivable is not posted to the Rent Payable account. It is important to keep income and expenditure in separate accounts.

Transaction 11 April 15. Abdul pays wages by cheque, $1200.

Bank			
	$		$
Apr 1 Abdul – Capital	10 000	Apr 2 Motor Vehicles	2000
Apr 4 Sales	800	Apr 3 Purchases	3000
Apr 8 Purchases Returns	100	Apr 7 Sales Returns	40
Apr 11 Tania – Loan	5 000	Apr 10 Motor Vehicles	4000
Apr 14 Rent Receivable	300	Apr 12 Rent Payable	1000
		Apr 15 Wages	1200

Wages			
	$		$
Apr 15 Bank	1 200		

Transaction 12 April 16. Abdul withdraws $600 from the business Bank account for personal use.

Bank				
	$			$
Apr 1 Abdul – Capital	10 000	Apr 2	Motor Vehicles	2000
Apr 4 Sales	800	Apr 3	Purchases	3000
Apr 8 Purchases Returns	100	Apr 7	Sales Returns	40
Apr 11 Tania – Loan	5 000	Apr 10	Motor Vehicles	4000
Apr 14 Rent Receivable	300	Apr 12	Rent Payable	1000
		Apr 15	Wages	1200
		Apr 16	Drawings	600

Drawings			
	$		$
Apr 16 Bank	600		

Note. Money drawn out of a business by the owner for personal use is debited to a Drawings account, not to the owner's Capital account.

EXERCISE 1

Open the necessary ledger accounts and post the following transactions to them. All transactions took place in the bank account.

May 1 Martine started business as a florist by paying $300 into a business Bank account.
   2 Charline lent the business $1000.
      Martine then had the following transactions.
   3 Paid rent, $100.
   4 Purchased shop fittings, $400.
      Purchased flowers $300, paying by cheque.
   5 Received refund of $20 for flowers returned to supplier.
   6 Sold some flowers and received $40.
   7 Paid wages, $60.
   8 Withdrew $100 for personal use.

EXERCISE 2

Complete the entries for the following table. The first item has been done for you.

	Debit account	Credit account
1. Noel pays a cheque into his business Bank account as capital	Bank	Noel – Capital
2. Purchases some goods for resale and pays by cheque		
3. Sells some goods and banks the takings		
4. Pays rent by cheque		
5. Purchases shop fittings and pays by cheque		
6. Cashes cheque for personal expenses		
7. Pays wages by cheque		
8. Returns goods to supplier and banks refund		
9. Receives rent from tenant and banks cheque		
10. Refunds money to customer by cheque for goods returned		
11. Motor vehicle purchased and paid for by cheque		
12. Pays for petrol for motor vehicle and pays by cheque		

HINTS

- All transactions are recorded from the point of view of the business, not from those of its customers and suppliers.
- When recording transactions, think very carefully about which account 'gives' and which account 'receives'. Credit the account that 'gives' and debit the account that 'receives'.
- Make sure you complete the double entry for every transaction before starting to record the next one.
- Date every entry and enter the name of the other account in which the double entry is completed in the details column.
- If you make a mistake in an exercise, study the answer given at the end of the book and make sure you understand what you should have done *and why*.
- The golden rule is that for every debit entry there must be an equal credit entry.

MULTIPLE-CHOICE QUESTIONS

1. Joel occupies part of Natasha's business premises. Which entries in Natasha's books record the rent Joel pays her by cheque?

	Debit account	Credit account
A.	Bank	Rent Payable
B.	Bank	Rent Receivable
C.	Rent Payable	Bank
D.	Rent Receivable	Bank

2. Yasmina purchased some office equipment for use in her business. The equipment was faulty and she returned it to the supplier who refunded the cost to Yasmina.
Which entries in Yasmina's books record the return of the equipment?

	Debit account	Credit account
A.	Bank	Purchases Returns
B.	Bank	Office Equipment
C.	Purchase Returns	Bank
D.	Office Equipment	Bank

3. A trader withdraws money from his business Bank account for personal expenses.
Which entries record this in his books?

	Debit account	Credit account
A.	Bank	Capital
B.	Bank	Drawings
C.	Capital	Bank
D.	Drawings	Bank

4. A trader returns goods to the supplier and receives a refund.
Which entries record the refund in the trader's books?

	Debit account	Credit account
A.	Bank	Purchases
B.	Bank	Purchases Returns
C.	Purchases	Bank
D.	Purchases Returns	Bank

ADDITIONAL EXERCISES

1. Open the necessary ledger accounts and post the following transactions to them.

June 1 Farook commenced business by paying $15 000 into his business Bank account.
Amna lent the business $5000.
Farook then had the following business transactions.
2 Purchased premises and paid $8000.
3 Bought office furniture for $2000 and paid by cheque.
4 Paid $5000 by cheque for goods for re-sale.
5 Sold some goods for $1500 and banked the proceeds.
6 Paid insurance premium by cheque, $600.
7 Bought motor van and paid $3000 by cheque.
8 Drew cheque for $50 to pay for petrol for motor van.
9 Bought some goods costing $2000 for re-sale and paid by cheque.
10 Sold goods for $2400 and banked the proceeds. Drew cheque for wages, $400.
11 Repaid $1200 by cheque to customers for goods returned.
12 Received a refund of $900 from suppliers for goods returned.
13 Received a refund of insurance of $100.
Withdrew $200 from business Bank account for personal expenses.
14 Returned some office furniture that was damaged and received a refund of $800.
15 Repaid $1000 of the loan from Amna.

2. Complete the entries for the following table with information taken from the accounts of a trader.

	Debit account	Credit account
1. Local taxes paid by cheque		
2. Bank pays interest to trader		
3. Sundry expenses paid by cheque		
4. Postage and stationery paid by cheque		
5. Telephone bill paid by cheque		
6. Carriage inwards* paid by cheque		
7. Carriage outwards** paid by cheque		
8. Interest paid by cheque to brother in respect of a loan received from him		
9. Interest paid to bank		

* Carriage inwards is the delivery cost of bringing the goods from the supplier to the buyer.
** Carriage outwards is the cost of delivering goods to a customer.

2 Double-entry bookkeeping: credit transactions

In this chapter you will learn:

- how to record transactions which do not involve immediate cash payments in ledger accounts
- the difference between trade and cash discounts and how to treat them.

2.1 What are credit transactions?

Many transactions take place without any money being paid or received at the time. For example, Lai sells goods to Chin for $500 on 31 May and gives Chin until 30 June to pay. The transaction is 'on credit'. The sale has taken place on 31 May and must be recorded in the books of both Lai and Chin at that date. No entries to record payment are made in their books until Chin pays Lai.

2.2 How to record credit transactions

In a seller's books A sale on credit is credited to Sales account and debited to an account opened in the name of the customer. When the customer pays, his or her account is credited, and the Bank account debited.

In a customer's books A purchase on credit is debited to Purchases account and credited to an account opened in the name of the supplier. When the supplier is paid, his or her account is debited, and the Bank account credited.

Example

Lai sells goods to Chin for $500 on 31 May and gives Chin until 30 June to pay.

In Lai's books Credit the sale to Sales account and debit it to an account for Chin.

Sales			
	$		$
		May 31 Chin	500

Chin			
	$		$
May 31 Sales	500		

The debit entry in Chin's account shows that he is a **debtor** in Lai's books; that is, Chin owes Lai $500 until he pays for the goods.

In Chin's books Debit the purchase to Purchases account and credit it to an account for Lai.

Purchases			
	$		$
May 31 Lai	500		

Lai			
	$		$
		May 31 Purchases	500

The credit entry in Lai's account shows that he is a **creditor** in Chin's books.

Goods returned

On 4 June Chin returns some of the goods costing $100 to Lai because they are damaged.

In Lai's books Credit Chin's account and debit Sales Returns account.

Chin

	$			$
May 31 Sales	500	Jun 4	Sales Returns	100

Sales Returns

	$		$
Jun 4 Chin	100		

In Chin's books Debit Lai's account and credit Purchases Returns account.

Lai

	$		$
Jun 31 Purchases Returns	500	May 31 Purchases	500

Purchases Returns

	$		$
		Jun 4 Lai	100

2.3 How to record payments for goods bought or sold on credit

Trade discount

Trade discount is an allowance made by one trader to another. In the above example, the goods which Lai sold to Chin may have been sold normally for $625. Lai knows that Chin, also a trader, must make a profit on the goods when he sells them. He has allowed Chin a **trade discount** of $125 (20% of $625) so that if Chin sell the goods for $625 he will make a profit of $125.

Note. Although the normal price of the goods was $625, the transaction was for $500 only, and only $500 is entered into the books of both Lai and Chin. Trade discount is *never* recorded in ledger accounts.

Cash (or settlement) discount

Lai has given Chin one month to pay for the goods. To encourage Chin to pay by 30 June, Lai may allow Chin to pay less than the amount due. This allowance is a cash (or settlement) discount. (Notice the difference between cash discount and trade discount: trade discount is not dependent on payment being made promptly, or even at all.)

Note. Cash discounts are *always* recorded in ledger accounts.

Suppose Lai has allowed Chin a cash discount of 5% provided Chin pays by 30 June, and Chin pays Lai on 28 June. Chin owes Lai $400 ($500 − $100), 5% of $400 = $20. He will, therefore, pay only $380.

In Lai's books Debit the discount to Discounts Allowed account.

Chin

	$		$
May 31 Sales	500	Jun 4 Sales Returns	100
		Jun 28 Bank	380
		Jun 28 Discounts Allowed	20

Bank

	$		$
Jun 28 Chin	380		

Discounts Allowed

	$		$
Jun 28 Chin	20		

In Chin's books Credit the discount to Discounts Received account

Lai

	$		$
Jun 4 Purchases Returns	100	May 31 Purchases	500
Jun 28 Bank	380		
Jun 28 Discounts Received	20		

Bank

	$		$
		Jun 28 Lai	380

Discounts Received

	$		$
		Jun 28 Lai	20

Example

Andrew had the following transactions in May.

May 1 Purchased goods from David. The goods cost $1000 less 10% trade discount.

2 Purchased goods from Rodney for $1600 less 15% trade discount.

3 Purchased a computer for the office on credit from Bernard for $2000.

4 Sold goods to Mario for $800.

5 Returned goods which had cost $100 after trade discount to David.

6 Purchased goods from Ludovic for $700 less trade discount at 20%.

7 Sold goods to Ravin for $500.

8 Mario returned goods which had been sold to him for $40.

9 Received cheque from Ravin for amount owing, less cash discount of 5%.

10 Paid amount owing to David, less cash discount of 5%.

11 Paid amount owing to Rodney, less cash discount of 5%. Paid Bernard for computer.

12 Received cheque from Mario for amount owing, less 5% cash discount.

   Paid amount owing to Ludovic, less 5% cash discount.

These transactions are recorded as follows:

David

	$		$
May 5 Purchases Returns	100	May 1 Purchases	900
May 10 Bank	760		
May 10 Discounts Received	40		

Rodney

	$		$
May 11 Bank	1292	May 2 Purchases	1360
May 11 Discounts Received	68		

Bernard

	$		$
May 11 Bank	2000	May 3 Office Computer	2000

Ludovic

	$		$
May 12 Bank	532	May 6 Purchases	560
May 12 Discounts Received	28		

Mario

	$		$
May 4 Sales	800	May 8 Sales Returns	40
		May 12 Bank	722
		May 12 Discounts Allowed	38

Ravin

	$		$
May 7 Sales	500	May 9 Bank	475
		May 9 Discounts Allowed	25

Purchases

	$		$
May 1 David	900		
May 2 Rodney	1360		
May 6 Ludovic	560		

Purchases Returns

	$		$
		May 5 David	100

Sales

	$		$
		May 4 Mario	800
		May 7 Ravin	500

Sales Returns

	$		$
May 8 Mario	40		

Discounts Allowed

	$		$
May 9 Ravin	25		
May 12 Mario	38		

Discount Received

	$		$
		May 10 David	40
		May 11 Rodney	68
		May 12 Ludovic	28

Office Computer

	$		$
May 3 Bernard	2000		

Bank

	$		$
May 9 Ravin	475	May 10 David	760
May 12 Mario	722	May 11 Rodney	1292
		May 11 Bernard	2000
		May 12 Ludovic	532

Calculations

Purchases:	Amount before trade discount	Trade discount	Cost to Andrew
	$	$	$
From: David	1000	(10%) 100	900
Rodney	1600	(15%) 240	1360
Ludovic	700	(20%) 140	560

Cash settlements:	Amount before cash discount	Cash discount (5%)	Amount paid
	$	$	$
By: Ravin	500	25	475
Mario	760	38	722

EXERCISE 1

Post the following transactions in the books of Geraud.

June 1 Purchased goods from Khor which cost $3000 less trade discount of 10%.
5 Sold goods to Lai for $600.
10 Returned goods which had cost Geraud $200 to Khor.
15 Purchased goods from Lim which cost $2800 before trade discount of 10%.
20 Sold goods to Chin for $1300.
25 Lai returned goods which had cost him $200.
30 Geraud paid Khor and Lim the amounts due to them after deducting 5% cash discount.
Lai and Chin paid Geraud the amounts they owed him after deducting 5% cash discount.

HINTS

- Remember to record all transactions from the point of view of the business, not from those of its customers and suppliers.
- Where trade discounts are given, record all amounts net of trade discount.
- Note carefully whether cash discount is to be deducted from settlements.
- Remember to complete the entries for cash discounts to the correct Discount accounts.
- Be accurate in all your calculations.

MULTIPLE-CHOICE QUESTIONS

1. Davina bought goods on credit from Sharon for $600 less trade discount of $120.
Which entries record this transaction in Davina's books?

	Account to be debited	Account to be credited
A.	Purchases $480	Sharon $480
B.	Purchases $480	Sharon $600
	Discounts Allowed $120	
C.	Purchases $600	Sharon $600
D.	Purchases $600	Sharon $480
		Discounts Received $120

2. Kristal bought goods on credit from Prisca. The goods had a list price of $1000 but Prisca allowed

Kristal trade discount of 10% and cash discount of 4%.

How much did Kristal have to pay Prisca?

A. $860   **B.** $864   **C.** $900   **D.** $960

3. Shirley bought goods from Corrine. The goods had a list price of $800. Corrine allowed Shirley trade discount of 20% and cash discount of 5%.
In Corrine's books, which entries record the cheque she received from Shirley?

	Account to be debited	Account to be credited
A.	Bank $608 Discounts Allowed $32	Shirley $640
B.	Bank $608 Discounts Received $32	Shirley $640
C.	Bank $608 Discounts Allowed $152	Shirley $760
D.	Bank $608 Discounts Received $152	Shirley $760

ADDITIONAL EXERCISES

1. Fleming had the following transactions.

July 1 Purchased goods from Adams for $5000 less trade discount of 15%. Adams allowed Fleming 4% cash discount.
4 Purchased goods from Bond for $2500 less trade discount of 10%. Bond allowed Fleming 4% cash discount.
5 Returned goods which had cost $600 to Adams.
7 Purchased goods from Astle for $7000 less trade discount of 20%. Astle allowed Fleming 5% cash discount.
9 Returned goods which had cost $800 to Astle.
10 Purchased goods from Cairns for $4200 less 10% trade discount. Cairns allowed Fleming 5% cash discount.
14 Fleming settled all accounts owing to his suppliers by cheque, taking advantage of the cash discount in each case.

Required

Post the transactions listed above in Fleming's books in good form.

2. Streak had the following transactions in March.

Mar 1 Sold goods to Blignaut for $2500 less trade discount of 10%, and allowed him cash discount of 4%.
4 Sold goods to Ebrahim for $4000 less trade discount of 15%, and allowed him cash discount of 5%.
6 Ebrahim returned goods which had cost him $200.
8 Sold goods to Friend for $3200 less trade discount of 20%, and allowed him cash discount of 5%.
12 Sold goods to Flower for $2000 less trade discount of 10%, and allowed him cash discount of 4%.
14 Flower returned goods which had cost him $350.
15 Blignaut, Ebrahim, Friend and Flower settled their accounts by cheque, each taking advantage of cash discount.

Required

Post the transactions listed above in Streak's books in good form.

3 Books of prime (or original) entry

In this chapter you will learn:

- the purpose of books of prime entry
- how to enter transactions in books of prime entry
- how to post transactions from the books of prime entry to ledger accounts.

3.1 What is a book of prime entry?

A **book of prime entry** is used to list all transactions of a similar kind *before* they are posted to ledger accounts. They are sometimes known as books of first (or original) entry but for convenience they will be referred to as books of prime entry in this text. Because they list transactions before they are posted to ledger accounts they are *outside* the double-entry model. *It is important to remember that they are not part of double-entry bookkeeping.* There is, however, one exception to this rule, and that is the cash book, as explained later in §3.4.

The names of the books of prime entry and their uses are:

Book of prime entry	Use
Sales journal (or sales day book)	To record all sales made on credit. The entries are made from copies of invoices sent to customers.
Sales returns book (or sales returns journal, or returns inwards journal)	To record all goods returned from customers. When customers return goods that were bought on credit they are sent credit notes showing the amount credited to their account for the returns. The sales returns book is prepared from the copies of credit notes sent to customers.
Purchases journal (or purchases day book)	To record all purchases of stock in trade (goods for resale) made on credit. These are entered in the purchases journal from suppliers' invoices.
Purchases returns journal (or purchases	To record all goods returned to suppliers. The purchases returns journal is

Book of prime entry	Use
returns book, or returns outwards journal)	prepared from credit notes received from suppliers.
Cash book	To record all cash and bank transactions. (But see §3.4)
Journal (or general journal)	To record all transactions for which there is no other book of prime entry. (Also see HINTS.)

3.2 How to write up books of prime entry

Example

Jayasuriya has sent and received the following invoices and credit notes.

Invoices sent to customers		Amount of invoice $
May 1	Atapattu	2350
May 4	de Silva	1746
May 6	Arnold	520

Credit notes sent to customers		Amount of credit note $
May 3	Atapattu	350
May 5	de Silva	146
May 7	Arnold	60

Invoices received from suppliers		Amount of invoice $
May 2	Vaas	5000
May 5	Fernando	3600
May 7	Mubarak	2200

Credit notes received from suppliers		Amount of credit note $
May 6	Vaas	1000
May 7	Fernando	600

The transactions will be entered in the books of prime entry as follows:

Sales journal		$	Sales Returns journal		$
May 1	Atapattu	2350	May 3	Atapattu	350
May 4	de Silva	1746	May 5	de Silva	146
May 6	Arnold	520	May 7	Arnold	60
		4616			556

Purchases journal		$	Purchases returns journal		$
May 2	Vaas	5 000	May 6	Vaas	1000
May 5	Fernando	3 600	May 7	Fernando	600
May 7	Mubarak	2 200			1600
		10 800			

3.3 How to post from books of prime entry to ledger accounts

Example

Use the information in the books of prime entry in §3.2.

Step 1. Post each item in the books of prime entry to the supplier's or customer's account in the ledger following the procedure already learned in chapter 2, but do *not* post the individual items to the Purchases, Purchases Returns, Sales or Sales Returns accounts.

Atapattu					
		$			$
May 1	Sales	2350	May 3	Sales Returns	350

de Silva					
		$			$
May 4	Sales	1746	May 5	Sales Returns	146

Arnold					
		$			$
May 6	Sales	520	May 7	Sales Returns	60

Vaas					
		$			$
May 6	Purchases Returns	1000	May 2	Purchases	5000

Fernando					
		$			$
May 7	Purchases Returns	600	May 5	Purchases	3600

Mubarak				
	$			$
		May 7	Purchases	2200

Step 2. Post the *total* of each book of prime entry to the Sales, Sales Returns, Purchases or Purchases Returns accounts, as appropriate.

Sales				
	$			$
		May 7	Sales journal total	4616

Sales Returns				
		$		$
May 7	Sales returns journal total	556		

Purchases				
		$		$
May 7	Purchases journal total	10 800		

Purchases Returns				
	$			$
		May 7	Purchases returns journal total	1600

3.4 The cash book

A **cash book** is the book of prime entry for all cash and bank transactions; but we have already seen in chapter 1 that it is also an account. It is the only book of prime entry that is also part of the double-entry model.

The cash book is also used as the book of prime entry for cash discounts. A column is provided on the debit side of the Bank account to record discounts allowed, and a column on the credit side to record discounts received.

Bank					
Discounts (allowed)	Bank			Discounts (received)	Bank
$	$			$	$

The words 'allowed' and 'received' are sometimes omitted because bookkeepers know which is which.

3.5 How to enter discounts in the cash book

When a payment is received from a customer who has deducted cash discount, enter the amount of the discount in the discounts allowed column next to the amount received in the bank column.

Enter discounts received from suppliers in the discounts received column next to the amount paid in the bank column.

Example

All payments due from customers and all payments to suppliers in §3.2 were settled on 7 May. In each case, cash discount of 5% was allowed or received.

Bank

	Discounts (allowed) $	Bank $			Discounts (received) $	Bank $
May 7 Attapattu	100	1900	May 7 Vaas		200	3800
May 7 de Silva	80	1520	May 7 Fernando		150	2850
May 7 Arnold	23	437	May 7 Mubarak		110	2090
	203				460	

Atapattu

	$			$
May 1 Sales	2350	May 3	Sales Returns	350
		May 7	Bank	1900
		May 7	Discounts Allowed	100

de Silva

	$			$
May 4 Sales	1746	May 5	Sales Returns	146
		May 7	Bank	1520
		May 7	Discounts Allowed	80

Arnold

	$			$
May 6 Sales	520	May 7	Sales Returns	60
		May 7	Bank	437
		May 7	Discounts Allowed	23

Vaas

	$			$
May 6 Purchases Returns	1000	May 2	Purchases	5000
May 7 Bank	3800			
May 7 Discounts Received	200			

Fernando

	$			$
May 7 Purchases Returns	600	May 5	Purchases	3600
May 7 Bank	2850			
May 7 Discounts Received	150			

Mubarak

	$			$
May 7 Bank	2090	May 7	Purchases	2200
May 7 Discounts Received	110			

3.6 How to post discounts from the cash book to the Discounts Allowed and Discounts Received accounts

The periodic totals of the discount allowed column in the cash book are posted to the **debit** of the Discounts Allowed account; the periodic totals of the discounts received column are posted to the **credit** of the Discounts Received account. The discount columns in the cash book are not part of the double-entry model.

Discounts Allowed

	$		$
May 7 Cash book total	203		

Discounts Received

	$		$
		May 7 Cash book total	460

Exercise 1

Murgatroyd had the following transactions, all on credit, in March.

March 1	Purchased goods from Tikolo for $10 000 less trade discount of 20%. Tikolo allowed him 5% cash discount.
4	Sold goods to Snyman for $1200 less trade discount of 10%. He allowed Snyman 4% cash discount.
6	Purchased goods from Walters for $8000 less trade discount of 10%. Walters allowed Murgatroyd 5% cash discount.
10	Sold goods to Karg for $2500 less trade discount of 10%. He allowed Karg 4% cash discount.
11	Snyman returned goods which had cost him $200.
12	Returned goods which had cost $400 to Tikolo.
13	Purchased goods from Burger for $7000 less trade discount of 25%. Burger allowed him cash discount of 4%.
17	Sold goods to Kotze for $3000 less trade discount of 10%. He allowed Kotze 5% cash discount.
18	Purchased goods from Tikolo for $6000 less trade discount of 20%. Tikolo allowed him 5% cash discount.
20	Karg returned goods which had cost him $300.
22	Returned to Burger goods which had cost $1000.
25	Sold goods to Snyman for $1800 less trade discount of 10%. Murgatroyd allowed Snyman 5% cash discount.
31	Received cheques from Snyman, Karg and Kotze respectively in full settlement of their accounts, and sent cheques in full settlement of their accounts to Tikolo, Walters and Burger.

Required

Enter the transactions for March in Murgatroyd's books of prime entry and post them in good form to the proper accounts.

3.7 Three-column cash book

Most businesses receive cash that they do not bank and pay some of their expenses out of the unbanked cash. An account for this cash is kept in the cash book. It is usually found convenient to have columns for cash next to those for the Bank account for cash receipts and payments. The account is then a combined Bank and Cash account.

Bank and Cash						
Disc $	Cash $	Bank $		Disc $	Cash $	Bank $

3.8 How to write up a three-column cash book

The cash columns are entered in exactly the same way as the bank columns, cash received being debited, and cash payments credited, in the cash columns. When cash is banked, the cash column must be credited and the bank column debited with the amount. When cash is drawn from the bank, the bank column must be credited and the cash column must be debited.

Example

On 1 May Cassius received $700 in cash from a customer. On 3 May he paid sundry expenses of $40 out of cash. On 4 May his takings were $2000. On 5 May he banked $1500 cash.

On 7 May he paid cash, $70, on sundry items. On May 8 he withdrew $500 from the bank to pay wages.

Bank and Cash						
	Disc $	Cash $	Bank $		Disc $	Cash $	Bank $
May 1 Sales		700		May 3 Sundry exps.		40	
May 4 Sales		2000		May 5 Bank ¢		1500	
May 5 Cash ¢			1500	May 7 Sundry exps.		70	
May 8 Bank ¢		500		May 8 Cash ¢			500
				May 8 Wages		500	

Note. ¢ is an abbreviation for 'contra', indicating that the double entry is completed on the opposite sides of the Bank and Cash accounts.

Exercise 2

Enter the following transactions in Joshua's three-column cash book.

March 1	Received takings from cash sales, $1100.
2	Paid electricity in cash, $130.
3	Received takings from cash sales, $900.
4	Banked cash, $1700.
5	Paid sundry expenses in cash, $25.
6	Drew $800 from bank for the office cash float.
7	Paid for stock by cash, $750.

3.9 The journal

All transactions should be recorded in one of the books of prime entry before being posted to ledger accounts. The journal is the book of prime entry for transactions for which there is no other book of prime entry. Items which will require entries in the journal are

- corrections of posting errors
- adjustments to accounts (which are dealt with later)
- transfers between accounts
- purchase and sale of items other than stock-in-trade (e.g. machinery, delivery vans, etc. used in the business) on credit
- opening entries in a new set of ledgers (e.g. when there is no more room in the existing ledgers and the balances on the accounts are transferred to new ledgers or to make the opening entries at the start of a new accounting period).

Each journal entry shows the account to be debited, and the account to be credited. It follows that the debits should always equal the credits. The journal is ruled as follows:

Date	Accounts	Dr*	Cr*

*Dr is short for debit and Cr is short for credit.

3.10 How to make journal entries

Always state the account to be debited before the one to be credited. Every entry should have a brief but informative explanation of the reason for the entry; this is called the **narrative**.

Example

1. Jonah discovered that he had credited $100 that he had received from A. Burger on 1 April to an account for L. Burger in error. The journal entry to correct the error will be:

Date	Accounts	Dr	Cr
		$	$
April 1	L. Burger	100	
	A. Burger		100

Correction of an error. A remittance from A. Burger on this date was posted incorrectly to L. Burger's account.

2. On 4 May Jonah bought office furniture from A. Whale on credit for $400.

Date	Accounts	Dr	Cr
		$	$
May 4	Office Furniture	400	
	A. Whale		400

Purchase of office furniture from A. Whale. See A. Whale's invoice no. 123 dated 4 May.

Note. The narrative gives Jonah the information he needs to enable him to check on the details later if needs be.

3. On 13 May Jonah bought a delivery van for $3000 and paid by cheque.

   (The book of prime entry for this cash transaction is the cash book but, by also entering the purchase in the journal, Jonah will be able to see more detail about this important item than if he had entered it in the cash book only.)

Date	Accounts	Dr	Cr
		$	$
May 13	Delivery Van account	3000	
	Bank		3000

Purchase of delivery van, registration no. G1234PYD. See Wheeler's invoice no. 6789 dated 13 May.

Exercise 3

Prepare journal entries in proper form to correct the following.

1. Credit note no. 964, for $120, received from A & Co., a supplier, has been posted to A. Cotter's account in error.
2. Invoice no. 104, for $400, received from Hussain, a supplier, has not been entered in the purchases journal.
3. Invoice no. 6789, for $150, sent to Maya, a customer, has been entered in the sales journal as $105.
4. The purchase of a machine for use in the business, and costing $2300, has been debited to Purchases account in error.
5. Credit note no. 23, for $68, sent to Hanife, a customer, has been omitted from the sales returns journal.

HINTS

- Remember that books of prime entry, *except the cash book,* are not part of the double-entry model.
- Recognise the correct book of prime entry for every transaction you record in ledger accounts.
- Enter invoices *net of trade discount* in the books of prime entry.
- Post the periodic totals of the sales journal, sales returns journal, purchases journal and purchases returns journal to the Sales, Sales Returns, Purchases and Purchases Returns accounts respectively.
- Remember that the discount columns in the cash book are memorandum columns only and not part of the double-entry model.
- Prepare cash books in columnar form if possible. (See §3.8.)
- Show the debit entry before the credit entry in the journal.
- Add a suitable narrative with proper detail to every entry in the journal.
- Prepare journal entries only to ledger accounts, *never to other books of prime entry.*

MULTIPLE-CHOICE QUESTIONS

1. Tania purchased goods for $1000 less 25% trade discount. She was allowed cash discount of 10%. Which amount should she enter in her purchases journal?

   A. $650   B. $675   C. $750   D. $1000

2. Lara purchased goods costing $1800 less trade discount of 30%. He was allowed cash discount of 5%.
   How much should Lara have to pay for the goods?

   A. $1080   B. $1197   C. $1260   D. $1800

3. Cora sent an invoice to Maria for $2000 less 20% trade discount. Cora has omitted to enter the invoice in her sales journal.

   What effect will this have on her accounts?

	Maria's account		Sales account	
	Debit	Credit	Debit	Credit
A		understated $1600	understated $1600	

	Debit	Credit	Debit	Credit
B	understated $1600			understated $1600
C		understated $2000	understated $2000	
D	understated $2000			understated $2000

4. Cheung has received a cheque for $1540 from Raju in full settlement of a debt of $1700.
   How should this be recorded in Cheung's books of account?

	Debit	$	Credit	$
A	Bank	1540	Raju	1540
B	Bank	1700	Raju	1700
C	Bank	1540	Raju	1700
	Discounts Allowed	160		
D	Bank	2000	Raju	1540
			Discounts Received	160

ADDITIONAL EXERCISES

1. Adeel's transactions for the month of April were as follows:

   April 1 Bought goods from Bilal for $3000 less 20% trade discount. Bilal allowed Adeel 5% cash discount.
   2 Sold goods to Imran for $800 less 10% trade discount. He allowed Imran 5% cash discount.
   3 Bought goods from Asad for $1300 less 20% trade discount. Asad allowed Adeel 5% cash discount.
   5 Purchased a delivery van on credit from Syed for $6000. The invoice for the van was no. 324.
   8 Returned goods which had cost $100 to Bilal.
   10 Sold goods to Raza for $1100 less 20% trade discount. He allowed Raza 5% cash discount.
   13 Imran returned goods which had cost him $60.
   15 Purchased goods from Asma for $4000 less 25% trade discount. Asma allowed Adeel 5% cash discount.
   16 Sold goods to Amna for $1500 less 20% trade discount. He allowed Amna 5% cash discount.
   17 Sold goods to Raza for $1600 less 20% trade discount. He allowed Raza 5% cash discount.
   21 Returned goods which had cost him $600 to Asma.
   24 Amna returned goods which had cost her $300.
   26 Purchased goods from Bilal for $4000 less 20% trade discount. Bilal allowed Adeel 5% cash discount.
   30 Adeel settled all accounts he owed by cheque, and received cheques for all amounts owing by his customers. All discounts were taken.

   Required
   (a) Enter all the transactions for April into the books of prime entry.
   (b) Post the books of prime entry to the ledger accounts.

2. Prepare journal entries with suitable narratives to record the following:
   (a) Received from Mumtaz invoice no. 506 dated 3 March for $10 000. This was in respect of the purchase of a machine on credit.
   (b) Invoice no. 495 dated 6 March for $675 for goods sold to Wayne. The invoice has been entered twice in the sales journal.
   (c) Invoice no. 998 dated 7 March for $4250 in respect of a delivery van purchased from Younas and paid for by cheque.
   (d) Credit not no. 103 dated 10 March for $190 sent to Browne but omitted from the sales returns journal.
   (e) Invoice no. 854 dated 15 March for $1300 for goods purchased from Sandra. The invoice has been posted to Geeta's account in error.

4 Balancing accounts

In this chapter you will learn:

- how to find and record a balance on a ledger account
- what debit balances and credit balances mean.

4.1 Why accounts need to be balanced

The cash book must be balanced periodically to find how much money is left in the bank account or how much cash the business has left. Similarly, the ledger accounts are balanced to find how much the business owes other people, how much it is owed, and how much has been received from, or spent on, the various activities.

4.2 How to balance an account

Add each side of the account to find which has the lesser total. Insert on that side the amount needed to make both sides equal, or, in other words, balance. Insert the total on each side of the account and carry the balance down to the other side of the account on the next day.

Example 1

Bank					
		$			$
Apr 1	Abdul – Capital	10 000	Apr 2	Motor Vehicles	2 000
Apr 4	Sales	800	Apr 13	Purchases	3 000
Apr 8	Purchases Returns	100	Apr 7	Sales Returns	40
Apr 11	Tania – Loan	5 000	Apr 10	Motor Vehicles	4 000
Apr 14	Rent Receivable	300	Apr 12	Rent Payable	1 000
			Apr 15	Wages	1 200
			Apr 16	Drawings	600
			Apr 10	Balance carried down	4 360
		16 200			16 200
Apr 11	Balance brought down	4 360			

Notes

- The account has been balanced at 10 April.
- The balance was entered on the credit side to make it balance with the debit side, and carried down to the debit side on the next day.
- The account has a *debit balance* showing how much money is left in the Bank account on 10 April.
- The totals are placed level with each other although there are more items on the credit side than on the debit side.

Example 2

Charley is a customer whose account has been balanced and is as follows:

Charley					
		$			$
Jun 4	Sales	1040	Jun 6	Sales Returns	400
Jun 10	Sales	3105	Jun 14	Bank	600
Jun 19	Sales	900	Jun 14	Discount	40
			Jun 30	Balance c/d	4005
		5045			5045
Jul 1	Balance b/d	4005			

Notes

- Charley's account has a debit balance which shows that he owes the business $4005; he is a 'debtor' of the business.
- c/d is short for 'carried down' and b/d is short for 'brought down'. These abbreviations are quite acceptable in accounting.
- The credit entry on 14 June is described simply as 'discount' because it is understood that it is discount allowed.

Example 3

Sara (who supplies goods to the business)					
		$			$
May 8 Purchases Returns	1000	May 1	Balance	b/d	1940
May 29 Bank	2005	May 12	Purchases		7330
May 29 Discount	125				
May 31 Balance c/d	6140				
	9270				9270
		June 1	Balance	b/d	6140

Notes
- The credit balance shows that Sara is owed $6140; she is a creditor of the business.
- When Sara's account was balanced on the previous 30 April, a balance of $1940 was carried down and appears as an opening credit balance on her account at 1 May.

If an account has only one entry on each side and they are of equal amount, the account is simply ruled off.

Gerald				
	$			$
Mar 4 Sales	1000	Mar 23	Bank	1000

An account with an entry on one side only is balanced without the insertion of totals.

Paula				
	$			$
Mar 31 Balance c/d	1500	Mar 22	Purchases	1500
		Apr 1	Balance b/d	1500

A three-column cash book is balanced as follows:

Bank and Cash									
		Disc	Cash	Bank			Disc	Cash	Bank
		$	$	$			$	$	$
May 1	Sales		700		May 3	Sundry exps.		40	
May 4	Sales		2000		May 5	Bank	¢	1500	
May 5	A & Co.	100		2080	May 6	Z & Sons	50		600
May 5	Cash	¢		1500	May 7	Sundry exps.		70	
May 7	P Ltd	80		450	May 8	Q Bros.	40		160
May 8	Bank	¢	500		May 8	Cash	¢		500
					May 8	Wages		500	
					May 8	Balance	c/d	1090	2770
		180	3200	4030			90	3200	4030
May 9									
Balances		b/d	1090	2770					

Note. The discount columns are not balanced. The totals are carried to the Discounts Allowed and Discounts Received accounts respectively.

4.3 When are accounts balanced?

The cash book will usually be balanced at frequent intervals because it is always important to know how much money is in the Bank account. It will be balanced at weekly intervals in small businesses, daily in large ones.

Accounts for customers and suppliers are balanced monthly because of the practice of sending and receiving statements of account. The statements are copies of the accounts of customers in the sellers' books and are sent to customers so that they can reconcile their ledger accounts with those of their suppliers. Any differences can be enquired into and agreement reached between supplier and customer. The statements also remind customers that payment of outstanding balances is due.

The other accounts are usually balanced as and when required; this will always be when a trial balance is being prepared. Trial balances are explained in chapter 6.

HINTS
- Remember that balances carried down on accounts should always be shown as brought down on the accounts on the next day. Marks may be lost in an examination if this is not done.

5 The classification of accounts and division of the ledger

In this chapter you will learn:

- that accounts are classified as either personal or impersonal
- about the division of impersonal accounts into real accounts and nominal accounts.

5.1 The classification of accounts

All accounts fall into one of two classes: **personal** or **impersonal**. Each of these classes can be further divided into subgroups.

Personal accounts are those for persons (including sole traders, partnerships and companies). The subgroups are as follows:

- **Accounts for debtors**, persons who owe the business money. They are usually the customers of the business, and their accounts have debit balances. These accounts are collectively known as current assets. (Other current assets include cash in hand, cash at bank and stock, as explained below under Impersonal accounts.)
- **Accounts for creditors**, persons to whom the business owes money. They are usually those who supply goods or services to the business, and their accounts have credit balances. This group includes Loan accounts. Creditors who have to be paid within one year are **current liabilities**. Creditors who do not have to be paid within one year (e.g. for a long-term loan) are **long-term liabilities**.
- The owner's **Capital and Drawings accounts**.

Impersonal accounts are all accounts other than personal accounts. The subgroups are as follows:

- **Accounts with debit balances**. These are further divided into asset accounts (real accounts) and expenses accounts (nominal accounts).

- **Asset accounts** (real accounts) are things that the business owns. This group may be further subdivided into
  - **fixed or non-current assets**, which are things acquired for use in the business and not for re-sale, such as premises, plant and machinery, vehicles, office furniture and equipment. These assets are intended to be used in the business for a number of years. Expenditure on fixed assets is **capital expenditure**.
  - **current assets**, in addition to the debtors referred to above, are those that arise in the course of trading, such as stock-in-trade, stocks of stationery, stocks of fuel, cash at bank and in hand.
- **Expenses accounts** (nominal accounts) include rent payable, wages, salaries, heating and lighting, postage and stationery, etc. This type of expenditure is **revenue expenditure**.
- **Accounts with credit balances**. These accounts record **revenue** (sales) and **other income** (rent receivable, discounts received and interest receivable). These are also nominal accounts.

The distinction between the types of accounts is very important. Care must always be taken to ensure that capital expenditure is not confused with revenue expenditure. The cost of purchasing a motor vehicle is capital expenditure and must be debited to the Motor Vehicles account. The cost of running the vehicle is revenue expenditure and must be debited to Motor Vehicles Running Expenses account.

As a result, you will always find capital expenditure on the balance sheet (statement of financial position) of a business (see chapter 8). Revenue expenditure, on the other hand is always found in the Profit and Loss Account (Income Statement) for a business (see chapter 7).

Exercise 1

Copy and complete this table, ticking the boxes which correctly describe the given accounts in the books of a bakery.

Account	Personal	Fixed asset	Current asset	Revenue or other income	Expense
Capital					
Sales Returns					
Delivery Vans					
Purchases					
Rent Payable					
Debtors					
Stock-in-trade					
Discounts Allowed					
Drawings					
Bank					
Rent Receivable					
Creditors					
Computer					
Wages					
Discounts Received					

5.2 Division of the ledger

Except in very small businesses there are too many accounts to be kept in a single ledger. It is usual to divide the accounts among several ledgers as follows:

- sales ledger for the accounts of customers
- purchase ledger for the accounts of suppliers
- general (or nominal) ledger for the impersonal accounts for assets, revenue, other income, and expenses
- private ledger for accounts of a confidential nature—the owner's Capital and Drawings accounts and Loan accounts; also the Trading and Profit and Loss Accounts (Income Statements) and Balance Sheets (Statements of Financial Position) (see chapters 7 and 8).
- cash book containing the Bank and Cash accounts.

The division of the ledger as above is essential in a business which employs several bookkeepers; the work may be divided between them so that they do not all need to be working on the same ledger at the same time. It helps to detect and prevent errors occurring in the books of account. It may also help to detect and prevent fraud by the accounts staff. This is known as internal control.

6 The trial balance

In this chapter you will learn:

- the purpose of trial balances
- how to prepare a trial balance
- the limitations of trial balances
- six types of error which do not affect the agreement of the two sides of a trial balance.

6.1 What is a trial balance?

A **trial balance** is a list of all the balances extracted from the ledgers at a particular date. Its purpose is to check that the total of the debit balances equals the total of the credit balances. The principle of double entry ensures that the two totals should agree. If the totals do not agree there must be an error somewhere in the bookkeeping.

6.2 How to prepare a trial balance

First balance all the ledger accounts including the cash book. Then list the balances with the debit balances and credit balances in separate columns. The total of the debit balances should equal the total of the credit balances. If the totals are equal, the trial balance agrees.

Example

The following trial balance has been extracted from the books of Zabine at 31 March 2010.

Account	Debit balances $	Credit balances $
Premises	70 000	
Machinery	10 000	
Office Furniture	5 000	
Sales		100 000
Sales Returns	700	
Purchases	6 900	
Purchases Returns		1 000
Trade receivables*	1 100	
Trade payables*		1 575
Rent Payable	1 600	
Wages and Salaries	4 080	
Heating and Lighting	960	
Sundry Expenses	1 430	
Cash	500	
Bank	12 600	
Loan from Ludmilla		2 000
Capital – Zabine		13 000
Drawings	2 705	
	117 575	117 575

* The balances on the accounts in the sales ledger are listed and totalled separately; the total is entered in the trial balance as trade receivables.

** The balances on the accounts in the purchase ledger are listed and totalled separately; the total is entered in the trial balance as trade payables.

Exercise 1

Prepare a trial balance from the following balances that have been extracted from the books of Achilles, a grocer, at 31 December.

Account	$
Premises	50 000
Motor Vans	8 000
Office Furniture	2 000
Computer	3 000
Sales	60 000
Sales Returns	700
Purchases	4 000
Purchases Returns	500
Motor Vehicle Running Expenses	4 200
Wages	1 800
Rent	2 000
Bank	1 650
Capital	20 000
Drawings	3 150

6.3 Limitations of a trial balance

As stated above, if a trial balance does not agree, there must be a mistake somewhere in the bookkeeping. Unfortunately, even if a trial balance agrees, it does not mean that there are no errors because there are six types of error that do not affect the agreement of the trial balance. They are as follows:

1. **Errors of omission**. A transaction omitted completely from the books results in there being neither debit nor credit entry for the transaction. This could happen if a transaction is not entered in a book of prime entry.

2. **Errors of commission**. A transaction is posted to the wrong account, but the account is of the same class as the account to which the posting should have been made. Example: the payment of a telephone bill is posted in error to Heating and Lighting account. Telephone account and Heating and Lighting account are both expense accounts.

3. **Errors of principle**. A transaction is posted to a wrong account which is not of the same type as the correct account. Example: revenue expenditure treated as capital expenditure. For instance, payment for petrol for a vehicle has been debited to Motor Vehicles account (a fixed asset account) instead of to Motor Vehicles Running Expenses account (an expense account).

4. **Errors of original entry**. A wrong amount is entered in a book of prime entry for a transaction. Example: a sales invoice for $200 is entered in the sales journal as $20.

5. **Complete reversal of entries**. An account which should have been debited has been credited, and the account which should have been credited has been debited. Example: a payment received from Hussain is debited to Hussain's account and credited to Bank account.

6. **Compensating errors**. Two or more errors cancel each other out. Example: an invoice for $1100 in the sales journal is posted to the customer's account as $1000. At the same time, the sales journal total is understated by $100. The debit balance on the customer's account and the credit balance on Sales account will both be understated by $100.

Exercise 2

State which type of error each of the following represents.

(a) Payment of rent has been debited to the Bank account and credited to the Rent Payable account.

(b) The purchase of a computer has been debited to the Office Expenses account.

(c) A supplier's invoice has been omitted from the purchases journal.

(d) The total of Wages account has been overstated by $1000 and rent received of $1000 has been posted twice to the Rent Received account.

(e) Discount allowed to Amna has been credited to Asma's account.

(f) A purchase of goods for $960 has been entered in the purchases journal as $690.

HINTS

- Learn the six types of error which do not affect the trial balance.
- Look for the cause of a difference on a trial balance by carrying out the following simple checks before spending a lot of time checking all your postings:
  - check the additions of the trial balance
  - if the difference is divisible by 2, look for a balance equal to half the difference which may have been entered on the wrong side.
  - if the difference is divisible by 9, two figures may have been transposed in a balance; for example $269 may have been copied as $296.

MULTIPLE-CHOICE QUESTIONS

1. Which of the following accounts normally has a credit balance?
   A. Discounts Allowed
   B. Discounts Received
   C. Purchases
   D. Sales Returns.

2. After which error will a trial balance still balance?
   A. An invoice for $400 in the sales journal not posted to the customer's account in the sales ledger.
   B. A purchase of goods from Ratna for $1000 credited to Ravin's account in the purchases ledger.
   C. Payment of $60 to Josan entered correctly in the Bank account and credited to Josan's account.
   D. Rent paid $660 entered correctly in the cash book but posted to Rent Payable account as $600.

3. A business has paid rent of $800. The payment has been entered in the books as follows:

Account debited	Account credited
Bank $800	Rent $800

   Which type of error is this?
   A. Commission
   B. Compensating
   C. Complete reversal
   D. Principle.

4. Discounts allowed of $160 for one month have been posted to the credit of the Discounts Received account. What effect has this had on the trial balance?
   A. $160 too much credit
   B. $160 too little debit
   C. $160 too little debit and $160 too much credit
   D. $320 too much credit

ADDITIONAL EXERCISES

1. The following balances at 31 December 2010 have been extracted from Hassan's books.

	$
Sales	160 000
Sales Returns	2 600
Purchases	84 000
Purchases Returns	3 400
Wages	26 000
Heating and Lighting	3 160
Rent Payable	5 000
Rent Receivable	1 000
Advertising	2 900
Postage and Telephone	2 740
Discount Allowed	6 100
Discounts Received	5 900
Plant and Machinery	50 000
Delivery Van	9 000
Bank	2 300
Trade Receivables	7 400
Trade Payables	3 700
Drawings	8 800
Capital	?

Required

Prepare a trial balance at 31 December 2010 from the balances extracted from Hassan's books and calculate the balance on his Capital account.

2. An inexperienced bookkeeper has extracted a trial balance at 31 December 2010 from Andrea's books. It contains some errors and does not balance.

	$	$
Premises	70 000	
Plant and Machinery	30 000	
Office Equipment	5 000	
Wages	7 600	
Rent Payable		4 000
Heating and Lighting	1 500	
Sundry Expenses	1 720	
Sales		133 000
Purchases	57 000	
Discounts Allowed		2 450
Discounts Received	1 070	
Bank	2 910	
Trade Receivables	14 000	
Trade Payables		10 140
Purchases Returns	2 400	
Sales Returns		3 150
Rent Receivable	1 200	
Capital		80 000
Drawings		28 480
	194 400	261 220

Required

Re-write the trial balance and correct the errors so that it balances.

Part II
Financial accounting

7 Income Statements for sole traders

In this chapter you will learn:

- how to prepare Income Statements
- what the purpose of the Stock account is.

7.1 What is an Income Statement?

Most people carry on business in order to make a living. They depend upon the profit of the business for their income to enable them to buy food, clothes and other necessities. They compare the revenue earned by the business with its expenses. If the revenue exceeds expenses the business has made a profit. On the other hand, if the expenses exceed the revenue the business has made a loss and the trader has no income. Profit or loss is found by the preparation of an Income Statement covering a period of time, usually one complete year. Until now, double-entry bookkeeping may have seemed a tiresome and largely pointless exercise, but it is the only system that enables the Income Statements to be prepared.

7.2 How to prepare an Income Statement for a sole trader

Step 1

All ledger accounts must be balanced and a trial balance prepared at the date to which the Income Statement is to be prepared.

Example

Andrew commenced business on 1 January 2010. The following trial balance has been extracted at 31 December 2010 from his books.

Account	$	$
Sales		126 000
Sales Returns	2 000	
Purchases	55 200	
Purchases Returns		2 200
Discounts Received		2 340
Discounts Allowed	3 260	
Wages	28 000	
Rent	16 000	
Heating and Lighting	3 400	
Postage and Stationery	1 070	
Motor Van Expenses	9 830	
Interest on Loan	800	
Sundry Expenses	920	
Premises	40 000	
Motor Vans	18 000	
Office Furniture	5 000	
Trade Receivables	7 400	
Trade Payables		3 420
Bank	2 160	
Loan from Marie (repayable in 2012)		10 000
Andrew – Capital		60 000
Drawings	10 920	
	203 960	203 960

Income Statements are part of the double-entry model. Balances on the nominal (revenue, income and expense) accounts are transferred to them by journal entries.

Step 2 Trading section of the Income Statement

The Trading section of the Income Statement calculates the profit on the activity of buying and selling goods. The balances on the Sales, Sales Returns, Purchases and Purchases Returns accounts are *transferred* to the Income Statement by journal entry:

	$	$
Sales	126 000	
Income Statement		126 000
Income Statement	2 000	
Sales Returns		2 000
Income Statement	55 200	
Purchases		55 200
Purchases Returns	2 200	
Income Statement		2 200

(Narratives have been omitted.)

These journal entries produce a Trading section of the Income Statement as follows:

Andrew
Trading section of the Income Statement for the year ended 31 December 2010

	$		$
Sales returns	2 000	Sales	126 000
Purchases	55 200	Purchases returns	2 200

The Trading section of the Income Statement is improved if sales returns are deducted from sales to show the revenue actually earned (called **revenue** or **turnover**). Similarly, it is better to deduct purchases returns from purchases.

Andrew
Trading section of the Income Statement for the year ended 31 December 2010

	$		$
Purchases	55 200	Sales	126 000
Less Purchases returns	2 200	Less Sales returns	2 000
	53 000*		124 000

*$53 000 is the cost of the goods which were available for selling.

Under IAS stock will be referred to as **INVENTORY** when presenting the accounts of a limited company. However, here we will still refer to it as stock in order to show the bookkeeping entries for it in the ledger. In later chapters, the stock of materials the business trades in will only be referred to as inventory.

Closing stock. It is unlikely that Andrew has sold all his stock by 31 December, therefore some remains to be sold next year. This 'closing stock' must be deducted from the cost of the goods that were available for selling in the Trading section of the Income Statement to arrive at the cost of the goods sold. The double entry for this requires a journal entry to open a Stock account.

	$	$
31 December 2010 Stock	5000	
Income Statement		5000
Transfer of closing stock at 31 December 2010 to Income Statement		

Note. The debit to the Stock account creates a new asset that is not in the trial balance.

The closing stock is credited to the Trading section of the Income Statement. This is done by *deducting* it on the debit side from net purchases. The Trading section of the Income Statement now shows the cost of the goods which have been sold. The debit side of the account is therefore headed with the words 'Cost of goods sold' or 'Cost of sales' (in this case $48 000):

Andrew
Trading section of the Income Statement for the year ended 31 December 2010

	$		$
Cost of sales		Sales	126 000
Purchases	55 200	Less Sales returns	2 000
Less Purchases returns	2 200		124 000
	53 000		
Less Closing stock	5 000		
Cost of sales	48 000		
Gross profit	76 000		
	124 000		124 000

Note. The balance on the Trading section of the Income Statement is *gross profit*, or the profit made on buying and selling goods before any other expenses are taken into account.

Step 3

The Profit and Loss section follows the Trading section without a break. The Profit and Loss section begins with the gross profit, to which is added other income, if any. Next, the overhead expenses included in the trial balance are deducted. (The balances on the ledger accounts are transferred to the Income Statement by journal entries.) The Income Statement is now as follows:

Andrew
Income Statement for the year ended 31 December 2010

	$		$
Cost of sales		Sales	126 000
Purchases	55 200	Less Sales returns	2 000
Less Purchases returns	2 200		124 000
	53 000		
Less Closing stock	5 000		
Cost of sales	48 000		
Gross profit	76 000		
	124 000		124 000
Less Overheads		Gross profit brought	
Wages	28 000	down	76 000
Rent	16 000	Discounts received	2 340
Heating and lighting	3 400		78 340
Postage and Stationery	1 070		
Motor van expenses	9 830		
Discounts allowed	3 260		
Sundry expenses	920		
Interest on loan	800		
Net profit	15 060		
	78 340		78 340

Andrew
Income Statement for the year ended 31 December 2010

	$	$
Sales		126 000
Less Sales returns		2 000
		124 000
Less Cost of sales		
Purchases	55 200	
Less Purchases returns	2 200	
	53 000	
Less Stock at 31 December	5 000	48 000
Gross profit		76 000
Add Discount received		2 340
		78 340
Less Overheads		
Wages	28 000	
Rent	16 000	
Heading and lighting	3 400	
Postage and stationery	1 070	
Motor van expenses	9 830	
Discounts allowed	3 260	
Sundry expenses	920	
Loan interest	800	63 280
Net profit		15 060

Income Statements like this have debit and credit sides like ledger accounts and are described as being in *horizontal* form. Many people reading these accounts are not accountants; they know nothing about debits and credits and find the accounts difficult to understand. It is now normal to prepare these accounts in *vertical* forms, which is easier for non-accountants to understand.

Andrew's Income Statement in vertical form is shown on the right.

Notes

- Give the Income Statement a proper heading including the name of the business.
- The account is known as a period statement because it covers a period of time; it must be described as 'for the year (or other period) ended (date) (month) (year)'.
- It is part of the double-entry model and the balances on the accounts are transferred to it by journal entry.
- 'Sales less sales returns' is the **revenue** or **turnover** of the business (in this case $124 000).
- The words 'Cost of sales' or 'Cost of goods sold' are important and should always be shown.
- A trader may take some stock from the business for personal use. The goods taken should be deducted from purchases at cost price and added to the trader's drawings.

- The words 'Gross profit' are important and must be shown. The gross profit is the profit earned on selling goods before any other expenses are taken into account.
- Trading sections of the Income Statement should only be prepared for traders, that is, people who trade in (buy and sell) goods. People who sell their services, such as accountants, lawyers, dentists and gardeners, only require Income Statements.
- Any other income should always be added to the gross profit figure.
- There is no particular order in which overheads should be shown in the Income Statement of a sole trader, but it is often best to place the larger amounts before the smaller.
- It is also a good plan to group similar kinds of expenses, for example, property expenses (rent, heating and lighting, and insurance) together.
- Net profit is the trader's income after all expenses have been taken into account.
- A net loss arises if the overheads exceed the gross profit.
- Always describe the final balance as 'net profit' (or 'net loss').

• *Examiners expect Income Statements to be prepared in vertical form: marks may be lost if they are prepared in horizontal form. You should study the vertical form carefully until you are quite familiar with it.*

Exercise 1

Corrine began trading on 1 January 2010. The following trial balance as at 31 December 2010 has been extracted from her books.

Account	$	$
Sales		200 000
Sales Returns	6 300	
Purchases	86 500	
Purchases Returns		5 790
Rent Received		3 000
Discounts Received		3 210
Discounts Allowed	5 110	
Wages	61 050	
Rent Paid	12 000	
Electricity	5 416	
Insurance	2 290	
Motor Van Expenses	11 400	
Sundry Expenses	3 760	
Loan Interest	1 000	
Land and Buildings	84 000	
Plant and Machinery	22 000	
Motor Van	19 000	
Trade Receivables	12 425	
Trade Payables		4 220
Bank	5 065	
Loan (repayable in 2014)		20 000
Drawings	25 904	
Capital at 1 January 2010		127 000
	363 220	363 220

Corrine had unsold stock of $10 000 at 31 December 2010.

Required
Prepare Corrine's Income Statement for the year ended 31 December 2010 in good form.

Save your answer; it will be required again in chapter 8.

7.3 Opening stock

One year's closing stock is the next year's opening stock and it must be included in the cost of sales for that year. The debit balance on the Stock account is transferred by journal entry to the Trading section of the Income Statement.

Example

When Andrew (see §7.2) prepares his Trading section of the Income Statement for the year ended 31 December 2011 the opening stock will be transferred from the Stock account to the Trading section of the Income Statement:

Journal		$	$
31 Dec 2011	Income Statement	5000	
	Stock		5000

Stock		$			$
31 Dec 2010	Income Statement	5000	31 Dec 2011	Income Statement	5000

In the year ended 31 December 2011 Andrew's sales totalled $150 000 and his purchases were $62 000. Stock at 31 December 2011 was $8000. Andrew's Trading section of the Income Statement will be as follows:

Andrew
Income Statement for the year ended 31 December 2011

	$	$
Sales		150 000
Less Cost of sales		
Opening stock	5 000	
Purchases	62 000	
	67 000	
Less Closing stock	8 000	59 000
Gross profit		91 000

Note. In almost every case, stock shown in a trial balance is opening stock. The exception occurs when the trial balance has been extracted from the books *after* a Trading section of the Income Statement has been prepared, in which case the trial balance will not include Sales, Sales Returns, Purchases or Purchases Returns accounts.

Exercise 2

The following balances have been extracted from Khor's books at 31 December 2010.

	$	$
Sales		48 000
Sales Returns	1 600	
Purchases	21 000	
Purchases Returns		900
Stock at 1 January 2010		4 000

Stock at 31 December 2010 was $7500.

Required
Prepare Khor's Trading section of the Income Statement for the year ended 31 December 2010.

Exercise 3

The following trial balance has been extracted from the books of Perkins, a sole trader, at 31 March 2011.

	$	$
Premises	60 000	
Plant and Machinery	12 000	
Sales		104 000
Sales Returns	3 700	
Purchases	59 000	
Purchases Returns		2 550
Stock at 1 April 2010	6 000	
Wages	13 000	
Rent Payable	2 000	
Rent Receivable		1 800
Heating and Lighting	2 700	
Repairs to Machinery	4 100	
Interest on Loan	750	
Discounts Allowed	1 030	
Discounts Received		770
Trade Receivables	1 624	
Trade Payables		1 880
Bank	5 000	
Drawings	10 096	
Long-term Loan		15 000
Capital		55 000
	181 000	181 000

Stock at 31 March 2011 was $10 000.

Required
Prepare Perkins' Income Statement for the year ended 31 March 2011.

Save your answer; it will be required again in chapter 8.

7.4 Carriage inwards and carriage outwards

When goods are purchased, the supplier may make an additional charge to cover the cost of delivery. This charge is carriage inwards and adds to the cost of the goods. Carriage inwards is added to the cost of purchases in the Trading section of the Income Statement.

The cost of delivering goods to a customer is carriage outwards and is debited in the Income Statement as an overhead. Carriage inwards and carriage outwards are both expense items but it is important to treat them correctly in Income Statements.

Example

A. Trader
Income Statement for the year ended 31 December 2010

	$	$	$
Sales			93 000
Less Sales returns		2 700	90 300
Less Cost of sales			
Stock at 1 January 2010		3 000	
Purchases	45 200		
Less Purchases returns	3 400		
	41 800		
Carriage inwards	4 000	45 800	
		48 800	
Less Stock at 31 December 2010		7 000	41 800
Gross profit			48 500
Less Overheads			
Wages		12 000	
Rent		5 600	
Carriage outwards		2 220	
Sundry		1 760	21 580
Net profit			26 920

Double check the treatment of Carriage inwards and Carriage outwards. Marks could be lost in an examination if you put them in the wrong place.

Exercise 4

Sara's trial balance at 31 March 2011 was as follows:

Account	$	$
Sales		40 000
Stock	5 000	
Purchases	20 500	
Wages	6 000	
Rent	10 000	
Electricity	2 600	
Carriage inwards	1 320	
Carriage outwards	1 080	
Sundry Expenses	1 250	
Plant and Machinery	8 000	
Office Equipment	1 000	
Trade Receivables	1 900	
Trade Payables		800
Bank	820	
Drawings	6 330	
Capital		25 000
	65 800	65 800

Stock at 31 March 2011 was $3000.

Required

Prepare Sara's Income Statement for the year ended 31 March 2011.

7.5 Wages treated as cost of sales

Goods purchased may not be in a suitable condition for selling to customers. Further work may be required on them before they are sold. The wages paid to employees for performing this work should be debited as part of cost of sales in the Trading section of the Income Statement.

Example

The following balances are extracted from a trial balance at 30 April 2011.

	$	$
Sales		80 000
Stock at 1 May 2010	5 000	
Purchases	35 000	
Wages	16 000	

Stock at 30 April 2011 was $6000, and 25% of the wages were paid to staff who prepared the stock for sale to customers.

Trading section of the Income Statement for the year ended 30 April 2011		
	$	$
Sales		80 000
Cost of sales		
Stock at 1 May 2010	5 000	
Purchases	35 000	
	40 000	
Less Stock at 30 April 2011	6 000	
	34 000	
Wages (25% of $16 000)	4 000	38 000
Gross profit		42 000

The examiner will tell you if any of the amounts paid for wages should be entered in the Trading section of the Income Statement. If no instructions are given then always show wages as an expense in the Income Statement.

● If you refer to opening and closing stock as opening and closing inventory, the examiner will still mark it as being correct.

MULTIPLE-CHOICE QUESTIONS

1. Which of the following does not appear in Income Statement?
A. Motor vehicles
B. Carriage outwards
C. Discounts allowed
D. Discounts received

2. The following information has been extracted from the trial balance of a business:

	$
Sales	100 000
Purchases	60 000
Wages	21 000

Closing stock was $3000 more than opening stock.
One third of the wages was charged to cost of sales in the Trading section of the Income Statement.
What was the gross profit?
A. $30 000
B. $33 000
C. $36 000
D. $37 000

3. The Carriage inwards of a business amounted to $6000, and the Carriage outwards was $7000. The Carriage outwards was charged in the Trading section of the Income Statement in error, and the Carriage inwards was debited in the Income Statement.
What has been the effect of these errors?

Gross profit	Net profit
A. understated by $1000	understated by $1000
B. overstated by $1000	overstated by $1000
C. understated by $1000	not affected
D. overstated by $1000	not affected

4. Discounts received amount to $10 500 and discounts allowed to $13 000. The discounts received have been debited, and the discounts allowed have been credited in the Income Statement.
What has been the effect of these errors on net profit?
A. understated by $2500
B. overstated by $2500
C. understated by $5000
D. overstated by $5000

5. Carriage inwards in a trial balance is $2300. It has been entered in the Trading section of the Income Statement as $3200. In addition, motor expenses of $600 been posted to the Motor Vans account.
What effect has this had on the Income Statement?

Gross profit	Net profit
A. understated by $900	understated by $300
B. overstated by $900	overstated by $300
C. understated by $900	overstated by $1500
D. overstated by $900	understated by $1500

ADDITIONAL EXERCISES

1. The following trial balance has been extracted from Hadlee's books at 31 December 2010.

	$	$
Plant and Machinery	25 000	
Office Furniture	6 000	
Stock at 1 January 2010	11 000	
Trade Receivables	4 740	
Trade Payables		1976
Bank	3 327	
Loan, repayable in 2012		5 000
Sales		72 800
Purchases	28 540	
Sales Returns	1 600	
Purchases Returns		2 144
Wages	3 100	
Rent	4 000	
Heating and Lighting	5 120	
Advertising	2 400	
Sundry Expenses	2010	
Loan Interest	250	
Drawings	4 833	
Capital		20 000
	101 920	101 920

Stock at 31 December 2010 cost $9000.

Required

Prepare Hadlee's Income Statement for the year ended 31 December 2010.

Keep your answer; it will be needed again in chapter 8.

2. The trial balance extracted from Tikolo's books at 31 March 2011 is as follows:

Amount	$	$
Sales		204 000
Sales Returns	3 600	
Purchases	120 000	
Purchases Returns		4 440
Stock at 1 April 2010	18 000	
Carriage inwards	5 000	
Carriage outwards	3 724	
Discounts Received		3 160
Discounts Allowed	5 020	
Wages	36 800	
Rent	8 000	

Amount	$	$
Heating and Lighting	6 450	
Sundry Expenses	1 143	
Fixtures and Fittings	9 000	
Office Furniture	2 000	
Trade Receivables	1 970	
Trade Payables		2 130
Bank	2 496	
Drawings	20 527	
Capital		30 000
	243 730	243 730

During the year, Tikolo had taken goods costing $2000 for his own use. This had not been recorded in the books.

Stock at 31 March 2011 cost $20 000.

Required

Prepare Tikolo's Income Statement for the year ended 31 March 2011.

Keep your answer; it will be needed again in chapter 8.

8 Statements of Financial Position for sole traders

In this chapter you will learn:

- what a Statement of Financial Position is and why Statements of Financial Position are prepared
- how to prepare a Statement of Financial Position for a sole trader.

8.1 What is a Statement of Financial Position?

A **Statement of Financial Position** is a list of the assets and liabilities of a business at a particular date. A trader needs to know if his business will continue to provide an income for the foreseeable future. A Statement of Financial Position can provide a good indication of the answer to this question.

Unlike an Income Statement, a Statement of Financial Position is not part of the double-entry model. After the nominal account balances have been transferred to the Income Statement, the only balances left in the ledger are those for assets and liabilities. The Statement of Financial Position is a list of these balances.

Although a Statement of Financial Position is not an account, the Income Statement and Statement of Financial Position are known collectively as the **final accounts** of a business. Together these two documents are also known as the **financial statements** of a business. This may also include the Statement of cash flow (see chapter 24), and is a term you will see included in examination papers. You will find both terms used throughout the book.

8.2 How to prepare a Statement of Financial Position

The changes to final accounts resulting from the International Accounting Standards (IAS) mean that some of the headings in the Statement of Financial Position will change. The table below shows the terms you may have come across before and their equivalent terms under International Accounting Standards alongside:

Traditional Balance Sheet headings	Headings under the International Accounting Standards
Fixed assets	Non-current assets
Current assets	Current assets
Current Liabilities	Current Liabilities
Long-term liabilities	Non-current liabilities
Capital	Capital

Notice that not all of the headings have been changed. In the examination you should become familiar with the IAS headings and use them in your answers to the questions. List and group the assets and liabilities of the business under these headings.

Example

The following is the Statement of Financial Position for Andrew's business at 31 December 2010. It is prepared from the trial balance given in §7.2 and lists all the balances remaining in the ledger after the Income Statement has been prepared.

Andrew
Statement of Financial Position at 31 December 2010

	$	$
Non-current assets		
Premises		40 000
Motor vans		18 000
Office furniture		5 000
		63 000
Current assets		
Inventory (Stock)	5 000*	
Trade Receivables	7 400	
Bank	2 160	
	14 560	
Less Current liabilities		
Trade Payables	3 420	11 140
		74 140
Less Non-current liabilities		
Loan from Marie		10 000
		64 140
Represented by:		
Capital at 1 January 2010		60 000
Add net profit for the year		15 060
		75 060
Deduct drawings		10 920
		64 140

* Stock: see page 32.

Notes

- A Statement of Financial Position is a 'position' statement showing the position of a business at a particular moment in time. It is not a period statement like an Income Statement. The date at which the Statement of Financial Position is prepared must be included in the heading 'Statement of Financial Position at …'.
- The Statement of Financial Position has been prepared in vertical form. Study it carefully until you are quite familiar with it and prepare all your Statements of Financial Position in similar style.
- The non-current assets are grouped together and totalled. The assets which are likely to have the longest useful life are placed first.
- Current assets are grouped next in the inner column and totalled. The order in the Statement of Financial Position is: Inventory, Trade receivables, bank and cash (if any). A **liquid asset** is one which is in the form of cash (cash in hand) or nearly so (cash at bank). Inventory is not a liquid asset because it has not been sold and no money has been, or will be received for it until it is sold. Trade receivables should soon become a liquid asset when they pay the business.
- The current assets are not added to the non-current assets at this stage.
- Current liabilities are those that are due to be settled within one year of the date of the Statement of Financial Position. They are deducted from the total of current assets to give the **working capital**. In the example above, the working capital is $11 140. This figure is also known as the **net current assets**. If the current liabilities are greater than the current assets then the figure is known as **net current liabilities**.
- Working capital is a very important item. The liquid current assets should exceed the current liabilities and show that the business resources adequately cover the payments it must make to its creditors. If the current assets are insufficient to meet the current liabilities, the trader may be forced to sell fixed assets to pay his creditors and that could be the beginning of the end of the business.
- Non-current (or Long-term liabilities) are those which are not due to be settled within one year of the date of the Statement of Financial Position. They are deducted from the total of non-current assets and working capital.
- The assets less the liabilities are represented by the owner's capital. The capital shown in the trial balance is the balance on the Capital account brought forward from the previous year. The net profit shown by the Income Statement is added to the opening capital, but a net loss must be deducted. Profit increases capital and losses reduce capital. When the drawings are deducted, the balance on the Capital account will be carried forward as the opening capital next year.
- At the end of the year, the balances on the Income Statement and Drawings account are transferred to the Capital account (by journal entry) as shown.
- The total of the non-current and current assets $(63 000 + 14 560) less the total of the current and non-current liabilities $(3420 + 10 000) equals the closing balance on the Capital account, $64 140. This is always true, and the formula 'assets – liabilities = capital' is known as the **accounting equation** or **Statement of Financial Position equation**. If the total of the non-current and current assets is greater than the total of the non-current and current liabilities, this is known as the **net assets** of the business.

Andrew – Capital				
2010		$	2010		$
Dec 31	Drawings	10 920	Jan 1	Balance brought down	60 000
	Balance carried down	64 140	Dec 31	Income Statement	15 060
		75 060			75 060
			2011		
			Jan 1	Balance brought down	64 140

Exercise 1

Prepare a Statement of Financial Position at 31 December 2010 for Corrine from the trial balance given in exercise 1 of chapter 7 (page 34).

Exercise 2

Prepare a Statement of Financial Position at 31 March 2011 for Perkins from the trial balance given in exercise 3 of chapter 7 (page 35).

HINTS

- Marks may be awarded in an examination for good presentation of Statements of Financial Position.
- Give every Statement of Financial Position a proper heading which should include the name of the business and the date. (If the Statement of Financial Position follows an Income Statement which is headed with the name of the business, the name need not be repeated for the Statement of Financial Position).
- Prepare Statements of Financial Position as shown in this chapter, with headings for non-current assets, current assets, current liabilities and non-current liabilities. Show the total of each group.

MULTIPLE-CHOICE QUESTIONS

1. The purchase of an office computer has been debited to Office Expenses instead of to Office Equipment.
What effect will this have on the Statement of Financial Position?

	Non-current asset	Profit	Capital
A.	no effect	understated	no effect
B.	no effect	understated	understated
C.	understated	no effect	understated
D.	understated	understated	no effect

2. The owner of a business has taken goods for his own use but no entry has been made in the books to record this. What is the effect of this on the Statement of Financial Position?

	Inventory	Capital
A.	no effect	no effect
B.	no effect	overstated
C.	overstated	no effect
D.	overstated	overstated

3. The following information has been extracted from a Statement of Financial Position at 31 December 2010.

	$
Non-current assets	310 000
Working capital	30 000
Long-term loan	20 000
Profit for the year	35 000
Drawings	25 000

What was the balance on Capital account at 31 December 2010?
A. $300 000   B. $320 000
C. $340 000   D. $350 000

4. Which of the following statements is **not** correct?
A. assets = liabilities + capital
B. capital = assets – liabilities
C. capital – liabilities = assets
D. liabilities = assets – capital

ADDITIONAL EXERCISES

1. Prepare the Statement of Financial Position at 31 December 2010 for Hadlee from the trial balance given in Additional Exercise 1 (page 37).
2. Prepare the Statement of Financial Position at 31 March 2011 for Tikolo from the trial balance given in Additional Exercise 2 (page 38).

9 Accounting principles or concepts

In this chapter you will learn:

- why it is necessary to have generally accepted rules for accounting
- the most important rules and what they aim to achieve
- why the rules should be applied to answers to exercises and examination questions.

9.1 What are principles or concepts?

Accounting principles are basic rules that are applied in recording transactions and preparing financial statements. They are also known as concepts. These rules are necessary to ensure that accounting records provide reliable information. All businesses should apply the rules in their financial statements. The most important of these rules are now described, and should be learned, understood and applied when preparing financial statements.

9.2 Business entity

Every business is regarded as having an existence separate from that of its owner. This has already been recognised when an owner's capital has been debited in the business Bank account and credited to the owner's Capital account. The credit in the Capital account shows that the owner is a creditor of the business, which owes him the money. This can only be the case if the business is regarded as being separate from the owner as no one can owe himself money. When the owner withdraws money from the business, the amount is debited to his Drawings account. The business accounts do not show if he spends the money on food, clothes, or holidays because these are not business transactions.

(It is important to remember that this is only an accounting concept. Anyone who has a grievance against a business may legally sue a sole trader or a partner in a firm. The business is not a separate entity for that purpose.)

9.3 Money measurement

Only transactions that can be expressed in monetary terms are recorded in ledger accounts. Goods, non-current assets, trade receivables and expenses etc. may be recorded in ledger accounts because they have resulted from transactions that can be expressed in monetary terms.

Although there are obvious advantages in being able to record things in monetary terms, it has disadvantages. Things which cannot be expressed in monetary terms, such as the skills of workers or their satisfaction with their working conditions, are not recorded in the accounts. Some people think it would be good if these and some other 'non-monetary' items could be included in financial statements.

9.4 Historic cost

Transactions are recorded at their cost to the business. Cost cannot be disputed as invoices or other documentary evidence may be produced to support it. This treatment is said to be objective because it is based on fact and not on opinion.

The opposite of objectivity is subjectivity, which is based upon personal opinion. For example, somebody may give his friend a watch that cost $50. The friend may already have a good watch or perhaps several watches. He would not have paid

$50 for another. He would probably value the gift at less than $50. On the other hand, if the friend had not already got a watch and his life depended on him having one, he might value the watch at much more than $50. Values based on personal opinions are said to be subjective and are not reliable bases on which to record transactions.

While the principle of recording transactions at their historic cost has obvious advantages, it has two disadvantages.

- It ignores the changing value of money. An item that was purchased five years ago for $100 might have been sold then for $200 making a profit of $100. If inflation since then has been 25%, today's selling price would be $250 giving an apparent profit of $150. A more realistic calculation of the profit would be to express the original cost at today's prices, $125, giving a profit of $125, which would be enough to buy no more than $100 would have bought five years ago! Historic cost may produce misleading results unless its limitations are understood.
- Like the concept of money measurement, historic cost does not allow things that cannot be expressed in monetary terms to be recorded in accounting.

as it prevents revenue from being credited in the accounts before it has been earned.

Goods on sale or return. When a trader sends goods on sale or return to a customer, no sale takes place until the customer informs the seller that he has decided to buy them. The customer has the right to return the goods to the trader. The goods remain the property of the seller until the sale actually takes place. Goods on sale or return must be treated as stock or inventory when the final accounts are being prepared. If they have been wrongly treated as sold the accounting treatment must be reversed. Sales and trade receivables must be reduced by the selling price, and closing inventory must be increased by the cost price of the goods.

Example

George has sent goods on sale or return to Helen for $500 and treated the transaction as a sale. Helen has not yet accepted the goods. The goods cost George $350. The following balances have been extracted from George's trial balance: Sales $30 000; trade receivables $1000. Inventory on hand has been valued at $900. The following adjustments must be made for the final accounts.

Sales	$	Trade Receivables	$	Stock or Inventory	$
Per trial balance	30 000	Per trial balance	1 000	As given	900
Less	500	Less	500	Add	350
Trading Account	29 500	Statement of Financial Position	500	Income Statement and Statement of Financial Position	1 250

9.5 Realisation

When accountants speak of realisation, they mean that something becomes an actual fact, or that something has been converted into money. For example, if a man goes into a shop and says that he will return tomorrow and buy a pair of shoes, there is no sale yet; but if the man returns the next day and buys the shoes, the sale has become a fact. By selling the shoes, the shopkeeper has converted goods into money. The sale has been **realised**. Transactions are realised when cash or a debtor replace goods or services. This principle is important

9.6 Duality

The concept of **duality** recognises that there are two aspects for each transaction – represented by debit and credit entries in accounts. The concept is the basis of the accounting equation:

$$assets = capital + liabilities$$

The equation is also expressed in its other form: assets – liabilities = capital. Statements of Financial Position are prepared in this form.

The accounting equation is a very useful tool for solving some accounting problems.

9.7 **Consistency**

Transactions of a similar nature should be recorded in the same way (that is, consistently) in the same accounting period and in all future accounting periods. For example, the cost of redecorating premises should always be debited to an expense account for the redecoration of premises and charged to the Income Statement. It would not be correct, the next time the offices were redecorated, to debit the cost to the Premises (non-current assets) account.

Consistency in the treatment of transactions is important to ensure that the profits or losses of different periods, and Statements of Financial Position, may be compared meaningfully.

9.8 **Materiality**

Sometimes a business may depart from the generally accepted principles for recording some transactions. They may do this when the amounts involved are not considered **material** (or significant) in relation to the amounts of the other items in their Income Statements and Statements of Financial Position.

A company may prepare its Statement of Financial Position showing all amounts rounded to the nearest $000 or even $m. It would treat the purchase of any asset not exceeding, say, $1000 as revenue expenditure instead of adding it to its non-current assets, as it would not make any noticeable difference to the figure of non-current assets in the Statement of Financial Position. It would not be considered a material item.

On the other hand, the same amount of expenditure in a small business may be very significant and would need to be treated as capital expenditure in order not to distort profit and the assets in the Statement of Financial Position.

An amount may be considered material in the accounts if its inclusion in, or omission from, the Income Statement or Statement of Financial Position would affect the way people would read and interpret those financial statements.

9.9 **Accruals (matching)**

If the final accounts of a business are to give reliable information, the revenue and other income must be no more and no less than the business has earned in the period covered by the Income Statement. The expenses in the Income Statement should fairly represent the expenses incurred in earning that revenue. The difference between an Income Statement prepared on a cash basis and one prepared on an accruals basis will be apparent from the following example:

A business occupies premises at an annual rental of $2000. In one year it has paid $2500 because it has paid one quarter's rent in advance. It has also used $2100 worth of electricity but it has paid only $1200 because it has not paid the latest bill for $900. Its gross profit for the year is $10 000.

Income Statements prepared on (a) a 'cash basis', that is, on the actual payments made, and (b) on an accruals basis, would look as follows:

	(a) Cash basis		(b) Accruals basis	
	$	$	$	$
Gross profit		10 000		10 000
Less Rent	2500		2 000	
Electricity	1200	3 700	2 100	4 100
Net profit		6 300		5 900

The accruals basis is the correct one as it records the actual costs incurred in the period for rent and electricity.

Income Statements should be prepared on the **accruals**, or matching, basis so that expenses are matched to the revenue earned; that is, expenses should be shown in the Income Statement as they have been *incurred* rather than as they have been paid.

9.10 **Prudence**

The prudence concept is intended to prevent profit from being overstated. If profit is overstated, a trader may believe that his income is more than it really is, and he may withdraw too much money from the business. That would lead to the capital invested in the business being depleted. If it happens too often the business will collapse because there will not be enough money to pay creditors or to renew assets when they are worn out. The principle is sometimes know as the **concept of conservation**. It is safer for profit to be understated rater than overstated.

The rule is:
- profits should not be overstated
- losses should be provided for as soon as they are recognised.

Students often make the mistake of saying that the prudence concept means that profits must be understated. That is not so; the concept is meant to ensure that profits are realistic without being overstated.

9.11 Going concern

A business is a going concern if there is no intention to discontinue it in the foreseeable future. If it is short of working capital and the owner is unable to put more money into it, or to find somebody who will be prepared to lend it money, it may be unable to pay its creditors and be forced to close.

Unless stated to the contrary, it is assumed that the accounts of a business are prepared on a going concern basis. If the business is not a going concern, the assets should be valued in the Statement of Financial Position at the amounts they could be expected to fetch in an enforced sale, which could be much less than their real worth. Statements of Financial Position should always show a realistic situation, bearing in mind the weakness of the business.

9.12 Substance over form

These words are used to describe the accounting treatment of something that does not reflect the legal position.

For example, a machine bought on hire purchase remains the property of the seller until the final instalment has been paid. If the purchaser fails to pay the instalments as they become due, the seller may reclaim the machine. That is the legal position, or the 'form'.

However, the machine is being used in the purchaser's business in the same way as the other machines that have not been bought on hire purchase. From an accounting point of view and for all practical purposes, the machine is no different from the other machines; that is the 'substance' of the matter.

The practical view (the substance) is preferred to the legal view (the form) in the accounting treatment. This is known as 'substance over form'.

Example

Antonio bought a machine on hire purchase on 1 January 2010. The cash price of the machine was $50 000. Antonio paid $10 000 on 1 January 2010. The balance was to be settled by four payments of $10 100 (including interest of $100) on 1 April 2010, 1 July 2010, 1 October 2010 and 1 January 2011. The following entries should appear in Antonio's final accounts at 31 December 2010.

Income Statement: Interest on hire purchase $400
Statement of Financial Position: Non-current assets $50 000 (the cash price although only $40 000 has been paid) Current liabilities $10 100 (the final instalment) not paid until 1 January 2011.

HINTS
- Learn all the concepts and make sure you understand them.
- Watch for the application of the concepts when you answer examination questions.
- Make sure you identify the correct concept when asked which one has been applied to a particular situation. (Prudence is not always the right answer!)
- Read questions carefully. Questions may require you to give a definition, or to explain, or to discuss. Each of those requirements must be met with an appropriate response.
- When asked for a definition, do not give an example instead. If asked to define 'substance over form', an answer such as 'substance over form is when an asset is bought on hire purchase' is unlikely to gain any marks because

the definition is missing. The following is better: 'Subject over form is the treatment accorded to a transaction so that the real effect on the business is recorded in the accounts, rather than the strictly legal position. For example, an asset bought on hire purchase is treated as though it already belongs to the purchaser although it legally remains the property of the seller until the final instalment has been paid.' This answer gives a definition as required. (The example develops the answer further and may gain an additional mark.)

'Explain...' requires an explanation of the way a concept is applied and an explanation as to why it is necessary or important.

'Discuss...' invites an answer which includes a discussion of the advantages **and** disadvantages of a concept. *Examiners choose their words carefully and expect candidates to take note of the wording of questions.*

MULTIPLE-CHOICE QUESTIONS

1. A trader who sells food does not include food that is past its 'sell by' date in his inventory in the Statement of Financial Position. Which concept has he applied in valuing his inventory?
   A. matching
   B. prudence
   C. realisation
   D. going concern

2. A business is about to be closed down as it has insufficient funds to pay its creditors. The owner places a very low value on his inventory in the Statement of Financial Position. Which concept is being applied?
   A. going concern
   B. materiality
   C. money measurement
   D. subjectivity

3. The owner of a business paid his private telephone bill from the business bank account. The amount was debited to his Drawings account. Which concept was applied?
   A. business entity
   B. matching
   C. prudence
   D. realisation

4. A trader has included rent which is due but not paid in his Income Statement. Which accounting concept has been applied?
   A. historic cost
   B. matching
   C. money measurement
   D. prudence

5. The balances in a sales ledger total $16 000. A debtor who owes $800 is known to be in financial difficulty. The figure of debtors shown in the Statement of Financial Position is $15 200. Which concept has been applied?
   A. matching
   B. prudence
   C. realisation
   D. substance over form

6. A trader sends goods on sale or return to a customer. When the trader prepares his Statement of Financial Position at 31 March 2010, the customer has still not indicated that he has accepted the goods. Which concept should the trader apply when he prepares his accounts at 31 March 2010?
   A. consistency
   B. matching
   C. prudence
   D. realisation

10 Accruals and prepayments (the matching concept)

In this chapter you will learn:

- the practical application of the accruals (matching) principle
- how to record accruals and prepayments in ledger accounts
- how to adjust trial balances for accruals and prepayments
- how to show accruals and prepayments in Statement of Financial Position.

10.1 What are accruals and prepayments?

Accruals are expenses that have been incurred but not paid for. For example, an unpaid electricity bill is an accrued expense; the electricity has been consumed (the cost has been incurred), but not paid for.

Prepayments are payments made in advance of the benefits to be derived from them. Rent is an example because it usually has to be paid in advance.

10.2 How to treat an accrued expense in an account

An accrued expense is an amount that is owed to somebody; that somebody is a creditor. The creditor must be represented in the expense account by a credit balance carried down on the account.

Example

The accounting year of a business ended on 31 December 2010. In the 11 months ended 30 November 2010 payments for electricity amounted to $900. At 31 December 2010 there was an unpaid electricity bill for $130. That amount is carried down on the account as a credit balance. The electricity account is prepared as follows:

Electricity						
2010			$	2010		$
Jan–Nov	Sundry payments		900	Dec 31	Income	
Dec 31	Electricity				Statement	1030
	owing	c/d	130			
			1030			1030
				2011		
				Jan 1	Balance b/d	130

Notes

- Only $900 has been paid but the Income Statement has been debited with the full cost of electricity for the year, $1030.
- A creditor for the amount owing for electricity has been created on the account by a credit balance carried down.
- The creditor will be shown in the Statement of Financial Position under current liabilities as an 'accrued expense', as an 'expense creditor' or other trade payables to distinguish it from trade payables.

10.3 How to treat a prepaid expense in an account

The person to whom a payment has been made in advance is a debtor of the business. The debtor is represented on the expense account by a debit balance carried down.

Example

Yousif occupies premises at a rental of $2000 per annum, the rent being payable in advance on 1 January, 1 April, 1 July and 1 October. In 2010, Yousif paid the rent on each of those dates, but on 31 December he paid the rent due on 1 January 2011. At 31 December, the landlord is a debtor for the amount of the prepayment.

Rent Payable					
2010		$	2010		$
Jan 1	Bank	500	Dec 31	Income	
Apr 1	Bank	500		Statement	2000
Jul 1	Bank	500	Dec 31	Rent paid in	
				advance c/d	500
Oct 1	Bank	500			
Dec 31	Bank	500			
		2500			2500
2011					
Jan 1	Balance b/d	500			

Notes

- Payments during the year amount to $2500, but the Income Statement has been debited with the rent for one year only.
- The debtor (the landlord) is represented by the debit balance on the account.
- The debit balance will be included in the Statement of Financial Position under current assets as a prepayment or other trade receivables to distinguish it from trade receivables.

10.4 How to record inventory (stock) of stores on expense accounts

Some expense accounts represent stocks of consumable stores. Examples are stationery, heating fuel and fuel for motor vehicles. Stocks of consumable stores may be unused at the year-end. According to the matching principle, these stocks should not be charged against the profit for the year; they are an asset and not an expense at the year-end. Carry them down as a debit balance on the account. This may result in an expense account having debit and credit balances at the year-end.

In the Statement of Financial Position the stocks of unused consumable will appear under current assets. They should be shown under their own headings of say, stocks of unused stationery. They should *never* be included with the closing trading stock or inventory in the Statement of Financial Position.

Example

In the year ended 31 December 2010, Prospero had paid $1200 for stationery. At 31 December 2010, he owed $270 for stationery and had a stock (inventory) of unused stationery which had cost $400.

Stationery					
2010		$	2010		$
Jan 1			Dec 31	Income	
Dec 31	Bank	1200		Statement	1070
Dec 31	Amount owing				
	c/d	270	Dec 31	Inventory c/d	400
		1470			1470
2011			2011		
Jan 1	Inventory b/d	400	Jan 1	Balance b/d	270

Note. Closing balances are the opening balances of the next financial period. In the Statement of Financial Position at 31 December 2010 the stock of unused stationery, $400, will be shown under current assets.

10.5 How to adjust income for accruals and prepayments

Some income accounts such as rents or interest receivable may need to be adjusted for income received in advance or in arrears. Income received in advance of its due date indicates the existence of a creditor (trade payable) and requires a credit balance equal to the prepayment to be carried down on the account. Income accrued at the date it is due indicates the existence of a debtor (trade receivable) and a debit balance equal to the amount should be carried down on the account.

Example

In the year ended 31 January 2011, Elizabeth had received $500 for rent from a tenant and $160 for interest on a loan. At that date, the rent prepaid amounted to $100, and $40 interest was due from the borrower. The entries in the Rent Receivable and Interest Receivable accounts at 31 January 2011 are as follows:

Rent Receivable					
2011		$	2011		$
Jan 31	Income Statement	400	Jan 31	Bank	500
Jan 31	Rent prepaid c/d	100			
		500			500
			Feb 1	Balance b/d	100

Interest Receivable

2011		$	2011		$
Jan 31	Income Statement	200	Jan 31	Bank	160
			Jan 31	Interest accrued c/d	40
		200			200
Feb 1	Balance b/d	40			

Exercise 1

In the year ended 31 December 2010, Alex made the following payments: rent $1000; electricity $630; stationery $420. In addition he had received $300 rent from a tenant.

At 31 December 2010, Alex had prepaid rent of $200. Accrued expenses were electricity $180 and stationery $130. The stock (inventory) of stationery was $140. The tenant owed rent of $100.

Required

Show how the accounts concerned will appear in Alex's books after the adjustments for accruals and prepayments have been made. Show clearly the amounts to be transferred to the Income Statement.

10.6 How to adjust a trial balance for accruals and prepayments

Examination questions often include trial balances that require to be adjusted for accruals and prepayments. A reliable examination technique (or method) to deal with this situation is important for success. Adjustments may be made on the question paper but the workings should be shown on your examination script. Two good methods are suggested here. You should try both methods, decide which one you prefer, and stick to it in your preparations for the exam.

Example

The following is an extract from a trial balance at 31 December 2010.

	$	$
Rent Payable	2400	
Heating and Lighting	1860	
Stationery	1100	
Interest Receivable		600
Rent Receivable		1200

The following amounts were owing at 31 December 2010: heating and lighting $290; stationery $100. Rent receivable of $200 had been received in advance.

At 31 December 2010, rent payable of $400 had been paid in advance; interest receivable of $120 was due but had not been received.

There was an unused stock (inventory) of stationery, $230, at 31 December 2010.

Method 1. Adjust the items in the trial balance in the question. Make lists of the debtors (trade receivables) and creditors (trade payables) you create. Insert stock (inventory) of stationery in the trial balance. (The adjustments are shown in *italics*.)

Show your workings with your answer.

	$	$	Debtors $	Creditors $
Rent Payable	2400 – *400*		*400*	
Heating and Lighting	1860 + *290*			*290*
Stationery	1100 + *100* – *230*			*100*
Stock (inventory) of stationery 230				
Interest Receivable	600 + *120*		*120*	
Rent Receivable	1200 – *200*			*200*
			520	590

Method 2. Delete the items on the trial balance after cross-referencing them to calculations shown as workings with your answer (TB Trial Balance; Inc. St. Income Statement).

W1	Rent Payable	$	W2	Heat & Light	$	W3	Stationery	$
	Per TB	2400		Per TB	1860		Per TB	1100
	Less prepaid	(400)*		Add owing	290†		Add owing	100†
	Inc. St.	2000		Inc. St.	2150		Less stock (inventory)	(230)
							Inc. St.	970

W4	Interest Receivable	$	W5	Rent Receivable	$
	Per TB	600		Per TB	1200
	Add due	120*		Less prepaid	(200)†
	Inc. St.	720		Inc. St.	1000

Items marked * will be listed as debit balances as in method 1. Items marked † will be listed as credit balances as in method 1.

Exercise 2

Devram extracted a trial balance at 31 December 2010 from his books after he had prepared the Trading Account section of his Income Statement for the year ended on that date. It was as follows:

	$	$
Non-current assets	40 000	
Inventory at 31 December 2010	7 000	
Trade receivables	1 600	
Trade payables		1 400
Bank	2 524	
Long-term Loan		10 000
Gross profit		30 000
Rent	2 600	
Electricity	926	
Stationery	405	
Motor Expenses	725	
Interest on Loan	500	
Drawings	5 120	
Capital		20 000
	61 400	61 400

Further information

1. At 31 December 2010, rent had been prepaid in the sum of $300.
2. The following amounts were owing at 31 December 2010: electricity $242; stationery $84; motor expenses $160.
3. The long-term loan was made to the business on 1 January 2010. Interest at the rate of 10% per annum is payable on the loan.
4. The stock (inventory) of unused stationery on hand at 31 December 2010 was valued at cost: $100.

Required

(a) Prepare Devrams's Income Statement for the year ended 31 December 2010.
(b) Prepare the Statement of Financial Position at 31 December 2010.

(**Note**. Inventory shown in the trial balance is the closing inventory.)

HINTS

- Read questions carefully before starting to answer them. Note any adjustments required for accruals and prepayments.
- Calculate adjustments carefully and show your workings. Even if your answer is wrong, you may gain some marks for partially correct answers if the examiner can follow your workings.
- Take care to complete the double entry for each adjustment you make to the trial balance.
- As you make each adjustment, tick the item on the question paper. Before starting to copy out the answer, check that all adjustments have been ticked on the question paper. Many candidates lose marks because they have missed some of the adjustments.

MULTIPLE-CHOICE QUESTIONS

1. A trader prepares his accounts annually to 30 April. He pays annual rent of $12 000 and makes the payments quarterly in advance on 1 January, 1 April, 1 July and 1 October. Which amount should be included in his accounts for the year ended 30 April 2011?
   A. $1000 accrual   B. $1000 prepayment
   C. $2000 accrual   D. $2000 prepayment

2. A trader commenced business on 1 February 2010. He paid rent on his premises as follows:

Date	Period	Amount
1 Feb 2010	1 Feb – 31 Mar	$1200
1 Apr 2010	1 Apr – 30 Jun	$1800
1 Jul 2010	1 Jul – 31 Sept	$1800

| 1 Oct 2010 | 1 Oct – 31 Dec | $2100 |
| 1 Jan 2011 | 1 Jan – 31 Mar | $2100 |

Which amount for rent should be shown in the Income Statement for the year ended 31 January 2011?
   A. $6900   B. $7600
   C. $7800   D. $9000

3. A business has an accounting year that ends on 30 September. Its insurance premiums are paid in advance on 1 July each year. Premiums have been paid in the past three years as follows:

Year 1 $1800
Year 2 $2000
Year 3 $2400

How much will be debited in the Income Statement for insurance in Year 3?

A. $2000   B. $2100   C. $2300   D. $2400

4. The accounts of a business have been prepared, but no adjustments have been made for accrued expenses at the end of the year.
   What effect will these omissions have on the accounts?

	Net profit	Current assets	Current liabilities
A.	overstated	no effect	understated
B.	understated	no effect	overstated
C.	overstated	understated	no effect
D.	understated	overstated	no effect

ADDITIONAL EXERCISES

1. Antonia's trial balance at 31 December 2010 was as follows:

	$	$
Sales		120 000
Purchases	62 400	
Sales Returns	7 300	
Purchases Returns		4 190
Wages	17 310	
Rent	3 200	
Heating and Lighting	2 772	
Motor Expenses	1 284	
Interest on Loan	500	
Inventory	5 660	
Trade Receivables	12 440	
Trade Payables		6 167
Bank	5 055	
Loan		10 000
Premises	24 000	
Motor Vehicles	7 400	
Drawings	7 036	
Capital		16 000
	156 357	156 357

Further information
1. Inventory at 31 December 2010 was valued at $8000.
2. The loan was received on 1 April 2010 and is repayable in 2013. Interest is charged at 10% per annum.
3. Expenses owing at 31 December 2010 were as follows:

	$
Wages	558
Heating and Lighting	328

4. Rent in the sum of $800 was prepaid at 31 December 2010.

Required
(a) Prepare the Income Statement for the year ended 31 December 2010.
(b) Prepare the Statement of Financial Position at 31 December 2010.

2. Desmond's trial balance at 31 March 2011 was as follows:

	$	$
Plant and Machinery	36 000	
Motor Vehicles	17 000	
Inventory	9 000	
Trade Receivables	7 060	
Bank	5 400	
Trade Payables		3 950
Capital		70 000
Drawings	22 088	
Sales		219 740
Purchases	100 100	
Sales Returns	17 420	
Purchases Returns		8 777
Wages	67 000	
Rent Payable	8 000	
Rent Receivable		2 600
Interest Receivable		840
Discounts Allowed	2 826	
Discounts Received		1 040
Carriage Inwards	5 170	
Carriage Outwards	7 920	
Sundry Expenses	1 963	
	306 947	306 947

Further information
1. Inventory at 31 March 2011 was valued at $11 000.
2. Expenses owing at 31 March 2011 were: rent payable $2000; carriage inwards $330; carriage outwards $280.
3. Sundry expenses of $200 had been paid in advance; interest receivable of $160 had accrued.
4. At 31 March 2011, rent receivable of $200 had been received in advance.

Required
(a) Prepare Desmond's Income Statement for the year ended 31 March 2011.
(b) Prepare the Statement of Financial Position at 31 March 2011.

11 Provisions for the depreciation of non-current assets

In this chapter you will learn:

- what depreciation is and why it must be provided for in accounts
- how to calculate it by the straight-line and reducing-balance methods
- how to account for the disposal of non-current assets.

11.1 What is depreciation?

Depreciation is the part of the cost of a non-current asset that is consumed during the period it is used by a business. For example, a motor purchased for $10 000 may be worth only $8000 one year later because it is not as good as new after a year's use. The asset has suffered depreciation of $(10 000 − 8000) = $2000.

Assets may depreciate for a number of reasons.

- **Wear and tear**: assets become worn out through use.
- **Obsolescence**: assets have to be replaced because new, more efficient technology has been developed; or machines which were acquired for the production of particular goods are of no further use because the goods are no longer produced.
- **Passage of time**: an asset acquired for a limited period of time, such as a lease of premises for a given number of years, loses value as time passes. Accountants refer to this as **effluxion of time** and speak of **amortising** rather than 'depreciating' these assets.
- **Using up, or exhaustion**: mines, quarries and oil wells depreciate as the minerals etc. are extracted from them.

11.2 How does depreciation of non-current assets affect accounts?

The accounting treatment of capital expenditure, which is expenditure on non-current assets, is different from the treatment of revenue expenditure. Revenue expenditure is debited to the Income Statement as it is incurred. Capital expenditure, on the other hand, is on assets that are intended for use in a business for more than one year, usually for many years. It would be wrong to debit the whole of the cost of a non-current asset to the Income Statement in the year it was acquired; it would be against the matching principle. Nevertheless, the cost of *using* non-current assets to earn revenue must be charged in the Income Statement; that cost is the depreciation suffered in the accounting period.

11.3 How to account for depreciation

There are several methods used to calculate depreciation. The two most common are:

- straight line
- reducing balance.

Straight-line depreciation

With this method the total amount of depreciation that an asset will suffer is estimated as the difference between what it cost and the estimated amount that will be received when it is sold or scrapped at the end of its useful life. The total depreciation is then spread evenly over the number of years of its expected life.

Calculation: (cost − estimated proceeds on disposal) ÷ estimated useful life in years

Example 1

A machine cost $20 000. It is expected to have a useful life of five years at the end of which time it is expected to be sold for $5000 (its **residual value**). The total depreciation over five years is $(20 000 – $5000) = $15 000. The annual depreciation is $15 000 ÷ 5 = $3000.

Ledger entries for depreciation. Debit the Income Statement and credit a Provision for Depreciation account with the annual depreciation each year.

In the above example, the bookkeeping entries in each of the five years will be as follows:

Income Statement	$
Overheads	
Year 1	
Provision for depreciation of machine	3000
Year 2	
Provision for depreciation of machine	3000
Year 3	
Provision for depreciation of machine	3000
Year 4	
Provision for depreciation of machine	3000
Year 5	
Provision for depreciation of machine	3000

Machinery at Cost			
	$		$
Year 1 Bank	20 000		

Provision for Depreciation of Machinery				
		$		$
Year 1	Balance c/d	3 000	Year 1 Income Statement	3 000
Year 2	Balance c/d	6 000	Year 2 Balance b/d	3 000
			Income Statement	3 000
		6 000		6 000
Year 3	Balance c/d	9 000	Year 3 Balance b/d	6 000
			Income Statement	3 000
		9 000		9 000
Year 4	Balance c/d	12 000	Year 4 Balance b/d	9 000
			Income Statement	3 000
		12 000		12 000
Year 5	Balance c/d	15 000	Year 5 Balance b/d	12 000
			Income Statement	3 000
		15 000		Income Statement	15 000

Notes

- The non-current asset account continues to show the machine at cost each year of its life.

Non-current asset accounts sometimes include the words 'at cost' in their titles to emphasise this point.

- The balance on the Provision for Depreciation of Machinery account increases each year.
- A provision in accounting is an amount set aside for a particular purpose.
- A separate Provision for Depreciation account must be opened for each *class* of non-current asset.
- The balance on the Provision for Depreciation account is deducted from the cost of the non-current asset in the Statement of Financial Position:

		Cost $	Depreciation $	Net book value $
Year 1:	Machinery	20 000	3 000	17 000
Year 2:	Machinery	20 000	6 000	14 000
Year 3:	Machinery	20 000	9 000	11 000
Year 4:	Machinery	20 000	12 000	8 000
Year 5:	Machinery	20 000	15 000	5 000

The balance remaining after depreciation has been deducted from cost is known as the **net book value** (NBV) or **written down value** (WDV) of the asset. It is the amount of the cost of the asset which has not yet been charged against profit in the Income Statement. The net book values of assets at which the assets are 'carried' in the Statement of Financial Position are known as **carrying amounts**.

Note: The non-current assets at cost, the balances on the Provisions for Depreciation accounts, and net book values should now be shown in Statement Financial Position under headings as shown in the example above.

Exercise 1

A motor vehicle cost $18 000. It is expected to have a useful life of seven years and to be sold for $4000 at the end of that time.

Required

(a) Prepare the Provision for Depreciation of Motor Vehicles account for each year.

(b) Prepare a Statement of Financial Position extract to show the cost, depreciation and net book value of the Motor Vehicles at the end of each year.

Reducing balance depreciation

In this method, depreciation is calculated as a fixed percentage of the written down value of the asset each year.

Example 2

A machine cost $20 000. It is expected to have a useful life of five years. Depreciation is to be calculated at the rate of 25% per annum on the reducing balance.

Calculation:	$
Cost	20 000
Year 1 (25% × 20 000)	(5 000)
	15 000
Year 1 (25% × 15 000)	(3 750)
	11 250
Year 1 (25% × 11 250)	(2 813)
	8 437
Year 1 (25% × 8437)	(2 109)
	6 328
Year 1 (25% × 6328)	(1 582)
	4 746

The bookkeeping entries for the reducing-balance method are similar to those for straight-line; only the amounts differ.

Exercise 2

A machine costing $40 000 and with an expected useful life of five years is to be depreciated by the reducing-balance method. The annual rate of depreciation is 30%.

Required

(a) Prepare the Provision for Depreciation of Machinery account for years 1 to 5.

(b) Prepare a Statement of Financial Position extract to show the cost, depreciation and net book value of the machinery at the end of each of the five years.

Notes

- Always calculate depreciation to the nearest $.
- The percentage used for the reducing-balance method is much higher than that used for straight-line.
- In the early years of an asset's life, the annual charge for depreciation for the reducing-balance method is higher than for straight-line.

Example: A machine cost $50 000. It is expected to have a useful life of 10 years at the end of which time it will have no residual value. The annual depreciation for each year is compared in the following table.

		Annual charge for depreciation	
		Straight line (10%)	Reducing balance (40%)
		$	$
Year	1	5000	20 000
	2	5000	12 000
	3	5000	7 200
	4	5000	4 320
	5	5000	2 592
	6	5000	1 555
	7	5000	933
	8	5000	560
	9	5000	336
	10	5000	202

A much higher rate of depreciation has had to be used for the reducing-balance method, and the annual depreciation for the first three years is very much higher than under the straight-line method. In fact, using the reducing-balances method, 50% of cost is provided for within the first 18 months but the machine has not been completely depreciated at the end of 10 years – there is still a residual balance of $302.

- The net book values of assets may be reduced to zero if straight-line depreciation is used. They will never be written down to zero with the reducing-balance method unless a small residual value is deliberately transferred to the Income Statement.
- Provision for depreciation of an asset should cease to be made once it has been completely written off. Assets that have been completely written off in the books may still be of use to the business, but no further depreciation will be provided for them.

11.4 Which assets should be depreciated?

All assets that have finite useful lives should be depreciated. Therefore depreciation should be provided on all assets except freehold land, which does not have a finite useful life. Freehold buildings will eventually need to be replaced and should be depreciated. Land that is used in an extractive industry, such as quarries and mines, will lose value as the mineral etc. is extracted and should be depreciated.

11.5 Choice of depreciation method

Providing for depreciation is an application of the matching principle, and the method chosen for any particular type of asset should depend upon the contribution the asset makes towards earning revenue. Some general principles may be explained as follows:

- The **straight-line method** should be used for assets that are expected to earn revenue evenly over their useful working lives. It is also generally used where the pattern of an asset's earning power is uncertain. It should always be used to amortise the cost of assets with fixed lives such as leases.
- The **reducing-balance method** should be used when it is considered that an asset's earning power will diminish as the asset gets older. This method is also used when the asset loses more of its value in the early years of its life, for example a car.

A common excuse for using the reducing-balance method rather than straight-line method is that the reducing charges for depreciation compensate for increases in the cost of maintaining and repairing assets as they get older. It is highly improbable that the two costs will balance each other out. The proper way of dealing with this situation would be to depreciate the asset on the straight-line method and to create a Provision for Repairs and Maintenance by equal transfers annually from the Income Statement. The costs of repairs are debited to this provision as and when they arise.

11.6 More important points about depreciation

Provision for depreciation in the year of acquisition of an asset

Businesses vary in the way they depreciate non-current assets in the year in which they are acquired.

The two possibilities are:

- a full year's depreciation is taken in the year of acquisition, but none in the year of disposal
- depreciation is calculated from the date of acquisition; in the year of disposal, depreciation is calculated from the commencement of the year to the date of disposal, that is, only a proportion of the annual depreciation will be provided.

In an examination, follow the instructions given in the question. If the question gives the dates of acquisition and disposal, calculate depreciation on a time basis for the years of acquisition and disposal. Otherwise, calculate depreciation for a full year in the year of acquisition, but not for the year of disposal.

Consistency

The chosen method of depreciating an asset should be used consistently to ensure that the profits or losses of different periods of account can be compared on a like-for-like basis.

A change in the method of calculating depreciation should only be made if it will result in the financial results and position of the business being stated more fairly. A change should never be made in order to manipulate profit.

Exceptional depreciation

Sometimes an event may occur that causes the amount that may be recovered on the disposal of non-current asset to fall below its net book value (carrying amount). In this case the asset is said to be **impaired**. When this happens, the asset should immediately be written down to the amount which could be received if it was sold. This is known as its **recoverable amount**. The loss should be charged as an expense in the Income Statement.

The remaining useful life of the asset should now be reviewed, in order to calculate the depreciation to be charged for the remainder of the asset's useful life. This is calculated by dividing the new carrying amount by the number of years of useful life remaining.

Example

A machine was purchased in 2005 at a cost of $30 000. It had an estimated useful life of 10 years and a residual value of $2000. Straight-line depreciation of $2800 was provided each year until 31 December 2009 when the machine had a written down value of $16 000. At 31 December 2010 it was then found that the recoverable amount of the machine was only $9000 and that it had only three years' useful life left and no residual value.

In the year ended 31 December 2010, the Income Statement should be debited with $7000, $(16 000 − 9000), and the annual depreciation for the next three years should be $9000 ÷ 3 = $3000.

11.7 How to account for the disposals of non-current assets

When a non-current asset is sold, the difference between its net book value and the proceeds of sale represents a profit or loss on disposal, which is transferred to the Income Statement. The profit or loss is calculated in a Disposal account. The bookkeeping entries are as follows:

Debit the Disposal account and **credit** the Non-current asset account with the original cost of the asset.
Debit the Provision for Depreciation account and **credit** the Disposal account with the depreciation provided to date on the asset.
Debit the Bank account and **credit** the Disposal account with the proceeds (if any) of the disposal.
A debit balance remaining on the Disposal account is a loss on disposal. A credit balance is a profit on disposal. The balance is transferred to the Income Statement.

Example 1

At 1 December 2010, a machine which had cost $20 000 was sold for $500. A total of $18 000 had been provided for depreciation on the machine. The bookkeeping is as follows:

Machinery at Cost

2010		$	2010		$
Jan 1	Balance b/d	20 000	Dec 1	Machinery Disposal	20 000

Provision for Depreciation of Machinery

2010		$	2010		$
Dec 1	Machinery Disposal	18 000	Jan 1	Balance b/d	18 000

Machinery Disposal

2010		$	2010		$
Dec 1	Machinery at Cost	20 000	Dec 1	Provision for Depreciation	18 000
				Bank	500
			31	Income Statement (loss on disposal)	1 500
		20 000			20 000

Notes
- The cost of the machine exceeds the accumulated depreciation + the sale proceeds; there is a loss on disposal.
- The debit entry in the Income Statement is really an adjustment to previous years' depreciation charges, which have proved to be insufficient.

Part exchange

A new asset may be acquired in part exchange for one that is being disposed of. The part exchange value of the asset being disposed of is debited to the non-current asset account and credited to the Disposal account as the proceeds of disposal.

Example 2

On 5 March 2011 a motor vehicle X100 was purchased for $15 000. The cost was settled by a payment of $13 000 and the part exchange of motor vehicle Z23 for the balance.

Motor vehicle Z23 cost $11 000 and had a net book value of $800 at 5 March 2011.

Motor Vehicles at Cost

2011		$	2011		$
Jan 1	Balance b/d (Z23)	11 000	Mar 5	Motor Vehicles Disposal A/c	11 000
Mar 5	Bank (X100)	13 000			
	Motor Vehicles Disposal A/c	2 000			
		15 000			

Provision for the Depreciation of Motor Vehicles

2011		$	2011		$
Mar 5	Motor Vehicles Disposal A/c	10 200	Jan 1	Balance b/d	10 200

Motor Vehicles Disposal

2011		$	2011		$
Mar 5	Motor Vehicles at Cost Income Statement (Profit on disposal)	11 000	Mar 5	Provision for Depreciation of Motor Vehicles (see note below)	10 200
		1 200		Motor Vehicles at Cost	2 000
		12 200			12 200

Notes
- No depreciation has been charged in the year of disposal.
- The profit of $1200 is credited in the Income Statement and is, in effect, an adjustment of over-depreciation of the motor vehicle in previous years.

Exercise 3

The following balances have been extracted from Joel's books at 31 December 2010. Machinery at Cost $18 000; Provision for Depreciation of Machinery $9600.

Joel's transactions in 2011 included the following:

May 7	Sold machine No. 1 for $1500. This machine cost $6000 when purchased in 2007.
June 3	Purchased machine No. 3 which was priced at $10 000. Joel paid $7000 and gave machine No. 2 in part exchange. Machine No. 2 cost $12 000 when purchased in 2005.

Joel depreciates his machinery using the straight-line method and the rate of 10% per annum. He provides for a full year's depreciation in the year of purchase, but none in the year of disposal.

Required

Prepare the following accounts to show the transactions on 7 May and 3 June:
(a) Machinery at Cost
(b) Provision for Depreciation of Machinery
(c) Machinery Disposal.

11.8 How to adjust a trial balance for depreciation

Examination questions frequently provide a trial balance that has to be adjusted to provide for a further year's depreciation of the non-current assets.

The amount that has to be debited in the Income Statement should be inserted in the debit column of the trial balance and added to the credit side.

Example

The following extract is taken from a trial balance.

	$	$
Leasehold Premises	30 000	
Provision for Depreciation of Leasehold Premises		6 000
Plant and Machinery	40 000	
Provision for Depreciation of Plant and Machinery		23 120

Further information
1. Leasehold premises are to be amortised over the term of the lease of 10 years on the straight-line basis.
2. Plant and machinery are to be depreciated at the rate of 25% per annum on the reducing-balance method.

Adjust the trial balance as follows (adjustments shown in *italics*):

	$	$
Leasehold Premises	30 000	
Provision for Depreciation of Leasehold Premises	*3 000*	6 000 + *3 000*
Plant and Machinery	40 000	
Provision for Depreciation of Plant and Machinery	*4 220**	23 120 + *4 220*
* 25% of (40 000 – 23 120)		

The result of this will be to charge the depreciation on the premises ($3 000) and the depreciation on the plant and machinery ($4 220) as expenses in the Income Statement.

The accumulated depreciation figures of $9 000 ($6 000 + 3 000) for premises and $27 340 ($23 120 + $4 220) for plant and machinery will be shown in the Statement of Financial Position. They will be deducted from the cost of their respective assets to show the net book value.

11.9 Provisions for depreciation and the accounting concepts

Provisions for depreciation are made to comply with the following concepts:

Matching. The cost of using non-current assets to earn revenue should be matched in the Income Statement to the revenue earned.

Prudence. If the cost of using non-current assets was not included in the Income Statement, profit would be overstated.

HINTS

- Read questions carefully to make sure you understand which method of depreciation you should use.
- If required to prepare ledger accounts for depreciation or disposals of non-current assets, be sure to include in each posting the name of the other account in which the double entry is completed. The examiner needs to see that you understand the double entry involved.
- When calculating straight-line depreciation, include any residual value in your calculation.
- Be sure to complete the double entry for each adjustment on the trial balance.
- Show all workings on your answer paper.
- As you make the adjustments to the trial balance, tick the instructions on the question paper. Check that all instructions are ticked before copying out your answer.
- Show non-current assets in Statement of Financial Position with cost, depreciation and net book value presented in columnar form.

MULTIPLE-CHOICE QUESTIONS

1. Why is depreciation on non-current assets charged in the accounts of a business?
   A. to ensure that assets are replaced when they are worn out
   B. to make sure that cash is available to replace assets when they are worn out
   C. to show what assets are worth in the Statement of Financial Position
   D. to spread the cost of assets over their useful lives.

2. A business purchased a crane for $40 000 on 1 January 2008. The crane was depreciated at the rate of 30% per annum using the reducing-balance method. The crane was sold on 31 December 2010 for $7750. A full year's depreciation was charged in the year of disposal. What was the profit or loss on disposal?
   A. $3750 loss   B. $3750 profit
   C. $5970 loss   D. $5970 profit

3. The following information relates to the non-current assets of a business.

	$
Cost at 1 April 2010	32 000
Accumulated depreciation at 1 April 2010	13 600
Non-current assets purchased in year ended 31 March 2011	7 000
Depreciation charged for the year ended 31 March 2011	4 200

Depreciation is calculated on the reducing balance basis at the rate of 30%. What was the net book value of the assets that were disposed of in the year ended 31 March 2011?
   A. $11 400   B. $16 800
   C. $18 400   D. $25 400

4. The following information is extracted from the books of a business.

	At 31 Dec 2009 $	At 31 Dec 2010 $
Non-current assets (at cost)	230 000	275 000
Less accumulated depreciation	85 000	98 000

Further information for the year ended 31 December 2010 is as follows:

	$
Depreciation charged in the Income Statement	25 000
Additions to non-current assets (at cost)	60 000
Loss on sale of non-current assets	1 000

How much was received from the sales of non-current assets?
   A. $2000   B. $3000   C. $4000   D. $5000

ADDITIONAL EXERCISES

1. The following trial balance was extracted from the books of Piccolo at 31 May 2011.

	$	$
Freehold Land and Buildings at cost	100 000	
Provision for Depreciation of Freehold Buildings		40 000
Plant and Machinery at cost	76 000	
Provision for Depreciation of Plant and Machinery		32 000
Trade receivables	14 000	
Trade payables		6 300
Bank	5 500	
Sales		300 000
Purchases	190 000	
Inventory	30 000	
Wages	56 000	
Heating and Lighting	17 600	
Repairs to Plant and Machinery	5 100	
Advertising	7 000	
Drawings	27 100	
Capital		150 000
	528 300	528 300

Further information

1. Inventory at 31 May 2011: $42 000.
2. Freehold land and buildings at cost is made up as follows: land $20 000; buildings $80 000.
3. Freehold buildings are depreciated at 4% per annum on the straight-line basis.
4. Plant and machinery are depreciated at 25% per annum on the reducing-balance basis.
5. At 31 May 2011, $1800 was owing for heating and lighting. $6000 of the cost of advertising related to the year beginning 1 June 2011.
6. In the year ended 31 May 2011, Piccolo had taken inventory costing $4000 for his personal use. No entry had been made in the books for this.

Required

(a) Prepare Piccolo's Income Statement for the year ended 31 May 2011.
(b) Prepare the Statement of Financial Position at 31 May 2011.

2. Wilhelmina is a trader whose financial year ends on 31 March. Her trial balance at 31 March 2011 was as follows:

	$	$
Leasehold Property at cost	45 000	
Provision for Depreciation of Leasehold Property		13 500
Plant and Machinery at cost	21 000	
Provision for Depreciation of Plant and Machinery		9 200
Office Equipment at cost	7 000	
Provision for Depreciation of Office Equipment		2 400
Trade receivables	1 526	
Trade payables		973
Inventory	13 000	
Bank	1 964	
Wages	13 017	
Electricity	1 012	
Repairs to Machinery	643	
Sundry Expenses	1 234	
Interest on Loan	1 000	
Sales		80 600
Sales Returns	1 590	
Purchases	50 914	
Purchases Returns		825
Long-term Loan		20 000
Drawings	18 598	
Capital		50 000
	177 498	177 498

Further information

1. Inventory at 31 March 2011 cost $16 000.
2. The loan was received in 2008 and is repayable in 2013. Interest on the loan is at the rate of 10% per annum.
3. Plant and machinery at cost include $6000 for a machine bought on hire purchase on 1 January 2011. The cash price of the machine is $30 000. The balance is payable in four quarterly instalments of $6200, including interest, on 1 April 2011, 1 July 2011, 1 October 2011 and 1 January 2012.
4. The leasehold property was acquired on 1 October 2009 for a period of 15 years. It is being amortised on the straight-line basis.
5. Plant and machinery are depreciated on the reducing-balance method using the annual rate of 25%.

6. Office equipment is depreciated at 15% per annum on the straight-line basis.
7. At 31 March 2011, $300 was owing for electricity, and sundry expenses of $180 had been prepaid.

Required

(a) Prepare Wilhelmina's Income Statement for the year ended 31 March 2011.
(b) Prepare the Statement of Financial Position at 31 March 2011.

Bad and doubtful debts

In this chapter you will learn:

- the difference between bad debts and doubtful debts
- how to account for bad debts and bad debts recovered
- how to provide for doubtful debts.

12.1 Bad debts

When somebody owes money but is unable to pay, the debt is a bad one. As soon as debts are known to be bad, they should be cleared from the sales ledger by transferring them by journal entry to a Bad Debts account.

Example

Samuel is owed $1200 by H. Ardup and $850 by Tony Broke. Both of these debtors have become bankrupt on 1 November 2010 and are unable to pay their debts. Samuel writes the debts off as bad.

Journal entries:

2010		$	$
Nov 1	Bad Debts account	1200	
	H. Ardup		1200
H. Ardup has become bankrupt and unable to pay amount due.			
Nov 1	Bad Debts account	850	
	Tony Broke		850
T. Broke has become bankrupt and unable to pay amount due.			

Sales ledger accounts:

H. Ardup					
2010		$	2010		$
Nov 1	Balance b/d	1200	Nov 1	Bad Debts	1200

Tony Broke					
2010		$	2010		$
Nov 1	Balance b/d	850	Nov 1	Bad Debts	850

General ledger: Bad debts				
2010		$	2010	$
Nov 1	H. Ardup	1200		
	Tony Broke	850		

When Samuel prepares his annual accounts, he will transfer the balance on the Bad Debts account to the Income Statement as an expense.

12.2 Bad debts recovered

A debt that has been written off as bad may be recovered at a later date if the debtor becomes able to pay. The debt must be recorded once more on the sales ledger account by a journal entry. The debtor's account will be debited and a Bad Debts Recovered account credited with the amount recovered. The amount received from the debtor may then be credited to his account and debited in the cash book.

Example

On 6 January 2011, Tony Broke had sufficient funds to enable him to pay Samuel and sent him a cheque for $850.

Journal entry:

2011		$	$
Jan 6	Tony Broke	850	
	Bad Debts Recovered		850
An amount of $850 received from Tony Broke. This debt was previously written off as a bad debt on 1 November 2010.			

On 8 January 2011, Samuel received a cheque for $300 being a dividend (or part payment) of 25% of H. Ardup's debt.

Journal entry:

2011		$	$
Jan 8	H. Ardup	300	
	Bad Debts Recovered		300

$300 received in respect of a dividend of 25% of H. Ardup's debt of $1200, which was written off as a bad debt on 1 November 2010.

Sales ledger accounts:

H. Ardup

2010		$	2010		$
Nov 1	Balance b/d	1200	Nov 1	Bad Debts	1200
2011			2011		
Jan 8	Bad Debts Recovered	300	Jan 8	Bank	300

Tony Broke

2010		$	2010		$
Nov 1	Balance b/d	850	Nov 1	Bad Debts	850
2011			2011		
Jan 6	Bad Debts Recovered	850	Jan 6	Bank	850

General ledger accounts:

Bad Debts Recovered

2011		$	2011		$
			Jan 6	Tony Broke	850
			8	H. Ardup	300

The balance on Bad Debts Recovered account will be credited to the Income Statement.

Sometimes, only the difference between the balances on the Bad Debts account and the Bad Debts Recovered account will be included in the Income Statement.

12.3 Provisions for doubtful debts

Although a debt may not actually have become bad, there may be doubt as to whether it will be paid; it may turn out eventually to be a bad debt. It would be misleading to include that debt as an asset in the Statement of Financial Position pretending that the amount is not in doubt. On the other hand, since it has not yet become bad, it would be wrong to write it off. A provision is made to cover that and other doubtful debts.

12.4 How to create and maintain a provision for doubtful debts

When the provision is first created, debit the Income Statement and credit a Provision for Doubtful Debts account with the full amount of the provision.

In the years that follow, the entries in the accounts will only be for increases or decreases in the amounts required for the provision:

Debit the Income Statement and credit the Provision for Doubtful Debts with increases in the Provision.
Debit the Provision for Doubtful Debts and credit the Income Statement with decreases in the provision.

The Provision for Doubtful Debts is deducted from trade receivables in the Statement of Financial Position.

Example

The following information is extracted from Jonah's accounts.

	Total of all receivables	Doubtful debts
	$	$
At 31 December: 2008	12 000	900
2009	14 000	1100
2010	10 000	800

Jonah had not previously made a provision for doubtful debts. The following entries will be made in his accounts.

Income Statement (extracts) for the year ended 31 December		
	Debit	Credit
	$	$
2008 Provision for Doubtful Debts	900	
2009 Provision for Doubtful Debts	200	
2010 Provision for Doubtful Debts		300

Provision for Doubtful Debts (3 years ended 31 December 2008/2009/2010)

2008			$	2008			$
Dec 31	Balance	c/d	900	Dec 31	Income Statement		900
2009				2009			
Dec 31	Balance	c/d	1100	Jan 1	Balance	b/d	900
				Dec 31	Income Statement		200
			1100				1100
2010				2010			
Dec 31	Income Statement		300	Jan 1	Balance	b/d	1100
	Balance	c/d	800				
			1100				1100
				2011			
				Jan 1	Balance	b/d	800

Jonah's Statement of Financial Position at 31 December (extracts)		
	$	$
2008 Trade receivables	12 000	
Less Provision for Doubtful Debts	900	11 100
2009 Trade receivables	14 000	
Less Provision for Doubtful Debts	1 100	12 900
2010 Trade receivables	10 000	
Less Provision for Doubtful Debts	800	9 200

12.5 How to calculate the amount of a provision for doubtful debts

The calculation of a provision for doubtful debts depends upon the type of provision required. There are three kinds of provision:

- specific
- general
- specific and general.

Specific. Certain debts are selected from the sales ledger as doubtful. The provision will be equal to the total of those debts.

General. The provision is calculated as a percentage of the total trade receivables. The average percentage of debts by amount that prove to be bad is usually taken for this purpose.

Specific and general. The provision is made up of the debts that are thought to be doubtful plus a percentage of the remainder.

Example

Job maintains a specific and general provision for doubtful debts. The general provision is based on 4% of trade receivables after deducting doubtful debts.

At 31 December	Total receivables (a) $	Doubtful debts (b) $	Provision Specific (c) $	Provision General (c) $	Total $
2007	31 000	4500	4500	1060	5560
2008	37 000	5000	5000	1280	6280
2009	34 200	3700	3700	1220	4920
2010	35 640	4090	4090	1262	5352

Note

- Specific provisions must be deducted from trade receivables before the general provision is

calculated. In the above example:
[column (a) – column (b)] × 4% = column (c).

- Never refer to a Provision for Bad debts. Bad debts are never provided for; they should always be written off as soon as they become bad.

Exercise 1

Saul maintains a provision for doubtful debts in his books. It is made up of a specific provision for doubtful debts and a general provision equal to 5% of the remainder. The following information is extracted from Saul's books.

At 31 March	Total trade receivables $	Doubtful debts (included in total trade receivables) $
2007	27 000	4000
2008	33 900	6400
2009	30 000	7500
2010	28 000	3000
2011	36 700	8300

Required

(a) Calculate the total provision for doubtful debts for each of the above years.
(b) Prepare the Provision for Doubtful Debts account for each of the years. (Assume that Saul had not made a provision for doubtful debts before 31 March 2007.)

12.6 How to adjust a trial balance for bad and doubtful debts

The adjustments to a trial balance for bad and doubtful debts are demonstrated in the following example.

Example

A trial balance includes: Trade receivables $40 650 (including $400 which are bad debts), and a Provision for Doubtful Debts of $1900. A provision of 8% is to be made for doubtful debts. (The adjustments are shown in *italics*.)

	Trial balance	
	$	$
Trade receivables	40 650 – 400	
Bad debts	*400*	
Provision for Doubtful Debts	*1 320*	1900 + *1320*

Step 1. Deduct the bad debts, $400, from Trade receivables. Insert 'Bad debts 400' as a new debit balance; this will be debited in the Income Statement.

Step 2. Calculate the new provision for doubtful debts and deduct the provision brought forward: $(40\,650 - 400) \times 8\% - \$1900 = \$1320$. Add the result to both sides of the trial balance.

12.7 Provisions for doubtful debts and the concepts

A provision for doubtful debts complies with the following accounting concepts.

Prudence. Amounts expected to be received from trade receivables should not be overstated in Statement of Financial Position. The Income Statement should provide for the loss of revenue and not overstate profit.

Matching. The possible loss of revenue should be provided for in the period in which the revenue was earned, not in a later period when the debt becomes bad.

HINTS

- Read questions carefully and make sure you know exactly what you are required to do.
- Make sure you calculate doubtful debt provisions on trade receivables after you have deducted any bad debts.
- Debit an increase, but credit a decrease, in a provision to the Income Statement.
- Be sure to complete the double entry for each adjustment.
- Show your workings with your answer.
- Tick the adjustments on the question paper. This will ensure you do not overlook them.
- Deduct the new balance on the Provision for Doubtful Debts account from the trade receivables in the Statement of Financial Position.

MULTIPLE-CHOICE QUESTIONS

1. Kapil has decided to maintain a Provision for Doubtful Debts.
   Which of the following concepts should he apply in his accounts?

1. going concern	2. matching
3. prudence	4. realisation
A. 1 and 3	B. 1 and 4
C. 2 and 3	D. 2 and 4

2. The following information is available about a business.

	$
Provision for Doubtful Debts at 1 April 2010	1 100
Trade receivables at 31 March 2011	24 800
Bad debt included in trade receivables at 31 March 2011	600
Charge to Income Statement for bad and doubtful debts, including bad debt of $600	2 294

   Which percentage was used to calculate the Provision for Doubtful Debts at 31 March 2011?
   A. 6.8   B. 7   C. 9.25   D. 9.5

3. At 31 December 2009 a business had a Provision for Doubtful Debts of $1200. At 31 December 2010 the provision was adjusted to $900.
   How did this affect the final accounts?

	Net profit	Net trade receivables
A.	decrease by $300	decrease by $300
B.	decrease by $300	increase by $300
C.	increase by $300	decrease by $300
D.	increase by $300	increase by $300

4. Before any end-of-year adjustments had been made, the trial balance of a business at 31 May 2011 included the following.

	Debit	Credit
	$	$
Trade receivables	13 400	
Provision for Doubtful Debts		500

At 31 May 2011 it was found that trade receivables included a bad debt of $650. It was decided to adjust the Provision for Doubtful Debts to 4% of trade receivables. A debt of $420, which had been written off as bad in January 2010 was recovered in January 2011.

What was the effect of these events on the Income Statement for the year ended 31 May 2011.

A. Debit $384
B. Debit $410
C. Credit $430
D. Credit $456

ADDITIONAL EXERCISES

1. David's trial balance at 31 March 2011 was as follows:

Account	$	$
Sales		210 000
Sales Returns	9 240	
Purchases	84 000	
Purchases Returns		5 112
Wages	37 000	
Rent	7 600	
Electricity	1 027	
Telephone	900	
Postage and Stationery	359	
Carriage inwards	1 840	
Carriage outwards	1 220	
Discounts Allowed	6 015	
Discounts Received		2 480
Leasehold Premises at cost	70 000	
Provision for Depreciation of Leasehold Premises		5 000
Delivery Vans at cost	18 000	
Provision for Depreciation of Delivery Vans		3 600
Office Furniture at cost	3 000	
Provision for Depreciation of Office Furniture		1 500
Inventory	4 000	
Bank	1 245	
Trade receivables	19 800	
Provision for Doubtful Debts		800
Trade payables		7 200
Drawings	20 446	
Capital		50 000
	285 692	285 692

Further information

1. Inventory at 31 March 2011: $5000.
2. Sales include goods sent on sale or return to a customer who has not yet indicated acceptance of the goods. The goods cost $3000 and the customer has been invoiced for $4000.
3. Trade receivables includes debts totalling $1700 which are known to be bad. The Provision for Doubtful Debts is to be adjusted to include a specific provision of $3100 and a general provision of 5%.
4. The following expenses are to be accrued: wages $400, electricity $360 and telephones $100.
5. Rent of $1600 has been prepaid.
6. Depreciation is to be provided on the following bases: leasehold premises at 5% straight line; delivery vans at 25% reducing balance; office furniture at 10% straight line.

Required

(a) Prepare David's Income Statement for the year ended 31 March 2011.
(b) Prepare the Statement of Financial Position at 31 March 2011.

2. Saul is a trader and his trial balance at 31 May 2011 was as follows:

Account	$	$
Freehold Property at cost	180 000	
Provision for Depreciation of Freehold Property		45 000
Plant and Machinery at cost	97 000	
Provision for Depreciation of Plant and Machinery		53 000
Motor Vehicles at cost	41 000	
Provision for Depreciation of Motor Vehicles		27 000
Trade receivables	34 600	
Provision for Doubtful Debts		1 200
Trade payables		5 720
Bank	11 374	
Sales		700 000
Sales Returns	6 670	
Purchase	410 890	
Purchases Returns		3 112
Wages	137 652	
Rent Payable	10 000	
Rent Receivable		1 020
Heating and Lighting	4 720	
Telephone and Postage	3 217	
Stationery	6 195	
Repairs to Machinery	17 600	
Discounts Allowed	3 220	
Discounts Received		2 942
Carriage inwards	4 240	
Carriage outwards	1 819	
Inventory	40 000	
Drawings	28 797	
Capital		200 000
	1 038 994	1 038 994

Further information
1. Inventory at 31 May 2011 cost $58 000.
2. Depreciation is to be calculated as follows: freehold property at 4% per annum, straight line; plant and machinery at 15% per annum; motor vehicles at 30% per annum on the reducing balance.
3. Included in trade receivables is a bad debt of $1800; the provision for doubtful debts is to be 5% of trade receivables.
4. $400 was owing for heating and lighting, and $220 for stationery. The inventory of unused stationery at 31 May 2011 had cost $450.
5. Rent paid in advance was $2000; rent receivable was owing in the sum of $280.
6. Saul had taken goods for his own use. The goods had cost $2400. No entries for this had been made in the books.

Required
(a) Prepare Saul's Income Statement for the year ended 31 May 2011.
(b) Prepare the Statement of Financial Position at 31 May 2011.

13 Bank reconciliation statements

In this chapter you will learn:

- what a bank reconciliation statement is
- how to ensure that the bank balance in the cash book equals the correct balance of cash at bank
- how to adjust a trial balance after the cash book has been reconciled to the bank statement.

13.1 What is a bank reconciliation statement?

A **bank reconciliation statement** shows the correct balance on a bank account. The balance on the bank account in a cash book may not agree with the balance on the bank statement at any particular date. This may be because of

- timing differences (the delay between items being entered in the cash book and their entry on the bank statement)
- items on the bank statement that have not been entered in the cash book (for example, bank charges and interest, direct debits and other items).

Note. A bank statement is a copy of a customer's account in the books of a bank. Consequently items debited in the customer's own cash book appear as credits in the bank statement, and items credited in the cash book are debited in the bank statement. A debit balance in the cash book will appear as a credit balance in the bank statement. If a bank account is overdrawn, the customer owes the bank money. The bank is now a creditor represented by a credit balance in the cash book; the customer is the bank's debtor and is shown as a debit balance on the bank statement.

When the balances in the cash book and bank statement do not agree, the correct balance must be found by preparing a bank reconciliation statement.

13.2 How to prepare a bank reconciliation statement

Follow these three steps.

1. Compare the entries in the cash book with the bank statements. Tick items that appear in both the cash book *and* the bank statement. Be sure to tick them in both places.
2. Enter in the cash book any items that remain unticked in the bank statement. Then tick those in both places. Calculate the new cash book balance.
3. Prepare the reconciliation statement. Begin with the final balance shown on the bank statement and adjust it for any items that remain unticked in the cash book. The result should equal the balance in the cash book.

The cash book balance will now be the correct balance of cash at bank.

Example 1

After step 1 has been completed, A.J. Belstrode's cash book and bank statement appear as follows at 31 March 2011. (Note the items which have been ticked.)

Cash book
Bank account

2011		$	2011	Cheque No.	$
Mar 1	Balance brought forward	1250	Mar 8	1022 Electricity	300✓
7	Cash banked	700✓	10	1023 Wages	600✓
12	P. Witte	200✓	11	1024 Rent	400✓
			14	1025 T. Bone	920✓

15	Cash banked	600✓	15	1026 Wages	440✓
20	T. Bagge	430✓	28	1027 A. Cape	120
31	T. Cake	594	29	1028 F. Goode	96
			31	1029 H. Ope	300
			31	Balance c/d	598
		3774			3774
April 1	Balance b/d	598			

Bank statement
THE REDDYPAY BANK

Account: A.J. Belstrode

		Money out $	Money in $	$
March 1	Balance brought forward			1250 Cr
7	Paid in		700✓	1950 Cr
10	Paid by cheque 1023	600✓		1350 Cr
11	Paid by cheque 1022	300✓		1050 Cr
12	Paid in		200✓	1250 Cr
14	Direct debit: I. Taikeit	227		1023 Cr
15	Paid in		600✓	1623 Cr
	Paid by cheque 1026	440✓		1183 Cr
6	Paid by cheque 1024	400✓		783 Cr
	Paid by cheque 1025	920✓		137 Cr
20	Paid in		430✓	293 Cr
25	Bank Giro credit – Invest dividend		200	493 Cr
31	Bank charges	112		381 Cr

Step 2. The unticked items in the bank statement are entered in the cash book and ticked.

Cash book
Bank account

2011		$	2010		$
Apr 1	Balance b/d	598	Mar 14	D/d I. Taikeit	227✓
Mar 25	Invest – dividend	200✓	Mar 31	Bank charges	112✓
			Mar 31	Balance c/d	459
		798			798
April1	Balance b/d	459			

Note. Do not re-write the whole cash book to enter the new items.

Step 3. A bank reconciliation statement is prepared commencing with the bank statement balance which is adjusted for the items remaining unticked in the cash book.

Bank reconciliation statement at 31 March 2011

		$	$
Balance per bank statement			381
Add: Item not credited in bank statement			594
			975
Deduct cheques not presented:	1027	120	
	1028	96	
	1029	300	516
Balance per cash book			459

The correct bank balance, $459, has been calculated and, if a Statement of Financial Position at 31 March 2011 is prepared, $459 will be the amount included in it as the bank balance.

Example 2

At 30 June 2011 Eliza's bank statement shows a balance at bank of $1000. When Eliza checks her cash book she finds the following:

- A payment of $200 into the bank on 30 June does not appear in the bank statement.
- Cheques totalling $325 sent to customers on 29 June do not appear in the bank statement.
- The bank statement shows that Eliza's account has been debited with bank charges of $40. These have not been recorded in the cash book.

Required

(a) Prepare Eliza's bank reconciliation at 30 June 2011.

(b) Calculate Eliza's cash book balance at 30 June 2011 before it was corrected.

Answer

(a) Bank reconciliation statement at 30 June 2011

	$
Balance per bank statement	1000
Add amount paid in not credited	200
	1200
Deduct cheques not presented	325
Balance at 30 June 2011	875

(b) Cash book balance before correction

Correct balance at bank at 30 June 2011	875
Add bank charges not debited in cash book	40
Cash book balance before it was corrected	915

13.3 Uses of bank reconciliation statement

- They reveal the correct amount of the cash at bank. Without a reconciliation, the cash book and bank statement balances may be misleading.
- They ensure that the correct bank balance is shown in the Statement of Financial Position.
- They are an important system of control:
  - unintended overdrawing on the bank account can be avoided
  - a surplus of cash at bank can be highlighted and invested to earn interest
  - if reconciliations are prepared regularly, errors are discovered early
  - if the reconciliation is prepared by somebody other than the cashier, the risk of fraud or embezzlement of funds is reduced. This division of duties is called **internal check**.

Exercise 1

The balance on a bank statement at 31 January 2011 was $1220 Credit. The following items had been entered in the cash book in January but did not appear on the bank statements:

(i) amount paid into the bank $300.

(ii) cheques sent to customers $1045.

Required

Calculate the cash book balance at 31 January 2011.

Exercise 2

The bank balance in a cash book at 31 July 2011 was $310 (debit). The following items did not appear in the bank statement at that date:

(i) cheques totalling $1340 which had been paid into the bank on 31 July 2011.

(ii) cheques sent to customers in July, totalling $490.

Required

Calculate the bank statement balance at 31 July 2011.

Exercise 3

At 31 March 2011 a cash book showed a balance of $80 at bank. On the same date the bank statement balance was $650 (credit). When the cash book was compared with the bank statement the following were found:

(i) a cheque sent to a supplier for $1000 had not been presented for payment

(ii) a cheque for $220 paid into the bank had not been credited on the bank statement

(iii) bank charges of $210 were omitted from the cash book.

Required

(a) Calculate the corrected cash book balance at 31 March 2011.

(b) Prepare a bank reconciliation statement at 31 March 2011.

Exercise 4

The following balances were extracted from the trial balance of a business at 31 December 2010.

	$	$
Trade receivables	1055	
Trade payables		976
Rent	800	
Bank	1245	

	$
Payment to a supplier by direct debt	360
Amount received from a customer by bank giro	420
Rent paid by standing order	200
Customer's cheque returned, dishonoured	323

When the bank statement for December was received it was discovered that the following items had not been entered in the cash book.

Required

Prepare the adjusted trial balance to include the items omitted from the cash book.

HINTS

- Remember the three steps required to reconcile a bank account.
- Note carefully if the balances given for the cash book or bank statement are overdrafts.
- Complete the double entry for all items entered in the cash book. Amend the other balances in the trial balance.
- Show bank overdrafts as current liabilities in Statements of Financial Position, never as current assets.

MULTIPLE-CHOICE QUESTIONS

1. At 30 April 2011 the balance in X's cash book was $1740. At the same date the balance on his bank statement was $2240. Comparison of the cash book and bank statement showed the following:
   (i) a dividend, $200, credited to X in the bank statement had not been entered in the cash book
   (ii) cheques totalling $300 sent to suppliers in April had not been entered in the bank statement.
   Which amount should be shown in the Statement of Financial Position at 30 April 2011?
   A. $1640 **B.** $1740 **C.** $1940 **D.** $2240

2. A cash book balance at 31 October 2010 was $1600. When the bank statement was received the following were discovered:
   (i) a cheque for $425 sent to a supplier had been entered in the cash book as $452.
   (ii) a cheque for $375 sent to a supplier had not been presented for payment.
   (iii) a cheque for $400 paid into the bank had not been credited in the bank statement.
   What was the balance on the bank statement at 31 October 2010?
   A. $1548 **B.** $1575 **C.** $1602 **D.** $1652

3. Y's bank statement showed a credit balance of $2170 at 31 May 2011. An examination of the statement showed the following:
   (i) a direct debit for $300 had been debited twice in the bank statement

   (ii) a cheque for $1015 sent to a supplier had not been presented for payment
   (iii) a cheque for $600 paid into the bank had not been credited in the bank statement
   What was the cash book balance at 31 May 2011.
   A. $1455 **B.** $2055 **C.** $2285 **D.** $2885

4. A bank statement at 31 January 2011 showed a balance of $1000 Dr. The following did not appear on the statement:
   (i) cheques not presented for payment, $230
   (ii) a cheque for $400 banked on 31 January 2011
   (iii) bank charges of $200 had not been entered in the cash book
   What was the original balance in the cash book at 31 January 2011 before it was amended?
   A. $630 Cr   **B.** $630 Dr
   C. $970 Cr   **D.** $970 Dr

5. A bank statement showed an overdraft of $360 at 31 July 2011. The following discoveries were made:
   (i) cheques totalling $2100 banked in July had not been credited in the bank statement.
   (ii) cheques drawn for $875 in the cash book in July had not been entered on the bank statement.
   What was the balance in the cash book at 31 July 2011?
   A. $865 Cr   **B.** $865 Dr
   C. $1585 Cr   **D.** $1585 Dr

ADDITIONAL EXERCISES

1. The following balances have been extracted from a trial balance at 30 June 2011.

	$	$
Trade receivables	400	
Trade payables		380
Rent receivable		750
Bank changes	100	
Bank	990	

After the preparation of the trial balance a bank statement was received and revealed that the following had not been entered in the cash book.

	$
Bank interest receivable credited to account	10
Bank charges	130
Standing order payment to supplier	298
Amount received from customer by direct debit	78
Rent received by bank giro	150

Required

Prepare an amended trial balance extract at 30 June 2011 to take account of the amounts not entered in the cash book.

14 Control accounts

In this chapter you will learn:

- what Control accounts are and how to prepare them
- how to reconcile Control accounts and ledgers
- how to calculate revised net profit per draft accounts after the Control and ledger accounts have been reconciled
- how to revise the current assets and current liabilities in a draft Statement of Financial Position.

14.1 What is a Control account?

A **Control account** contains the totals of all postings made to the accounts in a particular ledger.

Control accounts are usually maintained for the sales and purchase ledgers. The totals are the periodic totals of the books of prime entry from which postings are made to the ledger.

The balance on a Control account should equal the total of the balances in the ledger it controls. Because the entries in the Control accounts are the totals of the books of prime entry they are also known as Total accounts. Control (or Total) accounts are kept in the nominal (or general) ledger.

Just as a trial balance acts as a check on the arithmetical accuracy of *all* the ledgers, a Control account checks the arithmetical accuracy of a single ledger. A difference between a Control account balance and the total of the balances in the ledger it controls shows where a cause of a difference on a trial balance may be found. Any difference between the Control account and the total of the balances in the ledger must be found without delay. The Sales Ledger Control account is also known as the Debtors' or Trade Receivables Control account, and the Purchase Ledger Control account is also known as the Creditors' or Trade Payables Control account.

The following examples show how postings are made from the books of prime entry to the ledgers and the Control accounts, and how the balances on the Control accounts should equal the totals of the balances on the accounts in the ledgers.

14.2 The purchase ledger and its Control account

Books of prime entry

Purchases journal		Purchases returns journal		Cash book		
	$		$	$		$
AB	100	PQ	8		AB	80
PQ	50	XY	10		PQ	40
XY	240		18		XY	200
	390					320

Purchase ledger
AB

	$			$
Cash book	80	Purchases		100
Balance c/d	20*			
	100			100
		Balance	b/d	20

PQ

	$			$
Purchases returns	8	Purchases		50
Cash book	40			
Balance c/d	2*			
	50			50
		Balance	b/d	2

XY

	$			$
Purchases returns	10	Purchases		240
Cash book	200			
Balance c/d	30*			
	240			240
		Balance	b/d	30

Nominal (general) ledger
Purchase Ledger Control account

	$			$
Purchases returns journal	18	Purchases journal		390
Cash book	320			
Balance c/d	52* =	*20 +2 +30		
	390			390
		Balance	b/d	52

*Balancing figure

14.3 How to prepare a Purchase Ledger Control account

Enter items in the Control account as follows:

Debit side	Credit side
Total of purchase ledger debit balances (if any) brought forward from the previous period	Balance on the account brought forward from the previous period
Total of goods returned to suppliers (from purchases returns journal)	Total of purchases on credit (from purchases journal)
Total of cash paid to suppliers (from cash book)	Refunds from suppliers (from cash book)
Cash discounts received (from discount column in cash book)	Interest charged by suppliers on overdue invoices (from purchases journal)
Purchase ledger balances set against balance in sales ledger (from journal)	Total of debit balances (if any) at end of period in purchase ledger, carried forward
Balance carried forward (to agree with total of credit balances in purchases ledger)	

Note. Debit balances in the purchase ledger must *never* be netted against (deducted from) the credit balances.

* **Warning**. Only credit purchases are entered in the Purchase Ledger Control account. Do not enter cash purchases in it.

14.4 The sales ledger and its Control account

Books of prime entry

Sales journal		Sales returns journal		Cash book		
	$		$	$	$	$
Bali	300			Bali	180	
Carla	520	Bali	50	Carla	480	
Paula	140	Paula	10	Paula	100	
	960		60		760	

Sales ledger
Bali

	$			$
Sales	300	Sales returns		50
		Cash book		180
		Balance	c/d	70*
	300			300
Balance	b/d	70		

Carla

	$			$
Sales	520	Cash book		480
		Balance	c/d	40*
	520			520
Balance	b/d	40		

Paula

	$			$
Sales	140	Sales returns		10
		Cash book		100
		Balance	c/d	30*
	140			140
Balance	b/d	30		

*Balancing figure

Nominal (general) ledger
Sales Ledger Control account

	$		$	
Sales journal	960	Sales returns journal	60	
		Cash book	760	
		Balance c/d	140	= *70
				+ 40
				+ 30
	960		960	
Balance	b/d	140		

14.5 How to prepare a sales ledger Control account

Enter items in the Control account as follows:

Debit side	Credit side
Balance brought forward from previous period	Total of sales ledger credit balances (if any) brought forward from previous period
Credit sales for period (total sales journal)	Sales returns for the period (total of sales returns journal)
Refunds to credit customers (from cash book)	Cash received from credit customers (from cash book)
Dishonoured cheques (from cash book)	Cash discounts allowed (discounts columns in cash book)
	Bad debts written off (journal)
Interest charged to customers on overdue accounts (sales journal or cash book)	Cash from bad debts recovered, previously written off (cash book)

Debit side	Credit side
Bad debts previously written off, now recovered (journal)	Sales ledger balances set against balances in purchase ledger (journal)
Total of credit balances (if any) in sales ledger at end of period carried forward	Balance carried forward to agree with total of debit balances in sales ledger

Note. Do not 'net' credit balances in the sales ledger against the debit balances.

* Warning. Do not enter the following in a Sales Ledger Control account:
- cash sales
- provisions for doubtful debts.

14.6 Control accounts and the double-entry model

Control account duplicate the information contained in the purchase and sales (personal) ledgers. Control accounts *and* personal ledgers cannot both be part of the double-entry model. It is usual to treat the Control accounts as part of the double entry and to regard the personal ledgers as memorandum records containing the details which support the Control accounts.

Example

The following information has been extracted from the books of Useful Controls Ltd.

		$
At 1 June 2011 Purchase ledger balances brought forward	– debit	900
	– credit	16 340
Sales ledger balances brought forward	– debit	30 580
	– credit	620
Month to 30 June 2011		
Purchases journal total		65 000
Purchases returns journal total		3 150
Sales journal total		96 400
Sales returns journal total		1 980
Cash book: Payments to suppliers		59 540
Cheques received from customers (see note below)		103 900
Discounts received		2 670
Discounts allowed		4 520
Dishonoured cheques		3 300
Journal: Bad debts written off		1 220
Sales ledger balances set against purchase ledger balances		4 800
At June 30 Debit balances on purchase ledger accounts		600
Credit balances on sales ledger accounts		325

Note. The cash received from customers includes $800 relating to a bad debt previously written off.

Required

Prepare a Purchase Ledger Control account and a Sales Ledger Control account for Useful Controls, for the month of June 2011.

Answer

Purchase Ledger Control account

2011		$	2011		$
Jun 1 Balance b/d		900	Jun 1 Balance b/d		16 340
30 Purchases returns			30 Purchases journal		65 000
journal		3 150	30 Balance c/d		600
Cash book		59 540			
Discounts received		2 670			
Sales ledger-contra		4 800			
Balance c/d					
(Balancing figure)		10 880			
		81 940			81 940
July 1 Balance b/d		600	July 1 Balance b/d		10 880

Sales Ledger Control account

2011		$	2011		$
Jun 1 Balance b/d		30 580	Jun 1 Balance b/d		620
30 Sales journal		96 400	30 Sales returns		
Bad debt			journal		1 980
recovered		800	Cash book		103 900
Bank —			Discounts allowed		4 520
dishonoured			Bad debts written		
cheques		3 300	off		1 220
Balance c/d		325	Purchase ledger —		
			contra		4 800
			30 Balance c/d		
			(Balancing figure)		14 365
		131 405			131 405
Jul 1 Balance b/d		14 365	Jul 1 Balance b/d		325

Exercise 1

The following information has been obtained from the books of Byit Ltd.

		$
At 1 March 2011 Purchase ledger balances		
brought forward	(credit)	10 000
	(debit)	16
In the month to 31 March 2011		
Total of invoices received from suppliers		33 700
Goods returned to suppliers		824
Cheques sent to suppliers		27 500
Discounts received		1 300
At 31 March 2011 Debit balances in purchase ledger		156
Credit balances in purchase ledger		?

Required

Prepare the Purchase Ledger Control account for the month of March 2011.

Exercise 2

Information extracted from the books of Soldit Ltd is as follows:

		$
At 1 May 2011 Sales ledger balances		
brought forward	(debit)	27 640
	(credit)	545
In the month to 31 May 2011		
Total of invoices sent to customers		109 650
Goods returned by customers		2 220
Cheques received from customers		98 770
Discounts allowed		3 150
Cheque received in respect of bad debt previously written off (not included above)		490
Sales ledger balance set against balance in purchase ledger		2 624
At 31 May 2011 Credit balances in sales ledger		800
Debit balance carried down		?

Required

Prepare the Sales Ledger Control account for the month of May 2011.

14.7 Uses and limitations of Control accounts

Uses

- They are an important system of control on the reliability of ledger accounts.
- They warn of possible errors in the ledgers they control if the totals of the balances in those ledgers do not agree with the balances on the Control accounts.
- They may identify the ledger or ledgers in which errors have been made when there is a difference on a trial balance.
- They provide totals of trade receivables and trade payables quickly when a trial balance is being prepared.
- If a business employs several accounting staff, the Control accounts should be maintained by somebody who is not involved in maintaining the sales or purchase ledgers. This increases the likelihood of errors being discovered and reduces the risk of individuals acting dishonestly. This division of duties is called **internal check**. For this reason Control accounts are kept in the general ledger and not in the sales and purchase ledgers.

Limitations

- Control accounts may themselves contain errors. [See (1) and (2) in §14.8.]
- Control accounts do not guarantee the accuracy of individual ledger accounts, which may contain compensating errors, for example items posted to wrong accounts.

14.8 How to reconcile Control accounts with ledgers

When there is a difference between the balance on a Control account and the total of the balances in the ledger it controls, the cause or causes must be found and the necessary corrections made. This is known as reconciling the Control accounts.

It is helpful to remember the following.

1. If a transaction is omitted from a book of prime entry, it will be omitted from the personal account in the sales or purchase ledger *and* from the Control account. Both records will be wrong and the Control account will not reveal the error.
2. If a transaction is entered incorrectly in a book of prime entry, the error will be repeated in the personal account in the sales or purchase ledger *and* in the Control account. Both records will be wrong and the Control account will not reveal the error.
3. If an item is copied incorrectly from a book of prime entry to a personal account in the sales or purchase ledger, the Control account will *not* be affected, and it will reveal that an error has been made.
4. If a total in a book of prime entry is incorrect, the Control account will be incorrect *but* the sales or purchase ledgers will not be affected. The Control account will reveal that an error has been made.

Example

The following information has been extracted from Duprey's books at 31 December 2010.

		$
Total of sales ledger balances	(debit)	17 640
	(credit)	110
Balance on Sales Ledger Control account (debit)		18 710
Total of purchase ledger balances	(credit)	6 120
	(debit)	80
Balance on Purchase Ledger Control account (credit)		6 330

The following errors have been discovered.

1. A sales invoice for $100 has been omitted from the sales journal.
2. A credit balance of $35 in the sales ledger has been extracted as a debit balance in the list of sales ledger balances.
3. The sales journal total for December has been overstated by $1000.
4. A balance of $250 on a customer's account in the sales ledger has been set against the amount owing to him in the purchase ledger but no entries have been made for this in the Sales and Purchase Ledger Control accounts.
5. A supplier's invoice for $940 has been entered in the purchases journal as $490.
6. An item of $340 in the purchases returns journal has been credited in the supplier's account in the purchase ledger. There was a credit balance of $800 on the supplier's account at 31 December.
7. Discounts received in December amounting to $360 have been credited to the Purchase Ledger Control account.

Further information

Duprey's draft accounts for the year ended 31 December 2010 show a net profit of $36 000. He makes a provision for doubtful debts of 6%.

Required

(a) Calculate the following at 31 December 2010:
  (i) the revised sales ledger balances
  (ii) the revised purchase ledger balances
(b) Prepare the amended Sales Ledger and Purchase Ledger Control accounts.
(c) Prepare a statement of the revised net profit for the year ended 31 December 2010.
(d) Prepare an extract from the Statement of Financial Position at 31 December 2010 to show the trade receivables and trade payables.

Answer

(a) (i) Revised sales ledger balances

	Debit $	Credit $
Before adjustment	17 640	110
Invoice omitted from sales journal	100	
Credit balance listed as a debit	(35)	35
Revised balances	17 705	145

(ii) Revised purchase ledger balances.

	Debit $	Credit $
Before adjustment	80	6120
Error in purchases journal $(940 – 490)		450
Adjustment of return credited to supplier $(340 × 2)*		(680)
Revised balances	80	5890

* An adjustment for an item placed on the wrong side of an account must be twice the amount of the item.

(b)

Amended Sales Ledger Control account

2010	$	2010	$
Dec 31 Balance brought forward	18 710	Dec 31 Correction of sales journal total	1 000
Invoice omitted from S J	100	Contra to purchase ledger ¢	250
Balance c/d	145	Balance c/d	17 705
	18 955		18 955
2011		2011	
Jan 1 Balance b/d	17 705	Jan 1 Balance b/d	145

Amended Purchase Ledger Control account

2010	$	2010	$
Dec 31 Contra to sales ledger ¢	250	Dec 31 Balance brought forward	6330
Correction of discounts $(360 × 2)	720	Error in purchase journal	450
Balance c/d	5890	Balance c/d	80
	6860		6860
2011		2011	
Jan 1 Balance b/d	80	Jan 1 Balance b/d	5890

(c) Revised net profit for the year ended 31 December 2010.

	Decrease $	Increase $	$
Net profit per draft accounts			36 000
Sales invoice omitted from sales journal		100	
Overcast of sales journal	1000		
Purchase invoice understated	450		
Increase in provision for doubtful debts 6% of (17 705 – 17 640)	4		
	1454	100	(1 354)
Revised net profit			34 646

(d) Statement of Financial Position extracts at 31 December 2010.

	$	$
Trade receivables		
Sales ledger	17 705	
Deduct provision for doubtful debts	1 062	
	16 643	
Purchase ledger (debit balances)	80	16 723
Trade payables		
Purchase ledger	5 890	
Sales ledger (credit balances)	145	6 035

Notes

- Trade receivables should never be deducted from trade payables, or trade payables from trade receivables in a Statement of Financial Position.
- Do not provide for doubtful debts on debit balances in the purchase ledger.

Exercise 3

The following information has been extracted from the books of Rorre Ltd at 31 December 2010.

	$
Total of purchase ledger balance	64 (debit)
	7 217 (credit)
Total of sales ledger balances	23 425 (debit)
	390 (credit)
Purchase Ledger Control account	7 847 (credit)
Sales Ledger Control account	22 909 (debit)

Draft accounts show a net profit of $31 000 for the year ended 31 December 2010. The following errors have been discovered.

1. An invoice for $100 has been entered twice in the purchases journal.
2. A total of $84 has been omitted from both the Discounts Received account and the Purchase Ledger Control account.
3. A debit balance of $50 has been entered in the list of purchase ledger balances as a credit balance.
4. An amount of $710 owing to Trazom, a supplier, has been offset against their account in the sales ledger, but no entry has been made in the Control accounts.
5. An invoice in the sales journal for $326 has been entered in the sales ledger as $362.
6. The sales journal total for December has been understated by $800.

Required

(a) Prepare a statement to show the corrected purchase and sales ledger balances.
(b) Prepare corrected Purchase and Sales Ledger Control accounts.
(c) Calculate the amended net profit for the year ended 31 December 2010.
(d) Prepare a Statement of Financial Position extract at 31 December 2010 to show the trade receivables and trade payables.

MULTIPLE-CHOICE QUESTIONS

1. The debit balance on a Sales Ledger Control Account at 30 September 2010 is $104 000. The following errors have been discovered.

	$
Total of sales journal overstated	1300
Discounts allowed omitted from Sales Ledger Control account	870
Bad debts written off not recorded in Sales Ledger Control account	240
Increase in provision for doubtful debts	600

What is the total of the balances in the sales ledger?

A. $100 990   B. $101 590

C. $102 070   D. $103 330

2. The credit balance on a Purchase Ledger Control account at 31 October is $28 000. The following errors have been found.

	$
Amount transferred from Calif's account in the sales ledger to his account in the purchase ledger not recorded in the Control accounts	1 400
A debit balance in the purchase ledger at 31 October not carried down in the Purchase Ledger Control account	300
A refund to a cash customer debited in Purchase Ledger Control account	150

What is the total of the credit balances in the purchase ledger?

A. $26 450   B. $26 750

C. $27 050   D. $28 950

3. A Purchase Ledger Control account has been reconciled with the purchase ledger balances as shown.

	$
Balance per Control account	76 000
Total of purchases journal for one month not posted to general ledger	4 000
Cash paid to trade payables not posted to purchase ledger	5 000
Total of balances in purchase ledger	85 000

Which figure for trade payables should be shown in the Statement of Financial Position?

A. $75 000   B. $77 000

C. $80 000   D. $85 000

ADDITIONAL EXERCISES

1. The following information was taken from Peter's books.

2011		$
March 1	Sales Ledger Control account balance	55 650 Dr
	Purchase Ledger Control account balance	34 020 Cr
31	Sales for March	47 700
	Purchases for March	21 840
	Cheques received from credit customers	36 900
	Payments to trade payables	24 300
	Customers' cheques returned unpaid	1 920
	Bad debts written off	2 250
	Discounts received	600
	Discounts allowed	930
	Returns inwards	580
	Returns outwards	330
	Credit balance in purchase ledger transferred from sales ledger	810

Required

Prepare the Sales Ledger Control account and the Purchase Ledger Control account for the month of March 2011.

2. The following information was extracted from the books of Colombo for the year ended 30 April 2011.

	$
Purchase ledger balances at 1 May 2010	64 680
Credit purchases	1 236 210
Credit purchases returns	18 600
Cheques paid to trade payables	1 118 970
Cash purchases	13 410
Discount received on credit purchases	47 100
Credit balances transferred to sales ledger accounts	7 815

Required

(a) Prepare the Purchase Ledger Control account for the year ended 30 April 2011.
The total of the balances extracted from Colombo's purchase ledger amounts to $101 490, which does not agree with the closing balance in the Control account. The following errors were then discovered.
1. The total of discount received had been overstated by $1500.
2. A purchase invoice for $3060 had been completely omitted from the books.
3. A credit balance in the purchase ledger account had been understated by $150.
4. A credit balance of $1275 in the purchase ledger had been set off against a contra entry in the sales ledger, but no entry had been made in either Control account.
5. A payment of $2175 had been debited to the creditor's account but was omitted from the bank account.
6. A credit balance of $4815 had been omitted from the list of trade payables.

(b) (i) Extract the necessary information from the above list and draw up an amended Purchase Ledger Control account for the year ended 30 April 2011.
(ii) Beginning with the given total of $101 490, show the changes to be made in the purchase ledger to reconcile it with the new Control account balance.

3. At 31 December 2010 the balance on Sellit's Sales Ledger Control account was $17 584 (debit). It did not agree with the total of balances extracted from the sales ledger. The following errors have been found.
1. The total of the discount allowed column in the cash book has been overstated by $210.
2. A receipt of $900 from P. Ford, a customer, has been treated as a refund from B. Ford, a supplier.
3. An invoice for $1200 sent to P. Williams, a customer, has been entered in the sales journal as $1020.
4. The total of the sales journal for December has been understated by $600.
5. Goods with a selling price of $578 were sent to Will Dither, a customer, in December, and he has been invoiced for that amount. It has now been discovered that the goods were sent on sale or return and the customer has not yet indicated whether he will purchase the goods.

6. An invoice for $3160 sent to W. Yeo, a customer, has been entered correctly in the sales journal but has been entered in the customer's account as $3610.

Required

(a) Prepare the Sales Ledger Control account showing clearly the amendments to the original balance.

(b) Calculate the total of the balances extracted from the sales ledger before the errors listed above had been corrected.

(c) Prepare the journal entries to correct the sales ledger accounts. Narratives are required.

4. At 31 May 2011 the debit balance on a Sales Ledger Control account was $18 640. This balance did not agree with the total of balances extracted from the sales ledger. The following errors have now been found.

1. Cash received from trade receivables entered in the Control account included $400 in respect of a debt which had previously been written off. This fact had not been recognised in the Control account.

2. A debit balance of $325 in the sales ledger had been set off against an account in the purchase ledger. This transfer had been debited in the Sales Ledger Control account and credited in the Purchase Ledger Control account.

3. Cash sales of $1760 had been recorded in the cash book as cash received from trade receivables.

4. Cash received from K. Bali, $244, had been entered in the account of B. Kali in the sales ledger.

5. Credit balances in the sales ledger totalled $436.

Required

Prepare the corrected Sales Ledger Control account at 31 May 2011.

5. (a) Outline *three* reasons for keeping control accounts.

(b) The following information was extracted from the books of William Noel for the year ended 30 April 2011.

	$
Purchase Ledger Balance at 1 May 2010	43 120
Credit purchases for the year	824 140
Credit purchases returns	12 400
Cheques paid to Trade payables	745 980
Cash purchases	8 940
Discount received on credit purchases	31 400
Credit balances transferred to sales ledger accounts	5 210

Draw up the Purchase Ledger Control account for the year ended 30 April 2011. The total of the balances in William Noel's purchase ledger amounts to $67 660, which does not agree with the closing balance in the Control account.

The following errors were then discovered.

1. Discount received had been overstated by $1000.

2. A credit purchases invoice for $2040 had been completely omitted from the books.

3. A purchases ledger account had been understated by $100.

4. A credit balance of $850 in the purchases ledger had been set off against a contra entry in the sales ledger, but no entry had been made in either Control account.

5. A payment of $1450 had been debited to the creditor's account but was omitted from the bank account.

6. A credit balance of $3210 had been omitted from the list of Trade payables.

(c) (i) Extract the necessary information from the above list and draw up an amended Purchase Ledger Control account for the year ended 30 April 2011.

(ii) Beginning with the given total of $67 660, show the changes to be made in the Purchase Ledger to reconcile it with the new Control account balance.

15 Suspense accounts

In this chapter you will learn:

- what the purpose of Suspense accounts is, and how to prepare them
- how to prepare journal entries to correct errors
- how to revise the net profit per draft accounts after errors have been corrected
- how to revise the working capital in a draft Statement of Financial Position.

15.1 What is a Suspense account?

Suspense accounts are sometimes used when transactions are recorded in the books before any decision has been made about their proper accounting treatment. For example, an invoice may contain a mixture of capital and revenue expenditure. The expenditure may be recorded in a Suspense account until it is decided how much is capital expenditure and how much revenue.

This chapter is concerned with Suspense accounts that are opened when the causes of differences on trial balances cannot immediately be found and corrected.

15.2 When a Suspense account should be opened

A Suspense account should be opened only when attempts to find the cause of a difference on a trial balance have been unsuccessful. The following checks should be carried out before opening a Suspense account.

1. Check the additions of the trial balance.
2. If the difference is divisible by 2, look for a balance of half the difference which may be on the wrong side of the trial balance. (Example: a difference of $1084 may be caused by 'discounts allowed $542' being entered on the credit side of the trial balance.)
3. If the difference is divisible by 9, look for a balance where digits may have been reversed. (Example: a difference of $18 may be caused by $542 entered in trial balance as $524.)
4. Check the totals of sales ledger balances and purchase ledger balances to the Control accounts, if these have been prepared.
5. Check the extraction of balances from the ledgers.

If the cause of the difference has still not been found, and an Income Statement and a Statement of Financial Position are required urgently, a Suspense account may be opened.

15.3 How to open a Suspense account

A Suspense account is opened in the general ledger with a balance on whichever side of the account will make the trial balance agree when the balance is inserted in it. For example, if the total of the credit side of a trial balance is $100 less than the total of the debit side, the Suspense account will be opened with a credit balance of $100. When the Suspense account balance is inserted in the trial balance, the latter will balance. A Statement of Financial Position may then be prepared.

15.4 When a Suspense account has been opened

The cause or causes of the difference on the trial balance must be investigated at the earliest opportunity and the errors corrected.

In real life, if there is still a small balance on a Suspense account after all reasonable attempts have been made to find the difference, a business may decide that the amount involved is not material. It will save further time and expense in searching for errors by writing the balance off to the Income Statement. However, there may be a danger that a small difference hides large errors which do not quite cancel each other out.

The types of error which will require Suspense account to be opened will include:

- When only half of the transaction has been posted. For example, the payment of wages has been entered as a credit in the bank account, but no other entry has been made on the debit side of an account.
- When both entries have been made on the same side of two separate accounts. For example, when the payment of wages has been credited to both the bank account and the wages account.
- When the entries have been made on the correct side of the account, but the figures differ. For example the payment of wages has been correctly entered in the bank account as a credit of $230. However, the debit in the wages account is $320.

There are other instances, as you will see in some of the exercises.

15.5 How to correct errors

The correction of errors will require journal entries which will be posted to the Suspense (and other) accounts *unless* they are errors that do *not* affect the trial balance, which are as follows:

- errors of omission
- errors of commission
- errors of principle
- errors of original entry
- errors caused by the complete reversal of entries
- compensating errors.

(These types of errors have been explained more fully in §6.3.)

To decide how to correct an error, ask the following three questions.

(i)   How has the transaction been recorded?
(ii) How should the transaction have been recorded?
(iii) What adjustments are required to correct the error?

Remember the following.

- An item on the wrong side of an account must be corrected by an adjustment equal to *twice* the amount of the original error (once to cancel the error and once to place the item on the correct side of the account).
- Some errors do not affect the double entry; an example would be a balance on a sales ledger account copied incorrectly onto a summary of balances for inclusion in the trial balance. The summary of balances should be amended and a one-sided entry in the journal prepared to correct the Suspense account. Such errors do not require to be corrected by debit *and* credit entries.

Example

Kadriye extracted a trial balance from her ledgers on 31 December 2010. The trial balance totals were $23 884 (debit) and $24 856 (credit). She placed the difference in a Suspense account so that she could prepare a draft Income Statement for the year ended 31 December 2010, and a Statement of Financial Position at that date.

Kadriye then found the following errors.

1. The debit side of the Telephone account had been overstated by $200.
2. An invoice sent to Singh for $240 had been completely omitted from the books.
3. A cheque for $124 received from X and Co. had been posted to the debit of their account.
4. The purchase of some office equipment for $1180 had been debited to Office Expenses account.
5. Discounts received, $90, had been posted to the purchase ledger but not to the Discounts Received account.
6. Rent paid, $800, had been credited to Rent Receivable account.
7. A refund of an insurance premium, $60, had been recorded in the cash book but no other entry had been made.

8. A purchase of office stationery, $220, had been debited to Purchases account in error.
9. A credit balance of $30 in the purchase ledger had been omitted from the list of balances extracted from the ledger. The total of the list had been included in the trial balance. Kadriye does not keep control accounts in the nominal ledger.
10. Goods returned to Speedsel had been credited to Speedsel's account and debited to Purchases Returns account. The goods had cost $400.

Required

(a) Prepare journal entries to correct errors 1 to

10. (Narratives are required.)

(b) Prepare the Suspense account showing the opening balance and the correcting entries.

The draft Income Statement showed a net profit for the year ended 31 December 2010 of $8400 and the Statement of Financial Position at that date showed working capital (current assets less current liabilities) of $1250.

Required

(c) Calculate the revised net profit for the year ended 31 December 2010.
(d) Calculate the revised working capital at 31 December 2010.

Answer

(a)

Journal entries		
	$	$
1. *Note. The debit side of the Telephone account is overstated by $200. Reduce this by crediting the account and debiting the Suspense account with $200*		
Suspense account	200	
Telephone account		200
Correction of the overcast of $200 of the Telephone account.		
2. *Note. This transaction has been omitted from the books entirely. It has not affected the trial balance and the Suspense account is not involved.*		
Singh	240	
Sales		240
Recording invoice for $240 sent to Singh but omitted from books.		
3. *Note. $124 has been posted to the wrong side of X and Co.'s account. This is corrected by crediting their account with double that amount.*		
Suspense account	248	
X and Co. account		248
Correction of $124 received from X and Co. debited to their account in error.		
4. *Note. This is an error of principle; do not adjust through the Suspense account.*		
Office Equipment (asset) account	1180	
Office Expenses account		1180
Purchase of office equipment treated as revenue expense in error.		
5. *Note. This is not an error of complete omission; correct through the Suspense account.*		
Suspense account	90	
Discounts Received account		90
Discounts received, $90, omitted from Discounts Received Account.		
6. *Note. Rent Receivable account must be debited to cancel error; Rent Payable must be debited to record payment correctly. Note separate debit entries must be made.*		
Rent Receivable account	800	
Rent Payable account	800	
Suspense account		1600
Correction of rent paid incorrectly treated as rent received.		
7. *Note. This refund has not been completely omitted from the books. Adjust through the Suspense account.*		
Suspense account	60	
Insurance account		60
Refund of insurance premium omitted from the Insurance account.		

			$	$
8.	*Note. This is an error of commission. Do not adjust through the Suspense account.*			
	Office Stationery account		220	
	Purchases account			220

Purchase of office stationery treated as inventory for re-sale in error.

9. *Note. This is not a double-entry error but it has affected the trial balance. The list of balances must be corrected and a one-sided entry in the Suspense account is required. This is quite a tricky problem and requires some further explanation. When the list of balances was extracted form the purchase ledger one of the balances amounting to $30 was not included in the list. This incorrect total was used in the trial balance, so the trial balance would not balance by $30 as a result. In order to correct the error, $30 must be debited in the suspense account. The total of the purchase ledger balances in the trial balance must also be increased by $30. However, no entry needs to be made on the credit side of any of the balances in the purchase ledger as they have been correctly added to arrive at their individual totals.*

			$	$
	Suspense account		30	
10.	Speedsel		800	
	Purchases Returns account			800

Goods returned to Speedsel, $400, credited to their account and debited to Purchases Returns account in error.

Note. This is a complete reversal of entries. The correcting entry is twice the original amount and the Suspense account is not involved.

(b)

Suspense account

	$		$
Difference on trial balance	972	Rent receivable	800*
Telephone	200	Rent payable	800*
X and Co.	248		
Discounts received	90		
Insurance	60		
Correction of trade creditors	30		
	1600		1600

*These two entries should be shown separately as the double entry is completed in different accounts.

Note. The Suspense account is opened with the difference on the trial balance and then posted from the journal entries in (a).

(c)

Calculation of corrected net profit for the year ended 31 December

	Decrease (Dr) $	Increase (Cr) $	$
Net profit per draft Income Statement			8400
(1) Decrease in telephone expense		200	
(2) Increase in sales		240	
(4) Decrease in office expenses		1180	
(5) Increase in discounts received		90	
(6) Reduction in rent receivable	800		
Increase in rent payable	800		
(7) Reduction in insurance premium		60	
(8) No effect on net profit			
(10) Increase in purchases returns		800	
	1600	2570	
	(1600)	970	
Revised net profit for the year		9370	

Note. Set the calculation out as shown above. Untidy, 'straggly' calculations do not commend themselves to examiners. Debit entries to nominal accounts in the journal decrease profit, and credit entries to nominal accounts increase profit.

Calculation of Working capital at 31 December

	Decrease (Dr) $	Increase (Cr) $	$
Working capital per draft Statement of Financial Position			1250
(1) Singh invoice omitted	240		
(3) X and Co. $124 cheque misposted		248	
(9) Credit balance omitted		30	
(10) Goods returned to Speedsel	800		
	1040	278	
	(278)		762
Revised working capital			2012

Note. The layout of the answer given above is a good one and should be followed whenever possible. Adjust working capital by journal postings to personal accounts and by personal accounts omitted from the trial balance.

Exercise 1

Lee's trial balance at 30 June 2011 fails to agree and he places the difference in a Suspense account. Lee then discovers the following errors.

1. The total of the sales journal for one month was $5430. This had been posted to the Sales account as $5340.

2. An invoice for $150 for the purchase of goods for resale from Bilder had been entirely omitted from the books.
3. A cheque for $75 from Doyle, a customer, had been credited to his account as $57.
4. A debt of $50 in the sales ledger had been written off as bad but no entry had been made in the Bad debts account.
5. An improvement to a machine at a cost of $400 had been debited to Machinery Repairs account. (Lee depreciates machinery by the straight-line method over 10 years; a full year's depreciation is calculated for the year of purchase.)

Required

(a) Prepare the Suspense account in Lee's ledger showing clearly the difference on the trial balance at 30 June as the first entry and the entries required to adjust the errors.
(b) Prepare journal entries for errors 2 and 5. (Narratives are *not* required.)

Lee's draft Income Statement for the year ended 30 June 2011 showed a net profit of $3775.

Required

(c) Calculate the corrected net profit for the year ended 30 June 2011.

Exercise 2

When Jayesh extracted a trial balance from his books at 31 December 2010 he found that it did not balance. He entered the difference in a Suspense account and then prepared a draft Income Statement which showed a net profit of $2500. Jayesh later found the following errors.

1. The balance of opening inventory $8500 had been entered in the trial balance as $5800.
2. The inventory at 31 December 2010 had been understated by $2000.
3. Repairs to a machine, $3500, had been posted to Machinery at Cost account as $5300.
4. An invoice in the sum of $800 for the sale of goods to Bane had been posted to Bane's account but had not been entered in the sales Account.
5. A credit balance of $63 in the sales ledger had been extracted as a debit balance. Jayesh does not maintain Control accounts.

Required

(a) Prepare the journal entries to correct the errors. (Narratives are *not* required.)
(b) Prepare the Suspense account showing the trial balance difference and the correcting entries.

Jayesh's draft Statement of Financial Position at 31 December 2010 showed working capital of $3200.

Required

(c) Calculate Jayesh's corrected working capital at 31 December 2010.

HINTS

- Remember the six types of error that do not affect the trial balance. These are not corrected through the Suspense account.
- Prepare correcting journal entries in proper form. (Revise §3.10.) Note whether narratives are required.
- The first entry in a Suspense account is the difference on the trial balance. Enter it on the same side of the account as it will be entered in the trial balance.
- Post the Suspense account from journal entries. If these have not been required by the question it may be helpful to prepare them in rough.
- The Suspense account should not have a balance on it when you have posted the journal entries to it.
- Calculate revised profit or loss from the nominal account entries in the journal.
- Calculate revised working capital from the journal entries affecting current assets and current liabilities.
- Do not make journal entries to other books of prime entry. Postings from the journal should always be to named accounts in the ledgers.

MULTIPLE-CHOICE QUESTIONS

(In each of the following cases, a trial balance has failed to agree and the difference has been entered in a Suspense account.)

1. A credit balance in the sum of $93 has been omitted from the list of balances extracted from the sales ledger.
   What is the effect on the trial balance?
   A. The credit side is understated by $93.
   B. The credit side is overstated by $93.
   C. The debit side is understated by $93.
   D. The debit side is overstated by $93.

2. A credit note for $46 sent to A. Moses has been debited to A. Mason's account in the sales ledger. What effect will this have on the trial balance?

Debit total	Credit total
A. none	none
B. $46 overstated	$46 understated
C. none	$92 understated
D. $92 overstated	none

3. The total of the sales journal for one month is $9160. It has been entered in the Sales account as $9610. Which entries are required to correct the error?

Debit		Credit	
A. Sales account	$450	Sales journal	$450
B. Sales journal	$450	Sales account	$450
C. Sales account	$450	Suspense account	$450
D. Suspense account	$450	Sales account	$450

4. An invoice for repairs to machinery, $500, has been entered in the Machinery at Cost account. Which entries are required to correct the error?

Debit		Credit	
A. Machinery at Cost account	$500	Repairs to Machinery account	$500
B. Repairs to Machinery account	$500	Machinery at Cost account	$500
C. Repairs to Machinery account	$500	Suspense account	$500
D. Suspense account	$500	Machinery at Cost account	$500

5. Which of the following will cause a difference on a trial balance?
   A. An invoice omitted from the sales journal
   B. An invoice for $415 entered in the Sales journal as $451
   C. An invoice for $600 entered in the sales journal not included in the monthly total
   D. A credit note entered in the sales journal.

6. After which error will a trial balance still balance?
   A. Wages paid, $1500, was entered correctly in the bank account but debited to the wages account as $2500
   B. Rent receivable of $200 was debited to the Rent Payable account
   C. Goods returned to supplier, $150, were entered in purchases returns journal as $105
   D. The sales journal was undercast by $200.

7. A trial balance failed to agree and a Suspense account was opened. It was then found that rent received of $500 had been debited to the Rent Payable account. Which entries are required to correct this error?

	Rent Received account		Rent Payable account		Suspense account	
		$		$		$
A.	credit	500	credit	500	debit	1000
B.	credit	500	debit	500	no entry	
C.	debit	500	credit	500	debit	1000
D.	debit	500	credit	500	no entry	

1. Bastien does not maintain Control accounts. His trial balance does not balance and he has opened a Suspense account. The following errors have now been discovered.
   1. Discount received from Veeraj, amounting to $70, has been included in the discount column of the cash book but has not been posted to Veeraj's account.
   2. Goods have been sold on credit to Bernard for $1400 less 25% trade discount. Correct entries have been made in the sales journal but $1000 has been posted to Bernard's ledger account.
   3. A cheque for $400 received from Rodney has been debited in the cash book and also debited in Rodney's ledger account.
   4. A motor vehicle costing $12 000 has been bought on credit from Nedof Motors. The Purchases account has been debited and Nedof Motor's account credited.
   5. $60 spent by Bastien on his personal expenses has been posted to the Sundry Expenses account.

Required
Prepare the entries in Bastien's journal, with suitable narratives, to correct the above errors.

2. Boulder's trial balance at 31 March 2011 did not balance and the difference was entered in a Suspense account. Boulder does not maintain Control accounts. The following information was later discovered.
   1. A receipt of $313 from Head, a customer, has been entered correctly in the cash book but has been debited to Head's account in the sales ledger as $331.
   2. Goods sold to Joey for $100 have been returned by him and entered correctly in the Sales Returns account. No entry has been made for the return in Joey's account in the sales ledger.
   3. The purchase of a second-hand motor vehicle costing $3000 has been debited to the Motor Vehicle Expenses account.
   4. The total of the Discount Allowed column in the cash book has been overcast by $300.

5. A dishonest employee has stolen $700 from the business and the cash will not be recovered. No entry to record the theft has been made in the accounts.

Required
(a) Prepare journal entries to correct errors 1 to 5. Narratives are required.
(b) Prepare a Suspense account commencing with the trial balance difference.
The working capital shown in the Statement of Financial Position at 31 March 2011 before the errors were corrected was $2400.

Required
(c) Calculate the working capital after the errors have been corrected.

3. Amber's trial balance at 31 December failed to agree and the difference was entered in a Suspense account. The total of the purchase ledger balances had been entered as creditors in the trial balance but it did not agree with the credit balance of $5419 on the Purchase Ledger Control account. The following errors were found.
   1. No entry had been made in the books to record a refund by cheque of $90 from Victor, a supplier.
   2. A cheque for $420 sent to Shah, a supplier, had been entered correctly in the cash book but debited to General Expenses account as $240.
   3. Goods returned, $900, by Amil, a customer, had been credited in Amil's account and debited in the Purchases account.
   4. Goods which cost $350 had been returned to Hussein, a supplier. No entry had been made in the books for this.
   5. The discount received column in the cash book had been undercast by $600.

Required
(a) Prepare journal entries to correct errors 1 to 5. Narratives are *not* required.
(b) Prepare the Suspense account commencing with the difference on the trial balance.

4. Logan has prepared the following trial balance at 31 March 2011.

	$	$
Sales		131 940
Purchases	33 000	
Sales returns	260	
Purchase returns		315
Opening inventory	6 900	
Debtor's Control (Trade receivables)	14 125	
Creditor's Control (Trade payables)		16 070
Discount allowed	700	
Discount received		614
Wages and salaries	20 600	
Advertising	1 000	
General expenses	2 340	
Bank	13 710	
Premises	70 000	
Motor vehicles	5 000	
Equipment	3 500	
Capital		25 000
Drawings	3 000	
Suspense		196
	174 135	174 135

Logan is unable to find the difference on the trial balance and has entered the difference in the Suspense Account. The following errors have been made in the accounts.

1. Discount allowed of $55 has been posted to the credit of Discount received.
2. Purchase returns of $108 have been posted to the debit of Sales returns.
3. A cheque for $400 from a customer has been dishonoured, but no record has been made of this in the accounts. There is no reason to believe that payment will not be made in April 2011.
4. Equipment bought during the year for $4400 has been debited to Purchases account.
5. During the year Logan had taken goods for resale which cost $800 for his own personal use.
6. $90 of the general expenses related to an amount paid out of the business bank account for one of Logan's private expenses. In his attempt to correct the accounts, Logan made another debit entry of $90 in the General Expenses account, with no other entry being made.

Required

(a) Prepare journal entries to correct errors 1 to 6 (narratives are not required).
(b) Prepare the Suspense account to show the correcting entries.
(c) Prepare a corrected trial balance at 31 March 2011.

The net profit per the draft accounts, prepared before the above errors were corrected, was $25 000.

Required

(d) Prepare a statement of corrected net profit showing the effect of each error on the net profit per the draft accounts.

16 Incomplete records

In this chapter you will learn:

- how to calculate profit or loss from statements of affairs
- how to prepare Income Statements and Statements of Financial Position from incomplete records
- the relationship between mark-up and margin
- how to calculate the cost of inventory lost by fire or theft.

16.1 What are incomplete records?

The term **incomplete records** describes any method of recording transactions that is not based on the double-entry model. Often, only a cash book, or only records of debtors and creditors, are kept, so that only one aspect of each transaction is recorded. This is **single-entry bookkeeping**. Incomplete records also describe situations where the only records kept may be invoices for purchases, copies of sales invoices, cheque counterfoils and bank statements. In all these cases, Income Statements and Statements of Financial Position cannot be prepared in the normal way.

16.2 How to calculate profit or loss from statements of affairs

When records of transactions are insufficient to enable an Income Statement to be prepared, the profit or loss of a business for a given period may be calculated if the assets and liabilities of the business at both the start and end of the period are known. The method is based upon two principles:

1. the accounting equation,
   capital = assets – liabilities
2. profit increases capital; losses reduce capital.

The difference between the opening and closing capitals, after making adjustments for new capital

introduced and the owner's drawings in the period, will reveal the profit or loss. Capital is calculated by listing the assets and liabilities in a **statement of affairs**.

Example

Fatima is a hair stylist who has been in business for some time. She has never kept records of her takings and payments. She wishes to know how much profit or loss she has made in the year ended 31 December 2010. Her assets and liabilities at 1 January and 31 December 2010 were as follows:

	1 January 2010	31 December 2010
	$	$
Equipment	800	1000
Stock of hair styling sundries	70	45
Amounts owing from clients	50	70
Rent paid in advance	100	120
Balance at bank	150	160
Creditors for supplies	25	30
Electricity owing	40	50

Fatima has drawn $100 per week from the business for personal expenses.

Required

Calculate Fatima's profit for the year ended 31 December 2010.

Answer

	Statements of affairs at	
	1 January 2010	31 December 2010
	$	$
Equipment	800	1000
Stock of hair styling sundries	70	45
Amounts owing from clients	50	70
Rent paid in advance	100	120
Balance at bank	150	160
	1170	1395

Less			
Creditors for supplies	25	30	
Electricity owing	40 65	50 80	
Net assets (= capital)	1105	1315	
Add drawings in year to 31 December 2010			
(52 × $100)		5200*	
		6515	
Deduct capital at beginning of year		1105	
Profit for the year ended 31 December 2010		5410	

* Drawings have been added back as the capital at 31 December 2010 would have been greater if Fatima had not taken this money out of the business.

Note. When an asset is valued at more or less than cost, it should be included in a statement of affairs at valuation.

Exercise 1

Lian has run a business repairing motor vehicles for some years but has not kept proper accounting records. However, the following information is available.

	at	at
	1 January 2010	31 December 2010
	$	$
Premises at cost	4000	4000
Motor van at cost	5000	5000
Motor car at cost	–	3000
Plant and equipment	1100	1300
Stock of parts	400	200
Debtors for work done	700	800
Balance at bank	1300	900
Owing to suppliers for parts	170	340

The premises were bought some years ago and were valued at $9000 at 31 December 2010. At the same date, the motor van was valued at $4000. The motor car was Lian's own car, which he brought into the business during the year at its original cost. Lian's weekly drawings were $120.

Required

Calculate Lian's profit or loss for the year ended 31 December 2010.

16.3 How to prepare an Income Statement and a Statement of Financial Position from incomplete records

Most businesses keep records of receipts and payments. The records may consist of bank paying-in-book counterfoils, cheque-book counterfoils and bank statements in addition to suppliers' invoices and copies of sales invoices. From these records it may be possible to prepare an Income Statement and a Statement of Financial Position. The steps are as follows:

Step 1 Prepare an opening statement of affairs for this business. This is, in effect the preparation of a balance sheet and will allow the opening capital to be calculated.

Step 2 Prepare a receipts and payment account. This is similar to preparing a bank account and a cash account for the business. You may need this to calculate the closing bank/cash balances for the closing balance sheet.

Step 3 Prepare Control accounts for debtors (trade receivables) and creditors (trade payables), if necessary, to calculate sales and purchases. These will be the amounts required to make the Control accounts balance.

Step 4 Adjust the receipts and payments for accruals and prepayments at beginning and end of the period.

Step 5 Calculate provisions for doubtful debts, depreciation and any other matters not mentioned above.

Step 6 Prepare the Income Statement and Statement of Financial Position from the information now available.

Example

The only records that Aasim has kept for his business are bank paying-in-book counterfoils, cheque-book counterfoils and records of debtors (trade receivables) and creditors (trade payables). From these it is possible to summarise his transactions with the bank in the year ended 31 December 2010 as follows:

Takings paid into the bank: $8000.
Cheques drawn: payments to suppliers $2430; rent $600; electricity $320; postage and stationery $80; purchase of shop fittings $480; cheques drawn for personal expenses $2700.

Aasim banked all his takings after paying the following in cash: creditors for supplies $400 and sundry expenses $115.

Aasim estimated his assets and liabilities at 1 January 2010 to be: shop fittings $1600; inventory $1960; trade receivables $240; rent prepaid $80; bank balance $1500; cash in hand $50; creditors (trade payables) for goods $420; electricity owing $130.

At 31 December 2010 Aasim listed his assets and liabilities as follows: shop fittings $1800; inventory $1520; trade receivables $380; rent prepaid $50; bank balance $2640; cash in hand $50; creditors for goods (trade payables) $390; electricity owing $225.

Required

Prepare Aasim's Income Statement for the year ended 31 December 2010 and his Statement of Financial Position at that date.

Answer

Step 1. Opening statement of affairs

	$	$
Assets		
Shop fittings		1600
Inventory		1960
Trade receivables		240
Rent prepaid		80
Bank		1500
Cash in hand		50
		5430
Less Liabilities		
Creditors for goods (Trade payables)	420	
Electricity owing	130	550
Capital at 1 January		4880

Step 2. Receipts and Payments account. This includes only those amounts actually received and spent. It is a cash book summary with columns for cash and bank.

	Cash $	Bank $		Cash $	Bank $
Jan 1 Balance b/f	50	1500	Trade creditors	400	2430
Takings (800 + 400 + 115)	8515		Rent		600
Cash		8000	Electricity		320
			Postage and stationery		80
			Shop fittings		480
			Sundry expenses	115	
			Drawings (2700 + 250†)		2950
			Bank	8000	
			Balance c/f	50	2640
	8565	9500		8565	9500

† $250 is money not accounted for and is treated as Aasim's drawings.

Step 3. Debtors and Creditors Control accounts

Debtors Control

	$		$
Jan 1 Balance b/f	240	Dec 31 Takings[1]	8515
Dec 31 Sales[3]	8655	Balance c/f	380
	8895		8895

1 From Receipts and Payments account.
2 From Receipts and Payments account.
3 Balancing figures.

Creditors Control

	$		$
Dec 31 Bank and cash[2]	2830	Jan 1 Balance b/f	420
Balance c/f	390	Dec 31 Purchases[3]	2800
	3220		3220

Step 4. Adjust for prepayment and accruals.

	$		$
Rent paid	600	Electricity paid	320
Add prepaid at 1 Jan	80	Less owing at 1 Jan	(130)
Deduct prepaid at 31 Dec	(50)	Add owing at 31 Dec	225
Rent payable for the year	630	Electricity payable for the year	415

Step 5. Calculate depreciation of shop fittings.

	$
Shop fittings at valuation at 1 Jan	1600
Add fittings purchased in year	480
	2080
Shop fittings at valuation at 31 Dec	1800
Depreciation for the year	280

Step 6.

Aasim Income Statement for the year ended 31 December 2010	$	$
Sales		8655
Less cost of sales		
Inventory at 1 January	1960	
Purchases	2800	
	4760	
Less inventory at 31 December	1520	3240
Gross profit		5415
Less		
Rent	630	
Electricity	415	
Postage and stationery	80	
Sundry expenses	115	
Depreciation of shop fittings	280	1520
Net profit		3895

Aasim Statement of Financial Position at 31 December 2010	$	$	$
Non-current assets: Shop fittings			1800
Current assets			
Inventory		1520	
Trade receivables		380	
Rent prepaid		50	
Bank		2640	
Cash		50	
		4640	
Current liabilities			
Trade payables	390		
Electricity owing	225	615	4025
			5825
Capital at 1 January			4880
Profit for the year			3895
			8775
Less Drawings			2950
			5825

16.4 Margin and mark-up

Ability to calculate margin and mark-up may be necessary to solve some incomplete record problems. **Margin** is gross profit expressed as a percentage or fraction of selling price.

Example

	$
Cost price of goods	100
Profit	25
Selling price	125

The margin is profit/selling price × 100

$$= \frac{25}{125} \times 100$$

$$= 20\% = \frac{1}{5}$$

Mark-up is gross profit expressed as a percentage or fraction of cost of sales.

In the above example, mark-up is profit/cost price of goods × 100 $= \frac{25}{100} \times 100 = 25\% = \frac{1}{4}$.

There is a close relationship between margin and mark-up. In the above examples:

$$\text{margin} = \frac{1}{5} \left(\text{or } \frac{1}{4+1}\right); \text{mark-up} = \frac{1}{4} \text{ or } \left(\frac{1}{5-1}\right).$$

From this, a general rule will be observed:

When margin is $\frac{a}{b}$, mark-up is $\frac{a}{b-a}$ and, when mark-up is $\frac{a}{b}$, margin is $\frac{a}{b+a}$.

Examples

If margin is $\frac{1}{3}$, mark-up is $\frac{1}{3-1} = \frac{1}{2}$; if mark-up is $\frac{1}{6}$, margin is $\frac{1}{6+1} = \frac{1}{7}$.

If margin is $\frac{2}{5}$, mark-up is $\frac{2}{5-2} = \frac{2}{3}$; if mark-up is $\frac{2}{5}$, margin is $\frac{2}{5+2} = \frac{2}{7}$.

Conversion of percentage to fractions. Enter the *rate* percentage as the numerator of the fraction and 100 as the denominator, and reduce to a common fraction, for example $25\% = \frac{25}{100} = \frac{1}{4}$.

Conversion of fraction to a percentage. Multiply the numerator of the fraction by 100, cancel top and bottom of the fraction and add 'per cent' or % sign, for example $\frac{2}{5} = \frac{200}{5} = 40\%$.

Most useful examples to remember

$12\frac{1}{2}\% = \frac{1}{8}$; $20\% = \frac{1}{5}$; $25\% = \frac{1}{4}$; $33.3\% = \frac{1}{3}$;

$40\% = \frac{2}{5}$; $50\% = \frac{1}{2}$; $66.7\% = \frac{2}{3}$; $75\% = \frac{3}{4}$;

$80\% = \frac{4}{5}$

Examples

1. Cost of sales: $300. Margin is 25%. Calculate the sales revenue.

Answer Margin is $\frac{1}{4}$, mark-up is $\frac{1}{3}$, i.e. $3000 \times \frac{1}{3} = \$1000$.

Therefore sales revenue = $(3000 + 1000) = $4000.

2. Sales revenue: $7000. Mark-up is 40%. Calculate the gross profit.

Answer Mark-up is $\frac{2}{5}$; margin is $\frac{2}{7}$.

Therefore gross profit = $\frac{2}{7} \times \$7000 = \$2000$.

3. Maheen provides the following information for the year ended 31 December 2010.

	$
Inventory 1 January 2010	9 000
Inventory at 31 December 2010	11 000
Sales in the year ended 31 December 2010	84 000

Maheen sells her goods at a mark-up of $33\frac{1}{3}\%$.

Prepare the Trading section of Maheen's Income Statement for the year ended 31 December 2010 in as much detail as possible, clearly showing the sales, cost of sales and gross profit for the year.

Answer This a typical example of problem that is solved by working backwards.

Maheen: Trading account for the year ended 31 December 2010

		$	$
Sales (*given*)			84 000
Less			
Inventory at 1 January (*given*)		9 000	
Step 4	Purchases (balancing figure 3)	65 000	
Step 3	(balancing figure 2)	74 000	
Inventory at 31 December (*given*)		11 000	
Step 2	Cost of sales (balance figure 1)		63 000
Step 1	Gross profit $\frac{1}{4} \times \$84\,000$		21 000

Exercise 2

Ammar provides the following information for the year ended 30 June 2011.

	$
Opening inventory	4 000
Closing inventory	7 000
Cost of goods sold	28 000

Ammar's margin on all sales is 20%.

Required

Prepare the Trading section of Ammar's Income Statement for the year ended 30 June 2011 in as much detail as possible, clearly showing the sales, cost of sales and gross profit for the year.

16.5 Inventory lost in fire or by theft

The methods used for preparing accounts from incomplete records are also used to calculate the value of inventory lost in a fire or by theft when detailed inventory records have not been kept, or have been destroyed by fire.

Solve this problem by preparing a 'pro forma' Trading section of the Income Statement. (It is described as 'pro forma' because it is not prepared by transferring balances from the ledger accounts.)

Example

Shahmir's warehouse was burgled on 10 April 2011. The thieves stole most of the goods but left goods which cost $1250. Shahmir supplies the following information.

Extracts from Shahmir's Statement of Financial Position at 31 December 2010:

	$
Inventory	30 000
Trade receivables	40 000
Trade payables	20 000

Extracts from cash book, 31 December 2010 to 10 April 2011:

	$
Receipts from customers	176 000
Payments to suppliers	120 000

Other information:

	$
Trade receivables at 10 April 2011	24 000
Trade payables at 10 April 2011	26 000

Shahmir sells his goods at a mark-up of 25%.

Required

Calculate of the cost of the stolen goods.

Answer

Shahmir Pro forma Trading section of the Income Statement for the period 1 January to 10 April		
	$	$
Sales (see working 1 below)		160 000
Cost of sales: Inventory at 1 January 2011	30 000	
Purchases (see working 2 below)	126 000	
	156 000	
Inventory at 10 April 2011 (balancing figure)	28 000	128 000
Gross profit (mark-up is 25% so margin is 20%;		
$160 000 × 20%)		32 000

Cost of goods stolen: $(28 000 − 1250) = $26 750

Working 1

Debtors Control account			
	$		$
1 January Trade receivables	40 000	10 April Cash	176 000
10 April Sales (balancing figure)	160 000	Trade receivables	24 000
	200 000		200 000

Working 2

Creditors Control account			
	$		$
10 April Cash	120 000	1 January Trade payables	20 000
Trade payables	26 000	10 April Purchases (balancing figure)	126 000
	146 000		146 000

Exercise 3

Neha's warehouse was damaged by fire on 5 November 2010 and most of the goods was destroyed. The goods that was salvaged was valued at $12 000.

Neha has provided the following information to enable the cost of the goods lost to be calculated.

Extracts from Statement of Financial Position at 30 June 2010:	
	$
Inventory	47 000
Trade receivables	16 000
Trade payables	23 000
Further information for the period 30 June 2010 to 5 November 2010.	
	$
Receipts from debtors	122 000
Cash sales	17 000
Payments to suppliers	138 000
At 5 November: Trade receivables	37 000
Trade payables	28 000

Neha's mark-up on goods sold is $33\frac{1}{3}$ %.

Required

Calculated the cost of the inventory lost in Neha's fire.

HINTS

- A question that gives only assets and liabilities requires the preparation of statements of affairs to find the profit or loss of the business. The 'requirement' usually begins with 'calculate'.
- If required to prepare an Income Statement and Statement of Financial Position, prepare them in as much detail as possible.
- Be careful to distinguish between 'mark-up' and 'margin'. Learn how to convert mark-up to margin, and vice versa.
- Include all your workings with your answer. If your workings are not quite right, you may still gain some marks; but 'no workings – no marks' for a wrong answer.
- Tick each item in the question as you deal with it; check that everything has been ticked before writing your answer to ensure you have not missed anything.
- Incomplete records questions test a whole range of candidates' accounting knowledge and skills. For that reason they are frequently set in examinations. Some candidates fear these questions unnecessarily. Keep calm and follow the steps taught in this chapter carefully. If your Statement of Financial Position does not balance first time, don't panic. Do not spend valuable time looking for the difference if this time is better spent answering the next question. You have probably done enough to gain useful marks, anyway.

MULTIPLE-CHOICE QUESTIONS

1. Jackson commenced business with $10 000 that he had received as a gift from his aunt and $8000 that he had received as a loan from his father. He used some of this money to purchase a machine for $15 000. He obtained a mortgage for $20 000 to purchase a workshop.

How much was Jackson's capital?

A. $3000   **B.** $10 000

C. $18 000   **D.** $38 000

2. At 1 January 2010 Robert's business assets were valued at $36 000 and his liabilities amounted to $2000. At 31 December 2010 Robert's assets amounted to $57 000 and included his private car which he had brought into the business on 1 November 2010 when it was valued at $9000. His trade payables at 31 December 2010 totalled $17 000 and his drawings during the year were $19 000. What was Robert's profit for the year ended 31 December 2010?

A. $6000   **B.** $16 000

C. $24 000   **D.** $33 000

3. At 1 April 2010 Tonkin's business assets were: motor van valued at $5000 (cost $8000), tools $1600, inventory $700, trade receivables $168, cash $400. His trade payables totalled $1120. At 31 March 2011 his assets were: workshop which had cost $20 000 and on which a mortgage of $16 000 was still outstanding, motor van $4000, tools $1900, inventory $1000, trade receivables $240 (of which $70 were known to be bad), cash $500. His trade payables amounted to $800. During the year Tonkin's drawings amounted to $5200. What was Tonkin's profit for the year ended 31 March 2011?

A. $6222   **B.** $6292

C. $9222   **D.** $9292

4. At 1 March 2010 Allen's trade receivables amounted to $12 100. In the year ended 28 February 2011 he received $63 500 from trade receivables and allowed them cash discounts of $3426. At 28 February 2011 his trade receivables totalled $14 625. How much were Allen's sales for the year ended 28 February 2011?

A. $62 599   **B.** $64 401

C. $66 025   **D.** $69 451

5. At 1 October 2010 Maria's trade receivables amounted to $7440. Of this amount $384 is known to be bad. In the year to 30 September 2011 she received $61 080 from trade receivables. Her trade receivables at 30 September 2011 were $8163. How much were Maria's sales for year ended 30 September 2011?

A. $60 741   **B.** $61 419

C. $61 803   **D.** $62 187

6. All of Graysons's inventory was stolen when his business was burgled on 4 March 2011. His inventory at 31 December 2010 was $23 000. From 1 January to 4 March 2011 sales totalled $42 000 and purchases were $38 000. Grayson's mark-up on goods is $33\frac{1}{3}$% to arrive at selling price. What was the cost of the inventory that was stolen?

A. $28 000   **B.** $29 500

C. $33 000   **D.** $40 000

ADDITIONAL EXERCISES

1. Seng commenced business on 1 January 2010 when he paid $40 000 into the bank together with $20 000 which he had received as a loan from his brother. At 31 December 2010 Seng's assets and liabilities were as follows:

	$
Shop premise	20 000
Motor van	8 000
Shop fittings	3 000
Inventory	4 000
Trade Receivables	1 000
Bank balance	5 000
Trade Payables	6 000
Loan from brother	16 000

Seng's drawings were $100 per week.

Required

(a) Prepare Seng's statements of affairs at

(i) 1 January 2010 and (ii) 31 December 2010.

(b) Calculate Seng's profit or loss for the year ended 31 December 2010.

2. Saeed does not keep proper books of account for his business but he has provided the following details of his assets and liabilities.

	At 1 July 2010 $	At 30 June 2011 $
Land and buildings at cost	60 000	60 000
Fixtures and fittings	10 000	12 000
Office machinery	8 000	7 000
Inventory	17 000	21 000
Trade receivables	4 000	5 000
Rent prepaid	1 000	600
Bank balance	14 000	16 000
Trade payables	3 000	1 600
Wages owing	2 000	1 000

Further information

1. Land and buildings have been revalued at $90 000 at 30 June 2011.
2. Office machinery at 30 June 2011 included a computer costing $1400, which Saeed had paid for from his personal bank account.
3. Saeed had withdrawn $200 per week from the business in cash, and a total of $2000 of goods for his own use during the year to 30 June 2011.

Required

Calculate Saeed's profit or loss for the year ended 30 June 2011.

3. Ahmed carries on business as a general trader. He has not kept proper accounting records and he asks you to help him prepare his Income Statement for the year ended 30 September 2011 and his Statement of Financial Position at that date. Ahmed's assets and liabilities at 30 September 2010 were as follows:

	$
Premises	60 000
Motor van	8 000
Inventory	6 250
Trade receivables	3 200
Rent paid in advance	400
Balance at bank	9 450
Cash in hand	50
Trade payables	1 800
Electricity owing	600
Interest on loan owing	150
Loan from brother	2 000

The loan carries interest at 10% per annum payable in arrears annually on 31 December each year.

Ahmed's transactions in the year ended 30 September 2011 were as follows:

Bank summary	$
Receipts	
Receipts from trade receivables	29 400
Cash banked	17 000
Payments	
Suppliers	23 000
Electricity	2 200
Rent	4 000
Motor van expenses	1 800
Interest on loan	200
Wages	7 400
Telephone and stationery	1 650
Purchase of fixtures and fittings	3 000
Drawings	11 800

Cash summary	$
Receipts	
Cash sales	21 750
Payments	
Goods for resale	3 140
Stationery	300
Motor van expenses	600
Sundry expenses	400

Further information

1. The balance of cash in hand has been maintained at $50.
2. At 30 September 2011, the closing inventory was $8000. Trade receivables were $1600 and trade payables for supplies were $1300.
3. Bad debts written off in the year were $250.
4. Discounts received from suppliers in the year were $420.
5. At 30 September 2011 electricity owing was $320 and rent of $450 had been prepaid.
6. At 30 September 2011 the motor van was valued at $6000.
7. Fixtures and fittings are to be depreciated on the reducing balance method using the rate of 25% per annum. A full year's depreciation is to be taken in the year ended 30 September 2011.
8. Ahmed does not provided for depreciation on the premises.
9. Ahmed has taken goods costing $800 from the business for his own use during the year.
10. Ahmed states that he paid some private bills out of the cash takings, but cannot remember how much is involved.

Required

(a) Prepare Ahmed's Income Statement for the year ended 30 September 2011.
(b) Prepare Ahmed's Statement of Financial Position at 30 September 2011.

4. Nurvish, who does not keep proper records for his business, supplies the following information.

	1 July 2010	30 June 2011
	$	$
Inventory of goods	16 000	11 000
Trade Payables for goods	3 600	5 200

In the year ended 30 June 2011, Nurvish paid suppliers $54 000.

Nurvish sells his goods at a gross profit margin of 40%.

On 17 January 2011, Nurvish's premises were flooded and inventory that cost $5000 was damaged and could only be sold at half cost price. In the year ended 30 June 2011, Nurvish took goods which cost $1300 for his personal use.

Required

Prepare the Trading section of Nurvish's Income Statement for the year ended 30 June 2011, clearly showing the sales, cost of sales and gross profit for the year.

5. Nadia was ill when her inventory should have been counted on 31 December 2010. The stock count did not take place until 8 January 2011 when it was carried out by an inexperienced member of staff. The inventory was valued at $62 040 at 8 January 2011.

Nadia was sure that the inventory had been overvalued and discovered the following errors.

1. The inventory had been valued at selling price instead of at cost. The gross profit margin on all goods sold is 20%.
2. Goods had been sent on sale or return to a customer who had not yet accepted the goods. The customer had been sent an invoice for $2000. This had been treated as a sale.
3. Goods sold to a customer on 3 January 2011 had been overcharged by $240.
4. The following transactions had taken place between 1 January and 8 January 2011 but had not been taken into account in the stock taking:
   (i) goods costing $4400 had been received from suppliers.
   (ii) sales of goods for $12 000 (not including goods sent on sale or return).

Required

Calculate the value of her inventory at cost at 31 December 2010.

6. Korn, a retailer, does not keep proper books of account but he has provided the following information about his business.

Balance at	30 April 2010 $	30 April 2011 $
Land and buildings at cost	60 000	70 000
Fixtures and fittings	8 000	10 000
Motor vehicles	10 000	8 000
Trade payables	7 500	6 900
Trade receivables	20 400	32 000
Rent owing	800	1 000

Balance at	30 April 2010 $	30 April 2011 $
Wages and salaries owing	800	600
Inventory	22 400	21 923
Bank	39 000	To be calculated

Korn's bank account transactions for the year ended 30 April 2011 were as follows:

Receipts	$
Trade receivables	170 430
Cash sales	103 000
Sales of non-current assets [see note (4) below]	2 400
Payments	
Trade payables	227 668
Wages	17 200
Rent	8 000
Electricity	9 670
General expenses	5 150
Purchases of fixed assets (see point 4 below)	27 000

Further information

1. Korn banks his receipts from cash sales after taking $300 each week as drawings.
2. During the year ended 30 April 2011, Korn had taken goods costing $1350 for his own use.
3. Korn normally valued his inventory at cost but on the advice of a friend he decided to value his inventory at 30 April 2011 at selling price. His normal mark-up on inventory was 30%.
4. Korn had borrowed $30 000 from his brother on a long-term basis on 1 May 2010. He had not recorded this transaction. Interest on the loan at 10% per annum is payable on 1 May each year.

During the financial year ended 30 April 2011 the following transactions had taken place.

	$
Purchases	
Freehold land and buildings	10 000
Motor vehicles	10 000
Fixtures and fittings	7 000
Sales	
Motor vehicles	2 000 (net book value at 30 April 2010 $3500)
Fixtures and fittings	400 (net book value at 30 April 2010 $800)

Required

(a) Prepare Korn's Income Statement for the year ended 30 April 2011.

(b) Prepare the Statement of Financial Position at 30 April 2011.

(c) Comment on the suggestion by Korn's friend that inventory should be valued at selling price, and refer to any relevant accounting principle.

7. Cornelius commenced business on 1 April 2009. He has not kept complete records of his transactions but he supplies the following information.

	1 April 2009 $	31 March 2010 $	31 March 2011 $
Balance at bank	30 000	116 000	111 110
Equipment	15 000	28 000	45 900
Inventory of goods at cost	37 500	52 000	74 250
Long-term loan from father	20 000	20 000	20 000
Premises		80 000	80 000
Trade receivables		22 400	34 200
Trade payables		56 000	67 410
Sundry expenses in arrears		2 280	875
Sundry expenses in advance		700	4 050

Further information

1. Cornelius made payments of $371 340 to suppliers in the year ended 31 March 2011.

2. Complete records of takings are not available but goods are sold at a mark-up of 30%.

3. Taking were banked after deduction of the following.

(i) From 1 April 2009 to 31 March 2010, Cornelius drew $400 per week from takings for his personal expenses. From 1 April 2010 the weekly amounts drawn were increased to $500.

(ii) On 1 July 2010, Cornelius paid $5000 out of takings to pay for a family holiday.

(iii) Cornelius has taken various other amounts from takings for personal expenses, but he has not kept a record of these.

4. Cornelius purchased the business premises on 1 October 2009. He paid $40 000 for these from his own private bank account. The balance was obtained as a bank loan on which interest is payable at 15% per annum on 31 December each year.

5. Cornelius' father has agreed that his loan to the business will be free of interest for the first year. After that, interest will be at the rate of 8% per annum, payable annually on 31 March.

6. Cornelius purchased additional equipment costing $24 000 in the year ended 31 March 2011.

7. Sundry expenses paid in the year ended 31 March 2011 amounted to $27 000.

Required

(a) Calculate Cornelius' profit or loss for the year ended 31 March 2010.

(b) Prepare in as much detail as possible an Income Statement for the year ended 31 March 2011.

(c) Prepare a Statement of Financial Position as at 31 March 2011.

17 Non-profit-making organisations (clubs and societies)

In this chapter you will learn:

- new terms used for non-profit-making organisations
- new forms of financial statements for non-profit-making organisations
- how to apply the techniques used for incomplete records to prepare accounts for non-profit-making organisations.

17.1 What are non-profit-making organisations?

Non-profit-making organisations exist to provide facilities for their members. Examples are: sports and social clubs, dramatic societies, music clubs, etc. Making a profit is not their main purpose, although many carry on fund-raising activities to provide more or better facilities for the members. The organisation is 'owned' by all of its members and not by just one person or partnership. Records of money received and spent are usually kept by a club member who is not a trained bookkeeper or accountant. Usually no other records are kept. This topic is, therefore, an extension of the work of the previous chapter, which deals with incomplete records.

It follows from the above that a business which is *meant* to make profits is not a non-profit-making organisation, even if it keeps making losses.

Non-profit-making organisations are a different type of enterprise from trading organisations. As a result, they have their own terms for some of the items you will come across (see 17.2).

17.2 Special features of the accounts of non-profit-making organisations

- An **Income and Expenditure Account** takes the place of the Income Statement.

- The words **surplus of income over expenditure** are used in place of 'net profit'.
- The words **excess of expenditure over income** are used in place of 'net loss'.
- The terms **Accumulated fund** is used in place of 'Capital account'.
- A **Receipts and Payments Account** takes the place of a Bank Account.
- **Subscriptions** take the place of Sales as the main source of income in the Income and Expenditure Account. Other types of club income may come from dances or the sale of tickets for a particular activity.
- Items are grouped together, or matched in the Income and Expenditure Account, so that it is possible to see whether a particular activity, say a dance has made a surplus or deficit.
- A Trading Account is only prepared for an activity that is in the nature of trading and is carried on to increase the club's funds, for example a café. Any profit or loss calculated will be transferred to the Income and Expenditure account. If it is a profit it will be added to the income. If it is a loss it will be added to the expenditure. A loss should never be shown as a negative under the income column of the Income and Expenditure account.

17.3 The treatment of income

Income of a club (which is the term that will be used in the rest of this chapter to cover all non-profit-making organisations) should be treated in the club's accounts as follows:

Subscriptions

The amount credited to the Income and Expenditure Account should equal the annual subscription per member multiplied by the number of members. It may be helpful to prepare a Subscriptions account as workings to decide how much should be credited to the Income and Expenditure Account.

Subscriptions in arrears and **subscriptions in advance** should *normally* be treated as accruals and prepayments. However, each club has its own policy for treating subscriptions in arrears or in advance. The two possible policies are as follows:

- **Cash basis**. The amount actually received in the year is credited to the Income and Expenditure Account. This may include subscriptions for a previous year or paid in advance for the next year.
- **Accruals basis**. All subscriptions due for the year, including those not yet received, are credited to the Income and Expenditure Account. It will usually be the club's policy to write off, as bad debts, subscriptions that are not received in the year after they were due.

Life subscriptions and entry fees

Life subscriptions and entry fees are received as lump sums but should not be credited in full to the Income and Expenditure Account when received. The club should have a policy of spreading this income over a period of, say, five years. The amounts received should be credited to a Deferred Income account and credited to the Income and Expenditure Account in equal annual instalments over a period determined by the club committee.

Donations

Donations and legacies to a club are usually made for particular purposes, for example towards the cost of a new pavilion or a piece of equipment. Such donations should be credited to an account opened for the purpose, and expenditure on it debited to the account. Money received for special purposes should be placed in a separate bank account to ensure that it is not spent on other things.

Ancillary activities

Ancillary activities are incidental to a club's main purpose. They raise money to supplement income from subscriptions. If they involve some sort of trading, a Trading Account should be prepared for them as part of the annual accounts, and the profit or loss should be transferred to the Income and Expenditure Account.

Non-trading activities, such as socials, outings and dinner-dances, may be dealt with in the Income and Expenditure Account with the income and costs being grouped together as follows:

	$	$
Annual dinner-dance		
Sale of tickets	600	
Less: Hire of band	(100)	
Catering	(240)	
Net receipts/net surplus on dinner-dance		260

17.4 How to prepare club accounts

The preparation of club accounts follow the same procedures as those used for businesses whose records are incomplete (see chapter 16) together with the principles explained in §§17.2 and 17.3.

Example

The Star Sports and Social Club provides recreational activities, refreshments and social events for its members. It sells sports equipment to its members at reduced prices. Its assets and liabilities at 31 December 2010 were as follows:

	$
Fixed or Non-current assets	
Pavilion	120 000
Club spots equipment	40 000
Motor roller	2 000
Current assets	
Inventory of equipment for sale to members	4 000
Annual subscriptions owing	1 200
Bank balance	6 730
Current liabilities	
Creditors for equipment for sale to members	1 300
Annual subscriptions received in advance	800
Life subscriptions fund	1 750

In the year ended 31 December 2011 the club's cash receipts and payments were as follows:

	$
Receipts	
Annual subscriptions	18 000
Proceeds from sale of equipment	12 000
Sale of tickets for dinner-dance	4 400
Refreshment bar takings	2 660
Life member subscriptions	400
Payments	
Caretaker's wages	8 000
Repairs to club equipment	1 700
Purchase of sports club equipment	2 000
Equipment for sale to members	4 000
Heating and lighting	1 800
Dinner-dance expenses	
Hire of band	200
Catering	1 000
Food for refreshment bar	1 400
Secretary's expenses	840

Further information

1. At 31 December 2011.
   annual subscription in arrears were $1400
   annual subscriptions received in advance were $900.
2. Inventory of equipment for sale to members: $2000.
3. Creditors for equipment for sale to members: $900.
4. A member donated $5000 to a fund to encourage young people to train for sport. This donation was invested immediately in savings bonds.
5. The club transfers life subscriptions to the Income and Expenditure Account in equal instalments over five years.
6. Depreciation is to be provided on fixed assets by the reducing-balance method as follows:
   Pavilion   6%
   Sports equipment   20%
   Motor roller   20%

Required

(a) Prepare the Star Sports and Social Club's Income and Expenditure Account for the year ended 31 December 2011.
(b) Prepare the club's Statement of Financial Position as at 31 December 2011.

Note. Often the amount of information given in questions such as this looks terrifying but don't let

that worry you. Keep calm. Read the question carefully two or three times, making sure you understand it, and underline important points. Decide what workings are required and which must be shown in your answer. Then proceed as follows:

Step 1. Prepare an opening statement of affairs. This will give the balance on the Accumulated fund at 1 January 2011 and will be the starting point for recording the transactions during the year.

Statement of affairs at 31 December 2010		
		$
Fixed or Non-current assets		
Pavilion		120 000
Club sports equipment		40 000
Motor roller		2 000
Current assets		
Inventory of equipment for sale to members		4 000
Annual subscriptions owing		1 200
Bank balance		6 730
Total assets		173 930
Current liabilities		
Creditors for equipment for sale to members	1300	
Annual subscriptions received in advance	800	
Life subscriptions fund	1750	3 850
Accumulated fund at 1 January 2011		170 080

Step 2. Prepare Receipts and Payment account. This will summarise all the transactions affecting the Income and Expenditure Account and Statement of Financial Position and calculate the bank balance at 31 December 2011.

Receipts and Payments account for the year ended 31 December 2011				
		$		$
1 Jan Balance brought forward		6 730	31 Dec Caretaker's wages	8 000
31 Dec Annual subscriptions		18 000	Repairs: club equipment	1 700
Sales of equipment		12 000	Purchase: club equipment	2 000
Sales of tickets Dinner-dance		4 400	Purchase of equipment for resale	4 000
Takings - refreshments		2 660	Heating and lighting	1 800
Life membership subscriptions		400	Dinner-dance hire of band	200
			catering	1 000
			Food for refreshment bar	1 400
			Secretary's expenses	840
			Balance c/f	23 250
		44 190		44 190

Step 3. Prepare workings to adjust for accruals, prepayments, depreciation and any other items. Show these workings with your answer.

You may show your workings as ledger ('T') accounts or as calculations. Decide which method is best for you and practise it in all your exercises. Both methods will be shown here.

'T' accounts				**Calculations**	

1. Purchase of equipment for resale

	$		$		$
Cash paid	4 000	Creditors b/f	1 300	Cash paid	4 000
Creditors c/f	900	I & E A/c	3 600	less creditors b/f	(1 300)
	4 900		4 900		2 700
				add creditors c/f	900
				Trading A/c	3 600

2. Annual subscriptions

	$		$		$
Owing at 1 Jan	1 200	Prepaid at 1 Jan	800	Received in year	18 000
Prepaid at 31 Dec	900	Cash	18 000	less owing 1 Jan	(1 200)
I & E A/c	18 100	Owing at 31 Dec	1 400	prepaid 31 Dec	(900)
	20 200		20 200		15 900
				add prepaid 1 Jan	800
				owing 31 Dec	1 400
				I & E A/c	18 100

3. Life subscriptions

	$		$		$
I & E A/c $\frac{1}{5} \times 2150$	430	B/f	1 750	Balance b/f	1 750
C/f	1 720	Cash received	400	Cash received	400
	2 150		2 150		2 150
				I & E A/c $(\frac{1}{5})$	430

4. Club sports equipment

	$		$		$
B/f	40 000	I & E (20%)	8 400	Balance b/f	40 000
Cash	2 000	c/d	33 600	Cash	2 000
	42 000		42 000		42 000
				I & E A/c (20%)	8 400
				Net book value	33 600

Step 4. The Income and Expenditure Account and Statement of Financial Position may now be copied out from steps 1, 2 and 3. As the sale of equipment to members is trading, a Trading Account should be prepared even though one is not asked for in the question.

If steps 1, 2 and 3 have been carried out with care, preparing the Income and Expenditure Account and Statement of Financial Position is now little more than a copying exercise and can be completed in little time.

(a)

Sales of equipment		
	$	$
Sales		12 000
Less cost of sales		
Inventory at 1 January 2011	4000	
Purchase (working 1)	3600	
	7600	
Less inventory at 31 December 2011	2000	5 600
Profit transferred to Income & Expenditure Account		6 400

Star Sports and Social Club			
Income and Expenditure Account for the year ended 31 December 2011			
	$	$	$
Annual subscriptions (working 2)			18 100
Life subscriptions (working 3)			430
Profit on sale of equipment			6 400
Dinner/dance*			
Sale of tickets		4 400	
Less hire of band	200		
catering	1 000	1 200	3 200
Refreshment bar*			
Takings		2 660	
Less cost of food		1 400	1 260
			29 390
Less expenses			
Caretaker's wages		8 000	
Repairs to club equipment		1 700	
Heating and lighting		1 800	
Secretary's expenses		840	
Depreciation: Pavilion (6% of $120 000)		7 200	
Equipment (working 4)		8 400	
Motor roller (20% of $2000)		400	28 340
Surplus of income over expenditure			1 050

*Expenses of dinner-dance and refreshment bar are grouped with the income from those activities to help members see how those activities have contributed to the club's funds.

(b)

Statement of Financial Position at 31 December 2011

	$	$	$
Fixed or Non-current assets at net book value			
Pavilion			112 800
Club equipment			33 600
Motor roller			1 600
			148 000
Current assets			
Inventory of equipment for sale to members		2 000	
Subscriptions owing		1 400	
Bank		23 250	
		26 650	
Less Current liabilities			
Trade receivables	900		
Subscriptions prepaid	900		
Life subscriptions	1 720	3 520	23 130
			171 130
Represented by			
Accumulated fund at 1 January 2011			170 080
Add surplus of income over expenditure			1 050
Accumulated fund at 31 December 2011			171 130
Fund to encourage young people to train for sport*			5 000
Represented by savings bonds			5 000

* See Note 4 in further information.

Exercise 1

The Wellington Drama Club has 120 members. The annual subscription is $20 per member. Subscriptions not paid in one year are written off if not paid by the end of the next year.

The Club presents two plays a year, each play being performed over ten days. The Club hires a local hall for the performance and the dress rehearsals, which take place over three days before the presentation of each play. The Club donates half of its net surpluses to the Actors Benevolent Fund.

The receipts and payments of the Club in the year ended 31 December 2011 were as follows:

Receipts	$
Sales of tickets	20 000
Sales of programmes	3 000
Sales of refreshments	3 500
Subscriptions for the year ended 31 December 2011	2 000
Subscriptions for the year ended 31 December 2010	280

Subscription for the year ending 31 December 2012	360
Payments	
Hire of hall	2 600
Printing of posters, tickets and programmes	180
Hire of costumes	4 700
Cost of refreshments	2 200
Payments for copyrights	1 400

At 31 December 2010, members subscriptions of $280 were owing.

Required

(a) Prepare The Wellington Drama Club's Income and Expenditure Account for the year ended 31 December 2011.

(b) Prepare a Statement of Financial Position extract at 31 December 2011 to show the items for subscriptions.

Exercise 2

The Hutt River Dining Club is funded partly by the member's annual subscriptions ($20 per member), partly by restaurant takings and partly from profits from the sale of books on dieting, healthy eating and cooking.

At 31 December 2010, the club's Statement of Financial Position showed the following:

	$	$
Catering equipment at cost	11 000	
Depreciation of catering equipment	3 000	8000
Inventory of food		200
Inventory of books		1100
Subscriptions owing		180
Cash at bank		1520
Amount owing for supplies of food		40
Subscriptions in advance		60

Receipts and payments for the year ended 31 December 2011 were as follows:

Receipts	$
Annual subscriptions	5 000
Restaurant takings	73 760
Sales of books	12 150
Payments	
Restaurant staff wages	39 000
Cost of food	24 980
Purchase of books	4 840
New catering equipment	3 750
Heating and lighting	8 390
Sundry expenses	2 270

Further information

1. Subscriptions owing at 31 December 2011: $40.
2. Subscriptions paid in advance at 31 December 2011: $140.
3. Inventories at 31 December 2011: food $270; books $965.
4. Creditors at 31 December 2011: for food $360; for books $200.
5. Annual depreciation of catering equipment is 10% on cost.

Required

(a) Calculate the Accumulated fund at 1 January 2011.

(b) Prepare a Receipts and Payments Account for the year ended 31 December 2011.
(c) Prepare the Members Subscriptions Account for the year ended 31 December 2011.
(d) Prepare a Trading Account for the year ended 31 December 2011 for the sale of books.
(e) Prepare a Restaurant Account for the year ended 31 December 2011.
(f) Prepare The Hutt River Dining Club's Income and Expenditure Account for the year ended 31 December 2011.
(g) Prepare the Statement of Financial Position as at 31 December 2011.

HINTS

- Club accounts often look difficult, but they need not be so. Keep calm and follow carefully the steps taught in this and the previous chapter.
- Always follow carefully whatever instructions are given in an examination question.
- Even if your answer is not perfect, you can earn many useful marks if you show the examiner what you can do.
- Ensure you always use the correct terms for a non-profit-making organisation.
- Include all your workings with your answer.
- Tick each item in the question as you deal with it; check that everything has been ticked to ensure you have not missed anything.

MULTIPLE-CHOICE QUESTIONS

1. Which of the following will *not* be found in the accounts of a club?
   A. Accumulated fund   **B.** Drawings account
   C. Receipts and Payments account
   D. Statement of Financial Position

2. The following information for a year is extracted from a sports club's accounts.

	$
Subscriptions received	10 000
Sales of equipment to members	7 000
Opening inventory of equipment	1 300
Closing inventory of equipment	800
Purchases of equipment	5 000

What was the club's surplus of income over expenditure for the year?

   A. $10 000   **B.** $11 500
   C. $12 500   **D.** $17 000

3. The following information relates to a club for a year.

Number of members	60
Annual subscription	$20
Subscriptions owing at beginning of year	$100
Subscriptions owing at end of year	$60

How much should be credited to the club's Income and Expenditure Account for annual subscriptions for the year?

   A. $1100   **B.** $1160
   C. $1200   **D.** $1260

4. A club's records provide the following information for a year.

	$
Annual subscriptions received in the year	4000
Annual subscriptions received in advance at end of year	50
Balance on Life Subscriptions account at beginning of year	500
Life subscriptions received during the year	100

The club's policy is to credit life subscriptions to the Income and Expenditure Account over five years.
How much should be credited to the Income and Expenditure Account for subscriptions for the year?

A. $4050 B. $4070
C. $4150 D. $4170

ADDITIONAL EXERCISES

1. The Civic Athletics Club's Receipts and Payments Account for the year ended 31 May 2011 is as follows:

Receipts	$	Payments	$
Balance at bank 1 June 2010	4 650	Refreshment supplies bought	2 654
Subscriptions received	7 970	Wages	4 000
Sales of tickets for dance	1 897	Rent of rooms	540
Refreshment bar takings	4 112	Purchase of new equipment	1 778
Sale of old equipment	94	Teams' travelling expenses	995
Donation	90	Balance at bank at 31 May 2011	8 846
	18 813		18 813

Further information
1. Refreshment bar inventories were valued at $150 at 1 June 2010, and at $180 at 31 May 2011.
2. Trade payables for refreshment bar inventories were: at 1 June 2010 $15; at 31 May 2011 $40.
3. At 1 June 2010, subscriptions owing were $330, of which $310 was paid in the year to 31 May 2011. It is club's policy to write off subscriptions if they have not been received by the end of the year following their due date. Subscriptions owing at 31 May 2011 were $275.
4. Of the wages paid, $900 was paid to staff serving refreshments.
5. On 1 June 2010 the club's equipment was valued at $4700. The equipment sold during the year had a book value of $70 at the date of sale. At 31 May 2011, the equipment was valued at $6000.

Required
(a) Calculate the Accumulated fund as at 1 June 2010.
(b) Prepare the refreshments Trading Account for the year ended 31 May 2011.

(c) Prepare the Income and Expenditure Account for the year ended 31 May 2011.
(d) Prepare the club's Statement of Financial Position as at 31 May 2011.

2. The members of The Howzidun Magic Club meet to demonstrate their conjuring skills and to entertain visitors, who pay an entrance fee at the door. The club also has a shop for the sale of conjuring tricks and props.
The club's Bank account for the year ended 30 June 2011 was as follows:

	$		$
Balance at 1 July 2010	16 800	Purchases of tricks and props	8 220
Subscriptions received	10 730	Shop wages	6 000
Cash taken at door	9 456	Cost of annual dance	2 600
Shop takings	12 348	Purchase of equipment	5 000
Annual dance receipts	3 720	Secretary's expenses	2 125
Grant from local council	4 000	Transfer to Deposit account	20 000
Donations to the Disappeared Wizards Memorial Fund	666	Balance at 30 June 2011	13 775
	57 720		57 720

The club has 200 members. The annual subscription was $30 until 1 July 2010 when it was increased to $40.

At 1 July 2010, 20 members had not paid their subscriptions for the year ended 30 June 2010 but, of these, 15 had paid their arrears of subscriptions by 30 June 2011. By 30 June 2011, all members had paid their subscriptions for the year up to date and some had paid their subscriptions for the year to 30 June 2012.

Other assets and liabilities were:

	At 1 July 2010 $	At 30 June 2011 $
Shop inventory	1 600	1 850
Trade payables for shop purchases	400	210
Equipment at cost	7 000	12 000
Deposit account	10 000	30 000
Disappeared Wizards Memorial Fund	–	666

The equipment at 1 July 2010 had been depreciated for five years by $1400 per annum. The new equipment is to be depreciated at the same annual percentage rate.

The grant from the local council was the first instalment of an annual grant of $8000.

The transfer to the Deposit account was made on 1 January 2011. Interest at 4% per annum is payable on 30 June each year.

Required

(a) Calculate the Accumulated fund at 1 July 2010.
(b) Prepare the Club Shop Trading Account for the year ended 30 June 2011.
(c) Prepare the Club Subscriptions Account for the year ended 30 June 2011.
(d) Prepare the Club Income and Expenditure Account for the year ended 30 June 2011.
(e) Prepare the Club Statement of Financial Position at 30 June 2011.

3. The Taupo Sailing Club provides its members with a number of activities:
(i) hire of boats for members; non-members are charged an extra 20% for boat hire
(ii) yacht racing competitions
(iii) a clubhouse with a refreshment bar which is also used for social functions
(iv) a sailing training school for all age groups.
The following financial information relates to 1 April 2010.

	$
Fixed or Non-current assets at net book value	
Freehold premises	350 000
Yacht maintenance shop	42 000
Boatyard and launch facilities	74 000
Fixtures and fittings	28 000
Boats and yachts	465 000

Other items

Members' subscriptions:	$
in arrears	3 000
in advance	6 000
Balance at bank	94 000
Inventories of refreshments	1 250
Trade payables for refreshments	1 030

The following financial information relates to the year ended 31 March 2011.

Receipts	$	Payments	$
Hire of yachts and boats		Repairs and maintenance	
to members	43 000	of yachts	23 400
to non-members	34 000	Purchase of new boats	
Receipts from		and yachts	61 000
training school	34 500	Wages of training-	
Members'		school staff	16 500
subscriptions	186 000	Wages of	
Refreshments		refreshment-	
and social		bar staff	14 000
events	77 000	Purchase of	
Receipts from		refreshment-bar	
yacht racing		food	53 000
competition	28 900	Expenses of	
		yacht racing	
		competition	13 000
		Sundry	
		expenses	26 000

Further information

1. At 31 March 2011, members' subscriptions owing amounted to $2000; members' subscriptions in advance for next year were $3400.
2. The club's depreciation policy is as follows:
   ● Freehold premises, boatyard and launch facilities, and boats and yachts: 5% per annum on net book value
   ● Fixtures and fittings, and yacht maintenance shop: 10% per annum on net book value.
3. Trade payables at 31 March 2011 were as follows:

	$
Repairs and maintenance of yachts	1350
Refreshments	970
Wages: training-school staff	700
refreshment bar staff	400

Refreshment bar inventory at 31 March 2011 was valued at $1600.

Required

(a) Prepare Taupo Sailing Club's Income and Expenditure Account for the year ended 31 March 2011 in good format. A Trading Account should be prepared for the refreshment bar.

(b) Prepare the club's Statement of Financial Position as at 31 March 2011.

4. The Abracamagic Club's Bank Current account for the year ended 30 September 2011 was as follows:

	$		$
Balance at		Purchases	
1 October 2010	8 400	for shop	3 745
Subscriptions		Shop wages	4 000
received	6 435	General	
Donations	600	expenses	1 500
Cash taken		Cost of Annual	
at door	3 500	Dance	1 490
Grant from		Transfer to	
local council	6 000	Deposit account	16 000
Annual Dance		New equipment	2 000
receipts	1 400	Rent	8 000
Shop takings	7 168		
Balance at			
30 Sept. 2011	3 232		
	36 735		36 735

In order to increase funds the club has a shop which sells magic tricks. In addition to an annual membership subscription, members pay $1 each time they visit the club. This is referred to as 'Cash taken at door'.

The annual membership subscription was $40 until 30 September 2011 when it was raised to $45. There were 150 members at 1 October 2010. At that date 15 of them had not paid their subscriptions for the year ended 30 September 2010 and 12 had already paid their subscriptions for the year ended 30 September 2011.

By 30 September 2011, all members had paid their due subscriptions, and some had paid in advance for the year ending 30 September 2012, but the Treasurer had not yet calculated how many.

Other balances were as follows:

	At 1 October 2010 $	At 30 September 2011 $
Shop inventory	500	850
Cash float for shop	50	70
Trade payables for shop	1 450	1 260
Deposit account	15 000	31 000
Equipment at cost	8 000	10 000

The equipment at 1 October 2010 had been depreciated by $1600 per annum for five years. The new equipment is to be depreciated at the same annual percentage rate.

The local council's grant was for $10 000 and the remainder of this has yet to be received. This will be treated as revenue income in the final accounts. Interest of $800 is due on the deposit account for the year ended 30 September 2011.

At 30 September 2011, general expenses of $65 were due and unpaid.

Required

(a) Calculate the Accumulated fund at 1 October 2010.

(b) Prepare the Club Shop Trading Account for the year ended 30 September 2011.

(c) Prepare the Club Subscriptions Account for the year ended 30 September 2011.

(d) Prepare the Club Income and Expenditure Account for the year ended 30 September 2011.

 **Departmental accounts**

In this chapter you will learn:

- how to allocate or apportion expenses to the departments of a business
- how to prepare departmental Income Statements in columnar form.

18.1 What are departmental accounts?

Departmental accounts are Income Statements for businesses that have more than one department. A business may sell furniture, electrical appliances and clothing. It may also provide a restaurant for its customers. Each of these activities will be carried on in a separate department and will make its own contribution to the profit of the business. To find the profit of each department, separate Income Statements are prepared. This will require entries in the books of prime entry to be analysed between the departments, or separate books to be kept for each department.

18.2 How to prepare departmental Income Statements

The Trading Sections of the Income Statement

The Trading sections of the Income Statement should be prepared in columnar form, that is, with a separate column for each department, and one for totals.

Example 1

Omnimart sells furniture, clothing and electrical goods. The following information has been extracted from its books for the year ended 31 December 2010.

		$
Sales:	Furniture	272 000
	Clothing	138 000
	Electrical	110 000
Purchases:	Furniture	112 000
	Clothing	76 000
	Electrical	50 000
Inventory at 1 January 2010:		
	Furniture	28 000
	Clothing	19 000
	Electrical	22 000
Inventory at 31 December 2010:		
	Furniture	35 000
	Clothing	23 000
	Electrical	26 000

The Trading section of the Income Statement is prepared in columnar form as follows:

Omnimart								
Trading section of the Income Statement for the year ended 31 December 2010								
	Furniture		Clothing		Electrical		Total	
	$	$	$	$	$	$	$	$
Sales		272 000		138 000		110 000		520 000
Less Cost of sales								
Opening inventory	28 000		19 000		22 000		69 000	
Purchases	112 000		76 000		50 000		238 000	
	140 000		95 000		72 000		307 000	
Closing inventory	35 000	105 000	23 000	72 000	26 000	46 000	84 000	223 000
Gross profit		167 000		66 000		64 000		297 000

Income Statements

Overheads are allocated to departments if the actual amounts to be debited to them are known. Wages and salaries can be allocated to departments if the payroll is analysed. Electricity can be charged to each department if separate meters are provided for each department.

Overheads which cannot be allocated to departments must be apportioned to them on suitable bases. Examples of the ways in which overheads may be apportioned are:

Expense	Basis of apportionment
Heating and lighting (when not separately metered)	in proportion to the respective floor areas of the departments
Rent	
Insurance of buildings	
Advertising, distribution	in proportion to departmental sales
Insurance of plant, machinery and other assets	on the replacement values of assets in each department
Depreciation	on the cost of assets in each department
Administration costs	on number of employees in each department, or on departmental turnover

Commission paid to an employee, based on profit

The commission is usually calculated as a percentage of the profit after charging the commission. Calculate the commission using the following formula:

$$\frac{\text{percentage of commission}}{100 + \text{percentage of commission}}$$

Example 2

A manager is entitled to 5% commission calculated on profit after charging the commission. The profit before charging commission is $84 000. What is the profit after commission?

The commission is

$$\$(84\,000 \times \frac{5}{105}) = \$4000.$$

Profit after commission = $80 000.

Note. Make all calculations of apportionment to the nearest dollar.

Example 3

(Continuing Omnimart as shown above.)
In the year ended 31 December 2010, Omnimart's expenses were as follows:

		$
Salaries and wages:	Furniture	35 000
	Clothing	28 000
	Electrical	25 000
Rent		60 000
Heating and lighting		15 000
Advertising		6 000
Delivery expenses		4 000
Depreciation of fixed assets		10 000
Administration		30 000

Further information

1. Delivery and advertising costs are to be apportioned in proportion to departmental sales.
2. Administration costs are to be divided equally between the three departments.
3. Departmental statistics are:

	Furniture	Clothing	Electrical
Area occupied in metres²	150	90	60
Non-current assets at cost	$50 000	$30 000	$20 000

4. The manager of each department is entitled to a commission of 5% of his departmental net profit after charging the commission.

Required

Prepare a Departmental Income Statement for the year ended 31 December 2010 in as much detail as possible, clearly showing the gross profit made by each department.

Answer

	Furniture		Clothing		Electrical		Total	
	\$	\$	\$	\$	\$	\$	\$	\$
Gross profit		167 000		66 000		64 000		297 000
Salaries and wages	35 000		28 000		25 000		88 000	
Rent[1]	30 000		18 000		12 000		60 000	
Heating[1]	7 500		4 500		3 000		15 000	
Advertising[2]	3 139		1 592		1 269		6 000	
Delivery[2]	2 092		1 062		846		4 000	
Depreciation[3]	5 000		3 000		2 000		10 000	
Administration	10 000	92 731	10 000	66 154	10 000	54 115	30 000	213 000
		74 269		(154)		9 885		84 000
Managers' commission ($\frac{5}{100}$)		3 537				471		4 008
Net profit/(loss)		70 732		(154)		9 414		79 992

Omnimart
Departmental Income Statement for the year ended 31 December 2010

1 Apportioned on basis of area occupied.
2 Apportioned on basis of sales.
3 Apportioned on basis of cost of fixed assets.

Exercise 1

Geeta owns a shoe shop. The shop has three departments: ladies', men's and children's. Information extracted from Geeta's books for the year ended 31 March 2011 is given:

	Ladies'	Men's	Children's
	\$	\$	\$
Sales	100 000	120 000	80 000
Inventory at 1 April 2010	14 000	17 000	5 000
Purchases	50 000	63 000	42 000
Inventory at 31 March 2011	18 000	22 000	4 000
Wages	20 000	20 000	12 000

Other balances at 31 March 2010:

	\$
Rent	28 000
Heating and lighting	6 000
Advertising	5 000
Administration	27 000
Depreciation	7 200

Further information

	Ladies'	Men's	Children's
Area occupied	$\frac{2}{5}$	$\frac{2}{5}$	$\frac{1}{5}$
Cost of fixed assets (\$000)	30	25	15
Number of staff	4	3	2

Advertising is to be apportioned on the basis of departmental sales.

Administration is to be apportioned in the ratio of departmental staff numbers.

Managers are entitled to a commission of 5% of their departmental profit after charging the commission.

Required

Prepare Geeta's Departmental Income Statement for the year ended 31 March 2011 in as much detail as possible, clearly showing the gross profit made by each department.

Note. Make all calculations to the nearest dollar.

18.3 A loss-making department

If a department is unprofitable, there are courses of action that may be taken to make it profitable. These include:

- increase prices, provided this does not adversely affect sales volume
- negotiate cheaper prices with suppliers, or find alternative suppliers
- advertise the department's products in order to increase its sales
- offer discounts or other incentives to increase turnover, provided these do not cancel out the additional revenue

- offer more attractive products
- reduce the department's overheads.

If the loss-making department cannot be made profitable, closure may have to be considered. Two factors should be considered before the department is closed:

(i) the effect of the closure of a department on the fixed overheads

(ii) any other effect of closure on the remaining departments.

Fixed overheads

Some overheads are fixed; that is, they must still be paid even if the business does not trade. Examples are: rent and insurance of premises, depreciation of non-current assets and some other administration expenses. The fixed overheads of a department may still have to be paid even if it is closed; the remaining departments will have to bear additional costs, which will affect their profitability.

Example

Hiatus is a retail store with three departments: A, B and C. Its Income Statement for the year ended 31 January 2011 is as follows:

	Department A		Department B		Department C	
	$	$	$	$	$	$
Gross profit		80 000		48 000		30 000
Wages	24 000		18 000		13 000	
Rent	5 000		6 000		4 000	
Electricity	1 500		1 800		1 200	
Advertising	5 000		3 000		4 000	
Administration	16 000	51 500	16 000	44 800	16 000	38 200
		28 500		3 200		(8 200)

Wages have been allocated on an actual basis. Rent and electricity have been apportioned on the basis of floor areas occupied. Advertising has been apportioned on the basis of relative sales.

Each department is debited with one-third of the administration expenses. No administration expenses will be saved if department C is closed.

At present, the business is making a profit of $(28 500 + 3200 − 8200) = $23 500.

Closure of department C would reduce the total profit of the business as departments A and B would have additional administration expenses: $(28 500 + 3200 − 16 000) = $15 700. The business will be worse off by $7800. This is department C's contribution to the overall profit before it has been charged with administration ($30 000 − $22 200). It would be better to keep department C open and to benefit from its contribution to the overall profitability.

The way in which administration costs have been apportioned to the departments should be questioned. The costs have been spread evenly over the three departments, but examination of the apportionment of the other expenses suggests that department C is smaller than the others. It would be more reasonable to reflect the differences in the sizes of the departments in the apportionment of administration costs.

The situation might be different if administration costs could be reduced by the closure of department C.

Other factors

It may sometimes be desirable to keep a loss-making department open regardless of the effect that closure would have on the fixed overheads. Department C in the above example may be necessary for the operations of the other departments. Or it may attract customers if, for example, it is a restaurant situated where customers have to pass through the other departments to get to it. The sales of those departments may benefit as a result.

MULTIPLE-CHOICE QUESTIONS

1. Which basis is suitable for apportioning advertising cost between departments?
   A. departmental cost of goods sold
   B. departmental gross profit
   C. departmental turnover
   D. number of staff in each department

2. Which basis should be used to apportion the cost of insuring plant and machinery between departments?
   A. net book value
   B. original cost
   C. present disposable value
   D. replacement cost

3. A manager is paid a commission of 5% based on net profit after charging the commission. The profit before commission is $157 500.
   How much commission is paid to the manager?
   A. $1500   B. $1575   C. $7500   D. $7875

4. The administration expenses of a business amount to $30 000. They are apportioned to three departments as follows: department A $\frac{3}{6}$, department B $\frac{2}{6}$, department C $\frac{1}{6}$. It has been decided to close department C but there will not be any reduction in administration costs.
   How will the administration expenses be apportioned to departments A and B after department C has been closed?

	Dept A $	Dept B $
A.	15 000	10 000
B.	18 000	12 000
C.	21 000	14 000
D.	22 200	14 800

ADDITIONAL EXERCISES

1. Mason is a retailer selling furnishings, kitchen equipment and clothing. The following information has been extracted from his books for the year ended 30 April 2011.

	Furnishings $000	Kitchen equipment $000	Clothing $000
Sales	912	696	552
Inventory at 1 May 2010	350	306	94
Purchases	491	406	402
Inventory at 30 April 2011	394	222	65

	Furnishings $000	Kitchen equipment $000	Clothing $000
Salaries for the year ended 30 April 2011	58	42	60
Fixtures and fittings at cost at 30 April 2011	300	200	200

Further information

1. Mason incurred the following expenses for the year ended 30 April 2011.

	$
Rent	94 000
Heating and lighting	75 000
General expenses	62 000

2. The premises cost $800 000.
3. Floor space occupied: Furnishings 40%
   Kitchen equipment 35%
   Clothing 25%
4. Depreciation is to be calculated as follows:

Premises 4% per annum on cost.
Fixtures and fittings 15% per annum on cost.

5. General expenses are to be apportioned between the departments in proportion to their respective turnovers.

	Kitchen Equipment		Radios & TVs		Home Computers	
	$000	$000	$000	$000	$000	$000
Sales		200		90		60
Less Cost of sales		110		40		35
Gross profit		90		50		25
Variable expenses	30		25		18	
Fixed expenses	40	70	18	43	12	30
Net profit		20		7		(5)

Further information
1. Year-end inventory taking reveals that damaged stock has been included in cost of sales as follows:

	$
Kitchen Equipment	4000
Radios and TVs	5000

The goods have no disposable value.
2. Computer equipment sales includes goods which have been sent to a customer on sale or return for $3000. The equipment cost $2000. It is not known if the customer is going to buy the equipment.
3. Administration expenses of $30 000 have been divided equally between the three departments and included in fixed expenses.

Required
Prepare departmental Income Statements for the year ended 30 April 2011 in as much detail as possible, clearly showing the gross profit made by each department. (Where necessary, calculations should be made to the nearest $000.)

2. Spicer sells electrical goods from three departments: Kitchen Equipment, Radios and TVs, and Home Computers. The following is the summarised Income Statement for the year ended 30 April 2011.

4. All other fixed expenses have been allocated as wholly attributable to the departments concerned.

Required
(a) Calculate revised net profit figures for
    (i) Kitchen Equipment
    (ii) Radios and TVs
    (iii) Home Computers
    (iv) Spicer.
(b) Calculate the contribution which Home Computers has made to Spicer's profit.

Spicer has decided to close the Home Computer department. This will not result in any reduction of administration expenses.

Required
(c) Calculate Spicers' profit for the year ended 30 April 2011 if the Home Computers department had been closed at 30 April 2010.

19 Manufacturing Accounts

In this chapter you will learn:

- how to prepare a Manufacturing Account
- how to calculate manufacturing profit in the Income Statement
- how to provide for unrealised profit inventories of finished goods.

19.1 What is a Manufacturing Account?

Manufacturing Accounts are prepared by manufacturing companies to show the cost of producing goods.

The Manufacturing Accounts are prepared before the Income Statements. The cost of goods manufactured is transferred to the Trading section of the Income Statement and replaces the figure for Purchases which would be found if the business is buying and selling wholly completed goods.

Trading companies purchase finished goods, but a manufacturing company's purchases consist of materials it uses in its manufacturing process. A large part of a manufacturing company's wages will most probably be paid to employees engaged on making goods, and some of the overheads will relate to the manufacturing process. A Manufacturing Account groups all the manufacturing expenses together as factory expenses. If the goods are produced more cheaply than they can be purchased from an outside supplier, the factory may be considered to have made a profit and will be credited with **factory profit**.

Manufacturing companies' inventories include raw materials, work in progress and finished goods. Any factory profit included in the inventory of finished goods must be excluded from the value of inventory shown in the Statement of Financial Position.

19.2 How to prepare a Manufacturing Account

Select from the trial balance those expenses that relate to the company's manufacturing operation. The expenses are either direct (e.g. the cost of materials from which the goods are made, and the wages of the workers who actually make the goods) or indirect (all other manufacturing expenses).

The following outline shows how expenditure is allocated to Manufacturing Accounts.

Sample Example Ltd Manufacturing Account for the year ended 31 December 2011		
	$000	$000
Direct costs		
Direct material[1]		200
Direct labour[2]		380
Other direct expenses[3]		60
Prime cost[4]		640
Factory overheads		
Indirect materials[5]	95	
Indirect wages[6]	120	
Other overheads[7]	330	545
		1185
Work in progress at 1 January 2011[8]	78	
Work in progress at 31 December 2011[9]	(53)	25
Factory cost of finished goods		
(or cost of production)[10]		1210
Factory profit[11]		242
Cost of goods transferred to Trading Account[12]		1452

1. **Direct material:** material from which goods are made. The cost includes carriage inwards on raw material.

2. **Direct labour:** the wages of the workers who actually make the goods.
3. **Direct expenses:** royalties, licence fees, etc. which have to be paid to other persons for the right to produce their products or to use their processes. The payment is a fixed sum for every unit of goods produced.
4. **Prime cost:** the total of the direct costs. This description must *always* be shown.
5. **Indirect materials:** all materials purchased for the factory but which do not form part of the goods being produced, for example cleaning materials, lubricating oil for the machinery.
6. **Indirect wages:** the wages of all factory workers who do not actually make the goods, for example factory managers, supervisors, stores staff, cleaners, etc.
7. **Other overheads:** overheads relating exclusively to the factory and production, for example factory rent, heating and lighting, depreciation of the factory building and machinery, etc.
8. **Work in progress:** goods in the process of being made at the end of the previous year but which were not finished are brought into the current year as an input to this year's production.
9. Goods that are not completely finished at the end of the current year must be deducted from the year's costs in order to arrive at the cost of finished goods.
10. **Factory cost of finished goods:** either these words or the alternative, **cost of production**, should be shown at this point in the account.
11. **Factory profit:** the percentage to be added to cost of production as profit. The amount is decided by management and will always be given in questions if necessary. It is debited in the Manufacturing Account and credited in the Profit and Loss Account (see below).
12. The total of the Manufacturing Account is debited in the Trading section of the Income Statement under the heading 'Cost of Sales'.

Example

The following balances have been extracted from Makeit & Co.'s trial balance at 31 December 2011.

	$000	$000
Inventories at 1 January 2011:		
Direct materials	10	
Work in progress	38	
Finished goods	40	
Purchases (direct materials)	140	
Carriage inwards	24	
Direct wages	222	
Direct expenses	46	
Indirect materials	45	
Indirect labour	72	
Rent:		
factory	100	
offices	90	
Heating, lighting and power:		
factory	45	
offices	35	
Sales		1 300
Administration salaries and wages	173	

Further information

1. Inventory at 31 December 2011 was as follows:

	$000
Direct materials	18
Work in progress	20
Finished goods	69

2. Depreciation is to be provided on fixed assets as follows:

	$000
Factory building	20
Factory machinery	36
Office equipment	24

3. Factory profit is to be calculated at 15% on cost of production.

Required

Prepare the Manufacturing Account and Income Statement for the year ended 31 December 2011.

Answer

Makeit & Co.
Manufacturing Account and Income Statement
for the year ended 31 December 2011

	$000	$000
Direct materials Inventory at 1 January 2011	10	
Purchases	140	
Carriage inwards	24	
	174	
Less Inventory at 31 December 2011	18	156
Direct labour		222
Direct expenses		46
Prime cost		424
Indirect materials	45	
Indirect labour	72	
Rent of factory	100	
Heating, lighting and power	45	
Depreciation: factory	20	
machinery	36	318
		742
Work in progress 1 January 2011	38	
Work in progress 31 December 2011	(20)	18
Factory cost of finished goods		760
Factory profit (15%)		114
Transferred to Trading Account		874
Sales		1300
Cost of sales		
Inventory of finished goods at 1 January 2011	40	
Transferred from factory	874	
	914	
Inventory of finished goods at 31 December 2011	69	845
Gross profit		455
Wages and salaries	173	
Rent of offices	90	

Heating and lighting	35	
Depreciation of office equipment	24	322
Net profit on trading[1]		133
Add factory profit[2]	114	
Less Unrealised profit on closing stock		
of finished goods[3]	9	105
Net profit		238

1. Net profit on trading is the profit that has been made from the trading activity and does not include factory profit.
2. Factory profit (after deducting unrealised profit) is added to the net profit on trading to show Makeit & Co.'s total profit.
3. See §19.3.

Note. The Income Statement follows on from the Manufacturing Account without a break. It is included in the heading to the Manufacturing Account.

19.3 Unrealised profit included in the inventories of finished goods

The figure of closing inventory in Makeit & Co.'s Income Statement includes factory profit. This profit will not be realised until the goods are sold and must be excluded to arrive at the realised factory profit. (The concept of realisation must be applied.) Makeit & Co's. unrealised profit is calculated as follows. The inventory of $69 000 is 115% of the cost of manufacture

and the unrealised profit is $69\,000 \times \dfrac{15}{115} = \$9000$.

The double entry for unrealised profit, $9000, debited in the Profit and Loss Account is completed by a credit to a Provision for Unrealised Profit.

In future years, it will be necessary only to adjust the Provision for Unrealised Profit for increases or decreases in the closing inventories of finished goods. For example, if Makeit & Co.'s finished goods inventory one year later, at 31 December 2012, is $92 000, the provision required

for unrealised profit will be $92\,000 \times \dfrac{15}{115} = \$12\,000$.

Only the increase of $3000 in the provision will be debited in the Profit and Loss Account and credited to the Provision for Unrealised Profit.

The Provision for Unrealised Profit account is as follows:

Provision for Unrealised Profit Account				
2012	$	2012		$
Dec 31 Balance c/f	12 000	Jan 1 Balance b/f		9 000
(92 000 ×		Dec 31 Income		
15/115)		Statement		3 000
	12 000			12 000

An increase in the provision is recorded as follows:

> **Debit** Income Statement
> **Credit** Provision for Unrealised Profit
> with the amount of the increase

A decrease in the provision is recorded as follows:

> **Debit** Provision for Unrealised Profit
> **Credit** Income Statement
> with the amount of the decrease.

(The accounting for a Provision for Unrealised Profit is similar to that of a Provision for Doubtful Debts; see §12.4.)

19.4 Manufacturing Statement of Financial Position

The Statement of Financial Position of a manufacturing business includes the inventories of materials, work in progress and finished goods at cost.

The inventories appear in Makeit & Co.'s Statement of Financial Position at 31 December 2011 as follows:

Current assets		$000	$000
Inventory: Materials			18
Work in progress			20
Finished goods		69	
Less unrealised profit		9	60
			98

Exercise 1

The Fabricating Company carries on a manufacturing business. Information extracted from its trial balance at 31 March 2011 is as follows:

	$000	$000
Sales		700
Inventory at 1 April 2010		
Raw materials	10	
Work in progress	12	
Finished goods	24	
Purchase of raw materials	130	
Carriage inwards	14	
Direct labour	170	
Other direct expenses	16	
Factory overheads	128	
Office overheads	96	

The following further information is given.

	$000
Inventory at 31 March 2011	
Raw materials	20
Work in progress	22
Finished goods	36
Depreciation charges for the year:	
Factory	12
Office	3

Completed production is transferred to the warehouse at a mark-up on factory cost of 20%.

Required
Prepare a Manufacturing Account and Income Statement for the year ended 31 March 2011.

Exercise 2

The following balances have been extracted from the books of Glupersoo at 30 April 2011.

	$
Sales	800 000
Purchase of raw materials	132 000
Direct wages	146 250
Indirect wages	19 500
Rent	45 000
Heating and lighting	42 300
Insurance	3 150
Office salaries	51 450
Carriage inwards	11 505
Carriage outwards	2 520
Advertising	7 000
Motor van expenses	6 000
Inventories at 1 May 2010:	
Raw materials	11 250
Work in progress	18 000
Finished goods	27 000

Further information
1. Inventories at 30 April 2011:

	$
Raw materials	13 125
Work in progress	15 750
Finished goods	24 000

2. The following expenses must be accrued at 30 April 2011.

	$
Rent	3750
Heating and lighting	2700

3. The following expenses have been prepaid at 3 April 2011.

	$
Insurance	900
Advertising	3500

4. Expenses are to be apportioned as follows:

Rent: Factory 75%; Office 25%

Heating and lighting: Factory $\frac{2}{3}$, Offices $\frac{1}{3}$

Insurance: Factory $\frac{9}{10}$, Offices $\frac{1}{10}$

Motor costs: Factory 50%

5. Provision for depreciation is to be made as follows:

	$
Factory building	3 000
Factory machinery	10 000
Office machinery and equipment	4 000
Motor vans	8 000

6. Completed production is transferred to the warehouse at a mark up on factory cost of 20%.

Required
Prepare a Manufacturing Account and Income Statement for the year ended 30 April 2011. (Make all calculations to the nearest $.)

HINTS

- Adjust for accruals and prepayments, where necessary, **before** apportioning overhead expenses between the Manufacturing Account and the Income Statement.
- Take care to calculate the provision for unrealised profit, based on closing inventory, correctly. The fraction to be used is

$$\frac{\text{percentage of mark-up}}{100 + \text{percentage of mark-up}}$$

(see §16.4)
- The entry in the Income Statement for unrealised profit is the increase or decrease in the amount of the provision brought forward from the previous year.
- Ensure that the closing inventory of finished goods is shown in the Statement of Financial Position at cost by deducting the balance on the Provision for Unrealised Profit Account.

MULTIPLE-CHOICE QUESTIONS

1. Goods are transferred from the Manufacturing Account to the Income Statement at factory cost of production plus a mark-up of 20%.
   The transfer prices of the closing inventories of finished goods were as follows:

Year 1	$39 600
Year 2	$42 000
Year 3	$45 600

   What was the provision for unrealised profit charged against the profit for Year 3?

   A. $400   **B.** $600   **C.** $720   **D.** $1200

2. Goods are transferred from the factory to the warehouse at a mark-up of $33\frac{1}{3}$%. At 1 April 2010, the balance on the Provision for Unrealised Profit was $17 000. At 31 March 2011, the closing inventory of finished goods was $60 000.
   What was the effect on profit of the entry in the Provision for Unrealised Profit on 31 March 2011?

   A. decrease of $2000   **B.** decrease of $3000
   C. increase of $2000   **D.** increase of $3000

3. The following items appear in the accounts of a manufacturing company:
   (i) carriage inwards
   (ii) carriage outwards
   (iii) depreciation of warehouse machinery
   (iv) provision for unrealised profit.
   Which items will be included in the Manufacturing Account?

   A. (i) and (ii)   **B.** (i) and (iii)
   C. (ii) and (iii)   **D.** (ii) and (iv)

4. A manufacturing company adds a factory profit of 25% to its cost of production. The following information is available:

	$
Inventory of finished goods at 1 April 2010 (per Statement of Financial Position at that date)	30 000
Cost of goods produced (per Manufacturing Account for the year ended 31 March 2011)	300 000
Closing inventory of finished goods (per Income Statement for the year end 31 March 2011)	60 000

   How much will be credited as factory profit in the Income Statement for the year ended 31 March 2011?

   A. $67 500   **B.** $69 000
   C. $70 500   **D.** $71 500

ADDITIONAL EXERCISES

1. The following balances have been extracted from the books of Spinners & Co. at 31 December 2010.

	$
Inventories at 1 January 2010	
Raw materials	8 000
Work in progress	12 000
Factory expenses	
Direct wages	40 000
Indirect wages	28 000
Patent fees paid to patent holder	16 000
Heating and lighting	5 000
General factory expenses	14 000
Insurance of plant and machinery	6 000
Purchases of raw materials	140 000
Plant and machinery at cost	70 000

   Further information

   1. Inventories at 31 December 2010:

	$
Raw materials	10 000
Work in progress	9 700

   2. Expenses owing at 31 December 2010:

	$
Direct wages	600
Indirect wages	400
General expenses	300

   3. Expenses prepaid at 31 December 2010:

	$
Insurance	400
Heating and lighting	180

4. Plant and machinery are to be depreciated at the rate of 10% on cost.
5. A factory profit of 10% is added to the factory cost of goods produced.

Required

Prepare the Manufacturing Account for the year ended 31 December 2010.

2. The following balances have been extracted from the books of the Uggle Box Manufacturing Company at 30 April 2011.

	$
Premises at cost	250 000
Plant and machinery (net book value)	70 000
Motor vehicles at cost	40 000
Inventories at 1 May 2010	
Raw materials	42 000
Work in progress	50 000
Finished goods	48 000
Factory wages (direct)	280 000
Royalties based on production	40 000
Factory expenses	20 000
Selling expenses	42 000
Administrative expenses	62 000
Sales	1 240 000
Purchases of raw materials	390 000
Carriage inwards	26 000

Further information

1. Inventories at 30 April 2011:

	$
Raw materials	36 000
Work in progress	46 000
Finished goods	62 400

2. Finished goods are transferred to the Trading Account at factory cost plus a mark-up of 20%.

3. Depreciation is to be provided as follows:

Premises: 5% per annum on cost
Plant and machinery: 20% per annum on the written down value
Motor vehicles: 20% per annum on cost

4. Depreciation charges are to be apportioned as followed:

Premises:	Factory	50%
	Administration	50%
Plant and machinery:	Factory	80%
	Administration	20%
Motor vehicles:	Factory	90%
	Administration	10%

Required

Prepare a Manufacturing Account and Income Statement for the year ended 30 April 2011.

3. The following balances have been extracted from Yendor's books at 31 March 2011.

	$000	$000
Inventories at 1 April 2010:		
Raw materials	450	
Work in progress	375	
Finished goods	390	
Factory wages		
Direct	900	
Indirect	90	
Purchases		
Direct materials	2250	
Indirect materials	45	
Carriage inwards	162	
Other factory overheads	245	
Sales		6075
Office salaries	391	
Other administration expenses	675	
Provision for Unrealised Profit		65
Freehold premises at cost	1000	
Provision for Depreciation of Freehold Premises		160
Manufacturing Plant and Machinery at cost	600	
Provision for Depreciation of Manufacturing Plant and Machinery at 31 March 2010		350
Office equipment at cost	300	
Provision for Depreciation of Office Equipment at 31 March 2010		100

Further information

1. Inventories at 31 March 2011 were as follows (in $000s): raw materials $440; work in progress $562; finished goods $594.

2. Carriage inwards relates wholly to the purchase of raw materials.

3. Finished goods are transferred from the factory to the warehouse at a mark-up of 20%.

4. The factory occupies $\frac{3}{4}$ of the freehold premises; the administrative offices occupy the remainder.

5. Depreciation should be provided as follows:

Freehold premises 4% per annum on cost
Plant and machinery 30% per annum on net book value
Office equipment 15% per annum on net book value

Required

Prepare Yendor's Manufacturing Account and Income Statement for the year ended 31 March 2011.

Valuation of inventory

In this chapter you will learn:

- the importance of valuing inventory in accordance with recognised accounting principles
- valuation of inventory on the First In, First Out (FIFO) basis
- valuation of inventory on Weighted Average Cost (AVCO) basis
- the merits and defects of each method
- what continuous and periodic inventories are
- the importance of IAS 2 and inventory valuation.

20.1 The importance of valuing inventory in accordance with recognised accounting principles

Opening and closing inventories are included in the trading section of the Income Statement to calculate cost of sales and gross profit. Closing inventory is included as a current asset in Statements of Financial Position as part of working capital. The value placed upon inventory is therefore of very great importance. Three possible ways in which stock may be valued are:

- at its cost price
- at its selling price
- at what it is considered to be worth.

The third way, at the inventories worth, should be ruled out immediately because 'worth' is a very subjective term; it can mean different things to different people, and even different things to the same person at different times and in different circumstances. This aspect has already been discussed in §9.4. Obviously 'profit' and 'working capital' should not mean different things at different times.

Selling price is also an unsatisfactory way of valuing inventory as the following example shows.

Aykbourne makes up his accounts to 31 December each year and values his closing inventory at selling price. He purchased goods for $800 on 30 November 2011. He sold the goods on 30 January 2012 for $1000.

If these were Aykbourne's only transactions, the trading section of his Income Statement for the years ended 31 December 2011 and 2012 would be as follows:

Year ended 31 December 2011			Year ended 31 December 2012		
	$	$		$	$
Sales		0	Sales		1000
Cost of sales			Cost of sales		
Opening inventory	0		Opening inventory	1000	
Purchases	800		Purchases	0	
	800			1000	
Less closing inventory	1000	(200)		0	(1000)
Net profit		200	Net profit		0

This example shows Aykbourne making a profit of $200 in the year ended 31 December 2011 although he had not sold the goods, but not making any profit in the next year when he sold them. Valuing the inventory at selling price has offended against three important accounting principles:

- realisation – no profit was realised in the year ended 31 December 2011 because no sale had taken place
- matching – the profit has not been matched to the time the sale took place
- prudence – the profit was overstated in 2011; it was not even certain then that the goods could be sold at a profit.

It is an important principle that inventory should never be valued at more than cost. Valuing inventory at historic cost observes the principles of realisation, matching and prudence.

Another important principle is that the method used to value inventory should be used consistently from one accounting period to the next. The methods are considered next.

20.2 Two methods of valuing inventory at cost

In a very few cases, it may be possible to value goods at the price actually paid for them. For example, the owner of an art gallery may be able to say from whom she bought each of the pictures in her gallery and how much she paid for them because there would probably be a limited number of paintings and she would be able to recall how much she paid for them.

A manufacturer of computers, however, would not find it easy to say how much he paid for the parts he needed for the computers. Purchases of hard drives, for example, would be in bulk and made at different times and at different prices. It would be impossible to say at the year-end how much had been paid for any particular hard drive remaining at the year end. The problem is solved by assuming that inventory movements occur in a particular pattern, even if that is not strictly so. This is often called a convention: something that is assumed to happen even if it is not strictly true, at least all the time. The two methods considered here are:

- **First In, First Out (FIFO)**, which assumes that goods are used or sold in the same order in which they were received
- **Weighted average cost (AVCO)**, which involves calculating the weighted average cost of inventory after every delivery to the business. Closing inventory at any given time, and inventory sold or issued, is valued at weighted average cost.

20.3 How to value inventory

FIFO

Goods are assumed to be used in the order in which they are received from the supplier.

Example 1

At 31 May the inventory of a certain material

consisted of 80 kilograms which had cost $0.60 per kilogram. The receipts and issues of the material in June were as follows:

	Receipts Quantity kg	Price per kg $	Issues Quantity kg
June 1 Inventory brought forward from May 31	80	0.60	
3	100	1.00	
7			70
16	200	1.20	
23			200
25	50	1.40	
30			80

Required
Calculate the value of inventory at 30 June based on FIFO.

Answer

June		1	3	16	25
	Price per kg	$0.60	$1.00	$1.20	$1.40
	Inventory (kg)	80			
	Receipts (kg)		100	200	50
7	Issued	(70)			
		10			
23	Issues	(10)	(100)	(90)	
		–	–	110	
30	Issued			(80)	
	Closing inventory			30	50
	Valuation at cost			$36	$70 Total $106

This example shows how FIFO works. The same result can be quickly calculated as follows:

Units available (80 + 100 + 200 + 50)	430
Units issued (70 + 200 + 80)	350
Balance of units	80
Valuation: 50 at latest price $1.40	$70
30 at previous price $1.20	$36 $106

Exercise 1

At 30 September Fiford Ltd had an inventory of 100 kg of fifolium, which had cost $5 per kilogram. In October, it made the following purchases and sales of fifolium.

October		Purchases kg	Price per kg $	Sales kg
	3			40
	10	80	5.20	
	12			75
	14			50
	15	50	5.24	
	17			45
	22	70	5.28	
	29	100	5.32	
	30			70

Required

Calculate the quantity and value of the inventory of fifolium at 31 October using the FIFO method.

AVCO

The weighted average cost of inventory is calculated every time new goods are received.

Example 2

(Data as for example 1, FIFO)

June		Units	Price $	Weighted average cost ($)	Balance ($)
1	Balance b/f	80	0.60	0.60	48
3	Received	100	1.00		100
	Balance	180		0.822	148
7	Issued	(70)			58
	Balance	110			90
16	Received	200	1.20		240
	Balance	310		1.065	330
23	Issued	(200)			213
	Balance	110			117
25	Received	50	1.40		70
	Balance	160		1.169	187
30	Issued	(80)			(94)
	Balance	80		1.163*	93

* Rounded calculations may result in an adjustment being made to the average price of closing inventory.

The weighted average cost at 3 June is calculated by dividing the total cost of stock at that point ($ 148) by the total number of items in stock (180). This calculation is made each time a new delivery of goods is received.

Exercise 2

A.V. Co. had a stock of 200 digital hammers at 31 May. The hammers were valued at $5 each.

Transactions in digital hammers in the month of June were as follows:

Date received	Quantity	Price per hammer ($)	Sold Quantity
June 4	100	5.20	
10			75
13	100	5.35	
20			150
26	80	5.40	
30			90

Required

Calculate the closing inventory of digital hammers at 30 June showing quantity and total value based on weighted average cost.

20.4 Perpetual and periodic inventories

A **stock inventory** is a record of goods received by, and used or sold by, a business. A **perpetual inventory** maintains a running balance of inventory-on-hand after each transaction. The example given above for AVCO is a typical perpetual inventory.

A periodic inventory shows the balance of stock-on-hand only at intervals, for example at the end of each month. The total of items used in the period is deducted from the total of items received to give the balance of items in stock. The 'quick' method, shown above, of calculating the value of closing stock on the FIFO basis is an example of a periodic inventory.

20.5 The effect of the methods of inventory valuation on profits over the whole life of a business

The profit made over the whole life of a business is not affected by the choice of method of valuing inventory. This is demonstrated in the following examples.

Quad Ltd began business in year 1 and stopped trading at the end of year 4. The following information is given for each of the four years.

	Year 1 $	Year 2 $	Year 3 $	Year 4 $
Sales	1000	1400	1600	800
Purchases	600	800	700	400
Closing inventory:				
FIFO	80	100	90	–
AVCO	70	90	80	–

Trading Account (using FIFO for valuing inventory)												
	Year 1			Year 2			Year 3			Year 4		
	$	$		$	$		$	$		$	$	
Sales		1000			1400			1600			800	
Opening inventory	–			80			100			90		
Purchases	600			800			700			400		
Closing inventory (FIFO)	(80)	(520)		(100)	(780)		(90)	(710)		—	(490)	
Gross profit		480			620			890			310	
										Total gross profit $2300		

Trading Account (AVCO)												
	Year 1			Year 2			Year 3			Year 4		
	$	$		$	$		$	$		$	$	
Sales		1000			1400			1600			800	
Opening inventory	–			70			90			80		
Purchases	600			800			700			400		
Closing inventory (AVCO)	(70)	(530)		(90)	(780)		(80)	(710)		—	(480)	
Gross profit		470			620			890			320	
										Total gross profit $2300		

20.6 FIFO and AVCO compared

It is important to compare the advantages and disadvantages of FIFO and AVCO in order to decide which method is the right one to use in particular circumstances.

FIFO

Advantages

1. It is a relatively simple system to use.
2. It is generally realistic. Materials are normally used in FIFO order, and goods will be sold in that order, especially if they are perishable.
3. Prices used are those that have actually been paid for goods.
4. Closing inventory is valued on current price levels.
5. FIFO is an acceptable method of inventory valuation for the purposes of the Companies Act 2006, Accounting Standards (Statement of Standard Accounting Practice, SSAP 9) and International Accounting Standard (IAS) 2.

Disadvantages

1. Manufacturing businesses usually prefer to charge materials to production at current purchase prices or selling prices, but use FIFO to value inventories for their financial accounts.

2. Identical items of stock from batches bought at different times may be used for similar jobs with the result that job A may be charged for the item at a different price from job B. The customer for job B may be unfairly treated as a result. Quotations for jobs when materials are based on FIFO may be unreliable.
3. In times of rising prices, the closing stock in the financial accounts will be priced at the latest (high) prices. This results in lowering cost of sales and increasing gross profit. It may be considered that this is not consistent with the concept of prudence. However, as stated above, the method is acceptable under SSAP 9 and IAS 2.

AVCO

Advantages

1. The use of average prices avoids the inequality of identical items being charged to different jobs at different prices.
2. AVCO recognises that identical items purchased at different times and prices have identical values. Averaged prices are truer to this concept than actual prices used for FIFO.
3. Averaging costs may smooth variations in production costs, and comparisons between the

results of different periods more meaningful.

4. Averaged prices used to value closing stock may be fairly close to the latest prices.
5. AVCO is acceptable for the purposes of SSAP 9 and the Companies Act 2006 and IAS 2.

Disadvantages

1. The average price must be re-calculated after every purchase of stock.
2. The average price does not represent any price actually paid for stock.

20.7 Net realisable value

Net realisable value is the price that may be expected to be received from the sale of goods, less the cost of putting them into a saleable condition. The costs involved include completion of the goods (if they are being manufactured), and marketing, selling and distribution costs.

Example 1

Some bales of fabric that cost $800 have become damaged by flood water entering the warehouse. If they are cleaned and treated for the damage at a cost of $300, they can be sold for $1000. The net realisable value is what the trader will be left with after they have been sold, which is $(1000 − 300) = $700.

Valuation of inventory at the lower of cost and net realisable value

As we saw in chapter 19, firms have inventories in various forms:

- Raw materials for use in a manufacturing process.
- Work in progress, partly manufactured goods.
- Finished goods, completed goods ready for sale to customers.
- Finished goods which the business has bought for resale to customers.

The principle of inventory valuation is set out in International Accounting Standard 2 (**IAS 2**). So far we have seen that inventory can be valued using one of two different methods, FIFO or AVCO. These are the only two methods of stock valuation which IAS 2 allows to be used. We have also seen that

whichever method is chosen can affect the gross profit which the company makes.

The standard states that **inventories should be valued at the lower of cost and net realisable value.** This is the price that may be expected to be received from the sale of the goods, less the cost of putting them into a saleable condition. The costs involve include the costs of completing the goods if they are manufactured, plus the marketing, selling and distribution costs.

Notice the exact wording. It is the lower of cost **and** net realisable value, **not** the lower of cost **or** net realisable value.

The term net realisable value can be compared to the selling price of the product. If the expected selling price is **lower** than the cost price, then inventory should be valued at their selling price.

Inventory is **never** valued at selling price when the selling price is greater than the cost. By using the lowest price possible to value stock it means that inventory valuation follows the **prudence** concept.

Similarly, inventories which are similar in nature and use to the company will use the same valuation method. Only where inventories are different in nature or use can a different valuation method be used.

Once a suitable method of valuation has been adopted by a company then it should continue to use that method unless there are good reasons why a change should be made. This is in line with the **consistency** concept.

Example 2

Goods were bought at a cost of $1300. They have become damaged and will cost $400 to be put into a saleable condition. They can then be sold for $1900. Net realisable value is $(1900 − 400) = $1500. As this is more than cost, the goods should be valued inventory at cost ($1300).

Example 3

Details as in example 2 but, after repair, the goods can be sold for only $1500. The net realisable value is $(1500 − 400) = $1100. This is less than cost and is the value to be placed upon the goods.

20.8 The valuation of individual items of inventory or groups of similar items

Individual items or groups of items of inventory should be considered separately when deciding whether they should be valued at cost or net realisable value. This is to ensure that losses on individual items or groups of items are not 'hidden'.

Example

A company sells six different grades of compact discs for computers. The following are the cost to the company and the net realisable values (NRVs) of the inventories of the six grades of discs.

	Cost	NRV	Value to be used for inventory valuation
	$	$	$
Grade 1	2 000	2 400	2 000
Grade 2	4 500	3 800	3 800
Grade 3	3 000	3 100	3 000
Grade 4	5 750	5 000	5 000
Grade 5	1 250	2 000	1 250
Grade 6	2 500	2 200	2 200
	19 000	18 500	17 250

If the inventories were valued as a whole without taking the individual items into consideration, it would be valued at NRV ($18 500) as this is less than cost; but the items where NRV is more than cost are hiding the losses made on grades 2, 4 and 6. The items must be valued separately at $17 250 as this recognises the losses.

20.9 Closing inventories for a manufacturing organisation

In chapter 19 we saw that a manufacturer may hold three categories of inventory:
- raw materials
- work in progress
- finished goods

Valuing raw materials

A comparison is made between the cost of the raw materials (applying either FIFO or AVCO) and their realisable value. Whichever is the lower will be used to value the inventory for the annual accounts.

Valuing work in progress and finished goods

IAS 2 requires that the valuation of these two items includes not only their raw or direct material content, but also includes an element for direct labour, direct expenses and production overheads.

The cost of these two items, therefore, consists of:
- direct materials
- direct labour
- direct expenses
- production overheads, these are costs to bring the product to its present location and condition
- other overheads which may be applicable to bring the product to its present location and condition

The cost of these two items excludes:
- abnormal waste in the production process
- storage costs
- selling costs
- administration costs not related to production.

Example 1

The XYZ Manufacturing Company manufactures wooden doors for the building trade. For the period under review it manufactured and sold 10,000 doors. At the end of the trading period there were 1000 completed doors ready for despatch to customers and 200 doors which were half completed as regards direct material, direct labour and production overheads.

Cost for the period under review were

	$
Direct material used	20 000
Direct labour	5 000
Production overheads	8 300
Non-production overheads	10 000
Total Costs for the period	43 300

Calculate the value of work in progress and finished goods.

Total units sold	10 000
Finished goods units	1 000
Half completed units (200 × 0.5)	100
Production for the period	11 100
Attributable costs	$33 300
Cost per unit	33 300 / 11 100 = $3

Value of work in progress:
$200 \times 0.5 \times \$3 = \$300$

Value of finished goods:
$1000 \times 3 = \$3000$

Note that non-production overheads are **excluded** from the calculations.

The value of finished goods will be compared with their net realisable value when preparing the annual accounts. Whichever is the lower will be used.

20.10 Replacement cost

Replacement cost is the price that will have to be paid to replace goods used or sold. The replacement cost may be the latest price of the good, or an estimate of what the price will be at some future date.

Replacement cost is not acceptable as a basis for valuing inventory under IAS 2. However, replacement cost may be used to estimate the cost of a particular job when quoting for an order.

Using a price based on historic cost may lead to an underestimate of the price for the job and a lower profit. Replacement cost is usually more realistic for this purpose.

Replacement cost should also be used when preparing budgets (see chapter 34).

HINTS

- Read questions carefully to see which method or methods of inventory valuation are required.
- Some questions are about the value of closing inventory, but others are concerned with the cost of goods issued to production or sold. Make sure you understand the point of the question or you may provide the wrong answer.
- Perform all calculations with the utmost care.
- Be prepared to answer questions on the principles governing inventory valuation and the advantages and disadvantages of each method.
- Questions on inventory valuation may require you to use techniques and knowledge gained from your studies on any part of the syllabus.

MULTIPLE-CHOICE QUESTIONS

1. How should inventory be valued in a Statement of Financial Position?
   A. at the lower of net realisable value and selling price
   B. at the lower of replacement cost and net realisable value
   C. at lower of cost and replacement cost
   D. at lower of cost and net realisable value

2. A company bought and sold goods as follows:

		Bought		Sold
		Units	Unit price ($)	Units
March	1	20	2.00	
	3	10	2.50	
	4			12
	5	20	3.00	
	6			16

What is the value of the inventory at 6 March based on FIFO?
A. $44   B. $45   C. $65   D. $66

3. A company had the following inventory transactions in June.

June 1 Purchased 50 units at $3 per unit
    14 Purchased 100 units at $4.50 per unit
    23 Sold 70 units
    30 Purchased 62 units at $5 per unit

What is the value of inventory at 30 June based on AVCO?
A. $4.292   B. $4.437   C. $4.50   D. $5.00

4. At the end of its financial year a company provides the following information in respect of its inventory:

Item	Cost Price $	Net Realisable Value $	Selling Price (when new) $
New dresses	1 000	1 500	2 000
Children's clothes	2 000	3 000	3 000
Bargain Fashions	1 200	900	2 000

What is the total inventory value to be included in the final accounts?

A. $3 900   **B.** $4 200

C. $4 700   **D.** $5 400

ADDITIONAL EXERCISES

1. Discuss how the concept of prudence might be relevant when considering the valuation of inventory.

2. Janice Jersey's first 6 months of trading showed the following purchases and sales of inventory.

2011	Purchases	Sales
January	280 @ $65 each	
February		140 @ $82 each
March	100 @ $69 each	
April		190 @ $85 each
May	220 @ $72 each	
June		200 @ $90 each

Calculate Janice's profit for the 6 months ended 30 June 2011 using the following methods of inventory valuation:

(a) FIFO (First In First Out)

(b) AVCO (Weighted Average Cost). Calculate to 2 decimal places.

3. Because of illness, Achmed's annual stocktaking, which should have taken place on 31 March 2011, was not completed until 7 April 2011, and was undertaken by an inexperienced member of the staff. Achmed felt that the inventory figure of $92 050 was too low and ordered an investigation. It was discovered that the following had occurred during the week ended 7 April 2011 and had not been accounted for in the closing inventory calculation:

1. Goods with a selling price of $1040 had been sent to a customer on approval.
2. Goods costing $9400 were received and invoiced.
3. Sales of $18760 had been made and invoiced to customers.
   These sales included
   (i) an overcharge of $160;
   (ii) sales of $6000 on special offer at a margin of 10%;
   (iii) damaged goods which had cost $2500 and were sold for $2800.

Achmed's standard rate of gross profit is 25% of sales. Calculate the correct value of closing inventory at 31 March 2011.

 **Partnership accounts**

In this chapter you will learn:

- what a partnership is
- how profits are shared when there is a partnership agreement
- how to apply the Partnership Act of 1890 when there is no partnership agreement
- how to prepare partnership accounts
- the advantages and disadvantages of partnerships.

21.1 What are partnerships?

A partnership is formed when two or more people carry on business together with the intention of making profit.

Partners must agree on how the partnership is to be carried on, including how much capital each partner is to contribute to the firm and how profits and losses are to be shared. These, and other important matters, are decided in a **partnership agreement**. The agreement will usually be in writing, possibly by deed (a formal legal document), or verbally. If the partners do not make an agreement and a dispute arises regarding their rights and duties as partners, the Court may assume that past practice constitutes an 'implied' agreement, and resolve the dispute according to what the partners have done previously.

The **Partnership Act 1890** governs partnerships and states the rights and duties of partners. The Act includes the following provisions, which are important and apply to partnerships *unless* the partners have agreed to vary the terms.

- All partners are entitled to contribute equally to the capital of the partnership.
- Partners are not entitled to interest on the capital they have contributed.
- Partners are not entitled to salaries.
- Partners are not to be charged interest on their drawings.
- Partners will share profits and losses equally.

- Partners are entitled to interest at 5% per annum on loans they make to the partnership.

The Appropriation Account

The Appropriation Account is a continuation of the Income Statement. It begins with the net profit or loss brought down from the Income Statement. The following methods of dividing profits between partners must be treated as appropriations of profit in the Appropriation Account.

Partners' salaries. A partnership agreement may entitle one or more partners to be paid a salary. This may be paid in addition to a further share of profit. A salary guarantees a partner an income, even if the firm does not make a profit. Partners' salaries are **never** debited in the Profit and Loss Account.

Interest on capital and drawings. Interest on capital recognises that if partners do not invest their capital in the partnership, their money could earn interest in some other form of investment. The partnership agreement should state the rate of interest to be paid. Interest on capital is payable even if the firm does not make a profit.

Interest charged to partners on their drawings is intended to encourage the partners to leave their shares of profit in the business as additional temporary capital, rather than take them as drawings.

Interest on partners' loans to the firm

Interest on a loan made by a partner to a firm is *not* an appropriation of profit – it is an expense to be debited in the Income Statement, *not in the Appropriation Account.*

Profit/loss sharing

Any balance of profit or loss on the Appropriation Account after charging interest on capitals and partners' salaries is shared between the partners in their agreed profit-sharing ratios. If there is no partnership agreement, the profit or loss will be shared equally.

It is important to remember that interest on capitals and partners' salaries is a method of sharing profit so that a partner's total share of profit includes these items.

Read questions carefully and note what the partners have agreed. If a question does not state what the partners have agreed about any of the matters in the Partnership Act listed above, apply the terms of the Act in your answer to the question.

21.2 How to prepare partnership accounts

Open the following accounts for each partner:

      Capital
      Drawings
      Current

The capital account will record the capital introduced by the partner and any capital withdrawn by them. This may be in the form of cash or assets such as a car or equipment. Capital introduced is credited in the account. Capital withdrawn is debited in the account. There are other items of a special nature which are entered in the capital account, such as goodwill and profit on revaluation of assets. These are dealt with fully in chapter 22.

The Current account is used to complete the double entry from the partnership Profit and Loss and Appropriation Account for the partner's share of profits, losses, interest and salary. It is also credited with interest on a partner's loan to the firm, if any, from the Profit and Loss Account. At the end of the year, the balance on the partner's Drawings account is transferred to the debit of his Current account.

Note. If partners do not maintain Current accounts, the double entry for interest, their salaries and shares of profit must be completed in their Capital accounts.

However, it is likely in your examination that partners will have both capital and current accounts. Familiarise yourself with the information each contains.

Example 1

(No partnership agreement regarding interest, partners' salaries or sharing of profits/losses)

Michael and Charles began to trade as partners on 1 January 2010. Michael introduced $60 000 into the business as capital, and Charles contributed $40 000.

On 1 July 2010, Charles lent $10 000 to the business. The partnership trial balance at 31 December 2010 was as follows:

	$	$
Sales		300 000
Purchases	120 000	
Staff wages	42 000	
Rent	10 000	
Electricity	7 000	
Sundry expenses	5 400	
Premises at cost	60 000	
Fixtures and fittings at cost	28 000	
Trade receivables	5 460	
Trade payables		2 860
Bank balance	94 000	
Capital accounts: Michael		60 000
Charles		40 000
Drawings Michael	24 000	
Charles	17 000	
Loan from Charles		10 000
	412 860	412 860

Further information
1. Inventory at 31 December 2010: $18 000.
2. Depreciation is to be provided as follows:
   Premises: 5% per annum on cost
   Fixtures and fittings: 12½% per annum on cost.
3. The partners had not made any agreement regarding interest on capital and drawings, salaries or sharing of profits and losses.

Required
(a) Prepare the Income Statement and Appropriation Account for the year ended 31 December 2010.
(b) Prepare the partners' Current accounts at 31 December 2010.
(c) Prepare the Statement of Financial Position at 31 December 2010.

Answer

(a)

Michael and Charles
Income Statement and Appropriation Account for the year ended 31 December 2010

	$	$	$
Sales			300 000
Less Cost of sales			
Purchases		120 000	
Less Inventory at 31 December 2010		18 000	102 000
Gross profit			198 000
Staff wages		42 000	
Rent		10 000	
Electricity		7 000	
Sundry expenses		5 400	
Depreciation: Premises	3000		
Fixtures and fittings	3500	6 500	
Interest on loan (6 months at 5% p.a.)*		250	71 150
Net profit			126 850
Shares of profit Michael $(\frac{1}{2})$		63 425	
Charles $(\frac{1}{2})$		63 425	126 850

* Note that the interest on Charles' loan is charged as an expense in the profit and loss account, *before* splitting the net profit between the partners. It is, however, entered in Charles' Current Account as Charles is entitled to withdraw it from the business. As no Partnership Agreement exists, the rate of interest on the loan is 5%.

The Appropriation Account begins at the point where the net profit of $126 850 is shown.

(b)

Partners' Current accounts

2010		Michael $	Charles $	2010		Michael $	Charles $
Dec 31	Drawings	24 000	17 000	Dec 31	Interest on loan*	–	250
	Balances c/d	39 425	46 675		Share of profit	63 425	63 425
		63 425	63 675			63 425	63 675
				2011			
				Jan 1	Balance b/d	39 425	46 675

(c) Showing the Partners' Current Accounts side by side like this is known as showing them in *Columnar form*. Often, questions will ask for the partners' current accounts (and sometimes their capital accounts) in this format. Even if the question does not ask for the accounts in columnar form, it is still a good way to show them.

Statement of Financial Position at 31 December 2010

	Cost $	Dep. $	NBV $
Non-current assets			
Premises	60 000	3 000	57 000
Fixtures and fittings	28 000	3 500	24 500
	88 000	6 500	81 500
Current assets: Inventory	18 000		
Trade receivables		5 460	
Bank	94 000		
	117 460		
Current liabilities: Trade payables	2 860	114 600	
		196 100	

Non-current liability: Loan from Charles		10 000
		186 100
Capital accounts: Michael	60 000	
Charles	40 000	100 000
Current accounts: Michael	39 425	
Charles	46 675	86 100
		186 100

Example 2

(Partnership agreement in place)

Data as in example 1 above, with the following additional information.

The partnership agreement includes the following terms.

- Interest on capitals and annual drawings: 5% per annum.
- Partnership salaries (per annum): Michael $20 000; Charles $10 000.

- The balance of profits and losses is to be shared as follows: Michael $\frac{2}{3}$; Charles $\frac{1}{3}$.
- Charles is to be credited with interest on his loan to the partnership at a rate of 8% per annum.

Required

(a) Prepare the Income Statement and Appropriation Account for the year ended 31 December 2010.
(b) Prepare the partners' Current accounts at 31 December 2010.

Answer

(a)

Michael and Charles
Income Statement and Appropriation Account
for the year ended 31 December 2010

	$	$	$
Sales			300 000
Less Cost of sales			
Purchases		120 000	
Less Inventory at 31 December 2010		18 000	102 000
Gross profit			198 000
Staff wages		42 000	
Rent		10 000	
Electricity		7 000	
Sundry expenses		5 400	
Depreciation:			
Premises	3 000		
Fixtures and fittings	3 500	6 500	
Interest on loan (6 months)		400	71 300
Net profit			126 700
*Add Interest on drawings:			
Michael		1 200	
Charles		850	2 050
			128 750
*Less Interest on capitals:			
Michael		3 000	
Charles		2 000	
		5 000	
*Partners' salaries:			
Michael		20 000	
Charles		10 000	35 000
			93 750
Shares of profit			
Michael ($\frac{2}{3}$)		62 500	
Charles ($\frac{1}{3}$)		31 250	93 750

* Adjustments are made for interest on drawings, interest on capital and partner's salaries *before* the remaining net profit is split in the profit sharing ratios.
This is an important point. The net profit is *never* split until these adjustments have been made.

(b)

Partners' Current accounts

2010		Michael $	Charles $	2010		Michael $	Charles $
Dec 31	Drawings	24 000	17 000	Dec 31	Interest on capital	3 000	2 000
	Interest on drawings	1 200	850		Interest on loan	–	400
					Salary	20 000	10 000
	Balanced c/d	60 300	25 800		Share of profit	62 500	31 250
		85 500	43 650			85 500	43 650
				2011			
				Jan 1	Balance b/d	60 300	25 800

Note: The Statement of Financial Position will be the same as Example 1 except for the different balance on the partners' current accounts: Michael $60 300 and Charles $25 800.

Exercise 1

(No partnership agreement)

Tee and Leef are trading in partnership. Their trial balance at 31 March 2011 is as follows:

	$	$
Capital accounts at 1 April 2010: Tee		100 000
Leef		50 000
Current accounts at 1 April 2010: Tee		5 000
Leef		10 000
Drawing accounts: Tee	29 000	
Leef	31 000	
Sales		215 000
Purchases	84 000	
Inventory at 1 April 2010	16 000	
Selling expenses	30 000	
Administration expenses	42 000	
Fixtures and fittings at cost	48 000	
Provision for depreciation of fixtures and fittings		8 000
Office equipment at cost	27 000	
Provision for depreciation of office equipment		5 000
Trade receivables	24 000	
Trade payables		11 000
Bank balance	85 000	
Loan from Leef		12 000
	416 000	416 000

Further information

1. Inventory at 31 March 2011: $20 000.
2. Selling expenses prepaid at 31 March 2011: $6000.
3. Administration expenses accrued at 31 March 2011: $4000.
4. Depreciation is to be provided as follows: on fixtures and fittings 10% of cost; on office equipment 20% of cost.
5. Leef made the loan to the business on 1 April 2010.
6. The partners had not made any agreement regarding interest, salaries or profit sharing.

Required

(a) Prepare the partnership Income Statement and Appropriation Account for the year ended 31 March 2011.
(b) Prepare partners' Current Account at 31 March 2011 in columnar form.
(c) Prepare the partnership Statement of Financial Position at 31 March 2011.

Exercise 2

(Partnership agreement in place)

The facts are as in exercise 1, but Tee and Leaf have a partnership agreement which includes the following terms.

1. Leef is to be credited with interest on his loan to the partnership at the rate of 10% per annum.
2. The partners are allowed interest at 10% per annum on capitals and are charged interest at 10% per annum on drawings.
3. Leef is entitled to a salary of $4000 per annum.
4. The balance of profit/loss is to be shared as follows:

Tee $\frac{3}{5}$; Leef $\frac{2}{5}$.

Required

(a) Prepare the partnership Income Statement and Appropriation Account for the year ended 31 March 2011.
(b) Prepare the partners' Current accounts at 31 March 2011 in columnar form.
(c) Prepare the partnership Statement of Financial Position at 31 March 2011.

21.3 Advantages and disadvantages of partnerships

Advantages

- The capital invested by partners is often more than can be raised by a sole trader.
- A greater fund of knowledge, experience and expertise in running a business is available to a partnership.
- A partnership may be able to offer a greater range of services to its customers (or clients).
- The business does not have to close down or be run by inexperienced staff in the absence of one of the partners; the other partner(s) will provide cover.
- Losses are shared by all partners.

Disadvantages

- A partner has not the same freedom to act independently as a sole trader has.
- A partner may be frustrated by the other partner(s) in his or her plans for the direction and development of the business.
- Profits have to be shared by all partners.
- A partner may be legally liable for acts of the other partner(s).

HINTS

- Learn the provisions of the Partnership Act 1890 as they affect partners' rights to salaries, interest and sharing of profits and losses.
- Read each question carefully to see if you have to apply the terms of a partnership agreement or the provisions of the Partnership Act 1890.
- Debit interest on a partner's loan to the firm in the Income Statement and credit it to the partner's Current account.

- Do not debit partners' drawings to the Appropriation Account.
- Complete the double entries from the Appropriation Account to the partners' Current accounts.
- Transfer the end-of-year balances on the partners' Drawings accounts to their Current accounts.
- If partners do not maintain Current accounts, the entries to Current accounts referred to above must be made in their Capital accounts instead.
- Tick every item in the question as you give effect to it. Check that all items are ticked before copying out your answer.

MULTIPLE-CHOICE QUESTIONS

1. Cue and Rest are partners sharing profits and losses in the ratio of 2 : 1. They are allowed interest at 10% per annum on capitals and loans to the partnership.
   Other information is as follows:

	Cue	Rest
	$	$
Capitals	20 000	8000
Loan to firm	3 000	–

   The partnership has made a net profit for the year of $40 000.
   How much is Cue's total share of the net profit?
   A. $24 800   **B.** $25 100
   C. $26 800   **D.** $27 100

2. Stump and Bail are in partnership. Stump has lent the partnership $10 000 on which he is entitled to interest at 10%. He is also entitled to a salary of $12 000 per annum. Profits and losses are shared equally. The partnership has made a net profit of $25 000.
   How much is Stump's share of the net profit?
   A. $500   **B.** $5500
   C. $6000   **D.** $6500

3. Gohl and Poast are partners sharing profits and losses equally. Gohl has lent the partnership $8000 on which he is entitled to interest at 10% per annum. The partners are entitled to annual salaries as follow: Gohl $6000; Poast $4000. The partnership has made a profit of $17 000. How much is Gohl's share of the profit?
   A. $3500   **B.** $3900
   C. $8500   **D.** $9300

ADDITIONAL EXERCISES

1. The following trial balance has been extracted from the books of Bell and Binn at 30 April 2011.

	$	$
Sales		425 000
Purchases	200 000	
Inventory at 1 May 2010	30 000	
Wages	98 000	
Rent	25 000	
Heating and lighting	16 000	
Office expenses	12 600	
Vehicle expenses	5 510	
Advertising	3 500	
Bad debts written off	416	
Plant and machinery at cost	125 000	
Provision for Depreciation of Plant and Machinery		36 000
Motor vehicles at cost	41 000	
Provision for Depreciation of Motor Vehicles		22 000
Trade receivables and payables	45 750	18 000
Provision for Doubtful Debts		1 000
Bank balance	15 724	
Loan from Bell		60 000
Capital accounts:		
Bell		50 000
Binn		40 000
Current accounts:		
Bell		7 000
Binn		3 000
Drawing accounts:		
Bell	30 000	
Binn	13 500	
	662 000	662 000

Further information

1. Inventory at 30 April 2011 is valued at $27 000.
2. Bell is to be credited with interest on the loan at a rate of 10% per annum.
3. The bank reconciliation shows that bank interest of $314 and bank charges of $860 have been debited in the bank statements. These amounts have not been entered in the cash book.
4. At 30 April 2011, rent of $1500 and advertising of $2000 have been paid in advance.
5. Depreciation is to be provided as follows:
   (i) Plant and machinery: 10% per annum on cost
   (ii) Motor vehicles: 20% per annum on their written down values
6. The partners are to be charged interest on drawings and allowed interest on capitals at a rate of 10% per annum.
7. Partnership salaries are to be allowed as follows: Bell $10 000 per annum; Binn $8000 per annum.
8. The balance of profits and losses is to be shared as follows: Bell $\frac{3}{5}$; Binn $\frac{2}{5}$.

Required

(a) Prepare the partnership Income Statement and Appropriation Account for the year ended 30 April 2011.
(b) Prepare the partners' Current accounts for the year ended 30 April 2011.
(c) Prepare the Statement of Financial Position at 30 April 2011.

2. Mill has been a second-hand car dealer for some years. His Income Statment for the year ended 31 December 2010 was as follows:

	$	$
Sales		160 000
Less Cost of sales		95 000
Gross profit		65 000
Wages	31 000	
Rent	7 000	
Heating and lighting	4 000	
Advertising	1 000	

Sundry expenses	2 400	45 000
Net profit		19 600

Mill's net profits for the previous two years were as follows:

		$
Year ended:	31 December 2008	30 000
	31 December 2009	24 000

Mill's friend, Grist, has also been trading for some years repairing and servicing motor vehicles. Grist's net profits for the past three years have been as follows:

		$
Year ended:	31 December 2008	11 600
	31 December 2009	14 500
	31 December 2010	18 000

The lease on Grist's premises is about to expire, and Grist has suggested to Mill that the two businesses should be combined and that he and Mill should become partners.

Mill estimates that combining the businesses will immediately improve his net profit by 10% and that the improvement will be maintained in future years. Grist estimates that his net profit will be increased by 20% and that this increase will also be maintained in the future.

The proposed partnership agreement would provided as follows:

Capitals: Mill $20 000; Grist $30 000
Interest on capitals to be allowed at 10% per annum.
The balance of profits and losses to be shared equally.

Required

(a) Prepare a forecast Income Statement and Appropriation Account of the partnership for the year ending 31 December 2011, assuming the partnership is formed on 1 January 2011.
(b) State, with reasons, whether Mill should agree to Grist becoming a partner in the combined businesses.

3. Senter and Harf have prepared their draft Statement of Financial Position as at 30 June 2011 as follows:

	$	$
Non-current assets		
Fixtures and fittings at cost	45 000	
Less Depreciation to date	34 500	10 500
Current assets		
Inventory	28 500	
Trade payables	24 000	
Bank	9 000	
	61 500	
Less Current liabilities		
Trade receivables	12 000	49 500
		60 000
Less Non-current liability		
Senter		15 000
		45 000
Capital accounts:		
Senter	22 000	
Harf	14 000	36 000
Current accounts:		
Senter	7 500	
Harf	1 500	9 000
		45 000

It has now been discovered that the following errors and omissions have been made.

1. Some fixtures and fittings were sold for $3500 in January 2011. These items had cost $15 000 and their net book value at 30 June 2010 was $4500. The sale proceeds were credited to the Fixtures and Fittings at Cost account. No further entries had been made in the books for this sale.
   (The partnership provides for depreciation on the straight-line basis at a rate of 10% on the balance on the Fixtures and Fittings account at the end of each financial year.)
2. Interest at the rate of 10% per annum is to be provided on the long-term loan from Senter for the year ended 30 June 2011.
3. The accounts for the year ended 30 June 2010 included inventory at 30 June 2010 in the sum of $20 000. The correct value of the stock should have been $30 000. The partners have agreed that this error should be corrected in the partnership accounts.
4. The partners have decided that a provision for doubtful debts equal to 4% of the debtors should be provided in the accounts.
5. An adjustment should be made for the prepaid rent at 30 June 2011 in the sum of $750.
6. During the year ended 30 June 2011, Harf had taken goods costing $1075 for his personal use.

Further information

In addition to the interest allowed on Senter's loan, the partners are allowed interest at 10% per annum on their Capital account balances. The balance of profits and losses are divided between Senter and Harf in the ratio of 3 : 2.

Required

Prepare a corrected Statement of Financial Position as at 30 June 2011 for the partnership.

 **Partnership changes**

In this chapter you will learn:

- how to prepare partnership accounts when a partner joins or leaves the firm
- how to account for the revaluation of assets when there is partnership change
- how to account for partnership Goodwill
- how to account for the realisation of a partnership.

22.1 What is a partnership change?

A change in a partnership occurs:

- when partners agree to change the way in which profits and losses are to be shared
- when a new partner joins a firm, or an existing partner leaves
- death or retirement of a partner.

22.2 How to account for changes in the allocation of profits or losses between partners

Partners may change the way in which profits and losses are to be shared. The change may occur at any date, and the partnership continues whether the change takes place at the start of a new financial year or during the year.

All profits that have been earned and losses that have been incurred before the change must be shared in the old profit/loss-sharing ratio. Subsequent profits and losses must be shared in the new profit/loss-sharing ratio. In each case, profits and losses include realised *and* unrealised profits and losses.

Realised profits and losses are those that are recognised in the Income Statement. They are usually apportioned on a time basis, but there may be exceptional circumstances. For example, the new partnership agreement may provide for the rate of interest on a partner's loan to be changed; or for a partner to make a loan to the firm; or for the repayment of a loan. The interest on the loan, in these cases, must be apportioned on an actual and not on a time basis.

Unrealised profits and losses are gains and losses arising from the revaluation of assets and liabilities at the date of the change in the profit/loss-sharing agreement and will result in adjustments to the partners' capitals.

Assets and liabilities may have different values at the date of a change in the profit/loss-sharing ratio from the values shown in the last available Statement of Financial Position. Some assets may not even be shown in the Statement of Financial Position; an example is **Goodwill** (see §22.4). The partners' Capital accounts will not show their actual interest in the firm unless they are adjusted to reflect the real net asset value of the business. This is a matter of importance when the partnership is dissolved (ceases trading) or there is a change in the composition of the partnership.

Unrealised profits and losses must be attributed to the period in which they arose (matching concept). In what follows, the accounting procedures will be explained for:

- adjusting partners' Capital accounts for unrealised profits and losses

• apportioning realised profits and losses in Income Statements.

22.3 How to account for the revaluation of assets in a partnership

At certain times throughout the life of the partnership, the partners may revalue the assets and liabilities of the business. They may do this because they realise that some of the assets, probably land is now well below the market value. The partners will also revalue the assets just before the admission of a new partner. This is done to reward the existing partners for their efforts in building up the business over its life. When one of the partners retires then it is only fair that they too are rewarded for their efforts in building up the business over the years. The assets of the partnership may be revalued at that time and the retiring partner credited with their share of the profit on revaluation. This will increase the amount they can take from the business on their retirement.

The principle is that any revaluations are passed through a Revaluation account.

Step 1 – debit the Revaluation account with the book value any assets being revalued. The opposite entry is to credit the asset account.

Step 2 – credit the revaluation account with the book value of any liabilities being revalued. The opposite entry is to debit the liability account.

Step 3 – credit the revaluation account with the new value of the assets. The opposite entry is to debit the asset account.

Step 4 – debit the revaluation account with the new value of the liabilities. The opposite entry is to credit the liability account.

The remaining balance on the revaluation account will represent a profit or loss on revaluation. This is shared between the partners in their **profit sharing ratio**. Any profit or loss should be entered in the partner's Capital accounts. If it was entered in their current account then the

partners could draw cash from the business equal to the amount of any profit. As the adjustment is simply an entry in the books with no cash coming into or going out of the business, allowing them to draw any profit would result in cash leaving the business which could result in the business suffering financial difficulty.

Example

Abdul and Bashir are in business sharing the profits and losses equally. Their summarised Statement of Financial Position at 31 October 2011 is as follows:

	$000	$000
Non-current assets		
Property		60
Plant and machinery		30
		90
Current assets		
Inventory	7	
Trade receivables	6	
Bank account	2	
	15	
Current liabilities		
Trade payables	4	11
		101
Capital accounts		
Abdul	40	
Bashir	40	80
Current accounts		
Abdul	11	
Bashir	10	21
		101

They decide to revalue their assets to bring them in line with their latest values. The revised values are:
- Property $90 000
- Plant and machinery $24 000
- Inventory $6000 and Trade receivables $5000.

Required

(a) Prepare the Revaluation account to reflect the change in values.
(b) Prepare the partners' Capital accounts after the changes have taken place.

(c) Prepare a revised Statement of Financial Position showing the new values of the assets and liabilities.

Revaluation account

	$000		$000
Property (old value)	60	Property (new value)	90
Plant and machinery (old value)	30	Plant and machinery (new value)	24
Inventory (old value)	7	Inventory (new value)	6
Trade receivables (old value)	6	Trade receivables (new value)	5
Profit on revaluation – Abdul	11		
Profit on revaluation – Bashir	11		
	126		126

Capital accounts

	$000 Abdul	$000 Bashir		$000 Abdul	$000 Bashir
Balance c/f	51	51	Opening balances	40	40
			Profit on revaluation	11	11
	51	51		51	51

Statement of Financial Position at 31 October 2011 following revaluation.

	$000	$000
Non-current assets		
Property		90
Plant and machinery		24
		114
Current assets		
Inventory	6	
Trade receivables	5	
Bank account	2	
	13	
Current liabilities		
Trade payables	4	9
		123
Capital accounts:		
Abdul	51	
Bashir	51	102
Current accounts:		
Abdul	11	
Bashir	10	21
		123

Notice that the balance at the bank has remained unchanged. If the partners had drawn the profit on revaluation from the business it would have resulted in an overdraft.

Exercise 1

Ann and John are in partnership sharing the profits and losses in the ratio of 2 : 1. Their summarised Statement of Financial Position at 31 October 2011 is as follows:

		$000	$000
Non-current assets			
Property			120
Plant and machinery			60
			180
Current assets			
Inventory		20	
Trade receivables		30	
Bank account		1	
		51	
Current liabilities			
Trade payables		24	27
			207
Capital accounts:	Ann	120	
	John	60	180
Current accounts:	Ann	17	
	John	10	27
			207

They decide to revalue their assets to bring them in line with their latest values. The revised values are:

- Property $150 000
- Plant and machinery $51 000
- Inventory $17 000 and Trade receivables $28 000
- Trade payables $22 000

Required
(a) Prepare the Revaluation account to reflect the changes in value of the assets.
(b) Prepare the partners' Capital accounts after the changes have taken place.
(c) Prepare a revised Statement of Financial Position showing the new values of the assets and liabilities.

In some cases, the partners may decide to change their profit sharing ratios part of the way through the trading year. At that time they may also revalue the partnership assets. As we have seen, any increase or decrease is adjusted through a Revaluation account with any profit or loss transferred to the partners' Capital accounts. If the changes take place part way through the year the profit or loss on revaluation must be shared in the old profit sharing ratios because any gain or loss in values has occurred before the ratios were changed.

Example

Grace and Grant are in partnership, sharing profits and losses in the ratio of 2 : 1. On 1 July 2011 they agree to change the profit-sharing ratio so that they will share profits and losses equally in future. The partnership Statement of Financial Position at 31 December 2010 was as follows:

	$	$
Non-current assets at net book values		
Freehold premises		60 000
Plant and machinery		35 000
Motor vehicles		23 000
		118 000
Current assets		
Inventory	29 000	
Trade receivables	13 000	
Bank	8 000	
	50 000	
Current liabilities		
Trade payables	7 000	43 000
		161 000
Capitals		
Grace		90 000
Grant		71 000
		161 000

The partners agree that the assets shall be revalued at 30 June 2011 as follows:

	$
Freehold premises	100 000
Plant and machinery	30 000
Motor vehicles	20 000
Inventory	25 000
Trade receivables	12 000

Required

(a) Prepare the journal entries to give effect to the revaluation of the assets in the partnership books.

(b) Prepare a redrafted Statement of Financial Position as at 30 June 2011 after the assets have been revalued.

Answer

(a)

Journal	$	$
Freehold premises	40 000	
Plant and machinery		5 000
Motor vehicles		3 000
Inventory		4 000
Debtors control		1 000
Revaluation account		27 000
Revaluation of assets at 30 June 2011		
Revaluation account	27 000	
Capital accounts: Grace		18 000
Grant		9 000

Profit on revaluation of assets credited to the partners' Capital accounts in their former profit sharing ratios: Grace $\frac{2}{3}$, Grant $\frac{1}{3}$.

(b)

Grace and Grant
Statement of Financial Position at 30 June 2011

	$	$
Non-current assets at net book values		
Freehold premises (*60 000 + 40 000*)		100 000
Plant and machinery (*35 000 – 5000*)		30 000
Motor vehicles (*23 000 – 3000*)		20 000
		150 000
Current assets		
Inventory (*29 000 – 4000*)	25 000	
Trade receivables (*13 000 – 1000*)	12 000	
Bank	8 000	
	45 000	
Current liabilities		
Trade payables	7 000	38 000
		188 000
Capitals		
Grace (*90 000 + 18 000*)		108 000
Grant (*71 000 + 9000*)		80 000
		188 000

Exercise 2

Tom and Tilly shared profits and losses equally until 1 September 2011 when they agreed that Tilly would be entitled to a salary of $10 000 per annum from that date. Profits and losses would continue to be shared equally.

The partnership Statement of Financial Position at 31 March 2011 was as follows:

Non-current assets at net book values	$	$
Freehold premises		40 000
Fixtures and fittings		18 000
Office equipment		7 000
		65 000
Current assets		
Inventory	17 000	
Trade receivables	4 000	
Bank	6 000	
	27 000	
Current liabilities		
Trade payables	3 000	24 000
		89 000
Capitals accounts		
Tom		48 000
Tilly		41 000
		89 000

The partners agreed that the assets should be revalued at 1 September 2011 as follows:

	$
Freehold premises	65 000
Fixtures and fittings	15 000
Office equipment	5 000
Inventory	14 000
Trade receivables	3 000

Required

(a) Prepare journal entries to give effect to the revaluation of the partnership assets at 1 September 2011.

(b) Prepare the partnership Statement of Financial Position as at 1 September 2011 to include the effects of revaluation of the assets.

22.4 How to account for Goodwill

Goodwill is the amount by which the value of a business as a going concern exceeds the value its net assets would realise if they were sold separately. It is an intangible asset; that is, it cannot be touched and felt as buildings, plant and machinery and other 'tangible' assets can be touched and felt.

There are two types of goodwill to consider:

- **Purchased goodwill**. This arises when one business buys another. If the purchaser pays more for the business than the net book value of

its assets then the difference is goodwill. The international accounting standards allow this type of goodwill to be shown as an intangible non-current asset in the Statement of Financial Position. It is usually depreciated each year until it is written off. This is dealt with more fully in chapter 26.

- **Inherent goodwill**. This has not been paid for and so does not have an objective value. This is immediately written off in the accounts when a change in the partnership occurs and will be dealt with in §22.5.

Example

Will and Wendy are partners who have shared profits and losses in the ratio of Will $\frac{2}{3}$ and Wendy $\frac{1}{3}$.

On 1 January 2011 they agree to share profits and losses equally in future. At that date the partnership assets and liabilities are recorded in the books at the following valuations.

	$
Premises	100 000
Fixtures and fittings	48 000
Motor vehicles	35 000
Inventory	12 000
Trade receivables	6 000
	201 000
Less Trade payables	3 250
Net assets	197 750

Will and Wendy have recently been informed that they can expect to receive $230 000 for their business if they decide to sell it. They have agreed to record Goodwill in the partnership books as from 1 January 2011, and to value the business at $230 000 for the purpose of valuing Goodwill. Goodwill is valued at $(230 000 – 197 750) = $32 250. The journal entry to record the Goodwill is:

	Dr $	Cr $
Goodwill account	32 250	
Capital accounts: Will ($\frac{2}{3}$)		21 500
Wendy ($\frac{1}{3}$)		10 750

Goodwill recorded at valuation and credited to partners in their old profit-sharing ratios.

An account for Goodwill is opened in the partnership books.

Exercise 3

Vera and Ken are partners who have shared profits and losses equally. On 1 July 2011 they decide to change the profit-sharing ratio to: Vera $\frac{3}{5}$ and Ken $\frac{2}{5}$. The partnership assets and liabilities at book values at 1 July 2011 are as follows:

	$
Premises	140 000
Fixtures and fittings	65 000
Motor vehicles	35 000
Office equipment	15 000
Inventory	6 500
Trade receivables	11 800
Bank	3 620
Trade payables	5 830

The partners have been informed that the value of the business as a going concern is $300 000 and have decided to value Goodwill on this figure.

Required
(a) Calculate the value of Goodwill.
(b) Calculate the amounts to be credited to the partners' Capital accounts for Goodwill.

22.5 How to account for Goodwill when no Goodwill account is opened

Partners often do not wish to record Goodwill in their books for two reasons:
- the value placed on Goodwill is usually very difficult to justify, being a matter of opinion; it may not even exist
- if Goodwill is shown in a Statement of Financial Position at, say, $20 000 it would be very difficult to persuade a prospective purchaser of the business to pay more, even if the value had increased since Goodwill was first introduced into the books.

When there is a partnership change and the partners decide not to open a Goodwill account, the procedure to be followed is as follows:

Step 1. Credit the partners' Capital accounts with their share of Goodwill *in their old profit-sharing ratio.*
Step 2. Debit the partners' Capital accounts with their share of the Goodwill *in their new profit-sharing ratio.*

Steps 1 and 2 can be combined in a single operation, as shown in the following example.

Example 1

Noat and Koyn have shared profits and losses in the ratio of 2 : 1 but have now agreed they will share profits and losses equally in future. Goodwill is valued at $30 000, and the partners' Capital accounts will be adjusted as follows:

Working :	Column A Goodwill shared in *old* profit-sharing ratio (credit Capital accounts)	Column B Goodwill shared in *new* profit-sharing ratio (debit Capital accounts)	Adjustment to Capital accounts (column A − column B)
	$	$	$
Noat	20 000	15 000	5000 Credit
Koyn	10 000	15 000	5000 Debit
	30 000	30 000	

The Capital account of a partner who loses a share of Goodwill is credited with the amount of the loss. The Capital account of a partner who gains a share of Goodwill is debited with the amount of the gain.

Thus, a partner who loses a share of Goodwill is compensated by a partner who gains a share.

In the example, Koyn has 'purchased' his increased share of Goodwill from Noat. A Goodwill account has not been opened.

At first glance this seems strange. It seems that Koyn is being penalised by debiting his Capital account, even though he will be partly responsible for building up the business.

It is done to ensure that if the partnership is sold immediately after the adjustments take place then, providing all the assets and liabilities included goodwill are old at their values then no partner will lose out.

Example 2

Alan and Brian are in partnership sharing profits and losses equally. Their Statement of Financial Position is:

	$000
Non-current assets	50
Current assets	30
Current liabilities	(20)
	60
Capital – A	30
Capital – B	30
	60

They admit Colin into the partnership and all three now share the profits and losses equally. Goodwill is valued at $30 000. No goodwill account is to be kept in the books.

Immediately after the change the partners decide to sell the business. All the assets and liabilities realise their book values, including Goodwill.

Show the partners' Capital accounts to reflect these transactions.

Capital Accounts

	A	B	C		A	B	C
	($000)				($000)		
				Opening Balance	30	30	–
Goodwill	10	10	10	Goodwill	15	15	–
Balance payable			—	Profit on sale	10	10	10
to each partner	45	45	—				
	55	55	10		55	55	10

The profit on the sale is the value of the net assets $60 000 plus the value of the Goodwill $30 000 = $90 000 minus the value of the net assets $60 000. Each partner receives a one-third share of this profit ($10 000 each).

Notice that only Alan and Brian receive any money from the sale. The two partners who built up the Goodwill are rewarded for their efforts. The new partner gains no benefit, as Colin does not receive any payment.

Exercise 4

Punch and Judy have shared profits and losses in the ratio of 2 : 1. On 1 October 2011 they agree to share profits and losses as follows in future: Punch $\frac{3}{5}$, Judy $\frac{2}{5}$. Goodwill is valued at $18 000. The balances on their Capital accounts before the change in the profit/loss-sharing ratio are: Punch $36 000; Judy $14 000. A Goodwill account is *not* to be opened in the books.

Required

(a) Calculate the adjustments to be made to the Capital accounts.
(b) Prepare the partners' Capital accounts to show the adjustments for Goodwill.

22.6 **Apportionment of profit**

Partnership changes often occur in the middle of a firm's financial year. If an Income Statement is not prepared at the time of the change, the profit or loss for the financial year must be apportioned between the periods before and after the change.

If the profit is assumed to have been earned evenly throughout the year, it should be divided between the old and new partnerships on a time basis. However, some expenses may not have been incurred on a time basis and these must be allocated to the period to which they belong. Such expenses will be specified in a question. Apportionment of profit or loss is shown in an Income Statement prepared in columnar form as in the following example.

Example

Old and New are partners sharing profits and losses equally after allowing Old a salary of $10 000 per annum. On 1 January 2011 their Capital and Current account balances were as follows:

	Old	New
	$	$
Capital accounts	25 000	20 000
Current accounts	7 500	5 000

On 1 July 2011, the partners agree to the following revised terms of partnership.
1. Old to transfer $5000 from his Capital account to a Loan account on which he would be entitled to interest at 10% per annum.
2. New to bring his private car into the firm at a valuation of $12 000.
3. New to receive a salary of $5000 per annum.
4. Profits and losses to be shared: Old $\frac{3}{5}$, New $\frac{2}{5}$.

Further information for the year ended 31 December 2011 is as follows:

	$
Sales (spread evenly throughout the year)	200 000
Cost of sales	87 500
Rent	25 000
Wages	35 000
General expenses	15 000

Of the general expenses, $5000 was incurred in the six months to 30 June 2011.

New's car is to be depreciated over four years on the straight-line basis and is assumed to have no value at the end of that time.

All sales produce a uniform rate of gross profit.

Required

(a) Prepare the Income Statement and Appropriation Accounts for the year ended 31 December 2011.

(b) Prepare the partners' Current accounts for the year ended 31 December 2011.

Answer

Old and New
Income Statement and Appropriation
Account for the year ended 31 December 2011

							$
Sales							20 000
Less Cost of sales							87 500
Gross profit carried down							112 500

	6 months to 30 June 2011		6 months to 31 December 2011		Year to 31 December 2011	
	$	$	$	$	$	$
Gross profit brought down		56 250		56 250		112 500
Rent	12 500		12 500		25 000	
Wages	17 500		17 500		35 000	
General expenses	5 000		10 000		15 000	
Interest on loan	–		250		250	
Depreciation — car	–		1 500		1 500	
		35 000		41 750		76 750
Net profit		21 250		14 500		35 750
Less						
Salary: Old	5 000		–		5 000	
New	–		2 500		2 500	7 500
		16 250		12 000		28 250
Share of profit:						
Old $(\frac{1}{2})$ 8 125			$(\frac{3}{5})$ 7 200		15 325	
New $(\frac{1}{2})$ 8 125		16 250	$(\frac{2}{5})$ 4 800	12 000	12 925	28 250

(b)

Partners' Current Accounts

2011	Old $	New $	2011		Old $	New $
Dec 31 Bal c/d	28 075	20 425	Jan 1	Bal b/d	7 500	5 000
			Dec 31	Salary	5 000	2 500
				Loan interest	250	
				Share of profit	15 325	12 925
	28 075	20 425			28 075	20 425
			2012			
			Jan 1	Bal b/d	28 075	20 425

Exercise 5

Hook, Line and Sinker have shared profits and losses in the ratio 3 : 2 : 1 for a number of years. On 1 July 2011, the partners agreed that, from that date,

1. Hook will be entitled to a salary of $6000 per annum
2. profits and losses will be shared equally.

Information extracted from their books for the year ended 31 December 2011 was as follows:

	$
Sales	129 500
Cost of sales	66 500
Wages	14 000
General expenses	5 250
Depreciation of fixed assets	1 750

Two thirds of the General expenses were incurred in the six months ended 31 December 2011.

On 1 April 2011, Hook made a loan of $8000 to the partnership. Interest on the loan is at a rate of 10% per annum.

Sales have accrued evenly throughout the year and all sales have earned a uniform rate of gross profit.

Required

Prepare an Income Statement for the year ended 31 December 2011 in columnar form to show the appropriation of profit before and after the change.

22.7 How to account for the introduction of a new, or the retirement of an existing, partner

When a partner leaves a firm, or a new partner joins, it marks the end of one partnership and the beginning of a new one. As in the case of a simple change in profit-sharing ratios, a change in partners may occur at any time in a firm's financial year, and no entries may be made in the books to record the change until the end of the year.

The procedures are similar to those already described in §22.2. Account must be taken of:
● asset revaluation
● Goodwill
● changes in the profit/loss-sharing ratios.

If a partnership change occurs on the first day of a firm's financial year, the procedure is so straightforward that it is unlikely to form the basis of an examination question. There is no reason why partners should join on the first day of a firm's financial year, or why one should leave on the last day of the financial year. In practice, changes usually occur during a financial year and the accounting records are continued without interruption; final accounts are not produced until the end of the year.

Example 1

(Admission of a new partner)
Grey and Green have shared profits and losses in the ratio of 3 : 2. On 1 October 2011 they decided to admit Blue as a partner. No entries to record Blue's admittance as a partner were made in the books before the end of the financial year on 31 December 2011.

Information extracted from the books for the year ended 31 December 2011 included the following.

	$
Turnover	400 000
Cost of sales	240 000
Wages	40 000
Rent	8 000
General expenses	9 600
Depreciation of fixed assets:	
1 January to 30 September 2011	6 000
1 October to 31 December 2011	4 350 (based on asset revaluation as shown below)

At 31 December 2010 the balances on Grey and Green's Capital and Current accounts were as follows:

	Capital accounts $	Current accounts $
Grey	50 000	2000
Green	30 000	3000

On 1 October 2011, the partnership assets were revalued as follows:

	$	
Freehold premises	50 000	increase
Other non-current assets	14 000	decrease
Current assets	3 000	decrease

The partners agreed the value of Goodwill at 1 October 2011 at $40 000 and decided that no Goodwill account should be opened in the books.

On 1 October 2011 Blue paid $20 000 into the firm's bank account as capital. On the same day, Grey lent the partnership $20 000. He is entitled to interest at a rate of 10% per annum on the loan.

The balances on the partners' Drawings account at 31 December 2011 were as follows:

	$
Grey	23 000
Green	17 000
Blue	3 000

The new partnership agreement provided for the following as from 1 October 2011.

(i) Interest was allowed on the balances on Capital accounts at 31 December each year at a rate of 5% per annum.

(ii) Green was entitled to a salary of $12 000 per annum.

(iii) The balance of profits and losses were to be shared: Grey $\frac{2}{5}$; Green $\frac{2}{5}$; Blue $\frac{1}{5}$.

Required

(a) Prepare the Capital accounts of Grey, Green and Blue at 31 December 2011.

(b) Prepare the Partnership Income Statement and Appropriation Account for the year ended 31 December 2011.

(c) Prepare the partners' Current accounts at 31 December 2011.

Answer

Working: Goodwill		Before 1Oct 2011 $		After 1Oct 2011 $	Capital accounts $
Grey ($\frac{3}{5}$)		24 000	($\frac{2}{5}$)	16 000	8000 credit
Green ($\frac{2}{5}$)		16 000	($\frac{2}{5}$)	16 000	no change
Blue		–	($\frac{1}{5}$)	8 000	8000 debit

(a)

Partners' Capital accounts

2011		Grey $	Green $	Blue $	2011		Grey $	Green $	Blue $
Dec 1	Green – Goodwill			8 000	Jan 1	Balance b/d	50 000	30 000	–
Dec 31	Balance c/d	77 800	43 200	12 000	Oct 1	Bank	–	–	20 000
						Profit on revaluation	19 800	13 200	–
						Goodwill	8 000		
		77 800	43 200	20 000			77 800	43 200	20 000
					2012				
					Jan 1	Balance b/d	77 800	43 200	12 000

(b)

Grey, Green and Blue Income Statement and Appropriation Accounts for the year ended 31 December 2011						
						$
Turnover						400 000
Less Cost of sales						240 000
Gross profit carried down						160 000
	9 months to 30 June 2011		3 months to 31 December 2011		Year to 31 December 2011	
	$	$	$	$	$	$
Gross profit brought down		120 000		40 000		160 000
Wages	30 000		10 000		40 000	
Rent	6 000		2 000		8 000	
General expenses	7 200		2 400		9 600	
Interest on loan	–		500		500	
Depreciation	6 000	49 200	4 350	19 250	10 350	68 450
Net profit		70 800		20 750		91 550
Interest on capitals:						
Grey			973			
Green			540			
Blue			150			
			1 663			
Salary: Green			3 000	4 663		4 663
				16 087		86 887
Profit shares:						
Grey	$(\frac{3}{5})$ 42 480		$(\frac{2}{5})$ 6 435		48 915	
Green	$(\frac{2}{5})$ 28 320		$(\frac{2}{5})$ 6 435		34 755	
Blue	–	70 800	$(\frac{1}{5})$ 3 217	16 087	3 217	86 887

(c)

Partners' Current accounts								
2011	Grey $	Green $	Blue $	2011		Grey $	Green $	Blue $
Dec 31 Drawings	23 000	17 000	3 000	Jan 1 Balance b/d		2 000	3 000	–
Dec 31 Balance c/d	29 388	24 295	367	Dec 31 Loan interest		500	–	–
					Interest on capital	973	540	150
					Salary	–	3 000	–
					Profit	48 915	34 755	3 217
	52 388	41 295	3 367			52 388	41 295	3 367
				2012				
				Jan 1 Balance b/d		29 388	24 295	367

Note: The interest on capital is only payable for three months, in other words from the date it was set up by the partnership agreement.

Exercise 6

Bell and Booker have been partners for some years, making up their accounts annually to 31 December. The partnership agreement contained the following provisions.

- Interest was allowed on capitals at 10% annum.
- Booker was entitled to a salary of $15 000 per annum.
- Profits and losses were to be shared: Bell $\frac{2}{3}$; Booker $\frac{1}{3}$.

At 31 December 2010 the partners' Capital and Current account balances were as follows:

	Capitals	Current accounts
	$	$
Bell	100 000	16 000
Booker	60 000	12 000

On 1 September 2011, Bell and Booker admitted their manager, Candell, as a partner. Candell had been receiving a salary of $24 000.

The revised partnership agreement provided as follows:

- Partner's salary: Booker $18 000 per annum.
- Interest on capitals at 10% per annum.
- Profits and losses shared: Bell $\frac{2}{5}$, Booker $\frac{2}{5}$, Candell $\frac{1}{5}$.

The partnership's non-current assets at cost at 31 December 2010 were as follows:

	At cost	Depreciation to date	Net book value
	$	$	$
Freehold premises	180 000	45 000	135 000
Plant and machinery	90 000	60 000	30 000
Motor cars	30 000	25 000	5 000
Office equipment	21 000	14 000	7 000

No additions to, or disposals of, non-current assets had taken place between 31 December 2010 and 31 August 2011.

The assets were revalued at 1 September as follows:

	$
Freehold premises	210 000
Plant and machinery	27 000
Motor cars	5 000
Office equipment	6 000

Depreciation of fixed assets is calculated on cost and is provided as follows: freehold premises 4% per annum; plant and machinery 20% per annum; motor cars 25% per annum; office equipment 10% per annum.

Goodwill was valued at $60 000, but no Goodwill account was to be opened in the books.

On 1 September 2011, Candell paid $50 000 into the firm's bank account as capital, and also brought his private car, valued at $7000, into the business. On the same day, Bell transferred $20 000 from his Capital account to a loan account on which interest is to be paid at a rate of 12% per annum.

The following information is available from the partnership books for the year ended 31 December 2011.

	$
Turnover	600 000
Cost of sales	330 000
Wages and salaries	106 000
Rent	42 000
Heating and lighting	6 000
Sundry expenses	12 000

Note. Sales were spread evenly throughout the year and earned a uniform rate of gross profit.

Drawings in the year ended 31 December 2011 were: Bell $30 000; Booker $40 000; Candell $4000.

Required
(a) Prepare an Income Statement and Appropriation Account for the year ended 31 December 2011.
(b) Prepare the partners' Capital and Current accounts for the year ended 31 December 2011.

Example 2

(Partner retires)
Norman, Beard and David have traded in partnership for some years. Norman decided to retire on 30 September 2011 but no accounts were prepared for the partnership until the end of the financial year on 31 December 2011.

The following balances have been extracted from the trial balance at 31 December 2011.

	$	$
Sales		720 000
Purchases	400 000	
Inventory at 1 January 2011	20 000	
Wages	100 000	
Rent	26 000	
Heating and lighting	21 000	
Sundry expenses	120 000	

Further information
1. Inventory at 31 December 2011 cost $24 000.
2. At 31 December 2011 rent of $2000 had been prepaid and $1200 had accrued for heating and lighting.
3. Non-current assets at 1 January 2011 at cost were as follows:

	$
Plant and machinery	80 000
Office equipment	10 000

   Additional machinery was purchased on 1 October 2011 for $12 000.
4. Depreciation of non-current assets is to be provided at 10% per annum on cost.
5. Goodwill was valued at $45 000, but no Goodwill was to be recorded in the books.
6. The partners' Capital and Current account balances at 1 January 2011 were as follows:

	Capital accounts $	Current accounts $
Norman	50 000	8 000 (Cr)
Beard	40 000	9 000 (Cr)
David	20 000	3 000 (Cr)

7. The partners' drawings were as follows:

	$
Norman (up to 30 September 2011)	30 000
Up to 31 December 2011	
Beard	50 000
David	32 000

8. Norman left $60 000 of his capital in the business as a loan with interest at 10% per annum. The interest was payable on 30 June and 31 December each year.
9. The partnership agreement up to 30 September 2011 allowed for the following:

   Interest on capitals: 8% per annum (based on balances on Capital accounts at 1 January 2011).
   Salary: David $6000 per annum.
   Profits and losses to be shared: Norman ($\frac{1}{2}$), Beard ($\frac{1}{3}$), David ($\frac{1}{6}$).

   The agreement was amended on 1 October 2011 as follows:

   Interest on capitals: 10% per annum (based on balances on Capital accounts at 1 October 2011).
   Salary: David $10 000 per annum.
   Profits and losses to be shared Beard ($\frac{3}{5}$), David ($\frac{2}{5}$).

10. The assets were not revalued at 30 September 2011.
11. It is assumed that gross profit has been earned evenly throughout the year.

Required
(a) Prepare the partners' Capital accounts.
(b) Prepare the partnership's Income Statement and Appropriation Accounts for the year ended 31 December 2011.
(c) Prepare the partners' Current accounts for the year ended 31 December 2011.

Answer
(a)

Partners' Capital accounts

2011		Norman $	Beard $	David $	2011		Norman $	Beard $	David $
Sep 30	Goodwill		27 000	18 000	Jan 1	Balance b/d	50 000	40 000	20 000
	Loan a/c	60 000			Sep 30	Goodwill	22 500	15 000	7 500
	Bank	46 750				Current a/c	34 250*		
Dec 31	Balance c/d		28 000	9 500					
		106 750	55 000	27 500			106 750	55 000	27 500
					2012				
					Jan 1	Balance b/d		28 000	9 500

* The balance on the outgoing partner's Current account is transferred to Capital account.

(b)

Norman, Beard and David					
Income Statement and Appropriation Accounts for the year ended 31 December 2011					

	$		$		
Sales			720 000		
Less Cost of sales					
Inventory at 1 Jan 2001	20 000				
Purchases	400 000				
	420 000				
Less Inventory at 31 Dec 2011	24 000		396 000		
Gross profit			324 000		

	9 months to 30 Sep 2011		3 months to 31 Dec 2011		Total	
	$	$	$	$	$	$
Gross profit		243 000		81 000		324 000
Wages	75 000		25 000		100 000	
Rent (26 000 – 2000)	18 000		6 000		24 000	
Heating and lighting						
(21 000 + 1200)	16 650		5 550		22 200	
Sundry expenses	9 000		3 000		12 000	
Depreciation:						
Plant and machinery	6 000		2 300		8 300	
Office equipment	750		250		1 000	
Interest on loan	–	125 400	1 500	43 600	1 500	169 000
Net profit		117 600		37 400		155 000
Interest on capital:						
Norman	3 000		–		3 000	
Beard	2 400		700*	–	3 100	
David	1 200		238*		1 438	
	6 600		938		7 538	
Salary						
David	4 500	11 100	2 500	3 438	7 000	14 538
		106 500		33 962		140 462
Shares of profit						
Norman	53 250		–		53 250	
Beard	35 500		20 377		55 877	
David	17 750	106 500	13 585	33 962	31 335	140 462

* On capitals of $28 000 and $9500 respectively.

(c)

Partners' Current accounts								
	Norman	Beard	David			Norman	Beard	David
2011	$	$	$	2011		$	$	$
Sep 30 Drawings	30 000			Jan 1	Balance b/d	8 000	9 000	3 000
Capital a/c	34 250*			Sep 30	Int. on Capital	3 000		
					Profit	53 250		
Dec 31 Drawings		50 000	32 000	Dec 31	Int. on Capital		3 100	1 438
Balance c/d		17 977	10 773		Salary			7 000
					Profit		55 877	31 335
	64 250	67 977	42 773			64 250	67 977	42 773
				2012				
				Jan 1	Balance b/d		17 977	10 773

* The balance on the outgoing partner's Current account is transferred to Capital account.

Exercise 7

Wilfrid, Hide and Wyte were partners sharing profits and losses in the ratio of 3 : 2 : 1 after charging interest on capitals at 10% per annum. Their Capital and Current account balances at 1 July 2011 were as follows:

	Capital a/cs $	Current a/cs $
Wilfrid	80 000	12 000
Hide	50 000	3 000
Wyte	30 000	4 000

Wilfrid decided to retire on 31 December 2011. He left $75 000 of the balance on his Capital account as a loan to the firm, with interest at 10% per annum. The balance on his Capital account was paid to him by cheque.

At 31 December 2011, Goodwill was valued at $60 000 but Goodwill was not to be shown in the books. It was also agreed that the partnership assets should be revalued at $21 000 less than their current book values.

Hide and Wyte continued in partnership from 1 January 2012, with interest allowed on capitals at 10% per annum and with profits and losses being shared equally.

The partners' drawings in the year ended 30 June 2012 were as follows:

	$
Wilfrid (6 months to 31 December 2011)	23 000
Hide (12 months to 30 June 2012)	28 000
Wyte (12 months to 30 June 2012)	18 000

Further information

1.

	$	
Gross profit for the year ended 30 June 2012	187 000	(assumed to have been earned evenly throughout the year.)
Expenditure for the year ended 30 June 2012:		
Wages	91 000	
Rent paid	14 000	
Electricity paid	7 000	
Sundry expenses	9 000	

2. At 30 June 2012, rent of $2000 had been paid in advance, and electricity in the amount of $14 000 had accrued.

Required

(a) Prepare the partnership Income Statement and Appropriation Account for the year ended 30 June 2012.

(b) Prepare the Capital and Current accounts of the partnership for the year ended 30 June 2012.

Some examination question will combine the revaluation of assets with the introduction of a new partner. In this case, work through the revaluation account, transferring any profit or loss on revaluation to the old partners in their old profit sharing ratios. Then introduce the new partner and adjust the Capital accounts for goodwill in line with section 22.7.

22.8 How to account for the realisation of a partnership

There may come a time in the life of any business when the owner or owners no longer wish to run the firm any more. When this decision is made, one of two things can happen. All the business assets and liabilities can be sold to a new business. This is a business purchase and is dealt with in chapter 26.

Alternatively, the assets may be sold to several people and the money raised used to pay off the liabilities, such as trade payables. The owner or owners then retire and the balance on the business bank account transferred to them.

When the business is sold the accounting treatment is to open an account called a **Realisation account**. Like the Revaluation account, all the assets to be sold are debited to the Realisation account at their book values. All the liabilities to be paid are credited to the Realisation account at their book values. Any money received or paid is credited or debited to the realisation account. Any expenses arising from the realisation are also debited to the Realisation account.

This hopefully will result in a profit on realisation. In the case of a partnership, this profit is split between the partners in their **profit sharing ratios** and credited to their Capital accounts. If it results in a loss on realisation then this loss is debited to their Capital accounts in their **profit sharing ratios**.

The balances on the partners' current accounts are transferred to their capital accounts. Finally, their capital accounts are then closed by debiting them with the money from the business bank account.

Sometimes one of the partners may decide to take one of the assets of the partnership rather than sell it. In this case, the Realisation account is credited with the agreed value of the asset to be taken by the partner. The opposite entry is to debit the Capital account of the partner taking the asset.

Example

Colin and John are in business sharing the profits and losses equally. Their summarised Statement of Financial Position at 31 December 2011 is as follows:

	$000	$000
Non-current assets		
Property		40
Motor vehicles		20
		60
Current assets		
Inventory	16	
Trade receivables	14	
Bank account	1	
	31	
Current liabilities		
Trade payables	13	18
		78
Capital accounts:		
Colin	30	
John	30	60
Current accounts:		
Colin	10	
John	8	18
		78

The partners are unable to work together any more and decide to sell the business.

- The property is sold for $70 000.
- Colin agrees to take one of the vehicles at a value of $5000. The remaining vehicles are sold for $12 000.
- The inventory is sold for $13 000 and the partners collect $11 000 from the trade receivables.
- They pay their trade suppliers $12 000.

- The expenses of realising the partnership amount to $2000.

Required

(a) Prepare the partnership Realisation account.
(b) Prepare the partners' Capital accounts.
(c) Prepare the partnership bank account, showing the closing entries to close the account.

Realisation account

	$000		$000
Property (book value)	40	Bank — sale of property	70
Motor vehicles (book value)	20	Colin's Capital account	
Inventory (book value)	16	value of car taken	5
Trade receivables (book value)	14	Bank – sale of vehicles	12
Bank – pay'ts to trade		Bank – sale of inventory	13
payables	12	Bank – from trade	
Bank – expenses of sale	2	receivables	11
Profit on realisation:		Trade payables (book value)	13
Colin	10		
John	10		
	124		124

Capital accounts

	Colin $000	John $000		Colin $000	John $000
Vehicle taken	5	–	Opening balances	30	30
Bank	45	48	Current accounts	10	8
			Profit on realisation	10	10
	50	48		50	48

Bank account

	$000		$000
Opening balance	1	Trade payables	12
Sale of property	70	Expenses of sale	2
Sale of vehicles	12	Colin – Capital account	45
Sale of inventory	13	John – Capital account	48
From trade receivables	11		
	107		107

Exercise 8

Raul and Samir are in business sharing the profits and losses in the ratio of 3 : 2. Their summarised Statement of Financial Position at 31 August 2011 is as follows:

	$000	$000	$000
Non-current assets			
Property			80
Motor vehicles			20
			100
Current assets			
Inventory		19	
Trade receivables		16	
		35	

	$000	$000	$000
Current liabilities			
Trade payables	10		
Bank overdraft	4	14	21
			121
Capital accounts:			
Raul		60	
Samir		55	115
Current accounts:			
Raul		10	
Samir		(4)	6
			121

The partners decide to sell the business.

- The property is sold for $106 000.

- Samir agrees to take one of the vehicles at a value of $7000. The remaining vehicles are sold for $9000.

- The inventory is sold for $18 000 and the partners collect $13 000 from the trade receivables.

- They pay their trade suppliers the full amount owed.

- The expenses of realising the partnership amount to $3000.

Required
(a) Prepare the partnership Realisation account.
(b) Prepare the partners' Capital accounts.
(c) Prepare the partnership bank account, showing the closing entries to close the account.

HINTS

- Read questions involving partnership changes very carefully two or three times before starting to answer them. Highlight or underline important information and instructions. Tick every item as you give effect to it in your answer.
- Treat partnership changes as the ending of one partnership and the commencement of a new one.
- A partnership change requires separate Income Statements to be prepared for the old and new firms. It will normally be assumed that revenue has been earned evenly over the whole period before and after the change. Apportion expenses in the Income Statement on a time basis unless any expense has to be apportioned on some other basis. Perform your arithmetical calculations carefully and show your workings.
- Adjust for accrued and prepaid expenses before apportioning them.
- Partners' salaries, interest on drawings and capital will be stated in the question on an annual basis. These must be apportioned on a time basis.
- Read partnership questions very carefully to see whether or not a Goodwill account is to be opened when there is a partnership change.
- If a Goodwill account is not to be opened, Goodwill is credited to the partners' Capital accounts before the change in their old profit-sharing ratio, and debited after the change to the partners' Capital accounts in their new profit-sharing ratio.
- When assets are revalued on a partnership change, they are retained in the books of the new partnership at their new values.
- The balance on an outgoing partner's Current and Drawings accounts must be transferred to his Capital account. Make sure you treat the final balance on his Capital account exactly as required by the question.
- If partners do not maintain Current accounts in their books, the entries that would normally be posted to the Current accounts must be posted to the Capital accounts.
- Before beginning to copy out your answer, make sure that you have ticked every piece of information and every instruction on the question paper.

MULTIPLE-CHOICE QUESTIONS

1. The summarised Statement of Financial Position for F and G in partnership is given.

	$		$
Goodwill	12 000	Capital accounts	
Net assets	28 800	Partner F	24 000
		Partner G	16 800
	40 800		40 800

F and G have previously shared profits and losses in the ratio of 2 : 1 but have now decided to change the ratio to 3 : 2.
Goodwill is to be revalued and shown in the Statement of Financial Position at $30 000.
What is the new balance on F's Capital account?

A. $23 800   B. $24 000
C. $34 800   D. $36 000

2. J and K are partners sharing profits and losses equally. They do not record Goodwill in the firms' books.
L joins the partnership, paying $24 000 for his share of the Goodwill. Profits and losses are to be shared equally between J, K and L.

Which of the following, shows the increases in the partners' accounts on the admission of L as a partner?

	J $	K $	L $
A	12 000	12 000	-
B	12 000	12 000	24 000
C	36 000	36 000	-
D	36 000	36 000	24 000

3. L and M are in partnership sharing profits and losses in the ratio of 3 : 2. They admit N as a partner on 1 January. On the same date the partnership net assets are revalued and show a loss on revaluation of $40 000. The new profit/loss-sharing ratio is: $L\frac{2}{5}, M\frac{2}{5}, N\frac{1}{5}$.
How will the revaluation of the net assets be recorded in the partners' Capital accounts?

Capital accounts			
	L	M	N
	$	$	$
A.	Credit 16 000	Credit 16 000	Credit 8000
B.	Debit 16 000	Debit 16 000	Debit 8000
C.	Credit 24 000	Credit 16 000	–
D.	Debit 24 000	Debit 16 000	–

4. P, Q and R were partners, sharing profits and losses equally. P retired and Q and R continued in partnership sharing profits and losses equally. Goodwill was valued at $60 000 but was not shown in the books.

Which entries will record the adjustments for P's retirement in the books?

Capital accounts			
	P	Q	R
	$	$	$
A.	–	Credit 10 000	Credit 10 000
B.	Credit 20 000	Debit 10 000	Debit 10 000
C.	Debit 20 000	Credit 10 000	Credit 10 000
D.	–	Credit 30 000	Credit 30 000

5. S and T are partners sharing profits and losses in the ratio of 1 : 2. They admit V as a partner and revise the profit-sharing ratio to: $S\frac{2}{5}, T\frac{2}{5}, V\frac{1}{5}$.
Goodwill is valued at $60 000 but no Goodwill is to be recorded in the books.
Which entries will be made in the partners' Capital accounts?

Capital accounts			
	S	T	V
	$	$	$
A.	Debit 4 000	Credit 16 000	Debit 12 000
B.	Credit 24 000	Credit 24 000	Debit 48 000
C.	Credit 4 000	Debit 16 000	Credit 12 000
D.	Debit 24 000	Debit 24 000	Credit 48 000

1. Ali and Siri are in partnership sharing the profits and losses equally. Their Statement of Financial Position at 31 October 2011 is as follows:

Statement of Financial Position at 31 October 2011

	$000	$000	$000
Non-current assets			
Property			40
Motor vehicles			20
			60
Current assets			
Inventory		12	
Trade receivables		10	
		22	
Current liabilities			
Trade payables	8		
Bank overdraft	2	10	12
			72
Capital accounts: Ali		36	
Siri			36
			72

On 1 November 2011 they admit Bill as a partner, taking an equal share of the profits. Bill will pay $30 000 into the bank as his capital. The goodwill is valued at $24 000. No goodwill account is to appear in the books.

Ali and Siri also revalue the assets at the same date. The property is revalued at $60 000 and the inventory revalued at $10 000.

Required

(a) Prepare the Revaluation account for the partnership.

(b) Prepare partner's Capital accounts after the revaluation and the introduction of Bill as a partner.

(c) Prepare the Statement of Financial Position immediately after the above transactions have taken place.

(d) All the partners then agree that the balances on their Capital accounts should be equal. Calculate how much additional capital Bill must introduce to achieve this.

2. Wilson, Keppel and Betty were in partnership and shared profits and losses equally. They did not operate Current accounts and on 30 April 2010 their Capital accounts showed the following balances.

Wilson	$40 000
Keppel	$30 000
Betty	$15 000

(a) Keppel retired from the partnership on 1 May 2010 and at that time Goodwill was valued at $24 000. Non-current assets were revalued as follows:

Premises increased in value by $10 000
Fixtures increased in value by $4000
Vehicles decreased in value by $2000

It was agreed that neither a Goodwill account nor a Revaluation account would be shown in the partnership books. Keppel received cash for his share of the partnership and Wilson and Betty continued to run the partnership still sharing the profits equally. Drawings during the year ended 30 April 2011 were Wilson $46 000 and Betty $45 000. Net profit for that year was $120 000.

Required

Draw up the partners' Capital accounts for the year ended 30 April 2011 in columnar form.

(b) Imogen joined the partnership on 30 November 2011, bringing in capital of $12 000 and $8000 as her share of Goodwill. No Goodwill account was opened. Profits were now to be shared on the following basis:

Wilson $\frac{3}{7}$
Betty $\frac{3}{7}$
Imogen $\frac{1}{7}$

During the year ended 30 April 2012 profits amounted to $140 000 and partners' drawings were Wilson $52 000, Betty $48 000 and Imogen $20 000. Profits accumulated at a regular rate throughout the year. The partnership was sold on 1 May 2012 for $126 000. The partnership was dissolved and all of the partners took the money due to them.

Draw up the partners' Capital accounts for the period 1 May 2011 to 1 May 2012, in columnar form.

3. Dellow and Coucom are in partnership in a business which has three retail departments, Television, Computing and Telephones. The following balances were extracted from the business accounts at 30 April 2011.

	Dr $	Cr $
Purchases and Sales		
Television	120 000	214 000
Computing	220 000	428 000
Telephones	40 000	107 000
Wages	56 000	
Inventory at 1 May 2010		
Television	8 000	
Computing	19 000	
Telephones	3 000	
Sales staff salaries	147 000	
General expenses	5 000	
Office salaries	35 000	
Advertising	14 000	
Rent	40 000	
Electricity	9 000	
Insurance	5 000	
Motor Vehicles at cost	45 000	
Furniture & Fittings at cost	30 000	

Notes

The following must now be taken into consideration. Inventories at 30 April 2011:

Television	$17 000
Computing	$40 000
Telephones	$5 000

Inventory is recorded on a computer and is based solely on sales and purchases. No physical check of the inventory has been taken.
Accruals at 30 April 2011:

General expenses	$2000
Electricity	$1000
Rent	$2000

Number of sales staff employed:

Television	3
Computing	4
Telephones	1

Commission is paid to sales staff at 1% of Sales. Depreciation is charged to Motor Vehicles and Furniture & Fittings at 20% per annum on cost. Floor space (square metres):

Television	2000
Computing	2500
Telephones	500

Expenses are apportioned as follows:

Expense	Basis of apportionment
Wages	Sales
General expenses	Sales
Office salaries	Sales
Sales staff salaries	Number of sales staff
Advertising	Sales
Rent and rates	Floor area
Electricity	Floor area
Insurance	Floor area
Depreciation	Equally between departments

Dellow and Coucom share profits in the ratio of their Capital accounts, which at 1 May 2010 were: Dellow $60 000, Coucom $40 000.

Interest on capital is payable at 1% of opening capital. Cash drawings for the year were Dellow, $15 000 and Coucom, $4 000.

Interest is chargeable on drawings at 2% of total drawings for the year.

Coucom is paid a Partnership salary of $7600. During the year Coucom took from stock for her own use a Television costing $1000. No entries were made for this in the accounts.

Required

(a) Prepare, in columnar format, Departmental Trading Accounts and Income Statements for the year ended 30 April 2011.

(b) Prepare the Partnership Appropriation Account for the year ended 30 April 2011.

(c) It has been suggested that any department that is making a loss should be closed. Comment on this suggestion.

23 An introduction to the accounts of limited companies

In this chapter you will learn:

- what limited companies are and how they differ from partnerships
- the Companies Acts 1985, 1989 and 2006 and some of the legal requirements for companies
- the format of final accounts: Income Statement and Statement of Financial Position in line with IAS 1
- types of share capital and reserves
- which profits are distributable in cash as dividends and how the dividends are calculated
- what debentures are and how they differ from shares.

23.1 What is a limited company?

A limited company differs from other organisations because it is a *separate legal entity;* its existence is separate from that of its shareholders (the people who own it). It is important to distinguish between the *accounting concept of entity,* which, as explained in §9.2, applies to every business for the purposes of bookkeeping and accounting, and the concept of *legal entity,* which applies only to limited companies. If Mr S. Ossidge, a sole trader, is a butcher, a customer who wishes to sue him for food poisoning will be able to sue him as a person; the *accounting concept* will not protect Mr Ossidge from a legal action. But, if Mr Ossidge has formed his business into a limited company, S. Ossidge Limited, the concept of *separate legal entity* applies and the customer must sue the company and not Mr Ossidge because the goods were purchased from the company and not from Mr Ossidge!

23.2 The growth of limited companies

The concept of limited liability goes back to the sixteenth century but it became important in the eighteenth century because of the Industrial Revolution. Before that, people earned their living by farming, or from cottage industries that did not require large sums of capital. With the invention of machinery powered by steam engines, increased productivity led to manufacturing being concentrated in factories. Larger amounts of capital were needed to construct the factories and equip them with machinery. This capital could be raised by inviting people to buy shares (or invest) in the business without taking part in its management. These investors were the **shareholders** or members of the companies. By the middle of the nineteenth century, limited companies had become very important as business organisations.

Limited companies are sometimes known as **limited liability companies** because the liability of their shareholders is limited to the amounts they have paid, or have agreed to pay, for their shares. For example, a shareholder owning 100 shares of $1 each cannot be compelled to pay more than the $100 he has already paid for his shares if the company cannot pay its creditors; the creditors may be the losers. (It is possible to have limited partnerships in which the liability of some, but not all, of the partners for the firm's debts is limited. Limited partnerships are outside the scope of this book.)

23.3 The Companies Acts of 1985, 1989 and 2006

Two characteristics of limited companies have now been identified:

1. creditors risk not being paid if a company has insufficient funds, that is, the company is insolvent
2. shareholders are not entitled to help manage a company simply because they own shares in it; they rely on directors to manage the company for them.

The Companies Act 1985, as amended by the Companies Act 1989, is designed to protect the interests of creditors and shareholders, including those who might in future become creditors or shareholders. Some of the provisions of the Companies Act 1985 are as follows:

Formation. A company is formed when certain documents are registered by people, known as its 'founders', with the Registrar of Companies and various fees and duties are paid to the Registrar.

Memorandum and Articles of Association. These are two of the documents which must be filed with the Registrar of Companies.

The Memorandum defines the relationship of the company to the rest of the world. It contains information about:

1. the name of the company, which must end with the words **Public limited company** or **Plc** if it is a public company, or **Limited** or **Ltd** if it is a private company (the difference between the two types of company will be explained later)
2. a statement that the liability of the company is limited
3. what activities the company can carry out. These are referred to as its objects.

Note: Before the Companies Act of 2006, a company used to have to state its **authorised share capital**. However, the 2006 Companies Act has abolished the need for a company to have an authorised share capital. Thus there is no longer any need to show this in any answers in your examinations and questions should not include it anymore.

The Articles of Association is a document that defines the rights and duties of a company's shareholders and directors. It contains regulations for calling meetings of shareholders, members' voting rights, the forfeiture of shares by members who fail to pay the amounts called upon them, and the appointment of directors to manage the company. Another clause fixes the directors' **qualification**, that is the number of shares that directors must hold. This ensures that the directors have a financial stake in the company, giving some sort of insurance that they will manage the company well for the shareholders. It is important to remember that the directors manage the company because they are voted into office by the shareholders, and not simply because they own shares.

Public and private companies. Companies register as either public companies or private companies.

Public companies may offer their shares to the public and the shares may be bought and sold on the Stock Exchange.

Private companies are not allowed to offer their shares to the public and shares cannot, therefore, be bought and sold on the stock exchange.

The distinction between public and private companies applies in the United Kingdom, but may not apply in all other countries. To cater for this situation, companies will be described as 'Limited' or 'Ltd' in this text, but will be assumed to be public companies unless they are specifically stated to be private companies or the context implies that they are private.

23.4 Partnerships and limited companies compared

	Partnerships	Limited companies
Number of partners/ shareholders	Not less than 2. Not more than 20 (except in certain professional firms such as accountants, lawyers, etc.).	Note less than 2. Maximum number depends on the number of shares permitted by the authorised capital.
Liability of partners/ shareholders	Unlimited. The private assets of partners may be seized to pay the firm's creditors (except in the case of limited partners in a limited partnership).	Shareholders' liability is limited to the amount they have paid, or agreed to pay on their shares.
Capital	Determined by the partnership agreement.	The share capital for a public limited company is unlimited. The share capital for a private limited company will depend on how much money the shareholders have to invest in the business.
Management	All partners (except those with limited liability) may manage the firm's affairs.	Shareholders are not entitled to manage the affairs. This must be left to the directors. (The directors act because they have been appointed directors, not because they are shareholders.)
Taxation	Firms are not liable to pay tax on their profits. The liability to pay tax on their shares of profit rests with the partners individually.	Companies are liable to pay tax on their profits. The tax payable is treated as an appropriation of profit.
Distribution of profit	Partners share profits and losses.	Profits are distributed as dividends. Undistributed profits may be retained in the company.

23.5 Income Statement for a limited company

The way the final accounts of limited companies are prepared is set out in the **International Accounting Standard 1 (IAS 1)**. The statement allows income and expenses of a company to be presented in one of two ways:

(a) in a single Income Statement covering the accounting period, or

(b) in two separate statements, (i) a separate income statement and (ii) a statement of other comprehensive income.

For the remainder of the text an **Income Statement** will be used. The example given contains all that is required for the CIE examinations.

The format of the Income Statement is extremely important and should be learned. In an examination students should follow this format as far as possible.

Example 1

Exhibit Co. Limited
* Income Statement
for the year ended ....

	*This year $000	*Last year $000
Revenue[1]	100 000	80 000
Cost of sales[2]	(60 000)	(45 000)
Gross profit	40 000	35 000
Other income[3]	2 000	1 500
Distribution costs[4]	(8 000)	(7 000)
Administrative expenses[5]	(11 000)	(10 000)
Other expenses[6]	(1 000)	(500)
Profit/(Loss) from Operations	22 000	19 000
Finance Costs[7]	(3 000)	(2 000)
Profit/(Loss) Before Tax	19 000	17 000
Tax[8]	(5 000)	(4 000)
Profit/(Loss) for the year attributable to equity Holders[9]	14 000	13 000

* In practice and in examinations dates would be included. This is an example of the expenses being classified by function, Distribution, Administrative and so on and is the one most likely to appear in the examination.

1. Revenue is the income generated by the company from its trading activities. In other words, its sales for the year.

2. Cost of sales. The detail does not have to be shown here, but show as a working: opening inventory + purchases − closing inventory.
3. Other income would include such things as profit on disposal of non-current assets, or rental income, where renting property or equipment is not the main object of the company.
4. Distribution costs include expenses such as salesperson's salaries or expenses, warehousing costs, carriage outwards, depreciation of warehouses or delivery vans or any other expenses associated with the transfer of goods from the company to its customers.
5. Administrative expenses would include office salaries or costs, selling costs not treated as part of the distribution expenses, general depreciation of cars or office equipment. It may also include discount allowed, provision for doubtful debts and bad debts.
6. Other expenses would include items not included under either 3 or 4 above. It may include, say leasing costs or loss on disposal of non-current assets.
7. Finance costs would include bank overdraft or loan interest, debenture interest or interest on loans from other companies. It also includes dividends paid on redeemable preference shares. These type of shares are regarded as a long-term loan of the business.
8. The tax is payable on the profits the company earns. In an examination this figure will be given in the question.
9. Profit attributable to equity holders. The equity holders are the owners of the company: the shareholders. All the profit earned by the company belongs to them.

In an examination it is likely that you will be given figures for the total distribution and administrative expenses. You may also be asked to make adjustments for accruals and prepayments of certain individual expenses. You may be told whether they are administrative or distribution expenses, but you may have to make a judgement. As in all cases, show the examiner all the workings.

Remember also that the layout above is for accounts which will be published by the company and available for the general public to look at. It is likely that the company will produce internal accounts which are much more detailed than the statement shown above. It may, for instance, list each individual expense rather than group them under two or three headings. This is to allow managers to look in more detail at the performance of the company. It is possible that the examination may require all the expenses listed rather than put into function. If this is the case, then a format similar to the one below will be acceptable.

Example 2

Exhibit Co. Limited Income Statement for the year ended		
	$000	$000
Revenue		100 000
Opening inventories	20 000	
Purchases	55 000	
	75 000	
Closing inventories	(15 000)	
Cost of sales		(60 000)
Gross profit		40 000
Rental income		2 000
		42 000
Overheads:		
Office salaries	4 100	
Selling expenses	4 000	
Delivery costs	800	
Salesman's salary	4 300	
Provision for bad debts	900	
Loss on sale of non-current assets	1 000	
Depreciation:		
Delivery vehicles	2 900	
Office equipment	2 000	
		(20 000)
PROFIT FROM OPERATIONS		22 000
Finance costs (bank interest)		(3 000)
PROFIT BEFORE TAX		19 000
Tax		(5 000)
PROFIT FOR THE YEAR ATTRIBUTABLE TO EQUITY HOLDERS		14 000

In this illustration only one year is shown. Dates should also be included in the heading.

23.6 Dividing up the profit for the year

Having generated a profit for the year and paying tax on it, what does the company do with it? Unlike a sole trader where all the profit belongs to the owner, a limited company can have a large number of owners in the form of shareholders. They will be rewarded for their investment by the company paying them a dividend. It would be unwise for a company to pay out all its profit to the shareholders. Indeed, most companies after paying some of the profit as dividend keep the balance as retained earnings. This is added to the retained earnings from previous years and shown as a separate figure on the Statement of Financial Position.

In other instances, after paying the dividend the company may transfer part of the remaining profit to a reserve. This could be a revenue reserve. This type of reserve may be a general reserve or a specific reserve, such as, a reserve for the replacement of machinery.

What is important to note is that profit and reserves are **not** cash funds as the next chapter will illustrate. They are represented by assets shown in the Statement of Financial Position. They record the fact that the assets belong to the owners of the business: the shareholders.

In IAS 1 the splitting of the profits is shown in a statement known as a **Statement of Changes in Equity.** This is shown below.

Example 3

Exhibit Co. Limited Statement of Changes in Equity for the year ended		
Retained Earnings	*This year $000	*Last year $000
Balance at start of year	43 000	34 000
Profit for the year	14 000	13 000
Transfers for other reserves	–	–
	57 000	47 000
Dividends Paid	(5 000)	(4 000)
Transfers to other reserves	–	–
Balance at end of year	52 000	43 000

* Note also that no dates are included. This would **not** be the case in practice where the actual date of the year end and previous year, say **31 December**, would be stated.

An alternative and more comprehensive presentation is shown below.

Statement of Changes in Equity for the year ended				
	Share capital and Reserves $000	Retained Earnings $000	Revaluation Reserve $000	Total Equity $000
Balance at start of year	52 000	43 000	×	95 000
Total profit for the year		14 000	×	14 000
Dividends paid		(5 000)		(5 000)
New share capital	×			×
Balance at end of the year	52 000	52 000	×	104 000

IAS 1 also requires a statement showing details of dividends **paid** during the year. An example of this is shown below. The important thing to note here is that only dividends paid during the year are included in the statement. This means that the statement of changes in equity could include the payment of the final dividend in respect of the previous year. Proposed dividends are usually voted on by the shareholders at the annual general meeting and approved by them at that time. This results in them being paid some months after the end of the financial year.

Proposed dividends are never shown in the financial statements. They are referred to by way of a note to the published accounts.

Example 4

*Dividends for the year ended .... (Note for the published accounts)		
	*This year $000	*Last year $000
Amounts recognised as distributions to Equity holders during the year:		
Final dividend for last year of $0.075 per share	3 000	2 200
Interim dividend for this year of $0.050 per share	2 000	1 800
	5 000	4 000
Proposed final dividend for this year of $0.095 per share	3 800	3 000

*Note also that no dates are included. This would **not** be the case in practice where the actual date of the year end and previous year, say **31 December**, would be stated.

The Statement of Changes in equity can be expanded further to include transfers to and from reserves and the issue or redemption of shares.

Example 5

Using the information from above, however:

1. During the year Exhibit Co. Limited issued 10 000 ordinary shares of $1 each at $1.20
2. At the end of the year the directors transferred $6 000 to the general reserve.

As a result of these actions the Statement of Changes in Equity would appear as shown below:

Statement of Changes in Equity for the year ended				
	Ordinary share capital	Share premium	General reserve	Retained earnings	Total equity
	$000	$000	$000	$000	$000
Balance at start of year	40 000	2 000	10 000	43 000	95 000
Profit for the year				14 000	14 000
Dividends paid				(5 000)	(5 000)
Issue of ordinary shares	10 000	2 000			12 000
Transfer to general reserve			6 000	(6 000)	—
Balance at end of year	50 000	4 000	16 000	46 000	116 000

IAS 1 allows for alternative ways of setting out the Statement of Changes in Equity. One such alternative is to prepare a **Statement of Recognised Income and Expenses**. This is much less detailed, as it includes such things as the profit for the year and gains on revaluation of non-current assets. It does not include dividends paid or issue of shares. For examination purposes, be aware of its existence and what it does and does not include.

The Statement of Changes in Equity set out above is an important part of the final accounts. Learn the layout and how to adjust the figures as a result of the changes, as it will be required for future examinations.

23.7 Statement of Financial Position for a limited company

IAS 1 specifies the minimum information which must be shown in the Statement of Financial Position for a limited company. The example which follows is the form students should use for examination purposes.

Example 6

*Statement of financial position as at		
	*This year $000	*Last year $000
Assets		
Non-current assets[1]		
Property, plant and equipment	100 000	92 100
Goodwill	7 700	8 000
	107 700	100 100
Current assets[2]		
Inventories	1 000	800
Trade receivables and other	5 000	4 000
Cash and cash equivalents	500	300
	6 500	5 100
Total assets[3]	114 200	105 200
Equity and Liabilities		
Capital and reserves[4]		
Share Capital	40 000	40 000
Share Premium	2 000	2 000
General Reserve	10 000	10 000
Retained Earnings	52 000	43 000
	104 000	95 000
Non-current liabilities[5]		
Bank Loan	5 500	5 200
Current liabilities[6]		
Trade and other payables	1 200	1 000
Tax liabilities	3 500	4 000
	4 700	5 000
Total Liabilities[7]	114 200	105 200

* Note that no dates are included. This would **not** be the case in practice where the actual date of the year end and previous year, say 31 **December**, would be stated.

1. Non-current assets
   This includes both tangible assets such as plant and machinery, motor vehicles and office equipment as well as non-tangible assets such as Goodwill. In this case, Goodwill should only be shown if it is purchased Goodwill; in other words, included in the purchase price of another business acquired by the company. Other intangible assets could include the cost of developing the company's products and acquiring patents and trade marks. Notice that only the net book value of the non-current assets is shown. Most companies provide a series of notes to accompany the final accounts. These would have the detailed breakdown of the cost of the assets, any additions or disposals made during the year and the depreciation charge for the year.
   It is also possible to show the non-current assets as intangible and tangible. For example:

Non-current assets	$000
Intangible	
Goodwill	7 700
Tangible	
Property, plant and equipment	100 000

2. Current assets
   This includes inventories, trade receivables and bank balances

identified as cash and cash equivalents. The figure for inventories would include raw materials work in progress and finished goods. In the case of trade receivables it is also acceptable to show the trade receivables as one figure, being the amount receivable from customers and other receivables, such as prepayments as a separate figure. Cash and cash equivalents include short term deposits as well as bank current accounts.

3. Total assets is simply the sum of non-current and current assets.
4. Equity
   The equity or capital of the company is analysed, showing separately the separate classes of paid up capital, share premium and reserves. Notice that the figure for Retained Earnings is the closing figure from the Statement of Changes in Equity. Unless this is calculated then the Statement of Financial Position will not balance.
5. Non-current liabilities
   These are amounts which fall due for payment more than twelve months after the end of the financial year. This would cover such items as long-term loans which the company owes. It would also include Debentures and Redeemable Preference Shares.
   Although not shown here it is also possible for a company to have non-current assets. This may be something such as a debt which is due to be received more than twelve months after the date of the statement. Such items would be shown as a separate heading in the statement.
6. Current liabilities
   This would include trade payables (amounts due to suppliers) and other payables such as accruals. It would also include other short-term borrowings such as a bank loan and the current portion of long-term borrowings such as that part of a long-term loan which is repayable within twelve months from the date of the statement of financial position.
7. Total liabilities is the sum of the equity, non-current and current liabilities.

23.8 Share capital

Issued capital is the total of the shares which have been issued to the shareholders.

Called-up capital is money required to be paid by shareholders immediately. A newly formed company may not require all the money due from shareholders immediately. If it has to have a factory built and then equip it with machinery, the money could lie idle in the company's bank account until those items have to be paid for. It may require the shareholders to pay only part of the amount due on their shares until further sums are required, when it will call on the shareholders to make further payments.

Uncalled capital is any amount of the share capital not yet called up by the company.

Paid-up capital is the money received from shareholders on the called-up capital. Some shareholders may be late in paying their calls, or may fail to pay them at all.

Calls in advance is money received from shareholders who have paid calls before they are due.

Calls in arrear is money due from shareholders who are late in paying their calls.

Forfeited shares are shares which shareholders have forfeited because they have failed to pay their calls. The shares may be re-issued to other shareholders.

23.9 Classes of shares

Shares may be **preference shares** or **ordinary shares**.

Preference shares

Preference shares are called so because they entitle holders of them to certain rights which ordinary shareholders do not enjoy. These shareholders are entitled to receive dividends at a fixed rate out of profits before the ordinary shareholders become entitled to dividends. The rate of the dividend is expressed as a percentage of the nominal value (see §23.10) in the description of the shares. When a company is **wound up** (ceases to exist), preference shareholders are entitled to have their capital repaid before any repayment is made to the ordinary shareholders. If there are insufficient funds after the preference shareholders have been repaid, the ordinary shareholders will lose some, if not all, of their money.

Non-cumulative preference shares. This class of preference share is not entitled to have any arrears of dividend carried forward to future years if the profit of any year is insufficient to pay the dividend in full.

Cumulative preference shares. This class of preference share is entitled to have arrears of dividend carried forward to future years when sufficient profits may become available to pay the arrears.

The following example shows the effect of fluctuating profits on non-cumulative preference shares and ordinary shareholders, and also shows the difference between cumulative and non-cumulative preference shares.

Example

Upandown Ltd was formed with a share capital of 10 000 8% non-cumulative preference shares of $1 each and 20 000 ordinary shares of $1 each.

The profits available for dividend were as follows: 2006 $1200; 2007 $900; 2008 $600; 2009 $1000; 2010 $700; 2011 $1300.

The dividends paid to the preference shareholders and the balances of profit available to pay dividends to the ordinary shareholders were as follows:

Year	2006 $	2007 $	2008 $	2009 $	2010 $	2011 $
Profit	1200	900	600	1000	700	1300
Preference dividend paid	800	800	600	800	700	800
Profit left for ordinary shareholders	400	100	nil	200	nil	500
Maximum ordinary dividend payable	2%	0.5%	0%	1%	0%	2.5%

If the preference shares in Upandown Ltd had been cumulative preference shares, the position would have been as follows:

Year	2006 $	2007 $	2008 $	2009 $	2010 $	2011 $
Profit	1200	900	600	1000	700	1300
Preference dividend for year	800	800	600	800	700	800
Arrears of dividend brought forward				200		100
Profit left for ordinary shareholders	400	100	nil	nil	nil	400
Maximum ordinary dividend payable	2%	0.5%	0%	0%	0%	2%

Exercise 1

Seesaw Ltd's share capital consists of 60 000 10% preference shares of $1 and 100 000 ordinary shares of $1. Profits for six years were as follow: 2006 $10 000; 2007 $5000; 2008 $7000; 2009 $4000; 2010 $7000; 2011 $12 000.

Required

Prepare tables showing the dividends payable to the preference shareholders and ordinary shareholders if the preference shares are (a) non-cumulative (b) cumulative.

Preference shares may also be **redeemable** or **non-redeemable**. If they are redeemable this means that the company can approach the preference shareholders and buy back the shares from them. If preference shares are redeemable then they will appear under non-current liabilities in the Statement of Financial Position. If, on the other hand, they are non-redeemable, in other words the company will not buy them back in the future, then they appear in the equity section of the statement, together with the ordinary shares, reserves and retained earnings. The dividends payable on non-redeemable preference shares will be disclosed in the statement of changes in equity, as will their par value. The examiner should indicate in the question if the preference shares are redeemable or otherwise.

Ordinary shares

The ordinary share capital is known as the **equity** of a company. The profit that remains after any dividend has been paid on preference shares belongs to the ordinary shareholders, and the ordinary dividend will be paid out of that. All the reserves (including retained profit) also belong to the ordinary shareholders. When a company is wound up, after all creditors (including the debenture holders) and the preference shareholders have been paid, the assets remaining belong to the ordinary shareholders, and the proceeds from the sale of the assets will be paid to them. The shareholders may receive more than their original investment in the company, but may receive less than they paid for their shares. It all depends upon the circumstances in which the company is wound up.

23.10 Shares issued at a premium

Shares have a **nominal (or par) value**. For example, shares of $1 have a nominal value of $1, and shares of $0.50 have a nominal value of $0.50. The directors of a company may issue shares at a price exceeding their nominal value if they believe that the issue will attract a lot of subscribers, or the shares are already being bought and sold on the Stock Exchange at a price higher than the nominal value. When shares are issued at a price above their nominal value they are said to be **issued at a premium**. If shares with a nominal value of $1 are issued at, say, $1.25 the premium on each share is $0.25. The premium on each share must be credited to a special account called Share Premium account. Only the nominal value of $1 may be credited to the Share Capital account. The balances on the Share Capital account and the Share Premium account are shown separately in the Statement of Financial Position.

Example

The directors of The Very Good Company Ltd issued 60 000 Ordinary Shares of $1 at $1.30 per share. All the shares were subscribed for and issued.

Required

Prepare journal entries to record the issue of the shares.

Answer

	$	$
Bank	78 000	
Ordinary Share Capital		60 000
Share Premium account		18 000
Issue of 60 000 ordinary shares of $1 at $1.30 per share.		

(The accounting entries for the issue of shares are actually more complex than those shown in this journal entry. The CIE syllabus does not require candidates to know the full accounting entries, and the journal entry given here is sufficient for the syllabus. The full accounting procedure produces exactly the same result in the end, in any case.)

Exercise 2

The directors of Premium Shares Ltd. offered 100 000 10% preference shares of $1 at $1.20 per share. All the shares were subscribed and paid for.

Required

Prepare journal entries to record the issue of the preference shares.

23.11 Reserves

There are two classes of reserves: **revenue reserves** and **capital reserves**. The differences between them are important.

Revenue reserves

Revenue reserves are created by transferring an amount from the profit attributable to the equity holders. The transfer is shown in the statement of changes in equity. Revenue reserves may be created for specific purposes (replacement of non-current assets, or planned expansion of the business) or generally to strengthen the financial position of the company. The creation of general reserves reduces the amount of profit available to pay dividends. If the reserves are later considered by the directors to be excessive and no longer required, they may be credited back to Retained earnings and become available for the payment of dividend. Again this adjustment is made in the statement of changes in equity.

Retained earnings shown in the Statement of Financial Position is one of the revenue reserves.

Capital Reserves

Capital reserves are *not normally* created by transferring profit from the Income Statement. They represent gains that arise from particular circumstances and usually represent gains which have not yet been realised. Capital reserves are part of the capital structure of a company; they may never be credited back to the Income Statement and can never be used to pay cash dividends to shareholders.

The most common capital reserves, and ones with which you should become familiar, are given below.

Share Premium account. This has already been explained in §23.10.

The Companies Act 1985 permits the Share Premium account to be used for certain specific purposes only:

- to pay up unissued shares to existing ordinary shareholders as fully paid-up bonus shares (these are dealt with in chapter 25)
- to write off preliminary expenses (i.e. expenses incurred in the formation of the company)
- to write off expenses incurred in the issue of shares or debentures of the company (this includes any commission payable on the issues)
- to provide any commission payable on the redemption of shares and debentures
- to provide for any premium payable on the redemption of debentures.

(These topics are covered later, and it will be seen that there are certain important restrictions on the use of the Share Premium account to provide for the premium payable on the redemption of shares.)

Capital Redemption Reserve. This reserve is created by transferring profit from the Income Statement. It will be explained more fully in another chapter, but suffice it to say at this point that this reserve must be created when a company redeems any of its shares otherwise than out of the proceeds of a new issue of shares.

The Capital Redemption Reserve may be used to pay up unissued shares to existing ordinary shareholders as fully paid-up bonus shares.

Revaluation Reserves. A company may revalue its non-current assets and any gain on the revaluation must be credited to a Revaluation Reserve; it is an unrealised profit and may not be credited to the Income Statement.

The Revaluation Reserve may be used to pay up unissued shares to members of the company as bonus shares.

Example

An extract from Premises Ltd's Statement of Financial Position is as follows:

	$
Freehold buildings: cost	60 000
Provision for depreciation	18 000
Net book value	42 000

The buildings have been professionally revalued at $100 000 and the directors have decided to revalue the buildings in the books. The entries in the books are shown by the following journal entry.

Journal	$	$
Freehold buildings at cost	40 000	
Provision for depreciation of freehold buildings	18 000	
Freehold Buildings Revaluation Reserve		58 000

Note. The buildings are being increased from a net book value $42 000 to $100 000, an increase of $58 000. The amount already provided for depreciation must be transferred to the Revaluation Reserve. The Freehold Premises at Cost account will now become Freehold Premises at Valuation account with a debit balance of $100 000.

Exercise 3

Freehold premises are shown in the Statement of Financial Position of a company as follows: Cost $60 000, Net Book Value $42 000. It has been decided to revalue the premises in the books of the company at $80 000.

Required

Prepare the journal entry for the revaluation of the premises in the company's books.

23.12 Calculation of the value of ordinary shares

The value of shares depends upon many factors. Shares are no different from other commodities, the prices of which depend upon supply and demand. The past performance and, more importantly, the future prospects of the company, economic, political and sociological factors at home and abroad may all influence the demand, and the price which has to be paid, for shares on the Stock Exchange. The aspect of share prices is outside the scope of this book.

The value of ordinary shares, however, may be of some importance. It is based on the fact that all the reserves of a company belong to the ordinary shareholders.

Example

The following is the summarised Statement of Financial Position of Appoggiatura Ltd.

	$000
Total assets less current liabilities	1400
Non-current liabilities: 10% debentures 2020	(300)
	1100
Equity	
1 000 000 ordinary shares of $0.50 each	500
Share premium	180
Capital redemption reserve	100
General reserve	200
Retained earnings	120
	1100

Required

Calculate the value of *one* ordinary share.

Answer

The total of the ordinary share capital and reserves = $1 100 000.

The value of one ordinary share is

$$\frac{\$1\,100\,000}{1\,000\,000} = \$1.10.$$

Exercise 4

The following is an extract from the Statement of Financial Position of Gracenote Ltd.

	$
Share capital and reserves	
200 000 ordinary shares of $1	200 000
Long-Term Loan	150 000
Share Premium account	50 000
General Reserve	100 000
Retained earnings	(40 000)
	460 000

Required

Calculate the value of 100 ordinary shares.

23.13 Liabilities, provisions and reserves

The differences between liabilities, provisions and reserves, including how they are created, are important and are summarised here.

Liabilities are amounts owing by a company to trade or other creditors when the amounts can be determined with substantial accuracy. They are created in the books by carrying down credit balances on personal or expense accounts. (See chapter 10.)

Provisions are created to provide for liabilities that are known to exist but of which the amounts cannot be determined with substantial accuracy, for example doubtful debt provisions. Provisions are also made for the depreciation of fixed assets and unrealised profit on stocks of manufactured goods.

Provisions are created by debiting the amounts to the Income Statement and crediting them to Provision accounts.

Reserves are any other amounts that are set aside and not included in the definition of provisions above. They may be created by debiting the appropriation section of a company's Income Statement and crediting reserve accounts. They may also be created by revaluing non-current assets.

23.14 Distributable profits and dividends

Distributable profit

The distributable profits of a company consist of
- its accumulated realised profits which have not already been distributed or used for any other purpose *less*
- its accumulated realised losses which have not previously been written off.

For our purposes, distributable profits are the profits attributable to the equity holders plus any retained earnings brought forward from last year.

Once the directors have decided how much, if any of this should be transferred to reserves the balance can be used to pay dividends to the shareholders.

Dividends

Dividends are the means by which shareholders share in the profits of a company. Directors may not pay dividends to shareholders except out of distributable profits as defined above.

Interim dividends may be paid to shareholders during a company's financial year provided the directors are satisfied that profits for the purpose have been earned and the cash resources of the company are sufficient to pay the dividend.

A final dividend is paid after the end of the financial year. However, the directors may only recommend the amount of dividend to be paid. Before it can be paid, the shareholders must approve payment by passing a resolution at the company's annual general meetings.

Interim dividends paid during the year are shown in the Statement of Changes in Equity. Final dividends approved after the end of the financial year appear as a note to the accounts.

Dividends are usually declared as so many cents per share or as a percentage of the nominal value of the shares.

Example

A company has issued 100 000 ordinary shares of $1 per share.
(a) The directors have recommended a dividend of $0.7 per share. The company will pay a total dividend of 100 000 × $0.07 = $7000.
(b) The directors have recommended a dividend of 5%. The company will pay a total dividend of 5% of $100 000 = $5000 (or $0.05 per share).

Dividend policy. Before paying or recommending dividends, directors of a company must consider the following important matters:
- whether sufficient distributable profits are available
- whether the company's funds will be sufficient to pay the dividend; a cash forecast is needed
- whether there is any need to transfer profits into revenue reserves to strengthen the business
- whether there is a proper balance between dividend growth and capital growth; unless dividends and share values increase,

shareholders' wealth is diminished by inflation in the economy (undistributed profit increases the company's reserves and the Statement of Financial Position value of the ordinary shares)

- a generous dividend policy may increase the value of shares on the Stock Exchange, and a 'mean' policy will have the opposite effect.

23.15 Debentures

A **debenture** is a document given by a company to someone who has lent it money. It states the amount of loan, the annual amount of interest payable, and the dates on which interest is to be paid. It also includes the date on which the loan is to be repaid by the company. Usually, repayment is spread over a period and the dates of commencement and end of the period are included in the description of the debenture.

Debentures are usually secured on all or some of the company's assets. If the company gets into financial difficulties, the assets on which the debentures are secured will be sold and the proceeds used to repay the loans to the debenture holders. This gives the debenture holders an advantage over other creditors of the company.

The difference between shares and debentures

Shares	Debentures
Shareholders are members of the company.	Debenture holders are not members of the company.
Share capital is shown in the Statement of Financial Position under *Equity*.	Debentures are shown in the Statement of Financial Position as *Non-current liabilities* unless they are due for redemption within one year, when they must be shown as *current liabilities*.
Shareholders are the last people to be repaid when a company is would up.	Debenture holders are entitled to be repaid before shareholders when a company is wound up.
Dividends may only be paid if distributable profits are available.	Interest on debentures must be paid even if the company has not made a profit.
Dividends are an appropriation of profit.	Debenture interest is an expense which is shown under Finance costs in the Income Statement.

A worked example

The trial balance of Dillydally Ltd at 30 April 2011 is as follows:

	$	$
Revenue		756 000
Purchases	446 000	
Inventory at 1 May 2010	32 000	
Sales staff salaries and commission	83 000	
Administration salaries	57 000	
Carriage outwards	24 000	
General expenses	45 000	
Interest on debentures	5 000	
Goodwill at cost	100 000	
Freehold premises at cost	240 000	
Provision for depreciation of freehold premises		71 000
Delivery vans at cost	75 000	
Provision for depreciation of delivery vans		30 000
Office machinery at cost	35 000	
Provision for depreciation of office machinery		10 000
Trade receivables	60 000	
Trade payables		42 000
Cash and Cash equivalent	66 000	
100 000 ordinary shares of $1		100 000
80 000 6% non-redeemable preference shares of $1		80 000
10% debentures 2018/2020		100 000
Share Premium account		30 000
General Reserve		40 000
Retained profit brought forward at 1 May 2010		13 900
Interim dividends paid:		
preference	2 400	
ordinary	2 500	
	1 272 900	1 272 900

Further information

1. Inventory at 30 April 2011: $54 000.
2. Depreciation for the year ended 30 April 2011 is to be provided as follows:
   Freehold warehouse $4000
   Freehold offices $12 000
   Delivery vehicles: 20% on cost
   Office machinery: 20% on cost
3. Debenture interest is payable half-yearly on 1 May and 1 November.
4. Provision is to be made for taxation on the year's profits in the sum of $25 000.
5. A transfer of $20 000 is to be made to General Reserve.
6. The directors have recommended a final dividend on the ordinary shares of $0.05 per share.

Required

(a) Prepare Dillydally Ltd's Income Statement for the year ended 30 April 2011 in as much details as possible.

(b) Prepare Dillydally Ltd's Income Statement for the year ended 30 April 2011, in line with IAS 1, classifying the expenses by function.

(c) Prepare Dillydally Ltd's Statement of Changes in Equity for the year ended 30 April 2011.

(d) Prepare Dillydally Ltd's Statement of Financial Position at 30 April 2011 in line with IAS 1.

Answer

(a)

Dillydally Ltd
Income Statement for the year ended 30 April 2011

	$	$	$
Revenue			756 000
Cost of Sales: Inventory at 1 May 2010		32 000	
Purchases		446 000	
		478 000	
Inventory at 30 April 2011		54 000	424 000
Gross profit			332 000
Selling and distribution			
Sales staff salaries and commissions	83 000		
Carriage out	24 000		
Depreciation: warehouse	4 000		
delivery vehicles	15 000	126 000	
Administration			
Administrative salaries	57 000		
General expenses	45 000		
Depreciation: office premises	12 000		
office machinery	7 000	121 000	247 000
Profit from operations			85 000
Debenture interest			10 000
Profit before taxation			75 000
Taxation			25 000
Profit for the year attributable to equity holders			50 000

(b)

Dillydally Ltd
Income Statement
for the year ended 30 April 2011
(In line with IAS 1)

	$
Revenue	756 000
Cost of sales	(424 000)
Gross profit	332 000
Other income	–
Distribution costs	(126 000)
Administrative expenses	(121 000)
Other expenses	–
Profit from Operations	85 000
Finance Costs	(10 000)

	$
Profit before Tax	75 000
Tax	(25 000)
Profit for the year attributable to equity holders	50 000

(c)

Dillydally Ltd
Statement of Changes in Equity for the year ended 30 April 2011

	Share capital $	Share premium $	General reserve $	Retained earnings $	Total equity $
Balance at start of year	180 000	30 000	40 000	13 900	263 900
Profit for the year				50 000	50 000
Dividends paid				(4 900)	(4 900)
Transfer to general reserve			20 000	(20 000)	–
Balance at end of year	180 000	30 000	60 000	39 000	309 000

(d)

Dillydally Ltd
Statement of Financial Position at 30 April 2011
(In line with IAS 1)

	$
Assets	
Non-current assets	
Intangible – Goodwill	100 000
Tangible – Property, plant and equipment	201 000
	301 000
Current assets	
Inventories	54 000
Trade receivables	60 000
Cash and cash equivalents	66 000
	180 000
Total assets	481 000
Equity and Liabilities	
Capital and reserves	
Share capital	180 000
Share premium	30 000
Reserves	60 000
Retained earnings	39 000
	309 000
Non-current liabilities	
Debentures	100 000
Current liabilities	
Trade payables	42 000
Other payables	5 000
Current tax payable	25 000
	72 000
	481 000

Exercise 5

Molly Coddle Ltd's trial balance at 30 April 2011 was as follows:

	$000	$000
Revenue		300
Inventory at 1 May 2010	20	
Purchases	113	
Sales office salaries	57	
Selling expenses	39	
General office wages	32	
Other general expenses	35	
Warehouse machinery at cost	70	
Provision for depreciation of warehouse machinery		30
Office machinery at cost	42	
Provision for depreciation of office machinery		20
Trade receivables	38	
Balance at bank	28	
Trade payables		11
10% debentures 2017/18		5
50 000 ordinary shares of $1		50
10 000 6% Non-redeemable preference shares of $1		10
Share Premium account		15
General Reserve		25
Retained earnings		8
	474	474

Further information
1. Inventory at 30 April 2011 was valued at $31 000.
2. Depreciation for the year is to be provided as followed.
   Warehouse machinery $8000;
   Office machinery $10 000
3. $10 000 is to be transferred to the General Reserve.

Required
(a) Prepare Molly Coddle Ltd's Income Statement for the year ended 30 April 2011 in as much detail as possible.
(b) Prepare Molly Coddle Ltd's Statement of Changes in equity for the year ended 30 April 2011.
(c) Prepare Molly Coddle Ltd's Statement of Financial Position at 30 April 2011 in as much detail as possible.

Exercise 6

The trial balance of Shillyshally Ltd at 30 June 2011 is as follows:

	$000	$000
Freehold premises at cost	1 000	
Provision for depreciation of freehold premises		60
Delivery vehicles at cost	80	
Provision for depreciation of delivery vehicles		28
Office machinery at cost	70	
Provision for depreciation of office machinery		21
Trade receivables	82	
Trade payables		33
Balance at bank	67	
12% debentures 2019/20		100
800 000 ordinary shares of $1		800
100 000 8% Non-redeemable preference shares of $1		100
General Reserve		50
Retained earnings		7
Revenue		1 000
Inventory at 30 June 2010	46	
Purchases	630	
Sales staff salaries	79	
Administration wages	36	
Delivery vehicle expenses	38	
Advertising	34	
Office expenses	24	
Debenture interest paid	6	
Interim dividends paid: preference	4	
ordinary	3	
	2 199	2 199

Further information
1. Inventory at 30 June 2011 was valued at $38 000.
2. Account is to be taken of the following at 30 June 2011.
   Accrued expenses: delivery vehicle expenses $2000
   Office expenses $3000
3. Freehold premises were revalued to $1 200 000 at 30 June 2011.
4. Depreciation is to be provided as follows for the year ended 30 June 2011.
   Delivery vehicles: 25% on the reducing balance
   Office machinery: 10% on cost
5. Debenture interest is payable half-yearly on 1 July and 1 January.
6. Taxation is to be provided for in the sum of $16 000.
7. $50 000 is to be transferred to the General Reserve.
8. The directors have recommended a final dividend of 3% on the ordinary shares.

Required

(a) Prepare Shillyshally Ltd's Statement of Financial Position for the year ended 30 June 2011.
(b) Prepare Shillyshally Ltd's Statement of Changes in Equity for the year ended 30 June 2011.
(c) Prepare Shillyshally Ltd's Income Statement for the year ended 30 June 2011.

HINTS

- Learn the differences between ordinary shares and preference shares.
- Learn the differences between liabilities, provisions and reserves.
- Learn the differences between capital reserves and revenue reserves.
- Learn the differences between debentures and shares.
- Remember that only the nominal account of the share capital is credited to the Share Capital account. Any premium on the issue of shares must be credited to the Share Premium account.
- Learn the restrictions on the uses of the Share Premium, Revaluation Reserve and the Capital Redemption Reserve.
- Learn how to record the revaluation of non-current assets and how to calculate the amount of the Revaluation Reserve.
- Remember that all the reserves of a company belong to the ordinary shareholders.
- Learn the differences between partnerships and limited companies.
- Prepare company Income Statements and Statements of Financial Position in the forms required by the Companies Act as far as possible. This is what the examiner means when he asks for them to be prepared 'in good form'.

MULTIPLE-CHOICE QUESTIONS

1. A company has ordinary shares of $0.05 each. It has issued 70 000 shares. The directors recommend a dividend of $0.06 per share. What will be the amount of the dividend?
   A. $2100   **B.** $3000   **C.** $4200   **D.** $6000

2. A company has 100 000 ordinary shares of $1 each. It also has $100 000 6% debentures. The profit for the year before finance costs is $20 000. The directors propose to transfer $10 000 to the general reserve.
   What is the maximum dividend per share that can be paid on the ordinary shares?
   A. $0.02   **B.** $0.04   **C.** $0.05   **D.** $0.07

3. A company's year end is 31 December 2011. The following information relates to dividends paid and proposed:
   6 April 2011 – paid final dividend of $7000 in respect of the year ended 31 December 2010.
   1 October 2011 – paid interim dividend $5000 in respect of the year ended 31 December 2011.

   1 January 2012 – the directors proposed a final dividend of $8000 in respect of the year ended 31 December 2011.
   How much will be included as dividends in the statement of changes in equity for the year ended 31 December 2011?
   A. $ 5 000   **B.** $12 000
   C. $15 000   **D.** $22 000

4. The following is a company's summarised Statement of Financial Position.

	$000
Share capital and reserves	
1 200 000 ordinary shares of $0.50	600
Long-term loan	100
Share premium	200
General Reserve	80
Retained earnings	20
	1000

What is the value of each ordinary share?

A. $0.75   **B**. $1.50   **C**. $0.83   **D**. $1.67

5. The following are extracts from a company's Statement of Financial Position.

| Non-current: | Freehold premises at cost $400 000 |
| | Provision for depreciation of freehold premises $160 000 |

Equity	$
Ordinary shares of $1	500 000
Long-Term Loan	100 000
Share premium	80 000
Retained earnings	40 000
	720 000

It has been decided to revalue the freehold premises to $500 000.

What will be the Statement of Financial Position value of the ordinary shares after the revaluation?

A. $1.44   **B**. $1.64   **C**. $1.76   **D**. $1.96

6. Ali holds 500 ordinary shares of $0.50 in Riski Ltd. He has paid in full the amount of $0.35 called up on each share. The company is unable to pay its creditors.

What is the maximum amount that Ali can now be required to pay on his shares?

A. $75   **B**. $250   **C**. $325   **D**. $500

7. Which of the following will **not** be shown as equity in the Statement of Financial Position?

A. debentures

B. retained earnings

C. revaluation reserve

D. share premium

8. Which is the safest form of investment in a limited company?

A. long-term debentures

B. ordinary shares

C. preference shares

D. short-term debentures

9. A shareholder sold 1000 ordinary shares of $1 for $1500. What effect will this have on the share capital of the company?

A. It will decrease by $1000.

B. It will decrease by $1500.

C. It will increase by $1500.

D. It will remain unchanged.

ADDITIONAL EXERCISES

1. The following is the summarised Statement of Financial Position of Bracket & Racket Ltd, a limited company wholly owned by its two shareholders, Bracket and Racket.

Statement of Financial Position as at 31 March 2011			
	$000	$000	$000
Non-current assets at net book value			
Buildings			250
Fixtures and fittings			100
			350
Current assets			
Inventory		1540	
Trade receivables		820	
Cash		3	2363
Current liabilities			
Trade payables		1210	
Accruals		192	
Bank		203	1605
			758
			1108
Share capital: Ordinary shares			25

	$000	$000	$000
Retained earnings			910
Loan accounts:			
Bracket		104	
Racket		69	173
			1108

The company accountant resigned at the beginning of April 2011 and proper records were not kept for the six-month period 1 April to 30 September 2011.

The following information is available for that six-months period.

	$000
Payments by cheque for purchases	1996
Payments by cheque for expenses	823
Interest changed on overdraft	20
Cash and cheques banked	2784

Included in the amount banked was $53 000 for the sale of an unused building, book value $70 000.

Prior to banking the takings,
(i) $25 000 was used to pay wages for the six months;
(ii) Bracket and Racket each reduced their loans to the firm by $45 000.

Depreciation on all non-current assets which remain in the company's books at the end of an accounting period is calculated at 25% per annum on the net book value.

At 30 September 2011 the following figures were available.

	$000
Trade payables	510
Accruals	103
Trade receivables	420
Inventory	704
Cash	8
Bank overdraft	195
Unpresented cheques	63

Doubtful debts are estimated at 5% at 30 September 2011 and a provision for doubtful debts at that date is to be created.

Required

(a) An Income Statement for Bracket and Racket Ltd for the six months ended 30 September 2011.

(b) A Statement of Financial Position for Bracket and Racket Ltd at 30 September 2011.

2. Pecnut Ltd's trial balance at 31 March 2011 was as follows:

	$000	$000
Issued share capital: ordinary shares of $1 each		600
General Reserve		120
10% debentures 2017/2018		360
Freehold buildings at cost	1500	

	$000	$000
Provision for depreciation of freehold buildings		180
Motor vehicles at cost	246	
Provision for depreciation of motor vehicles		162
Trade receivables	96	
Bank balance		51
Inventory at 1 April 2010	85	
Trade payables		60
Retained earnings		69
Sales		2683
Purchases	1152	
Selling and distribution	540	
Administration	648	
Debenture interest	18	
	4285	4285

Further information
1. Inventory at 31 March 2011: $105 000.
2. The freehold buildings are to be revalued to $2 000 000 at 31 March 2011.
3. The motor vehicles are to be depreciated at the rate of 25% using the reducing balance method.
4. $10 000 is to be transferred to General Reserve.
5. The directors have recommended a dividend of $0.25 per share.

Required

(a) Prepare Pecnut Ltd's Income Statement for the year ended 31 March 2011.
(b) Prepare the Statement of Financial Position as at 31 March 2011.
(c) Companies should prepare their annual accounts on the basis that they are going concerns. Explain what this means and how their annual accounts will be affected if they are not going concerns.

 # Statements of Cash Flows

In this chapter you will learn:

- what a statement of cash flows is and why it is an important addition to the annual financial statements of a business
- how and why companies are required to include a statement of cash flows in their annual accounts
- how to prepare a statement of cash flows in line with IAS 7
- how to prepare a statement of financial position with the aid of a statement of cash flow
- how to prepare a statement of cash flows for sole traders and partnerships.

24.1 What is a statement of cash flows?

A statement of cash flows is one that lists the cash flows of a business over a period of time, usually the same period as that covered by the Income Statement.

A cash flow is any increase or decrease in cash in a business. **Cash** includes cash in hand and deposits repayable on demand, less overdrafts that are repayable on demand. For our purpose, **deposits** and **overdrafts** will generally be balances at, and overdrafts with, banks. The words **on demand** mean either immediately (e.g. current accounts) or within 24 hours of giving notice of repayment.

24.2 Why statements of cash flows are important?

While it is necessary to know how much profit a business has made, profit is not cash in the bank. The business does not pay its creditors from the balance on the retained earnings account. Creditors are paid from the money the business has in its bank account. No business has ever been forced to close down by its creditors because it made an operating loss. But a business can be forced to close down because it has insufficient money in its bank account to pay its debts when they fall due. The amount by which the ready

money in a business exceeds its immediate liabilities is its **liquidity**. There is a big difference between profit and liquidity. A business may make a large profit but finish up with less money in its bank account at the end of its year than it started with!

Over a period of time a business needs to generate **cash inflows** that at least match its **cash outflows**.

Cash inflows include:

- money received from the sale of shares or capital put into the business by the owners
- money received from the sale of surplus non-current assets
- payments from its customers for goods received
- interest received on deposits with banks and other companies.

Cash outflows include:

- payment of creditors (as already mentioned) and the running costs of carrying on business (e.g. wages etc.)
- renewal of, and additions to, non-current assets
- interest on loans and debentures
- payment of tax on profits (companies)
- costs involved in the growth of the business (expansion and development)
- dividends payable to shareholders, or drawings of sole traders and partners
- repayment of loans or redemption of shares by the company.

24.3 Statements of cash flows and limited companies

The International Accounting Standard which covers the structure and layout of the statement of cash flows for a limited company is **IAS 7.** This statement requires that limited companies produce a statement of cash flows as part of the annual financial statements.

The statement provides guidelines for the format of Statements of Cash Flows. The statement is divided into three categories:

1. **Operating activities** – the main revenue generating activities of the business, together with the payment of interest and tax.
2. **Investing activities** – the acquisition and disposal of long-term assets and other investing activities.
3. **Financing activities** – receipts from the issue of new shares, payments for the redemption of shares and changes in long-term borrowings.

At the end of the statement the net increase in cash and cash equivalents is shown, both at the start and end of the period under review. For this purpose, cash is defined as: cash on hand and bank current accounts.

Cash equivalents are short-term investments that can easily be converted into cash, such as money held in a term deposit account that can be withdrawn within three months from the date of deposit. Bank overdrafts — usually repayable on demand — are also included as part of the cash and cash equivalents.

Format of the Statement

1. **Operating activities**
   The cash flow from operating activities is calculated as:
   - Profit from operations (profit before deduction of tax and interest)
   - Add: Depreciation charge for the year
   - Add: Loss on sale of non-current assets (or deduct gain on sale of non-current assets).
   - Add or deduct changes in inventories, trade and other receivables or payables
   - Less: Interest paid
   - Less: Taxes paid on income (usually corporation tax)

2. **Investing activities**
   This is calculated by including:
   - Inflows from:
     - proceeds from sale of non-current assets, both tangible and intangible, together with other long-term non-current assets.
   - Outflows from:
     - cash used to purchase non-current assets, both tangible and intangible, together with other long-term non-current assets.
   - Interest received
   - Dividends received

3. **Financing activities**
   This is calculated by including:
   - Inflows from:
     - cash received from the issue of share capital
     - raising or increasing loans
   - Outflows from:
     - repayment of share capital
     - repayment of loans and finance lease liabilities.
   - Dividends paid

Exhibit Co Ltd
*Statement of Cash Flows for the year ended ....

Cash flows from operating activities

	$	$
Profit from operations (before tax and interest)		50 000
Adjustments for:		
Depreciation charge for the year		12 000
Increase in inventories		(3 000)
Decrease in trade receivables		2 000
Increase in trade payables		4 000
Cash (used in)/from operations		65 000
Interest paid (during the year)		(5 000)
Tax paid (during the year)		(8 000)
Net cash (used in)/from operating activities		52 000
Cash flows from investing activities:		
Purchase of non-current assets	(20 000)	
Proceeds from the sale of non-current assets	1 000	
Interest received	2 000	
Dividends received	500	
Net cash (used in)/from investing activities		(16 500)
Cash flows from financing activities:		
Proceeds from issue of share capital	80 000	
(this would include both the share and share premium amounts)		
Repayment of long-term borrowings	(30 000)	
Dividends paid	(4 000)	
Net cash (used in)/from financing activities		46 000
Net increase/(decrease) in cash and cash equivalents		81 500
Cash and cash equivalents at the beginning of the year		10 000
Cash and cash equivalents at the end of the year		91 500

*Note also that no dates are included. This would **not** be the case in practice where the actual date of the year end and previous year, say **31 December**, would be stated.

IAS 7 allows some flexibility in the way some information can be shown. For example, cash flows from interest and dividends received and paid can be shown as above or in the first section relating to cash flows from operating activities. In the examination, either would be acceptable.

The above may seem a lot to understand and remember at this stage, but examples and practice with the exercises that follow should take away a lot of the pain and suffering with this topic — a favourite with examiners.

24.4 How to prepare a statement of cash flows from Statements of Financial Position

Statements of cash flows are prepared by comparing the amounts for items in the latest Statement of Financial Position with the amounts for the same items in the previous year's Statement of Financial Position. Some additional calculations for non-current asset details will be required. The following example, with explanatory notes, demonstrates the procedure.

Example

Hannibal Ltd's Statements of Financial Position at 30 June 2010 and 2011 and an extract from its Income Statement for the year ended 30 June 2011 are shown on page 177.

Further information
1. During the year ended 30 June 2011 the following transactions took place.
   (i) Plant and machinery which had cost $105 000, and on which depreciation of $85 000 had been provided, was sold for $24 000.
   (ii) Motor vehicles which had cost $60 000, and which had a net book value of $15 000 at the date of sale, were sold for $28 000.
   (iii) A bonus issue of shares was made on the basis of one bonus share for every two ordinary shares already held. This was done by using part of the balance on the Share Premium account.
   (iv) Following the bonus issue in (iii), the company issued a further 300 000 ordinary shares at $1.50 per share.
   (v) $50 000 of 10% debentures 2015/2016 were issued on 1 July 2010.
   (vi) The directors transferred $100 000 to the general reserve from the profit for the year.
2. There had been no additions to freehold property in the year to 30 June 2011.

Required

Prepare a statement of cash flows for the year ended 30 June 2011.

Statements of Financial Position

Non-current assets	as at 30 June 2010 $000 Cost	$000 Depn	$000 NBV	as at 30 June 2011 $000 Cost or valuation	$000 Depn	$000 NBV
Freehold property	900	300	600	1000	–	1000
Plant and machinery	700	300	400	800	400	400
Motor vehicles	450	180	270	500	200	300
	2050	780	1270	2300	600	1700
Current assets						
Inventories		200			300	
Trade receivables		260			215	
Short-term investments		500			800	
Cash and cash equivalents		98			200	
		1058			1515	
Current Liabilities						
Trade payables	336			163		
Taxation	90			86		
		426			249	
Net current assets			632			1266
			1902			2966
Non-current liabilities						
10% debentures 2015/2016			150			200
			1752			2766
Equity						
Ordinary shares of $1			600			1200
Share premium			350			200
Freehold Property Revaluation Reserve			–			400
General Reserve			700			800
Retained earnings			102			166
			1752			2766

Income Statement (extract)
for the year ended 30 June 2011

	$000
PROFIT FROM OPERATIONS	420
Finance costs (debenture interest)	(20)
PROFIT BEFORE TAX	400
Tax	(80)
PROFIT FOR THE YEAR ATTRIBUTABLE TO EQUITY HOLDERS	320

Note: During the year the company paid dividends of $156 000. This would be included in the statement of changes in equity, not shown here.

Answer
Step 1. Prepare workings: the following information will be required but will probably not be given in a question.

- Non-current assets: cash paid for new assets or received from the sale of old assets; amounts provided for depreciation in the Income Statement; profits and losses on the disposal of non-current assets.
- Dividends, interest and taxation paid.

This information is best discovered by preparing rough 'T' accounts as workings and calculating the missing information as balancing figures.

Plant and machinery (P & M) A/c			
Bal b/f	700	Disposal	105
Additions			
(bal. fig.)	205	Bal c/f	800
	905		905

Provn for depn P & M A/c			
Disposal	85	Bal b/f	300
Bal c/f	400	Charge for year (bal. fig.)	185
	485		485

Disposal of P & M A/c			
Cost	105	Depn.	85
Profit	4	Cash	24
	109		109

Motor vehicles (MV) A/c			
Bal b/f	450	Disposal	60
Additions			
(bal. fig.)	110	Bal c/f	500
	560		560

Provn for depn. MV A/c			
Disposal	45	Bal b/f	180
Bal c/f	200	Charge for year (bal. fig.)	65
	245		245

Disposal of MV A/c			
Cost	60	Depn	45
Profit	13	Cash	28
	73		73

The creation of the Freehold Property Revaluation Reserve shows that the increase in the freehold property was entirely due to revaluation, and no cash flow was involved.

Taxation			
Paid (bal. fig.)	84	Bal b/f	90
Bal c/f	86	Inc St	80
	170		170

Step 2 Prepare a Statement of Cash Flows for the year ended 30 June 2011.

Part 1 – Cash Flows from operating activities. Start with the profit from operations before tax and interest. Then adjust for:

Non-cash items in the income statement. That is those items which do not involve the movement of any cash, such as depreciation and profits or losses on the disposal of non-current assets. These figures will come from the workings above.

- Increases or decreases in inventories, trade receivables and trade payables. This is done by comparing the figures for each on the two statements of financial position. Remember that if the inventory has increased between the two years then the company must have spent cash acquiring the extra stock. This means that it will have a negative effect on the cash flow of the business and will appear in brackets in the statement. Likewise, if trade receivables have increased between the two years this means that the company has not received cash in from its customers, This, too will have a negative effect on the cash flow of the company and will appear in brackets in the statement. If, on the other hand the trade payables have increased between the years then the company will have saved its cash by not paying its suppliers. In this case the change will not appear in brackets in the statement, as the cash flow will have benefited from this action. If these situations are reversed then treat them the opposite way round in the statement.
- Interest payments made during the year. Take care as it may be that a loan was taken out part way through the year. Alternatively, perhaps not all the interest will have been paid

during the year. Check the closing statement of financial position to see if there is any accrual in the current liabilities.
- Tax paid during the year. This will come from the workings above.

Part 2 – Identify the items which form the cash flows from investing activities: purchase and sale of non-current assets, interest and dividends received.

Part 3 – identify the cash flows from investing activities: receipts from the issue of shares, cash spent on redemption of shares or repayment of loans and dividends paid.

Hannibal Ltd Statement of Cash Flows for the year ended 30 June 2011		
Cash flow from operating activities		
		$000
Profit from operations (before tax and interest)		420
Adjustments for:		
Depreciation charge for the year (185 + 65)		250
Profit on disposal of non-current asset		(17)
Increase in inventories (200 – 300)		(100)
Decrease in trade receivables (260 – 215)		45
Decrease in trade payables (336 – 163)		(173)
Cash (used in)/from operations		425
Interest paid (during the year)		(20)
Tax paid (during the year) from workings		(84)
Net cash (used in)/from operating activities		321
Cash flows from investing activities:	$000	
Purchase of non-current assets (205 + 110)	(315)	
Proceeds from the sale of non-current assets	52	
Interest received	nil	
Short-term investment	(300)	
Net cash (used in)/from investing activities		(563)
Cash flows from financing activities:		
Proceeds from issue of share capital	450	
Issue of debentures	50	
Dividends paid	(156)	
Net cash (used in)/from financing activities		344
Net increase/(decrease) in cash and cash equivalents		102
Cash and cash equivalents at the beginning of the year		98
Cash and cash equivalents at the end of the year		200

Note: The reconciliation of the figure for Retained earnings at 30 June 2011 is:

	$000
Balance at 30 June 2010	102
Add: profit for the year	320
	422
Less: dividends paid in the year	(156)
Transfer to general reserve	(100)
Balance at 30 June 2011	166

Exercise 1

Contraflo Ltd's Statement of Financial Position at 31 December 2010 and 2011 and an extract from its

Income Statement for the year ended 31 December 2011 were as follows:

Statement of Financial Position

	as at 31 December 2010			as at 31 December 2011		
	$000	$000	$000	$000	$000	$000
Non-current assets	Cost	Depn	NBV	Cost	Depn	NBV
Freehold property	400	–	400	364	–	364
Plant and machinery	80	35	45	150	39	111
Motor vehicles	120	90	30	160	95	65
	600	125	475	674	134	540
Current assets						
Inventory		100			85	
Trade receivables		40			52	
Cash and cash equivalents		55			36	
		195			173	
Current liabilities						
Trade payables	60			73		
Taxation	39			43		
		99			116	
Net current assets			96			57
			571			577
Non-current liabilities						
10% debentures 2017/2018			100			70
			471			527
Equity						
Ordinary shares of $1			250			300
Share Premium			20			25
General Reserve			100			100
Retained earnings			101			102
			471			527

Income Statement (extract) for the year ended 31 December 2010

	$000
Profit from operation	94
Interest paid	(7)
	87
Tax	(40)
Profit attributable to equity holders	47

Note. During the year the company paid dividends of $46 000.

Further information

During the year ended 31 December 2011 the following transactions took place.

1. Freehold buildings which had cost $36 000 were sold for $50 000. The premises had not been depreciated.

2. Plant and machinery which had cost $20 000, and on which depreciation of $16 000 had been provided, was sold for $1000. New plant and machinery had been purchased.

3. Motor vehicles which had cost $30 000, and which had a net book value of $5000 at the date of sale, were sold for $4000. New motor vehicles had been purchased.

4. 50 000 ordinary shares of $1 each were issued at a premium of $0.10 per share on 1 July 2011.

5. $30 000 of 10% debentures 2017/2018 were redeemed at par on 1 January 2011.

Required

Prepare a statement of cash flows for the year ended 31 December 2011.

24.5 How to prepare a Statement of Financial Position from a Statement of Cash Flows

Examination questions sometimes require Statement of Financial Position to be prepared from a statement of cash flows and the technique for doing this is shown in the next example.

Example 1

Hengist Ltd's Statement of Financial Position at 31 October 2010 was as follows:

Non-current assets	At cost $000	Depn $000	Net Book Value $000
Freehold premises	900	240	660
Plant and machinery	750	220	530
	1650	460	1190
Current assets			
Inventory		95	
Trade Receivables		77	
Cash and cash equivalents		40	
		212	
Current liabilities			
Trade payables	44		
Tax	26	70	142
			1332
Non-current liabilities			
10% debenture stock 2016/2017			200
			1132
Equity			
Share capital and reserves			
Ordinary shares of $1			830
Share premium			110
General Reserve			100
Retained earnings			92
			1132

An extract from Hengist Ltd's Income Statement for the year ended 31 October 2011 and the statement of cash flows for the year as follows:

Extract from Hengist Ltd's Income Statement for the year ended 31 October 2011	
	$000
Profit from operations	214
Finance costs	(15)
Profit before tax	199
Tax	(30)
Profit for the year attributable to equity holders	169

Note: The directors decided to transfer $100 000 to the General Reserve.

Hengist Ltd Statement of Cash Flows for the year ended 31 October 2011	
Cash flows from operating activities	
	$000
Profit from operations (before tax and interest)	214
Adjustments for:	
Depreciation charge for the year:	
Plant & machinery	50
Property	10
Profit on sale on non-current assets	(14)
Decrease in inventories	15
Increase in trade receivables	(18)
Decrease in trade payables	(6)
Cash (used in)/from operations	251
Interest paid (during the year)	(15)
Tax paid	(26)
Net cash (used in)/from operating activities	210
Cash flows from investing activities:	$000
Purchase of non-current assets (Plant)	(130)
Proceeds from the sale of Plant	50
Net cash (used in)/from investing activities	(80)
Cash flows from financing activities:	
Proceeds from issue of share capital	200
Repayment of debentures	(50)
Dividends paid	(56)
Net cash (used in)/from financing activities	94
Net increase/(decrease) in cash and cash equivalents	224
Cash and cash equivalents at the beginning of the year	40
Cash and cash equivalents at the end of the year	264

Note: 150 000 ordinary shares were issued during the year.

Note. The plant and machinery which was sold had cost $96 000.

Required

Prepare Hengist Ltd's Statement of Financial Position at 31 October 2011 in as much detail as possible.

Answer

Hengist Ltd Statement of Financial Position at 31 October 2011			
	Cost $000	Depn $000	NBV $000
Non-current assets			
Freehold premises	900	250	650
Plant & machinery	784	210	574
	1684	460	1224
Current Assets			
Inventory (95 – 15)		80	
Trade receivables (77 + 18)		95	
Cash and cash equivalents		264	
		439	
Current liabilities			
Trade payables (44 – 6)	38		
Tax	30	68	371

	Cost $000	Depn $000	NBV $000
Non-current liability			
10% Debentures 2016/2017			(150)
			1445
Equity			
Share capital (830 + 150)			980
Share premium (110 + 50)			160
General reserve (100 + 100)			200
Retained earnings			105
			1445
Workings			
Calculation of the figure for retained earnings			$000
Retained earnings at start of year			92
Profit for the year			169
			261
Transfer to reserves			(100)
Dividends paid			(56)
Retained earnings at 31 October 2011			105

Workings

Plant and machinery at cost				Depn plant and machinery						Disposal		
B/f	750	Disposal	96	Disposal	60	b/f	220	Cost	96	D'epn (bal. fig.)	60
Cash	130	c/d (bal. fig.)	784	c/d (bal. fig.)	210	Inc. St.	50	Profit	14	Cash	50
	880		880		270		270		110		110

Exercise 2

Horsa Ltd's Statement of Financial Position at 31 July 2010 was as follows:

Non-current assets

	At cost $000	Depn $000	Net Book Value $000
Freehold premises	300	130	170
Plant and machinery	125	75	50
Current assets			220
Inventory		36	
Trade receivables		79	
Cash and cash equivalents		42	
		157	
Current liabilities			
Trade payables	43		
Tax	18	61	96
			316
Non-current liabilities			
10% debenture stock 2017/2018			50
			266
Equity			
Ordinary shares of $1			150
Share Premium			20
General Reserve			40
Retained earnings			56
			266

An extract from Horsa Ltd's Income Statement for the year ended 31 July 2011 and the Statements of Cash Flows for that year are as follows:

Horsa Ltd's Extract from the Income Statement for the year ended 31 July 2011	
	$000
Profit from operations	69
Finance costs	(5)
Profit before tax	64
Tax	(25)
Profit for the year attributable to equity holders	39

Note: The directors decided to transfer $30 000 to the General Reserve.

Horsa Ltd.
Statement of Cash Flows for the year ended 31 October 2011

Cash flows from operating activities

	$000
Profit from operations (before tax and interest)	69
Adjustments for:	
Depreciation charge for the year	
– Plant & machinery	60
– Freehold premises	12
Loss on sale on non-current assets (cost $30 000)	7
Increase in inventories	(4)
Increase in trade receivables	(19)
Increase in trade payables	6
Cash (used in)/from operations	131
Interest paid (during the year)	(5)
Tax paid	(18)
Net cash (used in)/from operating activities	108

Cash flows from investing activities: ($000)

Purchase of non-current assets (Plant)	(48)
Proceeds from the sale of Plant	5
Net cash (used in)/from investing activities	(43)

Cash flows from financing activities:

Proceeds from issue of 20 000 shares of $1 each	40
Repayment of debentures	(20)
Dividends paid	(15)
Net cash (used in)/from financing activities	5
Net increase/(decrease) in cash and cash equivalents	70
Cash and cash equivalents at the beginning of the year	42
Cash and cash equivalents at the end of the year	112

Required

Prepare Horsa Ltd's Statement of Financial Position at 31 July 2011 in as much detail as possible.

24.6 Statements of Cash Flows for unincorporated businesses

Although sole traders and partnerships do not have to prepare statements of cash flows, they may well find the statements useful. Unlike the statements that must be prepared for companies, they may be prepared in any format, and the 'profit from operations' is the **net** profit for the year.

Example

Jaydee, a sole trader presents you with the following financial information in respect of his financial accounts for the year ended 31 December 2011 and 2010:

Statements of Financial Position at

	31 Dec 2010 $	31 Dec 2011 $
Assets		
Non-current assets		
Plant & machinery at cost	25 000	35 000
Depreciation	(12 000)	(14 000)
	13 000	21 000
Current assets		
Inventories	6 000	8 000
Trade receivables	7 000	10 000
Cash and cash equivalents	500	–
	13 500	18 000
Total Assets	26 500	39 000
Equity and liabilities		
Capital at start	15 000	10 000
Net profit	10 000	20 000
Drawings	(5 000)	(4 000)
	10 000	26 000
Non-current liabilities		
Long-term loan	10 000	8 000
Current liabilities		
Trade payables	6 500	4 000
Bank overdraft	–	1 000
	6 500	5 000
	26 500	39 000

Income statement (extract) for the year ended 31 December 2011

	$
Net profit before interest	21 000
Interest paid	(1 000)
Net profit for the year	20 000

Jaydee tells you that during the year he scrapped some plant which had cost $3000 and had a net book value of $500.

He cannot understand why he has an overdraft at 31 December 2011, despite making a profit for the year and asks for your help to explain the situation.

To help him the accountant prepares the following statement:

Jaydee Reconciliation of profit from operations to net cash flow from operating activities for the year ended 31 October 2011	
	$
Net profit for the year (profit from operations)	21 000
Adjustments for:	
Depreciation charge for the year	4 500
Loss on sale on non-current assets	500
Increase in inventories	(2 000)
Increase in trade receivables	(3 000)
Decrease in trade payables	(2 500)
Cash (used in)/from operations	18 500
Interest paid (during the year)	(1 000)
Net cash (used in)/from operating activities	17 500

Note the differences here. As Jaydee is a sole trader, it is perfectly acceptable to prepare a reconciliation statement of profit from operations (trading) to net cash flow from operations. The opening position is simply referred to as net profit for the year. As Jaydee is a sole trader all the profit belongs to him. There is also no adjustment for tax, as Jaydee will pay this personally. If he pays it from the business it will be included as part of his drawings figure.

The calculation of loss on the sale of the plant and machinery and the purchase of new machinery is as follows:

Plant and Machinery at cost account			
	$		$
Opening balance	25 000	Closing balance	35 000
Bank – purchases	13 000	Asset disposal	3 000
	38 000		38 000

Plant and Machinery Accumulated depreciation account			
	$		$
Asset disposal account	2 500	Opening balance	12 000
Closing balance	14 000	Charge for the year	4 500
	16 500		16 500

Asset disposal account			
	$		$
Cost of plant scrapped	3 000	Depreciation	2 500
		Loss on disposal	500
	3 000		3 000

Jaydee Statement of Cash Flows for the year ended 31 December 2011		
	$	$
Net cash (used in)/from operating activities		17 500
Cash flows from investing activities:		
Purchase of non-current assets (Plant)	(13 000)	
Net cash (used in)/from investing activities		(13 000)
Cash flows from financing activities:		
Repayment of loan	(2 000)	
Drawings	(4 000)	
Net cash (used in)/from financing activities		(6 000)
Net increase/(decrease) in cash and cash equivalents		(1 500)
Cash and cash equivalents at the beginning of the year		500
Cash and cash equivalents at the end of the year		(1 000)

Again, notice the differences from the statement for a limited company. As Jaydee is a sole trader, then no dividends are paid. Instead, he will take drawings from the business.

His accountant is now able to advise Jaydee why he has a bank overdraft at the end of the year, even though he has made a profit. It is because:

- He has purchased new plant and machinery
- He has repaid part of his loan
- He has increased his inventory. He has also allowed his trade payables to increase and reduced his trade receivables.
- All of these have led to cash leaving the business and resulted in the bank becoming overdrawn at 31 December 2011, despite Jaydee making a profit for the year.

Exercise

Janine, a sole trader presents you with the following financial information in respect of her financial accounts for the year ended 31 October 2011 and 2010:

Statements of Financial Position at

	31 Oct 2010			31 Oct 2011		
Assets	$000			$000		
Non-current assets	Cost	Depn	NBV	Cost	Depn	NBV
Freehold land			30			60
Plant & machinery at cost	39	21	18	55	25	30
	39	21	48	55	25	90
Current assets						
Inventories			11			16
Trade receivables			15			12
Cash and cash equivalents			3			–
			29			28
Total Assets			77			118
Equity and liabilities						
Capital at start			50			61
Capital introduced			–			10
			52			71
Net profit			20			50
Drawings			(9)			(21)
			61			100
Non-current liabilities						
Long-term loan			–			8
Current liabilities						
Trade payables			16			8
Bank overdraft			–			2
			16			10
			77			118

Income statement (extract) for the year ended 31 October 2011

	$
Net profit	25
Depreciation of Plant & machinery	(5)
Profit on disposal of Plant	1
Profit on revaluation of land	30
Interest paid	(1)
Net profit for the year	50

Janine tells you that during the year she scrapped some plant which had cost $6000.

She cannot understand why she has an overdraft at the 31 October 2011, despite making a profit for the year and asks for your help to explain the situation.

Required

Prepare a Statement of Cash Flows for Janine for the year ended 31 October 2011. Identify why she has made a profit for the year, yet her bank account is overdrawn.

24.7 Advantages of producing a Statement of Cash Flows

The statement of cash flows is an extremely useful addition to the annual accounts. The advantages to a business producing one are:

- It shows the movement of cash for the year. It also shows the business' ability to generate cash from its trading activities. The ability to generate cash is vital to the future survival of the business.
- Cash flow is easier for a non-accounting person to understand. We all look closely at our cash and bank position! This means it is easier to understand than an income statement and statement of financial position which rely on technical knowledge and are prepared using accounting conventions which do not apply to cash.
- Creditors are more interested in a business' ability to pay them than how much profit it makes. Remember, cash and profit are different things.
- It provides useful information as a backup to the income statement and statement of financial position.

The only real disadvantage of producing a statement is that it ignores the accruals and matching concepts. This means that the cash coming in or going out may relate to a previous accounting period. However, the advantages of producing a statement of cash flows are far more beneficial to the business. It allows another element to assess the overall performance of the firm.

HINTS

- Memorise the format in which Statements of Cash Flows should be prepared for companies, and the items which should be included under each heading.
- Tick each item in the question as you give effect to it, and show your workings.
- All non-cash items in the Income Statement must be adjusted in the reconciliation of operating profit to net cash flow from operating activities.
- Make sure you understand the effect of changes in inventory, trade receivables and trade payables on cash flow.
- Be prepared to draft a Statement of Cash Flows for a sole trader or a partnership.
- Get as much practice as you can at preparing Statement of Cash Flows.
- Good examination technique starts to earn marks as quickly as possible. Prepare the Statement of Cash Flows in outline, leaving plenty of space between the headings for details to be inserted. Start by filling in the easy items such as payments made to purchase non-current assets, proceeds of disposal, issues and redemptions of shares and debentures, movements in inventory, trade receivables and trade payables, etc. Then proceed to the items requiring more detailed calculations.
- If the cash flow in your answer in the examination does not equal the change in the cash balance in the question, do not spend time trying to trace the error(s) if this time is better spent tackling the next question. If you have studied the topic thoroughly before the examination, you will probably have done enough to earn useful marks anyway.

MULTIPLE-CHOICE QUESTIONS

1. An examination of a company's accounts at the end of the year revealed the following:

	$
Cash from operations	50 000
Increase in trade payables	3 000
Decrease in trade receivables	4 000
Increase in inventories	2 000
Depreciation charge for the year	14 000

What was the profit from operations before interest and tax for the year?

A. $31 000   B. $41 000
C. $69 000   D. $73 000

2. The following information has been extracted from the books of a limited company:

	At 31 Dec 2011 $000	At 31 Dec 2010 $000
Profit from operations	97	
Loss on disposal of non-current assets	3	
Inventories	35	41
Trade receivables	47	49
Trade payables	16	20

What was the cash from operating activities for the year?

A. $93 000   B. $97 000
C. $101 000   D. $115 000

3. The following relates to the plant and machinery for a limited company:

	At 31 Dec 2011 $	At 31 Dec 2010 $
Cost	80 000	50 000
Depreciation	(30 000)	(28 000)

During the year plant costing $10 000 was sold at a loss of $2000.
What figure will appear as purchase of non-current assets in statement of cash flows for the year?

A. $20 000   B. $30 000
C. $38 000   D. $40 000

4. The following figures have been extracted from the books of a limited company:

	At 31 Dec 2011 $000	At 31 Dec 2010 $000
Ordinary share capital	200	150
Share premium	30	10
Debenture 2018/2019	50	20
Dividends paid during the year	12	8

What is the cash from financial activities for the year?

A. $28 000   B. $32 000
C. $88 000   D. $92 000

5. The following relates to the motor vehicles for a limited company:

	At 31 Dec 2011	At 31 Dec 2010
	$	$
Cost	75 000	40 000
Depreciation	(35 000)	(25 000)

During the year a car costing $8000 was sold for $3000. This resulted in a loss of $1000.
What figure will appear as depreciation in statement of cash flows for the year?

A. $6 000   B. $10 000
C. $14 000   D. $18 000

6. A company purchased a motor vehicle for $25 000. Settlement was made by a payment of $22 000 and the part exchange of one of the company's own vehicles for $3000. The vehicle given in part exchange had a written down value of $7000, but had a re-sale value of $2000. Which amount should be shown in the statement of cash flows for the acquisition of the vehicle?

A. $22 000   B. $24 000
C. $25 000   D. $29 000

ADDITIONAL EXERCISES

1. The following is Winston plc's Statement of financial position at 31 October 2011.

Statement of Financial Position at 31 October 2011

	Cost	Depn	NBV
	$000	$000	$000
Non-current assets			
Freehold premises	850	90	760
Plant & machinery	1197	469	728
	2047	559	1488
Current Assets			
Inventory		191	
Trade receivables		82	
Cash and cash equivalents		25	
		298	
Current liabilities			
Trade payables	73		
Tax	40	113	185
Non-current liability			
10% Debentures 2010/2015			(300)
			1373
Equity			
Ordinary shares of $1 each		950	
Share premium		150	
General reserve		100	
Retained earnings		173	
		1373	

The company's accountant has prepared a budgeted Statement of cash flows for the year ended 31 October 2012:

Statement of Cash Flows for the year ended 31 October 2012

Cash flows from operating activities	$000
Profit from operations (before tax and interest)	243
Adjustments for:	
Depreciation charge for the year – Plant & machinery	200
Profit on sale of plant	(20)
Decrease in inventories	76
Increase in trade receivables	(15)
Decrease in trade payables	(26)
Interest paid (during the year)	(20)
Tax paid	(40)
Net cash (used in)/from operating activities	398
Cash flows from investing activities:	$000
Purchase of non-current assets (Plant)	(293)
Proceeds from the sale of Plant	41
Net cash (used in)/from investing activities	(252)

Cash flows from financing activities:

Proceeds from issue of 150 000 shares of $1 each	210	
Repayment of debentures	(100)	
Dividends paid	(30)	
Net cash (used in)/from financing activities		80
Net increase/(decrease) in cash and cash equivalents		226
Cash and cash equivalents at the beginning of the year		25
Cash and cash equivalents at the end of the year		251

Additional information:

1. The plant sold during the year had cost $110 000 when purchased.

2. The directors intended to transfer $80 000 to the general reserves at 31 October 2012.

3. The directors intended to revalue the Freehold premises to $1 000 000 during the year.

The company accountant also provided the following extract from the company's budgeted income statement for the year ended 31 October 2012:

	$000
Profit from operations	243
Debenture interest	(20)
Profit before tax	223
Tax	(60)
	163

Required

a) Prepare Winston plc's budgeted Statement of Financial Position at 31 October 2012.

b) Prepare Winston plc's budgeted Statement of Changes in equity for the year ended 31 October 2012.

25 Limited companies: more about share capital and debentures; capital reduction and reconstructions

In this chapter you will learn:

- the effect on the Statement of Financial Position of an issue of shares
- more about bonus shares and rights issues
- how to account for the redemption of shares
- the effect on the Statement of Financial Position of the redemption of shares, capital reductions and reconstructions
- the differences between shares and debentures
- what convertible loan stock is
- how to account for the redemption of debentures.

25.1 The Companies Act 1985 and share capital

In chapter 23 it was noted that under the 2006 Companies Act there is no longer any requirement for a company to have an authorised share capital. However, the following provisions of the 1985 Companies Act still apply to the share capital of a limited company.

- Public limited companies must have a minimum capital of £50 000 (stated thus in the Companies Act). At least one quarter of the nominal amount and the whole of any premium must have been paid up on the shares. The shares may be traded on the Stock Exchange.

- Private limited companies may have capital of less than £50 000. The shares may not be offered to the public generally. A private company may re-register as a public company if it fulfils the necessary requirements.

- A company may
  - increase its share capital by the issue of new shares
  - consolidate its shares into shares of a larger amount than its existing shares (e.g. if it has a

  share capital of 10 000 ordinary shares of $1, it can convert them into (say) 2000 shares of $5 or 1000 shares of $10)
  - divide its shares into shares of a lower denomination (e.g. convert its ordinary share capital of 10 000 ordinary shares of $1 into 20 000 shares of $0.50 or 40 000 shares of $0.25, etc.)
  - convert its paid-up shares into stock (Stock may be described as 'bundles of shares'. The advantage of stock is that it may be bought and sold in fractional amounts, e.g. $35.50 or $41.80. If the shares had not been converted into stock they could only be bought in multiples of $1.)
  - re-convert stock back into shares of any nominal value, e.g. shares of $1 may be converted into stock then, later, re-converted back into shares of, say, $0.25, $0.50, $5, $10 or any other amount
  - issue bonus shares
  - reduce its capital by redeeming or purchasing its shares provided it complies with strict conditions laid down under the Companies Act.

25.2 Share issues

Students will recall that a company **issues** its shares to people who wish to invest in it. (It is incorrect to say that it *sells* its shares.) The detailed procedure and accounting entries for the issue of shares are not required by the CIE syllabus.

Share premium. A company may issue its shares at a premium if it believes that there will be a good demand for them. This could be the case if the company has already issued shares which are being traded on the Stock Exchange at a price above their nominal value.

When shares are issued at a premium, only the amount received for the nominal value of the shares issued may be credited to the Share Capital account. The amount received for the premium must be credited to a Share Premium account. This topic has already been covered in §23.10, and students may wish to revise that section.

25.3 Bonus shares

The Companies Act gives companies the power to use their reserves to issues shares to the ordinary shareholders as fully paid-up shares. These shares are known as **bonus shares** because the shareholders do not have to pay for them; they own all the reserves, anyway, and are not being given anything they do not already own!

The main reason why companies issue bonus shares is because the issued share capital does not adequately represent the long-term capital of the company. Consider the following summarised Statement of Financial Position.

	$000
Non-current assets	1000
Net current assets	500
	1500
Equity	
Ordinary shares of $1	700
Share premium	200
General reserve	400
Retained earnings	200
	1500

The directors could, theoretically, distribute the revenue reserves of $600 000 (general reserve +

retained earnings) as a cash dividend to the shareholders. The problem with this suggestion is that the non-current assets are long-term assets which should be financed by long-term capital, but they exceed the share capital of the company by $300 000. In order to make the long-term capital of the company adequately support the long-term assets, the directors may transfer $300 000 of the reserves to the Share Capital account, making the balance on that account $1 000 000, equal to the non-current assets. The directors could use any of the reserves for the purpose, but will no doubt prefer to use the Share Premium account, $200 000, and $100 000 of the General Reserve. This would leave the revenue reserves almost intact and these may be used for other purposes including the payment of cash dividends. The reserves have been left in the most flexible form (see §23.11).

Revised Statement of Financial Position after the capitalisation of the Share Premium account	
	$000
Non-current assets	1000
Net current assets	500
	1500
Equity	
Ordinary shares of $1	1000
General reserve	300
Retained earnings	200
	1500

The balance on the Share Capital account has increased by $300 000, but the shareholders have share certificates for 700 000 shares. They must be issued with certificates for another 300 000 bonus shares on the basis of three shares for every seven shares they already hold.

Another reason for capitalising reserves is concerned with the payment of dividends to the ordinary shareholders. If the directors were to recommend paying the whole of the retained profit of $200 000 as a dividend on a share capital of $700 000, the shareholders would receive a dividend of more than 28%. This could cause problems with

(a) the workforce, who may have had little or no increase in their wages

(b) the company's customers, who think that the company should reduce its prices rather than

pay excessive dividends to the shareholders
(c) the cash reserves of the company.

In fact, the dividend does not represent 28% of the amount the shareholders have invested in the company; their investment includes the share capital and all the reserves and amounts to $1 500 000. The true return to the shareholders is therefore 13% on the amount invested. If the bonus shares were issued, a dividend payment of $200 000 would look a little more reasonable (20% on the issued capital).

Exercise 1

The following is the summarised Statement of Financial Position of Otago (Bonus Offers) Ltd.

	$000
Non-current assets	1400
Net current assets	350
	1750
Equity	
Ordinary shares of $1	800
Share premium	200
Revaluation reserve	600
General reserve	100
Retained earnings	50
	1750

The directors have decided to make a bonus issue of three new shares for every four already held. They wish to leave the reserves in the most flexible form.

Required
Redraft Otago (Bonus Offers) Ltd's Statement of Financial Position to show how it will appear following the bonus issue.

25.4 Rights issues

When a company needs to raise more capital, it may do so by issuing more shares. An invitation to the general public to subscribe for shares is an expensive process because the company must issue a prospectus which gives the past history of the company, its present situation and much other information in great detail. Preparation of a prospectus is very time consuming, requiring perhaps hundreds of labour hours. In addition, the company must employ lawyers, accountants and auditors to advise and check on the preparation of the prospectus.

If a company restricts the invitation to subscribe for shares to existing shareholders, the requirements are less stringent and less costly. In any case, if the company is a private company, it is not permitted to invite the general public to subscribe for shares; it must restrict the invitation to its existing shareholders. Such an issue of shares is known as a **rights issue** because the right to apply for the shares is restricted to existing shareholders.

A rights issue entitles existing shareholders to apply for a specified number of shares, depending on how many they already hold. For example, they may apply for one share (or any other number of shares) for every share they already hold. The offer price will be below the price at which shares are currently changing hands on the Stock Exchange, or their current valuation in the case of private companies.

Shareholders who do not wish to exercise their rights may sell the rights to some other person who might be willing to buy them, if the cost of the rights plus the share offer price is less than the price at which the shares are already being traded. For example, a rights issue may be offered at $1.20 per share. The current price at which shares are changing hands may be $1.60. If the rights can be bought for less than $0.40, the person buying the rights will be able to acquire the new shares at a price below that at which they are being traded.

The accounting entries for a rights issue are no different from those for an ordinary issue of shares. In any case, students are not required to know the bookkeeping entries for share issues, but it is important to note the differences between rights issues and bonus issues.

Rights and bonus issues compared	
Rights issue	**Bonus issue**
Subscribers pay for shares.	Shareholders do not pay for shares.
The company's net assets are increased by the cash received.	The net assets of the company are unchanged.
Shareholders do not have to exercise their right to subscribe for the new shares.	All the ordinary shareholders will receive their bonus shares.
Shareholders may sell their rights if they do not wish to exercise them.	Shareholders may sell their bonus shares if they do not wish to keep them.

25.5 How to record issues of bonus shares and rights issues

Example

Handout Ltd's Statement of Financial Position at 1 April 2011 is summarised as follows:

	$000
Net assets	1600
Equity	
Share capital and reserves	
Ordinary shares of $1	1000
Share premium	400
Retained earnings	200
	1600

On 1 April 2011, the directors made a bonus issue of shares on the basis of one new share for every two already held, leaving the reserves in the most flexible form.

Required

(a) Redraft Handout Ltd's Statement of Financial Position at 1 April 2011 after the issue of the bonus shares.

Answer

(a)

	$000
Net assets	1600
Equity	
Share capital and reserves	
Ordinary shares of $1	1500
Retained earnings	100
	1600

Following the bonus issue, Handout Ltd made a rights issue on 7 April 2011 of 150 000 ordinary shares of $1 at a price of $1.50. All the shares were subscribed for by the shareholders.

Required

(b) Redraft Handout Ltd's Statement of Financial Position at 7 April 2011 after the completion of the rights issue.

Answer

(b)

	$000
Net assets	1825
Equity	
Share capital and reserves	
Ordinary shares of $1	1650
Share premium	75
Retained earnings	100
	1825

Exercise 2

The summarised Statement of Financial Position of Bonarite Ltd at 30 June 2011 was as follows:

	$000
Net assets	2000
Equity	
Share capital and reserves	
Ordinary shares of $1	1000
Share premium	500
Revaluation reserve	300
General reserve	120
Retained earnings	80
	2000

On 1 July 2011, before any other transactions had taken place, the company made a bonus issue of shares on the basis of four new shares for every five already held. The directors wished to leave the reserves in the most flexible form.

Required

(a) Show how Bonarite Ltd's Statement of Financial Position will appear at 1 July 2011 immediately after the issue of the bonus shares.

Following the issue of the bonus shares, the company made a rights issue of one new share for every three shares already held. The shares were offered at $1.25 per share and all the shares were taken up.

Required

(b) Show how Bonarite Ltd's Statement of Financial Position will appear immediately after the rights issue has been completed.

25.6 Redemption and purchase of own shares by a company

The Companies Act 1985 permits a company to issue **redeemable shares** provided it has issued other shares which are not redeemable. Redeemable shares may later be bought back (redeemed) by the company. The Act also permits companies to purchase their own shares although they were not issued as redeemable shares. The treatment of such shares, whether redeemed or purchased by the company, is the same and no distinction between redemption and purchase will be made in what follows. The shares are cancelled on redemption or purchase so that the issued capital is reduced.

The Companies Act is concerned with the protection of creditors, who may suffer if the capital of companies is depleted. The Act requires companies to replace redeemed capital by:

(a) either using the proceeds of a new issue of shares
(b) or ensuring that revenue reserves (which could be distributed as cash dividends to shareholders) are converted into a capital reserve, known as a Capital Redemption Reserve, making them unavailable for cash distributions
(c) or a combination of both of the above.

Example 1

Split Coggs Ltd's summarised Statement of Financial Position at 30 June is as follows:

	$000
Non-current assets	1000
Net current assets	700
	1700
Equity	
Ordinary shares of $1	1300
General reserve	250
Retained earnings	150
	1700

The company has decided to redeem 300 000 ordinary shares. The redemption will be made from the issue of 200 000 ordinary shares of $1 each at a price of $1.50. After the redemption of the shares, the Statement of Financial Position will be as follows:

	$000
Non-current assets	1000
Net current assets	700
	1700
Equity	
Ordinary shares of $1	1200
Share premium	100
General reserve	250
Retained earnings	150
	1700

The share capital has been replaced by ordinary shares and the Share Premium account. The interests of the creditors have been protected. The $300 000 received from the issue of ordinary shares has been paid to the preference shareholders, and the net current assets have remained unchanged.

Example 2

Details as in example 1. The company decided that the shares in Split Coggs Ltd should be redeemed, but that no new ordinary shares should be issued.

	$000
Non-current assets	1000
Net current assets	400
	1400
Equity	
Ordinary shares of $1	1000
Capital Redemption Reserve	300
Retained earnings	100
	1400

The interests of the creditors have been protected by the transfer of revenue reserves to a Capital Redemption Reserve which cannot be used to pay cash dividends to the shareholders. Net assets have been reduced by the cash paid to the shareholders.

Exercise 3

Choppers Ltd's summarised Statement of Financial Position is as follows:

	$000
Non-current assets	1300
Net current assets	550
	1850
Equity	
Ordinary shares of $1	1300
Share premium	200
General reserve	200
Retained earnings	150
	1850

The company has decided to redeem 300 000 ordinary shares out of the proceeds of an issue of new ordinary shares of $1 each at a price of $2.00.

Required

(a) Prepare Choppers Ltd's Statement of Financial Position immediately after the redemption of the shares.

The company has decided to redeem the shares without the issue of any new shares.

Required

(b) Prepare Choppers Ltd's Statement of Financial Position immediately after the redemption of the shares.

Premium paid on the redemption of shares

Companies may pay a premium on shares when they redeem them. As an example, a company may redeem $1 shares at $1.20; shareholders will receive $1.20 for every share they hold, the $0.20 being the premium. The accounting treatment of the premium requires great care.

In some circumstances, the premium paid on redemption may be debited to the Share Premium account (see §23.11). However, the creditors must be protected against any improper reduction of a company's capital. The Companies Act places the following restrictions on the right of a company to debit the premium to Share Premium account:

- the shares being redeemed must have been issued at a premium
- the shares are being redeemed out of the proceeds of a fresh issue of shares made for the purpose
- the amount of the premium debited to Share

Premium account must be the lesser of:

- the amount of premiums received on the new issue of shares
- the balance on the Share Premium account (including the premiums received on the new issue of shares); this is to prevent a debit balance on the Share Premium account.

If the premium being paid on the redemption of shares exceeds the amount permitted to be debited to the Share Premium account (as explained above), the difference must be charged to the Retained Earnings Account.

If the shares being redeemed were not issued at a premium, or are not being redeemed out of the proceeds of a new issue made for the purpose, the whole of the premium on redemption must be charged to the Retained Earnings Account.

Example 3

Spin Ltd's summarised Statement of Financial Position is as follows:

	$000
Non-current assets	1100
Net current assets	600
	1700
Equity	
Ordinary shares of $1	1200
Share Premium Account	150
Retained earnings	350
	1700

The company has decided to redeem 200 000 ordinary shares at a premium of $0.20. No new issue of shares is to be made for the purpose.

Required

Show how Spin Ltd's Statement of Financial Position will appear immediately after the redemption of the ordinary shares.

Answer

	$000
Non-current assets	1100
Net current assets (600 – 240)	360
	1460
Equity	
Ordinary shares of $1	1000
Share Premium account	150
Capital Redemption Reserve	200
Retained earnings (350 – 240)	110
	1460

Example 4

Given the summarised Statement of Financial Position of Spin Ltd before the redemption of the shares as given in example 3 above, in this case the shares were redeemed partly out of the proceeds of a new issue of 100 000 ordinary shares of $1 issued at a premium of $0.15. The premium paid on the redemption of the preference shares was $0.20.

Required

Show how the Statement of Financial Position of Spin Ltd will appear immediately after the redemption of the ordinary shares.

Answer

	$000
Non-current assets	1100
Net current assets (600 + 115 – 240)	475
	1575
Equity	
Ordinary shares of $1	1100
Share Premium account (150 + 15 – 15)[1]	150
Capital Redemption Reserve[2]	100
Retained earnings [350 – (100 + 25)][3]	225
	1575

1. The Share Premium account has been increased by the amount of the premium received on the issue of the ordinary shares ($15 000), but the company has been allowed to apply this amount towards the premium payable on the redemption of the preference shares. The company cannot debit the whole of the premium paid on redemption ($40 000) to the Share Premium account as this exceeds $15 000.
2. The balance of the share capital not covered by the new issue of the ordinary shares must be covered by a transfer of $100 000 from the Retained Earnings Account to a Capital Redemption Reserve.
3. The amount of the premium paid on the redemption of the shares ($40 000) less the amount of the premium charged to Share Premium account ($15 000) is $25 000 and must be debited to the Retained Earnings Account.

Exercise 4

The summarised Statement of Financial Position of Twist Ltd is as follows:

	$000
Non-current assets	2000
Net current assets	800
	2800
Equity	
Ordinary shares of $1	2000
Share Premium account	450
Retained earnings	350
	2800

The company has decided to redeem 250 000 ordinary shares at $1.20 per share. When the shares were originally issued they were issued at a premium of $0.20. No new issue of shares is to be made for the purpose of the redemption.

Required

(a) Show how the Statement of Financial Position of Twist Ltd will appear after the redemption of the shares.

The shares are to be redeemed after a new issue of 200 000 ordinary shares of $1 has been made at $1.10 per share.

Required

(b) Show how the Statement of Financial Position of Twist Ltd will appear after completion of the new issue of ordinary shares and the redemption of the shares.

The shares are to be redeemed after a new issue of 250 000 ordinary shares of $1 has been made at $1.25.

Required

(c) Show how the Statement of Financial Position of Twist Ltd will appear after the new issue of ordinary shares and the redemption of the shares.

25.7 The redemption or purchase of own shares by a private company

The Companies Act recognises that the rules which apply to public companies may be too strict for private companies for the following reasons.

- As shares in private companies cannot be traded on the Stock Exchange, such companies are restricted in their ability to raise capital. Potential investors may hesitate to buy shares in private companies unless they can be certain that they can dispose of their shares in an emergency.
- Many private companies are 'family' concerns. If one of the shareholders dies, his or her family may need the money invested in the shares urgently, especially if death duties or taxes have to be paid out of the deceased's estate.

If a private company's distributable reserves are insufficient to create the Capital Redemption Reserve, the Act allows the company to use its capital reserves to make up the shortfall. If the company's total reserves (i.e. revenue and capital reserves) are insufficient to create the full amount of the Capital Redemption Reserve, the Act allows the Capital Redemption Reserve to be less than the nominal amount of the shares being redeemed.

25.8 Redemption of debentures

A debenture is a loan to a company and redemption of debentures by a company is simply the repayment of a loan. The rules applying to the redemption of shares do not apply to the redemption of debentures but the following should be noted:

- any premium payable to the debenture holders on redemption may be charged to Share Premium account if there is one
- it is not necessary to create a Redemption Reserve for debentures; if the directors consider it wise to create a reserve, it will be made by a transfer from the Retained Earnings Account, but should probably not be called a *Capital Redemption Reserve*.

25.9 Convertible loan stock

Convertible loan stock is similar to debentures, but it gives the holder of the stock the option to convert the stock into shares in the company on a pre-determined date at a pre-determined price. If, when the time arrives, the pre-determined price is less than the market price of the shares, it could be advantageous to exercise the option. If the pre-determined price is higher than the market price, the option will not be exercised.

25.10 Capital reduction and reconstruction

The Companies Act 1985 permits companies to reduce their share capital provided the interests of

creditors are preserved. Losses by the company can lead to a reduction of capital and, if the situation appears to be permanent, it will be necessary to recognise the fact by undertaking a scheme of capital reduction. A Capital Reduction account is opened in the books for this purpose.

Example

D. Pleet Ltd's summarised Statement of Financial Position at 31 September is as follows:

	$000
Non-current assets	
Intangible - Goodwill	100
Tangible	
Land and buildings	600
Plant and machinery	250
Motor vehicles	50
Net current assets	350
	1350
Equity	
1 600 000 ordinary shares of $1	1600
Retained earnings (debit balance)	(250)
	1350

Further information

1. Goodwill is now considered to have no value.
2. The non-current assets are considered to be overvalued and have been valued more realistically as follows:

	$000
Land and buildings	420
Plant and machinery	150
Motor vehicles	30

3. Inventory has been overvalued by $125 000. A major customer owing $25 000 has become bankrupt.

The company has not paid any dividends for some years but the directors believe that the company can become profitable again and start paying dividends once more. They propose to carry out a scheme of capital reduction with the agreement of the shareholders. The scheme of capital reduction:

The Statement of Financial Position value of the shares is $0.84375 [$(1 600 000 − 250 000) ÷ 1 600 000]. After taking the overvaluation of the assets into account, the value of the shares is $0.50.

	$000
Nominal value of share capital	1600
Less: Debit balance on Retained earnings	(250)
Reductions in value of: Goodwill	(100)
Land and buildings	(180)
Plant and machinery	(100)
Motor vehicles	(20)
Inventory	(125)
Trade receivables	(25)
Real value of share capital	800
($800 000 ÷ 1 600 000 = $0.50)	

Examination candidates may be required to prepare journal entries for a capital reconstruction but will not be required to prepare the Capital Reduction or other ledger accounts.

Journal entries

	$000	$000
Capital Reduction account	800	
Retained earnings		250
Goodwill		100
Land and buildings		180
Plant and machinery		100
Motor vehicles		20
Inventory		125
Bad debt written off		25
Reduction in asset values and writing off Goodwill.		
Ordinary Share Capital account	800	
Capital Reduction account		800
Reduction of share capital.		

The balance on the Share Capital account has now been reduced from $1 600 000 to $800 000, but the shareholders still hold share certificates for 1 600 000 shares of $1. The directors may correct this situation in various ways, but the two most likely are:

- to give the shareholders certificates for one ordinary share of $0.50 for every share of $1 they already hold.
- to give the shareholders a certificate for one share of $1 for every two shares they already hold.

Follow any advice given in the question. The student is advised to show the working for the reconstruction as follows:

	$000	$000	$000
Goodwill	100	−100	–
Non-current assets			
Land and buildings	600	−180	420
Plant and machinery	250	−100	150
Motor vehicles	50	−20	30
Net current assets	350	−(125 + 25)	200
	1350		800
Equity			
1 600 000 ordinary shares of $1	1600	−800	800
Retained earnings (debit balance)	(250)	+250	–
	1350		

The Statement of Financial Position can now be copied out as the answer.

D. Pleet Ltd
Statement of Financial Position immediately after the capital reduction

	$000
Non-current assets	
Land and buildings	420
Plant and machinery	150
Motor vehicles	30
Net current assets	200
	800
Equity	
1 600 000 ordinary shares of $0.50*	800

* Alternatively, 800 000 ordinary shares of $1

Exercise 5

The summarised Statement of Financial Position of Downsize Ltd is as follows:

	$000
Non-current assets	
Freehold property	400
Fixtures and fittings	100
Office furniture	80
	580
Net current assets	230
	810
Equity	
1 000 000 ordinary shares of $1	1000
Retained Earnings Account	(190)
	810

The directors propose to write off the debit balance on the Retained Earnings Account and to write the assets down to more realistic values as follows:

	$000
Freehold property	340
Fixtures and fittings	80
Office furniture	70

Inventory has been overvalued by $15 000 and a customer owing for $5000 has become bankrupt. The shareholders have agreed to a scheme of capital reduction on condition that they receive one new share for every share they already hold.

Required

Re-draft the Statement of Financial Position of Downsize Ltd as it will appear immediately after the completion of the capital reduction.

MULTIPLE-CHOICE QUESTIONS

1. A company redeems 60 000 $1 shares at a premium of $0.25 per share. The shares were originally issued at par. No new issue of shares was made to finance the redemption.
What effect does the redemption have on the Retained earnings and the Capital Redemption Reserve?

Retained earnings	Capital Redemption Reserve
A. decrease by $60 000	increase by $60 000
B. decrease by $60 000	increase by $75 000
C. decrease by $75 000	increase by $60 000
D. decrease by $75 000	increase by $75 000

2. A company issues bonus shares. How does this affect the Statement of cash flows?

A. It will increase the management of liquid resources.
B. It will increase financing.
C. It will increase cash flow from operating activities.
D. It will not appear in the cash flow statement.

3. A company has issued 300 000 ordinary shares of $0.50 each. It makes a bonus issue of two shares for every three already held. It follows that with a rights issue of one share for every two already held at $0.75 per share. The rights issue was fully taken up.
What was the increase in the Share Capital account as a result of the bonus and rights issues?

A. $150 000   B. $175 000
C. $225 000   D. $275 000

4. A company redeems its debentures at a premium. How may the company treat the premium on the redemption?
   A. debit Bank account
   B. debit Capital Redemption Reserve
   C. debit Share Capital account
   D. debit Share Premium account

5. A company, which has already issued ordinary shares of $1 each, issues 200 000 bonus shares and follows this with a rights issue of 100 000 ordinary shares at $1.50 per share.
   What is the increase in the share capital and reserves of the company after these transactions?
   A. $100 000   B. $150 000
   C. $300 000   D. $350 000

ADDITIONAL EXERCISES

1. The summarised Statement of Financial Position of Omicron Ltd at 31 December 2010 was as follows:

	$000
Non-current assets	1900
Net current assets	1500
	3400
10% debentures 2011/2012	400
	3000
Share capital and reserves	
Ordinary shares of $1	1800
Share Premium account	180
Retained Earnings Account	1020
	3000

On 1 January 2011 before any other transactions had taken place the following had occurred:
1. redemption of all the debentures at a premium of 5%
2. redemption of 800 000 ordinary shares at $1.25 per share.
The shares had originally been issued at $1.10 per share.

Required
A revised Statement of Financial Position at 1 January 2011 as it appeared after the redemption of the debentures and the ordinary shares.

2. Istaimy plc's summarised Statement of Financial Position at 30 April 2011 was as follows:

	$000
Non-current assets	1300
Net current assets	740
	2040

Ordinary shares of $1	1500
Share Premium account	200
Retained Earnings Account	340
	2040

On 1 May 2011, before any further transactions had taken place, it was decided to redeem 300 000 ordinary shares at a premium of $0.30. The shares had originally been issued at $1.20 per share. In order to provide funds for the redemption, the company issued a further 100 000 ordinary shares at a premium of $0.25.

Required
Prepare Istaimy plc's Statement of Financial Position as it will appear immediately after the issue of the additional ordinary shares and the redemption of the ordinary share capital.

3. The following is the Statement of Financial Position of Joloss plc at 30 April 2011.

	$000	$000
Intangible non-current asset – Goodwill		50
Tangible non-current assets		650
		700
Current assets		
Inventory	32	
Trade receivables	80	
Bank	6	
	118	
Current liabilities	42	76
		776
Share capital and reserves		
Ordinary shares of $1		1000
Retained Earnings Account		(224)
		776

Over the past few years Joloss plc has traded at a loss and no dividends have been paid to the shareholders during that time.

The directors are of the opinion that Goodwill now has no value. The tangible non-current assets are overvalued by $150 000. Some inventory which cost $10 000 now has no value. Included in trade receivables is an amount of $16 000 from a customer who has now become insolvent.

The directors are confident that, as a result of improved efficiency and the introduction of new products, the company can look forward to annual net profits of $50 000. They have proposed to the shareholders a scheme of capital reduction whereby each shareholder will receive one ordinary share with a nominal value of $0.55 for every $1 share presently held. This will enable the debit balance on the Retained Earnings Account to be eliminated and adjustments to be made to the company's assets to take account of the matters mentioned above.

The directors' policy in future will be to pay dividends which will be covered twice by earnings. The shareholders have agreed to the directors' proposals and the capital reduction was effected on 1 May 2011.

Required

(i) Prepare the Statement of Financial Position as it will appear immediately after the capital reduction.

(ii) Explain the reasons why the shareholders agreed to the reduction in the nominal value of their shares.

26 Business purchase

In this chapter you will learn:

- the difference between the purchase of a business and the purchase of the assets of a business
- Goodwill arising on the purchase of a business
- how to prepare a journal entry to record the purchase of a business in the books of the purchasing company
- the preparation of a Statement of Financial Position following the purchase of a business
- how to calculate the return on an investment in a new business.

26.1 What is the difference between the purchase of a business and the purchase of the assets of a business?

It is important to distinguish between a company buying the assets of another business, and the purchase by the company of that other business. Some students get confused between the two different kinds of purchase. A company may buy the assets of another business which may then cease to trade. That is very different from a company buying another business; the company takes over the assets *and* liabilities of that business together with its customers and carries on the trade of the business taken over. The distinction is important. The purchase only of assets does not involve any payment for Goodwill; the purchase of an entire business usually does involve payment for Goodwill.

When a limited company purchases another business it will usually pay for it partly by cash and partly by shares. The shares may be issued at a premium. However, the sellers of the business would not pay for the shares given to them.

Sometimes a sole trader or a partnership may decide to convert their business into a limited company. This is done by forming a new company which purchases the partnership business.

Example

Aiisha has traded for some years as a sole trader. On 1 October 2011 she decided to form a limited liability company to take over her business. She will hold ordinary shares of $1 in the company as her capital.

Aiisha's summarised Statement of Financial Position at 1 October 2011 was as follows:

	$
Non-current assets	20 000
Net current assets	14 000
	34 000
Capital account	34 000

The summarised Statement of Financial Position of the new company will appear as follows:

Aiisha Ltd	
	$
Non-current assets	20 000
Net current assets	14 000
	34 000
Share capital	
Ordinary shares of $1	34 000

26.2 Goodwill

When a company purchases a business, it will usually buy the assets less the liabilities at an agreed valuation. In addition, it usually pays for the advantage of acquiring an established trade. The company does not have to build up a new business from nothing; the business has been built up by the previous owner who will normally expect to be rewarded for their efforts.

Goodwill is the amount paid for the acquisition of a business in excess of the fair value of its separable net assets. The term 'separable net assets' is used to describe the sale of individual assets and using the money to settle the liabilities of the business.

It is important to distinguish between **purchased Goodwill** and **inherent Goodwill**. Purchased Goodwill has been paid for. Inherent Goodwill has not been paid for and will arise, for instance, if a trader decides that he wants to show the Goodwill of his business in his Statement of Financial Position; he debits a Goodwill account in his books and credits his Capital account with any amount that he wishes to show as Goodwill. International Accounting Standard **IAS 38** sets out how goodwill should be treated in the books. This was discussed in chapter 22, when it was seen that only purchased goodwill is shown in the Statement of Financial Position. Inherent goodwill is never shown in the final accounts.

If the amount paid for a business is less than the fair value of its separable net assets, the difference is called **negative Goodwill** (not Badwill!) and should be written off against the reserves in the equity section of the Statement of Financial Position.

26.3 How to make journal entries in the books of a company to record the purchase of a business

Before any entries for the purchase of a business are made in a company's ledger accounts, the transaction must be recorded in the journal. The entries should include the Bank and Cash accounts if these are taken over. However, the bank and cash balances of the business being acquired are not usually taken over unless a sole trader or a partnership converts their business into a limited company.

Example

Bortit Ltd purchased the business of A. Sellit, a sole trader, on 1 October 2011. Sellit's Statement of Financial Position at that date was:

	$	$
Non-current assets		
Land and buildings		60 000
Plant and machinery		35 000
Motor vehicles		21 000
		116 000
Current assets		
Inventory	7 000	
Trade receivables	4 000	
Cash and cash equivalents	5 000	
	16 000	
Less Current liabilities		
Trade Payables	2 000	14 000
		130 000
Equity		
Ordinary share capital		130 000

The assets were taken over at the following values:

	$
Land and buildings	80 000
Plant and machinery	28 000
Motor vehicles	16 000
Inventory	5 000
Trade Receivables	3 000
Trade Payables	2 000

Bortit Ltd did not take over Sellit's Bank account. Bortit Ltd paid A. Sellit $150 000, made up as follows: cash $20 000 and 100 000 ordinary shares of $1 each.

Required

Prepare the journal entries in Bortit Ltd's books to record the purchase of A. Sellit's business.

Answer

	Dr	Cr
	$	$
Land and buildings	80 000	
Plant and machinery	28 000	
Motor vehicles	16 000	
Inventory	5 000	
Trade Receivables	3 000	
Goodwill	20 000[1]	
Trade Payables		2 000
Cash and cash equivalents		20 000
Ordinary share capital		100 000
Share Premium account		30 000[2]
	152 000	152 000

The purchase of the business of A. Sellit on 1 October 2011 for the sum of $150 000 payable as follows: cash $20 000 and by the issue of 100 000 ordinary shares of $1 at $1.30 per share.

1 Goodwill = purchase consideration ($150 000) less value of net assets acquired ($130 000).

2 The shares were valued at $(150 000 − 20 000) = $130 000. $30 000 is the share premium.

Bortit Ltd's Statement of Financial Position at 1 October 2011 before it acquired the business of A. Sellit was as follows:

	$	$
Non-current assets		
Land and buildings		200 000
Plant and machinery		75 000
Motor vehicles		40 000
		315 000
Current assets		
Inventory	21 000	
Trade Receivables	16 000	
Cash and cash equivalents	32 000	
	69 000	
Current liabilities		
Trade Payables	7 000	62 000
		377 000
Equity		
Ordinary share capital		300 000
Retained profit		77 000
		377 000

Required

Prepare Bortit Ltd's Statement of Financial Position immediately after the purchase of the business of A. Sellit.

Answer

Add the journal entries to Bortit Ltd's assets, liabilities, share capital and reserves.

(Workings are shown in brackets.)

Bortit Ltd		
Statement of Financial Position at 1 October 2011		
after the acquisition of A. Sellit's business		
	$	$
Non-current assets		
Intangible – Goodwill		20 000
Tangible		
Land and buildings (200 000 + 80 000)		280 000
Plant and machinery (75 000 + 28 000)		103 000
Motor vehicles (40 000 + 16 000)		56 000
		459 000
Current assets		
Inventory (21 000 + 5 000)	26 000	
Trade Receivables (16 000 + 3 000)	19 000	
Cash and cash equivalents (32 000 – 20 000)	12 000	
	57 000	
Current liabilities		
Trade Payables (7000 + 2000)	9 000	48 000
		507 000
Equity		
Ordinary shares (300 000 + 100 000)		400 000
Share premium		30 000
Retained earnings		77 000
		507 000

Exercise 1

Hamil Ltd purchased the business of Abdul, a sole trader, on 30 June 2011. The Statements of Financial Position of both businesses at that date were as follows:

	Abdul		Hamil Ltd	
	$	$	$	$
Non-current assets				
Freehold property		40 000		100 000
Plant and machinery		15 000		60 000
Office equipment		–		14 000
Office furniture		7 000		–
		62 000		174 000
Current assets				
Inventory	4 000		10 000	
Trade Receivables	6 000		7 000	
Cash and cash equivalents	1 000		25 000	
	11 000		42 000	
Current liabilities				
Trade Payables	3 000	8 000	6 000	36 000
		70 000		210 000
Capital account		70 000		
Equity				
Ordinary shares of $1				150 000
Share Premium				20 000
Retained profit				40 000
				210 000

It was agreed that Abdul's assets should be valued as follows:

	$
Freehold property	70 000
Plant and machinery	12 000
Office furniture	4 000
Inventory	2 500
Trade Receivables	5 500

Hamil Ltd did not acquire Abdul's bank account. The consideration for the sale was $120 000 and was satisfied by the payment to Abdul of $20 000 in cash and the issue to him of 80 000 ordinary shares in Hamil Ltd.

Required

(a) Prepare the journal entries in Hamil Ltd's books to record the purchase of Abdul's business.
(b) Prepare Hamil Ltd's Statement of Financial Position immediately after the acquisition of Abdul's business.

26.4 Purchase of a partnership business

The purchase of a partnership business by a company follows a similar procedure to that for the purchase of a sole trader's business. When one of the partners has made a loan to the firm and the company takes the loan over, it is usual for the company to issue a debenture to the partner concerned. If the rate of interest on the debenture is different from the rate previously received by the partner on the loan, the amount of the debenture will usually ensure that the partner continues to receive the same amount of interest each year as previously. To calculate the amount of the debenture, find the capital sum which, at the new rate, will produce the same amount of interest. Multiply the amount of the loan by the rate paid by the partnership and divide by the rate of interest on the debenture, as shown in the following example.

(i) Partner's loan to partnership: $100 000 at 8% interest per annum. Annual interest = $8000. A 10% debenture producing annual interest of $8000 will be $100\,000 \times \dfrac{8}{10} = \$80\,000.$

(ii) If in (i) the rate of interest on the debenture is 5% the amount of debenture is: $100\,000 \times \dfrac{8}{5}$ = $160 000. (Interest on $160 000 at 5% per annum = $8000.)

Exercise 2

Carol has lent $60 000 at 5% interest per annum to the firm in which she is a partner. A company has offered to buy the partnership business. Part of the purchase price consists of a debenture to be issued to Carol to ensure that she continues to receive the same amount of interest annually as she had been receiving from the partnership.

Required

(a) Calculate the amount of the debenture to be issued to Carol if the debenture carries interest at 8% per annum.

(b) Calculate the amount of the debenture if it carries interest at 4% per annum.

Exercise 3

Spaid and Shuvell are partners in a business and their Statement of Financial Position at 31 December 2011 is as follows:

	$	$
Non-current assets		
Land and buildings		50 000
Fixtures and fittings		18 000
Office machinery		12 000
		80 000
Current assets		
Inventory	17 000	
Trade Receivables	8 000	
Cash and cash equivalents	4 000	
	29 000	
Current liabilities		
Trade Payables	12 000	17 000
		97 000
Non-current liability		
Loan from Spaid at 10% per annum		12 000
		85 000
Capital accounts		
Spaid		50 000
Shuvell		35 000
		85 000

The partners have accepted an offer from Digger Ltd to purchase the business for $118 000. The company will take over all the assets and liabilities of the partnership except the bank account. The partnership assets are to be valued as follows:

	$
Land and buildings	60 000
Fixtures and fittings	14 000
Office machinery	10 000
Inventory	15 000
Trade Receivables	6 000

Digger Ltd will settle the purchase price as follows:

- a payment of cash, $28 000.
- an 8% debenture issued to Spaid to ensure that he continues to receive the same amount of interest annually as he has received from the partnership
- the balance to be settled by an issue of ordinary shares of $1 in Digger Ltd at $1.25 per share.

Digger Ltd's Statement of Financial Position at 31 December 2011 is as follows:

	$	$
Non-current assets		
Land and buildings		90 000
Fixtures and fittings		30 000
Office machinery		15 000
		135 000
Current assets		
Inventory	20 000	
Trade receivables	5 000	
Cash and cash equivalents	60 000	
	85 000	
Current liabilities		
Trade payables	16 000	69 000
		204 000
Equity		
Ordinary shares of $1		200 000
Retained profit		4 000
		204 000

Required

Prepare Digger Ltd's Statement of Financial Position immediately after the company has acquired the partnership business.

Sometimes examination questions require that the entries showing the closure of the partnership books are shown. In this case, all the closing entries are shown in a Realisation account. The procedure is exactly the same as the dissolution of a partnership in chapter 22.

Example

Alan and Brian are in business sharing the profits and losses equally. Their summarised Statement of Financial Position at 31 July 2011 is as follows:

	$000	$000
Non-current assets		80
Current assets (including the bank balance of $6000)		40
		120
Current liabilities		(30)
		90
Capital accounts:		
Alan		45
Brian		45
		90

They accept an offer from Byit Ltd to purchase their business. The company will take over all the assets and liabilities of the partnership, with the exception of the bank account. Byit will pay the partners $50 000 in cash and 100 000 ordinary shares of $1 each.

Required

(a) Prepare the Realisation account in the partnership books.
(b) Prepare the partners' Capital and Bank accounts, showing the closure of the business.

Realisation account

	$000		$000
Non-current assets	80	Current liabilities	30
Current assets		Bank – cash paid	50
(40 000 – 6000)	34	Ordinary shares	100
Profit on realisation:			
Alan	33		
Brian	33		
	180		180

Capital accounts

	$000 Alan	$000 Brian		$000 Alan	$000 Brian
Bank	28	28	Opening bals	45	45
			Profit on		
Shares	50	50	realisation	33	33
	78	78		78	78

Bank account

	$000		$000
Opening balance	6	Alan	28
From Byit Ltd	50	Brian	28
	56		56

Notice that even though the business is sold at a figure higher than the net book value of the assets taken over, it is treated as a profit on realisation and not goodwill in the partnership books. In this case the shares are divided between the partners in the profit sharing ratios. This may not be the case in the question given.

The question may also include partners' Current accounts. The balances on these accounts should be transferred to the respective partner's Capital account. There may also be an asset taken over by a partner on the closure of the business, say a car at a valuation. In this case, credit the Realisation account and debit the partners' Capital account with the value of the asset taken over.

Exercise 4

Lee and Mick are in business sharing the profits and losses equally. Their summarised Statement of Financial Position at 31 October 2011 is as follows:

	$000	$000	$000
Non-current assets			
Property			50
Plant and machinery			20
			70
Current assets			
Inventory		8	
Trade receivables		12	
		20	
Current liabilities			
Trade payables	6		
Bank overdraft	2	8	12
Non-current liabilities			
Loan			(8)
			74
Capital accounts:			
Lee		30	
Mick		30	60
Current accounts:			
Lee		8	
Mick		6	14
			74

The partners accept an offer from Taykover Ltd for their business. The company will take over all the assets and liabilities of the business with the exception of the bank overdraft and loan. They will pay the partners $20 000 in cash and 100 000 ordinary shares of $1 each at a premium of $0.20.

Required

(a) Prepare the Realisation account in the partnership books.
(b) Prepare the partners' capital and bank accounts, showing the closure of the business.

26.5 Return on investment

It is important that a company purchasing another business succeeds in making the new business as profitable as its existing business. Profitability is measured by expressing profit as a percentage of capital invested. If a company has purchased a business for $100 000 and the business has made a profit of $12 000 in the first year, the profitability is 12%. This is the **return on capital invested**. If it is equal to, or more than, the return on capital the company was earning on its existing business, the investment may be considered to have been worthwhile. If it is less, overall profitability of the business will be **diluted** (or decreased). However, it is better to measure the profitability over a number of years to get a reliable picture.

The new business may have been merged with the existing business so closely that separate results for the new business are not available. In such a case, the incremental (that is, the additional) profit is measured against the additional capital invested in the business.

Example

X Ltd had a capital of $300 000. Its average annual profit was $54 000. Its return on capital was

$$\frac{\$54\ 000}{\$300\ 000} \times 100 = 18\%.$$

X Ltd purchased another business on 1 January 2011 for $100 000 which was settled by the issue to the vendor of shares in X Ltd. X Ltd's profit for the year ended 31 December 2011 was $84 000. The profitability of X Ltd has increased by 3% to 21%

$$(\frac{\$84\ 000}{\$400\ 000} \times 100).$$

A more reliable picture is obtained if the additional profit of $30 000 is calculated as a percentage of the price paid for the new business:

$$\frac{\$30\ 000}{\$100\ 000} \times 100 = 30\%.$$

X Ltd has benefited from the purchase of the new business.

HINTS

- Goodwill is the difference between the values of the net assets acquired and the purchase price paid.
- When a debenture is issued to a partner, and the partner is to receive the same amount of annual interest as he/she received before the sale of the firm; check that you have calculated the amount of the debenture correctly.
- If you are required to prepare journal entries in a company's books to record the purchase of a business, do *not* show the entries in the books of the business being taken over.
- Only purchased goodwill is shown in the books of account of the company buying the business.

- Make sure you prepare the journal entries in good form.
- Show all workings when preparing the company's Statement of Financial Position after the new business has been acquired.

MULTIPLE-CHOICE QUESTIONS

1. The following is information about the assets and liabilities of a business.

	Book value $	Market value $
Non-current assets	90 000	101 000
Current assets	32 000	29 000
	122 000	
Current liabilities	(14 000)	14 000
	108 000	

Goodwill is valued at $50 000.
What should be paid for the net assets of the business?
A. $116 000   B. $119 000
C. $166 000   D. $169 000

2. A company paid $1.8 million to acquire the business of a sole trader. The sole trader's assets and liabilities were valued as follows:

	$
Non-current assets	700 000
Current assets	300 000
Current liabilities	50 000
Non-current liability	100 000

How much was paid for Goodwill?
A. $650 000   B. $750 000
C. $850 000   D. $950 000

3. The Statement of Financial Position of a sole trader is as follows:

	$
Non-current assets	
Goodwill	30 000
Plant and machinery	100 000
Net current assets	50 000
	180 000

A company purchased the business, paying for the plant and machinery and the net current assets at the valuations shown above.
The company settled the purchase price by issuing 200 000 ordinary shares of $1 at $1.50 per share.
How much did the company pay for Goodwill?
A. $30 000   B. $50 000
C. $120 000   D. $150 000

ADDITIONAL EXERCISES

1. The following is the Statement of Financial Position of the Erchetai partnership at 30 April 2011.

Non-current assets	$	$
Intangible - Goodwill		50 000
Tangible		928 000
		978 000
Current assets		
Inventory	40 000	
Trade receivables	76 000	
Cash and cash equivalents	80 000	
	196 000	
Current liabilities: Trade payables	29 000	167 000
		1 145 000

Non-current liability		
Loan (carrying interest at 8% per annum)		100 000
		1 045 000
Partners' capitals		1 045 000

On 30 April 2011, Istaimy plc acquired the business of the Erchetai partnership. The following matters were taken into consideration in fixing the terms of the acquisition.
1. No depreciation had been provided on freehold buildings. It was agreed that a provision of $128 000 should have been made.

2. On 1 April 2011 Erchetai had purchased a machine. The cost was $60 000. $20 000 was paid immediately. The balance is payable by four equal instalments on 1 May, 1 June, 1 July and 1 August, together with interest at the rate of 12% per annum. Only the initial payment of $20 000 had been recorded in the partnership's books. It was Erchetai's policy to depreciate machinery at the rate of 15% per annum on cost, and to provide for a full year's depreciation in the year of purchase.

3. A customer owing $5000 at 30 April 2011 has since become bankrupt. Erchetai has been advised that it will receive $0.20 for every $1 the customer owes.

4. Inventory has been valued at cost. Investigation shows that if inventory had been valued at net realisable value it would have been valued at $28 000. If separate valuation at the lower of cost and net realisable value had been applied to each item of inventory it would have been valued at $30 000.

The purchase consideration was satisfied as follows:

- The long-term loan was satisfied by the issue of $80 of 10% debenture stock 2018/2020 for every $100 of the loan.
- The partners were issued, for every $50.00 of capital, with:
  3×8 percent non-redeemable preference shares at $1.20 per share, and 3 ordinary shares of $10.00 each at $12.50.

Required

Prepare the journal entry to record the purchase of the partnership business in the books of Istaimy plc. Your answer should include cash transactions.

2. On 1 April 2011 Joel Ltd acquired the partnership business of Kay and Ola. The partnership Statement of Financial Position at 31 March 2011 was as follows:

	$000	$000
Non-current assets		
Land and buildings		150
Plant and machinery		280
		430
Current assets		
Inventory	150	
Trade Receivables	141	
Cash and cash equivalents	69	
	360	
Current liabilities		
Trade Payables	130	230
		660
Non-current liability		
Loan from Kay at 12½% per annum		100
		560
Financed by capital accounts: Kay		300
Ola		260
		560

Further information

1. The assets (including the bank account) and current liabilities were taken over at the following valuations.

	$000
Land and buildings	220
Plant and machinery	170
Inventory	128
Trade Receivables	105
Trade Payables	138

2. Kay received sufficient 10% Convertible Loan Stock to ensure that she continued to receive the same amount of interest annually as she had received as a partner. The terms of this issue give Kay the option to have the debenture stock converted to ordinary shares in Joel Ltd on 1 June 2013 at $1.25 per share.

3. The balance of the purchase price was settled by the allocation of 300 000 shares in Joel Ltd to Kay and Ola at $1.50 per share.

Joel Ltd's Statement of Financial Position at 31 March 2011 was as follows:

	$000	$000	$000
Non-current assets			
Land and buildings			1425
Plant and machinery			803
			2228
Current assets			
Inventory		381	
Trade Receivables		519	
Cash and cash equivalents		420	
		1320	
Current liabilities			
Trade Payables	500		
8% debentures			
2011/2012	450	950	
			370
			2598
Equity			
Ordinary shares of $1			1350
Retained earnings			1248
			2598

Immediately following the acquisition of the partnership, Joel Ltd redeemed its 8% debentures 2011/2012 at a premium of 4%. In order to preserve the capital structure of the company, a reserve equal to the amount of the debentures redeemed was created.

Required

(a) Prepare Joel Ltd's Statement of Financial Position as it appeared immediately after it had acquired the partnership of Kay and Ola and redeemed the 8% debentures. (Show all workings.)

(b) Calculate the profit required on Joel Ltd's investment in the partnership business to produce a return of 25% on the investment. On 1 June 2013 the market price of Joel Ltd's shares was $1.37.

Required

(c) (i) State, with reason, whether Kay should convert her 10% convertible loan stock into ordinary shares in Joel Ltd.

(ii) State the effect that the conversion of Kay's 10% convertible loan stock into shares would have on Joel Ltd's Statement of Financial Position.

27 Published company accounts

In this chapter you will learn:

- the financial statements and reports that must be published and sent to shareholders
- reporting standards relating to Income Statement
- reporting standards relating to Statement of Financial Position
- the contents of directors' reports
- the importance of auditors' reports.

27.1 Introduction to published company accounts

Shareholders do not usually manage their company unless they are also directors of the company. The directors act as stewards of the shareholders' investments in the company; they are in a position of trust. The Companies Act 1985 ensures that the directors account to the shareholders regularly for their stewardship of the company. The documents which are required to be prepared and published annually are:

- Income Statement
- Statement of Financial Position
- Statement of Cash Flows
- Directors' report
- Auditors' report.

These documents must be sent to shareholders in advance of every annual general meeting. They must also be sent to debenture holders. The directors must file an annual return, which includes the annual accounts, with the Registrar of Companies, and the returns may be inspected by any member of the public. Apart from shareholders and debenture holders, other persons who may be interested in a company's accounts are:

- trade and other creditors
- providers of long-term finance such as banks and finance houses
- trade unions, representing the company's workforce
- financial analysts employed by the financial press

- fund managers managing client's investments
- the Stock Exchanges.

27.2 The Companies Act 1985

The overall objectives of a set of financial statements is that they provide a *true and fair view* of the profit or loss of the company for the year and that the Statement of Financial Position likewise gives a true and fair view of the state of affairs of the company at the end of the financial year. The word *true* may be explained in simple terms as meaning that, if financial statements indicate that a transaction has taken place, then it has actually taken place. If a Statement of Financial Position records the existence of an asset, then the company has that asset. The word *fair* implies that transactions, or assets, are shown in accordance with accepted accounting rules of cost or valuation.

Window dressing describes attempts by directors of a company to make a Statement of Financial Position to show the financial position of company to be better than it really is. For example, the directors may cause cheques to be drawn and entered in the books of account on the last day of the financial year but not send the cheques to the creditors until the next financial year. This would have the effect of artificially reducing a company's liabilities in the Statement of Financial Position, but it would not give a true and fair view because the creditors had not, in fact, been paid. An attempt to inflate the retained profit figure in the Statement of Financial Position by including unrealised profits in the Income Statement would not give a true and fair view. The Companies Act 1985 states that only profits which have been realised at the Statement of Financial Position date shall be included in the Income Statement.

The accounting principle of **substance over form** (see §9.12) is one accounting principle intended to give a true and fair view.

Schedule IV of the Companies Act 1985 sets out rules for the presentation of company accounts. If accounts prepared in accordance with those rules do not provide sufficient information to meet the requirement to present a true and fair view,

- any necessary information must be provided in the Financial Statements, or in notes to the accounts
- if necessary, because of special circumstances, the directors shall depart from the normal rules in order to present a true and fair view and state why they have departed from the normal rules.

These rules are also included in the Companies Act 2006.

27.3 Generally accepted accounting principles (GAAP)

Accounting standards have been published as Statements of Standard Accounting Practice (SSAPs) but, since 1991, as Financial Reporting Standards (FRSs), by the recognised professional accounting bodies in the United Kingdom. The purpose of the standards is to ensure compliance with the true and fair view concept, and they are officially recognised in the Companies Act 1985. All companies are required to comply with the standards, or to publish reasons for departing from them.

Company auditors are required to ensure that company accounts are prepared in accordance with the standards and to report any significant departure from the standards to the shareholders. The standards help to increase uniformity in the presentation of company accounts and to reduce the subjective element in the disclosure of information.

Students are not required to know the historical background to the origin of the accounting standards. It is very important, however, for students to learn the requirements of the standards referred to in this chapter.

Since 1991 Financial Reporting Standards have been issued by the recognised accounting bodies in

the United Kingdom. International accounting standards have been developed in the form of **International Accounting Standards (IASs)** and **International Financial Reporting Standards (IFRSs)** since 2005 with the aim of harmonising, or standardising financial reporting. It is only a matter of time before the IASs are adopted by all companies in the United Kingdom. Indeed, many of the multinational companies are now using them.

The CIE syllabus identifies a number of international accounting standards, the contents of which students need to be aware of. The following table identifies these. Some have already been covered in other chapters. The remaining ones and some aspects of the other not previously mentioned will be covered here. The full detail of the standards is far more than is required for the examination. Only the relevant parts of the standard will be covered.

IAS	Topic	Covered in
1	Presentation of financial statements	Chapter 23
2	Inventories	Chapter 20
7	Statement of cash flows	Chapter 24
8	Accounting policies	This chapter 27.5
10	Events after the Statement of Financial Position date	This chapter 27.6
16	Property, plant and equipment	This chapter 27.7
18	Revenue	This chapter 27.8
23	Borrowing costs	This chapter 27.9
33	Earnings per share	This chapter 27.10
36	Impairment of assets	This chapter 27.11
37	Provisions, contingent liabilities and contingent assets	This chapter 27.13
38	Intangible assets	This chapter 27.14

As we have seen throughout the sections on limited companies, Company law in the United Kingdom also plays an important part in the way financial accounts are presented. In particular, it makes it a requirement for companies to state that their accounts have been prepared in accordance with applicable accounting standards. If this has not been the case then details must be given as to why not.

27.4 FRS 18 Accounting policies

Although not an accounting standard, a *Framework* has been developed by the body which sets the International Accounting Standards. This sets out the principles which underlie the preparation and presentation of financial statements. The Framework identifies the main users of financial statements as:

The framework surrounding IAS identifies the typical user groups of accounting statements. The table below identifies these user groups (stakeholders) and gives likely reasons (by no means exhaustive) for them referring to financial statements:

Main users	Reasons for use
Investors	• To assess past performance as a basis for future investment.
Employees	• To assess performance as a basis of future wage and salary negotiations. • To assess performance as a basis for continuity of employment and job security.
Lenders	• To assess performance in relation to the security of their loan to the company.
Suppliers	• To assess performance in relation to them receiving payment of their liability.
Customers	• To assess performance in relation to the likelihood of continuity of trading
Government	• To assess performance in relation to compliance to regulations and assessment of taxation liabilities.
Public	• To assess performance in relation to ethical trading.

When preparing financial statements it is assumed that they are prepared on an accruals basis and that the business is a going concern. These have been mentioned previously in the text.

- **Accruals** (see §.9.9)
  Companies must compile their financial statements (except statements of cash flows) on an accruals basis. This means that transactions are recorded in the accounting period in which they occur and to which they relate, not when cash is received or paid. A good example here is a sale made on credit. The sale is recorded in the month it takes place. The cash may be received for it some months afterwards, perhaps even in another accounting year.

- **Going concern** (see §9.11)
  Financial statements are prepared on the basis and assumption that the business will continue trading for the foreseeable future. There is no intention that the business is to cease trading. If

that were the case, then the directors would have to prepare the financial statements on a different basis.

There are a number of other accounting concepts which should also be considered when preparing the financial statements. These have also been discussed elsewhere in the text. They are:

- Business entity (see §.9.2)
- Materiality (see §.9.8)
- Consistency (see §.9.7)
- Prudence (see §.9.10)
- Money measurement (see §.9.3)

All of these are designed to ensure that the information provided in the financial statements is useful to users with four objectives in mind:

- **relevance**
  Information should have the ability to influence the economic decisions of the users of the statements, and be provided in time to influence those decisions.

- **reliability**
  Information is reliable if it faithfully represents the facts and is free from bias and material error. It must be complete 'within the bounds of materiality' and prudently prepared.

- **comparability**
  It should be possible to compare information with similar information about the company in a previous period (trend analysis – see chapter 28) and with similar information about other companies (inter-firm comparison – see chapter 28).

- **understandability**
  Information should be able to be understood by users who have a reasonable knowledge of business and accounting, and who are willing to study the information reasonably diligently.

27.5 IAS 8

Accounting policies, changes in accounting estimates and errors

This statement deals with the treatment of changes in accounting estimates, changing in accounting policies and errors in the financial statements.

Accounting Policies

These are the principles, bases, conventions, rules and practices applied by a business when preparing and presenting its financial statements. These policies are selected by the directors of the business. In selecting them then they must make sure that where an accounting policy is given in an accounting standard then the policy they select must comply with the standard.

Where there is no accounting policy provided to give guidance then the directors must use their judgement to give information that is relevant and reliable. The directors must refer to any other standards or interpretations or to other standard setting bodies to assist them. However, they must ensure that their subsequent interpretation or recommended method of treatment for the transaction does not result in conflict with international standards or interpretations.

Accounting Principles

These are covered in the statement, although no formal definition is given for them, they are regarded as the broad concepts that apply to almost all financial statements. These would include such things as going concern, materiality, prudence and consistency, mentioned earlier.

Accounting Bases

These are the methods developed for applying the accounting principles to financial statements. They are intended to reduce subjectivity by identifying and applying acceptable methods.

The general rule is that once an entity adopts an accounting policy then it must be applied consistently for similar transactions. Changes in accounting policies can only occur if the change is required by a standard or interpretation, or if the change results in the financial statements providing more reliable and relevant information.

Once any changes are adopted then they must be applied retrospectively to financial statements. This means that the previous figure for equity and other figures in the income statement and statement of financial position must be altered, subject to the practicalities of calculating the relevant amounts.

Dealing with errors

If an error in the financial statements is discovered then the business must correct material errors from prior periods in the next set of financial statements. Comparative amounts from previous periods must be restated, subject to the practicalities of calculating the relevant amounts.

In this instance errors are omissions from or misstatements in the business financial statements covering one or more prior periods. They could be something as simple as a mathematical mistake made when preparing the accounts. They may also include the failure by directors to use reliable information which was available when the financial statements were prepared.

27.6 IAS 10

Events after the Statement of Financial Position date

These are events, either favourable or unfavourable, which occur between the Statement of Financial Position date and the date on which the financial statements are authorised for issue, having been approved by the shareholders at the Annual General Meeting. Such items may occur as a result of information which becomes available after the end of the year and, therefore need to be disclosed in the accounts. If they occur then amounts included in the financial statements must be adjusted; they may indicate that the going concern is not appropriate to the financial statements.

The key is the point in time at which changes to the financial statements can be made. Once the financial statements have been approved for issue by the board of directors they cannot be altered. For example, the accounts are prepared up to 31 December. They are approved for issue by the board of directors on 30 April in the following year. Between these two dates, changes resulting from events after 31 December can be disclosed in the accounts. After 30 April nothing can be changed until the next annual accounts are prepared.

The statement distinguishes between two types of events:

1. **Adjusting events**
   If, at the date of the Statement of Financial

Position, evidence of conditions existed that would **materially** affect the financial statements then the financial statements should be changed to reflect these conditions.

Examples of adjusting events could include:

- the settlement after the date of the statement of financial position of a court case which confirms that an obligation existed at the date of the statement of financial position.
- the purchase price or proceeds from the sale of a non-current asset bought or sold before the year end but are not known about at the date of the statement of financial position.
- inventories where the net realisable value falls below the cost price.
- assets where a valuation shows that impairment is required.
- trade receivables where a customer has become insolvent.
- the discovery of fraud or errors which show the financial statements to be incorrect.

2. **Non-Adjusting Events**

No adjustment is made to the financial statements for such events. If material, they are disclosed by way of notes to the financial statements.

Examples include:

- major purchase of assets.
- losses of production capacity caused by fire, floods or strike action by employees.
- announcement or commencement of a major reconstruction of the business.
- the company entering into significant commitments or contingent liabilities.
- commencing litigation based on events arising after the date of the statement of financial position.
- major share transactions, such as the issue of new shares and debentures or capital reductions or reconstructions.

There are three situations in addition to the above which require consideration:

(a) Dividends declared or proposed after the date of the statement of financial position are no longer recognised as a current liability in the final accounts. They are non-adjusting events and are now to be shown by way of a note to the accounts.

(b) If, after the date of the Statement of Financial Position, the directors determine that the business intends to cease trading and that there is no alternative to this course of action, then the financial statements cannot be prepared on a going concern basis.

(c) A business must disclose the date when the financial statements were authorised for issue and who gave that authorisation. If anyone had the power to amend the financial statements after their authorisation then this fact must also be disclosed.

27.7 **IAS 16**

Property, plant and equipment

This statement deals with the accounting treatment of the non-current assets of property, plant and equipment. The issues covered by the statement are:

- the recognition of the assets: when is the item recorded in the accounts.
- the determination of their carrying amounts: what value is placed on it in the financial statements
- their depreciation charges
- their impairment losses: what happens when the value of the asset is below than that shown in the accounts.

1. **Property, plant and equipment**

These are tangible assets held for use in the production or supply of goods and services, for rental to others and for administrative purposes. They are expected to be used by the business for more than a period of more than one year.

For example, an company may buy some plant and machinery at a cost of $15 000. It expects the plant to be used for 10 years and at the end of that time to be sold for $1000. The depreciable amount will be $14 000. Assuming the company uses the straight line method of depreciation, then each year $1400 will be recorded as an expense in the Income Statement. This example allows reference to be made to the definitions included in the standard. They are:

1. **Depreciation**

   This is the allocation of the cost of an asset over its useful life. This will be the $1400 written off each year.

2. **Depreciable amount**

   This is the cost or valuation of the asset, less any residual amount. This will be the figure of $14 000 ($15 000 – $1000).

3. **Useful life**

   This is usually the length of time for which an asset is expected to be used. This will be the period of 10 years for which the company intends to hold and use the plant. There is an alternative. If the asset is depreciated on the basis of the number of units it produces then the estimated output of the item over its useful life can be used.

4. **Residual value**

   The net amount the business expects to obtain for an asset at the end of its useful life, after deducting the expected costs of disposal. This will be the figure of $1000, which the company hopes to sell the asset for at the end of its useful life.

The standard also uses some other terms which you need to be aware of:

1. **Fair value**

   This is the amount for which an asset could be exchanged between knowledgeable, willing parties in an arm's length transaction. If, for example, after five years the company decided to sell the plant, it may offer it to a buyer at $5000. This would be regarded as a fair value for the item being sold.

2. **Carrying amount**

   This is the amount at which an asset is recognised in the statement of financial position, after deducting any accumulated depreciation and impairment loss. This is,

in effect the net book value of the asset shown in the statement of financial position.

At what point does an entity recognise the asset? Or put more simply, at what point is the asset to be recorded in the financial statements? This must be done when it is probable that the business will be able to use it to generate revenue and a cost can be assigned to it. Once an item of property, plant and equipment qualifies for recognition as an asset by meeting these criteria, then it is brought into the accounts and **initially valued at cost**.

Additional costs associated with the asset

The statement recognises that in addition to the initial purchase price of the asset, other amounts may also be spent on it. The statement provides the following guidelines to assist with the treatment of such expenditure:

1. Day-to-day costs of servicing or repairing the asset should be charged as expenditure in the Income Statement.

2. Where parts require replacement at regular intervals, say the seats in an aeroplane, then these costs can be added to the cost of the asset in the Statement of Financial Position and depreciated accordingly.

3. Where the asset requires regular inspections in order for the asset to continue operating, then the costs of such inspections can also be added to the cost of the asset in the Statement of Financial Position and depreciated accordingly.

When the asset is purchased, apart from its original cost a business may also pay other costs as part of the purchase price. The standard provides information as to what can be included as part of the cost in the statement of financial position:

- any import duties, taxes directly attributable to bring the asset to its present location and condition
- the costs of site preparation
- initial delivery and handling costs
- installation and assembly costs
- cost of testing the asset
- professional fees; say architects or legal fees.

Valuation of the asset

Once the asset is acquired the business must adopt one of two models for its valuation:
1. Cost less accumulated depreciation
2. Revaluation – the asset is included (carried) at a revalued amount. Revaluations are to be made regularly by suitably qualified people to ensure that the carrying amount does not differ significantly from the fair value of the asset at the date of the Statement of Financial Position. Revaluations should be undertaken by the business every three to five years, unless assets are bought and sold frequently. If an asset is revalued then every asset in that **class** must be revalued. Thus, if one parcel of land and buildings is revalued then all land and buildings must be revalued. Any surplus on revaluation is transferred to the equity section of the Statement of Financial Position as a Revaluation Reserve, this may not be used to pay dividends to the shareholders. Any loss on revaluation is recognised as an expense in the Income Statement.

Depreciation

The expected life and residual value of the asset are to be reviewed at least annually. If there is a difference from previous estimates this must be recognised as a change in an estimate under IAS 8 (Accounting policies, changes in accounting estimates and errors). Depreciation must also continue to be charged even if the fair value of an asset exceeds its carrying amount. However, depreciation need not be charged when the residual value is greater than the carrying amount. Depreciation is to be included as an expense in the Income Statement.

The business must choose a method of depreciation which reflects the pattern of its usage over its useful economic life. Ideally, once it has decided on the method this should not be changed. It is possible though to review the method and if a change in the pattern of usage of the asset has occurred then the method of depreciation should be changed to reflect this. Such a change would come under IAS 8.

When the asset is sold or no further future economic benefits are expected from its use. Any profit or loss on disposal is shown in the Income Statement.

Disclosure in the financial statements

For each class of property, plant and equipment the financial statements must show:
- the basis for determining the carrying amount
- the depreciation method used
- the useful life or depreciation rate
- the gross carrying amount at the beginning and end of the accounting period
- the accumulated depreciation and impairment losses at the beginning and end of the accounting period
- additions during the period
- disposals during the period
- depreciation for the period

These are likely to be shown by way of a non-current asset schedule and included as a note to the accounts.

Example

Non-current assets Cost	Premises	Plant and Machinery	Motor Vehicles	Total
	$000	$000	$000	$000
Cost at start of year*	800	400	230	1430
Revaluation	200			200
Additions during the year	–	246	170	416
Disposals during the year	–	(80)	(96)	(176)
Cost at end of year	1000	566	304	1870
Depreciation				
Balance at start of year*	400	256	164	820
Revaluation	(400)	–	–	(400)
Charge during year	–	115	70	185
Disposals	–	(70)	(80)	(150)
		301	154	455
Net Book Value				
At end of year*	1000	265	150	1415

*Dates at the start and end of the year would be provided in practice.

Note. A revaluation reserve of $600 000 (200 000 + 400 000) will have been created at the end of the year and recorded in the equity section of the Statement of Financial Position. The final figures for net book value will be recorded in the Statement of Financial Position.

27.8 IAS 18

Revenue

Revenue is defined in the statement as 'the gross inflow of economic benefits arising from the ordinary activities of an entity.' This means sales, either of goods or services. It also includes income from interest, say bank interest, dividends received and royalties received and gains from non-revenue activities, such as the proceeds from the disposal of non-current assets.

It does not include money collected by a business on behalf of another party, say where the business acts as an agent. However, any commission earned for collecting money as an agent is included as revenue.

When a transaction takes place the amount of revenue is usually decided by the agreement between the buyer and the seller. The amount of revenue measured will take into account any trade discounts, which will not be included as part of the revenue.

The sale of goods is to be accounted for when **all** of the following criteria have been met:

(a) the seller of the goods has transferred to the buyer the significant rewards of ownership. This is usually when the legal title to the goods transfer or possession of the goods passes from seller to buyer. This covers goods sold on a sale or return basis, where the title has not passed from seller to buyer.

(b) the seller retains no continual managerial involvement in and no effective control over the goods. The amount of revenue can be reliably measured.

(c) it is probable that the economic benefits will now flow to the seller.

(d) the costs incurred, or to be incurred in respect of the transaction can be reliably measured.

When the income is interest, the amount to be recognised is calculated using a time basis (accruals concept). If the income is dividends, these are brought into the Income Statement when the shareholder's right to receive payment is established. Dividends received are brought into the accounts when the shareholder's right to receive payment is established.

27.9 IAS 23

Borrowing costs

This covers such items in the accounts as interest on bank overdrafts and how they should be recognised in the Income Statement of the period for which they are incurred.

A borrowing cost is interest and other costs incurred by a business in connection with borrowing funds. This covers such things as bank loan or overdraft interest. The statement provides that borrowing costs are to be recognised as an expense in the Income Statement in the period in which they are incurred.

An alternative to this is when the borrowing relates to the acquisition, construction or production of a qualifying asset. In this instance the borrowing costs can be capitalised as part of the cost of the asset. For example, if an asset is being constructed and is financed by use of borrowed funds then any interest payable on the borrowings can also be capitalised. Suppose a company borrows $10 000 to construct a new building. Whilst the building is being constructed any interest payable on the $10 000 can be capitalised as part of the cost of the building. Once the building is completed then any interest payable on the $10 000 is entered in the Income Statement under Finance Costs.

If any of the funds borrowed are temporarily invested in the short term and generate interest, then this interest must be offset against the borrowing costs capitalised.

27.10 IAS 33

Earnings per share (EPS)

This is a ratio widely used by investors and analysts to measure the performance of a business and will be considered again in chapter 28. The earnings of a company are the profits (or losses) for the year that are attributable to the equity holders of the business.

IAS 33 sets out a basic method of calculating earnings per share, which is:

$$\frac{\text{Net profit attributable to the ordinary shareholders}}{\text{Number of ordinary shares issued}}$$

Example

For the year ended 31 December the Income Statement of a company shows the following:

	$000
Profit from operations before tax	1 500
Tax	(500)
Profit for the year attributable to equity holders	1 000

At the start of the year the entity had 2 million ordinary shares of $1 each.

The earnings per share are:

Profit for the year attributable to equity holders:

$$\frac{\$1\ 000\ 000}{2\ 000\ 000} = \$0.50 \text{ per share}$$

In published accounts earnings per share are always shown in the Income Statement for both the current year and the pervious year. They are always expressed in cents per share.

Dividends on non-redeemable preference shares should be deducted from the profit attributable to equity holders **before** calculating the earnings per ordinary share.

27.11 IAS 36

Impairment of assets

The purpose of this standard is to ensure that assets are shown in the Statement of Financial Position at no more than their value or **recoverable amount**. The term recoverable amount means the amount for which the asset can be sold on the open market (however, see below). If the recoverable amount is less than the amount, the asset is shown in the accounts (its **carrying amount,** in effect its net book value) then the carrying amount must be reduced. This is an **impairment loss** and must be recognised as an expense in the Income Statement.

The standard applies to most non-current assets such as land and buildings, plant and machinery, motor vehicles and so on. It also applies to intangible assets such as goodwill and investments.

It does not apply to inventories, which are the subject of their own standard, IAS 2.

Some of the terms in this standard have already been covered in the section on IAS 16. However, there are some other terms used in this standard which require explanation.

Amortisation — this usually refers to the write down of an intangible asset, such as goodwill.

Impairment loss — the amount by which the carrying amount of an asset exceeds its recoverable amount.

Fair value less costs to sell — the amount obtainable from the sale of an asset in an arm's length transaction between knowledgeable, willing parties, less the costs of the disposal.

Recoverable amount — In respect of the asset, 'the higher of its fair value less costs to sell and its value in use.'

Value in use — the present value of the future cash flows obtainable as a result of an asset's continued use, including cash from its ultimate disposal.

Useful life — this can be either the period of time which an asset is expected to be used by the business, or the number of units of output expected to be obtained from the asset.

The Impairment Review

Businesses are expected to undertake an impairment review of their assets. In other words, assess whether or not the asset's net book value in the financial statement is a fair representation of their true value to the business. The impairment review involves comparing the asset's carrying amount with the recoverable amount. It is carried out in three stages:

1. Calculate the asset's carrying amount – its net book value.
2. Compare this with the asset's recoverable amount. The recoverable amount will be the **higher** of:
   (a) the asset's fair value less costs to sell, and
   (b) the asset's value in use. This is the present value of future cash flows to the business generated as a result of using the asset.

Example

A company is reviewing its assets at the end of its financial year. It identifies that:

1. the net book value of the asset is $30 000 (cost minus accumulated depreciation).
2. the company could sell the asset for $25 000 but would have to pay costs when selling of $2 000.
3. The company estimates the net future cash flows of the asset as:

Year	Future cash flows from the asset $	Discount factors at 10%	Present values of future cash flows $
1	15 000	0.909	13 635
2	18 000	0.826	14 868
3	30 000	0.751	22 530
4	20 000	0.682	13 640

Total present value of future cash flows = $(13 635 + 14 868 + 22 530 +13 640) = $64 673.

The Impairment review will be carried out by comparing $30 000 with the higher of $23 000 (25 000 – 2 000) and $64 673.

As the net book value is lower than highest of the other two amounts ($64 673) then it will still be shown in the Statement of Financial Position at $30 000.

If the carrying value is greater than the recoverable amount then the asset is impaired. It must be written down to its recoverable amount in the Statement of Financial position. The amount of the impairment is recognised as an expense in the Income Statement as additional depreciation, or under its own heading of Impairment loss.

Example

An business has three non-current assets in use at its year end. Details of their carrying values and recoverable amounts are set out below:

Asset	Carrying amount $	Fair value less costs to sell $	Value in use $
1	30 000	10 000	50 000
2	15 000	12 000	14 000
3	20 000	15 000	9 000

In the Statement of Financial Position they should be shown at the following values:

Asset	Value in Statement of Financial Position $	Reason
1	30 000	The carrying amount is less than the recoverable amount, its value in use.
2	14 000	The carrying amount is greater than the recoverable amount, the highest of which is its value in use.
3	15 000	The carrying amount is greater than the recoverable amount, the highest of which is its fair value less costs to sell.

The difference between the carrying value and the value to include the assets in the Statement of Financial Position will be written off in the Income Statement. Their revised values will be included in the Statement of Financial Position.

27.12 IAS 37

Provisions, contingent assets and contingent liabilities

These items represent uncertainties at the time the final accounts are prepared. They need to be fully accounted for on a consistent basis so that readers and user of the accounts can have a better understanding of their effect on the accounts.

A **provision** can be defined as a liability of uncertain amount or timing. An example here would be provision for bad or doubtful debts. Provisions are only shown in the accounts when there are valid grounds for them. They should never be used as a way of window dressing the figures. If it is likely that a firm will have to make a payment for something and the amount it will have to pay can be reasonably estimated, then it can reasonably bring a provision into the accounts.

On the other hand, a **liability** is a present obligation a business has as a result of past events, where its settlement is expected to result in a payment being made. For example, a business has a liability to pay its suppliers for goods and services they have provided. There is also another class of liability known as a **contingent liability.** This is a possible liability to the business which arises from some past event. However, it may only result in the business having to pay for it when a decision is made which is outside the company's control. For example, someone may be suing the company for faulty goods supplied. There is a possibility that the company will have to pay damages to the other party. However, that decision will be made by the courts. This decision and the amount of the payment is outside the company's control.

A contingent liability is not recognised in the accounts, but is disclosed by way of a note to them. This will describe the nature of the contingent liability, an estimate of how much it is likely to cost and an indication of the uncertainties relating to the amount or timing of any outflow of funds.

There is also a **contingent asset** which may affect a company. This is a possible asset arising from past events which will materialise when something happens which is not entirely within the company's control.

A contingent asset should **never be recognised in the accounts**, as to do so may be to bring in revenue that may never be realised. However, when the profit is almost certain to arise it is no longer a contingent asset and it should then be recognised in the accounts.

In other words the accounts will include an amount which will be received.

The IAS uses three words when it talks about provisions, contingent assets and contingent liabilities. They are:

- Probable – more than a 50% chance that the event will occur.
- Possible – less than 50% chance that the event will occur.
- Remote – little or no chance of the event occurring.

The following provides guidance of how items falling within these headings should be treated.

1. **Provisions more that 50% likely to happen (Probable)**
   In this case the amount should be entered in the financial statements. There must also be a note to the accounts giving details of these figures.
2. **Contingent liabilities less than 50% likely to happen (Possible)**
   In this case no amount is included in the financial statements, but a note to the accounts is given about the contingent liability.
3. **Contingent liabilities which are remote, in other words most unlikely to happen**
   In this case no figures are shown in the accounts, neither is any note to the accounts included.
4. **Contingent assets with more than a 50% chance of occurring (Probable)**
   In this case no amount is included in the accounts. However, a note to the accounts is provided about the contingent asset.
5. **Contingent assets with less than a 50% chance of occurring (Both Possible and Remote)**
   In both cases no amount is included in the accounts, neither is a note to the accounts included.

27.13 IAS 38

Intangible assets

An intangible asset is a non-monetary asset without physical substance. The best example of an intangible asset is Goodwill. However patents and trade marks are also regarded as intangible assets. In other words, it is something which has value but, unlike, say plant and machinery, cannot be touched.

In terms of the definition given above, in order for it to be identifiable the asset must be capable of being sold separately from other parts of the business. Thus, for instance, a customer list could be an intangible asset as it can be sold separately by the entity. In an instance such as this, the entity has control of the asset and its use. The asset will also bring future economic benefits to the organisation.

Intangible assets can come from two sources. Firstly, they may be purchased. For instance a business may buy the patents of a particular product from another entity. Alternatively, when a business buys another at a figure in excess of the net book value of the assets taken over then it purchases Goodwill.

Alternatively, they are generated internally within the business. For instance, the Goodwill which is valued when a partner leaves a partnership or a new partner is introduced. In both cases the Goodwill has been internally generated by the efforts of the existing partners.

The general rule is that **only** purchased intangible assets are recognised in the accounts. The intangible asset is shown at cost less any accumulated amortisation (depreciation) and impairment losses. It may also be shown at a revalued amount, being its fair value, (see IAS 36, Impairment of Assets), less any amortisation or impairment losses. In this case any loss in value is shown as an expense in the Income Statement. Any surplus is credited to a Revaluation Reserve on the Statement of Financial Position.

In every case the business must identify the useful life of the intangible asset. In the case of those intangible assets having a finite life they should be amortised using the straight line method. In this case the residual value should be assumed as zero and the amount of the amortisation should be charged as an expense in the Income Statement. The amortisation period should be reviewed at least annually and any changes to the amounts charged made in line with such a review.

Where the asset is deemed to have an infinite life then it will not be amortised. Instead, it will undergo an annual impairment review. Part of the review must also consider whether or not an infinite life is still valid in respect of the asset. Any loss in value arising from such a review is charged as an expense in the Income Statement. It should be noted that strictly speaking no asset has an infinite life. Thus intangible assets should always be written off over a period of time.

The statement also provides guidance to businesses which undertake Research and Development. In doing so, it provides definitions of each.

Research is theoretical work undertaken to gain new knowledge. This may or may not have some commercial benefit in the future. In this case expenditure on research is to be written off as an expense in the Income Statement. Any non-current assets which are purchased as a result of the research can be capitalised and written off over their expected useful lives.

Development is moving on a stage. It is, perhaps using research to develop a product which the business can use to generate sales at some point in the future. A good example here is the automotive industry, where the research into green technology may result in the development of an emission-free car.

In this case, development expenditure can be written off as an expense in the Income Statement in the period in which it is incurred. Alternatively, the expenditure can be recognised as an intangible asset in the Statement of Financial Position of the business.

27.14 Directors' report

The directors of the company are required by the companies act to prepare a report for each financial year. The purpose of the report is to supplement the information given by the financial statements.

The directors' report contains the following information:

- A review of these activities over the past year, together with likely developments in the future including any research and development activities. The financial accounts only provide information which is expressed in monetary terms (the concept of money measurement). They cannot describe, for example the economic conditions under which the company has traded.
- A statement of the principal activities of the company and any significant changes in those activities during the year. In other words, what trading activities the company has carried out during the year.
- The names of the directors, together with their shareholdings in the company. The shareholders are entitled to know who have been stewards of their interests during the year.
- Proposed dividends payable by the company. These will be voted on for recommendation by the shareholders at the company's annual general meeting.
- Significant differences between the book value and market value of land and buildings.
- Political and charitable donations made by the company. Shareholders may not want their

money to be used for political purposes. Or wish that their money is used more for charitable purposes.

- Company policy on the employment of disable people. Legislation dictates that companies must not discriminate against employees on grounds of any disability.
- Health and safety at work of employees. The shareholders are entitled to be re-assured that company is abiding by current legislation on health and safety and is taking the welfare of its employees into account.
- What action the company has taken on employee involvement in the running of the business and consultation which has taken place between management and workers on the management and running of the business.
- Company policy on payment of suppliers. This requirement arose from the practice of many large companies delaying payments to creditors (especially those less powerful), whose cash flows suffered as a consequence. There is an ethical dimension to the requirement to disclose this information.

27.15 Auditors' report

Directors are stewards of the company in which shareholders have invested their capital. The shareholders are unable to inspect the company's books but they are, along with the debenture holders, entitled to receive copies of the annual accounts. It is important that shareholders and debenture holders can be sure that the directors can be trusted to conduct the company's business well and that the financial statements and directors' report are reliable.

The shareholders appoint auditors to report at each annual general meeting whether

- proper books of account have been kept
- the annual financial statements are in agreement with the books of account
- in the auditors' opinion, the Statement of Financial Position gives a true and fair view of the position of the company at the end of the financial year and the Income Statement gives a true and fair view of the profit or loss for the period covered by the account
- the accounts have been prepared in accordance with the Companies Acts and all current, relevant accounting standards.

If auditors are of the opinion that the continuance of a company is dependent on a bank loan or overdraft, they have a duty to mention that fact in their report as it is relevant to the going concern concept.

The auditors' responsibility extends to reporting on the directors' report and stating whether the statements in it are consistent with the financial statements. They must also report whether, in their opinion, the report contains misleading statements.

Auditors must be qualified accountants and independent of the company's directors and their associates. They report to the shareholders and not to the directors; as a result, auditors enjoy protection from wrongful dismissal from office by the directors.

HINTS

- Make sure you are familiar with the contents of the accounting standards covered in this chapter. They underpin and link in with everything you have learned so far and with the understanding and interpretation of accounts which will be covered in the next chapter.
- Multiple-choice questions are often based on a knowledge on this topic.
- Practise answering discursive-type questions based on published accounts. Answers should be clear, concise and relevant.

MULTIPLE-CHOICE QUESTIONS

1. On which amount are earnings per share calculated?
   A. profit after interest, tax and preference dividend
   B. profit after interest, tax, preference dividend and transfer to general reserve
   C. profit before interest, tax and preference dividend
   D. profit before interest, tax, preference dividend and transfer to general reserve.

2. Which of the following does **not** have to be shown in the directors' report?
   A. Charitable donations made by the company
   B. Directors' salaries
   C. Directors' shareholdings
   D. Donations to political parties

3. A company is undertaking a review of its non-current assets. It discovers that some items of plant and machinery should be shown at a value below their carrying amount. Others are valued above their carrying amount.
   Which of the following statements is true about the actions it should take as a result of this?
   A. It must revalue all its non-current assets.
   B. It must revalue all its non-current assets in that class
   C. It only needs to revalue those items which are above their carrying amount
   D. It only needs to revalue those items which are below their carrying amount.

4. A business carries out an impairment review of its assets. The following information is discovered about an item:

Cost when purchased	$20 000
Carrying amount	$12 000
Recoverable amount	$14 000
Value in use	$10 000

   What figure should it be shown as in the Statement of Financial Position?
   A. $10 000   B. $12 000
   C. $14 000   D. $20 000

5. A business carries out an impairment review of its assets. The following information is discovered about an item:

Cost when purchased	$25 000
Carrying amount	$14 000
Recoverable amount	$8 000
Value in use	$12 000

   What figure should it be shown as in the Statement of Financial Position?
   A. $8 000   B. $12 000
   C. $14 000   D. $25 000

6. Which of the following is a non-adjusting event?
   A. A non-current asset which is the subject of an impairment review loss.
   B. A major customer becoming insolvent three weeks after the end of the financial year.
   C. A discovery that the value of items of inventory have fallen below their cost.
   D. The purchase of a new machine costing $500 000 made one month after the end of the financial year.

ADDITIONAL EXERCISES

1. Explain what is meant by an adjusting event. Describe the action that needs to be taken when one occurs and explain why the action is necessary.

Part III
Financial reporting and interpretation

28 Interpretation and analysis

In this chapter you will learn:

- the limitations of financial statements
- how to analyse and interpret financial statements
- how to calculate ratios
- how to use ratios
- how to explain (and how not to explain) ratios.

28.1 The limitations of financial statements for shareholders and other interested parties

The purpose of financial statements such as Income Statement and Statement of Financial Position is to present information in a meaningful way. That is why items in financial statements are placed in groups of similar items: non-current assets, current assets, current liabilities, etc. It also explains why you should compile financial statements with every item in its correct place.

Accounting standards are intended to ensure that items included in financial statements and described in similar terms are calculated, as far as possible, on the same bases. The Companies Act and the accounting standards require companies to add numerous notes to their financial statements to throw more light on the items in the accounts.

To be useful, information must be clear, complete, reliable and timely. In spite of the efforts of the Companies Act and the numerous accounting standards to ensure some sort of uniformity in the preparation of financial statements, the published accounts of limited companies have a number of limitations as communicators of information.

- They are not clear to people who have an inadequate knowledge of accounting and finance.

- The information they give is not complete. Legislation and accounting standards recognise that companies are entitled to keep certain information confidential because publication would give competitors an unfair advantage.

- The reliability of financial statements is only relative because companies are permitted to exercise a fair degree of subjectivity in selecting their accounting policies. Depreciation, provisions for doubtful debts, inventory valuation and treatment of Goodwill are examples of areas where there is no uniformity.

- Companies are allowed to depart from accounting standards if such departure is justified by the nature of their business and will improve the quality of the information provided by the accounting statements.

- By their very nature, published accounts are of historic interest. They may not be published for many months after the end of the financial year they cover. In the meantime, many circumstances may have changed: the economy may have improved or worsened; the political scene may have altered; new technologies may have been developed; fashions may have changed. A company's performance may have improved or worsened between the date of the Statement of Financial Position and its publication.

The directors' report may help to overcome some of the limitations of the financial statements, but not completely.

Only people with some knowledge of accounting are able to make much sense of the mass of figures in a company's financial statements. Even accountants need to interpret the figures before they are able to understand their significance. As a useful tool for interpreting accounts, accountants calculate ratios that relate certain items in the accounts to other items where there should be some sort of sensible relationship.

The users of financial statements was covered in the previous chapter.

28.2 A pyramid of ratios

The ratios that accountants use may be represented as a pyramid, which classifies the ratios into useful types and shows how they relate to one another.

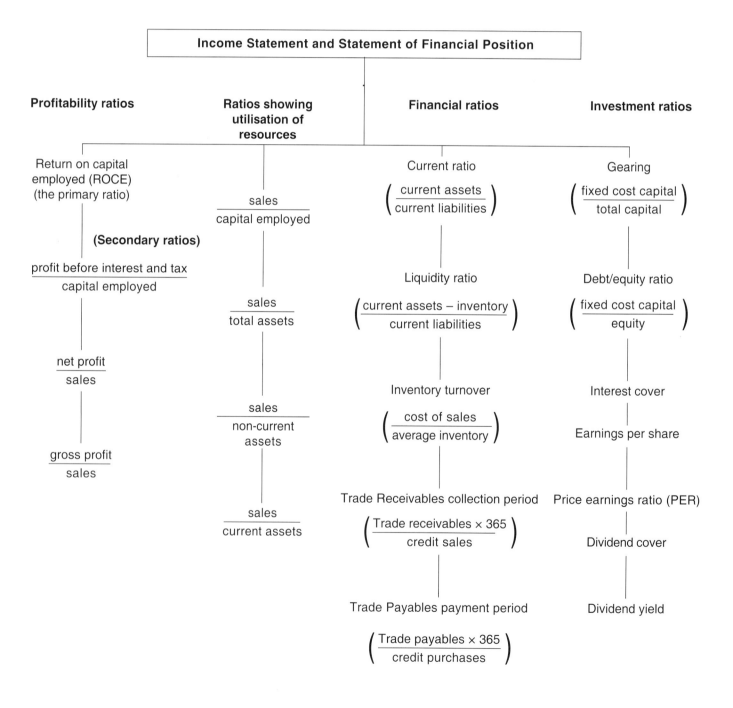

28.3 How to calculate and analyse ratios

All the ratios shown in the pyramid are explained in §§28.4 – 28.7 and illustrated with the aid of the following financial statements of Lladnar Ltd.

This chapter will cover the ratios usually asked for in the CIE examinations. They are contained in the syllabus, together with the basis on which they should be calculated. Other ratios not on the syllabus are also included in this chapter and can be used in an examination.

Note that these financial statements contain more detail than that required under IAS 1. This is done simply to help with identifying where information comes from in order to carry out the ratio analysis.

Lladnar Ltd
Income Statement
for the years ended 31 December

	2011		2010	
	$000	$000	$000	$000
Revenue		1600		1200
Cost of Sales				
Opening inventory	54		42	
Purchases	1166		800	
	1220		842	
Less: closing inventory	100	1120	54	788
Gross profit		480		412
Distribution costs		(184)		(160)
Administration costs		(80)		(70)
Profit from operations		216		182
Finance costs		(15)		(10)
Profit attributable to equity holders		201		172

Lladnar Ltd
Statement of Changes in Equity
for the years ended 31 December

	2011	2010
	$000	$000
Retained earnings at 1 January	118	11
Profit attributable to equity holders	201	172
Transfer to general reserve	(60)	(40)
Dividends paid	(30)	(25)
Balance at 31 December	229	118

Lladnar Ltd
Statements of Financial Position at 31 December

	2011			2010		
	$000	$000	$000	$000	$000	$000
Assets						
Non-current assets		924			670	
Current assets						
Inventory	100			54		
Trade receivables	200			115		
Cash & cash equivalents	29			100		
	329			269		
Total assets		1253			939	
Liabilities						
Current liabilities						
Trade payables		194			101	
Non-current liabilities						
10% Debenture 2018/2019		150			100	
Equity						
Ordinary shares		400			400	
General reserve		280			220	
Retained earnings		229			118	
		909			738	
Total liabilities		1253			939	

Most ratios are appropriate for both incorporated and unincorporated businesses.

The ratios explained and analysed in §§28.4 – 28.7 are calculated to three decimal places but rounded to two decimal places. This is the usual requirement in examinations, but the particular requirement of any question must be observed.

28.4 Profitability ratios

The primary ratio: return on capital employed (ROCE)

The test of a good investment is its profitability, that is, the reward it yields on the amount invested in it. (Profit and profitability should not be confused. Profit is expressed as an amount of money: $172 000 for 2010 and $201 000 for 2011 in Lladnar Ltd's case; profitability is a ratio that relates profit to the amount invested.) The **first (or primary) ratio** for investors in a business is the **return on capital employed**. It relates profit before interest and tax (profit from operations) to the capital employed in the business. The formula is:

$$\frac{\text{profit before interest and tax}}{\text{capital employed}} \times 100$$

(remember it easily as $\frac{\text{PROBIT}}{\text{capital employed}} \times 100$)

(PROBIT = profit before interest and tax)

Lladnar Ltd's return on capital employed is:

2011	2010
$\dfrac{216}{1059} \times 100 = 20.40\%$	$\dfrac{182}{838} \times 100 = 21.72\%$
$(150 + 909)$	$(100 + 738)$

Note. Debentures and other long-term loans are included in capital employed.

Comment. In 2010, $21.72 of every $100 of turnover was left on the bottom line as net profit. (The net profit is known as the 'bottom line'. Items in accounts may be described as 'above the line' or 'below the line'.) In 2011, the return has decreased by just over 1%, to 20.40%. Although only a small change, this contrasts with the preferred result which would have been to see an increase over the previous year. Whether or not a rate of return is satisfactory depends upon the return that may be expected on suitable alternative investments.

Return on Equity

This ratio identifies the return made by the business for the ordinary shareholders. The decision whether they should remain as ordinary shareholders in the company or look for a better return elsewhere can be based on this ratio. The formula is:

$$\frac{\text{Profit after tax and preference dividends}}{\text{Equity (Issued ordinary shares + reserves)}} \times 100$$

Profit attributable to equity holders

Lladnar Ltd's return on equity is:

2011	2010
$\dfrac{201}{909} \times 100 = 22.11\%$	$\dfrac{172}{738} \times 100 = 23.31\%$

Comment. In 2010 the company made a return of $0.23 on every $1 owned by the ordinary shareholders. In 2011 this decreased, or became slightly worse to $0.22, or by $0.01. This is only a small change and although the ordinary shareholders would have hoped to see an increase, they should not be worried. They should, however compare this with the return they could expect on a similar investment in a suitable alternative.

Profit before interest and tax as a percentage of sales (or Profit from operations as a percentage of sales)

Profit before interest and tax is calculated as a percentage of sales. For Lladnar Ltd this is:

2011	2010
$\dfrac{216}{1600} \times 100 = 13.50\%$	$\dfrac{182}{1200} \times 100 = 15.17\%$

Comment. Profit before interest and tax has fallen by 1.67%. When the gross profit percentage is calculated, that ratio will be seen to have fallen even more (by 4.33%). It is not surprising, therefore, to find that the profit before interest and tax has fallen although it should not fall by the same amount as most overheads are more or less fixed and do not vary with turnover.

Net profit percentage

Net profit can be related to sales by the following formula:

$$\frac{\begin{array}{c}\text{net profit attributable}\\ \text{to equity holders}\end{array}}{\text{sales}} \times 100. \text{ For Lladnar Ltd this is:}$$

2011	2010
$\dfrac{201}{1600} \times 100 = 12.56\%$	$\dfrac{172}{1200} \times 100 = 14.33\%$

Comment. The net profit percentage has fallen by 1.77% from 14.33% in 2010 to 12.56% in 2011, even though turnover has risen by $33\frac{1}{3}\%$ from $1 200 000 to $1 600 000. The causes for the change in the net profit percentage may be analysed by examining gross profit percentage and the overheads as a percentage of sales.

This ratio can be calculated by using either the net profit after interest and before tax or the net profit after tax (profit attributable to equity holders). In an examination the examiner is likely to require only one of them to be calculated. Look at the question to see what information is given and check what is asked for in the question.

Gross profit percentage

The formula for gross profit percentage is

$$\frac{\text{gross profit}}{\text{sales}} \times 100. \text{ For Lladnar Ltd this is:}$$

2011	2010
$\dfrac{480}{1600} \times 100 = 30.00\%$	$\dfrac{412}{1200} \times 100 = 34.33\%$

Comment. Gross profit percentage has decreased by 4.33% from 34.33% to 30.00%. In theory, the gross profit percentage should match the margin the business expects to make on all its sales. In practice, it is not as simple as that because most businesses sell more than one kind of good and a different mark up may be added to each kind. The gross profit percentage is affected by changes in the mix of the different products making up the turnover.

The reduction in the gross profit percentage may be explained by a number of factors:

- a rise in the price of goods purchased may not have been passed on to customers
- it may have been necessary to purchase the goods from a different supplier at a higher price
- the margin on sales may have been cut:
  - to increase the volume of sales
  - to fight competition from other businesses
  - as an introductory offer for a new product
  - as a result of seasonal sales
  - to dispose of out-of-date or damaged stocks
  - to increase cash flow when the business is short of cash
- the cost of sales may have been increased by the theft of stock.

Overheads (Operating expenses) expresed as a percentage of sales

Overheads expressed as percentage of sales are given as follows for Lladnar Ltd:

2011	2010
$\dfrac{279\,(184 + 80 + 15)}{1600} \times 100 = 17.44\%$	$\dfrac{240\,(160 + 70 + 10)}{1200} \times 100 = 20.00\%$

The overhead percentage is calculated more quickly by finding the difference between the gross and net profit percentages.

Comment. Although sales have increased in 2011 by $33\frac{1}{3}\%$, the ratio of overheads to sales has decreased from 20% to 17.44%. However, the decrease in overheads as a percentage of sales has not been enough to cover the decrease in gross profit margin. This, in turn, has led to a decrease in the net profit margin. Notice how this is a good example of how ratios are linked together and a decrease in one can lead to a decrease in others. Sometimes overheads may increase as a percentage of sales, but the increase may not match the increase in gross profit percentage. The reason is that most overheads,

such as rent, do not vary as a result of an increase in sales. Other overheads may vary, but not in proportion to sales. Salespeople's remuneration, for example, may consist of a fixed salary plus a bonus based on sales.

It is possible to analyse overheads further by expressing the individual items as percentages of sales but this is usually of very limited value because of the absence of any direct link between the individual overheads and sales.

28.5 Ratios showing the utilisation of resources

The profitability of a business depends on how efficiently it uses its resources, and the next group of ratios is designed to test this aspect of the business.

Sales as a percentage of capital employed

Capital invested in a business must be utilised efficiently if it is to produce a good ROCE. Capital of $100 producing sales of $300 is being used more efficiently than the same capital producing sales of only $200. Sales are expressed as a percentage of capital employed. For Lladnar Ltd, this is:

2011	2010
$\dfrac{1600}{1059} \times 100 = 151.09\%$	$\dfrac{1200}{838} \times 100 = 143.20\%$

Comment. In 2010, sales were only 1½ times the amount of capital employed. This is very low, but further comment would be unhelpful without knowing the kind of business being carried on by Lladnar Ltd. A low percentage may be normal for some businesses. The percentage for 2011 has only improved slightly.

The ratio of profit before tax and interest percentage, and sales as a percentage of capital employed, are known as **secondary ratios** because they help to explain the primary ratio (ROCE). If the two ratios are multiplied together, they give the primary ratio:

$$\frac{\text{net profit}}{\text{sales}} \times \frac{\text{sales}}{\text{capital employed}} = \frac{\text{net profit}}{\text{capital employed}}$$

(Sales in the denominator of the first fraction cancel out sales in the numerator of the second fraction to give the third fraction.) For Lladnar Ltd:

2011	2010
$13.5\% \times 151.09\% = 20.40\%$	$15.17\% \times 143.20\% = 21.72\%$

Some textbooks state that the net profit percentage is one of the secondary ratios, but this is only true if no interest is involved.

The ratio of sales to capital employed may be further refined by relating sales to total assets, then to non-current assets and current assets.

Utilisation of total assets

The number of times sales cover the capital invested in the assets of a business is calculated as follows:

$$\frac{\text{sales}}{\text{total assets}} = X \text{ times}$$

Lladnar Ltd's utilisation of total assets is as follows:

2011	2010
$\dfrac{1600}{924 + 329} = 1.28 \text{ times}$	$\dfrac{1200}{670 + 269} = 1.28 \text{ times}$

Comment. These ratios are on the low side but further comment is limited by lack of information about the nature of the business.

Notice that this 'ratio' is expressed as a 'number of times' the total assets are 'turned over'.

Return on total assets

This ratio identifies how much profit from operations has been generated by the company for every $1 of assets. The calculation is:

$$\frac{\text{Profit from operations}}{\text{Total assets} (\text{Non-current assets} + \text{current assets})} \times 100$$

For Lladnar Ltd these ratios are:

2011	2010
$\dfrac{216}{1253} \times 100 = 17.24\%$	$\dfrac{182}{939} \times 100 = 19.38\%$

Comment. In 2010 every $1 of the company's total assets generated $0.19 in profit. This fell, or deteriorated in 2011 to $0.17. Whilst this is slightly worrying it is not something about which shareholders and management should be concerned. It is, though, something which management should be working on. It could be a result of the company investing in more assets in 2011, which have yet to generate the level of profit required. Management should be trying to correct and improve this situation.

Non-current asset turnover

A business purchases non-current assets with the intention that they will earn revenue. Non-current asset turnover is calculated as $\dfrac{\text{sales}}{\text{total of non-curent assets}}$.

The ratios for Lladnar Ltd are:

2011	2010
$\dfrac{1600}{924} = 1.73 \text{ times}$	$\dfrac{1200}{670} = 1.79 \text{ times}$

Comment. There has not been a significant change in the ratio in 2011. Assets that are not owned for a full year will not earn a full year's revenue and, unless information is given about the dates the assets were purchased, further comment is impossible.

Current asset turnover

Current assets include inventory, trade receivables and cash and cash equivalents. The relationship of these to sales is of interest because inventory and trade receivables levels may well be determined by the level of sales. Current asset turnover is calculated as

$\dfrac{\text{sales}}{\text{total of current assets}}$. The ratios for Lladnar Ltd are:

2011	2010
$\dfrac{1600}{329} = 4.86 \text{ times}$	$\dfrac{1200}{269} = 4.46 \text{ times}$

Comment. There would appear to be very little change but other ratios, inventory turnover and trade receivables collection period (see below), will show if the situation is as satisfactory as it appears.

Net current assets (or working capital) to sales

This is another ratio that may be used to measure performance. It is calculated as $\dfrac{\text{turnover}}{\text{net current assets}}$.

For Lladnar Ltd:

2011	2010
$\dfrac{1600}{135} = 11.85 \text{ times}$	$\dfrac{1200}{168} = 7.14 \text{ times}$

Comment. The increase from 7.14 times to 11.85 times may appear to be a good result, but comment should be reserved until trade payables payment period (see below) have been calculated.

Net working assets to sales

This is a ratio which measures how effective management has been in generating sales from its 'working' current assets. Accruals and prepayments are excluded as they are simply accounting adjustments. Cash is also excluded from the calculation.

The formula is:

$$\frac{\text{Net working assets (Inventories} + \text{trade receivables} - \text{trade payables)}}{\text{Sales revenue}} \times 100$$

For Lladnar Ltd the calculation is

2011	2010
$\dfrac{106 \ (100 + 200 - 194)}{1600} \times 100 = 6.63\%$	$\dfrac{68 \ (54 + 115 - 101)}{1200} \times 100 = 5.67\%$

Comment. The ratio has improved in 2011, indicating that management has been more active and successful in generating sales from its working assets.

28.6 Financial ratios

Current ratio

Current assets are the fund out of which a business should pay its current liabilities; it should never have to sell non-current assets to pay its creditors. It follows that there should be a margin of safety between the current assets and the current liabilities. The current ratio expresses the margin in the form of a true ratio:

> current assets : current liabilities

Lladnar Ltd's current ratios are:

2011	2010
329 : 194 = 1.70 : 1	269 : 101 = 2.66 : 1

The right-hand figure in the ratio should always be expressed as unity (i.e. 1); divide the current liabilities into the current assets.

Comment. The ratios show that, although the current assets comfortably exceed the current liabilities, the safety margin has been reduced in 2011. Textbooks often state that the current ratio should be between 1.5 : 1 and 2 : 1 to take account of slow-moving inventory and slow-paying customers, but much depends upon the kind of business. While a low ratio could signal danger, a high ratio may indicate that a business has resources that are not being used efficiently. High levels of inventory, trade receivables and cash mean that capital is lying idle in the business instead of being used profitably.

The current ratio is sometimes described as an indication of liquidity but that is incorrect. The liquidity of a business depends upon the liquidity of its current assets. A **liquid asset** is one that is in the form of cash (cash and bank balances) or in a form that may become cash in the short term (trade receivables). Inventory is not a liquid asset – no buyer has yet been found for it! The current ratio calculation includes inventory, so is not a measure of liquidity. Liquidity is measured by the **liquidity ratio** (or acid test, quick ratio or liquid ratio).

Liquidity ratio (acid test, quick ratio or liquid ratio)

The liquidity ratio excludes inventory from the calculation and shows the proportion of liquid assets (trade receivables and cash) that is available to pay the current liabilities. The ratio is calculated as

> current assets – inventory : current liabilities

The liquidity ratios of Lladnar Ltd are:

2011	2010
(329 – 100) : 194 = 229 : 194 = 1.81 : 1	(269 – 54) : 101 = 215 : 101 = 2.13 : 1

Comment. The liquidity ratio has fallen in 2011. Textbooks often state that the liquidity ratio should not fall below 1 : 1, or perhaps 0.9 : 1. This is generally a good guide, but supermarkets' sales are on a cash basis while they enjoy a period of credit before they have to pay for their supplies. In the meantime, they have a constant inflow of cash from sales. Their liquidity ratio may not exceed 0.4 : 1.

Without knowing more about Lladnar Ltd's business, further comment may not be helpful. However, it would not appear to be supermarket.

Trade receivables, inventory and trade payables may be examined in a little more detail.

Trade receivables collection period (Trade receivables turnover)

A business should have set a limit on the amount of time it allows its customers to pay. Many customers take longer than the time allowed and the customers' ratio calculates the average time customers are taking to pay.

The formula is $\dfrac{\text{trade receivables} \times 365}{\text{credit sales}}$.

The accounts receivable collection period for Lladnar Ltd is:

2011	2010
$\dfrac{200 \times 365}{1600} = 45.63$ or 46 days	$\dfrac{115 \times 365}{1200} = 34.98$ or 35 days

As there is no information about any of Lladnar Ltd's sales being on a cash basis, it has been assumed that all sales were on credit. It is sensible to round all fractions of days up to the next day.

Comment. The customers are taking 11 more days in 2011 to pay their bills. It is usual in many businesses to allow customers 30 days, or 1 month, to pay. The company seems to be losing control over its customers' payments and to have a deteriorating cash flow. Customers' payments may be affected by a deterioration in the national economy or in the business sector. A business may try to attract new customers by offering more favourable payment terms. When customers are slow to pay there is an increased risk of incurring bad debts.

Inventory turnover

Inventory turnover is the rate of which the inventory is turned over, or the time that elapses before inventory is sold. This ratio is important for the following reasons.

- The more quickly inventory is sold, the sooner the profit on it is realised and the more times the profit is earned in the financial year.
- A slow inventory turnover may indicate that excessive stocks are held and the risk of

obsolete or spoiled stocks increases. Large quantities of slow-moving stocks mean that capital is locked up in the business and is not earning revenue.

However, different trades have their own expected rates of inventory turnover. Food shops will expect to have a fast inventory turnover if their food is not to deteriorate before it is sold. On the other hand, shops selling furniture, refrigerators, radios and television sets, etc. will have slower inventory turnovers, while manufacturers of large items of plant and shipbuilders will have very long inventory turnover period. Generally, fast-moving inventories have lower profit margins than slow-moving inventories. (Compare the profit margin to be expected on the sale of food with that expected on the sale of motor cars.)

The formula for calculating inventory turnover period is:

$$\frac{\text{cost of sales}}{\text{average inventory}}$$

where average inventory = (opening inventory + closing inventory) ÷ 2

It is important to take average inventory because closing inventory may not be representative of the normal inventory level. If opening inventory is not given, use closing inventory for the calculation.

It is usual to express the calculation as the number of times a year the inventory is turned over, but it is also acceptable to express it as the average number of days or months inventory remains in the business before it is sold.

The inventory turnover in times per year for Lladnar Ltd is:

2011	2010
$\dfrac{1120}{(54 + 100) \div 2} = 14.55$ times a year	$\dfrac{788}{(42 + 54) \div 2} = 16.4$ times a year
or $\dfrac{365}{14.55} = 26$ days	or $\dfrac{365}{16.4} = 23$ days

Comment. The rate of inventory turnover has slowed a little in 2011. Without more knowledge about the company's business further comment would only be speculation.

The cash at bank

It is not necessary to make up a formula for a cash ratio; it is sufficient to refer to the balances and, in the case of Lladnar Ltd, to draw attention to the fact that the bank balance has fallen from $100 000 to $29 000. When a balance at bank is converted into an overdraft, it may be appropriate to recognise the fact with a suitable comment. For example, the change here could be a result of the increase in the accounts receivable collection period increasing and a reduction in the number of times the inventory turns over. Both of these factors will cause cash to flow out of the business, resulting in a decrease in the bank balance over the two years.

The statement of cash flows will provide a figure for cash received from operating activities. It is possible to calculate ratios using this figure, for instance the cash margin on sales, the cash liquidity ratio or the interest and dividend cover on a cash basis. These ratios will identify how much cash is available to pay current liabilities or how many times the interest or dividends are covered by the cash generated from trading.

Trade payables payment period (Trade payables turnover)

This is calculated by using the formula

$$\frac{\text{Trade payables} \times 365}{\text{Purchases on credit}}$$

Assuming that all Lladnar Ltd's purchases were made on credit, the trade payables payment period are:

2011	2010
$\frac{194 \times 365}{1166} = 61$ days	$\frac{101 \times 365}{800} = 47$ days

Comment. The company is taking 14 days longer to pay its creditors and this is beneficial to its cash flow. However, it may be dangerous if it is greatly exceeding the period of credit allowed by suppliers as they may withdraw their credit facilities and require Lladnar Ltd to pay cash with orders in future.

Overtrading

Overtrading may occur when a business increases its turnover rapidly with the result that its inventories, trade receivables and trade payables also increase, but to a level that threatens its liquidity. The

business may become insolvent and unable to pay its creditors as they fall due. The result may be that the business is forced to close.

Lladnar Ltd has increased turnover by $33\frac{1}{3}$% in 2011. Inventory has increased by $46 000. Account receivable collection period has increased from 35 to 46 days (31%) suggesting poor credit control by the company. Inventory turnover has increased, but only slightly. Lladnar Ltd may be overtrading.

The cash operating cycle (Working capital cycle)

The cash operating cycle measures the time it takes for cash to circulate around the working capital system. It calculates the interval that occurs between the time a business has to pay its creditors (trade payables) and the time it receives cash from its customers. It is calculated using the following formula:

> inventory turnover period in days + trade receivables collection period in days – trade payables payment period in days

The cash operating cycle for Lladnar Ltd is found as follows:

	2011 days	2010 days
Inventory turnover period	26	23
Trade receivable collection period	46	35
	72	58
Trade payables payment period	61	47
Cash operating cycle	11	11

In both years the company received its money from sales, on average, 11 days after it had paid its suppliers. During this time, the company was financing its customers out of its own money!

28.7 Investment (stock exchange) ratios

Investment ratios are of particular interest to people who have invested, or are intending to invest, in a company. These people include shareholders and lenders such as debenture holders and banks.

Gearing ratio

Gearing is fixed-cost capital expressed as a percentage of total capital. Fixed-cost capital is the money that finances a company in return for a fixed return and includes debentures and preference share capital. Total capital includes the equity interests (ordinary share capital and reserves) plus the fixed-cost capital.

The formula is:

$$\frac{\text{debentures} + \text{preference share capital}}{\text{ordinary share capital} + \text{reserves}}$$

Lladnar Ltd's gearing is:

2011

$$\frac{\$150\,000}{\$909\,000} \times 100 = 14.16\%$$

2010

$$\frac{\$100\,000}{\$738\,000} \times 100 = 11.93\%$$

A company is described as highly geared if the gearing is more than 50%. If it is less than 50%, it is low geared. 50% is neutral gearing. Lladnar Ltd is low geared.

Comment. The key word in understanding the importance of gearing is risk. Lenders of money to a company may be concerned if it is highly geared; this may indicate that a large slice of profit is applied in the payment of interest. Risk arises if profits fall and fail to cover the interest payments. Banks approached by a highly geared company will question why, when the company is already heavily dependent upon loans, the shareholders are unwilling to invest more of their own money in their company. Perhaps they lack confidence in the company's future.

The risk to ordinary shareholders is increased in a highly geared company as the following example shows.

	Low geared company	Highly geared company
Gearing	20%	80%
	$	$
Ordinary share capital	800 000	200 000
10% debentures	200 000	800 000
	1 000 000	1 000 000
Year 1		
Profit before interest	100 000	100 000
Debenture interest	(20 000)	(80 000)
Profit left for ordinary shareholders	80 000	20 000
Profit as a percentage of ordinary share capital:	$\frac{80\,000}{800\,000}$ 10%	$\frac{20\,000}{200\,000}$ 10%

Year 2		
Profit before interest	150 000	150 000
Debenture interest	(20 000)	(80 000)
Profit left for ordinary shareholders	130 000	70 000
Profit as a percentage of ordinary share capital	$\frac{130\,000}{800\,000}$ 16.25%	$\frac{70\,000}{200\,000}$ 35%
Year 3		
Profit before interest	50 000	50 000
Debenture interest	(20 000)	(80 000)
Profit left for ordinary shareholders	30 000	(30 000)
Profit as a percentage of ordinary share capital	$\frac{30\,000}{800\,000}$ 3.75%	$\frac{(30\,000)}{200\,000}$ −15%

The above example shows that if profit varies by ± $50 000 (50%) in the low geared company, the profit left for the ordinary shareholders varies by ± 6.25%. In the highly geared company, the variation is ±25%. The swings in the fortunes of ordinary shareholders are greater (more risky) in a highly geared company than in a low geared company.

Debt/equity ratio

The formula for the debt/equity ratio is

$$\frac{\text{debentures} + \text{preference share capital}}{\text{ordinary share capital} + \text{reserves}}$$

Lladnar Ltd's debt/equity ratio is

2011

$$\frac{\$150\,000}{\$909\,000} \times 100 = 16.50\%$$

2010

$$\frac{\$100\,000}{\$738\,000} \times 100 = 13.55\%$$

Comment. This ratio is often taught as an alternative method of calculating the gearing ratio, but it is arguable whether expressing fixed-cost capital as a percentage of total capital employed. In contrast to the debt/equity ratio, the gearing ratio is consistent with the formula for return on capital employed.

If the debt/equity ratio is less than 100%, the company is low geared; if it exceeds 100% the company is highly geared; 100% is neutral gearing.

Interest cover

Debenture holders and other lenders to a company need to be sure that the profit before interest adequately covers the interest payments. Interest must be paid even if a company makes a loss, but it is reassuring if the profit before interest covers the interest payments several times; a good cover provides a safety margin against a fall in profits in the future. Shareholders are also concerned to see a good interest cover as their dividends can only be paid if profit is left after charging the interest in the Income Statement.

The formula for calculating interest cover is:

$$\frac{\text{profit before interest (profit from operations)}}{\text{interest payable}}$$

The interest cover for Llandar Ltd is

2011	2010
$\frac{216*}{15} = 14.4$ times	$\frac{182*}{10} = 18.2$ times
*201 + 15	*172 + 10

Comment. Lladnar Ltd's interest cover has decreased by 3.8 times in 2011, but is still very satisfactory.

Income gearing

Income gearing is the interest expressed as a percentage of the profit from operations. It shows to what extent a company can pay for its borrowings or what the interest is as a percentage of the profit from operations.

The formula is:

$$\frac{\text{Interest expense}}{\text{Profit from operations}} \times 100$$

For Lladnar Ltd the calculation is:

2011	2010
$\frac{15}{216} \times 100 = 6.94\%$	$\frac{10}{182} \times 100 = 5.49\%$

The same answer could have been obtained by dividing 100 by the number of times for interest cover calculated above:

2011	2010
$\frac{100}{14.4} = 6.94\%$	$\frac{100}{18.2} = 5.49\%$

Comment. In this case in 2011 the interest which Lladnar Ltd has to pay is a higher percentage of profit than 2010. However, it is not very high and unlikely to cause the company difficulty.

Earnings per share

Earnings are the profit left for the ordinary shareholders after interest, tax and preference dividends have been provided for in the Income Statement. Ordinary dividends are paid out of earnings, and any earnings not distributed increase the reserves and the Statement of Financial Position value of the shares. Earnings per share are expressed in cents ($0.00) per share, and are calculated using the formula:

$$\frac{\text{profit attributable to equity holders}}{\text{the number of ordinary shares issued}}$$

Lladnar Ltd's earnings per share are:

2011	2010
$\frac{\$201\,000*}{400\,000} = \$0.50$ per share	$\frac{\$172\,000*}{400\,000} = \$0.43$ per share
* Net profit less the preference dividend × 100	

Comment. Earnings per share have increased by $0.07 in 2011 and resulted in an increase in the retained earnings for the year.

Price earnings ratio (PER)

The price earnings ratio calculates the number of times the price being paid for the shares on the market exceeds the earnings per share; it is calculated using the formula:

$$\frac{\text{market price per share}}{\text{earnings per share}}$$

The market price of Lladnar Ltd's ordinary shares at 31 December 2010 was $1.80, and at 31 December 2011 it was $2.10. The price earnings ratios are:

2011	2010
$\frac{\$2.10}{\$0.50} = 4.20$	$\frac{\$1.80}{\$0.43} = 4.19$

Comment. The price earnings ratio has remained steady over both years. Shareholders have been prepared to pay just over 4 times the earnings per share. This is a measure of confidence in the ability of Lladnar Ltd to maintain its earnings in future. A PER of 4 is not particularly good for a long-term investment in a company. PER is an important ratio for investors as it gives a quick and easily understandable indicator of the market's assessment of a company's prospects.

Dividend cover

The formula for dividend cover is

$$\frac{\text{profit attributable to equity holders}}{\text{dividend on ordinary shares}}$$

Dividend cover is the number of times the profit out of which dividends may be paid covers the dividend. If the cover is too low, a decline in profits may lead to the dividend being restricted or not paid at all. On the other hand, if the cover is high, shareholders may decide that the directors are adopting a mean dividend policy.

This presents a slight problem with the way accounts are presented. The Statement of Changes in Equity shows dividends *paid* during the year. We have seen that this figure may include dividends paid in respect of a previous accounting period. The calculation of the ratio must be based on dividends in respect of the year in question. In the examination, the examiner will indicate the dividends for the year in question to enable the ratio to be calculated.

Assume that in the years in questions the dividends for Lladner Ltd were:

2011 – total dividend paid $35 000
2010 – total dividend paid $27 000

Notice that these are not the figures in the Statement of Changes in Equity.

The calculation of dividend cover for Lladnar Ltd is:

2011	2010
$\dfrac{\$201\,000}{\$35\,000} = 5.74$ times	$\dfrac{\$172\,000}{\$27\,000} = 6.37$ times

Comment In both years the level of cover is good. It may indicate that the company is retaining

profits for future expansion rather than paying it out as dividend. This will be of benefit to shareholders in the longer term.

An alternative to the above formula is:

$$\frac{\text{earnings per share}}{\text{dividends per share}}$$

2011	2010
$\dfrac{\$0.50}{\$0.0875} = 5.71$ times	$\dfrac{\$0.43}{\$0.0675} = 6.37$ times

The 2011 figure is slightly different as a result of rounding.

Dividend per share

Companies usually declare dividends as a certain number of cents per share, representing a certain percentage return based on the nominal value of the share. For example, a dividend of $0.03 per share paid on a share with a nominal value of $0.50 is a dividend of 6% on the share. Shareholders who have paid the market price for their shares need to know the return based on the price they have paid. The dividend yield is calculated using the following formula:

$$\text{dividend yield} =$$
$$\text{declared rate of dividend} \times \frac{\text{nominal value of share}}{\text{market price of share}}$$

Lladnar Ltd's declared rates of dividend per share are:

2011	2010
$\dfrac{\$35\,000}{\$400\,000} = \$0.0875$	$\dfrac{\$27\,000}{\$400\,000} = \$0.0675$

Comment. There is a slight increase in the amount of the dividend per share in 2011. This is positive for the shareholders, especially as the market price of the share has also increased.

Dividend yield

This is calculated as:

$$\frac{\text{dividend per share}}{\text{market price of a share}} \times 100\%$$

The market price of each share is $2.10 for 2011 and $1.80 for 2010.

The dividend yields are:

2011	2010
$\dfrac{\$0.0875}{\$2.10} \times 100 = 4.17\%$	$\dfrac{\$0.0675}{\$1.80} \times 100 = 3.75\%$

Comment. The small increase in the dividend yield in 2011 is the result of the share price increasing fractionally less than the increase in the dividend. There may be a connection between the increase in the market price and the small increases in the earnings per share and the dividend cover.

28.8 Trend analysis and inter-firm comparison

Individual ratios are usually of very limited value. The ratios of a business for past years are necessary if trends in progress or deterioration of performance are to be seen. The examples of Lladnar Ltd have given the results for 2010 and 2011 and some limited trends have been observed. Given the results for, say, four, five or six years, more reliable trends may be discerned.

Trends may signal to investors whether they should stay with their investment, or sell it and re-invest in a more promising venture.

Inter-firm comparison (IFC) is possible when information about the performance of other similar businesses is available. Trade associations collect information from their members and publish the statistics as averages for the trade or industry. It is thus possible to compare the results of one company with the averages for businesses of the same type. Comparisons, however, must be made with care. It is not realistic to compare the statistics of a small trader with results achieved by large companies. Comparison should always be on a like-for-like basis as far as possible.

Inter-firm comparison can inform shareholders whether they have invested their money in the most profitable and stable institutions.

28.9 The limitations of ratios

- To be useful and reliable, ratios must be reasonably accurate. They should be based on information in accounts and notes to the accounts.

Some useful information may not be disclosed in the accounts and some account headings may not indicate the contents clearly.
- Information must be timely to be of use. It may not be available until some long time after the end of a company's financial year.
- Ratios do not explain the cause of the changes in the results but may indicate areas of concern; further investigation is usually necessary to discover causes of the concern.
- Ratios usually do not recognise seasonal factors in business:
  - profit margins will be lower than normal during periods of seasonal sales.
  - inventory and trade receivables are unlikely to remain at constant levels throughout the year.
  - Companies, even in the same trade, will have different policies for such matters as providing for depreciation, doubtful debts, profit recognition, transferring profits to reserves, dividend policy, etc.

Such limitations should be borne in mind when making comparisons between businesses.

Exercise 1

(Based on the accounts of a sole trader)
Najim wants to analyse the results of his trading for the year ended 31 December 2011 and has prepared his Financial Statements. He compares these with the final accounts for the previous year.

Income Statement				
	for the year ended 31 Dec 2011		for the year ended 31 Dec 2010	
	$	$	$	$
Sales		187 500		172 308
Less cost of sales				
Opening inventory	16 000		12 000	
Purchases	125 500		116 000	
	141 500		128 000	
Closing inventory	14 000	127 500	16 000	112 000
Gross profit		60 000		60 308
Less expenses		32 678		38 769
Net profit		27 322		21 539

Statement of Financial Position				
	31 Dec 2011		31 Dec 2010	
	$	$	$	$
Non-current assets				
(net book values)		93 750		78 322
Current assets				
Inventory	14 000		16 000	
Trade receivables	12 511		9 914	
Cash and cash equivalents	7 185		4 851	
	33 696		30 765	
Current liabilities				
Trade payables	17 192	16 504	13 984	16 781
		110 254		95 103
Opening capital		95 103		81 176
Add profit		27 322		21 539
		122 425		102 715
Deduct drawings		12 171		7 612
		110 254		95 103

Further information

1. 60% of Najim's sales are on credit.
2. Najim purchases all his stock of goods on credit.
3. The only current assets are inventory, trade receivables and a bank balance.

Required

(a) Calculate the following ratios to *two* decimal places for each of the years ended 31 December 2010 and 2011.
   (i)   gross profit percentage
   (ii) net profit percentage
   (iii) non-current asset turnover
   (iv) inventory turnover
   (v)   trade receivables collection period
   (vi) trade payables payment period
   (vii) current ratio
   (viii) liquid (acid test) ratio

(b) Compare the performance of Najim's business in 2011 with its performance in 2010, using the ratios calculated in (a), and comment on the comparison.

Exercise 2

(Based on the accounts of limited companies).
A financial consultant has been asked by his client for advice on the relative performance of two companies, Dunedin Ltd and Wellington Ltd. Extracts from the financial statements for the year ended 31 December 2011 and the Statement of Financial Position at that date of the two companies are as follows:

Extract for Financial Statement for the year ended 31 December 2011		
	Dunedin Ltd	Wellington Ltd
	$000	$000
Operating profit	300	420
Debenture interest	(60)	(120)
	240	300
Transfer to General Reserve	(100)	(50)
Preference dividend paid	(6)	(60)
Ordinary dividend paid	(90)	(150)
Retained earnings	44	40

Statement of Financial Position extracts at 31 December 2011			
Dunedin Ltd		Wellington Ltd	
	$000		$000
Long-term liabilities		Long-term liabilities	
10% debentures 2014/15	600	12% debentures 2013/14	1 000
Ordinary shares of $1	200	Ordinary shares of $2	1 500
6% preference shares		8% preference shares	
of $1	100	of $1	750
General reserve	120	General reserve	200
Retained profit	80	Retained profit	350
	500		2 800

The market values of the ordinary shares at 31 December 2011 were as follows:
   Dunedin Ltd $2.70   Wellington Ltd $3.60

Required

(a) Calculate the following ratios to *two* decimal places for each company.
   (i)   gearing
   (ii) interest cover
   (iii) earnings per shares (EPS)
   (iv) dividend per share
   (v)   dividend cover
   (vi) price earnings ratio (PER)
   (vii) dividend yield

(b) Compare and comment on the performance of the two companies in 2011 using the ratios calculated in (a).

28.10 How to prepare an Income Statement and Statement of Financial Position from given ratios

The final accounts of a business may be prepared from a list of accounting ratios provided at least one item is given as a numerical term. The method begins with the given numerical term and progresses by steps from that.

Example

Pulchra's inventory at 31 December 2010 was $35 000, which was $5000 less than her inventory at 1 January 2010. Further information about her business for the year ended 31 December 2010 is as follows:

Inventory turnover 7 times
Gross profit/sales 44%
Net profit/sales 17½%
Distribution cost to administration expenses 1 : 3
Trade receivables collection period 32 days (70% of sales are on credit)
Trade payables payment period 65 days (all purchases were made on credit)
Non-current asset turnover 2½ times
Current ratio 1.8 : 1
Interest cover 12.2 times
The current assets consist of inventory, trade receivables and bank balance only.
Pulchra has received a long-term loan on which she pays interest at 10% per annum.
Pulchra has drawn $1000 from the business each week.

Required

Prepare Pulchra's Income Statement for the year ended 31 December 2010 and her Statement of Financial Position at that date in as much detail as possible. Make all calculations to the nearest $.

Answer

The inventory at 31 December 2010 is the starting point. Proceed as follows, in the order given by the numbered steps.

Pulchra
Income Statement
for the year ended 31 December 2010

			$	$
Step	6	Revenue (100/56* × 262 50)		468 750
		Cost of sales		
Step	2	Inventory at 1 Jan 2010 (35 000 + 5000)	40 000	
Step	5	Purchases (balancing figure)	257 500	
Step	4	(262 500 + 35 000)	297 500	
Step	**1**	Inventory at 31 Dec 10 (given)	35 000	
Step	3	(cost of sales $\frac{40\,000 + 35\,000}{2} = \times 7$)		262 500
Step	7	Gross profit (468 750 − 262 500)		206 250
Step	10	Distribution costs (124 219 × $\frac{1}{4}$)		31 055
Step	11	Administration expenses		
		(124 219 × $\frac{3}{4}$)		93 164
Step	9	(balancing figure)		124 219

Step	8	Profit from operations (17½% of 468 750)	82 031
Step	12	Interest on long-term loan	
		at 10% (82 031 ÷ 12.2)	6 724
Step	13	Profit attributable to equity holders	75 307

*Gross profit/sales = 44%, therefore cost of sales = 56% of sales.

Statement of Financial Position at 31 December 2010

			$	$
Step	14	Non-current assets (468 750 ÷ $2\frac{1}{2}$)		187 500
		Current assets		
Step	15	Inventory	35 000	
Step	16	Trade receivables		
		(468 750 × $\frac{7}{10}$ × $\frac{32}{365}$)	28 767	
Step	20	Bank balance (balancing figure)	18 774	
Step	19	(45 856 × 1.8)	82 541	
Step	17	Trade payables (257 500 × $\frac{65}{365}$)	45 856	
Step	18	(balancing figure)		36 685
Step	21			224 185
Step	22	Less long-term loan at 10% (6724 × 10)		67 240
Step	23			156 945
Step	28	Capital at 1 Jan 2011 (balancing figure)		133 638
Step	24	Profit for the year		75 307
Step	27			208 945
Step	26	Drawings (1000 × 52)		52 000
Step	25			156 945

Note. The steps show the order in which the items should be tackled but the step numbers do not form part of the answer and should not be shown in answers to questions. It is important in examinations to gain as many marks as possible as quickly as possible. It is a good idea to start with an outline for the financial statements (leaving spaces to insert additional items if necessary), and to fill in the items as soon as the figures are known. For example, inventory in the Statement of Financial Position can be inserted immediately it has been entered in the Income Statement. Similarly, net profit can be inserted in the Statement of Financial Position as soon as it has been calculated in the Income Statement.

Exercise 3

Patience has mislaid her final accounts for the year ended 31 December 2011 but has found the report, which her accountant has prepared, based on those accounts. She has decided to reconstruct the accounts from the information contained in the report.

The accountant's report contained the following data.

At 31 December 2011
Inventory $54 000. (This was 20% more than the inventory at 1 January 2011.)

For the year ended 31 December 2011

Inventory turnover	10 times
Gross profit margin	35%
Net profit margin	22%
Non-current asset turnover	4 times
Trade receivables collection period	34 days (based on 365 days in the year)
Trade payables payment period	42 days (based on 365 days in the year)
Current ratio	2.5 : 1

The current assets consist of inventory, trade receivables and bank balance.
All sales and purchases were made on credit.
Patience drew $140 000 from the business during the year.

Required

(a) Prepare, in as much detail as possible, Patience's Income Statement for the year ended 31 December 2011 and the Statement of Financial Position at that date. Make all calculations to the nearest $.

Virtue carries on a similar business to that of Patience and has the following data for the year ended 31 December 2011.

Inventory turnover	12 times
Gross profit margin	40%
Net profit margin	20%
Non-current asset turnover	5 times
Trade receivables collection period	31 days
Trade payables payment period	36 days

Required

(b) Compare Virtue's performance with that of Patience and indicate the ratios that show which business is the more efficient.

You should write your answer in sentence form and include supporting figures.

HINTS

- Learn the headings under which ratios are shown in the pyramid of ratios and which ratios are included under each heading.
- Remember how each ratio is calculated (the model).
- Take care to calculate ratios on the correct figures and check your arithmetic.
- Express every ratio in the correct terms, for example as a percentage, a number of times or days, a true ratio, etc. Marks will not be awarded in an examination if the correct terms are omitted.
- Make sure you understand what each ratio is intended to explain.
- Your comments on ratios should be based on the information you are given and justified by the ratios you have calculated. Do not assume facts you are not given.
- Avoid making definite statements that cannot be supported by the information given. You may *suggest* reasons for the comments you make.
- Your comments should be concise and relevant; avoid repetition of the same point. Long rambling answers that stray from the point do not impress the examiner.
- When you are asked by the examiner to comment on the ratios you have calculated, the wording of your answer is very important. Statements such as the gross profit percentage is higher this year than last year are not sufficient. The examiner wants you to tell them that this means the situation has *improved*, or the company's trading was *better* this year. Similarly, try to use words like *worse*, if that is what the results show. Bullet points in the answers are perfectly acceptable and will save your time.
- Always use the relevant sign or wording with the ratio. For example, a % sign after the calculation of gross profit, or the number of times for dividend cover.

MULTIPLE-CHOICE QUESTIONS

1. Information about a business is given in the following table.

	Year 1 $	Year 2 $
Turnover	200 000	250 000
Cost of sales	125 000	140 000
	75 000	110 000
Operating expenses	32 000	64 000
Profit from operations	43 000	46 000
Non-current assets	140 000	120 000
Net current assets	60 000	80 000
Long-term loans	(80 000)	(40 000)

Which of the following is true in year 2?

	Gross profit margin	Return on capital employed
A.	decreased	decreased
B.	increased	decreased
C.	decreased	increased
D.	increased	increased

2. Extracts from the Income Statement for two years for a business are given in this table:

	Year 1 $	Year 2 $
Sales	100 000	200 000
Gross profit	30 000	70 000

What might explain the change in the gross profit margin in year 2?

A. an increase in sales
B. an increase in the sales price
C. a reduction in inventory
D. suppliers offering higher cash discounts

3. What is the effect on the current ratio and quick ratio of a business if it uses cash to buy inventory?

	Current ratio	Quick ratio
A.	decrease	decrease
B.	decrease	increase
C.	no change	decrease
D.	no change	increase

4. The quick ratio (acid test) of a business has fallen. What is the reason for the fall?

A. a decrease in trade payables
B. a decrease in inventory
C. an increase in cash
D. an increase in the bank overdraft

5. The closing inventory of a business was $30 000 and the cost of goods sold was $600 000. Inventory turnover is based on the average value of the opening and closing inventories.

If the inventory turnover was 15 times, what was the opening inventory?
A. $10 000   B. $40 000
C. $50 000   D. $80 000

6. The following information is extracted from the final accounts of a business.

	$
Opening inventory	6 000
Purchases (all on credit)	220 000
Closing inventory	28 000
Trade payables at end of year	21 096

What is the period taken to pay the suppliers?
A. 31 days   B. 32 days
C. 34 days   D. 35 days

7. The following is an extract from the Income Statement of a company.

	$
Profit from operations	360 000
Debenture interest	24 000
Profit attributable to equity holders	336 000
Preference dividend paid	(16 000)
Ordinary dividend paid	(200 000)
Retained earnings	120 000

The company's share capital is as follows.

Issued: 200 000 8% preference shares of $1
800 000 ordinary shares of $1

What is the company's earnings per share?
A. $0.32   B. $0.40   C. $0.42   D. $0.45

8. A company has share capital of $1 each 500 000 shares. The following is an extract from its Income Statement.

	$
Profit from operations	400 000
Debenture interest	(60 000)

Profit attributable to equity holders	340 000
Transfer to general reserve	(100 000)
Ordinary dividend paid	(200 000)
Retained earnings	40 000

The current market price of the shares is $3.60. What is the price earnings ratio?

A. 5.29   **B.** 7.5   **C.** 8   **D.** 11.25

ADDITIONAL EXERCISES

1. On 1 October 2010 Manny Kyoor and his wife formed a limited company, Kyoor Ltd, to run a beautician's business, and each paid in $37 500 as share capital. The bank loaned the company a further $80 000 at 9% interest per annum.

At 30 September 2011 the business's final accounts were drawn up as follows:

Income Statement for the year ended 30 September 2011

	$	$
Sales and fees		350 000
Less Cost of sales		
Inventory	31 500	
Purchases	280 000	
	311 500	
Inventory at 30 September 2011	66 500	245 000
Gross Profit		105 000
Less Expenses		
Rent and Rates	3 950	
Advertising	1 750	
Wages	29 000	
Heat and Light	5 250	
Interest due	7 200	
Depreciation	12 000	59 150
Net Profit		45 850

Statement of Financial Position as at 30 September 2011

	Cost	Depreciation	NBV
Non-current assets	$	$	$
Premises	124 000		124 000

Fixtures and fittings	48 000	12 000	36 000
	172 000	12 000	160 000
Current assets			
Inventory	66 500		
Trade receivables	21 500	88 000	
Current liabilities			
Creditors	21 000		
Interest due	7 200		
Bank	18 950	47 150	40 850
			200 850
Non-current liabilities			
Long-term loan			80 000
			120 850
Equity			
75 000 ordinary shares of $1			75 000
Retained profit			45 850
			120 850

Industry average ratios and other relevant data concerning businesses similar to Kyoor Ltd were as follows.

(i)	Gross Profit percentage	30.00%
(ii)	Net Profit percentage	18.07%
(iii)	Current ratio	2.21 : 1
(iv)	Liquid (Quick) ratio	1.02 : 1
(v)	Inventory Turnover ratio	8 times
(vi)	Non-current Assets to Sales	50.18%
(vii)	Return to Total Assets	25.37%
(viii)	Return on Net Assets	34.93%
(ix)	Trade receivables collection period	25 days
(x)	Trade payables payment period	30 days

(a) Calculate each of the above ratios, to 2 decimal places, for Kyoor Ltd.

(b) Comment on the business's performance in the light of the data for the industry.

Note. It is not sufficient to say that a ratio is 'higher' or 'lower' than the industry average – it must be made clear whether you think it is *better* or *worse* than the industry average and you must give reasons for your comments.

2. The following information summarises the latest set of final accounts of Worky Tout & Co., a partnership.

At 30 April 2011
Inventory $45 000. (This was 50% more than the inventory at 30 April 2010.)
For the year ended 30 April 2011
Inventory turnover 12 times
Gross profit margin 40%
Net profit margin 18%
Non-current asset turnover 3 times
Average time taken by customers to pay: 36 days (based on a year of 365 days).
Average time taken to pay suppliers: 40 days (based on a year of 365 days).
The current ratio is 3 : 1.
The only current assets of the firm consist of inventory, trade receivables and balance at bank.
Partners' drawings for the year $125 000.
All sales and purchases were on a credit basis.

Required
(a) Prepare, in as much detail as possible, the Income Statement of Worky Tout & Co. for the year ended 30 April 2011 and a Statement of Financial Position as at that date. (All calculations should be made to the nearest $000.)

The following information is available for Zenapod, a similar business, for the year ended 30 April 2011.

Inventory turnover	10 times
Gross profit margin	45%
Net profit margin	20%
Non-current asset turnover	3½ times
Time taken by customers to pay	30 days (based on a year of 365 days)
Time taken to pay suppliers	28 days (based on a year of 365 days).

(b) Compare the performance of Worky Tout & Co. with that of Zenapod. Indicate the ratios which show that one business is more efficient than the other. Your answer should be in sentence form with supporting figures.

3. An extract from Oitar plc's Financial Statement for the year ended 30 April 2011 was as follows:

	$000	$000
Operating profit		1000
Debenture interest (12½%)		250
		750
Ordinary dividend paid and proposed for the year	350	
Preference dividend paid and proposed for the year	120	
Transfer to General Reserve	200	670
Retained profit for the year		80

Oitar plc's issued share capital and reserves at 30 April 2011 consisted of:

	$000
Ordinary shares of $10	4000
8% preference shares of $5	1500
Capital and revenue reserves	900

The market price of the ordinary shares at 30 April 2011 was $30.

Note
The information given is from the accounts prepared for internal use by the managers and is, therefore, different from the IAS format.

Required
(a) Calculate the following ratios for Oitar plc.
  (i) interest cover
  (ii) dividend cover
  (iii) earnings per share
  (iv) price earnings ratio
  (v) dividend yield
  (vi) gearing
(b) Explain why each of the ratios in (a) is important for investors in ordinary shares in the company.
Oitar plc's accounting ratios at 30 April 2010 were as follows:

interest cover	5.5 times
dividend cover	2.5 times
price earnings ratio	22
gearing (calculated as a percentage of long-term debentures and preference share capital to total long-term capital)	36%

Required

(c) Compare the ratios for 2010 with the same ratios in 2011 as calculated in (a), and comment on the changes that you find.

(d) State, with reasons, any further information you might require and what other documents you might wish to see to enable you to assess the likely future performance of Oitar plc.

29 Company financing

In this chapter you will learn:

- the sources of company financing
- principles that are important for the financing of companies
- the bases and limitations of modern financial reporting
- the critical appraisal of accounting reports
- what window dressing is
- the nature of company forecasts.

29.1 Source of company finance

As we have seen, every company must have share capital. A company may issue redeemable shares, but only if it has already issued shares which are not redeemable. This ensures that some part of a company's financing must be provided by the members of the company as an insurance for the creditors if the company gets into financial difficulties.

Besides share capital, other sources of finance are
- loans – debentures, bank loans, other loans
- bank overdrafts
- hire purchase and leasing of assets
- trade and other creditors.

Some forms of finance are more suitable than others; it depends upon the purpose for which the finance is required. It will be useful to recall the main features of each source.

29.2 Share capital

Ordinary shares, together with a company's reserves, are known as the **equity** of the company. Ordinary shareholders can be paid dividends only if there are profits available after all other claims by debenture holders and preference shareholders have been met. When a company ceases trading, the ordinary shareholders are entitled to the funds that remain after all creditors (including debenture holders and other lenders) and preference shareholders have been repaid. Thus ordinary shareholders may receive back more than they originally paid for their shares, or they may receive nothing at all. The Companies Act allows companies to convert their fully paid-up shares into stock. Stock may be thought of as 'bundles of shares' which may be bought and sold in fractional amounts. For example, shares with a nominal value of, say, $1 may only be traded in multiples of $1 (nominal value). It is not possible to buy, say, 100½ shares. Stock, however, may traded in any amounts and it is possible to trade in, say, $945.86 of stock. Companies may re-convert stock back into fully paid-up shares of any nominal value.

Preference shares entitle the holders to a fixed rate of dividend each year provided the company has made sufficient profit. **Participating preference shares** entitle the holders to have any arrears of dividend made good in later years when profits are sufficient. Preference shares are participating unless they are specifically described as non-participating. Preference dividends are payable before any dividends are payable to the ordinary shareholders, and holders of the preference shares are entitled to have their capital returned in priority to the ordinary shareholders when the company ceases trading, subject to funds being available.

Rights issues are shares offered to existing shareholders of a company at a price below the current market price. Shares may never be issued at a discount, that is, at a price below their nominal value. A rights issue ensures that existing shareholders do not lose control of the company, as could be the case if the shares were offered to the general public. A private company may only increase its capital by a rights issue because it is prevented from offering shares to the public.

Bonus issues are not a new source of funding as they do not create any additional cash for the company. Bonus shares are created by transferring the balance from a company's reserves to the Ordinary Share Capital account and issuing certificates for the new shares to the ordinary shareholders in proportion to their existing shareholdings.

29.3 Other sources of finance

Debentures

Debentures are loans to a company. Debenture holders are entitled to a fixed rate of interest on their loan regardless of whether or not the company has made a profit. If a company lacks the cash to pay debenture interest when it is due, and the loan is secured on the assets of the company, the debenture holders are entitled to have the assets sold to pay the interest and to repay the loan immediately. Debentures are usually repayable on a date or within a period of time specified at the time they are issued. They are a long-term, but not a permanent, form of finance.

Convertible loan stock

Convertible loan stock entitles the holders to a fixed rate of interest payable on defined dates, and the right to convert the stock into shares at a pre-determined price on a set date. Because of the option to convert, convertible loan stock usually carries a lower rate of interest than ordinary debentures and is usually not secured on the assets of the business.

If, when the time to convert arrives, the market price of the shares is higher than the pre-determined price, it will be advantageous to convert the stock into shares. The holder of the stock exchanges the right to a fixed income payable on settled dates for the uncertainty of receiving dividends which may be more or less than the interest on the stock. The company, on the other hand, is relieved of having to pay loan interest regardless of the profitability of the company, and need only pay dividends if profits are available. Conversion of the stock decreases the company's gearing.

Bank loans

Bank loans are available to a company provided it can satisfy the bank that the funds are required for a sound purpose such as capital investment or expansion, and that the company will be able to pay the interest on the due dates, and repay the loan in due course. The loan may be for a short term such as three months or for a longer term of a number of years depending on the purpose for which it is required. A bank will usually be unwilling to lend to a company that has got into difficulties through bad management. Loans will usually be secured on the assets of the company. The rate of interest charged may be fixed or variable. The interest is charged on the full amount of the loan whether it is used or not.

Bank overdrafts

Bank overdrafts are temporary facilities that allow companies to become overdrawn on their bank accounts. Interest is calculated on the overnight amount of the overdraft so that interest is only paid by a company on the amount of the facility it uses day by day. Banks may cancel overdraft facilities at any time without notice, exposing the borrower to the risk of financial embarrassment.

Hire purchase

Hire purchase enables a purchaser to have the beneficial use of an asset while the ownership of the asset remains with the hire purchase company. At the end of the hire purchase agreement the purchaser may become the owner of the asset on payment of a (usually) nominal sum. Under the principle of substance over form, the purchaser shows the asset as a non-current asset in the Statement of Financial Position at its normal cash price and shows the outstanding liability to the hire purchase company as a creditor.

Leasing

Leasing allows a company leasing an asset (the lessee) to use the asset while the ownership of the asset remains with the company from which it is leased (the lessor). The asset will never become the property of the lessee and the rental is shown in the lessee's Income Statement as an expense.

A company may raise money by selling some of its non-current assets to a leasing company and leasing them back, so retaining their use. This is known as 'sale and lease back'. It receives a capital sum for the sale and charges the leasing rental in its Income Statement.

Factoring

Some companies sell their book debts to a factoring company either with or without **recourse**. The factoring company makes a charge for collecting the debts and this is deducted from the book value of the debts sold. If the debts were sold *with recourse*, the factoring company will require the company that sold the debts to make good any loss resulting from bad debts. If the debts were sold *without recourse*, the factoring company will increase the charge for collecting the debts to allow for the risk of bad debts.

The advantage of factoring is that a company receives the money owing by debtors early and is relieved of the expense of credit control and debt recovery.

Trade payables

Some of a company's finance is provided by its trade and expense creditors. This is a short-term form of finance. However, a company that abuses this source of finance risks losing the goodwill of its suppliers and sacrificing advantageous credit terms. The

creditors may insist that future dealings are on a cash basis, or may even withdraw supplies or services altogether.

29.4 Important principles that should decide how companies are financed

The main principles that should decide how a company is financed are briefly explained below.

Long-term capital

Long-term requirements should be financed by long-term sources. Financing the acquisition of non-current assets, for example by short-term loans, runs the very great risk that the loans will have to be repaid before the assets in question have generated sufficient funds for the repayment. The non-current assets of a company should be adequately covered by share capital and reserves, and possibly by long-dated debentures.

An acquisition of a non-current asset may be financed by a bank loan for an agreed term to allow the asset to generate the funds for repayment by the time the term has expired. Alternatively the funds may be raised by an issue of debentures which will be repayable when the asset has started to earn revenue. This enables the shareholders to enjoy all the benefits accruing from the asset without having to share them with the provider of the capital used to purchase the asset.

Working capital

A positive current ratio (greater than 1 : 1) shows that the current assets are not wholly financed by the current liabilities (short-term trade payables). The possibility that inventory turnover may be low (slow-moving goods), and that customers may take a long time to pay means that some of the current liabilities could be funded by non-current finance. For example, the company may take a loan to pay its creditors or use it to buy stock.

The easiest way to show how a business finances itself is with the following diagram (no figures are included):

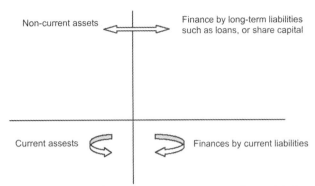

This shows that long-term assets **must** be paid for by long-term finance such as share capital, loans or debentures. The working capital of current assets and current liabilities are self financing. Under no circumstances should the arrows change. For example, long-term finance must never be used to buy inventory or pay creditors.

Share and debenture issues compared

- Issues of shares to the public are costly because of the need to meet the requirements of the Companies Act. Rights issues are less costly because they are limited to existing shareholders. A rights issue will fail if existing shareholders are not able to subscribe the additional funds required. Issues of debentures are less costly than issues of shares.

- An issue of ordinary shares to the public may result in a loss of control by existing shareholders. The shareholders' control will not be affected if the issue is one of preference shares or debentures, neither of which carry the right to vote in company meetings.

- Share dividends may be paid only if profits are available for the purpose. Debenture interest must be paid regardless of whether a company makes a profit or a loss.

- Issues of preference shares and debentures increase gearing. High gearing is associated with increased risk to the ordinary shareholders. However, very low or a 'nil' gearing is not necessarily good. When interest rates generally are low, the cost of servicing debenture interest may be less than the rate of dividend the company is paying on its shares. A company will fail its

shareholders if it does not take advantage of raising some of its capital cheaply.

- While shareholders may like to have a substantial amount of long-term capital raised by borrowing at cheap rates, banks and other providers of finance may be unwilling to provide further funds to companies in which the shareholders seem unwilling to risk more of their own money.

29.5 The critical appraisal of accounting reports

The basis of modern financial reporting and its limitations

The annual accounting reports of limited companies consist of an Income Statement, Statement of Financial Position, Statement of Cash Flows and the Directors' Report. These reports are prepared within an accounting framework made up of the requirements of the Companies Act and the various published accounting standards. These requirements are intended to ensure a degree of uniformity that will enable the users of the reports to interpret them in a generally accepted context. The framework has been considered in chapter 27.

Limitations of interpreting financial reports may be summarised as follows:

- While the accounting framework is intended to ensure that financial reports provide the information necessary for an understanding of a company's performance, the rules do not require confidential information which might provide an unfair advantage to competitors to be disclosed. The undisclosed information might, however, contain important clues to the better understanding of the company's performance.

- Companies are required to supplement the Income Statement and the Statement of Financial Position with additional notes to explain how the items in those financial statements are made up. However, companies differ in their classification of many items of income and expenditure, and the notes may not be in sufficient detail to identify the differences. This may cast doubt on the usefulness of some accounting ratios calculated from the financial statements.

- Where accounting standards do not fit a particular business, the directors may adapt them, or even ignore them, provided they have good reason for doing so.
- Companies have different policies for the treatment of expenditure on non-current assets; some will capitalise all such expenditure while others will treat the expenditure as revenue expenditure if it is not material compared with the size of the amounts shown in its Statement of Financial Position. For example, a multinational company may not capitalise any expenditure on a single item, say equipment, below $5000. However, to a small sole trade a new piece of equipment costing $5000 would almost certainly be treated as a non-current asset in the financial statements.
- A company may own its extensive properties or it may operate solely from rented accommodation. The one will pay no rent, while the other may be burdened with very high rental payments. One will show the item in the Statement of Financial Position, whist the other will show it in their Income Statement. This may make the comparison between the two companies using some ratios of little relevance.
- There are limits to the extent to which companies of considerably different sizes can be compared. For example, it would hardly be helpful to compare the performance of a company with an issued capital of $50 000 with the performance of a company with an issued capital of $5 million. There may also be difficulty in making a sensible comparison between a company with nil gearing and one that is very highly geared.
- Companies in the same line of business are often not comparable. For example, some may simply retail their goods while others manufacture and retail them. Some companies may act as manufacturers and wholesalers only.
- Financial reports may be too historical to be useful by the time they are published. There will be a time delay of several months between the end of the financial year and date on which the accounts are presented to shareholders at the annual general meeting.
- The interpretation of financial reports may be subject to external factors such as developments in the industry, general political and economic conditions at home and overseas, changes in fashion, market demand and so on.
- The financial accounts and reports of companies in countries where there is high inflation can be seriously misleading if the accounts have been based on historical costs.

Window dressing

Company directors naturally desire annual financial reports to present the company performance in as favourable a light as possible. Indeed their remuneration may well depend on the profit the company makes. This may lead to 'window dressing' which may take various forms, including:

- reducing trade payables in the Statement of Financial Position by drawing cheques at the end of the financial period to pay the creditors but not posting the cheques until the start of the next financial year, or even cancelling them on the first day of the next financial year.
- reducing the trade receivables in the Statement of Financial Position by pressing them to pay before the end of the financial period.

Other methods of window dressing, such as changing the bases of calculating depreciation of non-current assets and the provision for doubtful debts, of inventory valuation, etc. are not permissible and contravene accounting standards. They may even amount to fraud.

Income smoothing techniques

Income should be recognised as soon as it is realised and not before. A company carrying out work under a contract which spans two or more financial periods is required to spread the anticipated profit on the contract over the financial periods concerned. The amount of profit to be credited in each year is calculated on a formula which apportions the profit according to the amount deemed to have been earned in each period less a prudent provision for any future unanticipated losses. (A more detailed explanation of contract accounts is outside the scope of this text as students are not required to have a knowledge of the topic.)

When the directors of a company anticipate that a good trading year will be followed by a poor one, they may decide to delay invoicing some customers in the good year until the following one for the sake of appearances. This contravenes the concept of realisation and, if the financial statements are subject to audit, should not be allowed to happen without being reported.

Similarly, if customers are allowed to pay by instalments for work done or services rendered, and some of the instalments are payable in a subsequent financial period, any attempt to smooth income by partly deferring it until the instalments are received would be a contravention of the realisation principle.

29.6 The nature of company forecasts

Directors' reports and future developments

Directors' reports are required to include an indication of likely future developments in the business of the company. These statements are usually quite brief and lack sufficient detail to enable shareholders and others to form an accurate assessment of the future funding requirements of the business.

Company budgets

Every company, except some very small private companies, prepares budgets. Budgets are based on forecasts and express in money terms the plans and policies the directors intend to implement to achieve a company's long-term objectives. The budgets usually cover periods of five, ten or, for large companies, even more years ahead. Separate budgets are prepared for each of the company's activities: sales, production, purchasing, stock holding, etc. Cash budgets are prepared from these budgets to show if and when the company is likely to need additional cash. Master budgets, which take the form of forecast Income Statements and Statements of Financial Position, will indicate when additional long-term finance is required.

The budgets are for internal use within the company and are not published, but they are an essential management tool if the directors are to avoid the embarrassment, and possibly the catastrophe, of suddenly finding that the company has insufficient funds to continue in business. Banks and others approached to provide additional capital will require to see the budgets before deciding whether or not to lend to the business. Budgeting is covered in chapter 34.

EXERCISE 1

Explain the difference between stocks and shares.

EXERCISE 2

Explain the difference between debentures and convertible loan stock.

HINTS

- Learn the main short-, medium- and long-term sources of company financing and their advantages and disadvantages.
- Remember that long-term requirements for funds should be financed by long-term sources.
- Learn the limitations of financial reports and their effect upon interpretation.
- Be prepared to describe window dressing and income smoothing techniques.
- Note the importance of forecasting and budgeting as regards business financing.

MULTIPLE-CHOICE QUESTIONS

1. Information extracted from the Statements of Financial Position of company P and company Q is as follows.

	P	Q
	$000	$000
Ordinary share capital	500	600
12% debentures	400	200

Which of the following would experience the greatest degree of risk in times of declining profits?
   A. debenture holders in company P
   B. debenture holders in company Q
   C. ordinary shareholders in company P
   D. ordinary shareholders in company Q

2. Which of the following is a method of 'window dressing' financial statements?
   A. omitting a non-current asset acquired on hire purchase
   B. overstating Goodwill
   C. transferring a large amount to General Reserve
   D. writing off debts before they become bad

3. Which of the following may be used to smooth earnings per share from one year to another?
   A. non-current asset revaluation reserve
   B. capital redemption reserve
   C. General Reserve
   D. preference share dividend

4. A company proposes to purchase an expensive machine which will pay for itself in five years. General interest rates are low and the company wishes to avoid a change in the control. From which source of finance should it obtain the necessary funds?
   A. an issue of bonus shares
   B. an issue of convertible loan stock
   C. an issue of debentures
   D. an issue of ordinary shares

ADDITIONAL EXERCISES

1. Explain why the non-current assets of a company should be funded by long-term finance.
2. Explain why long-term finance should not exceed the amount of a company's long-term assets.
3. State *five* limitations that may be relevant to the appraisal of company financial reports.
4. Explain what is meant by 'window dressing' and why directors may wish to use it.
5. What means are available to enable directors to foresee future needs for additional funds?

Part IV
Elements of managerial accounting

30 Costing principles and systems: total (or absorption) costing

In this chapter you will learn:

- the nature and purpose of cost accounting
- how to analyse costs into direct and indirect costs
- how to record materials and labour
- how to allocate and apportion overheads
- how to calculate overhead absorption rates (OARs)
- the causes of over-/under-absorption of overheads.

30.1 The purpose and nature of total (absorption) costing

Cost accounting is one of the management tools included in a number of systems of accounting known as **management accounting**. Management accounting provides management with information which is not obtainable from the financial accounts of a business.

As a result, the way data is collected and, more especially presented in this section is completely different to the way it is collected an presented in financial accounting. Some larger businesses will have specific departments in the organisation dedicated to cost and management accounting. They provide a valuable addition to the organisation. So far in financial accounting we have been looking at a history book. The financial statements are prepared after the end of the financial year. There is nothing the organisation can do to change the results they disclose.

With cost and management accounting the organisation is looking forward. It is gathering and analysing information which will be used as a basis for making future decisions affecting the performance and profitability of the firm. Throughout this section how the information analysed can be used as a basis for decision making in the organisation will be considered. There is also some overlap with financial accounting, as information collected, particularly in relation to the cost of part completed units of product will allow it to accurately value inventory in the financial statements. Consider the following example.

Makeit & Co. Manufacturing Account for the year ended 30 June 2011			
		$000	$000
Direct materials	Inventory at 1 July 2010	10	
	Purchases	140	
	Carriage inwards	24	
		174	
Less	Inventory at 30 June 2011	18	156
Direct labour			222
Direct expenses			46
Prime cost			424
Indirect materials		45	
Indirect labour		72	
Rent of factory		100	
Heating, lighting and power		45	
Depreciation:	factory	20	
	machinery	36	318
			742
Work in progress 1 July 2010		38	
Work in progress 30 June 2011		(20)	18
Factory cost of finished goods			760

This manufacturing account has been prepared as part of the company's financial accounting system. It provides us with information about prime cost, overheads and the cost of producing goods. If only one type of goods has been produced, the unit cost can easily be found by dividing the factory cost by the number of units produced. The selling price for the good is fixed by adding the required amount of profit per unit. So far, so good, but it does not go far enough to help management make important decisions.

Assuming that Makeit & Co. manufactures only one type of product and that the output for the year was 1000 units of that product, each unit has cost $760 to produce. If the managers want to find the cost of producing 1001 units, the answer will not be

$$\$760\,000 \times \frac{1001}{1000} = \$760\,760, \text{ that is } \$(760\,000 + 760).$$

The additional unit will not result in additional costs of $760 because not all costs (rent and depreciation, for example) will be affected by the addition of one unit of output; they are **fixed costs**, which do not vary with the number of units produced. The effect on costs of increasing numbers of units produced is covered in chapter 33 on marginal costing.

The problem is even more complicated if Makeit & Co. manufactures more than one type of product, and each type requires different types and quantities of materials, different numbers of labour hours and different processes. Management must know how much it costs to make a single unit of each product if they are to fix selling prices. This problem is considered now.

30.2 **Direct and indirect costs**

In chapter 19 we saw that a distinction is made in manufacturing accounts between direct costs and indirect costs.

Direct costs include direct materials (those materials from which goods are made, and carriage inwards paid on the materials), direct labour (the wages of workers who actually make goods) and direct expenses (royalties, licence fees, etc.).

Indirect costs are indirect materials (purchased for the factory, e.g. cleaning materials, lubricating oil for the machinery), indirect wages (the wages of all factory workers who do not actually make the goods (factory managers, supervisors, stores staff, cleaners, etc.) and other overheads (rent, heating and lighting, depreciation, etc.). This distinction is very important in the following chapters. It is important that you are able to classify costs in this way.

30.3 **The behaviour of costs**

Direct costs are deemed to vary in proportion to the number of units produced. If 1 kg of material is required for one unit of production, 2 kg will be required for two units produced, 10 kg for ten units, and so on. It will be true for royalties and other direct expenses; if a royalty of $0.05 has to be paid for every unit produced, the royalties payable will always be equal to the number of units produced × $0.05. At one time, it might have been common for direct workers to be paid according to the amount they produced so that direct wages would be proportionate to output. Now, direct workers are usually paid a fixed or basic wage regardless of their output. This wage may or may not be supplemented by a productivity bonus. In practice, therefore, wages paid to direct labour will not be in relation to output, but we still tend to treat them in a theoretical way as being proportionate to production and thus direct and variable costs.

Indirect expenses may be **fixed** or **variable**. They are fixed if they are not linked directly to the level of activity. Rent is an example; it is fixed by a lease agreement. Straight-line depreciation is another fixed expense. However, it is important to remember that even fixed expenses are only fixed within certain limits. For example, it may be possible to increase the number of units produced only if additional machines are purchased, and that will increase the total depreciation charge. If production is increased still further and more machines have to be purchased, it may be necessary to lease more factory space and the rent will increase. Fixed costs then become 'stepped costs' and may be represented by a chart as follows:

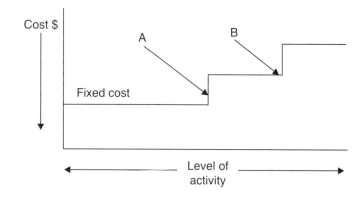

At A it has been necessary to buy an additional machine in order to increase production, and the depreciation of machinery charge has increased. At B, a further machine has been bought, and it has been necessary to rent additional factory space so that both the depreciation charge and the rent have increased.

30.4 Recording materials, labour and overheads

Cost accounting requires materials purchased and wages paid to be classified as direct or indirect. If expenditure has been incurred for particular departments within the business, it must be analysed by departments. Invoices for goods and services must be coded by the purchasing department to show the type of expenditure that has been incurred. The purchase journal must have additional columns so that the expenditure can be analysed according to the codes shown on the invoices. Analysed purchase journals have already been encountered in departmental accounts in chapter 18.

Wages are analysed into different departments and then classified into direct and indirect wages on payroll summaries.

If the systems of analysis outlined above have been carried out, all expenses can be posted in the ledger to appropriate accounts to enable the allocation and appropriation of expenses to **cost centres** as described below.

30.5 How to apportion overheads to cost centres

Cost centres

A **cost centre** is any location in a business to which costs may be attributed. A cost centre is usually a department or process, but may be an item of equipment (a machine) or even a person (e.g. a marketing manager). **Production cost centres** are directly involved in producing goods, for example moulding or shaping raw material, assembling components, painting, etc. **Service cost centres** are not involved in the production of goods, but provide services for the production cost centres, for example stores, building and plant maintenance, canteen, etc.

Allocation and apportionment of costs to production cost centres

Direct expenses and some overhead expenses can be identified with specific cost centres and are **allocated** to them.

Overheads which may be identified with, and allocated to, specific cost centres include:

- wood, metal, plastic, chemicals, components, etc. (production departments)
- paint (paints shop)
- packing materials (packing department)
- lubricating oil (the machine shop)
- maintenance of handling equipment (the stores or warehouse)
- food (the canteen).

Other overheads are incurred for the business generally and are **apportioned** to cost centres on suitable bases.

Overhead	Basis of apportionment
Heating and lighting (when not separately metered to the cost centres)	In proportion to the respective floor areas of the departments
Rent	
Insurance of buildings	
Power (if metered separately to cost centres)	Actual consumption (this is allocation rather than apportionment)
Insurance of plant, machinery and other assets	On cost or replacement values of assets in each department
Depreciation of non-current assets	On the cost or book value of assets in each department

Example 1

Oar Manufacturers & Co. has four production cost centres: moulding, machining, painting and packing. The following information is available.

Cost centres	Moulding	Machining	Painting	Packaging
Floor area (metres²)	1000	700	500	300
Plant and machinery at cost ($00)	50	40	20	10

Details of expenditure for the year ended 31 December 2011 are as follows:

	$
Direct materials: Moulding	50 000
Machining	7 000
Painting	9 000
Packaging	6 000
Direct labour: Moulding	96 000
Machining	80 000
Painting	40 000
Packaging	18 000
Indirect labour: Moulding	11 000
Machining	9 000

	$
Painting	4 000
Packaging	1 000
Factory rent	45 000
Repairs and maintenance of factory	5 000
Factory depreciation	6 000
Insurance of factory	2 500
Heating and lighting	5 500
Depreciation of plant and machinery	12 000
Maintenance of plant and machinery	18 000
Insurance of plant	3 000

The overhead apportionment will be as follows:

Expense	Basis	Total $	Moulding $	Machining $	Painting $	Packaging $
Indirect labour	allocation	25 000	11 000	9 000	4 000	1 000
Factory: rent	floor area	45 000	18 000	12 600	9 000	5 400
repairs and maintenance	floor area	5 000	2 000	1 400	1 000	600
depreciation	floor area	6 000	2 400	1 680	1 200	720
insurance	floor area	2 500	1 000	700	500	300
heating and lighting	floor area	5 500	2 200	1 540	1 100	660
Plant and machinery:						
depreciation	cost	12 000	5 000	4 000	2 000	1 000
maintenance	cost	18 000	7 500	6 000	3 000	1 500
insurance	cost	3 000	1 250	1 000	500	250
Total overhead		122 000	50 350	37 920	22 300	11 430

Note that direct expenses (materials and labour) are not entered in the overhead analysis. In an examination, you may also be given other ways in which Indirect costs could be apportioned to cost centres.

The total cost per cost centre includes direct expenditure:

Expense	Basis	Total $	Moulding $	Machining $	Painting $	Packaging $
Direct costs: materials	actual	72 000	50 000	7 000	9 000	6 000
labour	actual	234 000	96 000	80 000	40 000	18 000
Total direct cost		306 000	146 000	87 000	49 000	24 000
Apportionment of overhead		122 000	50 350	37 920	22 300	11 430
Total cost per cost centre		428 000	196 350	124 920	71 300	35 430

In an examination always spend a little time making sure that the totals across the bottom of any table always add up. For example in the apportionment chart above $50 350 + $37 920 + $22 300 + $11 430 = $122 000. This is important, as a mistake at this stage will probably affect the rest of the answer.

Exercise 1

Teepops Ltd manufactures a single product which passes through four stages of production: machining, painting, assembly and packing. The following expenditure has been incurred by the company in the year ended 31 March 2011.

		$000
Direct materials:	Machining	80
	Painting	20
	Assembly	5
	Packing	12
Direct labour:	Machining	136
	Painting	74
	Assembly	68
	Packing	45
Indirect labour:	Machining	51
	Painting	32
	Assembly	28
	Packing	14
Factory expenses:	Rent	90
	Heating and lighting	70
	Maintenance	30
	Insurance	20
Plant and machinery:	Depreciation	80
	Repairs	32
	Insurance	16

Further information

1. The floor areas of the departments are:

	metres^2
Machining	500
Painting	200
Assembly	200
Packing	100

2. Plant and machinery at cost is:

	$000
Machining	90
Painting	40
Assembly	10
Packing	20

Required

(a) Calculate the total overhead cost for each department.
(b) Calculate the total cost of production for each department.

Apportionment of service cost centre overheads to production cost centres

The total cost of goods produced includes all overhead expenditure, including the overheads of service departments; these must be apportioned to the production departments on suitable bases. The bases usually adopted are:

Service cost centre	Apportioned on
Stores	number or value of stores requisitions raised by production cost centre
Canteen	number of persons in each production cost centre
Building maintenance	area occupied by each production cost centre*
Plant and machinery maintenance	number or value of machines in each cost centre*

* However, records of actual maintenance costs may be kept and the costs allocated accordingly.

There are a number of ways of apportioning service cost centre overheads to production cost centres and they all usually produce very similar results. The simplest, and quickest, way is the elimination method.

Example 2

(Apportionment of service cost centre overheads by elimination)

Eliminator Ltd has three production and two service departments for which the following information is available.

	Foundry	Finishing	Assembly	Stores	Canteen
No. of stores requisitions	200	100	50	–	70
No. of staff	40	15	20	7	10
Overheads ($000)	110	60	50	35	30

The overheads are first tabulated under the cost centres. The overhead of one service department is then apportioned over the other cost centres and that service department is eliminated from future apportionments. If there are more than two service cost centres, there will be more steps until the last service cost centre is apportioned over the production cost centres.

	Foundry $000	Finishing $000	Assembly $000	Stores $000	Canteen $000
Overheads ($000)	110.00	60.00	50.00	35.00	30.00
First apportionment*	16.67	8.33	4.17	(35.00)	5.83
Second apportionment †	19.11	7.17	9.55	–	(35.83)
	145.78	75.50	63.72	–	–

* Based on 420 requisitions. † Based on 75 staff.

The Stores costs centre has been allocated first because it does work for the Canteen, whereas the Canteen does not do any work for the Stores.

Exercise 2

Luvlibix Foods has three production departments: mixing, bakery and packaging. It also has two service departments: stores and canteen. The following information is provided.

	Mixing	Bakery	Packaging	Stores	Canteen
Overheads ($000)	165	124	87	80	90
No. of staff	60	80	40	15	18
No. of stores requisitions	300	80	20	–	40

Required

Apportion the service department overheads to the production departments on appropriate bases.

30.6 How to calculate overhead absorption rates

Once overheads have been apportioned to cost centres, the next step is to calculate overhead absorption rates (OARs). The OARs are then used to calculate the amount of overhead to be attributed to each cost unit in each cost centre.

Cost units are units of production, for example:
a computer (computer manufacturer)
a garment (dress maker)
a thousand electric lamps (manufacturer of electric lamps)
a barrel of oil (oil well)
passenger-mile (freight transport)
a kilowatt-hour (electricity generation)
Overhead absorption rates are calculated for future periods because the cost of production must be known in advance to enable selling prices to be fixed. Calculations are based on planned volumes of output and budgeted overhead expenditure.

The amount of overhead absorbed by a cost unit is usually calculated by reference to the time taken to produce it. There are other methods but they are generally considered to be less satisfactory for reasons that will be discussed later. The two methods about to be described assume that a unit of production absorbs overheads (rent, heat and lighting, for example) proportionately to the time spent on processing it in the cost centres. This time is measured either in direct labour hours or machine hours.

Direct labour overhead absorption rate

A process is labour intensive when it requires the use of labour rather than machines, and the labour cost is greater than the cost of using machinery. The time is measured in direct labour hours.

Example 1

Manhour Ltd makes two products, P and Q. The output for September is budgeted as follows:

Product P	10 000 units
Product Q	8 000 units

Each unit of P requires 1½ direct labour hours to make, and each unit of Q requires ¾ direct labour hour.

The total number of direct labour hours required to produce 10 000 units of P and 8 000 units of Q is

$$(10\ 000 \times 1\tfrac{1}{2}) + (8\ 000 \times \tfrac{3}{4}) = 21\ 000$$

If Manhour Ltd's overheads for September are $131 250, the overhead absorption rate is

$$\frac{\text{total budgeted overhead expenditure}}{\text{total budgeted no. of direct labour hours}} = \frac{\$131\ 250}{21\ 000}$$
$$= \$6.25 \text{ per direct labour hour}$$

The amount of overhead absorbed by each unit of P is $6.25 × 1½ = $9.375 and the amount absorbed by Q is ¾ × $6.25 = $4.6875. The total overhead is therefore fully absorbed as follows:

	$
Product P: 10 000 × $9.375	93 750
Product Q: 8 000 × $4.6875	37 500
Total overhead absorbed	131 250

Exercise 3

Trimble Ltd manufactures two products, Dimbles and Gimbles.

The number of direct labour hours required for each unit is: Dimbles 1.3; Gimbles 0.7.

In July the company plans to produce 5000 Dimbles and 7000 Gimbles.

Trimble Ltd's estimated overhead expenditure for July is $129 276.

Required

(a) Calculate the direct labour overhead absorption rate:
   (i) per unit of Dimble (ii) per unit of Gimble.
(b) Show how the overhead for July is absorbed by the planned production for the month.

Machine hour overhead absorption rate

A cost centre is capital intensive when the operations carried out in the centre are mechanised and the machinery running cost is greater than the direct labour cost. Overhead should then be absorbed on a machine hour rate (machine hour OAR).

Example

Jigsaw Ltd has six machines which are used 9 hours each day in a five-day working week. The number of machine hours in a six-month period is $6 \times 9 \times 5 \times 26$ or 7020 machine hours.

If Jigsaw Ltd's overheads for the six months are $114 075, the machine hour absorption rate is

$$\frac{\$114\ 075}{7020} \text{ or } \$16.25 \text{ per machine hour.}$$

Exercise 4

Makeit-by-Robot Ltd uses 10 machines to produce its goods. The machines are used 7 hours a day for 6 days per week. In a period of 13 weeks it is planned to produce 1200 units, and the overheads are estimated to amount to $141 960.

Required

(a) Calculate the machine hour overhead absorption rate.
(b) Calculate the amount of overhead absorbed by each unit of production.

Example 2

Jenx Ltd manufactures two products, L and P, each of which requires processing in the company's three production departments, I, II and III.

The following information is available from the company's budget for the next six months.

Product		L	P
No. of units to be produced		4000	5000
Cost of direct materials per unit		$17	$16
Direct wages per unit		$10	$8
Machine hours per unit	Dept I	3	2
	Dept II	1	1
	Dept III	2	3
Direct labour hours per unit	Dept I	1	2
	Dept II	2	3
	Dept III	3	4
Production departments	I	II	III
Budgeted overheads	$95 920	$86 250	$96 000
Budgeted machine hours	22 000	9 000	23 000
Budgeted labour hours	14 000	23 000	32 000

Required

(a) Calculate an appropriate overhead absorption rate for each department.
(b) Calculate the overhead absorption for each unit of L and P, in each of the departments, and in total.
(c) Prepare a statement to show how the overhead of each department is absorbed by production.
(d) Calculate the total cost of each unit of L and P.

Answer

Department I is machine intensive and Departments II and III are labour intensive.

(a)

OARs	Dept I	Machine hour	$\frac{\$95\ 920}{22\ 000} = \$4.36$
	Dept II	Direct labour hours	$\frac{\$86\ 250}{23\ 000} = \$3.75$
	Dept III	Direct labour hours	$\frac{\$96\ 000}{32\ 000} = \$3.00$

(b)

OAR per unit	Dept	I		II		III	Total
Product L	($4.36 × 3)	$13.08	($3.75 × 2)	$7.50	($3 × 3)	$9.00	$29.58
Product P	($4.36 × 2)	$8.72	($3.75 × 3)	$11.25	($3 × 4)	$12.00	$31.97

(c)

Total overhead recovery	Dept	I		II		III	Total
		$		$		$	$
Product L	(4000 × $13.08)	52 320	(4000 × $7.50)	30 000	(4000 × $9)	36 000	118 320
Product P	(5000 × $8.72)	43 600	(5000 × $11.25)	56 250	(5000 × $12)	60 000	159 850
		95 920		86 250		96 000	278 170

(d)

Total cost per unit	Product L	Product P
	$	$
Direct material	17.00	16.00
Direct labour	10.00	8.00
Overhead	29.58	31.97
Total cost	56.58	55.97

Exercise 5

Egbert Ltd manufactures two products which it markets under the brand names 'Sovrin' and 'Ginny'. The following information is available for a six-month period.

No. of units	Sovrin 6000	Ginny 3000	
Production cost centres:	Moulding	Machinery	Paint shop
Direct materials per unit:			
Sovrin	$80	$10	$12
Ginny	$65	$5	$15
Direct labour per unit:			
Sovrin	$120	$40	$30
Ginny	$96	$40	$15
Machine hours per unit:			
Sovrin	2½	2	1
Ginny	2	2	½
Direct labour hours per unit:			
Sovrin	4	1	1
Ginny	3½	1¼	1
Budgeted overhead expenditure	$301 875	$115 200	$47 250
Budgeted machine hours	21 000	18 000	7 500
Budgeted direct labour hours	34 500	9 750	9 000

Required

(a) Calculate an appropriate overhead absorption rate for each department.

(b) Calculate the overhead absorption for each unit of Sovrin and Ginny, in each of the departments, and in total.

(c) Prepare a statement to show how the overhead of each department is absorbed by production.

(d) Calculate the total cost of each unit of Sovrin and Ginny.

30.7 Other bases for calculating OARs

The following bases for calculating overhead absorption rates are generally unsatisfactory, for the reasons stated, and are seldom used.

Direct material cost. Overhead absorption is not related to the cost of material. A product which is made of expensive material would be charged with a greater share of overheads than one which is made of cheap material but which requires the same time to make.

Direct labour cost. The labour cost incurred in making a product depends partly on the rate paid to the workers engaged on making it. A product made by highly skilled workers would be charged with a greater share of overheads than one which is made by unskilled workers but which takes the same time to make.

Prime cost. This method combines the disadvantages of the direct material cost and the direct labour cost.

Cost unit. This method is restricted to the production of one type of good which is made by a common process.

30.8 Under-/over-absorption of overheads

As explained above, overhead absorption rates are calculated on planned levels of production and budgeted overhead expenditure. It is most likely that the actual volume of goods produced and the actual overhead expenditure will turn out to differ from the forecasts. The result will be that overhead expenditure will be either under-absorbed or over-absorbed.

Under-absorption occurs when actual expenditure is more than budget and/or production is less than the planned level. In this case not enough overheads have been charged to production.

Over-absorption occurs when actual expenditure is less than budget and/or actual production is more than the planned level. In this case too much overhead has been charged to production.

Example

A company calculated its overhead absorption rates for the six months to 30 June and the next six months to 31 December as follows:

	6 months to 30 June	6 months to 31 December
Budgeted overhead expenditure	$200 000	$240 000
Budgeted direct labour hours	80 000	100 000
Actual expenditure	$215 000	$230 000
Actual direct labour hours	76 000	106 000

Budgeted OAR	$\dfrac{\$200\,000}{80\,000} = \$2.50$	$\dfrac{\$240\,000}{100\,000} = \$2.40$
Overhead recovered	$76\,000 \times \$2.50$ $= \$190\,000$	$106\,000 \times \$2.40$ $= \$254\,400$
(Under) / over absorption	$\$(215\,000 - 190\,000)$ $= (\$25\,000)$	$\$(230\,000 - 254\,000)$ $= \$24\,400$

Exercise 6

Upandown Ltd has provided the following information about its overhead expenditure for four quarterly periods ended 31 December.

	3 months to 31 March	3 months to 30 June	3 months to 30 September	3 months to 31 December
Budgeted overhead	$124 000	$128 000	$130 000	$131 000
Budgeted machine hours	1 000	1 000	1 000	1 000
Actual overhead	$128 000	$125 000	$129 500	$132 800
Actual machine hours	900	1 050	1 100	980

Required

Calculate the under-absorption or over-absorption of overhead in each of the four quarterly periods. State clearly in each case whether the overhead was under- or over-absorbed.

HINTS

- Learn the definitions of **cost centre** and **cost unit** and be prepared to explain them in examinations.
- Be prepared to apportion overheads to cost centres and to re-apportion service cost centre overheads to production cost centres.
- Practise calculating overhead absorption rates.
- Be prepared to state when direct labour OARs and machine hour OARs should be used and to explain why other methods of calculating OARs are normally unsuitable.
- Learn how to calculate under-absorption and over-absorption of overheads.
- Check all calculations carefully; arithmetical mistakes cost marks.
- Make sure you understand the causes of under-absorption and over-absorption. This is a weak spot for many candidates in examinations.

MULTIPLE-CHOICE QUESTIONS

1. A company provides the following information:

Actual direct labour hours worked	13 000
Actual overhead expenditure	$520 000
Budgeted direct labour hours	14 000
Budgeted overhead expenditure	$532 000

What is the overhead absorption rate based on direct labour hours?

A. $37.14 **B.** $38
C. $40 **D.** $40.42

2. Which of the following could cause an under-absorption of overhead expenditure?
1. absorption rate calculated on actual production and actual number of units produced
2. units produced exceeding the budgeted production
3. units produced being less than the planned production

4. overhead expenditure exceeding budget

A. 1 and 2 **B.** 1 and 3
C. 2 and 4 **D.** 3 and 4

3. The following information is provided by a company.

Actual direct labour hours	12 400
Actual overhead expenditure	$198 400
Budgeted direct labor hours	11 000
Budgeted overhead expenditure	$170 500

Which of the following correctly describes the overhead absorbed?

	Under-absorbed	Over-absorbed
A.	$6 200	
B.		$6 200
C.	$21 700	
D.		$21 700

ADDITIONAL EXERCISES

1. (a) Explain the following terms:
   (i) Cost Centre
   (ii) Cost Unit
(b) Julie and Cleary Ltd manufactures toy soldiers. The company has three production departments — Moulding, Sanding and Painting and two service departments — Canteen and Maintenance. Estimated indirect overheds for the year ended 30 April 2011 are as follows:

Overhead	Cost or Calculation	Basis of Apportionment or Allocation
Administration	$104 000	Number of employees
Electricity	$70 000	Kilowatt hours used
Depreciation	10%	Cost of non-current asset
Indirect wages	$360 000	Allocated
Rent	$80 500	Floor area (square metres)

Relevant information on the five departments is as follows:

	Moulding	Sanding	Painting	Canteen	Maintenance
No. of employees	40	50	40	38	40
Power (kW hours)	1400	1600	150	160	190
Cost of non-current asset	$162 000	$175 000	$40 000	$43 000	$80 000
Floor area (metre^2)	625	475	500	300	400
Indirect wages	$6 000	$11 250	$6 375	$18 750	$36 190
Direct Labour hours	8 000	7 800	7 500		
Direct Machine hours	7 750	5 625	1 250		

Canteen costs are shared among all the other departments on the basis of number of employees. Maintenance costs are shared among the three production departments on the basis of floor area.
  (i) Prepare an overhead analysis sheet for the year ending 30 April 2011 detailing the total overheads for Moulding, Sanding and Painting.
  (ii) Moulding and Sanding department overhead rates are calculated on a Direct Machine hour basis. Painting department overhead rate is calculated on a Direct Labour hour basis.

Calculate the Overhead absorption rate for each of the three production departments for the year ending 30 April 2011. Calculations should be shown to two decimal places.

2. Auckland (Manufacturers) Ltd has two manufacturing departments: (i) Machining and (ii) Assembly. It also has two service departments: (i) Maintenance and (ii) Power house. The information in the table below is available for the coming year.

Machining	Assembly	Maintenance	Power house	Total	
	$000	$000	$000	$000	$000
Indirect materials	298	482	132	152	1064
Indirect labour	706	918	282	672	2578
Rent and local taxes					1426
Supervision					660
Plant depreciation					1650
					7378

Further information is available as follows:

	Machining	Assembly	Maintenance	Power house
	$000	$000	$000	$000
No. of employees	40	80	20	10
Area (metrer²)	3 000	5000	1000	200
Plant valuation ($000s)	13 000	5000	2400	1600
Direct labour hours	3 200	4800		
Machine hours	11 080	2320		
Maintenance hours	1 800	600		
Units of power used	4 200	1200	600	

Required
(a) Analyse the above indirect costs between the four departments showing the bases of apportionment you have used.
(b) Re-apportion the costs of the service departments over the two production departments using appropriate bases.
(c) Calculate an overhead absorption rate for the machining department based on machine hours and an overhead absorption rate for the assembly department based on direct labour hours.

3. (a) Define the term 'overhead expenses'.

(b) Explain the meaning of the following terms as they relate to overhead expenditure:
  (i) allocation
  (ii) apportionment.
(c) Explain the meaning of the terms:
  (i) overhead absorption
  (ii) overhead under-absorption
  (iii) overhead over-absorption.
(d) State reasons why a company might recover more in overheads than the amount spent on overheads in the period.
(e) Explain why estimated figures are used to calculate overhead absorption rates.

Unit, job and batch costing

In this chapter you will learn:

● the difference between continuous and specific order operations
● what unit costing is
● what job costing is
● what batch costing is.

31.1 Continuous and specific order operations

Costing systems may be applied to every type of business including:

● public or privately owned organisations
● manufacturers of goods such as motor cars, breakfast cereals, etc.
● providers of services, for example hospitals, hotels, restaurants, lawyers, accountants, etc.

Each type of business must choose a costing system that suits its particular operation; no one system will serve every type of business.

The operations of a business may be classified as either **continuous** or **specific order**.

Continuous operations are typically those in which a single type of good is produced and the cost units are identical. Production may involve a sequence of continuous or repetitive operations. Examples are:

● manufacture of computers
● production of mineral water
● oil refining
● production of medicines
● passenger and freight transport.

Continuous operations will almost certainly involve a product passing through a number of processes. Process costing will be covered in chapter 32.

Specific order operations are those which are performed in response to special orders received from customers and may be classified according to whether the operations consist of individual jobs, or the production of batches of identical units for a customer.

31.2 Continuous costing

For a business with continuous operations, continuous costing is used to find the cost of a single unit of production or service (**unit costing**). A single unit may be a single item; but a manufacturer of large volumes of a single product may find it more convenient to regard a number of items as a single unit. For example, for a company producing hundreds of thousands of packets of breakfast cereal, the unit may be, say, 1000 packets. Other examples of cost units are a pallet of bricks in brick making (a pallet is a wooden platform on which a given number of bricks is stacked after manufacture), and barrels for the output of oil wells.

Example

The following information is given for a business producing a single type of product for a period of one year.

Number of units produced:	30 000
Expenditure: Direct labour	$108 000
Direct materials	$54 000
Indirect expenses	$66 000

The cost per unit is

$$\frac{\$(108\ 000 + 54\ 000 + 66\ 000)}{30\ 000} = \$7.60$$

Exercise 1

Luvlibrek manufactures breakfast cereal. Its cost unit is 1000 packets of the cereal. The following information is given.

Number of packets of cereal produced	425 000
Expenditure: Direct materials	$398 000
Direct labour	$996 000
Overheads	$1 687 250

Required
Calculate the cost of one cost unit of breakfast cereal.

31.3 Specific order costing

Job costing

For a company with specific order operations, that is, those which are performed in response to special orders received from customers, **job costing** can be carried out. Each order becomes a cost unit and can be costed as a separate job. Examples of jobs are:

- re-painting a house
- repairing a television set
- servicing a motor car.

Example 1

Jobbings Ltd is asked to quote a price to install central heating in a house. The quotation is based on estimated costs as follows:

	Estimated costs $
Materials*	3 000
Labour*	1 700
Overhead (200% of labour)	3 400
Total cost	8 100
Add profit (25% of cost)	2 025
Amount of quotation	10 125

*All the materials and labour are direct costs of the job.

If the quotation is accepted, the costs will be recorded on a job card as they are incurred by Jobbings Ltd.

Job No. 107 Installation of central heating at XXXXXX		
	Estimated $	Actual $
Materials*	3 000	2 740
Labour*	1 700	1 920

Overhead (200% of labour)	3 400	3 840
Total cost	8 100	8 500
Add profit (25% of cost)	2 025	1 625
Amount of quotation	10 125	10 125

*All the materials and labour are direct costs of the job.

When the job has been completed, the actual costs have been entered on the job card, which shows that actual cost exceeded the estimated cost by $400 and the profit made is only $1625 instead of $2025. The job card will provide useful information the next time Jobbings Ltd quotes for a similar job.

Exercise 2

Geoffrey Pannell is a professional researcher. He has been commissioned to conduct research into allegations that mobile phones are bad for public health. Geoffrey estimates that the project will require 200 hours of his time, which he charges at $100 per hour. He will also require the services of Susan, his research assistant, for 100 hours at $60 per hour. Overheads are recovered at the rate of $40 per labour hour.

Required
Prepare a statement to show the amount Geoffrey will charge for carrying out this research.

Batch costing

Batch costing is very similar to job costing and is applied when an order from a customer involves the production of a number of identical items. All the costs incurred are charged to the batch and the cost per unit is found by dividing the cost of the batch by the number of units in the batch.

Example 2

Evocation Ltd sells reproductions of antique furniture. It places an order with Fakerfabs Ltd for 500 dining chairs at an agreed price of $30 000 for the batch.

Fakerfabs Ltd has four production departments for which the following information is given.

Machining:	OAR $35 per machine hour
Finishing:	OAR $20 per direct labour hour
French polishing:	OAR $10 per direct labour hour
Assembly:	OAR $15 per direct labour hour

The costs incurred in the production of 500 dining chairs were:

Direct materials	$5000	
Direct labour:	Machining	125 hours at $10 per hour
	Finishing	180 hours at $9 per hour
	French polishing	220 hours at $12 per hour
	Assembly	100 hours at $8 per hour

160 machine hours were booked against the batch of chairs in the machining department.

Fakerfabs Ltd recovers its administration expenses at 15% on the total cost of production.

The batch cost, cost per chair and profit per chair are calculated as follows:

Costs for batch of 500 chairs			
		$	$
Direct materials			5 000
Direct labour:	Machining (125 × $10)	1250	
	Finishing (180 × $9)	1620	
	French polishing (220 × $12)	2640	
	Assembly (100 × $8)	800	6 310
Prime cost			11 310
Production overhead recovered			
	Machining (160 × $35)	5600	
	Finishing (180 × $20)	3600	
	French polishing (220 × $10)	2200	
	Assembly (100 × $15)	1500	12 900
Cost of production			24 210

Add administration costs		
recovered ($24 210 × 15%)		3 632
Total cost of batch of 500 chairs		27 842
Profit		2 158
		30 000

$$\text{Cost per chair} = \frac{\$27\ 842}{500} = \$55.684$$

$$\text{Profit per chair} = \frac{\$30\ 000}{500} - \$55.684 = \$4.316$$

Exercise 3

Wipup Ltd has received an order for 1000 packs of paper towels. Each pack contains six rolls of towels. The following information is given.

	$
Raw materials per roll of towels	0.08
Labour hourly rate	6.00
Cost of setting up machinery	30.00
Overhead absorption rate per labour/hour	9.35

100 packs of towels are manufactured per hour.

Required

(a) Calculate the cost of manufacturing the batch of 1000 packs of paper towels.
(b) Calculate the cost of one roll of paper towels.

HINTS

- Make sure you understand the difference between continuous operations and specific order operations.
- Learn the characteristics of job costing and be prepared to give examples.
- Be prepared to explain the difference between job costing and batch costing.
- Make sure you can calculate continuous costs, job costs and batch costs. Set all calculations out in a neat and orderly form.

MULTIPLE-CHOICE QUESTIONS

1. Which of the following operations would involve a system of continuous costing?
   A. painting walls of houses
   B. generating electricity
   C. hiring out boats in a fun park
   D. publishing newspapers

2. Retep Ltd hired a drilling machine for use on job 160. The machine was not used on any other job.

   Which of the following statements is true?
   A. Rent of the machine will be charged as a direct expense to job 160.
   B. Rent of the machine will be charged as an indirect expense to job 160.
   C. Rent and depreciation of the machine will be charged as a direct expense to job 160.
   D. Rent and depreciation of the machine will be charged as an indirect expense to job 160.

ADDITIONAL EXERCISES

1. Borlix Ltd makes a number of products, one of which is Super Borlix, which passes through three production departments, A, B and C. The following details are relevant to the production of Super Borlix.

Monthly production		4000 units
Direct material per unit		$8
Direct labour per unit	Dept A	1½ hours
	Dept B	1 hour
	Dept C	½ hour

Other information is as follows:

Direct labour rate (all depts.)		$8.75
Departmental overhead	Dept A	$36 000
	Dept B	$26 000
	Dept C	$24 000
Total direct labour hours	Dept A	24 000
	Dept B	20 000
	Dept C	8 000

Departmental overhead absorption is based on direct labour hours.

Required
Calculate the cost of one month's production of Supper Borlix.

2. Curepipe Successful Promotions Ltd has two departments: (i) Printing and (ii) Marketing and Promotion. The following information is available for the next six months.

	Printing	Marketing and Promotion
Direct wage rate per hour	$8	$12
Budgeted overheads	$127 400	$267 540
Budgeted labour hours	3640	6370

Departmental overhead is recovered on the basis of the number of direct labour hours.
The company has been asked to promote a new product under the brand name 'Port Louis Chox'. The cost of the job is based on the following estimates.

	Printing	Marketing and Promotion
Materials	$1300	$1600
Direct labour	120 hours	300 hours

Curepipe Successful Promotions Ltd charges to clients are based on cost plus 40%.

Required
Calculate the amount which Curepipe Successful Promotions Ltd will charge its client for the promotion of Port Louis Chox. Your answer should be prepared in the form of a fully itemised financial statement.

3. The Kelang Gum Boots Company has received a contract to manufacture 2000 pairs of children's boots. The boots pass through three departments: Moulding, Lining and Finishing. The following information is given.

	Moulding	Lining	Finishing
Direct material per pair of boots	$2	$3	–
Direct labour rate per hour	$7	$6	$6
Budgeted overhead expenditure	$21 840	$11 375	$4368
Budgeted machine hours	7280	–	–
Budgeted direct labour hours	–	4550	1820
Direct labour hours per pair of boots	0.25	0.5	0.25
Machine hours per pair of boots	0.5	–	–

Overhead absorption is calculated as follows:

Moulding: machine hours
Lining and finishing: direct labour hours

Required
(a) Calculate the total cost of producing the batch of 2000 pairs of children's boots.
(b) Calculate the cost of each pair of boots.

32 Process costing

In this chapter you will learn:

● when process costing is used
● how to prepare process accounts
● how to calculate the cost of work in progress
● what joint products, by-products and waste products are.

32.1 Process costing explained

Continuous production usually involves a product passing through a series of processes. Each process is a cost centre to which costs are allocated. The raw material of each process consists of the cost of the production transferred from the previous process. Further costs will be added in each process in the form of added material, labour and overheads. The following diagram illustrates the procedure.

Direct material $1000
Direct labour $1300   → Process 1 ......
Overhead $2400

Added material $800
Added labour $1100
Material transferred $4700   → Process 2 ...... Material transferred to finished goods
Added overhead $900 $7500 ....▶

An account is prepared for each process to show the cost of the output from the process.

Example

1000 units of a product passed through three processes for which the following information is available.

	Process 1	Process 2	Process 3
	$	$	$
Direct material	15 000	8 000	2 000
Direct labour	23 000	11 000	5 000
Overhead	19 000	16 000	12 000

All of the units of the product were completed. The process accounts are as follows:

Process 1			
	$		$
Direct material	15 000	Completed units	
Direct labour	23 000	transferred to	
Overhead	19 000	Process 2	57 000
	57 000		57 000

Process 2			
	$		$
Material transferred		Completed units	
from Process 1	57 000	transferred to	
Added material	8 000	Process 3	92 000
Direct labour	11 000		
Overhead	16 000		
	92 000		92 000

Process 3			
	$		$
Material transferred from Process 2	92 000	Completed units transferred to	
Added material	2 000	finished goods	111 000
Direct labour	5 000		
Overhead	12 000		
	111 000		111 000

The effect of this is to increase the cost per unit of product as it passes through each process. At the end of process 1 the 1000 units will have a cost of $57 000 / 1000 = $57.

At the end of process 2 that cost will increase by the amount of additional expenditure in process 2. $92 000 / 1000 = $92

By the end of the process the cost will have risen to $111 per unit ($111 000 / 1000).

This build up of cost will allow a firm to accurately value its inventory at the end of an accounting period. It will also give them the ability to quote a price to a customer who, say, wants to buy the product at the end of process 2 rather than the company complete it.

Exercise 1

The Sitrah Processing Company, which passes its product through three refining processes, provides the following information for one month.

	Process I $000	Process II $000	Process III $000
Direct material	10 000	4 000	7 000
Direct labour	400	350	275
Overhead	900	864	423

All the material which was input to process I completed processes II and III.

Required
(a) Prepare the cost accounts for processes I, II and III.
(b) Calculate the cost per unit at the end of process III if 2000 units are produced.

32.2 Work in progress

It is usual that at any particular time some units of production will not have been completely processed; these are **work in progress** and must be valued for accounting purposes. The incomplete units are expressed as **equivalent units** of production and valued according to the cost that has been incurred in processing them so far. For example, if 100 units are 60% complete, this is equivalent to 60 fully completed units.

Example

The budgeted cost of processing 1000 units of product X is made up as follows:

	$
Material transferred from a previous process (1000 units)	15 000
Added material	4 500
Direct labour in this process	20 000
Overhead (recovery based on 200% of direct labour)	40 000

Only 900 units have been completely processed. The other 100 are complete as to 80% material and 50% labour.

The cost of the 900 completed units is 90% of $(15 000 + 4500 + 20 000 + 40 000) = $71 550. The cost of 100 incomplete units is:

		$
Material transferred	$\frac{100}{1000} \times \$15\,000$	1500
Added material	$\frac{100}{1000} \times \$4500 \times 80\%$	360
Direct labour	$\frac{100}{1000} \times \$20\,000 \times 50\%$	1000
Overhead	$200\% \times \$1000$	2000
		4860

The incomplete units are carried down on the Process account as work in progress.

The Process account			
	$		$
Material transferred from previous process	15 000	Transferred to next process (or finished goods)	71 550
Added material (90% of $4500 + $360)	4 410	Work in progress c/d	4 860
Direct labour (90% of $20 000 + $1000)	19 000		
Overhead (90% of $40 000 + $2000)	38 000		
	76 410		76 410
Opening work in progress b/d	4 860		

Example

Gemmaton Ltd produces a single product. During the month the following production data is obtained:

	$
Input to Process 1:	
Direct material (1000 units)	19 950
Direct labour	9 500
Overheads	4 750
	34 200

At the end of the month 900 units are fully completed. The remaining 100 units are 50% complete as to material, labour and overheads.

Calculate the value of work in progress at the end of the month.

The 100 units are 50% complete. This is the equivalent of 50 fully completed units. The direct material cost per completed unit is $\frac{\$19\ 950}{950} = \$21$

The value of the direct material element of the work in progress is $\$21 \times 50 = \$1050$.

The direct labour cost per completed unit is $\frac{\$9\ 500}{950} = \$10$

The values of the direct labour element of the work in progress is $\$10 \times 50 = \$500$

The overhead cost per completed unit is $\frac{\$4\ 750}{950} = \$4\ 750 = \$5$

The value of the overheads element of work in progress is $\$5 \times 50 = \$250$.

The value of work in progress at the end of the month is, therefore ($\$1050 + \$500 + \$250 = \$1800$.

The value of the finished goods is ($\$34\ 200 - \$1800$) = \$32\ 400.

32.3 Joint products

A single process may yield two or more products known as **joint products**. They are not distinguishable when material enters the process, but at some stage in the process they become separately identifiable.

Examples of joint products are:
- oil refining, which results in the production of petrol, diesel oil, lubricating oil and paraffin
- cattle farming, which results in milk, cream, butter, meat and hides
- clay pits, which result in ceramics, bricks, roofing tiles and chemically resistant materials.

Joint products become recognisable at the point of separation. Up to that point they have shared all the processing costs. After separation each product will be charged with the further costs incurred in putting it into a saleable condition. The diagram at the bottom of the page illustrates the emergence of joint products in a process.

The joint costs up to the point of separation may be apportioned between the products on the basis of respective quantities, provided the products are measured in the similar terms, for example in kilograms, litres, etc.

Example

A process incurs the following costs.

	$
Common material input to process	30 000
Additional material	7 000
Direct labour	42 000
Overhead	51 000
Total cost of process	130 000

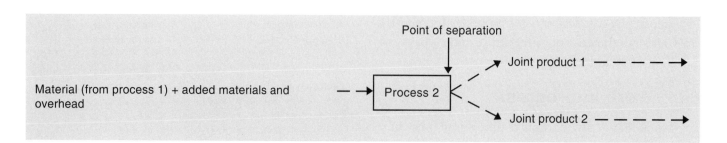

The process yielded two products:
A 17 000 kilograms, B 9000 kilograms.

After separation, A incurred further processing costs of $3400, and B incurred further processing costs of $13 500.

The cost of 17 000 kg of A up to the point of separation is $130\,000 \times \dfrac{17\,000}{26\,000} = \$85\,000$

The cost of 1 complete kilogram of A is

$$\frac{85\,000 + 3400}{17\,000} = \$5.20$$

The cost of 9000 kg of B up to the point of separation is $130\,000 \times \dfrac{9000}{26\,000} = \$45\,000$.

The cost of 1 complete kilogram of B is

$$\frac{45\,000 + 13\,500}{9000} = \$6.50.$$

Exercise 2

The Trinbago Refining Company produces two substances known as Animo and Lactino. In one week, 3400 litres of Animo and 5100 litres of Lactino were produced. The input to the process was as follows:

	$
Material: Animacto	21 000
Direct labour	11 000
Overheads	23 000

After separation, further processing costs to completion were: Animo $4624; Lactino $13 362.

Required
Calculate the cost of each complete litre of (a) Animo and (b) Lactino.

32.4 By-products and waste

A **by-product** is similar to a joint product except that its sales value is low compared with the sales value of the main product. The cocoa and chocolate industry provides a good example of a by-product: the shells of cocoa beans constitute about 8–10% of the weight of the beans and have to be removed. They are of no use in the chocolate industry but are used as fertiliser, and fuel. Other examples of by-products are remnants of material in garment manufacture, and wood off-cuts and sawdust in the timber industry.

Any income from the sale of by-products should be credited to the Process account to reduce the cost of the main or joint products.

Waste/Scrap describes material which has no value and therefore has no effect upon the Process accounts; nor will it be included in inventory.

In some cases the waste product is sold for scrap. The double entry for this transaction is to debit the bank account and credit the appropriate process account. This has the effect of reducing the overall cost per unit of the good production.

Example

Slag produced by an iron foundry is sold as scrap for $2000 to a firm of civil engineers. It is recorded in the foundry's Process accounts as follows:

	$
Material input to process	50 000
Direct wages	76 000
Overhead	94 000
	220 000
Less sale of scrap	2 000*
Cost attributed to main product	218 000

*The proceeds from the sale of the scrap were less than 1% of the process cost.

32.5 Normal losses in processing

Losses of material are unavoidable in many processes and the quantity of the product produced is less than the quantity of the material input to the process. If the loss is within the range expected for the process it is recognised as a **normal loss**. The unspoiled production will bear the cost of the loss.

Example

In a certain process, 1000 kg of material costing $4000 was used. The direct wages paid were $16 000 and overhead expenditure amounted to $24 100. The output from the process was 980 kg. The normal loss expected for the process is 2%. The output per kilogram will be valued at $(4000 + 16\,000 + 24\,100) \div 980 = \$45$.

The effect of this is to increase the cost per unit of the good production in the process.

Exercise 3

Okara Quality Carpets Ltd makes a product which involves two processes. Process 1 results in the production of a low-priced by-product which the company sells. 2000 units of the product were made in process 1 and transferred to process 2. Work in progress at the end of process 2 consisted of 800 units complete as to 75% material and 50% labour. Further production details are as follows:

Data per unit	Process 1	Process 2
Material	4 kg	2.5 kg
Cost of material	$12 per kg	$3.25 per kg
Labour hours per unit	3	5
Labour hourly rate	$14	$11
Production overhead absorption	$36 per labour hour	$27 per labour hour
Sale proceeds of scrap	$1630	–

Required

Prepare Process accounts 1 and 2 to show the cost of producing 2000 units. Show detailed workings for the valuation of finished units and work in progress in process 2.

HINTS

- Remember that the total cost of production in one process is the cost of material input to the next process.
- Make sure you can express partly completed work in terms of equivalent units.
- Learn how to apportion cost between joint products.
- Remember that the proceeds from the sale of by-products and scraps are credited in the Process accounts.
- Allow for waste when valuing completed production.

MULTIPLE-CHOICE QUESTIONS

1. Which of the following industries would use process costing?
A. building construction
B. chemical
C. hotel
D. road haulage

2. The following information is given about a process in which normal waste of 10% is incurred.

	$
Direct material	57 000
Direct labour	88 000
Overhead	79 000
Sale of waste	3 000

What is the prime cost of production?
A. $133 000   B. $142 000
C. $145 000   D. $148 000

3. The monthly production cost of a process was $156 400. Finished output was 16 000 completed units. There were 4000 units of work in progress which were 60% complete.

What was the cost per equivalent unit?
A. $7.82
B. $8.50
C. $8.89
D. $9.78

ADDITIONAL EXERCISES

1. The Taranaki Milk Products Company manufactures products which pass through three processes. The costing records for processes 1 and 2 give the following information.

	Process 1	Process 2
Materials per unit	2 litres	1 litres
Cost of materials per kg/litre	$1.25	$1.5
Materials used in process at cost	$60 000	

	Additional materials used in process	to be calculated
Direct labour per unit	30 minutes	15 minutes
Labour cost per hour	$12	$12
Variable overhead per unit	$5 per direct labour hour	$4 per direct labour hour
Fixed overhead absorption rate	$9 per direct labour hour	$6 per direct labour hour

Further information

Process 1. There were no opening or closing inventories of work in progress. All production from this process was passed to process 2.

Process 2. There was no opening inventory of work in progress. There was a closing inventory of work in progress consisting of 2000 units which were complete as to 80% materials and 60% labour.

Required

(a) Prepare the accounts for processes 1 and 2.
(b) Calculate the cost of:
   (i) one completed unit of production in process 1.
   (ii) one completed unit of production in process 2.
   (iii) one unit of work in progress in process 2.
10 000 units from process 2 were used in process 3 as a result of which two joint products X and Y were produced. The costs of this process were as follows: materials $9050; labour $18 500; variable overheads $5400; fixed overheads $10 800.
10% of production in process 3 was spoiled. X represented 75% of the good production, and Y the remainder. There were no opening or closing inventories of work in progress.

Required

(c) Calculate the quantities of (i) X and (ii) Y produced in process 3.
(d) Calculate the cost of each unit of output of process 3.
(e) Calculate the values of the finished inventories of (i) X and (ii) Y.
(f) (i) Explain what is meant by a by-product.
   (ii) State how by-products are accounted for in process cost accounting.

2. The Harare Metal Alloy Company manufactures two products which involve three processes. They pass through processes 1 and 2 as a single product and separate into product X and product Y in process 3.

The following information has been extracted from the cost records.

	Process 1	Process 2
Materials per unit	7 kg	4.5 kg
Cost of material per litre	$1.50	$2
Cost of materials used in process 1	$42 000	–
Cost of materials used in process 2	–	to be calculated
Direct labour hours per unit	4	3.5
Hourly labour cost	$8	$6
Variable overhead per unit	$16 per direct labour hour	$15 per direct labour hour
Fixed overhead absorption rate	$30 per direct labour hour	$29 per direct labour hour
Sale of by-product	$1 000	–
Opening inventory of work in progress	nil	nil
Closing inventory of work in progress	nil	1000 units

The closing inventory of work in progress in process 2 is complete as to 100% materials and 75% labour.

Required

(a) Prepare the ledger account for process 1.
(b) Prepare the ledger account for process 2.
The completed units in process 2 are transferred to process 3 where they separate into joint products, X and Y. 70% of the finished units are X and 30% are Y. The costs in process 3 are as follows:

Added materials: 3.5 kg per unit at $3 per kg
Direct labour: 2 hours per unit at $7 per hour
Variable overheads: $18 per direct labour hour
Fixed overhead absorption rate: $27 per direct labour rate.

10% of the production in process 3 was spoiled.

Required

(c) Prepare the ledger account for process 3.

33 Marginal costing

In this chapter you will learn:

- what marginal cost is and how it is used
- the importance of contribution and the C/S ratio
- what break-even is and how to calculate break-even point
- how to prepare a break-even chart
- how marginal costs are used to decide on a pricing policy
- when orders from customers may be accepted below normal selling price
- the use of marginal costs for make or buy decisions
- how to make the most profitable use of scarce resources
- the valuation of inventory using marginal and absorption costing
- the use of sensitivity analysis.

33.1 Marginal cost

In chapter 30 we saw how total costing can be used to determine price and profit but, beyond that, its uses are limited. For many management decisions it is necessary to know the **marginal cost** of a unit of production. Marginal cost can be described as the cost of making one extra unit of an item. It is based on the principle that an additional unit of production will only result an increase in the variable costs and that the fixed costs will not be affected. **Marginal cost of production** is the total of the variable costs of manufacture.

Example 1

The costs of producing 1000 units of a product are shown in the table on this page (with the unit cost shown in the second column).

The marginal cost of production for 1000 units is $150 000 (or $150 for a single unit). The difference between the total cost of production (i.e. including fixed overheads) and the selling price gives the profit of $40 000 (or $40 per unit – not shown). Fixed overheads + profit = $90 000, or $90 per unit. This is called the **contribution** because it is the contribution that each unit of production makes towards covering

the overheads and providing a profit. The contribution per unit is calculated as follows: selling price per unit less the total of the variable costs per unit or SP – VC (per unit). In this case $240 – $150 = $90.

	Cost of 1000 units $	Cost per unit $
Variable costs		
Direct material	30 000	30
Direct labour	100 000	100
Direct expenses	5 000	5
Prime cost	135 000	135
Variable overheads	15 000	15
Marginal cost of production	150 000	150
Fixed overheads	50 000	
Total cost of production	200 000	
Profit (20% of total cost)	40 000	
Contribution		90
Selling price	240 000	240

The cost of making 1001 units will be $(200\ 000 + 150) = \$200\ 150$, not $(200\ 000 \div 1000 \times 1001) = \$200\ 200$ as it might seem if we only had a total cost statement.

The ratio of the contribution to the selling price is known as the **C/S ratio**. In this example the C/S ratio is $\dfrac{90}{240} \times 100 = 37.5\%$. This is a very useful ratio that can be used to calculate the answers to many problems. The use of the C/S ratio can avoid the need to spend valuable time calculating marginal cost.

For example, if the sales increase to $300 000 then the total contribution will be $112 500 (300 000 × 37.5%). Assuming fixed costs remain the same at this level of output then the profit will be $62 500 ($112 500 – $50 000).

Example 2

The following is a summarised statement of producing 2000 units of product X.

	$
Marginal cost	81 900
Contribution	44 100
Sales	126 000
Fixed costs amount to $26 000	
Profit = contribution – fixed costs: $(44 100 – 26 000) = $18 100	

What will the profit or loss be if production is
(i) increased to 2400 units
(ii) reduced to 1800 units
(iii) reduced to 1100 units?

Answer

(i) The contribution from 1 unit is $44 100 ÷ 2000 = $22.05.
Therefore the contribution from 2400 units is 2400 × $22.05 = $52 920.

> Profit = contribution – fixed costs
> = $(52 920 – 26 000) = $26 920

(ii) The contribution from 1800 units will be 1800 × $22.05 = $39 690.

> Profit = $(39 690 – 26 000) = $13 690

(iii) The contribution from 1100 units will be 1100 × $22.05 = $24 255.

> Loss = $(26 000 – 24 255) = $1745

Exercise 1

The following is the marginal cost statement for the production of 3000 units of product Q.

	$
Marginal cost	178 750
Contribution	146 250
Sales	325 000

Fixed costs amount to $82 000.

Required

Calculate the profit or loss from the sale of (i) 3000 units (ii) 4000 units (iii) 1200 units of product Q.

33.2 The break-even point

The point at which a business or a product makes neither a profit nor a loss is the **break-even point**. Managers need to know the break-even point of a product when making decisions about pricing, production levels and other matters.

Break-even occurs when contribution equals fixed costs. It is found by dividing the total fixed costs by the contribution per unit. The calculation gives the number of units that have to be produced and sold before the fixed costs are covered.

Example

The following information relates to the production of a chemical.

	$
Marginal cost per litre	26
Selling price per litre	50
Total of fixed costs	72 000

The contribution per litre is $(50 – 26) = $24.

$$\text{Break-even point} = \frac{\$72\ 000}{\$24} = 3000 \text{ litres.}$$

The sales revenue at which the product will break even is 3000 × $50 = $150 000. This may also be found as follows:

$$\frac{\text{total fixed costs}}{\text{contribution per \$ of selling price}} = \frac{\$72\ 000}{\$0.48}$$

$$= \$150\ 000$$

(contribution per $ of selling price = $24 ÷ 50 = $0.48).

The C/S ratio in this case is $24 ÷ 50 × 100 = 48%. This can also provide the calculation of the break even point in terms of sales revenue by dividing the fixed costs by the C/S ratio. In this case it will be $7200 ÷ 48% = $150 000.

When the calculation of break-even point results in a fraction of a unit of production, the answer should be rounded up to the next complete unit, for example:

Contribution per unit of product $23; total fixed costs $32 000.

$$\text{Break-even} = \frac{\$32\,000}{\$23} = 1391.304, \text{ shown as 1392 units.}$$

The formula in §33.1 of selling price – variable costs can also be extended to calculate how many units need to be sold to earn a required level of profit.

Example

The break-even point is 3000 litres. However, how many litres need to be sold to earn a profit of $12 000?

This can be calculated by adding the required profit to the fixed costs and dividing the answer by the contribution per unit.

Fixed costs $72 000 + required profit $12 000 = $84 000.

$84 000 / $24 = 3500 litres.

This can be proved as follows:

	$
Sales revenue (3500 × $50)	175 000
Less marginal costs (3500 × $26)	91 000
Total contribution	84 000
Less fixed costs	72 000
Profit	12 000

The C/S ratio can also be used to calculate the revenue required to earn a target profit. In this case it will be $84 000 ÷ 48% = $175 000 (3500 unit × $50 each).

33.3 Break-even charts

A **break-even chart** is a diagrammatic representation of the profit or loss to be expected from the sale of a product at various levels of activity. The chart is prepared by plotting the revenue from the sale of various volumes of a

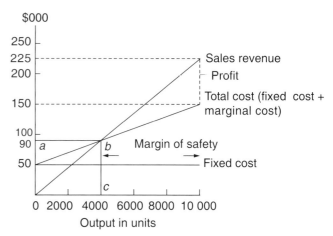

Break-even chart for product X

product against the total cost of production. The break-even point occurs where the sales line cuts the total cost line and there is neither profit nor loss.

Example

The marginal cost of product X is $10 per litre. It is sold for $22.50 per litre. Fixed costs are $50 000.

The line *ab* shows the revenue at break-even point ($90 000). The line *bc* shows the output in units at break-even point (4000). At 10 000 units, the sales revenue is $225 000 and total cost is $150 000. The distance between those two lines shows the profit of $75 000.

The area between the sales revenue line and the total cost line *before* the break-even point represents the loss that will be made if the output falls below 4000 units. The area *beyond* the break-even point represents profit.

The difference between the break-even point and 10 000 units is the **margin of safety**, or the amount by which output can fall short of 10 000 units before the business risks making a loss on product X. It may be expressed as a number of units, 6000, or as a percentage, $\dfrac{6000}{10\,000} \times 100 = 60\%$.

The break-even charts of two products, A and B, will now be compared. Both products have similar total costs and revenues, but product A has high fixed costs while product B has low fixed costs.

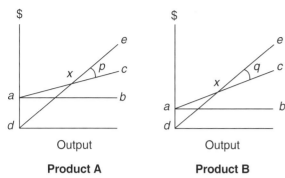

Product A   Product B

In each case, line *ab* represents fixed costs, line *ac* represents total cost, and line *de* represents sales revenue. The break-even point **X** for product A occurs further to the right of the chart (i.e. later) than that for product B. This shows that high fixed costs tend to result in high break-even points. Product B with a low fixed cost has a lower break-even point even though the marginal cost is greater.

The angle *p* at which the revenue line *de* intersects the total cost line *ac* for product A is greater than the angle *q* for product B. The size of the angle of intersection is an indication of the **sensitivity** of a product to variations in the level of activity. It can be seen that, as output increases for the two products, the profitability of product A increases at a faster rate than the profitability of product B. On the other hand, if output decreases for both products, the profitability of A decreases at a faster rate than for B. Product A is more sensitive to changes in output than product B. When the proportion of fixed cost to total cost is high, the risk to profitability is also high. Profit and break-even points are said to be sensitive to changes in prices and cost. This aspect will be considered later in §33.9.

Note. The CIE syllabus requires candidates to be able to prepare break-even charts from given information.

Exercise 2

Production of 5000 units of Product Q is planned. The following information is given.

	$
Variable cost per unit	65
Selling price per unit	95
Total of fixed costs	75 000

Required

(a) Calculate:
   (i) the break-even point of product Q in terms of units and revenue
   (ii) the margin of safety.
(b) Draw a break-even chart for product Q.

Profit/volume charts

Break-even charts may also be drawn to show only the profit or loss at each level of output. The cost and revenue lines are omitted. The break-even chart for product X given in the example above could be drawn as a profit/volume chart:

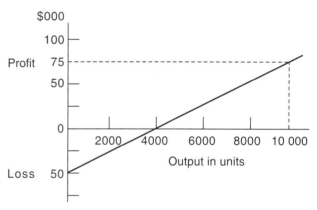

Profit/volume chart for product X

At zero output, the loss equals the total of the fixed costs, $50 000. At 10 000 units, the profit is equal to $75 000. A straight line joining the two points intersects the output line at the break-even point.

33.4 The limitations of break-even charts

Break-even charts are useful visual aids for the study of the effect of changes in output, costs and revenues on the break-even point, especially for managers with little accounting knowledge. The charts, however, have their limitations.

- Some costs are not easily classified as fixed or variable.
- Many fixed costs are fixed only within certain limits and may increase with the level of activity; they are 'stepped' costs (see §30.3).
- If sales revenue and costs are represented by straight lines they may be misleading. Maximum sales revenue may only be achieved if

customers are given attractive discounts, while variable costs may be affected by quantity discounts when output is increased. These factors would be more accurately represented on charts by curves than straight lines.

- Some costs may be semi variable. In other words, there is both an element of fixed cost and an element of variable cost included in the total. An example of this may be telephone. The fixed element may be the line rental, which must be paid whether any calls are made or not. The variable element would be the call charges which will increase each time a call is made. In order for break even to work then the fixed and variable element must be calculated and added in with the appropriate figures.
- The charts may mislead people whose accounting knowledge is limited, but trained accountants will know when to make allowances for the charts' limitations.

Example

Ken has collected the following data in relation to his output and costs and sales revenue.

Output	6000 units	8000 units
Sales revenue	$126 000	$168 000
Direct material	$30 000	$40 000
Direct labour	$18 000	$24 000
Other overheads	$48 000	$60 000
Fixed costs	$37 000	$37 000

At both levels of output the cost per unit for direct materials and direct labour are the same ($5 and $3 respectively). This means that they are wholly variable costs.

However, the cost per unit for other overheads is different at the two levels of output. For 6000 units of output the other overheads are $8 per unit. When 8000 units are produced the cost per unit is $7.50. This means that these costs are not variable costs. Neither are they fixed costs, as the total amount would be the same at both levels of output, either $48 000 or $60 000. This means that the other overheads are semi variable costs. Before the break-even point can be calculated, the amount of variable and fixed costs included in each must be calculated.

This is done by looking at the change in costs and the change in output.

	Output	Costs
	8000	$60 000
	6000	$48 000
Change	2000	$12 000

An increase in output by 2000 units has caused the costs to change by $12 000. The only type of cost which could cause this change is a variable cost. So the variable element of the costs = $12 000 / 2000 = $6 per unit.

For an output of 6000 units, this means that the total variable costs are $36 000 (6000 × $6). The fixed element must be $12 000 ($48 000 − $36 000).

This can be proved by carrying out the same procedure for an output of 8000 units.
Variable costs = 8000 × $6 = $48 000
Fixed costs are $60 000 − $48 000 = $12 000.
Ken can now work out his break-even point.

	$	$
Selling price per unit		21.00
Direct materials per unit	5.00	
Direct labour	3.00	
Other variable costs per unit	6.00	14.00
Contribution per unit		7.00

Break-even point = fixed costs ($37 000 + $12 000)/$7.00 = 7000 units.

Unless Ken had split out his other overheads into their fixed and variable element he would have been unable to calculate the break-even point.

33.5 Marginal costing and pricing

The price at which a good may be sold is usually decided by a number of factors:
- the need to make a profit
- market demand
- a requirement to increase market share for a product
- maximum utilisation of resources
- competition from other firms
- economic conditions
- political factors (price regulation etc.).

Marginal costing can help management to decide on pricing policy but first it is necessary to understand that some expenses, such as selling expenses, may be variable. An example is salespeople's commission based on the number of units sold. When variable selling expenses are included in marginal cost, the result is the **marginal cost of sales**:

	$000
Direct materials	100
Direct wages	80
Direct expenses	30
Marginal cost of production	210
Variable selling expenses	15
Marginal cost of sales	225
Other fixed expenses	175
Total cost	400

It is important to use the correct marginal cost when using marginal costing for decision making.

Example

(Increasing market share)
The Larabee Gamebusters Company produces and sells a computer game that sells at $30 per game.

Each year 6000 of the games are sold. The marketing director suggests that, if the price is reduced to $28, sales will increase to 8000 games. The sales manager thinks that sales will increase to 11 000 games if the price is reduced to $25.

The following information is available for 6000 computer games.

	$
Direct materials	48 000
Direct labour	66 000
Variable selling expenses (commission)	12 000
Fixed expenses	48 000

Required

Calculate the profit or loss from the sale of (i) 6000 (ii) 8000 (iii) 11 000 units and recommend which option should be adopted.

Answer

Every unit sold incurs a variable selling expense (commission) and the marginal cost of sales is used.

Per unit:	$	$	$
Selling price	30	28	25
Direct material	8		
Direct labour	11		
Variable selling expense	2		
Marginal cost of sales	21	21	21
Contribution	9	7	4

	6000 units	8000 units	11 000 units
	$	$	$
Total contribution	54 000	56 000	44 000
Fixed expenses	48 000	48 000	48 000
Profit/(loss)	6 000	8 000	(4 000)

The Larabee Gamebusters Company should reduce the price of the game to $28.

Exercise 3

Veerich Ardson Ltd makes and sells mobile phones. The following information is given.

Per phone:	$
Selling price	50
Direct materials	18
Direct labour	20
Variable selling expenses	3

Fixed overheads amount to $70 000.

Required

Calculate the profit or loss from the sale of (i) 10 000 phones at $50 each, (ii) 15 000 phones at $48 each, (iii) 20 000 phones at $42 each.

33.6 Acceptance of orders below normal selling price

There are occasions when orders may be accepted below the normal selling price. These may be considered when there is spare manufacturing capacity and in the following circumstances:
- when the order will result in further contribution to cover fixed expenses and add to profit
- to maintain production and avoid laying off a skilled workforce during a period of poor trading
- to promote a new product
- to dispose of slow-moving or redundant stock.
The selling price **must** exceed the marginal cost of production.

Example

K2 Altimeters Ltd makes altimeters that it sells at $80 each. It has received orders for:
  (i) 1000 altimeters for which the buyer is prepared to pay $60 per altimeter
  (ii) 2000 altimeters at $48 each.

The following information is available.

	$
Direct material per altimeter	21
Direct labour per altimeter	32

Fixed expenses will not be affected by the additional production.

Required
State whether K2 Altimeters Ltd should accept either of the orders.

Answer
Order for 1000 altimeters at $60 each:

Contribution per altimeter $(60 − 53) = $7
Additional contribution from order: $7000

K2 Altimeters Ltd should accept the order.
Order for 2000 altimeters at $48 each.

Contribution per altimeter $(48 − 53) = $5

K2 Altimeters Ltd would make a loss of $10 000 on the order and should not accept it.

Exercise 4

El Dugar Peach Ltd sells canned fruit for which the following information is given.

	$
Per 1000 cans of fruit:	
Direct materials	5500
Direct labour	8750

The company has received orders for:
(i)   5000 cans of fruit at $16 000 per 1000 cans
(ii) 3000 cans of fruit at $14 100 per 1000 cans.
The additional production will not require any additional fixed expenses.

Required
State which of the two orders, if any, El Dugar Peach Ltd should accept.

33.7 **Make or buy decisions**

We have already seen in §19.2 that a Manufacturing Account may suggest that it would be more profitable for a business to buy goods from another supplier than make the goods itself. This involves a **'make or buy' decision**. It may be relevant for goods that are already being produced, or to the introduction of a new product.

The decision will be based primarily on whether the cost of buying the goods from another supplier is more or less than the marginal cost of production. Notice that the marginal cost of sales is not relevant to this type of decision as any variable selling costs will have to be incurred whether the goods are manufactured or purchased.

Example
Uggle Boxes Ltd makes and sells uggle boxes for which the following information is available.

Per box	$
Selling price	25
Direct material	9
Direct labour	6
Variable selling expenses	7

Uggle Boxes Ltd's fixed overheads amount to $60 500.

The variable selling expenses are ignored as they will have to be incurred anyway. The marginal cost of production is $(9 + 6) = $15. The contribution per unit is ($(25 − 22) = $3. The current break-even point is $\frac{\$60\,500}{\$3} = 20\,167$ boxes.

Uggle boxes may be bought from Ockle Cockle Boxes Ltd for $13 per box, and from Jiggle Boxes Ltd for $16 per box.

Purchase of the boxes from Jiggle Boxes Ltd will increase the marginal cost to $23 and reduce the contribution to $2. Profit will be reduced and the break-even point will increase to $\frac{\$60\,500}{\$2}$ or 30 250 boxes. This option should not be considered.

If the boxes are bought from Ockle Cockle Boxes Ltd, the marginal cost will be $20 and the contribution will increase to $5. Profit will be increased and the break-even point will reduce to $\frac{\$60\,500}{\$5}$ or 12 100 boxes. This appears to be a good option.

The principle is that if the marginal cost of production is below the price quoted by the supplier then the offer should be rejected.

Note. There are other matters which Uggle Boxes Ltd should consider before finally deciding to buy the boxes from another supplier:

- How certain is it that Ockle Cockle Boxes Ltd will not increase the price above $13? If the price is increased to more than $15 it may not be easy for Uggle Boxes Ltd to recommence manufacturing the boxes if it has rid itself of its workers and other resources.
- Will Ockle Cockle Boxes Ltd supply boxes of the proper quality?
- Will Ockle Cockle Boxes Ltd deliver the boxes promptly? Uggle Boxes Ltd cannot afford to keep its customers waiting because it is out of stock.
- Has Uggle Boxes Ltd an alternative use for the resources which will become free when it ceases to make the boxes? Unless it can utilise the resources profitably to make another product it will either have to shed the resources (labour, machines, etc.) or increase its unproductive costs.
- Can Uggle Boxes Ltd afford to lose the services of a skilled and loyal workforce which it may be difficult to replace at a later date when the need arises?

As we shall see again in chapter 36 on capital investment appraisal, managers often need to take non-financial factors into account before deciding which course of action to take.

Exercise 5

Canterbury Planes Ltd supplies the following information for the production of 15 000 tools.

	$
Direct materials	45 000
Direct labour	37 500
Other direct expenses	15 000
Variable selling expenses	30 000

Fixed expenses total $74 000. The tools sell for $16 each.

Canterbury Planes Ltd has received the following quotations for the supply of the tools:

North Island Tool Co.	$6000 per 1000 tools
South Island Tool Co.	$6800 per 1000 tools

Required

(a) Calculate the effect on profit and the break-even point of the quotations of

(i) North Island Tool Co.
(ii) South Island Tool Co.

if either was awarded the contract to supply the tools to Canterbury Planes Ltd.

(b) State whether Canterbury Planes Ltd should continue to produce the tools or whether it should buy them, and if so, from whom. Support your answer with figures.

33.8 Making the most profitable use of limited resources

Anything which limits the quantity of goods that a business may produce is known as a **limiting factor**. Limiting factors include:

- shortage of materials
- shortage of labour
- shortage of demand for a particular product.

When faced with limited resources, a company making several different products should use the limited resources in a way that produces the most profit. The products must be ranked according to the amount of contribution they make from each unit of the scarce resource. Production will then be planned to ensure that the scarce resource is concentrated on the highest-ranking products.

Example 1

(Shortage of material)
Hillbilly Ltd makes three products: Hillies, Billies and Millies. All three products are made from a material called Dilly. Planned production is as follows: Hillies 2000 units; Billies 3000 units; Millies 4000 units. The following information is given for the products.

	Hillies	Billies	Millies
Selling price per unit	$54	$50	$105
Direct material per unit	2 kg	4 kg	5 kg
Direct labour hours per unit	3	2	6

Direct material costs $6 per kg; direct labour is paid at $10 per hour.

Fixed expenses amount to $72 000. To make the planned production Hillbilly Ltd will require (2000 × 2 kg) + (3000 × 4 kg) + (4000 × 5 kg) = 36 000 kg of material. If all the planned production was made, Hillbilly Ltd would make a profit of $30 000.

Hillbilly Ltd has discovered that the material Dilly is in short supply and only 30 000 kg can be obtained.

Required

Prepare a production plan that will make the most profit from the available material.

Answer

Calculation of contributions per kg of Dilly:

	Hillies	Billies	Millies
	$	$	$
Direct material per unit	12	24	30
Direct labour per unit	30	20	60
Marginal cost per unit	42	44	90
Selling price per unit	54	50	105
Contribution per unit	12	6	15
Contribution per kg of material	6	1.5	3
Ranking	1	3	2

Revised plan of production:

	Units	Direct material kg	Contribution $
Hillies	2000	4 000	24 000
Millies	4000	20 000	60 000
Billies	1500	6 000	9 000
		30 000	93 000
Deduct fixed expenses			72 000
Profit			21 000

Example 2

(Shortage of direct labour hours)
The data for the manufacture of Hillies, Billies and Millies is as given for example 1 but the number of direct labour hours available is limited to 33 000. There is no shortage of material.

Required

Prepare a production plan that will make the most profit from the available labour hours.

Answer

Calculation of contributions per direct labour hour:

	Hillies	Billies	Millies
	$	$	$
Contribution per unit (as above)	12	6	15
Contribution per direct labour hour	4	3	2.5
Ranking	1	2	3

Revised plan of production:

	Units	Direct labour hours	Contribution $
Hillies	2000	6 000	24 000
Billies	3000	6 000	18 000
Millies	3500	21 000	52 500
		33 000	94 500
Deduct fixed expenses			72 000
Profit			22 500

Exercise 6

Castries Ltd makes three products: Gimie, Gros and Petit. The budgeted production for three months is as follows:

	Gimie	Gros	Petit
No. of units	1000	2000	800
Selling price per unit	$14	$25	$20
Direct material per unit (litres)	2.5	3.25	4
Direct labour per unit (hours)	0.5	1.4	0.6

Direct material costs $2 per litre. Direct labour is paid at $10 per hour.

Fixed expenses are $10 000.

Castries Ltd has been informed that only 10 575 litres of material are available.

Required

Prepare a revised production budget that will produce the most profit from the available materials.

Exercise 7

Castries Ltd has been informed that supplies of material are not limited, but only 3395 direct labour hours are available. All the other information is as in exercise 6.

Required

Prepare a revised production budget that will produce the most profit from the available direct labour hours.

33.9 Sensitivity analysis

In §33.3 the sensitivity of profit and break-even points to changes in costs and revenue was mentioned. This topic will now be covered in more detail as errors in estimates of revenue and costs will affect profit. By definition, estimates are rarely likely to be accurate and allowances should be made in budgets for possible differences between estimates and actual costs and revenue. The point will be illustrated by taking the example of a high-risk situation.

Example

The following information relates to the budget for a certain product.

No. of units produced and sold: 10 000	$
Sales revenue	180 000
Variable costs	50 000
Fixed costs	100 000
Profit	30 000

(Break-even occurs at $\dfrac{\$100\ 000}{\$13} = 7692$ units)

If fixed costs rise by 10% and the increase is not passed on to customers, profit will be reduced by $10 000 to $20 000. Break-even will be increased to

$$\frac{\$110\ 000}{\$13} = 8462 \text{ units.}$$

If fixed costs do not increase but variable costs rise by 10%, and the increase is not passed on to customers, the profit will be reduced by $5000 to $25 000, and the break-even point will be increased to

$$\frac{\$100\ 000}{\$12.5} = 8000 \text{ units.}$$

If costs do not increase but the selling price per unit is only 90% of expectation, profit will be reduced by $18 000 to $12 000, and break-even will be increased to

$$\frac{\$100\ 000}{\$11.2} = 8929 \text{ units.}$$

If fixed costs increase by 10% and are not passed on to customers, and the selling price per unit is only 90% of expectation, profit will be reduced by $(10 000 + 18 000) to $2000, and break-even will be increased to

$$\frac{\$110\ 000}{\$11.2} = 9822 \text{ units.}$$

If all costs increase by 10% and are not passed on to customers, and the selling price per unit is only 90% of expectation, a loss of $3000 ($30 000 − $15 000 − $18 000) will be incurred, and break-even will be increased beyond the budgeted production at

$$\frac{\$110\ 000}{\$10.7} = 10\ 281 \text{ units.}$$

Exercise 8

The following budget has been prepared for the production and sales of 20 000 units of a product.

	$
Fixed costs	80 000
Variable costs	60 000
Total costs	140 000
Sales	175 000
Profit	35 000

Break-even occurs at $\dfrac{\$80\ 000}{\$5.75} = 13\ 914$ units.

Required
Calculate the profit and the break-even point if
  (i) fixed costs increase by 15% and are not passed on to customers
  (ii) variable costs increase by 15% and are not passed on to customers (there is no increase in fixed costs)
  (iii) fixed and variable costs increase by 15% and the increases are passed on to the customers.

Exercise 9

Cohort Ltd makes three products: Legion, Centurion and Praefect. All three products are made from the same material. The production budget for June is as follows:

	Legion	Centurion	Praefect
Budgeted production (units)	1000	2000	4000
Materials per unit (kg)	2	4	5
Direct labour per unit (hours)	3	5	6
Selling price per unit	$80	$130	$150

Material cost: $10 per kg Labour rate of pay: $12 per hour
Total fixed expenses for June: $115 000

Required
(a) Calculate the budgeted profit for June. Show your workings.

After the budget for June was prepared, Cohort Ltd learned that there was a shortage of the material and that it would not be able to obtain more than 28 000 kg in June.

Required
(b) Prepare a revised production budget which will ensure that Cohort Ltd obtains the maximum profit from the available material.
(c) Prepare a calculation to explain the difference between the original budgeted profit you have calculated in (a) and the revised profit you have calculated in (b).

Exercise 10

The Cockpit Country Industrial Co. Ltd has a maximum production capacity of 20 000 units. Each unit sells for $25.

The following are the costs for a single unit of production.

Direct materials	4 kilograms at $4.10 per kilogram
Direct labour	$12 per hour. 3 units are produced in one hour.
Variable expenses	$1.80 per unit for the first 16 000 units $1.70 per unit for all units in excess of 16 000 units
Fixed expenses	$1.50 per unit at full production

Required

(a) Using marginal costing, calculate the net profit if:
  (i) 15 000 units are produced and sold
  (ii) 18 000 units are produced and sold.
(b) Calculate the number of units required to break even.
(c) Calculate the profit at full production capacity if all production is sold at the reduced price of $24.
(d) State the possible advantages and disadvantages of reducing the normal selling price.
(e) State *five* assumptions which are made in the preparation of break-even charts, and state *one* limitation of each assumption.

33.10 Marginal costing vs absorption costing and inventory valuation

When we looked at FIFO and Average Cost we saw that any difference in valuing closing inventory will produce different profit figures. The two methods of costing, marginal and absorption will also produce totally different profits, as the closing inventory will be valued in two different ways.

Example

A company produces a single product. The results for the last month are as follows:

Quantity produced	400
Quantity sold	360
Selling price per unit	$100
Variable costs per unit	$60
Fixed overheads for the period	$2 000

Calculation of profit using each method of inventory valuation

Details	Marginal costing		Absorption costing	
	$	$	$	$
Sales Revenue		36 000		36 000
Variable costs	24 000		24 000	
Less: Closing Stock	2 400			
	21 600			
Fixed Overheads	2 000		2 000	
			26 000	
Cost of Sales		23 600		
Less: Closing Stock			2 600	
Cost of Sales				23 400
Gross Profit		12 400		12 600

The reason for this difference in gross profit is purely due to the way in which fixed overheads are treated. In marginal costing they are treated as period costs and written off in full in the month. No part of them is included in the closing inventory figure. Under this method the closing inventory is valued at $60 per unit to give a value of 40 × $60 = $2 400.

However, with absorption costing some of the fixed overheads are included in the closing inventory. Under this method total production cost of $26 000 are divided by the total production of 400 units to arrive at an inventory value per unit of $65 per unit. The closing inventory is, therefore, valued at 40 × $65 = $2 600.

Exercise 11

A company produces a single product, the Jonty. Details of its costs are as follows:

	$
Unit selling price	50
Unit variable costs	30
Fixed costs per month	15 000

Projected sales are 1000 units for month 1 and 1300 units for month 2. The company will produce 1500 units each month.

Required

(a) Calculate the net profit each month if the closing stock is valued using marginal costing.
(b) Calculate the net profit each month if the closing stock is valued using full absorption costing.
(c) Prepare a statement reconciling the net profit in each case.

HINTS

- Make sure you are able to distinguish between variable and fixed costs.
- Learn the definition of 'marginal cost'.
- The C/S ratio is most important and is certain to be required in marginal cost questions. Make sure you know how to calculate the ratio and when to use it.
- Learn how to calculate the break-even point and the margin of safety. Break-even point is calculated by dividing the total fixed costs by the contribution per unit. If you are given the fixed cost per unit, multiply it by the number of units to find the total fixed costs.
- Practise drawing break-even charts. Choose as large a scale as possible for the chart to achieve a good degree of accuracy. Give every chart a proper heading and label the x and y axes clearly. Indicate the break-even point and other features. Take a ruler, pencil and rubber to the exam.
- Make sure you know how to use limited resources most profitably. Product should be ranked according to the contribution per unit of the limited resource.

MULTIPLE-CHOICE QUESTIONS

1. Information about a product is given.

	per unit $
Selling price	110
Direct materials	50
Direct labour	40

Fixed costs total $50 000 and planned production is 2000 units. Which action is necessary to break even? Decrease cost of:

A. direct labour by 20% B. direct labour by 25%
C. direct material by 10% D. direct material by 20%

2. The annual results of a company with three departments are as follows:

Department	X	Y	Z
	$	$	$
Sales	210 000	100 000	140 000
Less: variable costs	100 000	80 000	90 000
head office			
fixed costs	75 000	35 000	50 000
Net profit (loss)	35 000	(15 000)	0

Head office fixed costs have been apportioned on the basis of the respective sales of the departments and will not be reduced if any department is closed. Which action should the company take, based on these results?

A. close department Y
B. close departments Y and Z
C. close department Z
D. keep all the departments open

3. A company makes three products, X, Y and Z, all of which require the use of the same material. Information about the products is as follows:

	Product X	Product Y	Product Z
	$	$	$
Per unit:			
Selling price	260	200	240
Direct material	96	80	90
Direct labour	50	40	50
Variable overhead	40	30	36
Fixed overhead	54	36	36
Profit	12	14	27

The material is in short supply. Which order of priority should the company give to the products to maximise profit?

	Order of priority		
	1	2	3
A.	Y	X	Z
B.	Y	Z	X
C.	X	Y	Z
D.	X	Z	Y

4. The following information relates to product Q.

	$
Sales revenue at break-even point	72 000
Unit sales price	24
Fixed costs	18 000

What is the marginal cost of each unit of product Q?

A. $4.00   B. $6.00   C. $10.00   D. $18.00

ADDITIONAL EXERCISES

1. Barkis & Co. Ltd manufactures specialised containers for use under water. The business uses two machines. These machines have different levels of efficiency. The following information applies to production and costs.

Machine	X	Y
Hourly rate of production	160	250
Material cost per unit	$5.00	$4.60
Hourly labour rate	$10	$10
Number of operatives	4	5
Fixed costs per order	$200	$500
Variable costs per order	$2.40	$2.60

Orders have been received from different customers for (a) 800 and (b) 1000 containers. Which machine should be used for each order, in order to minimise cost? Orders may not be split between machines, but the same machine may be used for more than one order.
(a) Order 123/P for 800 containers
(b) Order 382/Q for 1000 containers
(c) Calculate the contribution to be made for order 123/P to make a profit of 25% on total cost, using each machine.
(d) Barkis & Co. Ltd requires more funds to purchase an additional machine to complete further orders.
   Three methods of doing so have been discussed:
   (I)   a rights issue;
   (ii) an issue of shares to the public;
   (iii) an issue of debentures.
   Give one advantage and one disadvantage of each method.

2. Angelicus and Co. manufactures three different qualities of lock, Domestic, Commercial and Industrial. The company's results for the year ended 31 March 2011 were as follows:

	Domestic	Commercial	Industrial	Total
Sales (units)	120 000	45 000	56 250	221 250
	$000	$000	$000	$000
Sales (total value)	240	180	450	870
Total costs				
Direct material	108	66	84	258
Direct labour	60	30	150	240
Variable overheads	24	54	120	198
Fixed overheads	54	33	42	129
	246	183	396	825
Profit (loss)	(6)	(3)	54	45

Fixed overheads are absorbed on the basis of 50% of direct materials.

Required
(a) For the year ended 31 March 2011 calculate, for each type of lock,
   (i) the contribution per unit;
   (ii) the contribution as a percentage of sales.
   Give answers to a maximum of three decimal places. Show all workings.
(b) Calculate the break-even point for each type of lock in both units and dollars.
(c) Advise whether Angelicus should cease production of Domestic and Commercial locks. Give your reasons.

34 Budgeting

In this chapter you will learn:

- how budgets differ from forecasts
- how budgets help management to plan and control
- factors to be considered in the preparation of budgets
- how to prepare sales, production, purchasing, expense and cash budgets
- how to prepare master budgets
- what flexible budgets are.

34.1 The difference between a forecast and a budget

A business **forecast** is an estimate of the likely position of a business in the future, based on past or present conditions. For example, Cindy's sales over the past five years have been $100 000, $105 000, $110 250, $115 750 and $121 500; the sales have been increasing at the rate of about 5% each year. Based on this information, and assuming that trading conditions will continue unchanged, the forecast sales for the next year might be about $127 600.

A **budget** is a statement of *planned* future results which are expected to follow from actions taken by management to change the present circumstances. Cindy may want sales to grow by 10% each year in future by introducing new products, or by increasing advertising, or by offering improved terms of trading. Her budgeted sales for next year will then be $133 650 ($121 500 × 110%), and $147 000 and $161 700 for the following two years. A budget expresses management's plans for the future of a business in money terms.

A company may set its budget by analysing existing operations and justifying them on the basis of their use or need to the organisation. This is known as **zero** based budgeting. In effect the company starts with a blank piece of paper and builds up every cost from nothing.

An alternative to this is using last year's budgeted or actual figures and adding to it or subtracting from it to reflect changes. For example, from its accounts a company knows that its salaries figure last year was $50 000. It decides it will budget for a 5% increase this year so sets its salaries budget at $52 500. This is known as **incremental** budgeting.

There is an argument as to which is the best method. Using incremental budgeting may result in past inefficiencies being built into future plans. Whilst other would argue that using zero based budgeting is almost impossible without looking back to previous years.

34.2 Budgets as tools for planning and control

Planning

Managers are responsible for planning and controlling a business for the benefit of its owners, and budgets are essential tools for planning and controlling. Well-managed businesses have short-term budgets for, say, the year ahead. Small businesses may function well enough with these, but larger businesses need to plan further ahead and may prepare long-term budgets, in addition to the short-term ones, for the next five, ten or even more years ahead. These plans are often known as **rolling budgets** because, as each year passes, it is deleted from the budget and a budget for another year is added. A budget for one year ahead will be detailed, but budgets for the following years may be less precise because of uncertainty about future trading conditions.

The manager of each department or function in a business is responsible for the performance of his or her department or function. Separate operational, or functional, budgets must be prepared for each department or activity detailing the department's revenue (if any) and expenses for a given period. The budgets will be prepared for sales, production, purchasing, personnel, administration, treasury (cash and banking), etc. Opinions differ as to who should prepare these budgets.

Top-down budgets are prepared by top management and handed down to departmental managers, who are responsible for putting them into effect. Such budgets usually have the merit of being well co-ordinated so that they all fit together as a logical and consistent plan for the whole business. However, departmental managers may not feel committed to keeping to these budgets as they have had little or no say in their preparation and may be of the opinion that the budgets are unrealistic.

Bottom-up budgets are prepared by departmental managers and may be unsatisfactory because:

● they may not fit together with all the other departmental budgets to make a logical and consistent overall plan for the business
● managers tend to base their own budgets on easily achievable targets to avoid being criticised for failing to meet them; this will result in departments performing below their maximum level of efficiency and be bad for the business as a whole.

A budget committee, which should include the accountant, should co-ordinate the departmental budgets to ensure that they achieve top management's plans for the business.

The benefits of budgets may be summarised as follows.

1. They are formal statements in quantitative and financial terms of management plans.
2. Their preparation ensures the co-ordination of all the activities of a business.
3. Budgets identify limiting factors (shortages of demand or resources – see §33.8).
4. When managers are involved in the preparation of their budgets, they are committed to meeting them.
5. Budgets are a form of responsibility accounting as they identify the managers who are responsible for implementing the various aspects of the overall plan for the business.
6. Budgets avoid 'management by crisis', which describes situations in which managers have not foreseen problems before they arise and prepared for them in advance. These managers spend their time grappling with problems that should never have arisen had they been foreseen. The managers are sometimes described as 'fire fighters' when they should be 'fire preventers'.

Control

Control involves measuring actual performance, comparing it with the budget and taking corrective action to bring actual performance into line with the budget. It is important that deviations from budget are discovered early before serious situations arise. Annual departmental budgets are broken down into four-weekly or monthly, or even weekly, periods, and departmental management accounts are prepared for those periods. These management accounts compare actual performance with budget and must be prepared promptly after the end of each period if they are to be useful. If actual revenue and expenditure are better than budget, the differences (or variances) are described as **favourable** because they increase profit. On the other hand, if 'actual' is worse than budget, the variance is described as **adverse**.

Departmental management accounts usually contain many items of revenue and expenditure with a mixture of favourable and adverse variances. Managers should concentrate their attention on items with adverse variances and, to help managers focus their attention on these, management accounts may report only the items with adverse variances. This is known as **management by exception** or **exception reporting**.

Flexible budgets. Experience shows that sales and costs rarely conform to the patterns anticipated by management when they prepare a 'fixed' budget, that is, one that does not allow for different levels of activity and changing conditions. Fixed budgets may lose their usefulness as management tools as a result. If budgeted output is different from actual output we are not comparing like with like. Invariably, the number of units produced and sold is more or less than the number in a fixed budget. To overcome this, budgets may be 'flexed' to reflect various levels of activity and costs. Flexing budgets make use of marginal costing and is an important process when standard costing techniques (chapter 35) are employed. Flexing budgets are described in chapter 35.

34.3 Limiting (or principal budget) factors

Limiting factors, sometimes called **principal budget factors**, are circumstances which restrict the activities of a business. Examples are:

- limited demand for a product
- shortage of materials, which limits production
- shortage of labour, which also limits production.

Limiting factors must be identified in order to decide the order in which the departmental budgets are prepared. If the limiting factor is one of demand for the product, a sales budget will be prepared first. The other budgets will then be prepared to fit in with the sales budget. If the limiting factor is the availability of materials or labour, the production budget will be prepared first and the sales budget will then be based on the production budget.

34.4 How to prepare a sales budget

Sales budgets are based on the budgeted volume of sales. The volume is then multiplied by the selling price per unit of production to produce the sales revenue. For the sake of simplicity, the examples which follow assume that only one type of product is being sold.

Example

Xsel Ltd's sales for the six months from January to June are budgeted in units as follows:

January 1000; February 800; March 1100; April 1300; May 1500; June 1400.

The current price per unit is $15 but the company plans to increase the price by 5% on 1 May.

The sales budget will be prepared as follows:

	January	February	March	April	May	June	Total
				Xsel Ltd's Sales Budget for 6 month ending 30 June			
Units	1000	800	1100	1300	1500	1400	7100
Price	$15	$15	$15	$15	$15.75	$15.75	
Sales	$15 000	$12 000	$16 500	$19 500	$23 625	$22 050	$108 675

Exercise 1

Flannel and Flounder Ltd's sales budget in units for six months ending 30 June is as follows:

January 1000; February 1200; March 13000; April 1500; May 1700; June 1800.

The price per unit will be $20 for the three months to 31 March but will be increased to $22 from 1 April.

Required

Prepare Flannel and Flounder Ltd's sales budget for the new product for the six months ending 30 June. (Keep your answer; it will be needed later.)

34.5 How to prepare a production budget

Manufacturing companies require production budgets to show the volume of production required monthly to meet the demand for sales. It is important to check that production is allocated to the correct months.

Example

Xsel Ltd (see the example in §34.4) manufactures its goods one month before they are sold. Monthly production is 105% of the following month's sales to provide goods for stock and for free samples to be given away to promote sales. Budgeted sales for July are for 1800 units.

Answer

	December	January	February	March	April	May	June
Production for sales (units)	1000	800	1100	1300	1500	1400	1800
Add 5% for stock and samples	50	40	55	65	75	70	90
Monthly production	1050	840	1155	1365	1575	1470	1890

Exercise 2

Flannel and Flounder Ltd (see exercise 1, §34.4) manufactures their goods one month before the goods are sold. Monthly production is 110% of the following month's sales. Budgeted sales for July are 2000 units.

Required

Prepare Flannel and Flounder Ltd's production budget. (Keep your answer; it will be needed later.)

It is possible that there may be some loss in the production process. It is important that this is built into the production budget, as it will affect how much material needs to be purchased.

Example

Garden Ornaments Ltd manufactures clay animals.

Its budgeted sales for next month are 900 units. There is an opening inventory of 100 units and the company requires a closing inventory of 150 units.

How many units need to be produced?

Budgeted sales units	900
Opening inventory	(100)
Closing inventory	150
Production required	950

However, 5% of the production is lost due to damage in the production process. This loss will mean that more units have to be produced to cover the loss.

Production from above	950
Production to cover loss (950 / 95%)	1000

Notice that production is grossed up to achieve the required production. If 5% of 950 was taken as the amount of extra production the loss in process would not have been covered.

34.6 How to prepare a purchases budget

A purchases budget may be prepared for either
1. raw materials purchased by a manufacturer, or
2. goods purchased by a trader.

A manufacturing company's purchases budget is prepared from the production budget while a trader's purchases budget is prepared from the sales budget. The purchases budget is calculated as follows:

Units produced per production budget × quantity of material per unit produced × price per unit of material

Take care to ensure that the purchases are made in the correct month.

Example

Xsel Ltd (see the example in §34.5) purchases its raw materials one month before production. Each unit of production requires 3 kg of material, which costs $2 per kg.

Required

Prepare the purchases budget for the materials to be used in the production of goods for the period from December to June.

3

3

Answer

	November	December	January	February	March	April	May
No. of units	1050	840	1155	1365	1575	1470	1890
Material required (kg)	3150	2520	3465	4095	4725	4410	5670
Purchases ($2 per litre)	6300	5040	6930	8190	9450	8820	11340

Exercise 3

Flannel and Flounder Ltd (see exercise 2, §34.5) uses 2.5 litres of material in each unit of their product. The price of the material is currently $4.10 per litre, but the company has learned that the price will be increased to $4.25 in March. The raw materials are purchased one month before production; 2100 units are budgeted to be produced in July.

Required

Prepare Flannel and Flounder Ltd's purchases budget based on its production budget for the seven months from December to June. (Make all calculations to the nearest $.)

34.7 How to prepare an expenditure budget

An expenditure budget includes payments for purchased materials (from the purchases budget) plus all other expenditure in the period covered by the budget. Take care to ensure that:

- purchased materials are paid for in the correct month
- all other expenses are included in the budget in accordance with the given information.

Example

Xsel Ltd pays for its raw materials two months after the month of purchase (see §34.6). Its other expenses are as follows:

1. Monthly wages of $4000 are paid in the month in which they are due.
2. The staff are paid a commission of 5% on all monthly sales exceeding $15 000. The commission is paid in the month following that in which it is earned (see §34.4).
3. General expenses are paid in the month in which they are incurred and are to be budgeted as follows: January $6600; February $7100; March $6990; April $7000; May $7300; June $7500.
4. Xsel Ltd pays interest of 8% on a loan of $20 000 in four annual instalments on 31 March, 30 June, 30 September and 31 December.
5. A final dividend of $2000 for the year ended 31 December is payable in March.

Required

Prepare an expenditure budget for Xsel Ltd for the six months ending 30 June. All amounts should be shown to the nearest $.

Answer

	January $	February $	March $	April $	May $	June $
Purchases	6 300	5 040	6 930	8 190	9 450	8 820
Wages	4 000	4 000	4 000	4 000	4 000	4 000
Commission	–	–	–	75	225	431
General expenses	6 600	7 100	6 900	7 000	7 300	7 500
Loan interest	–	–	400	–	–	400
Dividend	–	–	2 000	–	–	–
Total expenditure	16 900	16 140	20 230	19 265	20 975	21 151

Exercise 4

Flannel and Flounder Ltd's overheads and other expenses for six months to 30 June are budgeted as follows:

1. Purchases are paid for in the following month.
2. Wages of $4000 per month are paid in the same month as they are earned.
3. Staff are paid a bonus equal to 4% of the amount by which monthly sales exceed $20 000. The bonus is paid in the month following that in which it is earned.
4. Electricity bills are expected to be received in January, for $2400, and in April for $1800. The bills will be paid in the month following their receipt.
5. Other expenses are expected to amount to $6000 per month. From April they are expected to increase by 10%. They are paid in the month they are incurred.
6. Flannel and Flounder Ltd has a loan of $20 000 on which interest at 10% is payable in four quarterly instalments on 31 March, 30 June, 30 September and 31 December.
7. The company will purchase a machine in May for $15 000.
8. A final dividend of $4000 for the year ended 31 December will be paid in April.

Required

Prepare Flannel and Flounder Ltd's expenditure budget for the six months ending 30 June. Save your answer; it will be needed later.

34.8 How to prepare a cash budget

Cash budgets are prepared from the sales and expenses budgets. Special care must be taken with respect to the following:

- Sales revenue must be allocated to the correct months. Receipts from credit customers who are allowed cash discounts must be shown at the amounts after deduction of the discounts. The discounts should not be shown separately as an expense.

- Payments to suppliers (purchases) must be shown in the correct months; read the question carefully.

Example

Xsel Ltd's sales in November were $18 000, and in December were $17 600.

Of total sales, 40% are on a cash basis; 50% are to credit customers who pay within one month and receive a cash discount of 2%. The remaining 10% of customers pay within two months.

$10 000 was received from the sale of a non-current asset in March. The balance at bank on 31 December was $12 400.

Required

Prepare Xsel Ltd's cash budget for the six months ending 30 June. All amounts should be shown to the nearest $.

Answer

(a)

	January $	February $	March $	April $	May $	June $
Receipts						
Cash sales[1]	6 000	4 800	6 600	7 800	9 450	8 820
Credit customers – 1 month[2]	8 624	7 350	5 880	8 085	9 555	11 576
Credit customers – 2 months[3]	1 800	1 760	1 500	1 200	1 650	1 950
Sales of non-current asset	–	–	10 000	–	–	–
Total revenue	16 424	13 910	23 980	17 085	20 655	22 346
Expenditure	January $	February $	March $	April $	May $	June $
Purchases	6 300	5 040	6 930	8 190	9 450	8 820
Wages	4 000	4 000	4 000	4 000	4 000	4 000
Commission	–	–	–	75	225	431
General expenses	6 600	7 100	6 900	7 000	7 300	7 500
Loan interest	–	–	400	–	–	400
Dividend	–	–	2 000	–	–	–
Total payments	16 900	16 140	20 230	19 265	20 975	21 151
Net receipts/(payments)	(476)	(2 230)	3 750	(2 180)	(320)	1195
Balance brought forward	12 400	11 924	9 694	13 444	11 264	10 944
Balance carried forward	11 924	9 694	13 444	11 264	10 944	12 139

1. Cash sales = 40% of sales for month.
2. Cash received from credit customers after one month = sales for previous month × 50% × 98%.
3. Cash received from credit customers after two months = 10% of sales for two months previously.

Note. At 30 June:

Trade receivables (Debtors) for sales:	$
10% of May sales ($23 625 × 10%)	2 363 (rounded)
50% of June sales ($22 050 × 50%)	11 025
10% of June sales ($22 050 × 10%)	2 205
	15 593

Trade payables (Creditors) for supplies: May purchases (paid for in July) = $11 340 + June purchases for production in July.

Accrued expenses: staff commission, 4% of $2050 = $82

Inventory: If information for July and August had been available the following would be known:

raw materials — purchased in June
finished goods — made in June

Exercise 5

Flannel and Flounder Ltd's sales in November were $18 000 and in December were $17 600.

Of total sales revenue, 50% is on a cash basis, 40% is received one month after sale. Cash discount of 2½% is allowed to customers who pay within one month. 10% of sales revenue is received two months after sale.

The company intends to sell plant and equipment for $12 000 in February. The balance at bank on 31 December was $31 750.

Required

(a) Prepare Flannel and Flounder Ltd's cash budget for the six months ending June. Make all calculations to the nearest $.

(b) State the amount of Flannel and Flounder Ltd's trade receivables and payables, and expense payables at 30 June.

34.9 How to prepare a master budget

A **master budget** is a budgeted Income Statement and Statement of Financial Position prepared from sales, purchases, expense and cash budgets. The purpose of the master budget is to reveal to management the profit or loss to be expected if management's plans for the business are implemented, and the state of the business at the end of the budget period.

It is important to remember that the Income Statement must be prepared on an accruals basis, and the information in the functional budgets must be adjusted for accruals and prepayments; it is advisable to identify these when preparing the cash budget. Much information additional to that required for the functional budgets mentioned above will usually be given. Details of non-current assets which are to be sold or purchased will often be supplied; this information will usually be included in a **capital budget**.

Example

Meadowlands Ltd's Statement of Financial Position at 31 December 2011 was as follows:

Non-current assets	Cost	Depreciation	Net
	$	$	$
Equipment	13 000	6 000	7 000
Motor vehicles	11 000	7 000	4 000
	24 000	13 000	11 000
Current assets			
Inventory		9 600	
Trade receivables		33 600	
Cash and cash equivalents		15 000	
		58 200	
Current liabilities			
Trade payables		6 200	52 000
			63 000
Equity			
Ordinary shares of $1			40 000
Retained earnings			23 000
			63 000

Further information

1. Goods are purchased one month before the month of sale.
2. Budgeted quarterly purchases and sales for the year ending 31 December 2012 are as follows:

	Purchases	Sales
	$	$
January – March	72 000	132 000
April – June	96 000	156 000
July – September	84 000	168 000
October – December	96 000	144 000

3. Meadowlands Ltd receives one month's credit on all purchases and allows one month's credit on all sales.

4. The following expenses will be incurred in the year ending 31 December 2012.

   (i) rent of $1600 per quarter paid in advance on 1 January, 1 April, 1 July, and 1 October

   (ii) wages of $7200 payable each month

   (iii) an insurance premium of $3000 for 15 months to 31 March 2013 paid on 1 January 2012.

   (iv) other expenses of $20 000 paid quarterly.

5. The company will purchase additional equipment costing $15 000 on 1 April 2012.

6. A new motor vehicle will be purchased on 1 April 2012 for $12 000.

7. A motor vehicle which cost $6000 and has a written down value of $3000 at 31 December 2011 will be sold for $2000 on 1 July 2012.

8. The company depreciates equipment at 10% per annum on cost. It depreciates motor vehicles at 12½% per annum on cost.

9. The company's inventory at 31 December 2012 will be valued at $32 000.

Required

(a) Prepare a cash budget for the year ending 31 December 2012.

(b) Prepare Meadowlands Ltd's budgeted Income Statement for the year ended 31 December 2012 in as much detail as possible.

(c) Prepare Meadowlands Ltd's budgeted Statement of Financial Position at 31 December 2012 in as much details as possible.

Answer

Meadowlands Ltd
Cash budget for the year ending 31 December 2012

	Jan/Mar $	Apr/Jun $	Jul/Sept $	Oct/Dec $
Receipts				
Sales	121 600[1]	148 000[2]	164 000[2]	152 000[2]
Proceeds from sale of van	–	–	2 000	–
	121 600	148 000	166 000	152 000
Payments				
Purchases	54 200[3]	88 000[4]	88 000[4]	92 000[4]
Rent	1 600	1 600	1 600	1 600
Wages	21 600	21 600	21 600	21 600
Insurance	3 000	–	–	–
Other expenses	20 000	20 000	20 000	20 000
Purchase of equipment	–	15 000	–	–
Purchase of motor vehicle	–	12 000	–	–
	100 400	158 200	131 200	135 200
Net receipts/(payments)	21 200	(10 200)	34 800	16 800
Balance brought forward	15 000	36 200	26 000	60 800
Balance carried forward	36 200	26 000	60 800	77 600

1 Trade receivables at 31 December 2011 + $\frac{2}{3}$ of sales for January/March.

2 $\frac{1}{3}$ of previous quarter's sales + $\frac{2}{3}$ of current quarter's sales.

3 Trade payables at 31 December 2011 + $\frac{2}{3}$ of purchases for January/March.

4 $\frac{1}{3}$ of previous quarter's purchases + $\frac{2}{3}$ of current quarter's purchases.

Budgeted Income Statement
for the year ending 31 December 2012

	$	$	$
Revenue			600 000
Less Cost of sales:			
Opening Inventory		9 600	
Purchases		348 000	
		357 600	
Closing Inventory		32 000[5]	325 600
Gross profit			274 400

Less expenditure			
Wages		86 400	
Rent		6 400	
Insurance ($\frac{12}{15}\times\$3000$)		2 400	
Other expenses		80 000	
Loss on sale of motor vehicle		1 000	
Depreciation:			
equipment	2800[6]		
motor vehicles	2125[6]	4 925	181 125
Profit attributable to equity holders			93 275

5 Goods purchased in December 2012 for sale in January 2013 ($\frac{1}{3}$ of $96 000).

6 See non-current assets in Statement of Financial Position.

Budgeted Statement of Financial Position
at 31 December 2012

Non-current assets	Cost $	Depreciation $	Net $
Equipment	28 000	8 800	19 200
Motor vehicles	17 000	6 125	10 875
	45 000	14 925	30 075
Current assets			
Inventory		32 000	
Trade receivables		48 000[7]	
Prepaid insurance (other receivables)		600	
Cash and cash equivalents		77 600	
		158 200	
Current liabilities			
Trade payables		32 000[8]	126 200
			156 275
Equity			
Ordinary shares of $1			40 000
Retained earnings (23 000 + 93 275)			116 275
			156 275

7 December sales.
8 December purchases.

Exercise 6

The directors of Greenfields Ltd have prepared functional budgets for the four months ending 30 April 2012. To discover the effect that the budgets will have on the company at the end of the four months, they require the accountant to prepare master budgets. The accountant is provided with the following data.

Greenfields Ltd's Statement of Financial Position at 31 December 2011

Non-current assets	Cost $	Depreciation $	Net $
Freehold premises	50 000	10 000	40 000
Plant and machinery	37 500	22 500	15 000
	87 500	32 500	55 000
Current assets			
Inventory		30 000	
Trade receivables		42 500	
Cash and cash equivalents		20 750	
		93 250	
Current liabilities			
Trade payables		22 500	70 750
			125 750
Non-current liability			
12% debentures 2019/2020			25 000
			100 750
Equity			
Ordinary shares of $1			65 000
General reserve			30 000
Retained earnings			5 750
			100 750

Further information

1. Sales and purchases for the four months from January to April 2012 are budgeted to be:

	Sales $	Purchases $
January	62 500	25 000
February	70 000	20 000
March	75 000	30 000
April	82 500	37 500

2. 40% of sales are to cash customers; one month's credit is allowed on the remainder.
3. The company pays for its purchases in the month following purchase.

4. Selling and distribution expenses amount to 10% of sales and are paid in the month in which they are incurred.

5. Administration expenses amount to $20 000 per month and are paid in the month in which they are incurred.

6. Inventory at the 30 April 2012 is estimated to be valued at $22 500.

7. Additional plant and machinery costing $60 000 will be purchased on 1 March 2012.

8. Annual depreciation of non-current assets is based on cost as follows: Freehold premises 3%; plant and machinery 20%. 50% of all depreciation is to be charged to selling and distribution expenses, and the balance to administration expenses.

9. Debenture interest is payable half-yearly on 30 June and 31 December.

10. A dividend of $0.10 per share will be paid on the ordinary shares on 30 April 2012.

11. $25 000 will be transferred to the General Reserve on 30 April 2012.

Required

(a) Prepare a cash budget for each of the four months from January 2012 to 30 April 2012.
(b) Prepare a budgeted Income Statement for the four months ending 30 April 2012 in as much detail as possible.
(c) Prepare a budgeted Statement of Financial Position as at 30 April 2012 in as much detail as possible.

HINTS

- Practise the preparation of the functional and master budgets. They are not too difficult provided you read questions carefully to ascertain exactly when transactions are to take place. Failure to allocate sales, purchases, receipts and payments to the correct periods is a common cause of the loss of valuable marks.
- Preparation of budgets is often an exercise in arithmetic, so be accurate; but note if the question states the degree of accuracy required (e.g. to nearest $ or nearest $000).

MULTIPLE-CHOICE QUESTIONS

1. A bedside table is made from 4 kg of raw material. Production for six months is based on the following data.

Budgeted sales	5000 tables
Budgeted decrease in stock of raw material	1200 kg
Budgeted increase in stock of tables	800 tables

How many kilograms of raw material will be purchased for the six months?
A. 18 000 kg B. 18 800 kg
C. 22 000 kg D. 23 200 kg

2. Trade receivables at the year-end are $40 000. It is planned to double turnover in the next year and to reduce the trade receivables' collection period from 45 days to 30 days.
What will the trade receivables be at the end of the next year?
A. $26 667 B. $53 334
C. $60 000 D. $80 000

3. The sales budget for four months from January to April is as follows.
January $80 0000
February $100 000
March $110 000
April $130 000

The cost of the raw material used in the goods is 40% of sales. The material is purchased one month before the goods are made, and manufacture takes place one month before sale. 50% of the material is paid for one month after purchase and the balance is paid for two months after purchase.

How much will be paid for raw materials in March?
A. $40 000 B. $42 000
C. $46 000 D. $48 000

4. A company plans to purchase a new machine costing $40 000. It will part exchange one of its existing machines for the new one. The existing machine has a net book value of $4000 and the part exchange will result in a loss on disposal of the machine of $1000. The company will pay the balance due on the new machine by cheque.
How will the transaction be recorded in the cash budget?

A. payment for new machine $37 000
B. payment for new machine $40 000
C. payment for new machine $40 000; cash received for old machine $3000
D. payment for new machine $40 000; cash received for old machine $4000

ADDITIONAL EXERCISES

1. The sales budget for Roh Ltd for the six months to 30 November 2012 is as follows:

	Units
June	600
July	800
August	1000
September	900
October	980
November	1020

Further information is as follows:
1. All units are sold for $60. Customers are allowed 1 month's credit.

2. Monthly production of the units is equal to the following month's sales plus 10% for inventory.
3. Costs per unit are as follows:

Material	3	kilograms
Cost of material	$4.00	per kilo
Labour	2	hours
Labour rate of pay	$8.00	per hour
Absorption rates		
Variable overhead	$14.00	
Fixed overhead	$3.50	

4. Materials are purchased one month before they are needed for production and are paid for two months after purchase.

5. Wages and variable overheads are paid in the current month.
6. Fixed overheads are paid in the following month.
7. The following information is to be taken into account:
   (i) cash book balance at 30 June 2012: $16 000;
   (ii) inventory of finished goods at 31 July 2012: $56 420.

Required

(a) The following budgets for the month of August 2012 *only*.
   (i)   Production budget (in units only)
   (ii) Purchases budget
   (iii) Sales budget
(b) Calculate the cash book balance at 31 July 2012.
(c) A cash budget for the month of August 2012 *only*.
(d) (i) Explain the advantages and uses of budgets.
     (ii) Explain how principal budget factors affect the preparation of budgets.

2. Banner Ltd's budget for the four months from January to April includes the following data.

1.

Month	Sales $000	Materials $000	Wages $000	Overheads $000
January	615	114.4	30	360
February	636	118.8	33	390
March	690	132.0	36	412
April	684	128.0	39	420

2. One-third of sales revenue is received one month after sale and the remainder is received two months after sale. The sales in the previous two months were: November $600 000; December $540 000.

3. One quarter of purchases of materials are paid for in the month of purchase. The remainder are paid for two months later. Purchases in the previous two months were: November $108 000; December $106 000.

4. Two-thirds of the wages are paid in the month in which they are earned, and the balance is paid in the following month. The wages for the previous December amounted to $30 000.

5. One half of the overhead expenditure is paid in the month in which it is incurred, and the balance is paid in the following month. The overheads for the previous December were $380 000.

6. Old machinery will be sold for $4000 in April. New machinery will be purchased in March for $90 000 but only one half of the price will be paid in that month. The balance will be paid in August.

7. Banner Ltd has an overdraft $63 000 at the bank at 31 December.

Required

(a) Prepare Banner Ltd's cash budget for each of the four months from January to April. The budget should be prepared in columnar form.
(b) Prepare a statement to show the accruals in part (a) which would appear in a Statement of Financial Position at 30 April.

35 Standard costing

In this chapter you will learn:

- what standard costing is and how standards are set
- how to flex budgets
- how to calculate sales, materials and labour variances
- how to reconcile the actual and budgeted profits
- how to recognise the possible causes of variances.

35.1 What is standard costing?

Standard costing is an accounting system that records the cost of operations at pre-determined standards. If the standards are realistic, the system informs managers of the material, labour and overhead costs that should be incurred if the business is managed efficiently. Standard costs are an essential tool for realistic budgeting. However, the costs actually incurred may differ from the standards for a variety of reasons:

- the quantity of goods produced may be more or less than budget
- the quantity of material used in each unit of production may be more or less than budget
- the cost of material many be more or less than budget because the price paid may have increased or decreased since the budget was prepared, or the material has been obtained from alternative suppliers
- workers may have been more or less efficient than expected in the budget
- the rates of pay for workers may be more or less than those on which the budget was based.

Standards are also set for sales revenue, and causes for differences between actual revenue and the standard may be highlighted.

The link between the profit calculated on standard cost and the profit shown in a traditional Income Statement is provided by the preparation of a reconciliation statement between the standard profit or loss and the actual profit or loss.

The differences between actual costs and budgeted costs are known as *variances*.

35.2 The advantages of standard costing

- The preparation of budgets is made easier if they are based on standard costs, and the budgets are likely to be more realistic. The standards are the building blocks of the budget.
- Differences between actual and budgeted results (**variances**) are easier to identify if standard costs are used.
- The activities that are responsible for variances are highlighted.
- Because it highlights activities that give rise to variances, standard costing is an essential part of responsibility accounting (see §34.2).
- Calculated standards facilitate the preparation of estimates for the costs of new products and quotations for orders.
- Although standard costing is usually associated in people's minds with manufacturing industries, it is of equal use in all kinds of businesses, including service industries such as hotels and hospitals.

35.3 Setting standards

Standards must be realistic if they are to be useful and not misleading. Unrealistic standards result in the loss of the advantages listed above in §35.2. The various types of standards may be described, as follows:

- **Ideal standards** are standards that can only be met under ideal conditions. Since the conditions under which business work are very rarely ideal, these standards are unrealistic and are never likely to be attained. As a result, they may actually demotivate managers and cause them to perform less, rather than more, efficiently. Ideal standards should not be used.

- **Current standards** are based on present levels of performance, which may be quite inappropriate for the future. They do not offer management or workers any incentive to perform more efficiently. Current standards should only be used when present conditions are too uncertain to enable more appropriate standards to be set.

- **Attainable standards** recognise that there is normally some wastage of materials and not all the hours worked are productive. Time spent unproductively by workers is called **idle time** and may occur when machinery breaks down or the machinery has to be 'set up' for a production run. The standards should take reasonable account of these factors and give the workers an incentive to use their time and materials efficiently. The standards set should, therefore, be attainable ones.

Standard hours of production are measures of quantity of work and should not be confused with a period of time. If, under normal, or standard, working conditions, 20 units of output can be produced in one hour, the standard hour is 20 units. This concept of standard hours is useful when budgets are being prepared for departments that produce two or more different products. For example, in one month a department's output may consist of:

	Standard hours
200 Xs which take 1 hour each to make:	200
400 Ys which take 1½ hours each to make	600
327 Zs which take 40 minutes each to make	218
Total standard hours of production	1018

The output of the department can conveniently be expressed as 1018 standard hours for budgeting purposes. Similarly, standard minutes are a quantity of work that can be done in a stated number of standard minutes.

35.4 How to flex budgets

The actual volume of goods produced is seldom the same as the volume on which a budget has been based. Sensible comparisons can only be made if 'like is compared with like', and the budget is based on the actual volume of output. This is done by **flexing** the budget.

The variable expenses in the budget must be adjusted to take account of the actual volume of goods produced.

Example 1

Variable Grommets Ltd produced the following budget for the production and sale of 10 000 grommets for the six months ending June.

Budget for 10 000 grommets Six months ending June	
	$
Variable expenses	
Direct materials	50 000
Direct labour	100 000
Production overheads	40 000
Selling and distribution	8 000
	198 000
Fixed expenses	
Production overheads	78 000
Selling and distribution	43 000
Administration	91 000
Total cost	410 000

The output for the six months ended 30 June was 12 000 grommets. The budget is flexed by multiplying the variable expenses by $\dfrac{12\ 000}{10\ 000}$, that is by 1.2.

Budget for 12 000 grommets Six months ending June	
	$
Variable expenses	
Direct materials	60 000
Direct labour	120 000
Production overheads	48 000
Selling and distribution	9 600
	237 600
Fixed expenses	
Production overheads	78 000
Selling and distribution	43 000
Administration	91 000
Total cost	449 600

Notice that it is the variable costs which change as a result of flexing the budget.

The fixed expenses have not changed. The flexed budget is the one that would have been prepared as the original budget if it had been known that the output would be 12 000 grommets.

Exercise 1

Brekkifoods Ltd's budget for the production of 100 000 packets of Barleynuts in the year ending 31 December was as follows:

	$
Variable expenses	
Direct materials	20 000
Direct labour	15 000
Production expenses	6 000
	41 000
Fixed expenses	
Production expenses	13 000
Administration	29 000
	83 000

The actual output for the year ended 31 December was 110 000 packets of Barleynuts.

Required

Prepare a flexed budget for the production of 110 000 packets of Barleynuts.

Flexing budgets with semi-variable expenses

Budgets may not show a distinction between fixed and variable expenses. In these cases, the distinction must be found by inspection.

Example 2

Obskure Ltd has prepared flexed budgets for the production of (i) 5000 and (ii) 6000 pairs of sun glasses.

	5000 pairs of glasses $	6000 pairs of glasses $
Direct materials	10 000	12 000
Direct labour	15 000	18 000
Production overheads	16 000	18 000
Selling and distribution	19 000	22 000
Administration	12 000	12 000
	72 000	82 000

8000 pairs of glasses were produced and a flexed budget for that output is required.

Answer

As we saw in chapter 33, some expenses vary directly with output: direct materials are $2 per pair of spectacles, and direct labour is $3 per pair. The cost of these items for 8000 pairs of glasses will be: direct materials $16 000; direct labour $24 000.

Production overheads and selling and distribution expenses have not increased proportionately with the increased production. Each of these items contains a fixed element. To find the variable elements of these costs, deduct the costs for 5000 units from the costs for 6000 units to find the variable costs for 1000 units, using the method described in chapter 33.

Production overheads

Production overheads for 1000 units = $(18 000 − 16 000) = $2000, or $2 per unit.

Fixed production costs are now found by deducting the variable cost for 5000 units from the total production cost: $(16 000 − 10 000) = $6000.

Production cost for 8000 pairs of spectacles is $6000 + (8000 × $2) = $22 000.

Selling and distribution

Selling and distribution for 1000 units = $(22 000 − 19 000) = $3000, or $3 per unit.

Fixed selling and distribution cost is found by deducting the variable cost for 5000 units from the total selling and distribution cost: $(19 000 − 15 000) = $4000.

Selling and distribution cost for 8000 pairs of spectacles is $4000 + (8000 × $3) = $28 000.

The flexed budget for 8000 pairs of spectacles is:

	$
Direct materials	16 000
Direct labour	24 000
Production overheads	22 000
Selling and distribution	28 000
Administration	12 000
	102 000

Exercise 2

Flexers Ltd has prepared the following budgets for the production of time locks.

No. of locks	6000	8000
	$	$
Direct materials	15 000	20 000
Direct labour	36 000	48 000
Production overhead	25 000	31 000
Selling and distribution	24 000	28 000
Administration	80 000	80 000
	180 000	207 000

Required

Prepare a flexed budget for the production of 9000 time locks.

35.5 Variances

A **variance** is the difference between a standard cost and an actual cost or, in the case of revenue, between budgeted revenue and actual revenue. Variances may be calculated for:

- sales
- direct materials
- direct labour
- overheads.

Variances highlight activities that may need management intervention if the budgeted profit is to be achieved or, at least, to limit any adverse effect on profit. The variances may be further analysed into sub-variances to indicate the activities or operations that are performing adversely. An adverse variance decreases profit while a favourable variance increases profit. Every variance must be described as either favourable (F) or adverse (A). Any variance not so described is meaningless and of no help to management. *No marks will be awarded in an examination for a variance that is not described as (F) or (A), even if it has been calculated correctly.*

35.6 Acrobat Ltd

Acrobat Ltd makes a product which it markets under the name of 'Capers'. The budget for one month is based on the following standards.

No. of Capers produced and sold: 20 000	
Per Caper:	
Selling price per Caper	$32
Direct material (kg)	1.25
Cost of material per kg	$4
Direct labour (minutes)	40
Labour rate per hour	$12

Production overhead:	
fixed	$30 000
variable per unit	$7
Selling and distribution:	
fixed	$16 000
variable per unit	$4
Administration (fixed)	$75 000

The master budget based on the above information is as follows:

	Master budget 20 000 Capers	Flexed budget 23 000 Capers
	$	$
Sales revenue	640 000	736 000
Direct materials	100 000	115 000
Direct labour	160 000	184 000
Production overhead	170 000	191 000
Selling and distribution	96 000	108 000
Administration	75 000	75 000
	601 000	673 000
Profit	39 000	63 000

The actual number of Capers sold was 23 000 and flexed budget for this number is shown next to the master budget.

Further information about the actual revenue and costs is as follows.

The increased sales resulted from a reduction in the selling price from $32 to $30.50.

The actual cost of the material was $4.15 and each Caper used 1.10 kg of the material.

The hourly rate paid to the workers was $10 but each Caper took 45 minutes to make.

Actual variable production overhead was $7.20 per Caper, and the variable selling and distribution overhead was $3.90 per Caper.

The actual outcome for the production and sale of 23 000 Capers was therefore:

	$
Sales revenue	701 500
Direct materials	104 995
Direct labour	172 500
Production overhead	195 600
Selling and distribution	105 700
Administration	75 000
	653 795
Profit	47 705

All the information is now available to enable variances to be calculated.

35.7 How to calculate sales variances

When a business sells more than one type of product, sales variances will occur when the mix of products sold differs from the budgeted mix and gives rise to a mix variance. However, it is only necessary in this text to consider situations involving a single product.

The sales variances for a single product are:

- **volume variance**, which equals the difference between the master budget and the flexed budget

Acrobat Ltd's sales volume variance is $(736 000 – 640 000) = $96 000 (F)

- **price variance**, which is the difference between the flexed budget sales and actual sales

Acrobat Ltd's sales price variance is $(736 000 – 701 500) = $34 500 (A)

Check: Actual sales – budgeted sales = $(701 500 – 640 000) = $61 500 (F)

Sales volume variance – sales price variance = $(96 000 – 34 500) = $61 500 (F).

35.8 How to calculate total cost variances

Cost variances may be summarised as follows:

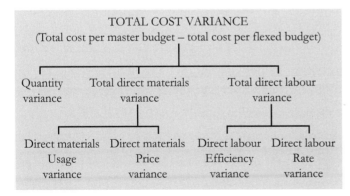

TOTAL COST VARIANCE
(Total cost per master budget – total cost per flexed budget)

Quantity variance — Total direct materials variance — Total direct labour variance

Direct materials Usage variance — Direct materials Price variance — Direct labour Efficiency variance — Direct labour Rate variance

The CIE syllabus does not require the calculation of overhead variances and these will not be covered in this text except as an overhead expenditure variance.

Note. When calculating cost variances, always start with the standard and deduct the 'actual'. A positive remainder will indicate that the variance is favourable, and a negative remainder will indicate that the variance is adverse. Always describe variances as favourable (F) or adverse (A).

Total cost variance. This is the difference between the total costs per the master budget and the actual total costs incurred. In the case of Acrobat Ltd the total cost variance is $(601 000 – 653 795) = $52 795 (A).

Quantity variance. This is the amount of the total cost variance which is due to the actual level of activity being more or less than budget. It is found by deducting the flexed budget costs from the master budget costs. Acrobat Ltd's quantity variance is $(601 000 – 673 000) = $72 000 (A).

Note. Once the quantity variance has been calculated, the master budget is not used to calculate the remaining variances; we shall calculate the all the variances which follow using the flexed budget.

Total direct materials variance. This is the difference between the flexed budget direct materials cost and the actual direct materials cost. Acrobat Ltd's total direct materials variance is $(115 000 – 104 995) = $10 005 (F).

Total direct labour variance. This is the difference between the flexed budget labour cost and the actual labour cost. Acrobat Ltd's total labour cost variance is $(184 000 – 172 500) = $11 500 (F).

The quantity, direct materials and direct labour variances can be reconciled to the total cost variance if the overhead expenditure variance is also taken into account:

	$	
Quantity variance	72 000	(A)
Direct materials variance	10 005	(F)
Direct labour variance	11 500	(F)
Overhead expenditure variance†	2 300	(A)
Total cost variance	52 795	(A)

† Production overhead $(191 000 – 195 600) = $4600 (A)
Selling and distribution $(108 000 – 105 700) = $2300 (F)
Net variance = $2300 (A)

Exercise 3

Enigma Ltd has prepared a budget based on standard

costs. It is shown below together with the actual results.

	Budget	Actual
No. of units	4000	4250
	$	$
Direct material	20 000	23 400
Direct labour	46 000	47 236
Variable overhead	10 000	10 500
Fixed overhead	50 000	50 000
Total costs	126 000	131 136

Required
(a) Prepare a flexed budget for 4250 units.
(b) Calculate:
  (i) total cost variance
  (ii) expenditure variance
  (iii) direct material variance
  (iv) direct labour variance.
(c) Reconcile the actual cost incurred with the budgeted costs, using the variances calculated in (b).

Exercise 4

Underpart Ltd has prepared a budget based on standard costs. It is shown below together with the actual results.

	Budget	Actual
No. of units	7000	6300
	$	$
Direct material	23 800	20 890
Direct labour	47 250	44 065
Variable overhead	3 500	3 250
Fixed overhead	62 000	62 000
Total costs	136 550	130 205

Required
(a) Prepare a flexed budget for 6300 units.
(b) Calculate:
  (i) total cost variance
  (ii) expenditure variance
  (iii) direct material variance
  (iv) direct labour variance.
(c) Reconcile the actual cost incurred with the budgeted costs, using the variances calculated in (b).

35.9 How to calculate material and labour sub-variances

Total material and labour cost variances reveal the main components of the difference between flexed budget total cost and actual total cost. However, this information is of limited use to management as it falls short of real responsibility accounting. A material variance may be caused by the price paid for material being more or less than standard, or by the quantity of material used for each unit made being more or less than standard. The purchasing manager is responsible for price, and the factory manager is responsible for usage. The total materials variance can be broken down into price and usage variances for which the purchasing and factory managers must give explanations.

Similarly, a total labour variance may be caused by the hourly rate being paid to workers being more or less than standard, or by the time taken in production being more or less than standard. The personnel manager is responsible for fixing rates of pay, and the factory manager is responsible for the time taken in production. A total labour variance is, therefore, broken down into rate and efficiency variances.

Direct material usage variance. The formula is (SM − AM) SP, where SM is the standard quantity of materials (per the flexed budget), AM is the actual quantity of materials used, and SP is the standard price of materials (per the master budget).

Example

The cost of direct material in Acrobat Ltd's (§35.6) flexed budget for 23 000 Capers was $115 000 based on a standard use of 1.25 kg of material per Caper at a cost of $4 per kg. Only 1.10 kg of material were used for each Caper and the cost per kg was $4.15. The usage variance is calculated as follows:

Standard materials (SM) = 23 000 × 1.25	28 750 kg
Actual materials used (AM) = 23 000 × 1.10 kg	25 300 kg
Variance (favourable)	3 450 kg (F)
Usage variance at standard price per kg ($4)	$13 800 (F)

Direct material price variance. The formula is (SP − AP) AM where SP is the standard price and AP is the price actually paid. In the example of Acrobat Ltd the standard price was $4 per kg, and the price actually paid was $4.15 per kg. The price variance is calculated as follows:

	$
Standard price (per kg)	4.00
Actual price	4.15
Variance (adverse)	0.15 (A)
Actual quantity of material	25 300 kg
Price variance (25 300 × $0.15)	$3 795 (A)

Check: Usage variance – price variance = total material variance: $13 800 (F) – $3795 (A) = $10 005 (F). This is equal to total standard direct material cost of $115 000 minus the total actual direct material cost of $104 995.

Exercise 5

Dandelion Ltd manufactures a health food known as 'Pickup'. The standard material cost of a packet of Pickup is as follows: 3 litres at $5 per litre. In one month Dandelion Ltd produced 12 000 packets of Pickup using 2.8 litres of material per packet at a total cost of $4.80 per litre.

Required

Calculate the direct material usage and price variances for 12 000 packets of Pickup.

Direct labour efficiency variance. This variance is calculated using the formula (SH – AH) SR where SH is the standard hours, AH is the actual hours taken and SR is the standard rate of pay.

Acrobat Ltd's standard hours were 40 minutes per Caper, or a total

of $\dfrac{40}{60} \times 23\,000 = 15\,333.33$ hours

The actual time taken was 45 minutes per Caper, or a total of

$\dfrac{45}{60} \times 23\,000 = 17\,250.00$ hours

Variance = 1916.67 hours (A)

1916.67 hours × Standard rate at $12 = $23 000 (A)

Direct labour rate variance. This is calculated using the formula (SR – AR) AH where AR is the actual hourly rate of pay.

Acrobat Ltd's actual hourly rate of pay was $10 and the rate variance is $(12 – 10) 17 250 = $34 500 (F).

Check: Efficiency variance – rate variance = total labour variance: $23 000 (A) – 34 500 (F) = $11 500 (F). This is equal to total standard direct labour cost of $184 000 minus the total actual direct labour cost of $172 500.

Exercise 6

Dandelion Ltd has a standard direct labour cost for the production of one packet of Pickup based on 1 labour hour at $10 per hour. The production of 12 000 packets of Pickup required 1.25 hours paid at $8.50 per hour.

Required

Calculate the direct labour efficiency and rate variances for 12 000 packets of Pickup.

35.10 How to comment on variances

Questions may require candidates to comment on variances they have calculated. This is not a difficult task if the following advice is heeded.

- Variances highlight operations that do not match standards. They do not explain the causes of differences but show management where further investigation is required if effective corrective action is to be taken.
- Without the further investigation mentioned above, it is not possible to do more than suggest possible reasons for variances. Some checks to support comments are suggested below.
- A favorable material usage variance may result from:
  1. use of material of a better quality than the standard: check for an adverse material price variance, or for a favourable labour efficiency variance (material easier to work with).
  2. the labour being of a higher skill than the standard skill, e.g. skilled labour used instead of semi-skilled; check for an adverse labour rate variance.
- An adverse material variance may indicate:
  1. the use of substandard material – check for a favourable material price variance or for an adverse labour efficiency variance

2. the employment of lower skilled labour –
check for a favourable labour rate variance.

- A favourable labour rate variance may result
from the employment of a lower grade of
labour than standard – check for an
unfavourable labour efficiency variance or an
adverse material usage variance.
- An unfavourable labour rate variance may result
from:
1. employment of a higher skill of labour than
standard – check for a favourable efficiency
variance
2. a wage increase (the standard should be
revised).
- A favourable sales volume variance may occur
because:
1. selling price has been reduced to increase
volume
2. seasonal sales have increased volume
3. special discounts have been given to selected
customers to increase orders
4. local competition from other firms has
disappeared.
- An adverse sales volume variance may occur
because:
1. selling price has been increased to pass
increased costs onto customers
2. the goods have become unfashionable or
obsolete
3. customers have heard that new, improved
products will be available soon and are waiting
for those
4. local competition from other firms may have
increased.
- A favourable sales price variance may occur
because:
1. increased costs have been passed onto
customers in the selling price
2. prices have been increased in line with
inflation
3. fewer discounts have been allowed to
favoured customers
4. improved products have allowed prices to be
increased.
- An adverse sales price variance may occur because:

1. local competition has necessitated a price
reduction
2. selling prices have been reduced in seasonal
sales
3. some favoured customers have been given
price concessions to increase volume of
orders
4. prices have been reduced generally to increase
sales volume.
- All comments should be consistent and not
contradict each other. Explain possible links
between variances. Be clear and concise.

Exercise 7

Larabee Ltd prepared a budget for the production of
300 units in April as follows:

	$
Direct materials (4 kg per unit)	7200
Direct labour ($11 per hour)	6600

The production for the month was 400 units and
the costs were as follows:

	$
Direct materials ($6.25 per kg)	9 000
Direct labour (2.25 hours per unit)	10 890

Required
(a) Calculate the following variances for April.
  (i)   direct material usage
  (ii) direct material price
  (iii) direct labour efficiency
  (iv) direct labour rate.
(b) Comment on the variances in (a) and suggest
possible causes.

35.11 Reconciliation of budgeted profit and actual profit

Actual profit should be reconciled to the budgeted
profit by summarising the variances.

Example

The actual profit made by Acrobat Ltd is reconciled
to the budgeted profit, using the variances that have
been calculated above, as follows:

	$	$
Profit per master budget		39 000
Add: favourable variances		
Sales volume		96 000
Materials usage		13 800
Labour rate		34 500
		183 300
Deduct: adverse variances		
Quantity	72 000	
Selling price	34 500	
Material price	3 795	
Labour efficiency	23 000	
Overhead expenditure (§35.8)	2 300	135 595
Actual profit (§35.6)		47 705

Exercise 8

Cantab Ltd's standard costing records provide the following information for three month's production and sales.

	$
Master budget profit	98 970
Variances	
Quantity	17 009 (A)
Sales volume	6 210 (F)
Sales price	3 730 (A)
Material usage	6 280 (A)
Material price	9 635 (F)
Labour efficiency	10 500 (F)
Labour rate	7 840 (A)
Overhead expenditure	5 760 (A)

Required

Prepare a statement to show the actual profit made by Cantab Ltd in the three months covered by the given information.

It is possible to work backwards from the variances to arrive at the actual and standard costs.

Example

Winston Ltd produces a single product. Details of the production and budget for month 5 are:

Actual output	10 000 units
Standard material cost 2 kg × $4	$80 000
Actual usage of material	18 000 kg
Total material variance	$6 200 favourable
Standard labour cost 3 hrs × $10	$300 000
Actual labour rate	$9.95 per hour
Total labour variance	$18 400 adverse

Required

(a) calculate the direct material price and usage variances

(b) calculate the direct labour rate and efficiency variances

(c) prepare a statement reconciling the actual direct material and direct labour cost of producing 10 000 units with the standard cost.

(a) Calculation of direct material variances

Before the variances can be calculated, some base data must be prepared:

Actual cost of direct material = $80 000 − $6200 = $73 800

Actual cost per kilogram of direct material = $73 800/ 18 000 = $4.10

Standard material required to produce 10 000 units = 10 000 × 2 = 20 000 kilograms.

The direct material price variance can now be calculated:

($4.00 − $4.10) × 18 000 = $1800 A

The direct material usage variance is

(20 000 − 18 000) × $4 = $8000 F

(b) Calculation of direct labour variances

Again, before the variances can be calculated some base data needs to be prepared:

Actual cost of direct labour = $300 000 + $18 400 = $318 400

Actual direct labour hours worked = $318 400/ $9.95 =32 000

Total standard direct labour hours for 10 000 units = 10 000 × 3 = 30 000 hours

The direct labour rate variance can now be calculated:

($10.00 − $9.95) × 32 000 = $1600 F

The direct labour efficiency variance is

(30 000 − 32 000) × $10 = $20 000 A

(c) statement reconciling the actual direct material and direct labour cost of producing 10 000 units with the standard cost.

	$	$
Actual direct material and labour costs ($73 800 + $318 400)		392 200
Direct material price variance	1 800 A	
Direct material usage variance	8 000 F	
Direct labour rate variance	1 600 F	
Direct labour efficiency variance	20 000 A	12 200 A
Standard direct material and labour costs ($80 000 + $300 000)		380 000

HINTS

- Learn the formulae for calculating the variances.
- Describe every variance as favourable (F) or adverse (A).
- Every variance must be shown with a $ sign, otherwise it is meaningless and will gain no marks in an exam.
- Use common sense when commenting on variances; remember that variances only indicate operations that require further investigation to reveal the causes.

MULTIPLE-CHOICE QUESTIONS

1. A company manufactures a product which requires 2 hours of direct labour per unit. Normal output is 1400 units and the standard labour rate is $6.50 per hour.
   In one month the company manufactured 1300 units of the product in 2500 direct labour hours costing $17 550.
   What is the direct labour efficiency variance?
   - A. $650 (favourable)
   - B. $675 (favourable)
   - C. $1300 (favourable)
   - D. $1350 (favourable)

2. A company makes a single product which requires two types of raw material: ionium and zetonium. The standard cost of materials to produce one unit of the product is shown:

Material	kg	Standard cost ($ per kg)
Ionium	30	2
Zetonium	45	3

   100 units of the product have been made using 3100 kg of ionium and 4400 kg of zetonium.
   What is the total material usage variance?
   - A. $100 (adverse)
   - B. $100 (favourable)
   - C. $500 (adverse)
   - D. $500 (favourable)

3. The following information is available for the sales of a product.
   Budgeted sales   40 000 units at $5 each
   Actual sales   42 000 at a total revenue of $189 000
   What is the sales volume variance?
   - A. $10 000 favourable
   - B. $11 000 favourable
   - C. $11 000 adverse
   - D. $21 000 adverse

4. The following information is available about a product.

Standard selling price per unit	$17
Budgeted sales (units)	45 000
Actual sales (units)	48 000
Total sales revenue	$744 000

   What is the sales price variance?
   - A. $51 000 (A)
   - B. $51 000 (F)
   - C. $72 000 (A)
   - D. $72 000 (F)

5. Details of direct material costs are as follows.

Budget	Actual
41 500 kg at $12 per kg	44 000 kg at $13.20 per kg

   What is the direct material price variance?
   - A. $49 500 (A)
   - B. $49 500 (F)
   - C. $52 800 (A)
   - D. $52 800 (F)

6. A company's cost of production is made up of the cost of direct materials and the cost of direct labour. The following variances have been calculated at the end of three month's production:

	$
Direct materials usage	1600 adverse
Direct materials price	1300 favourable
Direct labour efficiency	820 favourable
Direct labour rate	900 adverse

   The actual cost of production was $23 440.
   What was the standard cost of production?
   - A. $22 220
   - B. $23 020
   - C. $23 060
   - D. $24 580

ADDITIONAL EXERCISES

1. Kings Ltd makes an electronic device for finding lost keys, which it has patented under the trademark 'Gonkeys'. The product passes through two processes and the budget for the production of 10 000 Gonkeys is as follows:

	Process 1	Process 2
Costs per Gonkey		
Material	2 kg	4 litres
Cost of material per kg/litre	$8	$6
Labour hours per Gonkey	2	4
Labour rate per hour	$10	$12
Production overhead absorption	$20 per labour/hour	$23 per labour/hour

Required

(a) Prepare budgeted accounts for processes 1 and 2 to show the cost of producing 10 000 Gonkeys.

The actual production for process 1 was 10 000 Gonkeys. In process 2, completed production was 9000 Gonkeys, and 1000 Gonkeys were completed as to 50% of material and wages.

Required

(b) Prepare a flexed budget for process 2 based on actual production.

Actual costs per Gonkey were as follows:

	Process 1	Process 3
Material	2.22 kg	3.75 litres
Cost of material per kg/litre	$8.25	$6.2
Labour hours per Gonkey	2.25	4.5
Labour rate per hour	$11.50	$11.50
Production overhead absorption	$20 per labour/hour	$23 per labour/hour

Required

(c) Prepare ledger accounts for processes 1 and 2 based on actual expenditure.

(d) Calculate the following variances for process 1
  (i) material price
  (ii) material usage
  and the following variances for process 2
  (iii) labour efficiency
  (iv) labour rate.

(e) State *four* advantages of using a system of standard costs.

2. Pembroke Ltd makes an item of furniture known as a Tripos. The standard cost per Tripos is as follows:

Direct material: 2 kg at $7 per kg
Direct labour: 3 hours at $10 per hour
Production overhead: direct (variable) $14 per direct labour hour
indirect (fixed) based on overhead absorption rate of $30 per direct labour hour

Further information for the three months ending 30 June.
1. The budgeted amount for direct labour: $120 000.
2. Administration and selling overheads for three months ending 30 June : $32 000.
3. Factory profit is 20% of cost of production.
4. The budgeted selling price per Tripos: $250.
5. No stocks of raw materials, work in progress or finished goods are held.

Required

(a) Prepare a budgeted Manufacturing account and Income Statement for the three months ending 30 June to show the budgeted net profit or loss.

(b) Calculate, using the information in (a), the break-even point and margin of safety. The margin of safety should be shown as a percentage.

The actual production of Tripos and the related revenue and costs for the three months ended 30 June were as follows.

No. of Tripos produced	4180
Materials used	8990 kg
Cost of materials	$61 132
Direct labour hours	14 630
Direct labour cost	$138 985
Fixed overhead expenditure:	
Production	$372 000
Administration and selling	$42 000
Selling price per Tripos	$248

The overhead absorption rate for variable production overhead was not affected. All Tripos produced were sold.

Required

(c) Prepare

    (i) a flexed budget based on the actual number of Tripos produced and sold and

    (ii) a financial statement based on actual results.

(d) Calculate the following variances:

    (i) quantity (the additional profit arising from increased production)

    (ii) sales volume

    (iii) sales price

    (iv) direct materials usage

    (v) direct materials price

    (vi) direct labour efficiency

    (vii) direct labour rate.

(e) Calculate the break-even point based on actual revenue and expenditure. (Show your workings.)

(f) Prepare a financial statement to reconcile the original budgeted profit with the actual profit.

36 Investment appraisal

In this chapter you will learn:

- what investment appraisal is
- how to calculate accounting rate of return (ARR)
- how to calculate payback period
- how to calculate net present value (NPV)
- how to calculate internal rate of return (IRR)
- how to calculate the sensitivity investment to errors in estimates.

36.1 What is investment appraisal?

Investment appraisal is a process of assessing whether it is worthwhile to invest funds in a project. The project may be replacement of an existing asset, acquiring an additional asset, introducing a new product, opening a new branch of a business, etc. Funds invested in a project may include additional working capital as well as expenditure on non-current assets. These projects always involve making choices, including whether or not to proceed with the project, which assets to buy, which new products to introduce, and so on.

Accounting techniques are essential tools when these decisions have to be made. However, projects must sometimes be undertaken even when the accounting techniques appear to advise against them. For example, a business that is causing an environmental nuisance may face being closed down by health and safety inspectors unless it spends a considerable sum of money to abate the nuisance. It is well to remember that investment decisions should only be made after all relevant matters, economic, political, environmental, social, etc. have been considered.

This chapter is concerned principally with the financial techniques of appraisal:

- accounting rate of return (ARR)
- payback period

- net present value (NPV)
- internal rate of return (IRR).

These techniques are designed to assess the quality of projects, benefits arising from them, and degrees of risk involved. Only accounting rate of return is concerned with profitability; the others are based on cash flows. The net present value and internal rate of return take the time value of money into account. They are all based on **additional** benefits and costs which will arise from a project. These are referred to **incremental** profits and cash flows. Existing profit and cash flows are ignored as being irrelevant because they will continue whether the new project is undertaken or not. There are two new terms to learn.

- **Sunk costs** consist of expenditure that has been incurred before a new project has been considered. For example, a company plans to introduce a new product that will require the use of a machine it acquired some years ago and has used in the production of an existing product. The cost of the machine is a sunk cost because it has already been incurred and is not *incremental*. Its cost is a historical fact and cannot have any bearing on future decisions.

- **Opportunity costs** are the values of benefits that will be sacrificed if resources are diverted from their present uses to other applications. For example, if a machine that has been earning annual net revenue of $50 000 is to be used exclusively for another operation, it will cease to earn the $50 000. The lost revenue is an opportunity cost. If the machine will earn net revenue of $70 000 in its new capacity, the incremental net revenue will be $20 000 ($70 000 – $50 000).

36.2 How to calculate the accounting rate of return (ARR)

The **accounting rate of return** expresses average **profit** from the investment as a percentage of the average of the capital investment:

$$\frac{\text{average profit}}{\text{average investment}} \times 100.$$

Average profit is the average of the incremental profit (i.e. the profit arising from the investment) expected to be earned over the life of the project. For example, if the expected profit over a period of five years is: year 1 $26 000; year 2 $30 000; year 3 $33 000; year 4 $34 000; year 5 $35 000, the average profit for the purpose of calculating ARR is:

$(26 000 + 30 000 + 33 000 + 34 000 + 35 000) ÷ 5 = $31 600$

Non-current assets will be depreciated over the period in which they will be employed on a project and the average investment is therefore the average book value of the assets during that period. Unfortunately, there are different opinions as to how the average investment should be calculated. Students for the CIE exams need only be aware of the simplest method, which is $\dfrac{\text{the cost of the assets acquired}}{2}$.

Example

Baggins Ltd requires a new machine that will cost $160 000 and have a useful life of five years. The machine is expected to earn profits in those five years of $15 000, $18 000, $21 000, $21 000 and $20 000. The average profit is $95 000 ÷ 5 = $19 000. The average investment is $160 000 ÷ 2 = $80 000.

Average rate of return is $\dfrac{\$19\,000}{\$80\,000} \times 100 = 23.75\%$.

Baggins Ltd is able to compare 23.75% with the rate of return that it expects to earn on capital to decide whether the project will be worthwhile. If it is currently earning a return on capital employed (ROCE) of less than 23.75%, the project should improve its overall profitability; if the present ROCE is more than 23.75%, the project will dilute its profitability.

Notes

- ARR is the only technique being considered that takes depreciation of the investment into account.
- A project may require an increase in working capital because this may result in increased stock and debtors. Any increase in working capital will be assumed to remain constant throughout the life of the project and no calculation is required to find the average increase. For example, if a project involves the purchase of a machine at a cost of $60 000 and an increase in working capital of $40 000, the average investment is

$$\left(\frac{\$60\,000}{2} + \$40\,000\right) = \$70\,000.$$

Advantages of ARR

1. The expected profitability of a project can be compared with the present profitability of the business.
2. ARR is comparatively easy to calculate.

Disadvantages of ARR

1. The average annual profit used to calculate ARR is unlikely to be the profit earned in any year of the life of the project.
2. 'Profit' is a subjective concept. It depends upon a number of variable policies such as provisions for depreciation and doubtful debts, valuation of stock, and other matters.
3. The method does not take into account of the timing of cash flows. The initial outlay on the project is at risk until the flow of cash into the business has covered the initial cost.
4. ARR ignores the time value of money. Every $ received now is more useful to a business than a $ received at a later date.
5. No account is taken of the life expectancy of a project.

Exercise 1

Baseball Ltd intends to introduce a new product that is expected to produce the following incremental profits over a period of six years.

	$		$
Year 1	23 000	Year 4	26 000
Year 2	24 000	Year 5	29 000
Year 3	25 000	Year 6	23 000

The project will require the use of a machine that was purchased some years ago at a cost of $16 000 and the use of a second machine that will have to be purchased for $120 000. It is estimated that inventory held will increase by $10 000, and trade receivables will increase by $15 000.

Required

Calculate the accounting rate of return that will be earned from the new product.

36.3 How to calculate payback period

Until the initial expenditure on a project has been covered by net receipts (cash inflow – cash outflow) from the venture, a business is at risk of being worse off than if it had not launched the project. Calculation of the **payback period** indicates the time over which the business is at risk. Short payback periods are preferred especially in times of high inflation.

The payback method is concerned with cash flows, not with profitability; depreciation does not enter into the calculations.

In order to carry out the evaluation the net cash flows arising from the project must be calculated. This is the difference between the cash coming in from the project (this could be the sales revenue or savings) less the cash payments arising from the project. Profitability and depreciation do not enter into the calculations. It is important to consider when the cash comes in and goes out, not when sales or purchases are made. It may also be necessary to consider a build up of working capital. This needs to be shown at the start of the project as a cash outflow. At the end of the project it is brought back into the business as a cash inflow.

Example

Dumbells Ltd is proposing to market a new product which will involve the purchase of new plant costing $100 000. The net receipts from the new product are expected to be as follows: year 1 $30 000; year 2 $40 000; year 3 $50 000; year 4 $45 000.

The payback period is calculated as follows. In the first two years, net receipts will amount to $70 000. The balance of $30 000 will be received in the third year: $\frac{30\ 000}{50\ 000} \times 12 = 7.2$ months. The payback period is, therefore, 2 years 8 months. (It would be unrealistic to be more precise than this.)

Advantages of payback

1. It is relatively simple to calculate.
2. Payback can compare the relative risks of different projects.
3. Cash flow is less subjective than profitability.
4. Payback highlights the timing and size of cash flows.
5. Short payback periods result in increased liquidity and enable businesses to grow more quickly.

Disadvantages of payback

1. The life expectancy of the project is ignored. Once the payback period has been evaluated the net cash inflows after this time are ignored. This is a problem with this method of evaluation, as later in the life of the project net cash flows may be negative.
2. Projects with the same payback period may have different cash flows. For example:

	Project 1 $	Project 2 $
Year 0 Initial cost	(80 000)	(80 000)
Year 1 Net cash inflow	15 000	30 000
Year 2	25 000	40 000
Year 3	40 000	10 000

Both projects have a payback period of three years and similar amounts of cash inflows, but project 2 is more attractive as the cash flow is better in the early years.

Note. The initial outlay is shown as made in year 0 because it is assumed, simply as a matter of convenience, that cash flows occur on the last day of the year. The initial outlay should be shown as occurring on the first day of year 1, and the last day of year 0 is the nearest we can get to the first day of year 1. The use of the term 'year' should not be confused with the accounting year start or end. It relates solely to the start of the project (year 0), the year at which the project starts. This will be at any point during the accounting period.

3. The simple payback method ignores the time value of money, but it is possible to apply discounting techniques to it to overcome this failing.

Exercise 2

Mapleduck Ltd is planning to replace one of its machines. It has two choices of replacements: Duckbill and Kwak, each costing $90 000.

The following information is available for the machines.

	Duckbill		Kwak	
	Cash inflow	Cash outflow	Cash inflow	Cash outflow
	$	$	$	$
Year 0	–	90 000	–	90 000
1	80 000	50 000	60 000	20 000
2	90 000	54 000	68 000	28 000
3	100 000	60 000	72 000	32 000

Required

Calculate the payback periods for Duckbill and Kwak and state, with reasons, which machine Mapleduck Ltd should purchase.

36.4 How to calculate net present value (NPV)

Net present value recognises the time value of money. $1 received now is more useful than $1 received some time in the future because it can be used now. If, for example, $100 is invested now at 10% compound interest it will be worth $100 \times \dfrac{110}{100}$, or $110, in one year's time, and in two years it will be worth $121. To put it another way, $90.91 invested at 10% compound interest now will be worth $90.91 \times \dfrac{110}{100}$, or $100, in one year's time, and $100 receivable in one year's time has a present value of $90.91 when discounted at 10%.

The time value of money is important when future cash flows are compared with present cash flows because 'like should be compared with like'. Future cash flows are discounted to present day values so that they can be compared with the initial outlay on a realistic basis.

In addition, the full life of the project is considered. This is a positive advantage of using net present value over payback.

Future cash flows are the estimated cash receipts less the estimated cash payments attributable to an investment and will usually be known as **net receipts** or **net payments**. If assets purchased for the project are sold at the end of the venture, the proceeds of sale should be included in the net receipts in the last year.

The discounting rate taken for net present values is the cost of capital. For example, if money has to be borrowed at 8% interest per annum to finance the investment in a project, the cost of capital is 8% and the future cash flows will be discounted using the factors for that rate. A table of discounting factors can be found in Appendix 1 although the necessary rates are always given in examination questions.

Notes

- It is widely thought that cash flows are discounted to net present value to allow for inflation, but that is not so. The rate used for discounting is the cost of capital, not the rate of inflation.
- The payback period is sometimes calculated using the net present values of the cash flows.

Example

Netpres Ltd is undertaking a project which involves an initial outlay of $100 000. Its net receipts from the project for the next five years are estimated to be as follows:

Year 1	$40 000
Year 2	$42 000
Year 3	$48 000
Year 4	$46 000
Year 5	$38 000

Netpres Ltd's cost of capital is 10%. The discounting factors for the present value of $1 at 10% are: year 1 0.909; year 2 0.826; year 3 0.751; year 4 0.683; year 5 0.621.

Required

Calculate the net present value of the project.

Answer

Year	Net cash inflow/ (outflow) $	Factor	Net present value $
0	(100 000)	1.000	(100 000)
1	40 000	0.909	36 360
2	42 000	0.826	34 692
3	48 000	0.751	36 048
4	46 000	0.683	31 418
5	38 000	0.621	23 598
	Net present value		62 116

The net present value is positive, showing that the project may be undertaken. A negative NPV would mean that the net receipts in present day terms would not cover the initial outlay and the project should not be undertaken. The higher the net present value, the better the project. If two or more projects are being considered, the one with the higher or highest NPV would be preferred to the other(s).

Exercise 3

Nomen Ltd is considering buying a machine and has three options, machine A, B or C, only one of which it will buy. Each machine costs $135 000 and will have a five-year life with no residual value at the end of that time.

The net receipts for each machine over the five-year period are as follows:

	Machine A $	Machine B $	Machine C $
Year 1	50 000	38 000	26 000
2	50 000	38 000	26 000
3	38 000	38 000	38 000
4	26 000	38 000	50 000
5	26 000	38 000	50 000

Nomen Ltd's cost of capital is 12%.

The discounting factors at 12% are: year 1 0.893; year 2 0.797; year 3 0.712; year 4 0.636; year 5 0.567.

Required

Calculate the net present value of each option and state which machine Nomen Ltd should choose.

36.5 How to calculate initial rate of return (IRR)

Net present value compares future cash inflows with present cash outflow when the future cash flows are discounted to present day values, but it does not give the **rate of return** on investment based on discounted values. The internal rate of return enables managers to calculate the return on an intended investment and to compare it with the company's present return on capital.

The internal rate of return is the percentage required to discount cash flows to give a nil net present value. The percentage is found by selecting two discounting rates sufficiently wide apart to give positive and negative net present values. The results are then **interpolated** to find the percentage that will give a nil net present value. (**Interpolation** means finding an intermediate value between the two discounting rates.) Interpolation involves using the formula

$$P + \left[(P - N) \times \frac{p}{p + n} \right] = \text{IRR}$$

where P is the rate giving a positive net present value

N is the rate giving a negative net present value

p is the positive net present value

n is the negative net present value.

For example, if NPV at 10% is $14 000 and at 18% is $(6000), then

$$\text{IRR} = 10\% + (8\% \times \frac{14\,000}{14\,000 + 6000}) = 10\% + 5.6\% = 15.6\%$$

Therefore, discounted at 15.6%, the investment would have nil net present value.

Example

Netpres Ltd (see §36.4) has a net present value of $62 116 when discounted at 10%. To obtain a negative net present value it may be discounted at 40% as follows:

Year	$	at 40%	$
0	(100 000)	1.000	(100 000)
1	40 000	0.714	28 560
2	42 000	0.510	21 420
3	48 000	0.364	17 472
4	46 000	0.260	11 960
5	38 000	0.186	7 068
	Net present value		(13 520)

$$IRR = 10\% + (30\% \times \frac{62\,116}{62\,116 + 13\,520}) = 34.6\%$$

Exercise 4

The information is given as for Nomen Ltd in exercise 3 in §36.4, with the addition of the discounting factors for 20%: year 1 0.833; year 2 0.694; year 3 0.579; year 4 0.482; year 5 0.402.

Required
Calculate the internal rate of return for machines A and B.

Notes
- IRR can be calculated from two positive net present values but will be less accurate. The denominator of the fraction in the formula must be amended as follows: $P + \left[(P - N) \times \dfrac{p}{p - n} \right]$.
  If the discounting factors in a question produce only positive net present values, do *not* try to find another discounting rate; the examiner expects you to use the ones supplied in the question.
- When the receipts are constant for a number of consecutive years, the net present value of those receipts may be calculated quickly if the annual amount is multiplied by the sum of the factors for the years concerned. For example, if net receipts are $25 000 in each of the first five years and the cost of capital is 10%, the NPV for the five years is $25 000 × (0.909 + 0.826 + 0.751 + 0.683 + 0.621) = $25 000 × 3.790 = $94 750.

Exercise 5

Baxter Ltd requires a new machine to use in the manufacture of a new product. Two machines are available: Big Gee and Maxi-Shadbolt. Baxter Ltd depreciates machinery using the straight-line method. Baxter Ltd will obtain a bank loan at interest of 10% per annum to buy the machine.

Further information

	Big Gee	Maxi-Shadbolt
Cost of machine	$140 000	$180 000
	$	$
Additional receipts Year 1	98 000	101 000
2	112 000	118 000
3	126 000	126 000
4	126 000	140 000
5	100 000	110 000

Additional costs (including depreciation and bank interest):

		$	$
Year	1	70 000	84 000
	2	84 000	98 000
	3	91 000	105 000
	4	98 000	112 000
	5	95 000	100 000
Useful life of machine		5 years	5 years
Estimated proceeds of disposal after 5 years		$20 000	$30 000
Present value of $1		10%	40%
Year	1	0.909	0.714
	2	0.826	0.510
	3	0.751	0.364
	4	0.683	0.260
	5	0.621	0.186

Required
(a) Calculate for each machine:
   (i) the accounting rate of return (ARR) (ignore the sale proceeds of the machine)
   (ii) the payback period
   (iii) the net present value
   (iv) the internal rate of return (IRR).
(b) State, with reasons, which machine Baxter Ltd should purchase.

36.6 Sensitivity analysis

Appraisal of future capital expenditure is based on estimated future profitability and cash flows. Inaccuracies in the estimates may be very misleading, and acceptable margins of error must be recognised. **Sensitivity analysis** indicates the maximum acceptable margin of error; a greater margin might produce disastrous results especially as very large sums of money are involved.

The percentages of error that could produce unacceptable results must be determined and compared with the likely margins of error as shown by past forecasting experience.

Example

A project needs $100 000 to buy a machine. Net receipts in each of the four years of the project are expected to be $35 000. The cost of capital is 10%.

The net present value
$$= \$100\ 000 - \$(35\ 000 \times 3.169) = \$10\ 915. \text{ The}$$
net present value will be negative if:

- the cost of the machine exceeds $110 915, that is an increase of 11%; or
- the annual net receipts are less than $100 000 ÷ 3.169 = $31 555, that is a decrease of 9.8%.

The company should compare its past degrees of accuracy in estimating capital expenditure and forecasts of revenue with the percentages calculated above.

Exercise 6

The company proposes to replace an existing machine with a new one costing $150 000. It is estimated that the use of the new machine will result in net savings over the next four years of $50 000 per annum. The company will borrow $150 000 at an interest rate of 10% per annum to pay for the machine.

Required

Calculate the degrees of sensitivity as regards the cost of the machine and the annual operational savings.

36.7 Capital rationing

In some cases a company may evaluate a number of projects. However, because of the amount of capital it has, the company cannot invest in all the projects at the same time. It must ration its capital in such a way the projects it invests in maximises the net present value of the company over a period of time.

Example

Gemma has evaluated four projects with the following results.

Project	Capital cost $	Net present value $
A	300 000	80 000
B	500 000	250 000
C	200 000	180 000
D	300 000	100 000

However, she only has a maximum of $500 000 to spend. Which projects should she invest in to maximise the net present value?

She should invest in projects C and D, as these will yield a total net present value of $280 000. Any other combination will not achieve this amount.

An alternative is to calculate a 'profitability index' for each project. This is done by dividing the net present value of the project by its capital cost. The project with the highest figure is the most 'profitable' and should be considered first. Then the second most 'profitable', and so on. If this is done with the figures above, project C is the highest at 90% ($180 000 ÷ $200 000), then project C at 50%.

Exercise 7

A Co Ltd. is operating under capital rationing. It can only invest in any one of the following three projects at one time. Details of the projects are set out below.

Project	Capital cost $	Net present value $
A	400 000	70 000
B	500 000	60 000
C	600 000	120 000

Which order should the company invest in the projects to maximise the overall net present value?

HINTS

- Learn the methods of calculating ARR, payback periods, NPV and IRR.
- Remember that only ARR is calculated on profitability; payback, NPV and IRR are calculated on cash flows. Depreciation must be included for ARR but not for the other methods.
- Understand the importance of profitability and risk in investment, and why the time value of money is important.
- Be prepared to describe, explain or discuss the advantages and disadvantages of the various methods of investment appraisal.
- Take the utmost care to perform all calculations accurately.
- Look out for sunk cost and opportunity costs in problems.

MULTIPLE-CHOICE QUESTIONS

1. The net present value of a project has been calculated as follows:

	NPV ($)
at 10%	30 000
at 20%	(8 000)

What is the internal rate of return on the project?
A. 10%   **B.** 12.1%   **C.** 17.9%   **D.** 20%.

2. Why are cash flows discounted for investment appraisal?
A. $1 now is more useful that $1 receivable at a future time.
B. It is prudent to state future cash flows at a realistic value.
C. Money loses its value because of inflation.
D. The risk of not receiving money increases with time.

3. Which method of investment appraisal may be based on either actual cash flows or discounted cash flows?
A. accounting rate of return
B. internal rate of return
C. net present value
D. payback.

4. A company has $4 million to invest. Its investment opportunities are as follows:

Amount of investment for a period of 5 years	NPV ($)
1. $3 mill.	600 000
2. $2.5 mill.	350 000
3. $1.5 mill.	280 000
4. $1 mill.	50 000

In which opportunities should the company invest?
A. 1 and 3   **B.** 1 and 4
C. 2 and 3   **D.** 2 and 4

ADDITIONAL EXERCISES

1. The directors of Joloss plc intend to purchase an additional machine to manufacture one of their new products. Two machines are being considered: Milligan and Bentine. The company depreciates its machinery using the straight-line method.

Joloss plc will borrow the money required to purchase the machine and pay interest of 10% per annum on the loan.

Estimates for the machines are as follows:

		Milligan $	Bentine $
Cost of machine		100 000	130 000
Additional receipts	Year 1	70 000	72 000
	2	80 000	84 000
	3	90 000	90 000
	4	90 000	100 000
Additional costs (see note)	Year 1	50 000	60 000
	2	60 000	70 000
	3	65 000	75 000
	4	70 000	80 000

Note. These costs include the charges for depreciation and interest on the loans.

Useful life of the machine		4 years	4 years
Value at end of useful life		nil	nil
Present value of $1		10%	20%
Year	1	0.909	0.833
	2	0.826	0.694
	3	0.751	0.579
	4	0.683	0.482

Required
(i) Calculate the net present value of each machine. (Base your calculations on the cost of capital.)
(ii) State, with your reason, which machine Joloss plc should purchase.
The directors require the machine to produce a return on outlay of not less than 25%.

Required
(iii) Calculate the internal rate of return on the machine you have selected in (ii) to see if it meets the required return on outlay.

2. Jane Pannell Ltd proposes to purchase a new machine costing $120 000. It will be sold at the end of four years for $20 000. The company depreciates machinery using the straight-line method.

The machine will earn revenue of $80 000 per annum and involve additional expenditure of $46 000 each year. The company's cost of capital is 10%.

The present value of $1 is as follows:

Year	10%	15%
1	0.909	0.870
2	0.826	0.756
3	0.751	0.658
4	0.683	0.572

Required

Calculate:

(a) the accounting rate of return (ignore the sale proceeds of the machine)

(b) the net present value

(c) the internal rate of return.

Appendix 1: Table showing net present value of $1

Present value of $1

Years	5%	6%	7%	8%	9%	10%	11%	12%	13%	14%	15%	16%	17%
1	0.952	0.943	0.935	0.926	0.917	0.909	0.901	0.893	0.885	0.877	0.870	0.862	0.855
2	0.907	0.890	0.873	0.857	0.842	0.826	0.812	0.797	0.783	0.769	0.756	0.743	0.731
3	0.864	0.840	0.816	0.794	0.772	0.751	0.731	0.712	0.693	0.675	0.658	0.641	0.624
4	0.823	0.792	0.763	0.735	0.708	0.683	0.659	0.636	0.613	0.592	0.572	0.552	0.534
5	0.784	0.747	0.713	0.681	0.650	0.621	0.593	0.567	0.543	0.519	0.497	0.476	0.456
6	0.746	0.705	0.666	0.630	0.596	0.564	0.535	0.507	0.480	0.456	0.432	0.410	0.390
7	0.711	0.665	0.623	0.583	0.547	0.513	0.482	0.452	0.425	0.400	0.376	0.354	0.333
8	0.677	0.627	0.582	0.540	0.502	0.467	0.434	0.404	0.376	0.351	0.327	0.305	0.285
9	0.645	0.592	0.544	0.500	0.460	0.424	0.391	0.361	0.333	0.308	0.284	0.263	0.243
10	0.614	0.558	0.508	0.463	0.422	0.386	0.352	0.322	0.295	0.270	0.247	0.227	0.208

Years	18%	19%	20%	21%	22%	23%	24%	25%
1	0.847	0.840	0.833	0.826	0.820	0.813	0.806	0.800
2	0.718	0.706	0.694	0.683	0.672	0.661	0.650	0.640
3	0.609	0.593	0.579	0.564	0.551	0.537	0.524	0.512
4	0.516	0.499	0.482	0.466	0.451	0.437	0.423	0.410
5	0.437	0.419	0.402	0.386	0.370	0.355	0.341	0.328
6	0.370	0.352	0.335	0.319	0.303	0.289	0.275	0.262
7	0.314	0.296	0.279	0.263	0.249	0.235	0.222	0.210
8	0.266	0.249	0.233	0.218	0.204	0.191	0.179	0.168
9	0.225	0.209	0.194	0.180	0.167	0.155	0.144	0.134
10	0.191	0.176	0.162	0.149	0.137	0.126	0.116	0.107

Answers to exercises and multiple-choice questions

Chapter 1

Exercise 1. Martine

Bank					
	$				$
May 1 Martine Capital	3000	May 3	Rent Payable		100
May 2 Charline-Loan	1000	May 4	Shop Fittings		400
May 5 Purchases Returns	20	May 4	Purchases		300
May 6 Sales	40	May 7	Wages		60
		May 8	Drawings		100

Martine Capital			
	$		$
		May 1 Bank	3000

Charline-Loan			
	$		$
		May 2 Bank	1000

Rent Payable			
	$		$
May 3 Bank	100		

Shop Fittings			
	$		$
May 4 Bank	400		

Purchases			
	$		$
May 4 Bank	300		

Purchases Returns			
	$		$
		May 5 Bank	20

Sales			
	$		$
		May 6 Bank	40

Wages			
	$		$
May 7 Bank	60		

Drawings			
	$		$
May 8 Bank	100		

Exercise 2 Noel

	Debit account	Credit account
1. Noel pays his cheque into his business Bank account	Bank	Noel-Capital
2. Purchases goods for resale and pays by cheque	Purchases	Bank
3. Sells goods and banks the takings	Bank	Sales
4. Pays rent by cheque	Rent Payable	Bank
5. Purchases shop fittings	Shop Fittings	Bank
6. Cashes cheque for personal expenses	Drawings	Bank
7. Pays wages	Wages	Bank
8. Returns goods to supplier and banks refund	Bank	Purchases Returns
9. Receives rent from tenant	Bank	Rent Receivable
10. Refunds money to customer by cheque for goods returned	Sales Returns	Bank
11. Motor vehicle purchased and paid for by cheque	Motor Vehicles	Bank
12. Pays for petrol for motor vehicle	Motor Expenses*	Bank

*The costs of running motor vehicles (petrol, licence, insurance, repairs etc.) are not debited to the Motor Vehicles account. A new account, Motor Expenses, is opened to record them.

Multiple-choice questions

1. B   **2.** B   **3.** D   **4.** B

Chapter 2

Exercise 1. Geraud

Khor

	$			$
June 10 Purchases Returns	200	June 1	Purchases	2700
30 Bank	2375			
30 Discounts Received	125			

Lim

	$			$
June 30 Bank	2394	June 15	Purchases	2520
June 30 Discounts Received	126			

Lai

	$			$
June 5 Sales	600	June 25	Sales Returns	200
		June 30	Bank	380
		June 30	Discounts Allowed	20

Chin

	$			$
June 20 Sales	1300	June 30	Bank	1235
		June 30	Discounts Allowed	65

Purchases

	$		$
June 1 Khor	2700		
June 15 Lim	2520		

Purchases Returns

	$		$
		June 10 Khor	200

Sales

	$		$
		June 5 Lai	600
		June 20 Chin	1300

Sales Returns

	$		$
June 25 Lai	200		

Bank

	$		$
June 30 Lai	380	June 30 Khor	2375
June 30 Chin	1235	June 30 Lim	2394

Discounts Received

	$		$
		June 30 Khor	125
		June 30 LIm	126

Discounts Allowed

	$		$
June 30 Lai	20		
June 30 Chin	65		

Multiple-choice question

1. A   2. B   3. A

Chapter 3

Exercise 1. Murgatroyd

Purchases Journal		Sales Journal	
	$		$
March 1 Tikolo	8 000	March 4 Snyman	1080
March 6 Walters	7 200	March 10 Karg	2250
March 13 Burger	5 250	March 17 Kotze	2700
March 18 Tikolo	4 800	March 25 Snyman	1620
	25 250		7650

Purchases Returns Journal		Sales Returns Journal	
	$		$
March 12 Tikolo	400	March 11 Snyman	200
March 22 Burger	1000	March 20 Karg	300
	1400		500

Bank

	Discounts	Bank		Discounts	Bank
	$	$		$	$
March 31 Syman	100	2400	March 31 Tikolo	620	11 780
March 31 Karg	78	1872	March 31 Walters	360	6 840
March 31 Kotze	135	2565	March 31 Burger	170	4 080
	313			1150	

Purchases

	$		$
March 31 Purchases journal total	25 250		

Purchases Returns

	$		$
		March 31 Purchases returns journal total	1400

Sales

	$		$
		March 31 Sales journal total	7650

Sales Returns

	$		$
March 31 Sales returns journal total	500		

Discounts Allowed

	$		$
March 31 Cash book total	313		

Discounts Received

	$		$
		March 31 Cash book total	1150

Tikolo

	$		$
March 12 Purchases Returns	400	March 1 Purchases	8000
March 31 Bank	11 780	March 18 Purchases	4800
March 31 Discounts	620		

Walters

	$		$
March 31 Bank	6840	March 6 Purchases	7200
March 31 Discounts	360		

Burger

	$		$
March 22 Purchases Returns	1000	March 13 Purchases	5250
March 31 Bank	4080		
March 31 Discounts	170		

Snymn

	$		$
March 4 Sales	1080	March 11 Sales Returns	200
March 25 Sales	1620	March 31 Bank	2400
		March 31 Discounts	100

Karg

	$		$
March 10 Sales	2250	March 20 Sales Returns	300
		March 31 Bank	1872
		March 31 Discounts	78

Kotze

	$		$
March 17 Sales	2700	March 31 Bank	2565
		March 31 Discounts	135

Exercise 2. Joshua

Bank and Cash

	Disc $	Cash $	Bank		Disc $	Cash $	Bank
March 1 Sales		1100		March 2 Electricity		130	
March 3 Sales		900		March 4 Bank	¢	1700	
March 4 Cash	¢		1700	March 5 Sundry expenses		25	
March 6 Bank	¢	800		March 6 Cash	¢		800
				March 7 Purchases		750	

Exercise 3

	Dr $	Cr $
1. A and Co. Ltd.	120	
A. Cotter		120

Correction of credit note no. 964 received from A and Co. Ltd. in the sum of $120 debited to A. Cotter in error.

2. Purchases	400	
Hussain		400

Correction of invoice no. 104 in the sum of $400 received from Hussain omitted from the purchases journal.

3. Maya	45	
Sales		45

Correction of posting error: invoice no. 6789 in the sum of $150 sent to Maya entered in the sales journal as $105.

4. Machinery	2300	
Purchases		2300

Correction of purchase of machine posted in error to Purchases account.

5. Sales Returns	68	
Hanife		68

Correction of omission of credit note no. 23 for $68 and sent to Hanife, omitted from the sales returns journal.

Multiple-choice question

1. C   **2.** B   **3.** B   **4.** C

Chapter 5

Exercise 1. Capital – personal; Sales Returns – revenue; Delivery Vans – fixed asset; Purchases – expense; Rent Payable – expense; Debtors – personal (and current assets); Stock-in-trade – current asset; Discounts Allowed – expense; Drawings – personal; Bank – current asset; Rent Receivable – other income; Creditors – personal; Computer – fixed asset; Wages – expense; Discounts Receivable – other income.

Chapter 6

Exercise 1. Achilles' trial balance at 31 December 2010.

	$	$
Premises	50 000	
Motor Vans	8 000	
Office Furniture	2 000	
Computer	3 000	
Sales		60 000

	$	$
Sales Returns	700	
Purchases	4 000	
Purchases Returns		500
Motor Vehicle Running Expenses	4 200	
Wages	1 800	
Rent	2 000	
Bank	1 650	
Capital		20 000
Drawings	3 150	
	80 500	80 500

Exercise 2. (a) Complete reversal of entries (b) Error of principle (c) Error of omission (d) Compensating errors (e) Error of commission (f) Error of original entry.

Multiple-choice questions

1. B   **2.** B   **3.** C   **4.** C

Chapter 7

Exercise 1

Corrine Income Statement for the year ended 31 December 2010		
	$	$
Sales		200 000
Less Sales returns		6 300
		193 700
Cost of sales		
Purchases	86 500	
Less Purchases returns	5 790	
	80 710	
Less Stock at 31 December 2010	10 000	70 710
Gross profit		122 990
Add Rent received		3 000
Discounts received		3 210
		129 200
Less		
Wages	61 050	
Rent payable	12 000	
Electricity	5 416	
Insurance	2 290	
Motor van expenses	11 400	
Discounts allowed	5 110	
Sundry expenses	3 760	
Loan interest	1 000	102 026
Net profit		27 174

Khor Trading section of the Income Statement for the year ended 31 December 2010

	$	$	$
Sales			48 000
Less Sales returns			1 600
			46 400
Less Cost of sales			
Opening stock		4 000	
Purchases	21 000		
Less Purchases returns	900	20 100	
		24 100	
Less Closing stock		7 500	16 600
Gross profit			29 800

Perkins Income Statement for the year ended 31 March 2011

	$	$	$
Sales			104 000
Less Sales returns			3 700
			100 300
Less Cost of sales			
Opening stock		6 000	
Purchases	59 000		
Less Purchases returns	2 550	56 450	
		62 450	
Less Closing stock		10 000	52 450
Gross profit			47 850
Rent receivable			1 800
Discounts receivable			770
			50 420
Less Overheads			
Wages		13 000	
Rent payable		2 000	
Heating and lighting		2 700	
Repairs to machinery		4 100	
Discounts allowed		1 030	
Loan interest		750	23 580
Net profit			26 840

Sara Income Statement for the year ended 31 March 2011

	$	$	$
Sales			40 000
Less Cost of sales			
Stock at 1 April 2010		5 000	
Purchases	20 500		
Carriage inwards	1 320	21 820	
		26 820	
Less Stock at 31 March 2011		3 000	23 820
Gross profit			16 180
Less			
Wages		6 000	
Rent		10 000	
Electricity		2 600	
Carriage outwards		1 080	
Sundry expenses		1 250	20 930
Net loss			4 750

Multiple-choice question

1. A   2. C   3. C   4. D   5. A

Chapter 8

Exercise 1

Corrine Statement of Financial Position at 31 December 2010

	$	$
Non-current assets		
Land and buildings		84 000
Plant and machinery		22 000
Motor vans		19 000
		125 000
Current assets		
Stock	10 000	
Trade Receivables	12 425	
Bank	5 065	
	27 490	
Current liabilities		
Trade Payables	4 220	23 270
		148 270
Non-current liability		
Loan		20 000
		128 270
Represented by		
Capital at 1 January 2010		127 000
Add net profit		27 174
		154 174
Deduct Drawings		25 904
		128 270

Exercise 2

Perkins Statement of Financial Position at 31 March 2011

	$	$
Non-current assets		
Premises		60 000
Plant and machinery		12 000
		72 000
Current assets		
Stock	10 000	
Trade Receivables	1 624	
Bank	5 000	
	16 624	
Current liabilities		
Trade Payables	1 880	14 744
		86 744
Non-current liability		
Loan		15 000
		71 744
Represented by		
Capital at 1 April 2010		55 000
Net profit		26 840
		81 840
Drawings		10 096
		71 744

Multiple-choice questions

   1. D   **2.** A   **3.** A   **4.** C

Chapter 9

Multiple-choice questions

   1. B   **2.** A   **3.** A   **4.** B   **5.** B   **6.** D

Chapter 10

Exercise 1. Alex

Rent Payable				
2010		$	2010		$
Dec 31 Bank	1000	Dec 31 Profit and Loss	800
		Dec 31 Rent	
		prepaid c/d	200
	1000		1000
2011			
Jan 1 Balance b/d	200		

Electricity				
2010		$	2010		$
Dec 31 Bank	630	Dec 31 Profit and Loss	810
Dec 31 Amount			
owing c/d	180		
	810		810
		2011	
		Jan 1 Balance b/d	180

Stationery				
2010		$	2010		$
Dec 31 Bank	420	Dec 31 Profit and Loss	410
Dec 31 Amount		Dec 31 Stock c/d	140
owing c/d	130		
	550		550
2011		2011	
Jan 31 Balance b/d	140	Jan 31 Balance b/d	130

Rent Payable				
2010		$	2010		$
Dec 31 Profit and Loss	400	Dec 31 Bank	300
		Dec 31 Rent	
		owing b/d	100
	400		400
2011			
Jan 1 Balance b/d	100		

Exercise 2

(a)

Devram Income Statement for the year ended 31 December 2010		
	$	$
Gross profit b/d		30 000
Rent (2600 – 300)	2300	
Electricity (926 + 242)	1168	
Stationery (405 + 84 – 100)	389	
Motor expenses (725 + 160)	885	
Interest on loan	1000	5 742
Net profit		24 258

Note. Unpaid interest on the loan must be accrued although it is not mentioned in the question.

(b)

Statement of Financial Position at 31 December 2010			
	$	$	$
Non-current assets			40 000
Current assets			
Stock in trade	7000		
Stock of stationery	100	7 100	
Trade receivables		1 600	
Prepaid rent		300	
Bank		2 524	
		11 524	
Current liabilities			
Trade payables	1400		
Expense creditors	986	2 386	9 138
			49 138
Less Long-term loan			10 000
			39 138
Capital at 1 January 2010			20 000
Net profit			24 258
			44 258
Drawings			5 120
			39 138

Multiple-choice questions

   1. D   **2.** B   **3.** B   **4.** A

Chapter 11

Exercise 1.

(a)

Provision for Depreciation of Motor Vehicles

	$			$
Year 1 Balance c/d	2 000	Year 1	Profit and Loss	2 000
Year 2 Balance c/d	4 000	Year 2	Balance b/d	2 000
			Profit and Loss	2 000
	4 000			4 000
Year 3 Balance c/d	6 000	Year 3	Balance b/d	4 000
			Profit and Loss	2 000
	6 000			6 000
Year 4 Balance c/d	8 000	Year 4	Balance b/d	6 000
			Profit and Loss	2 000
	8 000			8 000
Year 5 Balance c/d	10 000	Year 5	Balance b/d	8 000
			Profit and Loss	2 000
	10 000			10 000
Year 6 Balance c/d	12 000	Year 6	Balance b/d	10 000
			Profit and Loss	2 000
	12 000			12 000
Year 7 Balance c/d	14 000	Year 7	Balance b/d	12 000
			Profit and Loss	2 000
	14 000			14 000
Year 8		Year 8	Balance b/d	14 000

(b)

Statement of Financial Position extracts

	Cost	Depreciation	Net book value
	$	$	$
Year 1 Motor vehicles	18 000	2 000	16 000
Year 2 Motor vehicles	18 000	4 000	14 000
Year 3 Motor vehicles	18 000	6 000	12 000
Year 4 Motor vehicles	18 000	8 000	10 000
Year 5 Motor vehicles	18 000	10 000	8 000
Year 6 Motor vehicles	18 000	12 000	6 000
Year 7 Motor vehicles	18 000	14 000	4 000

Exercise 2

(a)

Provision for Depreciation of Machinery

	$			$
Year 1 Balance c/d	12 000	Year 1	Profit and Loss	12 000
Year 2 Balance c/d	10 400	Year 2	Balance b/d	12 000
			Profit and Loss	8 400
	20 400			20 400

	$			$
Year 3 Balance c/d	26 280	Year 3	Balance b/d	20 400
			Profit and Loss	5 880
	26 280			26 280
Year 4 Balance c/d	30 396	Year 4	Balance b/d	26 280
			Profit and Loss	4 116
	30 396			30 396
Year 5 Balance c/d	33 277	Year 5	Balance b/d	30 396
			Profit and Loss	2 881
	33 277			33 277
Year 6		Year 6	Balance b/d	33 277

(b)

Statement of Financial Position extracts

	Cost	Depreciation	Net book value
	$	$	$
Year 1 Machinery	40 000	12 000	28 000
Year 2 Machinery	40 000	20 400	19 600
Year 3 Machinery	40 000	26 280	13 720
Year 4 Machinery	40 000	30 396	9 604
Year 5 Machinery	40 000	33 277	6 723

Exercise 3. Joel

(a)

Machinery at Cost

2011			$	2011			$
Jan	1	Balance b/d	18 000	May	7	Disposal of Machinery	6 000
Jun	3	Bank	7 000	Jun	3	Disposal of Machinery	12 000
		Disposal of Machinery	3 000	Dec	31	Balance c/d	10 000
			28 000				28 000
2012							
Jan	1	Balance b/d	10 000				

(b)

Provision for Depreciation of Machinery

2011			$	2011			$
May	7	Disposal of Machinery	2 400	Jan	1	Balance b/d (2400 + 7200)	9 600
Jun	3	Disposal of Machinery	7 200	Dec	31	Profit and Loss	1 000
Dec	31	Balance c/d	1 000				
			10 600				10 600
				2012			$
				Jan	1	Balance b/d	1 000

(c)

Disposal of Machinery

2011		$	2011		$
May 7	Machinery at Cost	6 000	May 7	Provision for Depreciation of Machinery	2 400
				Bank	1 500
				Profit and Loss (loss)	2 100
		6 000			6 000
Jun 3	Machinery at Cost	12 000	Jun 3	Provision for Depreciation of Machinery	7 200
				Part exchange	3 000
				Profit and Loss (loss)	1 800
		12 000			12 000

Multiple-choice questions

1. D   **2.** C   **3.** A   **4.** A

Chapter 12

Exercise 1. Saul

(a)   2007   : $(4000 + 1150) = \$5150$
      2008   : $(6400 + 1375) = \$7775$
      2009   : $(7500 + 1125) = \$8625$
      2010   : $(3000 + 1250) = \$4250$
      2011   : $(8300 + 1420) = \$9720$

(b)

Provision for Doubtful Debts

		$			$
31 Mar 2007	Balance c/d	5150	31 Mar 2007	Profit and Loss A/c	5150
31 Mar 2008	Balance c/d	7775	1 Apr 2007	Balance b/d	5150
			31 Mar 2008	Profit and Loss A/c	2625
		7775			7775
31 Mar 2009		8625	1 Apr 2008	Balance b/d	7775
			31 Mar 2009	Profit an Loss A/c	850
		8625			8625
31 Mar 2010	Profit and Loss A/c	4375	1 Apr 2009	Balance b/d	8625
	Balance c/d	4250			
		8625			8625
31 Mar 2011	Balance c/d	9720	1 Apr 2010	Balance b/d	4250
			31 Mar 2011	Profit and Loss A/c	5470
		9720			9720
			1 Apr 2011	Balance b/d	9720

Multiple-choice questions

1. C   **2.** B   **3.** D   **4.** B

Chapter 13

Exercise 1. $475 DR

Exercise 2. $540 Dr (overdrawn)

Exercise 3. (a)   Revised cash book balance: $80 − $210 = $130 overdrawn

        (b)   Bank reconciliation: Balance per bank statements $(650 + 220) Cr −

$1000 = $130 overdrawn (per cash book).

Exercise 4

	$	$
Trade receivables (1055 − 420 + 323)	958	
Trade payables (976 − 360)		616
Rent (800 + 200)	1000	
Bank (1245 − 360 + 420 − 200 − 323)	782	

Multiple-choice questions

1. C   **2.** C   **3.** B   **4.** A   **5.** B

Chapter 14

Exercise 1

Byit Ltd Purchase Ledger Control						
2011		$	2011			$
Mar 1	Balance b/d	16	Mar 1	Balance b/d		10 000
Mar 31	Purchases		Mar 31	Purchases		
	returns	824		journal		33 700
	Bank	27 500		Balance c/d		156
	Discounts					
	received	1 300				
	Balance c/d	14 216				
		43 856				43 856
Apr 1	Balance b/d	156	Apr 1	Balance b/d		14 216

Exercise 2

Soldit Ltd Sales Ledger Control					
2011		$	2011		$
May 1	Balance b/d	27 640	May 1	Balance b/d	545
31	Sales journal	109 650	31	Sales returns	2 220
	Bad debt			Bank	98 770
	recovered	490		Discounts	
	Balance c/d	800		allowed	3 150
				Bank-bad debt	
				recovered	490
				Purchases ledger	
				contra	2 624
				Balance c/d	30 781
		138 580			138 580
Jun 1	Balance b/d	30 781	Jun 1	Balance b/d	800

Exercise 3

(a)

Rorre Ltd	Purchases ledger balances				Sales ledger balances	
	Debit	Credit			Debit	Credit
	$	$			$	$
Before amendment	64	7 217	Before amendment		23 425	390
Deduct invoice entered twice		(100)	Correction of invoice $326 entered as $362		(36)	–
Debit balance incorrectly listed as credit balance	50	(50)	Corrected balances		23 389	390
Corrected balances	114	7 067				

(b)

Corrected Purchases Ledger Control					
2010		$	2010		$
Dec 31	Cancellation of		Dec 31	Balance b/d	7847
	invoice	100		Balance c/d	114
	Discounts				
	Received	84			
	Sales Ledger				
	contra-Trazom	710			
	Balance c/d	7067			
		7961			7961
2011			2011		
Jan 1	Balance b/d	114	Jan 1	Balance b/d	7067

(c)

Amended net profit	$
Profit per draft Profit	
and Loss Account	31 000
Add reduction in	
purchases	100
discounts received	
omitted	84
increase in sales	800
Amended net	
profit	31 984

(d)

Statement of Financial Position extract at 31 December		
	$	$
Trade Receivables		
Sales ledger	23 389	
Purchases ledger	114	23 503
Trade Payables		
Purchases ledger	7 067	
Sales ledger	390	7 457

Multiple-choice questions

1. B   **2.** C   **3.** C

Corrected Sales Ledger Control					
2010		$	2010		$
Dec 31	Balance b/d	22 909	Dec 31	Purchases Ledger	
	Sales journal	800		Contra-Trazom	710
	Balance c/d	390		Balance c/d	23 389
		24 099			24 099
2011			2011		
Jan 1	Balance b/d	23 389	Jan 1	Balance b/d	390

Chapter 15

Exercise 1. (a)

Lee Suspense account			
	$		$
Sales	90	Difference on trial balance	58*
Doyle	18	Bad debt	50
	108		108
*Balancing figure			

(b) Journal entries

	Debit $	Credit $
Purchases	150	
Bilder		150
Invoice from Bilder omitted from the books.		
Machinery at Cost	400	
Machinery Repairs		400
Capital expenditure incorrectly posted to Machinery Repairs account.		
Income Statement	40	
Provision for depreciation of machinery		40
Additional depreciation on machinery.		

(c) Calculation of corrected net profit for the year ended 30 June 2011.

	Decrease (Dr) $	Increase (Cr) $	$
Net profit per draft accounts			3775
(1) Increase in sales		90	
(2) Increase in purchases	150		
(4) Increase in bad debts	50		
(5) Decrease in machinery repairs		400	
(5) Increase in provision for depreciation of machinery	40		
	240	490	
		(240)	250
Correct net profit			4025

Exercise 2

(a) Journal entries

	Jayesh Dr $	Cr $
1. Suspense		2700
Note. No debit entry is required.		
2. *Note. The trial balance was not affected because the closing stock was not shown in it.*		
3. Repairs to machinery	3500	
Suspense	1800	
Machinery at cost		5300
4. Suspense	800	
Sales		800
5. Suspense	126	
Note. No credit entry is required.		

(b)

Suspense account			
	$		$
Machinery at cost	1800	Trial balance difference	26
Sales	800	Adjustment of opening	
Adjustment to creditors	126	stock	2700
	2726		2726

(c) Calculation of corrected net working capital at 31 December 2010.

	$
Net working capital per draft Statement of Financial Position	3200
Add Increase in closing stock	2000
Deduct: Credit balance $63 extracted as debit balance	(126)
Corrected net working capital at 31 December	5074

Multiple-choice questions

1. A   2. B   3. C   4. B   5. C
6. C   7. A

Chapter 16

Exercise 1. Lian

Statements of affairs	at 1 January $	at 31 December $
Premises at cost	4 000	9 000
Motor van at cost	5 000	4 000
Motor car at cost	–	3 000
Plant and equipment	1 100	1 300
Stock of parts	400	200
Debtors for work done	700	800
Balance at bank	1 300	900
	12 500	19 200
Less		
Owing to suppliers	170	340
Capital	12 330	18 860
Less capital introduced: motor car		(3 000)*
		15 860
Add drawings ($120 × 52)		6 240
		22 100
Deduct capital at 1 January		12 330
Profit for the year ended 31 December		9 770

*The cost of the car is deducted because it was capital introduced during the year.

Exercise 2. Ammar

Income Statement for the year ended 30 June		
	$	$
Sales (balancing figure)		35 000
Less		
Opening inventory	4 000	
Purchases (balancing figure)	31 000	
(balancing figure)	35 000	
Closing inventory	7 000	
Cost of sales		28 000
Gross profit (Margin 20%, so mark-up is 25%)		7 000

Exercise 3. Neha

Proforma Income Statement for the period 30 June 2010 to 5 November 2010		
	$	$
Sales (122 00 – 16 000 + 37 000 + 17 000)		160 000
Less Cost of sales		
Inventory at 30 June 2010	47 000	
Purchases (138 000 – 23 000 + 28 000)	143 000	
	190 000	
Less Stock at 5 November 2010		
(balancing figure)	70 000	120 000
Gross profit (25% of 160 000)		40 000

Cost of stock lost in fire: $(70 000 – 12 000)
= $58 000.

Multiple-choice questions

1. B	2. B	3. C	4. D	5. D
6. B				

Chapter 17

Exercise 1.

(a)

The Wellington Drama Club Income and Expenditure Account for the year ended 31 December 2011		
	$	$
Subscriptions		2 400
Sales of tickets		20 000
Sales of programmes		3 000
Sales of refreshments	3 500	

	$	$
Less Cost of refreshments	2 200	1 300
		26 700
Less		
Hire of costumes	4 700	
Hire of hall	2 600	
Copyright fees	1 400	
Printing	180	8 880
Surplus of income over expenditure		17 820
Donation to Actors Benevolent Fund (50%)		8 910
Balance carried to Accumulated Fund		8 910

(b)

Subscriptions Account				
2011			2011	
1 Jan Subscriptions owing b/f	280		31 Dec Bank	2 640
31 Dec Income & Expenditure a/c	2 400		Subs owing c/f	400
Subs prepaid c/f	360			
	3 040			3 040

Statement of Financial Position extracts at 31 December 2011		
Current asset	Subscriptions owing	$400
Current liability	Subscriptions in advance	$360

Exercise 2

(a)

The Hutt River Dining Club Statement of Affairs at 1 January 2011		
		$
Catering equipment		8 000
Stock of food		200
Stock of books		1 100
Subscriptions owing		180
Bank		1 520
		11 000
Less		
Creditors for supplies of food	40	
Subscriptions in advance	60	(100)
Accumulated fund at 1 January 2011		10 900

(b)

Receipts and Payments account for the year ended 31 December 2011					
2011		$	2011		$
Jan 1	Balance brought forward	1 520	Dec 31	Staff wages	39 000
Dec 31	Subscriptions	5 000		Purchase of food	24 980
	Restaurant takings	73 760		Purchase of books	4 840
	Sales of books	12 150		Catering equipment	3 750
				Heating and lighting	8 390
				Sundry expenses	2 270
				Balance carried forward	9 200
		92 430			92 430
2012					
Jan 1	Balance brought down	9 200			

(c)

Subscriptions					
2011		$	2011		$
Jan 1	Balance b/f	180	Jan 1	Balance b/f	60
Dec 31	Income and Expenditure	4 780	Dec 31	Bank	5 000
	Prepaid subscriptions c/d	140		Subscriptions owing c/d	40
		5 100			5 100
2012			2012		
Jan 1	Balance b/d	40	Jan 1	Balance b/d	140

(d)

Book Trading section of the Income Statement		
	$	$
Sales		12 150
Less		
Cost of sales		
Inventory at 1 January 2011	1100	
Purchases (4840 + 200)	5040	
	6140	
Inventory at 31 December 2011	965	5 175
Transferred to Income and Expenditure Account		6 975

(e)

Restaurant account		
	$	$
Takings		73 760
Less		
Cost of food		
Inventory at 1 January 2011	200	
Purchases (24980 + 360 – 40)	25 300	
	25 500	
Inventory at 31 December 2011	270	25 230
Gross profit		48 530
Staff wages	39 000	
Depreciation of catering equipment	1 475	40 475
Transferred to Income and Expenditure Account		8 055

(f)

The Hutt River Dining Club Income and Expenditure Account for the year ended 31 December 2011		
	$	$
Subscriptions		4 780
Profit on sales of books		6 975
Profit on restaurant		8 055
		19 810
Heating and lighting	8 390	
Sundry expenses	2 270	10 660
Surplus of income over expenditure		9 150

(g)

Statement of Financial Position at 31 December 2011			
	$	$	$
Catering equipment (800 + 3750)		11 750	
Less Depreciation		1 475	10 275
Current assets			
Stocks: Books		965	
Food		270	
		1 235	
Subscriptions owing		40	
Bank		9 200	
		10 475	
Current liabilities			
Creditors: Food	360		
Books	200		
Subscriptions in advance	140	700	9 775
			20 050
Accumulated fund at 1 January 2011			10 900
Surplus of income over expenditure			9 150
			20 050

Multiple-choice questions

  1. B   **2.** B   **3.** C   **4.** C

Chapter 18

Exercise 1.

	Ladies'		Men's		Children's		Total	
Geeta								
Income Statement for the year ended 31 march 2011								
	$	$	$	$	$	$	$	$
Sales		100 000		120 000		80 000		300 000
Less Cost of sales								
Stock at 1 April 2010	14 000		17 000		5 000		36 000	
Purchases	50 000		63 000		42 000		155 000	
	64 000		80 000		47 000		191 000	
Stock at 31 March 2011	18 000	46 000	22 000	58 000	4 000	43 000	44 000	147 000
Gross profit		54 000		62 000		37 000		153 000
Wages	20 000		20 000		12 000		52 000	
Rent	11 200		11 200		5 600		28 000	
Heating & lighting	2 400		2 400		1 200		6 000	
Advertising	1 667		2 000		1 333		5 000	
Administration	12 000		9 000		6 000		27 000	
Depreciation	3 086	50 353	2 571	47 171	1 543	27 676	7 200	125 200
		3 647		14 829		9 324		27 800
Managers' commission		(174)		(706)		(444)		(1 324)
Net profit		3 473		14 123		8 880		26 476

Multiple-choice questions

1. C   2. D   3. C   4. B

Chapter 19

Exercise 1

The Fabricating Company
Manufacturing Account and Income Statement for the year ended 31 March 2011

	$000	$000
Raw materials		
Inventory at 1 April 2010	10	
Purchases	130	
Carriage in	14	
	154	
Inventory at 31 March 2011	20	134
Direct labour		170
Direct expenses		16
Prime cost		320

	$000	$000
Factory overheads	128	
Depreciation of machinery	12	140
		460
Work in progress: 1 April 2010	12	
31 March 2011	(22)	(10)
Factory cost of goods produced		450
Factory profit (20%)		90
Transferred to Trading section of the Income Statement		540
Sales		700
Less Cost of sales		
Inventory of finished goods at 1 April 2010	24	
Transferred from Manufacturing Account	540	
	564	
Inventory of finished goods at 31 March 2011	36	528
Gross profit		172
Office overheads	96	
Office depreciation	3	99
Net profit on trading		73
Factory profit		90
Less Provision for unrealised profit $(36 - 24) \times \dfrac{20}{120}$	(2)	88
Net profit		161

Exercise 2

Glupersoo
Manufacturing Account and Income Statement
for the year ended 30 April 2011

	$	$
Direct materials:		
Inventory at 1 May 2010	11 250	
Purchases	132 000	
Carriage inwards	11 505	
	154 755	
Inventory at 30 April 2011	13 125	141 630
Direct labour		146 250
Prime cost		287 880
Indirect wages	19 500	
Rent $\frac{3}{4}$ (45 000 + 3750)	36 563	
Heating and lighting $\frac{2}{3}$(42 300 + 2700)	30 000	
Insurance $\frac{9}{10}$(3150 − 900)	2 025	
Motor vehicle expenses (6000 × $\frac{1}{2}$)	3 000	
Depreciation:		
Factory	3 000	
Machinery	10 000	
Motor vehicles (8000 × $\frac{1}{2}$)	4 000	108 088
		395 968
Work in progress:		
at 1 May 2010	18 000	
30 April 2011	15 750	2 250
Factory cost of goods produced		398 218
Factory profit (20%)		79 644
Transferred to Trading section of the Income Statement		477 862
Sales		800 000
Less Cost of sales		
Inventory of finished goods 1 May 2010	27 000	
Transferred from Manufacturing account	477 862	
	504 862	
Less Inventory of finished goods 30 April 2011	24 000	480 862
Gross profit		319 138
Office salaries	51 450	
Rent $\frac{1}{4}$ (45 000 + 3750)	12 187	
Heating and lighting $\frac{1}{3}$ (42 300 + 2700)	15 000	
Insurance $\frac{1}{10}$(3150 − 900)	225	
Carriage outwards	2 520	
Advertising (7000 − 3500)	3 500	
Motor vehicle expenses (6000 × $\frac{1}{2}$)	3 000	
Depreciation:		
Office machinery	4000	
Motor vans (8000 × $\frac{1}{2}$)	4000	8 000	95 882
Net profit on trading		223 256
Add Factory profit	79 644	
Reduction in Provision for Unrealised		
Profit $\frac{1}{6}$ (27 000 − 24 000)	500	80 144
Overall net profit		303 400

Multiple-choice questions
1. B   2. C   3. B   4. C

Multiple-choice questions
1. B   2. C   3. B   4. C

Chapter 20

Exercise 1. Fiford Ltd

Inventory of fifolium at 31 October

October		1	10	15	22	29
Price ($)		5.00	5.20	5.24	5.28	5.32
Quantity (kilos)		100	80	50	70	100
Sales						
3		(40)				
		60				
12		(60)	(15)			
		−	65			
14			(50)			
			15			
17			(15)	(30)		
			−	20		
30				(20)	(50)	−
31				−	20	100
Value					$105.60	$532.00

Total $637.60

Exercise 2. A.V. Co. Ltd

Inventory of digital hammers at 30 June

Date		Quantity	Price per unit ($)	Average price ($)	Balance $
Jun 1	Balance b/f	200	5.00	5.000	1000
4	Purchased	100	5.20		520
	Balance	300		5.067	1520
10	Sold	(75)			(380)
	Balance	225			1140
13	Purchased	100	5.35		535
	Balance	325		5.154	1675
20	Sold	(150)			(773)
	Balance	175			902
26	Purchased	80	5.40		432
	Balance	255		5.231	1334
30	Sold	(90)			(471)
	Balance	165		5.231	863

Multiple-choice questions
1. D   2. C   3. B   4. A

Chapter 21

Exercise 1. (a)

Tee and Leef Income Statement and Appropriation Account for the year ended 31 March 2011			
	$	$	$
Sales			215 000
Less Cost of sales:			
Inventory at 1 April 2010		16 000	
Purchases		84 000	
		100 000	
Less inventory at 31 March 2011		20 000	80 000
Gross profit			135 000
Selling expenses		24 000	
Administration expenses		46 000	
Depreciation			
Fixtures and fittings	4 800		
Office equipment	5 400	10 200	
Interest on loan		600	80 800
Net profit			54 200
Share of profit	Tee $(\frac{1}{2})$	27 100	
	Leef $(\frac{1}{2})$	27 100	54 200

(b)

Partners' Current accounts								
		Tee	Leef				Tee	Leef
2011		$	$	2010			$	$
Mar 31	Drawings	29 000	31 000	Apr 1	Balances b/d		5 000	10 000
				2011				
	Balance			Mar 31	Interest			
	c/d	3 100	6 700		on loan			600
					Share of			
					profit		27 100	27 100
		32 100	37 700				32 100	37 700
				Apr 1	Balance b/d		3 100	6 700

(c)

Statement of Financial Position at 31 March 2011			
	Cost	Depn.	NBV
	$	$	$
Non-current assets			
Fixtures and fittings	48 000	12 800	35 200
Office equipment	27 000	10 400	16 600
	75 000	23 200	51 800
Current assets			
Stock		20 000	
Trade receivables		24 000	
Prepayment		6 000	
Bank		85 000	
		135 000	
Current liabilities			
Trade payables	11 000		
Expense creditor	4 000	15 000	120 000
			171 800
Non-current liability: Loan-Leef			12 000
			159 800

		Cost $	Dep. $	NBV $
Capital accounts:	Tee	100 000		
	Leef	50 000		150 000
Current accounts:	Tee	3 100		
	Leef	6 700		9 800
				159 800

Exercise 2. (a)

Tee and Leef Income Statement and Appropriation Account for the year ended 31 March 2011			
	$	$	$
Sales			215 000
Less Cost of sales:			
Inventory at 1 April 2010		16 000	
Purchases		84 000	
		100 000	
Less Inventory at 31 March 2011		20 000	80 000
Gross profit			135 000
Selling expenses		24 000	
Administration expenses		46 000	
Depreciation:			
Fixtures and fittings	4 800		
Office equipment	5 400	10 200	
Interest on loan		1 200	81 400
Net profit			53 600
Interest on drawings:			
Tee		2 900	
Leef		3 100	6 000
			59 000
Interest on capitals			
Tee		10 000	
Leef		5 000	
		15 000	
Salary			
Leef		4 000	19 000
			40 600
Share of profit			
Tee $\frac{3}{5}$		24 360	
Leef $\frac{2}{5}$		16 240	40 600

Partners' Current accounts								
		Tee	Leef				Tee	Leef
2011		$	$	2010			$	$
Mar 31	Drawings	29 000	31 000	Apr 1	Balances b/d		5 000	10 000
	Interest on							
	drawings	2 900	3 100	2011				
	Balances			Mar 31	Interest on			
	c/d	7 460	2 340		capital		10 000	5 000
					Interest			
					on loan			1 200
					Salary			4 000
					Share of			
					profit		24 360	16 240
		39 360	36 440				39 360	36 440
				Apr 1	Balance b/d		7 460	2 340

(c)

Statement of Financial Position at 31 March 2011

	Cost $	Dep. $	NBV $
Non-current assets			
Fixtures and fittings	48 000	12 800	35 200
Office equipment	27 000	10 400	16 600
	75 000	23 200	51 800
Current assets			
Stock		20 000	
Trade receivables		24 000	
Prepayment		6 000	
Bank		85 000	
		135 000	
Current liabilities			
Trade payables	11 000		
Expense creditor	4 000	15 000	120 000
			171 800
Non-current liability: Loan-Leef			12 000
			159 800
Capital accounts: Tee	100 000		
Leef	50 000		150 000
Current accounts: Tee	7 460		
Leef	2 340		9 800
			159 800

Multiple-choice questions

1. C   **2.** D   **3.** A

Chapter 22

Exercise 1. Ann and John

(a)

Revaluation account

	$000		$000
Property (old value)	120	Property (new value)	150
Plant & machinery (old value)	60	Plant & machinery (new value)	51
Inventory (old value)	20	Inventory (new value)	17
Trade receivables (old value)	30	Trade receivables (new value)	28
Trade payables (new value)	22	Trade payables (old value)	24
Profit on revaluation – Ann	12		
Profit on revaluation – John	6		
	270		270

(b)

Capital accounts

	$000 Ann	$000 John		$000 Ann	$000 John
Balance c/f	132	66	Opening balances	120	60
			Profit on revaluation	12	6
	132	66		132	66

(c)

Statement of Financial Position at 31 October 2011 following revaluation

	$000	$000
Non-current assets		
Property		150
Plant and machinery		51
		201
Current assets		
Inventory	17	
Trade receivables	28	
Bank account	1	
	46	
Current liabilities		
Trade payables	22	24
		225
Capital accounts		
– Ann	132	
– John	66	198
Current accounts		
– Ann	17	
– John	10	27
		225

Exercise 2. Tom and Tilly

(a)

Journal entries	Dr $	Cr $
Freehold premises	25 000	
Fixtures and fittings		3 000
Office equipment		2 000
Inventory		3 000
Debtors Control		1 000
Revaluation account		16 000
Revaluation of assets at 1 September 2011 as agreed by partners.		
Revaluation account	16 000	
Tom Capital account		8 000
Tilly Capital account		8 000
Apportionment of profit on revaluation of assets to partners in profit-sharing ratios		

(b)

Tom and Tilly
Statement of Financial Position as at 1 September 2011

	$	$	$
Non-current assets at net book values			
Freehold premises			65 000
Fixtures and fittings			15 000
Office equipment			5 000
			85 000
Current liabilities			
Inventory		14 000	
Trade receivables		3 000	

	$	$	$
Bank		6 000	
		23 000	
Current liabilities			
Trade payables		3 000	20 000
			105 000
Capital accounts			
Tom			56 000
Tilly			49 000
			105 000

Exercise 3. Vera and Ken

(a) Value of net assets

	$
Premises	140 000
Fixtures and fittings	65 000
Motor vehicles	35 000
Office equipment	15 000
Inventory	6 500
Trade receivables	11 800
Bank	3 620
	276 920
Less	
Trade payables	5 830
Net asset value	271 090

Value of Goodwill: $(300 000 − 271 090)
= $28 910

Exercise 5

(b) Amounts to be credited to Capital accounts for Goodwill

Vera ($\frac{1}{2}$ of $28 910):	$14 455
Ken ($\frac{1}{2}$ of $28 910):	$14 455

Exercise 4. Punch and Judy

(a)

	Old profit-sharing ratios	New profit-sharing ratios	Capital accounts
	$	$	$
Punch	12 000	10 800	1200 credit
Judy	6 000	7 200	1200 debit
	18 000	18 000	

(b)

Capital accounts							
		Punch	Judy			Punch	Judy
2011		$	$	2011		$	$
Oct 1	Punch-Capital		1 200				
Oct 1	Balance b/f	36 000	14 000				
	Balance c/d	37 200	12 800		Judy-Capital	1 200	
		37 200	14 000			37 200	14 000
				Oct 1	Balance b/d	37 200	12 800

Hook, Line and Sinker
Income Statement and Appropriation
Account for the year ended 31 December 2011

						$
Sales						129 500
Less Cost of sales						66 500
Gross profit carried down						63 000

	6 months to 30 June 2011		6 months to 31 December 2011		Year to 31 December 2011	
	$	$	$	$	$	$
Gross profit brought down		31 500		31 500		63 000
Wages	7 000		7 000		14 000	
General expenses	1 750		3 500		5 250	
Interest on loan	200		400		600	
Depreciation	875	9 825	875	11 775	1 750	21 600
Net profit		21 675		19 725		41 400
Salary-Hook			3 000	3 000		3 000
				16 725		38 400

Share of profit:

Hook ($\frac{3}{6}$)	10 838		($\frac{1}{3}$) 5 575		16 413	
Line ($\frac{2}{3}$)	7 225		($\frac{1}{3}$) 5 575		12 800	
Sinker ($\frac{1}{6}$)	3 612	21 675	($\frac{1}{3}$) 5 575	16 725	9 187	38 400

Exercise 6

(a)

Bell, Booker and Candell
Income Statement and Appropriation
Account for the year ended 31 December 2011

						$
Turnover						600 000
Less Cost of sales						330 500
Gross profit carried down						270 000

	8 months to August 2011		4 months to 31 December 2011		Year to 31 December 2011	
	$	$	$	$	$	$
Gross profit brought down		180 000		90 000		270 000
Wages and salaries[1]	76 000		30 000		106 000	
Rent	28 000		14 000		42 000	
Heating and lighting	4 000		2 000		6 000	
Sundry expenses	8 000		4 000		12 000	
Interest on loan-Bell	–		800		800	
Depreciation						
Freehold premises	4 800		2 800		7 600	
Plant & Machinery	12 000		1 800		13 800	
Motor cars	5 000		1 000[2]		6 000	
Office equipment	1 400	139 200	200	56 600	1 600	195 800
Net profit		40 800		33 400		74 200
Interest on capitals						
Bell	6 667		5 444		12 111	
Booker	4 000		3 322		7 322	
Candell	–		1 567		1 567	
	10 667		10 333		21 000	
Salary-Booker	10 000	20 667	6 000	16 333	16 000	37 000
		20 133		17 067		37 200
Profit:						
Bell ($\frac{2}{3}$)	13 422		($\frac{2}{5}$) 6 827		20 249	
Booker ($\frac{1}{3}$)	6 711		($\frac{2}{5}$) 6 827		13 538	
Candell	–	20 133	($\frac{1}{5}$) 3 413	17 067	3 413	37 200

1. Wages and salaries: Paid $106 000, less paid to Candell for 8 months $16 000 = $90 000

                      January to August ($\frac{2}{3}$ × $90 000 + $16 000) = $76 000

                      September to December $30 000

2. Depreciation of motor cars September to December: $(5000 + 7000) \times 25\% \times \frac{4}{12} = \$1000$

(b)

Partners' Capital accounts

2011		Bell $	Booker $	2011		Bell $	Booker $
Aug 31	Balance c/d	187 333	103 667	Jan 1	Balance b/d	100 000	60 000
				Aug 31	Profit on revaluation[3]	47 333	23 667
					Goodwill	40 000	20 000
		187 333	103 667			187 333	103 667

3. Profit on revaluation: $(210 000 + 27 000 + 5000 + 6000) - $(135 000 + 30 000 + 5 000 + 7000) = $71 000

Partners' Capital accounts

2011		Bell $	Booker $	Candell $	2011		Bell $	Booker $	Candell $
Sep 1	Goodwill[4]		4 000	12 000	Sep 1	Blance b/d	187 333	103 667	–
	Loan a/c	20 000				Bank			50 000
Dec 31	Balance c/d	183 333	99 667	45 000		Motor cars			7 000
						Goodwill[4]	16 000		
		203 333	103 667	57 000			203 333	103 667	57 000
					2012				
					Jan 1	Balance b/d	183 333	99 667	45 000

4. Goodwill: Bell $(\frac{2}{5})$ $24 000 (reduction of $16 000); Booker $(\frac{2}{5})$ $24 000 (increase of $4 000); Candell entitled to $(\frac{1}{5})$ ($12 000).

Partners' Current accounts

2011		Bell $	Booker $	Candell $	2011		Bell $	Booker $	Candell $
Dec 31	Drawings	30 000	40 000	4 000	Jan 1	Blance b/d	16 000	12 000	
	Balance c/d	19 160	8 860	980	Dec 31	Int. on caps	12 111	7 322	1 567
						Int. on Loan	800		
						Salary		16 000	
						Profit	20 249	13 538	3 413
		49 160	48 860	4 980			49 160	48 860	4 980
					2012				
					Jan 1	Balance b/d	19 160	8 860	980

Exercise 7

(a)

	Wilfrid, Hide and Wyte Income Statement and Appropriation Account for the year ended 30 June 2012			
	6 months ended 31 Dec 2011		6 months ended 30 June 2012	
	$	$	$	$
Gross profit		93 500		93 500
Wages	45 500		45 500	
Rent	6 000		6 000	
Electricity	4 200		4 200	
Interest on loan	–		3 750	
Sundry expenses	4 500	60 200	4 500	63 950
Net profit		33 300		29 550
Interest on capital: Wilfrid	4 000		–	
Hide	2 500		1 650†	
Wyte	1 500	8 000	325†	1 975
		25 300		27 575
Share of profit Wilfrid $\frac{3}{6}$	12 650		–	
Hide $\frac{2}{6}$	8 433		$\frac{1}{2}$ 13 788	
Wyte $\frac{1}{6}$	4 217	25 300	$\frac{1}{2}$ 13 787	27 575

† $33 000 × 10% × 1/2 = 1650
† $6 500 × 10% × 1/2 = 325

(b)

	Wilfrid	Hide	Wyte			Wilfrid	Hide	Wyte
2011	$	$	$	2011		$	$	$
Dec 31 Goodwill		10 000	20 000	Jul 1 Blance b/d		80 000	50 000	30 000
Revaluation of assets	10 500	7 000	3 500	Dec 31 Goodwill		30 000		
Loan a/c	75 000			Current a/c		5 650		
Bank	30 150							
2012								
Jun 30 Balance c/d		33 000	6 500					
	115 650	50 000	30 000			115 650	50 000	30 000
				2012				
				Jul 1 Balance b/d			33 000	6 500

Partners' Capital accounts

Partners' Current accounts

	Wilfrid	Hide	Wyte			Wilfrid	Hide	Wyte
2011	$	$	$	**2011**		$	$	$
Dec 31 Drawings	23 000			Jul 1 Blance b/d		12 000	3 000	4 000
Capital a/c	5 650			Dec 31 Interest		4 000		
				Profit		12 650		
2012								
Jun 30 Drawings		28 000	18 000	**2012**				
Balance c/d		1 371	5 829	Jun 30 Interest			4 150	1 825
				Profit			22 221	18 004
	28 650	29 371	23 829			28 650	29 371	23 829
				2012				
				Jul 1 Balance b/d			1 371	5 829

Some examination questions will combine the revaluation of assets with the introduction of a new partner. In this case, work through the revaluation account, transferring any profit or loss on revaluation to the old partners in their old profit sharing ratios. Then introduce the new partner and adjust the capital accounts for goodwill in line with section 22.7.

Exercise 8. Raul and Samir

Realisation account

	$000		$000
Property (book value)	80	Bank - sale of property	106
Motor vehicles (book value)	20	Samir's capital account	
Inventory (book value)	19	value of car taken	7
Trade receivables		Bank – sale of vehicles	9
(book value)	16	Bank – sale of inventory	18
Bank – pay'ts to trade		Bank – from trade	
payables	10	receivables	13
		Trade payables	
Bank – expenses of sale	3	(book value)	10
Profit on realisation			
– Raul	10		
– Samir	5		
	163		163

Capital accounts

	Raul $000	Samir $000		Raul $000	Samir $000
Vehicle taken	7	–	Opening balances	60	55
Current account	–	4	Current accounts	10	–
Bank	73	56	Profit on realisation	10	5
	80	60		80	60

Bank account

	$000		$000
Sale of property	106	Opening balance	4
Sale of vehicles	9	Trade payables	10
Sale of inventory	18	Expenses of sale	3
From trade receivables	13	Capital account – Raul	73
		Capital account – Samir	56
	146		146

Multiple-choice questions

   1. D   **2.** A   **3.** D   **4.** B   **5.** A

Chapter 23

Exercise 1. Seesaw Ltd
(a) Non-cumulative preference shares

Year	2006 $	2007 $	2008 $	2009 $	2010 $	2011 $
Profit	10 000	5 000	7 000	4 000	7 000	12 000
Preference dividend paid	6 000	5 000	6 000	4 000	6 000	6 000
Profit left for ordinary share-holders	4 000	nil	1 000	nil	1 000	6 000
Maximum ordinary dividend payable	4%	–	1%	–	1%	6%

(b)

Year	2006 $	2007 $	2008 $	2009 $	2010 $	2011 $
Profit	10 000	5 000	7 000	4 000	7 000	12 000
Preference dividend for year	6 000	5 000	6 000	4 000	6 000	6 000
Arrears of dividend carried forward	–	–	1 000	–	1 000	1 000
Profit left for ordinary share-holders	4 000	nil	nil	nil	nil	5 000
Maximum ordinary dividend payable	4%	–	–	–	–	5%

Exercise 2. Premium Shares Ltd

Journal	$	$
Bank	120 000	
10% Preference Share Capital		100 000
Share Premium account		20 000
The issue of 100 000 10% preference shares of $1 at $1.20 per share.		

Exercise 3

Journal	$	$
Freehold Premises at Cost	20 000	
Provision for Depreciation of Freehold Premises	18 000	
Freehold Premises Revaluation Reserve		38 000
Revaluation of freehold premises from net book value of $42 000 to $80 000		

Exercise 4. Gracenote Ltd

Total of ordinary share capital and reserves:
$(200 000 + 50 000 + 100 000 – 40 000) = $310 000$

$$\text{Value of 100 ordinary shares} = \frac{\$310\,000}{200\,000} = \$1.55$$

Exercise 5
(a)

Molly Coddle Ltd
Income Statement
for the year ended 30 April 2011

	$000	$000
Revenue		300
Opening inventories	20	
Purchases	113	
	133	
Closing inventories	(31)	
Cost of sales		(102)
Gross profit		198
Overheads:		
Sales office salaries	57	
Selling expenses	39	
General office wages	32	
Other general expenses	35	
Depreciation		
– Warehouse machinery	8	
– Office machinery	10	(181)
PROFIT FOR THE YEAR ATTRIBUTABLE TO EQUITY HOLDERS		17

(b)

Molly Coddle Ltd
Statement of Changes in Equity for the year ended 30 April 2011

	Share capital $000	Share Premium $000	General Reserve $000	Retained Earnings $000	Total Equity $000
Balance at 30 April 2010	60	15	25	8	108
Profit attributable to equity holders				17	17
Transfer to general reserve			10	(10)	–
Balance at 30 April 2011	60	15	35	15	125

(c)

Molly Coddle Ltd Statement of Financial Position at 30 April 2011			
	$000	$000	$000
Assets			
Non-current assets	Cost	Dep'n	NBV
Warehouse machinery	70	38	32
Office machinery	42	30	12
	112	68	44
Current assets			
Inventories			31
Trade receivables			38
Cash and cash equivalents			28
			97
Total assets			141
Equity and Liabilities			
Capital and reserves			
Share capital			60
Share premium			15
General reserve			35
Retained earnings			15
			125
Non-current liabilities			
10 % Debentures 2017/2018			5
Current liabilities			
Trade payables			11
Total liabilities			141

Exercise 6

(a)

Shillyshally Ltd Income Statement for the year ended 30 June 2011		
	$000	$000
Revenue		1000
Opening inventories	46	
Purchases	630	
	676	
Closing inventories	(38)	
Cost of sales		(638)
Gross profit		362
Overheads:		
Sales office salaries	79	
Administration wages	36	
Delivery vehicle expenses (38 + 2)	40	
Advertising (34 – 6)	28	
Office expenses (24 + 3)	27	
Depreciation		
– Delivery vehicles	13	
– Office machinery	7	
		(230)
PROFIT FROM OPERATIONS		132
Finance costs (6 + 6)		(12)
PROFIT BEFORE TAX		120

	$000	$000
Tax		(16)
PROFIT FOR THE YEAR ATTRIBUTABLE TO EQUITY HOLDERS		104

(b)

Shillyshally Ltd Statement of Changes in Equity for the year ended 30 June 2011				
	Share capital $000	General Reserve $000	Retained Earnings $000	Total Equity $000
Balance at 30 April 2010	900	50	7	957
Profit attributable to equity holders			104	104
Transfer to general reserve		50	(50)	–
Dividends paid			(7)	(7)
Balance at 30 April 2011	900	100	54	1054

(c)

Shillyshally Ltd Statement of Financial Position at 30 June 2011			
	$000	$000	$000
Assets			
Non-current assets	Cost	Dep'n	NBV
Freehold premises	1200	–	1200
Delivery vehicles	80	41	39
Office machinery	70	28	42
	1350	69	1281
Current assets			
Inventories			38
Trade receivables			82
Other receivables			6
Cash and cash equivalents			67
			193
Total assets			1474
Equity and Liabilities			
Capital and reserves			
Ordinary Share capital			800
8% Preference shares			100
General reserve			100
Revaluation reserve (200 + 60)			260
Retained earnings			54
			1314
Non-current liabilities			
12 % Debentures 2019/2020			100
Current liabilities			
Trade payables			33
Other payables (2 + 3)			5
Debenture interest			6
Taxation			16
			60
Total liabilities			1474

Notes to the answer

1. The Preference shares are non-redeemable. Therefore they are part of the equity.
2. The recommended final dividend on the ordinary shares is shown by way of a note to the accounts.
3. Similarly, the unpaid preference dividend is not included in the accounts and is shown by way of a note.
4. However, the debentures are a long term loan and the unpaid interest on them is treated as an accrual.
5. Amounts prepaid are shown as other receivables.
6. Similarly, the amounts owing are shown as other payables.

Multiple-choice questions

| 1. C | 2. B | 3. B | 4. A | 5. C |
| 6. A | 7. A | 8. D | 9. D | |

Chapter 24

Exercise 1

Contraflo Ltd
Statement of Cash Flow for the year ended 31 December 2011

Cash flow from operating activities

	$000
Profit from operations (before tax and interest)	94

Adjustments for:	
Depreciation charge for the year	50
Profit less losses on sale on non-current assets	(10)
Decrease in inventories (100 – 85)	15
Increase in trade receivables (40 – 52)	(12)
Increase in trade payables (60 – 73)	(13)
Cash (used in)/from operations	150
Interest paid (during the year)	(7)
Tax paid (during the year) from workings	(36)
Net cash (used in)/from operating activities	107

Cash flows from investing activities:	$000	
Purchase of non – current assets	(160)	
Proceeds from the sale of non – current assets	55	
Net cash (used in)/from investing activities		(105)

Cash flows from financing activities:		
Proceeds form issue of share capital	55	
Repayment of debentures	(30)	
Dividends paid	(46)	
Net cash (used in)/from financing activities		(21)
Net increase/(decrease) in cash and cash equivalents		(19)
Cash and cash equivalents at the beginning of the year		55
Cash and cash equivalents at the end of the year		36

Workings
1. Fixed assets

Freehold buildings at cost	$000	Freehold building disposal	$000
At 31 December 2010	400	Cost	(36)
Disposal	(36)	Proceeds	50
At 31 December 2011	364	Profit on disposal	14

Plant and machinery at cost	$000	Plant and machinery depreciation	$000	Disposal	$000	Taxation	$000
At 31 December 2010	80	At 31 December 2010	35	Cost	20	At 31 December 2010	39
Disposals	(20)	On disposals	(16)	Depreciation	(16)	From Inc. Stat.	40
Additions (balancing figure)	90	Provided in year (balancing figure)	20	Proceeds	(1)	At 31 December 2011	(43)
At 31 December 2011	150	At December 2010	39	Loss on disposal	3 (3)	Tax paid	36

Motor vehicles at cost	$000	Motor vehicles depreciation	$000	Disposal	$000
At 31 December 2010	120	At 31 December 2010	90	Cost	30
Disposals	(30)	On disposals	(25)	Depreciation	(25)
Additions (balancing figure)	70	Provided in year (balancing figure)	30	Proceeds	(4)
At 31 December 2011	160	At 31 December 2011	95	Loss on disposal	1 (1)

Exercise 2

Horsa Ltd
Statement of Financial Position at 31 July 2011

	Cost $000	Depn $000	NBV $000
Non-current assets			
Freehold premises	300	142	158
Plant & Machinery	143	117	26
	1684	460	184
Current Assets			
Inventory (36 + 4)		40	
Trade receivables (79 +19)		98	
Cash and cash equivalents		112	
		250	
Current liabilities			
Trade payables (43 + 6)	49		
Tax	25	74	176
Non – current liability			
10% Debentures 2017/18 (50 – 20)			(30)
			330
Equity			
Share capital (150 + 20)			170
Share premium (20 + 20)			40
General reserve (40 + 30)			70
Retained earnings			50
			330

Workings

Calculation of the figure for retained earnings	$000
Retained earnings at start of year	56
Profit for the year	39
	95
Transfer to reserves	(30)
Dividends paid	(15)
Retained earnings	50

Exercise 3

Janine
Reconciliation of profit from operations to net cash flow from operating activities for the year ended 31 October 2011

	$000
Net profit for the year before interest	21
Adjustments for:	
Depreciation charge for the year	5
Profit on sale on non-current assets	(1)
Increase in inventories	(5)
Decrease in trade receivables	3
Decrease in trade payables	(8)
Cash (used in)/from operations	15
Interest paid (during the year)	(1)
Net cash (used in)/from operating activities	14

Workings

The net profit for the year before interest is:

	$000
Net profit from the Income Statement extract	25
Less – Depreciation	(5)
Add – Profit on disposal	1
Net profit for the year before interest	21

The profit on the revaluation of land is not included as this increases the value of the land and is included in Janine's capital on the Statement of Financial Position.

The calculation of loss on the sale of the plant and machinery and the purchase of new machinery is as follows:

Plant and Machinery at cost account

	$000		$000
Opening balance	39	Closing balance	55
Bank – purchases	22	Asset disposal	6
	61		61

Plant and Machinery Accumulated depreciation account

	$000		$000
Asset disposal account	1	Opening balance	21
Closing balance	25	Charge for the year	5
	26		26

Asset disposal account

	$000		$000
Cost of plant scrapped	6	Depreciation	1
Profit on disposal	1	Sale proceeds	6
	7		7

Janine
Statement of Cash Flows for the year ended 31 October 2011

		$000
Net cash (used in)/from operating activities		14
Cash flows from investing activities:	$000	
Purchase of non – current assets (Plant)	(22)	
Sale of non – current assets	6	
Net cash (used in)/from investing activities		(16)
Cash flows from financing activities:		
Capital introduced	10	
New loan	8	
Drawings	(21)	
Net cash (used in)/from financing activities		(3)
Net increase/(decrease) in cash and cash equivalents		(5)
Cash and cash equivalents at the beginning of the year		3
Cash and cash equivalents at the end of the year		(2)

The possible reasons why Janine has an overdraft are:

- The purchases of non – current assets $22 000 have been financed from the loan ($8000), capital introduced ($10 000) and the proceeds of the sale of non-current assets ($6000).

- The high drawings figure ($21 000) is higher than the cash generated from operations. This could be as a result of the mistaken belief that the revaluation of the land is a cash profit rather than a book adjustment.

- Although Janine has reduced her trade receivables she has increased her inventory and reduced her trade payables. The net effect of this has been to reduce the cash in the business.

- All these factors combined have resulted in more cash leaving the business than coming in.

Multiple-choice questions
1. A   2. C   3. D   4. C   5. C   6. A

Chapter 25

Exercise 1. Otago (Bonus Offers) Ltd

	$000
Non-current assets	1400
Net current assets	350
	1750
Equity	
Ordinary shares of $1	1400
Share Premium	200
General Reserve	100
Retained earnings	50
	1750

Note. The Share Premium account could have been used with $400 000 of the Revaluation Reserve, but the Share Premium account can be used for purposes not available to the Revaluation Reserve. (See chapter 23)

Exercise 2. Bonarite Ltd

(a)

	$000
Net assets	2000
Equity	
Share capital and reserves	
Ordinary shares of $1	1800
General reserve	120
Retained earnings	80
	2000

(b)

	$000
Net assets	2750
Equity	
Share capital and reserves	
Ordinary shares of $1	2400
Share premium	150
General Reserve	120
Retained earnings	80
	2750

Exercise 3. Choppers Ltd

(a)

Statement of Financial Position	
	$000
Non-current assets	1300
Net current assets	550
	1850
Equity	
Ordinary shares of $1	1150
Share premium	350
General reserve	200
Retained earnings	150
	1850

(b)

Statement of Financial Position	
	$000
Non-current assets	1300
Net current assets	250
	1550
Equity	
Ordinary shares of $1	1000
Share premium	200
Capital Redemption Reserve	300
Retained earnings	50
	1550

Exercise 4. Twist Ltd

(a)

Statement of Financial Position	
	$000
Non-current assets	2000
Net current assets (800 – 300)	500
	2500
Equity	
Ordinary shares of $1	2000
Share Premium account	200
Capital Redemption Reserve	250
Retained earnings[1]	50
	2500

1. The balance on the Retained earnings has been reduced by the transfer of $250 000 to Capital Redemption Reserve and a debit of $50 000 for the premium paid on redemption.

(b)

Statement of Financial Position	
	$000
Non-current assets	2000
Net current assets[1]	720
	2720
Equity	
Ordinary shares of $1[2]	2200
Share Premium account[3]	200
Capital Redemption Reserve[4]	50
Retained earnings[5]	270
	2720

1. Net current asset have been increased by the amount received on the new issue ($220 000) but reduced by the cost of redeeming the preference shares ($300 000).
2. Ordinary share capital has been increased by the nominal value of the new ordinary shares.
3. The Share Premium account has been credited with $20 000 premium received on the new issue and debited with $20 000 (the maximum amount permissible) of the premium paid on the redemption.
4. A Capital Redemption Reserve of $50 000 must be created to cover the difference between the nominal value of the redeemed shares and the nominal value of the new issue.
5. The Retained earnings have been reduced by the transfer to Capital Redemption Reserve and the amount of the premium on redemption that was not covered by the premium on the new issue.

(c)

Statement of Financial Position	
	$000
Non-current assets	2000.0
Net current assets[1]	815.5
	2812.5
Equity	
Ordinary shares of $1[2]	2250.0
Share Premium account[3]	212.5
Retained earnings[4]	350.0
	2812.5

1. Net current asset have been increased by the proceeds of the new issue ($312 500) but have been reduced by the cost of redeeming the shares ($300 000).
2. Ordinary share capital has been increased by the nominal amount of the new isse.

3. The Share Premium account has been increased by the premium on the new shares ($62 500) and reduced by the premium on the redemption ($50 000), all of which is allowed because it is less than the premium on the new issue.
4. The cost of redeeming the shares has been completely covered by the proceeds of the new issue; it has not been necessary to create a Capital Redemption Reserve, or to charge any of the premium on redemption to the Retained earnings.

Exercise 5

Downsize Ltd	
Statement of Financial Position after capital reduction	
	$000
Non-current assets	
Freehold property	340
Fixtures and fittings	80
Office furniture	70
	490
Net current assets	210
	700
Equity	
1 000 000 ordinary shares of $0.70[1]	700

1. It is important to show the nominal value of the new shares.

Multiple-choice questions
1. C   2. D   3. C   4. D   5. B

Chapter 26

Exercise 1. Hamil Ltd

(a)

Journal		
	$	$
Goodwill	29 000	
Freehold property	70 000	
Plant and machinery	12 000	
Office furniture	4 000	
Inventory	2 500	
Trade receivables	5 500	
Trade payables		3 000
Cash and cash equivalents		20 000
Ordinary share capital		80 000
Share Premium account		20 000
	123 000	123 000

Purchase of Abdul's business for $120 000 and settlement by $20 000 in cash and 80 000 ordinary shares if $1 in Hamil Ltd at $1.25.

(b)

Hamil Ltd
Statement of Financial Position at 30 June 2011
after the acquisition of Abdul's business

	$	$
Non-current assets		
Intangible		
Goodwill		29 000
Tangible		
Freehold property		170 000
Plant and machinery		72 000
Office equipment		14 000
Office furniture		4 000
		289 000
Current assets		
Inventory (10 000 + 2500)	12 500	
Trade receivables (7000 + 5500)	12 500	
Cash and cash equivalents (25 000 – 20 000)	5 000	
	30 000	
Current liabilities		
Trade payables (6000 + 3000)	9 000	21 000
		310 000
Equity		
Ordinary shares (150 000 + 80 000)		230 000
Share premium (20 000 + 20 000)		40 000
Retained earnings		40 000
		$310 000

Exercise 2. Carol

(a) $60\ 000 \times \dfrac{5}{8} = \$37\ 500$

(b) $60\ 000 \times \dfrac{5}{4} = \$75\ 000$

Exercise 3

Digger Ltd
Statement of Financial Position immediately
after the acquisition of Spaid and Shuvell

	$	$
Non-current assets		
Land and buildings (90 000 + 60 000)		150 000
Fixtures and fittings (30 000 + 14 000)		44 000
Office machinery (15 000 + 10 000)		25 000
Goodwill		25 000
		244 000
Current assets		
Inventory (20 000 + 15 000)	35 000	
Trade receivables (5000 + 6000)	11 000	
Cash and cash equivalents (60 000 – 28 000)	32 000	
	78 000	
Current liabilities		
Trade payables (16 000 + 12 000)	28 000	50 000
		294 000
Non-current liability		
8% Debenture (12 000 × 8/10)		15 000
		279 000

	$	$
Equity		
Ordinary shares (200 000 + 60 000[1])		260 000
Share premium (20 000 + 20 000)		15 000
Retained earnings		4 000
		279 000

		$	$
1 Shares issued: Purchase consideration			118 000
Less cash		28 000	
debenture		15 000	43 000
Value of shares			75 000

No of shares at $1.25 per share = 60 000
Share premium 60 000 × $0.25 = $15 000

Exercise 4

Lee & Mick
Realisation account

	$000		$000
Property	50	Trade payables	6
Plant & machinery	20	Bank – cash paid	20
Inventory	8	Ordinary shares	120
Trade receivables	12		
Profit on realisation			
– Lee	28		
– Mick	28		
	146		146

Capital accounts

	$000	$000		$000	$000
	Lee	Mick		Lee	Mick
Bank	6	4	Opening bals	30	30
			Current accounts	8	6
Shares	60	60	Profit on realisation	28	28
	66	64		66	64

Bank account

	$000		$000
From Taykover Ltd	20	Opening balance	2
		Loan	8
		Lee	6
		Mick	4
	20		20

Notice that in this case the partners take the shares in line with their profit sharing ratio. However, because of the difference in their current account balances the split of the remaining cash is not equal.

Multiple-choice questions

1. C   2. D   3. D

Chapter 27

Multiple-choice questions

1. B   **2.** A   **3.** B   **4.** B   **5.** B   **6.** D

Chapter 28

Exercise 1. Najim

(a)

(i) Gross profit percentage	2010	$\dfrac{\text{gross profit}}{\text{sales}} \times 100$ =	$\dfrac{60\,308}{172\,308} \times 100$	= 35%
	2011		$\dfrac{60\,000}{187\,500} \times 100$	= 32%
(ii) Net profit percentage	2010	$\dfrac{\text{net profit}}{\text{sales}} \times 100$ =	$\dfrac{21\,539}{172\,308} \times 100$	= 12.5%
	2011		$\dfrac{27\,322}{187\,500} \times 100$	= 14.57%
(iii) Non-current asset turnover	2010	$\dfrac{\text{sales}}{\text{non-current assets}}$ =	$\dfrac{172\,308}{78\,322}$	= 2.2 times
	2011		$\dfrac{187\,500}{93\,750}$	= 2 times
(iv) Inventory turnover	2010	$\dfrac{\text{cost of sales}}{\text{average inventory}}$ =	$\dfrac{112\,000}{(12\,000 + 16\,000) \div 2}$	= 8 times
	2011		$\dfrac{127\,500}{(16\,000 + 14\,000) \div 2}$	= 8.5 times
(v) Trade receivables collection period	2010	$\dfrac{\text{trade receivables}}{\text{credit sales}} \times 365$ =	$\dfrac{9914}{60\% \text{ of } 172\,308} \times 365$	= 35 days
	2011		$\dfrac{12\,511}{60\% \text{ of } 187\,500} \times 365$	= 40.59 days or 41 days
(vi) Trade payables payment-period	2010	$\dfrac{\text{trade payables}}{\text{credit purchases}} \times 365$ =	$\dfrac{13\,984}{116\,000} \times 365$	= 44 days
	2011		$\dfrac{17\,192}{125\,500} \times 365$	= 50 days
(vii) Current ratio	2010	current assets: current liabilities		= 30\,765 : 13\,984 = 2.2 : 1
	2011			= 33\,696 : 17\,192 = 1.96 : 1
(viii) Liquid ratio (acid test)	2010	current assets – stock: current liabilities		= 14\,765 : 13\,984 = 1.06 : 1
	2011			= 19\,696 : 17\,192 = 1.15 : 1

(b)

(i) Sales have increased by over $15\,000 or nearly 9% but gross profit percentage has decreased from 35% in 2010 to 32% in 2011, a reduction of 3%. This may be due to
- a reduction in selling prices to increase turnover.
- an increase in the cost of sales not passed on to customers.
- sales made at less than the normal mark-up (seasonal sales or disposal of old or damaged stock).
- some stock valued at less than cost because it is old or has deteriorated.
- stock which has been stolen.

Whether or not the gross profit percentage is acceptable depends upon the normal margin expected on sales, but information about this is not given in the question.

(ii) Net profit percentage has improved from 12.5% in 2010 to 14.57% in 2011. This is in spite of a reduction of 3% in the gross profit margin. This has been achieved by tighter control on overhead expenditure, down from $38 769 in 2010 to $32 678 in 2011, a reduction of 15.7% although sales have increased by 8.8%.

(iii) Non-current asset turnover has remained almost steady. Without further information about the nature of the business, it is not possible to comment on this ratio. There has been a considerable increase in the value of non-current assets employed in the business in 2011 and the additional assets would appear to have been brought into use early in the year for the full effect to have been felt.

(iv) Inventory turnovers has increased slightly from 8 times in 2010 to 8.5 times in 2011. The average time that goods remain in stock is 6.5 weeks which may seem reasonable, but as nothing is known about the type of business, further comment is not possible.

(v) Trade receivables collection period has increased by 6 days, from 35 in 2010 to 41 in 2011. This deterioration may be due to one or more of the following factors:
  - more lenient terms for debtors, to promote sales.
  - a deliberate policy to attract customers from competitors.
  - general economic conditions.
  - poor credit control.
  A deterioration in the debtors' ratio incurs the risk of an increase in bad debts as old debts usually become bad. Najim should monitor the situation carefully.

(vi) Trade payables payment period has increased by 6 days, from 44 days in 2010 to 50 days in 2011. While this may help the cash flow at a time when debtors are taking 6 days longer to pay, care must be taken to retain the goodwill of suppliers, otherwise the suppliers may insist that future orders will only be accepted on a cash basis and this would greatly harm Najim's cash flow.

(vii) The current ratio has decreased slightly from 2.2 : 1 in 2010 to 1.96 : 1 in 2011. It remains satisfactory by normal standards.

(viii) The liquid ratio has remained almost steady at 1.06 : 1 in 2010 and 1.15 : 1 in 2011. As 60% of sales are on credit, the very low ratios on which businesses such as supermarkets work are not appropriate for Najim's business and his present ratios may be considered satisfactory.

General comments. There are no indications that the business is not a going concern. Its cash position is positive and there are no bank loans or overdrafts that could cause embarrassment in the near future.

There is no sign of overtrading as stock and debtors are not excessive. Overtrading places businesses at great risk.

Note. Part (b) requires more than a simple repetition of the ratios already calculated in part (a) if marks are to be earned. It is necessary to *compare* the ratios and to recognise *trends* and their significance. Avoid irrelevant comments and repetition. Statements which cannot be supported by information given in the question should be avoided, but *possible* reasons for an improvement or deterioration in a trend may be *suggested*.

Exercise 2. Dunedin Ltd and Wellington Ltd

(a)

(i) Gearing

Dunedin Ltd $\dfrac{600 + 100}{400 + 600 + 100} \times 100 = 63.64\%$

Wellington Ltd $\dfrac{1000 + 750}{2050 + 1000 + 750} \times 100$
$= 46.05\%$

(ii) Interest cover
Dunedin Ltd $\dfrac{300}{60} = 5$ times
Wellington Ltd $\dfrac{420}{120} = 3.5$ times

(iii) Earnings per share
Dunedin Ltd $\dfrac{240 - 6}{200\ 000} = 117$ cents

Wellington Ltd $\dfrac{300-60}{750} = 32$ cents

(iv) Dividend per share

Dunedin Ltd $\dfrac{90}{200} = \$0.45\ (45\%)$

Wellington Ltd $\dfrac{150}{1500} = \$0.10\ (5\%)$

(v) Dividend cover

Dunedin Ltd $\dfrac{240-6}{90} = 2.6$ times

Wellington Ltd $\dfrac{300-60}{150} = 1.6$ times

(vi) Price earnings ratio

Dunedin Ltd $\dfrac{2.70}{1.17} = 2.31$ times

Wellington Ltd $\dfrac{3.60}{0.32} = 11.25$ times

(vii) Dividend yield

Dunedin Ltd $\dfrac{0.45}{2.70} \times 100 = 16.67\%$

Wellington Ltd $\dfrac{0.20}{3.60} \times 100 = 5.56\%$

(b)

(i) Gearing. Dunedin is highly geared (63.64%) and Wellington is low geared (46.05%). This makes Dunedin a little more risky from the point of view of shareholders and creditors, but neither company is far from neutral gearing (50%) and they are only separated by about 17½%.

(ii) Interest cover. Dunedin's interest is covered 5 times by the operating profit but Wellington's is only covered 3½ times. Both ratios are satisfactory. Dunedin's ordinary shareholders are at less at risk of having their dividend curtailed if profits fall than Wellington's shareholders.

(iii) Earnings per share. Dunedin's EPS is much higher at 117 cents than Wellington's at 32 cents. This is mainly due to Wellington having issued more shares than Dunedin

(3.75 times). This suggests that Dunedin is potentially the better company for dividend/capital growth.

(iv) Dividend per share. Dunedin is paying an ordinary dividend of $0.45 per $1 share, equal to 45% of the nominal value of the shares. Wellington is paying $0.10 per $2 share, equal to 5% of the nominal value of its shares. This makes Dunedin's shares seem the more attractive, but the yield on the amount invested is a better ratio.

(v) Dividend cover. Dunedin Ltd's dividend cover is 2.7 times, which is generally considered to be satisfactory. Wellington Ltd's dividend is covered 1.6 times and may be at risk if profits decline in the future.

(vi) Price earnings ratio. Dunedin Ltd's PER is 2.31 times and Wellington Ltd's PER is 11.25 times. This seems strange when the dividend covers of the two companies are compared. The share prices may be influenced by factors not mentioned in the question. Wellington Ltd's future trading prospects may be affected by various favourable factos not mentioned in the question.

(vii) Dividend yield. Dunedin's dividend yield based on the current market price is 16.67% compared with the yield of 5.56% on Wellington's shares. This makes Dunedin's shares more attractive from an income-earning view point. However, it should be considered along with the potential for capital growth and, as has already been stated, Dunedin's earnings per share has permitted adequate profits to be retained for capital growth especially if a conservative dividend policy is continued in future.

Conclusion. Every ratio except gearing is favourable to Dunedin Ltd and even the gearing should not give rise to serious concern. Although Dunedin's dividend policy is more conservative than Wellington's, it still offers a better return on capital invested.

Exercise 3

(a)

Patience Income Statement for the year ended 31 December 2011			
			$
Step 6	Revenue (495 000 × 100/65)		761 538
	Cost of sales		
Step 2	Inventory at 1 Jan 2011	(54 000 × 5/6)	45 000
Step 5	Purchases	*(balancing figure)*	504 000
Step 4		*(balancing figure)*	549 000
Step 1	Inventory at 31 Dec 2011 (given)		54 000
Step 3		*(65% of sales)*	495 000
Step 7	Gross profit	*(35% of 761 538)*	266 538
Step 9	Expenses	*(balancing figure)*	99 000
Step 8	Net profit	*(22% of 761 538)*	167 538

Statement of Financial Position at 31 December 2011				
			$	$
Step 10	Non-current assets (761 538 ÷ 4)			190 385
	Current assets			
Step 11	Inventory		54 000	
Step 12	Trade receivables	(761 538 × 34/365)	70 938	
Step 16	Bank	*(balancing figure)*	20 050	
Step 15		*(balancing figure)*	144 988	
Step 13	Trade payables	(504 000 × 42/365)	57 995	
Step 14				86 993
Step 17				277 378
Step 22	Capital at 1 Jan 2011 *(balancing figure)*			249 840
Step 18	Net profit			167 538
Step 21		*(balancing figure)*		417 378
Step 19	Drawings	*(given)*		140 000
Step 20		*(from step 17)*		277 378

(b) Virtue and Patience

 (i) Virtue's inventory turnover is 12 compared with 10 for Patience. Virtue earns his profit at a faster rate than Patience. His cash flow is improved by the higher stockturn.

(ii) Virtue's gross profit margin of 40% is more than Patience's 35% which indicates that he earns a higher margin on his sales. He may have cheaper sources of supply than Patience, or Patience's mark up may be lower than Virtue's. Without more information about their individual circumstances, further comment is not possible.

(iii) Virtue's net profit margin (20%) is 2% lower than Patience's (22%). This shows that Patience's overheads are comparatively lower than Virtue's. Not all overheads are easily controllable, and Virtue may have to pay higher rent, for example, because of the situation or size of his premises.

(iv) Virtue's turnover is 5 times his non-current assets but Patience's turnover is only 4 times. Virtue is using his non-current assets more efficiently and making them more profitable.

 (v) Virtue's Trade receivables collection period is 31 days, which is 3 days less than that of Patience (34 days). This indicates that Virtue controls his debtors more efficiently and his cash flow is improved as a result.

(vi) Virtue pays his creditors 6 days earlier than Patience pays hers (36 days compared to 42 days). No information is provided regarding the credit terms each receives. If Virtue obtains his goods more cheaply than Patience, as suggested in (ii), the period of credit he is allowed may be less than Patience receives. On the other hand, if Virtue is not taking the full period of credit he is allowed, he is not managing his cash flow to the best advantage.

Conclusion. With the exception of the net profit margin and the possible exception of his payment of creditors, Virtue appears to be running his business more efficiently than Patience.

Multiple-choice questions

1. D	2. B	3. C	4. D	5. C
6. D	7. B	8. A		

Chapter 29

Exercise 1. See §29.2
Exercise 2. See §29.3

Multiple choice questions

1. C	2. B	3. C	4. C

Chapter 30

Exercise 1. Teepops Ltd

(a)

Expense	Basis	Total $000	Machining $000	Painting $000	Assembly $000	Packing $000
Indirect labour	actual	125	51	32	28	14
Factory: Rent	floor area	90	45	18	18	9
Heating & lighting	floor area	70	35	14	14	7
Maintenance	floor area	30	15	6	6	3
Insurance	floor area	20	10	4	4	2
Plant & machinery:						
Depreciation	cost	80	45	20	5	10
Repairs	cost	32	18	8	2	4
Insurance	cost	16	9	4	1	2
Total overhead		463	228	106	78	51

(b)

Expense	Basis	Total $000	Machining $000	Painting $000	Assembly $000	Packing $000
Direct materials	allocation	117	80	20	5	12
Direct labour	allocation	323	136	74	68	45
Overhead	apportioned	463	228	106	78	51
Total cost		903	444	200	151	108

Exercise 2. Luvlibix Foods

	Mixing $000	Bakery $000	Packaging $000	Stores $000	Canteen $000
Overheads	165.00	124.00	87.00	80.00	90.00
Re-apportion stores	54.55	14.54	3.64	(80.00)	7.27
Re-apportion canteen	32.42	43.23	21.62	–	(97.27)
	251.97	181.77	112.26	–	–

Exercise 3. Trimble Ltd

(a) No. of direct labour hours required:
Dimbles: 5000 × 1.3 = 6500

$$\text{Gimbles: } 7000 \times 0.7 = \frac{4900}{11\ 400}$$

$$\text{OAR} = \frac{\$129\ 276}{11\ 400} = \$11.34 \text{ per hour}$$

(i) OAR per unit: Dimble $11.34 × 1.3
= $14.742 per unit

(ii) OAR per unit: Gimble $11.34 × 0.7
= $7.938 per unit

(b) Overhead absorbed:

	$
Dimbles 5000 × $14.742 =	73 710
Gimbles 7000 × $7.938 =	55 566
Total overhead	129 276

Exercise 4. Makeit-by-Robot Ltd

(a) Total number of machine hours in a 13 week
period = 10 × 7 × 6 × 13 = 5460

$$\text{Machine hour OAR} = \frac{\$141\ 960}{5460} = \$26$$

(b) Each unit requires $\dfrac{5460}{1200}$ machine hours to make

= 4.55 machine hours.

Therefore each unit absorbs $26 × 4.55, or $118.30 overhead.

(Proof: $118.30 × 1200 = $141 960)

Exercise 5. Egbert Ltd

(a) OARs

Moulding   Direct labour hourly rate $\dfrac{\$301\ 875}{34\ 500}$
= $8.75

Machining   Machine hourly rate $\dfrac{\$115\ 200}{18\ 000}$
= $6.40

Painting   Direct labour hourly rate $\dfrac{\$47\ 250}{9000}$
= $5.25

(b) Overhead absorbed per unit

	Sovrin $		Ginny $
Moulding (4 × $8.75)	35.00	(3½ × $8.75)	30.625
Machining (2 × $6.40)	12.80	(2 × $6.40)	12.800
Painting (1 × $5.25)	5.25	(1 × $5.25)	5.250
	53.05		48.675

(c) Total overhead recovery

	Sovrin $		Ginny $	Total $
Moulding				
(6000 × $35.00)	210 000	(3000 × $30.625)	91 875	301 875
Machining				
(6000 × $12.80)	76 800	(3000 × $12.800)	38 400	115 200
Painting				
(6000 × $5.25)	31 500	(3000 × $5.250)	15 750	47 250
	318 300		146 025	464 325

(d) Total cost per unit

	Sovrin $	Ginny $
Direct material	102.00	85.000
Direct labour	190.00	151.000
Overhead	53.05	48.675
	345.05	284.675

Exercise 6. Upandown Ltd

	3 months to 31 March	3 months to 30 June	3 months to 30 September	3 months to 31 December
OAR	$124	$128	$130	$131
Overhead recovered	$111 600	$134 400	$143 000	$128 380
Actual overhead	$128 000	$125 000	$129 000	$132 000
(Under-)/ over-recovery	($16 400)	$9 400	$13 500	($4 420)

Multiple-choice questions

   1. B   2. D   3. A

Chapter 31

Exercise 1. Luvlibrek

	$
Direct materials	398 000
Direct labour	996 000
Overheads	1 687 250
	3 081 250

Cost per unit of 1000 packets = $\dfrac{\$3\ 081\ 250}{425}$ = $7250

Exercise 2. Geoffrey Pannell

		$
Labour:	Geoffrey (200 × $100)	20 000
	Susan (100 × $60)	6 000
	Overhead recovery (300 × $40)	12 000
		38 000

Exercise 3. Wipup Ltd

No. of rolls = 6000 (1000 × 6)

No. of labour hours = 10 (6000/[100 × 6])

(a)

	$
Raw materials (6000 × $0.08)	480
Labour (10 × $6)	60
Setting up machinery	30
Machine hour overhead recovery	93.50
Cost of batch of 1000 rolls	663.50

(b) Cost of one roll: 663.50/6000 = $0.1106

Multiple-choice questions
   1. B   2. A

Chapter 32

Exercise 1. The Sitrah Processing Company

Process I			
	$000		$000
Direct material	10 000	Output transferred	
Direct labour	400	to process II	11 300
Overhead	900		
	11 300		11 300

Process II			
	$000		$000
Material transferred		Output transferred	
from process I	11 300	to process III	16 514
Added material	4 000		
Direct labour	350		
Overhead	864		
	16 514		16 514

Process III			
	$000		$000
Material transferred		Output transferred	
from process II	16 514	to finished stock	24 212
Added material	7 000		
Direct labour	275		
Overhead	423		
	24 212		24 212

(c) Cost per unit = $12.106 (24 212/2000)

Exercise 2
Total processing costs to separation:
$(21 000 + 11 000 + 23 000) = $55 000

(a) Joint cost of 3400 litres of Animo:

$$\$55\,000 \times \frac{3400}{8500} = \$22\,000.$$

Cost to completion of 1 litre of Animo:

$$\$\frac{22\,000 + 4624}{3400} = \$7.831$$

(b) Joint cost of 5100 litres of Lactino:

$$\$55\,000 \times \frac{5100}{8500} = \$33\,000.$$

Cost to completion of 1 litre of Lactino:

$$\$\frac{33\,000 + 13\,362}{5100} = \$9.091$$

Exercise 3. Okara Quality Carpets Ltd

Process 1 (2000 units)			
	$		$
Material		Sale of scrap	1 630
(2000 × 4 × $12)	96 000	Production transferred	
Labour		to process 2	394 370
(2000 × 4 × $14)	84 000		
Overhead			
(6000 × $36)	216 000		
	396 000		396 000

Process 2 (1200 complete units; 800 incomplete units)			
	$		$
Material from		Finished goods	474 372
process 1	394 370		
Added materials			
(9750 + 4875)	14 625		
Labour			
(66 000 + 22 000)	88 000		
Overhead			
(162 000 + 54 000)	216 000	Work in progress c/d	238 623
	712 995		712 995

Note	Finished goods		Work in progress
	$		$
Material from			
process 1			
($394 370 × $\frac{1200}{2000}$)	236 622	($394 370 × $\frac{800}{2000}$)	157 748
Added material		(800 × 2.5 ×	
(1200 × 2.5 × $3.25)	9 750	0.75 × $3.25)	4 875
Labour			
(1200 × 5 × $11)	66 000	(800 × 5 × 0.5 × $11)	22 000
Overhead			
(1200 × 5 × $27)	162 000	(800 × 5 × 0.5 × $27)	54 000
	474 372		238 623

Multiple-choice questions
   1. B   2. B   3. B

Chapter 33

Exercise 1
(i) Contribution from 1 unit = $146 250 ÷ 3000
      = $48.75.
      Contribution from 3000 units = $(48.75 × 3000)
      = $146 250.

Profit from 3000 units = $(146 250 – 82 000)
= $64 250

(ii) Contribution from 4000 units = $(48.75 × 4000)
= $195 000.
Profit from 4000 units = $(195 000 – 82 000)
= $113 000

(iii) Contribution from 1200 units = $(48.75 × 1200)
= $58 500.
Loss from 1200 units = $(82 000 – 58 500)
= $23 500

Exercise 2. Product Q

(a)

(i) Contribution per unit = $(95 – 65) = $30

$$\text{Break-even point} = \frac{\$75\,000}{\$30} = 2{,}500 \text{ units;}$$

$$\text{break-even revenue} = \frac{\$75\,000}{0.31579} = \$237\,500$$

(or 2500 × $95 = $237 500)

(ii) Margin of safety = $\dfrac{2500}{5000} \times 100 = 50\%$.

(b)

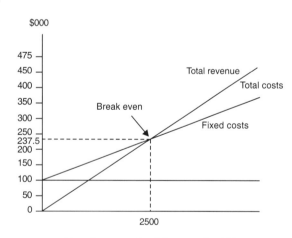

Break-even chart for product Q

Exercise 3. Veerich Ardson Ltd

No. of phones	(i) 10 000	(ii) 15 000	(iii) 20 000
	$	$	$
Contribution			
(50 – 41)	90 000	(48 – 41) 105 000	(42 – 41) 20 000
Fixed overheads	70 000	70 000	70 000
Profit/(loss)	20 000	35 000	(50 000)

Exercise 4. El Dugar Peach Ltd

Marginal cost per 1000 cans of fruit: $14 250

(i) Additional contribution from order for 5000 cans at $16 000 per 1000 cans:
5 × $(16 000 – 14 250) = $8750 profit
The order should be accepted.

(ii) Loss if order for 3000 cans at $14 100 is accepted:
3 × $(14 100 – 14 250) = $450 loss
The order should not be accepted unless it will prevent the company from having to lay off valuable skilled staff because of a temporary slump in trade.

Exercise 5. Canterbury Planes Ltd

Present position (tools produced by Canterbury Planes Ltd)	
	$
Selling price per tool	16.0
Direct costs: Material	3.0
Labour	2.5
Other expenses	1.0
Marginal cost of production	6.5
Variable selling expenses	2.0
Marginal cost of sales	8.5
Contribution	7.5

Contribution from sale of 15 000 tools = $112 500
Profit on sale of 15 000 tolls = $(112 500 – 74 000) = $38 500

Break-even point: $\dfrac{\$74\,000}{7.5} = 9867$ tools

(a)

(i) North Island Tool Co.
Cost per tool $6. This is $0.50 less than the present cost of production.
Effect on profit: Increase by (15 000 × $0.5) $7 500 to $46 000.
Effect on break-even point: $\dfrac{\$74\,000}{\$8} = 9250$ tools.

(ii) South Island Tool Co.
Cost per tool $6.80. This is $0.30 more than the present cost of production.
Effect on profit: Decrease by (15 000 × $0.3) $4 500 to $34 000.
Effect on break-even point: $\dfrac{\$74\,000}{\$7.2} = 10\,278$ tools.

(b) Tools should be purchased from Northern Island Tool Co. because

- the cost will be $0.50 less than the cost of production.
- profit will increase by $7500 to $46 000.
- the break-even point will be reduced from 9867 tools to 9250 tools.

Tools should not be purchased from South Island Tool Co. because

- the cost will be $0.30 more than the cost of production.
- profit will decrease by $4500 to $34 000.
- the break-even point will increase from 9867 tools to 10 278.

Exercise 6. Castries Ltd

Revised production budget to maximise profit

	Gimie $	Gross $	Petit $
Per unit			
Selling price	14	25	20
Direct material	5	6.50	8
Direct labour	5	14.00	6
Marginal cost	10	20.50	14
Contribution	4	4.50	6
Contribution per litre of material	1.6	1.38	1.5
Ranking	1	3	2

Revised production budget:

	Units	Litres	Contribution $
Gimie	1000	2 500	4 000
Petit	800	3 200	4 800
Gros	1500	4 875	6 750
		10 575	15 550
Less fixed expenses			10 000
Profit			5 550

Exercise 7. Castries Ltd

Revised production budget to maximise profit

	Gimie $	Gros $	Petit $
Contribution	4	4.50	6
Contribution per direct labour hour	8	3.21	10
Ranking	2	3	1

Revised production budget:

	Units	Labour hours	Contribution $
Petit	800	480	4 800.00
Gimie	1000	500	4 000.00
Gros	1725	2415	7 762.50
		3395	16 562.50
Less fixed expenses			10 000.00
Profit			6 562.50

Exercise 8

(i) Fixed costs increase by $12 000 and profit is reduced to $23 000.

$$\text{Break-even} = \frac{\$92\ 000}{\$5.75*} = 16\ 000 \text{ units;}$$

* contribution = $(8.75 − 3)

(ii) Variable costs increase by $9000 and profit is reduced to $26 000.

$$\text{Break-even} = \frac{\$80\ 000}{\$5.3*} = 15\ 095 \text{ units.}$$

* contribution = $(8.75 − 3.45)

(iii) Costs and revenue increase by $21 000 and profit is maintained at $35 000.

$$\text{Break-even} = \frac{\$92\ 000}{\$6.35*} = 14\ 489 \text{ units.}$$

* Costs have increased by $21 000; sales revenue becomes $196 000 ($9.80 per unit). Unit marginal cost is $3.45; contribution = $(9.80 − 3.45) = $6.35.

Exercise 9. Cohort Ltd

(a)

Products	Legion $	Centurion $	Praefect $
Per unit			
Material	20	40	50
Labour	36	60	72
Marginal cost	56	100	122
Selling price	80	130	150
Contribution	24	30	28
Budgeted contribution	24 000	60 000	112 000
	$		
Total contribution	196 000		
Less fixed expenses	115 000		
Profit	81 000		

(b) Revised production budget

Products ranked	Contribution	Units	Materials	Total
1. Legion	12.0	1000	2 000	24 000
2. Centurion	7.5	2000	8 000	60 000
3. Praefect	5.6	3600	18 000	100 800
			28 000	184 800
		Less	Fixed	
			expenses	115 000
			Profit	69 800

(c) Reconciliation of profit per revised budget with profit in original budget.

		$
Profit per original budget		81 000
Budgeted production of Praefect (units)	4000	
Revised budget for Praefect	3600	
Reduction in production	400	
Loss of contributions 400 × 28		11 200
Revised profit		69 800

Exercise 10. Cockpit Country Industrial Co. Ltd
(a)
(i)

15 000 units	
Per unit	$
Direct material (4 × $4.10)	16.4
Direct labour ($\frac{1}{3}$ × $12)	4.0
Variable overhead	1.8
Marginal cost	22.2
Selling price	25.0
Contribution	2.8

Profit: $(15 000 × 2.8) – $30 000* = $(42 000 – 30 000) = $12 000.
(*$1.5 × 20 000 = $30 000)

(ii)

18 000 units	
Per unit	$
Material	16.4
Labour	4.0
Variable overhead	1.7889*
Marginal cost	22.1889
Selling price	25.0000
Contribution	2.8111

*(16 000 × $1.8 + 2000 × $1.7) ÷ 18 000

Profit = (18 000 × $2.811) – $30 000 = $50 6000 (rounded) – $30 0000 = $20 6000.

(b) Break-even point

		$
Material per unit		16.4
Labour per unit		4.0
Variable overhead		
16 000 × $1.8	28 000	
4 000 × $1.7	6 800	
	35 600	
	per unit	1.79
Marginal cost		22.19
Selling price		25.00
Contribution per unit		2.81

Break-even point $= \dfrac{\$30\ 000}{\$2.81} = 10\ 677$ units;

(c)

20 000 units sold at $24 per unit		$	$
Sales revenue			480 000
Material (20 000 × 4 × $4.1)		328 000	
Labour (20 000 × $4)		80 000	
Variable overhead			
16 000 × $1.8	28 800		
4 000 × $1.7	6 800	35 600	443 600
			36 400
Less Fixed overheads			30 000
Profit			6 400

(d) A selling price may be lowered with advantage to:
   - increase demand for the good.
   - undercut the prices of competitors
   - maintain full production.
   - sell slow-moving stock
   - introduce a new product.
   Possible disadvantages are:
   - the start of a price war with competitors
   - fixed overheads may not be covered
   - the product may be sold below the cost of production if the marginal cost is not known.
(e) The following assumptions are made when break-even charts are prepared.
   - Fixed costs remain fixed at all levels of activity. *But* costs are only fixed within certain limits of activity and are more likely to be 'stepped' as activity increases.

- All costs may be classified as either fixed or variable. *But* many costs cannot easily be classed as fixed or variable.
- Variable costs vary directly with the output in units. *But* variable costs may decrease with the level of activity because quantity discounts are received on purchases of materials, or labour costs increase because overtime has to be paid to workers to achieve the level of activity.
- Sales revenue will increase proportionately to the volume of sales. *But* it may be necessary to discount prices to achieve the desired volume of sales.
- All the resources required for production will be available. *But* there may be limiting factors affecting materials, labour or demand for the product.

Exercise 11

(a)

Monthly profit using marginal costing		
	Month 1	Month 2
	$	$
Sales revenue	50 000	65 000
Less: Variable costs	30 000	39 000
Fixed costs	15 000	15 000
Monthly net profit	5 000	11 000

(b)

Monthly profit using full absorption costing		
	Month 1	Month 2
	$	$
Sales revenue	50 000	65 000
Opening stock	–	20 000
Cost of production:		
Variable costs: 1500 units x $30	45 000	45 000
Fixed costs	15 000	15 000
	60 000	80 000
Less closing stock	(20 000)	(28 000)
Cost of sales	40 000	52 000
Monthly net profit	10 000	13 000

Note1: Closing stock is valued at $40 per unit ($60 000 ÷ 1500 = $40)
Note 2: Closing stock at the end of month 1 is 500 units (1500 – 1000). At the end of month 2 the closing stock is (500 + 1500 – 1300) = 700 units.

(c)

Reconciliation of profit using each method		
	Month 1	Month 2
	$	$
Net profit using marginal costing	5 000	11 000
Add: fixed overheads in closing stock	5 000	7 000
Less: fixed overheads in closing stock	–	(5 000)
Net profit using full absorption costing	10 000	13 000

Note: The fixed overheads included in the closing stock is $15 000 ÷ 1500 = $10 per unit. The total overheads included in the closing stock at the end of each month are, therefore are: Month 1–500 units × $10 = $5000. In month 2–700 units × $10 = $7000.

Multiple-choice questions

1. C   2. D   3. D   4. D

Chapter 34

Exercise 1. Flannel and Flounder Ltd

Sales budget for 6 months ending 30 June						
	January	February	March	April	May	June
	$	$	$	$	$	$
Unit sold	1000	1200	1300	1500	1700	1800
Price	$20	$20	$20	$22	$22	$22
Sales revenue	$20 000	$24 000	$26 000	$33 000	$37 400	$39 600

Exercise 2. Flannel and Flounder Ltd

Production budget for the 7 months from December to 30 June							
	December	January	February	March	April	May	June
Sales (following month in units)	1000	1200	1300	1500	1700	1800	2000
Add 10%	100	120	130	150	170	180	200
Monthly production	1100	1320	1430	1650	1870	1980	2200

Exercise 3. Flannel and Flounder Ltd

Purchases budget for the period November to May								
	November	December	January	February	March	April	May	June
Units of production	1100	1320	1430	1650	1870	1980	2200	2100
Material required (litres)	2750	3300	3575	4125	4675	4950	5500	5250
Price per litre	$4.10	$4.10	$4.10	$4.10	$4.25	$4.25	$4.25	$4.25
Purchases	$11 275	$13 530	$14 658	$16 913	$19 869	$21 038	$23 375	$22 313

Exercise 4. Flannel and Flounder Ltd

Expenditure budget for six months ending June						
	January $	February $	March $	April $	May $	June $
Purchases	13 530	14 658	16 913	19 869	21 038	23 375
Wages	4 000	4 000	4 000	4 000	4 000	4 000
Bonus	–	–	160	240	520	696
Electricity	–	2400	–	–	1 800	–
Other expenses	6 000	6 000	6 000	6 000	6 600	6 600
Interest on loan	–	–	500	–	–	500
Dividend	–	–	–	4 000	–	–
Purchase of machine	–	–	–	–	15 000	–
	23 530	27 058	27 573	34 709	48 958	35 171

Exercise 5. Flannel and flounder Ltd

(a)

Cash budget for the six months ending 30 June						
	January $	February $	March $	April $	May $	June $
Receipts						
Cash sales	10 000	12 000	13 000	16 500	18 700	19 800
Debtors – 1 months	6 864	7 800	9 360	10 140	12 870	14 586
Debtors – 2 months	1 800	1 760	2 000	2 400	2 600	3 300
Proceeds from sale of plant	–	12 000	–	–	–	–
	18 664	33 560	24 360	29 040	34 170	37 686
Expenditure						
Purchases	13 530	14 658	16 913	19 869	21 038	23 375
Wages	4 000	4 000	4 000	4 000	4 000	4 000
Bonus	–	–	160	240	520	696
Electricity	–	2 400	–	–	1 800	–
Other expenses	6 000	6 000	6 000	6 600	6 600	6 000
Interest in loan	–	–	500	–	–	500
Dividend	–	–	–	4 000	–	–
Purchase of machine	–	–	–	–	15 000	–
	23 530	27 058	27 573	34 709	48 958	35 171
Net receipts/(payments)	(4 866)	6 502	(3 213)	(5 669)	(14 788)	2 515
Brought forward	31 750	26 884	33 386	30 173	24 504	9 716
Carried forward	26 884	33 386	30 173	24 504	9 716	12 231

(b) Trade receivables: $(19 800 + 3 740)
    = $23 540
Trade payables $22 313
Accrued commission on sales ($19 600 × 0.04)
    = $784

Exercise 6. Greenfields Ltd

(a)

Cash budget for the four months ending 30 April 2012

	January $	February $	March $	April $
Cash sales	25 000	28 000	30 000	33 000
Debtors	42 500	37 500	42 000	45 000
	67 500	65 500	72 000	78 000
Suppliers	22 500	25 000	20 000	30 000
Selling and distribution	6 250	7 000	7 500	8 250
Administration	20 000	20 000	20 000	20 000
Purchase of plant	–	–	60 000	–
Dividend	–	–	–	6 500
	48 750	52 000	107 500	64 750
Net receipts/(payments)	18 750	13 500	(35 500)	13 250
Balance b/fwd	20 750	39 500	53 000	17 500
Balance c/fwd	39 500	53 000	17 500	30 750

(b)

Greenfields Ltd
Budgeted Income Statement for the four months ending 30 April 2012

	$	$
Sales		290 000
Cost of sales		
Opening Inventory	30 000	
Purchases	112 500	
	142 500	
Closing Inventory	22 500	120 000
Gross profit		170 000
Selling and distribution expenses	32 500	
Administration expenses	83 500	116 000
Profit from operations		54 000
Interest on debentures		1 000
Profit attributable to equity holders		53 000
Ordinary dividend	6 500	
Transfer to General Reserve	25 000	31 500
Retained earnings for the year		21 500

Note: Although this is not the correct layout for published accounts, it is perfectly acceptable for management accounts and for an answer to an examination question.

(c)

Greenfields Ltd
Budgeted Statement of Financial Position at 30 April 2012

Non-current assets	Cost $	Depreciation $	Net $
Freehold premises	50 000	10 500	39 500
Plant and machinery	97 500	29 000	68 500
	147 500	39 500	108 000
Current assets			
Inventory		22 500	
Trade receivables		49 500	
Cash and cash equivalents		30 750	
		102 750	
Current liabilities			
Trade payables	37 500		
Debenture interest accrued	1 000	38 500	64 250
			172 250
Non-current liability			
12% debentures 2019/2020			25 000
			147 250
Equity			
Ordinary shares of $1			65 000
General reserve			55 000
Retained earnings			27 250
			147 250

Multiple-choice questions

1. C   2. B   3. B   4. A

Chapter 35

Exercise 1. Brekkifoods Ltd

Flexed Budget for the production of 110 000 packets of Barleynuts

	$
Variable expenses	
Direct materials	22 000
Direct labour	16 500
Production expenses	6 600
	45 100
Fixed expenses	
Production expenses	13 000
Administration	29 000
	87 100

Exercise 2. Flexers Ltd

No. of locks	9000
	$
Direct materials	22 500
Direct labour	54 000
Production overhead	34 000
Selling and distribution	30 000
Administration	80 000
	220 500

Exercise 3. Enigma Ltd

(a)

	Flexed budget
No. of units	4250
	$
Direct materials	21 250
Direct labour	48 875
Variable overheads	10 625
Fixed overhead	50 000
Total cost	130 750

(b)

(i)	Total cost variance	$5 136 (A)
(ii)	Quantity variance	$4 750 (A)
(iii)	Direct material variance	$2 150 (A)
(iv)	Direct labour variance	$1 639 (F)
		$5 261 (A)

(c)

Variable overhead variance	$ 125 (F)
	$5 136 (A)

Exercise 4. Underpar Ltd

(a)

	Flexed budget
No. of units	6300
	$
Direct materials	21 420
Direct labour	42 525
Variable overheads	3 150
Fixed overhead	62 000
Total cost	129 095

(b)

Total cost variance	$6345 (F)
Quantity variance	$7455 (F)
Direct material variance	$ 530 (F)
Direct labour variance	$1540 (A)
	$6445 (F)

(c)

Variable overhead variance	$ 100 (F)
	$6345 (A)

Exercise 5. Dandelion Ltd

Standard total material cost of 12 000 packets of Pickup = 3 litres × $5 × 12 000 = $180 000.

Actual material usage = 12 000 × 2.8 = 33 600 litres.

Direct material usage variance = (36 000 − 33 600) $5 = $12 000 (F).

Direct material price variance = ($5 − $4.80) 33 600 = $6720 (F).

(Check: Actual cost was 2.8 litres × $4.8 litres × 12 000 = $161 280; total material variance = $18 720 (F): $(12 000 + 6720) (as above)).

Exercise 6. Dandelion Ltd

The standard total direct labour cost for the production of 12 000 packets of Pickup = $10 × 12 000 = $120 000.

Actual hours taken 12 000 × 1.25 = 15 000.

The direct labour efficiency variance = (12 000 − 15 000) $10 = $30 000 (A).

The direct labour rate variance = $(10 − 8.50) 15 000 = $22 500 (F).

(Check: Actual labour cost of production of 12 000 packets of Pickup = 1.25 hours × $8.50 × 12 000 = $127 500; Total labour variance = $7500 (A) = $30 000 (A) − $22 500 (F) (as above)).

Exercise 7. Larabee Ltd

(a) Workings:

Direct material: standard cost per kg $\frac{\$7200}{300 \times 4}$ = $6

standard usage for 400 units: 4 × 400 kg = 1600 kg.

actual material per unit: $\frac{\$9000}{\$6.25 \times 400}$ = 3.6 kg.

actual usage 400 × 3.6 kg = 1440 kg

Direct labour: standard hours per unit $\frac{\$6600}{\$11 \times 300}$ = 2 hours

standard hours for 400 units = 800

actual hours for 400 units: 400 × 2.25 = 900

actual cost per hour $\frac{\$10\,890}{400 \times 2.25}$ = $12.10.

(i) Direct material usage variance: (1600 − 1440) $6 = $960 (F).

(ii)   Direct material price variance:
$(6.00 – 6.25) 1440 = $360 (A).
(iii) Direct labour efficiency variance:
(800 – 900) $11 = $1100 (A).
(iv)   Direct labour rate variance: $(11.00 – 12.10)
900 = $990 (A).

(b)   The favourable material usage variance may be
due to a better quality of material being used
resulting in less wastage during production. This
view may be supported by the adverse price
variance which suggests that a better quality of
material was more expensive than standard.

Both of the labour variances are adverse. The
higher hourly rate of pay has not resulted in a
favourable efficiency variance, even though the
workers may have been working with a better quality
of material. The adverse efficiency variance does not
suggest that the higher rate of pay was due to the
employment of a more skilled work force. It is
possible that a pay increase given to the workers was
below their expectation and they are poorly motivated
as a result. The reason for the adverse variances can
only be discovered by further investigation.

Exercise 8. Cantab Ltd

Calculation of actual profit made in a three month period		
	$	$
Profit per master budget		98 970
Add favourable variances		
Sales volume		6 210
Materials price		9 635
abour efficiency		10 500
		125 315
Deduct adverse variances		
Quantity	17 009	
Sales price	3 730	

	$	$
Materials usage	6 280	
Labour rate	7 840	
Overhead expenditure	5 760	40 619
Actual profit		84 696

Multiple-choice questions

1. A   2. B   3. C   4. C   5. C
6. C

Chapter 36

Exercise 1. Baseball Ltd
Ignore the machine that was acquired some years
earlier as it is a sunk cost.

Average profit = $150 000 ÷ 6 = $25 000.

$$\text{Average investment} = \$(\frac{120\ 000}{2} + 25\ 000)$$
$$= \$85\ 000.$$

$$\text{ARR} = \frac{25\ 000}{85\ 000} \times 100 = 29.4\%$$

Exercise 2. Mapleduck Ltd
Calculation of payback periods

Year		Duckbill $	Kwak $
	0	(90 000)	(90 000)
	1	30 000	40 000
	2	36 000	40 000
	3	24 000	10 000
Payback		$2\frac{24}{40}$ years	$2\frac{10}{40}$ years
		$2 + (\frac{24}{40} \times 12)$ years	
		2 years 7.2 months	
		2 years 8 months	2 years 3 months

Kwak should be chosen because it has the shorter
payback period and its pattern of cash flows will
benefit the liquidity of Mapleduck Ltd.

Exercise 3. Nomen Ltd

Year	Discounting factor 12%	Machine A $	A NPV $	B $	B NPV $	C $	C NPV $
0	1.000	(135 000)	(135 000)	(135 000)	(135 000)	(135 000)	(135 000)
1	0.893	50 000	44 650	38 000	33 934	26 000	23 218
2	0.797	50 000	39 850	38 000	30 286	26 000	20 722
3	0.712	38 000	27 056	38 000	27 056	38 000	27 056
4	0.636	26 000	16 536	38 000	24 168	50 000	31 800
5	0.567	26 000	14 742	38 000	21 546	50 000	28 350
Net present values			7 834		1 990		(3 854)

Nomen Ltd should choose machine A as it has the highest NPV. Machine C should not be considered because it has a negative NPV.

Exercise 4. Nomen Ltd

Year	Discounting factor 20%	Machine A $	A NPV $	B $	B NPV $
0	1.000	(135 000)	(135 000)	(135 000)	(135 000)
1	0.833	50 000	41 650	38 000	31 654
2	0.694	50 000	34 700	38 000	26 372
3	0.579	38 000	22 002	38 000	22 002
4	0.482	26 000	12 532	38 000	18 316
5	0.402	26 000	10 452	38 000	15 276
Net present values			(13 664)		(21 380)

IRR for machine A: $12\% + (8\% \times \dfrac{7834}{7834 + 13\,664}) = 14.9\%$

IRR for machine B: $12\% + (8\% \times \dfrac{1990}{1990 + 21\,380}) = 12.7\%$.

Exercise 5. Baxter Ltd

Workings

	Big Gee	Big Gee $	Maxi-Shadbolt	Maxi-Shadbolt $
Annual depreciation	$\dfrac{\$140\,000 - \$20\,000}{5} = \$24\,000$		$\dfrac{\$180\,000 - \$30\,000}{5} = \$30\,000$	
Cash outflows				
Year 1	$(70 000 – 24 000)	46 000	$(84 000 – 30 000)	54 000
2	$(84 000 – 24 000)	60 000	$(98 000 – 30 000)	68 000
3	$(91 000 – 24 000)	67 000	$(105 000 – 30 000)	75 000
4	$(98 000 – 24 000)	74 000	$(112 000 – 30 000)	82 000
5	$(95 000 – 24 000)	71 000	$(100 000 – 30 000)	70 000

Net receipts		Big Gee			Maxi-Shadbolt
		$			$
Year 1	$(98 000 – 46 000)	52 000	$(101 000 – 54 000)		47 000
2	$(112 000 – 60 000)	52 000	$(118 000 – 68 000)		50 000
3	$(126 000 – 67 000)	59 000	$(126 000 – 75 000)		51 000
4	$(126 000 – 74 000)	52 000	$(140 000 – 82 000)		58 000
5	$(100 000 – 71 000) plus $20 000	49 000	$(110 000 – 70 000) plus $30 000		70 000

Average profit		Big Gee			Maxi-Shadbolt
		$			$
Year 1	$(98 000 – 70 000)	28 000	$(101 000 – 84 000)		17 000
2	$(112 000 – 84 000)	28 000	$(118 000 – 98 000)		20 000
3	$(126 000 – 91 000)	35 000	$(126 000 – 105 000)		21 000
4	$(126 000 – 98 000)	28 000	$(140 000 – 112 000)		28 000
5	$(100 000 – 95 000)	5 000	$(110 000 – 100 000)		10 000
		124 000			96 000
	÷5	$24 800		÷5	$19 200

(a) (i)

	Big Gee	Maxi-Shadbolt
ARR =	$\frac{24\ 800}{70\ 000} \times 100 = 35.4\%$	$\frac{19\ 200}{90\ 000} \times 100 = 21.3\%$

(ii) Payback period

	$		$
Year 0	(140 000)		(180 000)
1	52 000		47 000
2	52 000		50 000
	36 000	Year 3	51 000
			32 000

Year 3 $\frac{36\ 000}{59\ 000} \times 12 = 8$ months   Year 4 $\frac{32\ 000}{58\ 000} \times 12 = 7$ months

Payback = 2 years 8 months   3 years 7 months

(iii) Net present values at 10%

		Big Gee		Maxi-Shadbolt	
Year	Factor	Net (payment)/ receipt	NPV	Net (payment)/ receipt	NPV
		$	$	$	$
0	1.000	(140 000)	(140 000)	(180 000)	(180 000)
1	0.909	52 000	47 268	47 000	42 723
2	0.826	52 000	42 952	50 000	41 300
3	0.751	59 000	44 309	51 000	38 301
4	0.683	52 000	35 516	58 000	39 614
5	0.621	49 000	30 429	70 000	43 470
	Net present values		60 474		25 408

(iv) IRR (40%)

		Big Gee		Maxi-Shadbolt	
Year	Factor	Net (payment)/ receipt	NPV	Net (payment)/ receipt	NPV
		$	$	$	$
0	1.000	(140 000)	(140 000)	(180 000)	(180 000)
1	0.714	52 000	37 128	47 000	33 558
2	0.510	52 000	26 520	50 000	25 500
3	0.364	59 000	21 476	51 000	18 564
4	0.260	52 000	13 520	58 000	15 080
5	0.186	49 000	9 114	70 000	13 020
	Net present values		(32 242)		(74 278)

IRR: Big Gee $10\% + (30\% \times \frac{60\ 474}{60\ 474 + 32\ 242})$
= 29.6%

Maxi-Shadbolt $10\% + (30\% \times \frac{25\ 408}{25\ 408 + 74\ 278})$
= 17.6%.

(b) Baxter Ltd should purchase Big Gee because
  • it has a higher accounting rate of return: 35.4% (Maxi-Shadbolt: 21.3%).
  • it has the shorter payback period: 2 years 8 months, lower risk (Maxi-Shadbolt: 3 years 7 months).
  • it has higher net present value: $60 474 (Maxi-Shadbolt: $25 408).
  • it has higher internal rate of return: 29.6% (Maxi-Shadbolt: $17.6%).

Exercise 6

Net present value: $150 000 – $(50 000 × 3.169) = $8450.

The net present value will become negative if:
1. the cost of the machine rises by $8450, i.e. an increase of 5.6%, or
2. the annual savings in operational costs fall below $47 333, i.e. they fall short by 5.3%.

Exercise 7

It should invest in the order C, A and B. By dividing the net present value by the capital cost C yields an net present value of 20%. Similarly, A yields 17.5% and C 12%. Thus C, A, B will be the most advantageous for the company.

Multiple-choice questions

   1. C   **2.** A   **3.** D   **4.** B

Index

Accounting principles
  accruals basis, 44
  business entity, 42
  conservation, concept of, 45
  consistency, 44
  definition, 42
  duality concept, 43
  going concern, 45
  for goods on sale or return, 43
  historic costs, 42–43
  materiality, 44
  in monetary terms, 42
  money measurement, 43
  prudence concept, 44–45
  realisation of accounts, 43
  substance over form, 45
Accounting rate of return (ARR),
    314–315
Accounts
  asset, 23
  capital and drawings, 23
  with credit balances, 23
  for creditors, 23
  with debit balances, 23
  for debtors, 23
  division of the ledger, 24
  impersonal, 23
  loan, 23
  Motor Vehicles Running
    Expenses, 23
  nominal, 23
Accruals
  as accounting principle, 44
  accrued expense,
    treatment of, 47
  income adjustment for, 48

inventory (stock) of stores on
    expense accounts, 48
  prepaid expense, treatment of,
    47–48
  trial balance adjustment for, 49
Apportionment of costs, 257, 259
Appropriation account, 128
Attainable standards, 302

Bad debts
  definition, 61
  recovered, 61–62
Balancing accounts
  examples, 21–22
  frequency of, 22
  method, 21
  need for, 21
Bank reconciliation statement
  definition, 67
  notes, 67
  preparation of, 67
  uses of, 69
Book of prime entry
  for cash discounts, 15
  definition, 14
  making entries in, 14–15
  posting in ledger accounts, 15
Budgeting
  bottom-up budgets, 290
  cash budget, 294
  difference with forecast, 289
  expenditure budget, 293
  flexible budgets, 290–291,
    302–304
  incremental, 289
  limiting factors, 291

master budget, 295–296
  principle budget factors, 291
  production budget, 291–292
  purchase budget, 292–293
  rolling budgets, 289–290
  sales budget, 291
  with semi-variable expenses, 303
  as tools for planning and control,
    289–291
  top-down budgets, 290
  zero-based, 289
Business entity, 42
Business purchase
  difference between the purchase
    of a business and purchase
    of the assets
    for business, 200
  Goodwill, 200–201
  journal entries, 201
  of a partnership business, 203
  return on investment, 205

Capital expenditure, 23
Carrying amounts, 52
Cash account, 3
Cash book
  definition, 15
  entering discounts in, 16
  posting in Discounts Allowed
    account, 16
  posting in Discounts Received
    account, 16
  three-column, 17
Cash operating cycle, 232
Cash (or settlement) discount, 10
Cash ratio, 232

Cash transactions, recording of, 3–6
Companies Act 1985, 209–210
Company finance
  appraisal of accounting reports, 248–250
  bank loans, 246
  bank overdrafts, 246
  basis of modern financial reporting, 248–249
  company budgets, 250
  convertible loan stock, 246
  debentures, 246
  directors' reports, 250
  factoring, 247
  hire purchase, 246–247
  income smoothing techniques, 249–250
  leasing, 247
  principles deciding, 247–248
  share and debenture issues compared, 248
  share capital, 245–246
  source of, 245
  trade payables, 247
  window dressing, 249
  working capital, 247–248
Compensating errors, 26
Conservation, concept of, 45
Control accounts
  definition, 72
  double-entry model and, 74–75
  purchase ledger and, 72–73
  reconciliation with ledgers, 76
  sales ledger and, 73–74
  uses and limitations of, 75–76
Cost accounting
  appropriation of expenses to cost centres, 257–259
  behaviour of costs, 256–257
  direct and indirect, 256
  overhead absorption rates (OARs), 260, 262
  purpose and nature of, 255–256

recording materials, labour and overheads, 257
  under-/over-absorption of overheads, 263
Cost centres, 257
Costing systems
  batch, 267
  for continuous operations, 266–268
  for continuous or specific order operations, 266
  for specific order operations, 266–267
Cost units, 260, 262
Credit side of account book, 3
Credit transactions
  cash (or settlement) discount, 10
  definition, 9
  goods returned, 9–10
  recording of, 9–10
  trade discount, 10
Current assets, 23
Current asset turnover, 230
Current liabilities, 23
Current ratio, 231
Current standards, 302
Customer's books, 9

Debit side of account book, 3
Debt/equity ratio, 234
Departmental accounts
  commission, 109
  definition, 108
  fixed overheads of a department, 111
  income statement, 109
  of loss-making department, 110–111
  preparation of, 108–109
  trading sections of the Income Statement, 108
Depreciation
  adjustment in trial balance, 57
  consistency and, 55

definition, 52
  for disposals of non-current assets, 56
  exceptional, 55
  identifying assets for, 54–55
  of non-current assets, 52
  part exchange value of the asset, 56
  provision in the year of acquistion of asset, 55
  provisions and accounting concepts, 57–58
  reasons for, 52
  reducing balance method of calculating, 54–55
  straight-line method of calculating, 52, 55
Direct labour cost, 262
Direct labour overhead absorption rate, 260
Direct material cost, 262
Discounts Allowed account, 10
Discounts Received account, 10
Dividend cover, 236
Dividend per share, 236
Dividend yield, 236–237
Division of the ledger, 24
Double-entry bookkeeping, 3
Doubtful debts
  accounting concepts for, 64
  adjustments to a trial balance for, 63–64
  calculation of a provision for, 63
  creating and maintaining provision of, 62
  provisions for, 62, 64
Duality concept principle, 43

Errors
  of commission, 26
  of omission, 26
  of original entry, 26
  of principle, 26

Final accounts of a business, 39

Financial statements, limitations of, 225–226
Financial statements of a business, 39
First in, first out (FIFO), 121
    advantages and disadvantages, 123–124
Fixed assets, 23
FRS 18 Accounting policies, 210–211

Gearing ratio, 233–234
Generally accepted accounting principles (GAAP) and, 210
Going concern principle, 45
Goods returned, recording of, 9–10
Gross profit percentage, 228–229

Ideal standards, 302
Income gearing, 235–236
Income statement, for a sole trader
    carriage inwards and carriage outwards, 35
    definition, 31
    opening stock, 34–35
    preparation, 31–34
    wages as an expense, 36
Income statement, using financial ratios, 238–239
Incomplete records
    calculate profit/loss from statements of affairs, 89–90
    definition, 89
    margin and mark-up in, 92–93
    preparing income statement and a statement of financial position from, 90–92
    value of inventory lost in a fire or by theft, 93
Initial rate of return (IRR), 317
Interest cover, 235
Internal control of accounts, 24
International Accounting Standard IAS 8, 211–212

IAS 10, 212–213
IAS 16, 213–215
IAS 18, 215–216
IAS 23, 216
IAS 33, 216–217
IAS 36, 217–218
IAS 37, 218–219
IAS 38, 219–220
Interpolation, 317
Inventory turnover, 232
Inventory valuation
    advantages and disadvantages of FIFO and AVCO, 123–124
    closing inventories for a manufacturing organisation, 125–126
    effects of methods on profits, 122
    important principle, 120–121
    of individual items or groups of items of inventory, 125
    International Accounting Standard 2 (IAS 2), 124–125
    at the lower of cost and net realisable value, 124
    methods of, 121–122
    net realisable value, 124
    of perpetual and periodic inventories, 122
    raw materials, 125
    replacement cost, 126
Investment appraisal
    accounting rate of return, 314–315
    capital rationing, 319
    definition, 313
    initial rate of return (IRR), 317
    net present value (NPV), 316
    payback period, 315–316
    sensitivity analysis, 318–319

Journal
    definition, 18
    making entries in, 18

Ledger accounts, 3
Limited company
    authorised share capital, 158
    bonus shares, 189–190
    calculation of value of ordinary shares, 166
    called-up capital, 163
    calls in advance, 163
    calls in arrear, 163
    Capital Redemption Reserve, 165–166
    capital reduction and reconstruction, 195–196
    capital reserves, 165–166
    Companies Acts of 1985, 1989 and 2006, 158, 166, 188
    convertible loan stock, 195
    cumulative preference shares, 163
    debentures, 168
    definition, 157
    differences between liabilities, provisions and reserves, 167
    distributable profits, 167
    dividends, 167–168
    dividing of profits, 160–161
    forfeited shares, 163
    growth of, 157–158
    income statements, 159–160
    Memorandum and Articles of Association, 158
    non-cumulative preference shares, 163
    notes, 158
    ordinary share capital, 164
    paid-up capital, 163
    partnerships, 159
    public and private, 158
    recording of bonus shares and rights issues, 191
    redeemable shares, 192–194
    redemption of debentures, 195
    redemption or purchase of own shares by a private company, 194–195

reserves, 165–166
Revaluation Reserves, 166
revenue reserves, 165
rights issues, 190
share capital, 163
share issues, 189
Share Premium account, 165
shares at a premium, 164–165
statement of changes in
   equity, 161
statement of financial position
   for, 162–163
uncalled capital, 163
Liquid asset, 40, 231
Liquidity ratio, 231–232
Long-term liabilities, 23

Machine hour OAR, 261
Management accounting, 255
Manufacturing accounts
   definition, 114
   factory profit, 114
   preparing of, 114–116
   statement of financial
      position, 116
   unrealised profit, 116
Marginal costing
   break-even chart, 278–279
   break-even point of a product,
      277–278
   limitations of break-even charts,
      279–280
   limiting factors, 283–284
   'make or buy' decisions, 282–283
   margin of safety, 278
   orders below normal selling price,
      281–282
   and pricing, 280–281
   profit/volume chart, 279
   ratio of the contribution to the
      selling price, 276–277
   sensitivity analysis of profit and
      break-even points,
      284–285
   sensitivity of a product, 279

vs absorption costing and
   inventory valuation, 286

Net book value (NBV) of the
   asset, 52
Net current assets (or working
   capital) to sales, 230–231
Net payments, 316
Net present value (NPV), 316
Net profit percentage, 228
Net receipts, 316
Net working assets to sales, 231
Non-current asset turnover, 230
Non-profit-making organisations
   accumulated fund, 99
   ancillary activities, 100
   definition, 99
   excess of expenditure over
      income, 99
   Income and Expenditure
      Account, 99
   life subscriptions and entry fees,
      treatment of, 100
   non-trading activities, 100
   preparation of club accounts,
      100–102
   Receipts and Payments Account,
      99
   special features of, 99
   subscriptions in arrears and
      subscriptions in advance,
      99–100
   surplus of income over
      expenditure, 99
   treatment of income, 100

Opportunity costs, 313–314
Overhead absorption rates (OARs),
   260
Overtrading, 232

Partnership Act 1890, 128
Partnership agreement, 128
Partnerships

account for changes in allocation
   of profits or losses
   between partners,
   136–137
account for Goodwill, 140
account for Goodwill when no
   Goodwill account is
   opened, 141–142
account for new or retirement of
   existing partner, 144–145
account for revaluation of assets
   in, 137–138
account for the realisation of,
   150–151
advantages, 132
apportionment of profit, 142
appropriation account, 128
changes, 136
definition, 128
disadvantages, 132
interest on a loan, 128–129
interest on capital and drawings,
   128
partners' salaries, 128
preparation of accounts for,
   129–131
profit/loss sharing, 129
Payback period, 315–316
Periodic inventory, 122
Perpetual inventory, 122
Prepayments, 47
   income adjustment for, 48
Price earnings ratio (PER), 235–236
Prime cost, 262
Process costing
   by-products and waste, 273
   explained, 270–271
   joint products, 272–273
   normal losses, 273–274
   work in progress, 271–272
Production cost centres, 257
Published company accounts
   accounting bases, 212
   accounting policies, 212

accounting principles, 212
additional costs associated with assets, 214
auditors' report, 221
borrowing costs, 216
contingent assets and contingent liabilities, 218–219
dealing with errors, 212
depreciation, 214–215
directors' report, 220–221
disclosure in the financial statements, 215
documents required to be prepared and published annually, 209
earnings per share (EPS), 216–217
events after the statement of financial position date, 212–213
impairment review of assets, 217–218
intangible asset, 219–220
provisions, 218
revenue, 215–216
treatment of changes in accounting estimates, 211
treatment of non-current assets of property, plant and equipment, 213–214
valuation of assets, 215

Rate of return on investment, 317
Ratios
calculation and analysis of, 227
financial, 231–233
investment (stock exchange), 233–237
limitations of, 237
profitability, 227–229
showing utilisation of resources, 229–231
trend analysis and inter-firm comparison, 237
useful, 226

Realisation of accounts, 43
Recoverable amount, 55
Replacement cost, 126
Return on capital employed (ROCE), 227–228
Return on equity, 228
Return on total assets, 230
Reversal of entries, 26

Sales as a percentage of capital employed, 229–230
Sales Returns account, 9
Sales variances, 305
Secondary ratios, 229
Seller's books, 9
Service cost centres, 257
Standard costing
advantages of, 301
definition, 301
material and labour cost variances, 306–307
reconciliation of budgeted profit and actual profit, 308–309
sales variances, 305
setting standards, 301–302
total cost variances, 305
variances, 304
Standard hours of production, 302
Statement of affairs, 89–90
Statement of cash flows
advantages of, 184
definition, 174
importance, 174
of limited companies, 175–176
from statements of financial position, 176–178
for unincorporated businesses, 182–183
Statement of financial position
definition, 39
notes, 40
objectives, 211
preparation of, 39–40

from statement of cash flows, 180
using financial ratios, 238–239
Window dressing, 209
Stock inventory, 122
Substance over form, accounting principle of, 45, 210
Sunk costs, 313
Suspense accounts
cause/causes of difference on the trial balance, 81–82
checks for opening, 81
correction of errors, 82–83
definition, 81
notes, 84
procedure for opening, 81
types of error and, 82

Trade discount, 10
Trade payables payment period, 232
Trade receivables collection period, 232
Trial balance
definition, 25
limitations, 26
preparing of, 25

Under-/over-absorption of overheads, 263
Utilisation of total assets, 230

Variances, 304
comments, 307–308
material and labour cost, 306–307
sales, 305
total cost, 305

Weighted average cost of inventory, 121
advantages and disadvantages, 123–124
Written down value (WDV) of the asset, 52